Lecture Notes in Computer Science   1857

Edited by G. Goos, J. Hartmanis and J. van Leeuwen

T0241065

Springer
*Berlin
Heidelberg
New York
Barcelona
Hong Kong
London
Milan
Paris
Singapore
Tokyo*

Josef Kittler   Fabio Roli (Eds.)

Multiple Classifier Systems

First International Workshop, MCS 2000
Cagliari, Italy, June 21-23, 2000
Proceedings

 Springer

Series Editors

Gerhard Goos, Karlsruhe University, Germany
Juris Hartmanis, Cornell University, NY, USA
Jan van Leeuwen, Utrecht University, The Netherlands

Volume Editors

Josef Kittler
University of Surrey
Centre for Vision, Speech and Signal Processing
Guildford GU2 7XH, United Kingdom
E-mail: j.kittler@eim.surrey.ac.uk

Fabio Roli
University of Cagliari
Department of Electrical and Electronic Engineering
Piazza D'Armi, 09123 Cagliari, Italy
E-mail: roli@diee.unica.it

Cataloging-in-Publication Data applied for

Die Deutsche Bibliothek - CIP-Einheitsaufnahme

Multiple classifier systems : first international workshop ;
proceedings / MCS 2000, Cagliari, Italy, June 21 - 23, 2000. Josef
Kittler ; Fabio Roli (ed.). - Berlin ; Heidelberg ; New York ;
Barcelona ; Hong Kong ; London ; Milan ; Paris ; Singapore ; Tokyo :
Springer, 2000
   (Lecture notes in computer science ; Vol. 1857)
   ISBN 3-540-67704-6

CR Subject Classification (1998): I.5, I.4, I.2.10, I.2, F.1

ISSN 0302-9743
ISBN 3-540-67704-6 Springer-Verlag Berlin Heidelberg New York

Springer-Verlag is a company in the BertelsmannSpringer publishing group.
© Springer-Verlag Berlin Heidelberg 2000
Printed in Germany

Typesetting: Camera-ready by author
Printed on acid-free paper   SPIN: 10722183   06/3142   5 4 3 2 1 0

Foreword

In the last decade, the theory of multiple classifier systems and related methods for combining classifiers has been developed within many diverse research communities including Machine Learning, Neural Networks, Pattern Recognition, and Statistics. This multiple genesis was useful since the same problems have been addressed from different perspectives and using different cultural backgrounds. On the other hand, the absence of common forums made difficult the exchange of results and cross-fertilization of the research carried out in the diverse communities. Researchers in one community often seem to be unaware of relevant results achieved in the other communities, and a unifying framework is clearly beyond the state of the art.

This international workshop on Multiple Classifier Systems was a first step towards the creation of a common international forum for researchers of the diverse communities working in the field of multiple classifier systems. The overwhelming response to the call for papers was a good starting point in establishing the forum. In addition, five world experts accepted to survey the state of the art, recent results, and directions of future research from the viewpoints of the machine learning, neural networks, and pattern recognition communities. We hope that this workshop will become the first in a series that will form a platform for future interactions between the respective research communities.

The present volume contains the proceedings of the First International Workshop on Multiple Classifier Systems (MCS 2000), held in Santa Margherita di Pula, Sardinia, Italy, June 21-23, 2000. The 33 papers selected by the scientific committee have been organized in sessions dealing with theoretical issues, methods for classifier fusion, design of multiple classifier systems, and applications. The significant number of papers dealing with real pattern recognition applications are proof of the practical utility of multiple classifier systems. The workshop program and this volume are enriched with five invited talks given by T.G. Dietterich (Oregon State University, USA), R.P.W. Duin (Delft Univ. of Technology, The Netherlands), A.J.C. Sharkey (University of Sheffield, UK), S.N. Srihari (CEDAR, State Univ. of New York, Buffalo, USA), and C.Y. Suen (CENPARMI, Concordia Univ., Montreal, Canada).

We wish to express our appreciation to all those who helped to organize MCS 2000. First of all, we would like to thank all the members of the scientific committee whose professionalism was instrumental in creating a very interesting technical program. A particular mention is due to G. Vernazza for his invaluable contribution to the scientific organization of MCS 2000. We also wish to thank J.A. Benediktsson and T.K. Ho who organized two special sessions. It would have been impossible to organize the workshop without the financial and technical support of the University of Cagliari and the Department of Electrical and Electronic Engineering and both forms of support are gratefully acknowledged. We also thank the International Association for Pattern Recognition for sponsoring MCS 2000 and the Italian companies and research centers listed on the next page for providing important financial support. Last but not least, special thanks are due to G. Giacinto and G. Fumera for their indispensable contributions to the local organization and proceedings preparation.

May 2000   Josef Kittler and Fabio Roli

Workshop Chairs

J. Kittler (Univ. of Surrey, United Kingdom)
F. Roli (Univ. of Cagliari, Italy)

Program Chair

G. Vernazza (Univ. of Genoa, Italy)

Scientific Committee

J. A. Benediktsson (Iceland)
H. Bunke (Switzerland)
L.P. Cordella (Italy)
B.V. Dasarathy (USA)
T.G. Dietterich (USA)
R.P.W. Duin (The Netherlands)
J. Ghosh (USA)
T.K. Ho (USA)
S. Impedovo (Italy)
N. Intrator (Israel)

A.K. Jain (USA)
D. Landgrebe (USA)
Dar-Shyang Lee (USA)
D. Partridge (UK)
C. Scagliola (Italy)
R. Schapire (USA)
A.J.C. Sharkey (UK)
S.N. Srihari (USA)
C.Y. Suen (Canada)
D. Wolpert (USA)

Local Committee

G. Armano (Univ. of Cagliari, Italy)
G. Fumera (Univ. of Cagliari, Italy)
G. Giacinto (Univ. of Cagliari, Italy)

Sponsored by

The International Association for Pattern Recognition

Supported by

CRS4 Center for Advanced Studies, Research and Development in Sardinia
COMPAQ
FST S.p.A.
ITC Irst Centre for scientific and technological research
STMicroelectronics
TECHSO S.p.A.
Telespazio

Table of Contents

Invited Papers

Ensemble Methods in Machine Learning 1
T.G. Dietterich

Experiments with Classifier Combining Rules 16
R.P.W. Duin, D.M.J. Tax

The 'Test and Select' Approach to Ensemble Combination 30
A.J.C. Sharkey, N.E. Sharkey, U. Gerecke, G.O. Chandroth

A Survey of Sequential Combination of Word Recognizers in Handwritten Phrase
Recognition at CEDAR 45
S. Srihari

Multiple Classifier Combination Methodologies for Different Output Levels 52
C.Y. Suen, L. Lam

Theoretical Issues

A Mathematically Rigorous Foundation for Supervised Learning 67
E.M. Kleinberg

Classifier Combinations: Implementations and Theoretical Issues 77
L. Lam

Some Results on Weakly Accurate Base Learners for Boosting Regression and
Classification 87
W. Jiang

Multiple Classifier Fusion

Complexity of Classification Problems and Comparative Advantages
of Combined Classifiers 97
T.K. Ho

Effectiveness of Error Correcting Output Codes in Multiclass Learning
Problems 107
F. Masulli, G. Valentini

Combining Fisher Linear Discriminants for Dissimilarity Representation . 117
Elżbieta Pękalska, M. Skurichina, R.P.W. Duin

A Learning Method of Feature Selection for Rough Classification 127
K. Takahashi, A. Sato

Analysis of a Fusion Method for Combining Marginal Classifiers 137
M.D. Happel, P. Bock

A Hybrid Projection Based and Radial Basis Function Architecture 147
S. Cohen, N. Intrator

Combining Multiple Classifiers in Probabilistic Neural Networks 157
J. Grim, J. Kittler, P. Pudil, P. Somol

Supervised Classifier Combination Through Generalized Additive
Multi-model 167
C. Conversano, R. Siciliano, F. Mola

Dynamic Classifier Selection 177
G. Giacinto, F. Roli

Bagging and Boosting

Boosting in Linear Discriminant Analysis 190
M. Skurichina, R.P.W. Duin

Different Ways of Weakening Decision Trees and Their Impact on Classification
Accuracy of DT Combination 200
P. Latinne, O. Debeir, C. Decaestecker

Applying Boosting to Similarity Literals for Time Series Classification ... 210
J.J. Rodríguez Diez, C.J. Alonso González

Boosting of Tree-Based Classifiers for Predicitve Risk Modeling in GIS ... 220
C. Furlanello, S. Merler

Design of Multiple Classifier Systems

A New Evaluation Method for Expert Combination in Multi-expert
System Designing 230
S. Impedovo, A. Salzo

Diversity Between Neural Networks and Decision Trees for Building
Multiple Classifier Systems 240
W. Wang, P. Jones, D. Partridge

Self-Organizing Decomposition of Functions in the Context of a Unified
Framework for Multiple Classifier Systems 250
N. Griffith, D. Partridge

Classifier Instability and Partitioning 260
T. Windeatt

Applications of Multiple Classifier Systems

Remote-Sensing Data Analysis

A Hierarchical Multiclassifier System for Hyperspectral Data Analysis ... 270
S. Kumar, J. Ghosh, M. Crawford

Consensus Based Classification of Multisource Remote Sensing Data 280
J.A. Benediktsson, J.R. Sveinsson

Combining Parametric and Nonparametric Classifiers for an Unsupervised
Updating of Land-Cover Maps 290
L. Bruzzone, R. Cossu, D.F. Prieto

A Multiple Self-Organizing Map Scheme for Remote Sensing
Classification 300
W. Wan, D. Fraser

Document Analysis

Use of Lexicon Density in Evaluating Word Recognizers 310
P. Slavík, V. Govindaraju

A Multi-expert System for Dynamic Signature Verification 320
V. Di Lecce, G. Dimauro, A. Guerriero, S. Impedovo, G. Pirlo, A. Salzo

A Cascaded Multiple Expert System for Verification 330
L. P. Cordella, P. Foggia, C. Sansone, F. Tortorella, M. Vento

Architecture for Classifier Combination Using Entropy Measures 340
K. Ianakiev, V. Govindaraju

Miscellaneous Applications

Combining Fingerprint Classifiers 351
R. Cappelli, D. Maio, D. Maltoni

Statistical Sensor Calibration for Fusion of Different Classifiers in a Biometric
Person Recognition Framework 362
B. Fröba, C. Rothe, C. Küblbeck

A Modular Neuro-fuzzy Network for Musical Instruments Classification . 372
A.M. Fanelli, G. Castellano, C. A. Buscicchio

Classifier Combination for Grammar-Guided Sentence Recognition 383
X. Jiang, K. Yu, H. Bunke

Shape Matching and Extraction by an Array of Figure-and-Ground
Classifiers 393
I. Kumazawa

Author Index 403

Ensemble Methods in Machine Learning

Thomas G. Dietterich

Oregon State University, Corvallis, Oregon, USA,
tgd@cs.orst.edu,
WWW home page: http://www.cs.orst.edu/~tgd

Abstract. Ensemble methods are learning algorithms that construct a set of classifiers and then classify new data points by taking a (weighted) vote of their predictions. The original ensemble method is Bayesian averaging, but more recent algorithms include error-correcting output coding, Bagging, and boosting. This paper reviews these methods and explains why ensembles can often perform better than any single classifier. Some previous studies comparing ensemble methods are reviewed, and some new experiments are presented to uncover the reasons that Adaboost does not overfit rapidly.

1 Introduction

Consider the standard supervised learning problem. A learning program is given training examples of the form $\{(\mathbf{x}_1, y_1), \ldots, (\mathbf{x}_m, y_m)\}$ for some unknown function $y = f(\mathbf{x})$. The $\mathbf{x}_i$ values are typically vectors of the form $\langle x_{i,1}, x_{i,2}, \ldots, x_{i,n} \rangle$ whose components are discrete- or real-valued such as height, weight, color, age, and so on. These are also called the *features* of $\mathbf{x}_i$. Let us use the notation x_{ij} to refer to the j-th feature of $\mathbf{x}_i$. In some situations, we will drop the i subscript when it is implied by the context.

The y values are typically drawn from a discrete set of classes $\{1, \ldots, K\}$ in the case of *classification* or from the real line in the case of *regression*. In this chapter, we will consider only classification. The training examples may be corrupted by some random noise.

Given a set S of training examples, a learning algorithm outputs a *classifier*. The classifier is an hypothesis about the true function f. Given new $\mathbf{x}$ values, it predicts the corresponding y values. I will denote classifiers by $h_1, \ldots, h_L$.

An ensemble of classifiers is a set of classifiers whose individual decisions are combined in some way (typically by weighted or unweighted voting) to classify new examples. One of the most active areas of research in supervised learning has been to study methods for constructing good ensembles of classifiers. The main discovery is that ensembles are often much more accurate than the individual classifiers that make them up.

A necessary and sufficient condition for an ensemble of classifiers to be more accurate than any of its individual members is if the classifiers are accurate and diverse (Hansen & Salamon, 1990). An accurate classifier is one that has an error rate of better than random guessing on new $\mathbf{x}$ values. Two classifiers are diverse if they make different errors on new data points. To see why accuracy and diversity are good, imagine that we have an ensemble of three classifiers: $\{h_1, h_2, h_3\}$ and consider a new case $\mathbf{x}$. If the three classifiers are identical (i.e., not diverse), then when $h_1(\mathbf{x})$ is wrong, $h_2(\mathbf{x})$ and $h_3(\mathbf{x})$ will also be wrong. However, if the errors made by the classifiers are uncorrelated, then when $h_1(\mathbf{x})$ is wrong, $h_2(\mathbf{x})$ and $h_3(\mathbf{x})$ may be correct, so that a majority vote will correctly classify $\mathbf{x}$. More precisely, if the error rates of L hypotheses h_ℓ are all equal to $p < 1/2$ and if the errors are independent, then the probability that the majority vote will be wrong will be the area under the binomial distribution where more than $L/2$ hypotheses are wrong. Figure 1 shows this for a simulated ensemble of 21 hypotheses, each having an error rate of 0.3. The area under the curve for 11 or more hypotheses being simultaneously wrong is 0.026, which is much less than the error rate of the individual hypotheses.

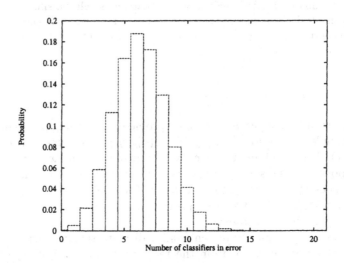

Fig. 1. The probability that exactly ℓ (of 21) hypotheses will make an error, assuming each hypothesis has an error rate of 0.3 and makes its errors independently of the other hypotheses.

Of course, if the individual hypotheses make uncorrelated errors at rates exceeding 0.5, then the error rate of the voted ensemble will *increase* as a result of the voting. Hence, one key to successful ensemble methods is to construct individual classifiers with error rates below 0.5 whose errors are at least somewhat uncorrelated.

This formal characterization of the problem is intriguing, but it does not address the question of whether it is possible in practice to construct good ensembles. Fortunately, it is often possible to construct very good ensembles. There are three fundamental reasons for this.

The first reason is statistical. A learning algorithm can be viewed as searching a space $\mathcal{H}$ of hypotheses to identify the best hypothesis in the space. The statistical problem arises when the amount of training data available is too small compared to the size of the hypothesis space. Without sufficient data, the learning algorithm can find many different hypotheses in $\mathcal{H}$ that all give the same accuracy on the training data. By constructing an ensemble out of all of these accurate classifiers, the algorithm can "average" their votes and reduce the risk of choosing the wrong classifier. Figure 2(top left) depicts this situation. The outer curve denotes the hypothesis space $\mathcal{H}$. The inner curve denotes the set of hypotheses that all give good accuracy on the training data. The point labeled f is the true hypothesis, and we can see that by averaging the accurate hypotheses, we can find a good approximation to f.

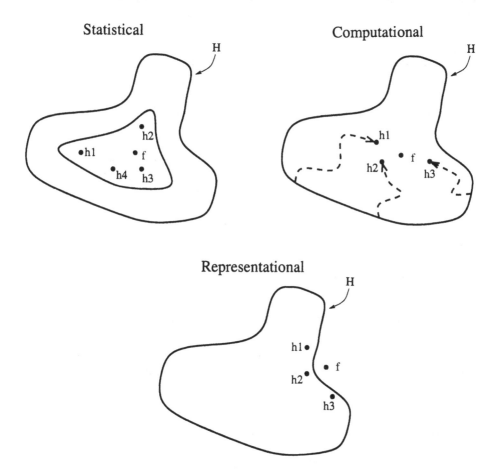

Fig. 2. Three fundamental reasons why an ensemble may work better than a single classifier

The second reason is computational. Many learning algorithms work by performing some form of local search that may get stuck in local optima. For example, neural network algorithms employ gradient descent to minimize an error function over the training data, and decision tree algorithms employ a greedy splitting rule to grow the decision tree. In cases where there is enough training data (so that the statistical problem is absent), it may still be very difficult computationally for the learning algorithm to find the best hypothesis. Indeed, optimal training of both neural networks and decisions trees is NP-hard (Hyafil & Rivest, 1976; Blum & Rivest, 1988). An ensemble constructed by running the local search from many different starting points may provide a better approximation to the true unknown function than any of the individual classifiers, as shown in Figure 2 (top right).

The third reason is representational. In most applications of machine learning, the true function f cannot be represented by any of the hypotheses in $\mathcal{H}$. By forming weighted sums of hypotheses drawn from $\mathcal{H}$, it may be possible to expand the space of representable functions. Figure 2 (bottom) depicts this situation.

The representational issue is somewhat subtle, because there are many learning algorithms for which $\mathcal{H}$ is, in principle, the space of all possible classifiers. For example, neural networks and decision trees are both very flexible algorithms. Given enough training data, they will explore the space of all possible classifiers, and several people have proved asymptotic representation theorems for them (Hornik, Stinchcombe, & White, 1990). Nonetheless, with a finite training sample, these algorithms will explore only a finite set of hypotheses and they will stop searching when they find an hypothesis that fits the training data. Hence, in Figure 2, we must consider the space $\mathcal{H}$ to be the effective space of hypotheses searched by the learning algorithm for a given training data set.

These three fundamental issues are the three most important ways in which existing learning algorithms fail. Hence, ensemble methods have the promise of reducing (and perhaps even eliminating) these three key shortcomings of standard learning algorithms.

2 Methods for Constructing Ensembles

Many methods for constructing ensembles have been developed. Here we will review general purpose methods that can be applied to many different learning algorithms.

2.1 Bayesian Voting: Enumerating the Hypotheses

In a Bayesian probabilistic setting, each hypothesis h defines a conditional probability distribution: $h(\mathbf{x}) = P(f(\mathbf{x}) = y|\mathbf{x}, h)$. Given a new data point $\mathbf{x}$ and a training sample S, the problem of predicting the value of $f(\mathbf{x})$ can be viewed as the problem of computing $P(f(\mathbf{x}) = y|S, \mathbf{x})$. We can rewrite this as weighted sum over all hypotheses in $\mathcal{H}$:

$$P(f(\mathbf{x}) = y | S, \mathbf{x}) = \sum_{h \in \mathcal{H}} h(\mathbf{x}) P(h|S).$$

We can view this as an ensemble method in which the ensemble consists of all of the hypotheses in $\mathcal{H}$, each weighted by its posterior probability $P(h|S)$. By Bayes rule, the posterior probability is proportional to the likelihood of the training data times the prior probability of h:

$$P(h|S) \propto P(S|h) P(h).$$

In some learning problems, it is possible to completely enumerate each $h \in \mathcal{H}$, compute $P(S|h)$ and $P(h)$, and (after normalization), evaluate this Bayesian "committee." Furthermore, if the true function f is drawn from $\mathcal{H}$ according to $P(h)$, then the Bayesian voting scheme is optimal.

Bayesian voting primarily addresses the statistical component of ensembles. When the training sample is small, many hypotheses h will have significantly large posterior probabilities, and the voting process can average these to "marginalize away" the remaining uncertainty about f. When the training sample is large, typically only one hypothesis has substantial posterior probability, and the "ensemble" effectively shrinks to contain only a single hypothesis.

In complex problems where $\mathcal{H}$ cannot be enumerated, it is sometimes possible to approximate Bayesian voting by drawing a random sample of hypotheses distributed according to $P(h|S)$. Recent work on Markov chain Monte Carlo methods (Neal, 1993) seeks to develop a set of tools for this task.

The most idealized aspect of the Bayesian analysis is the prior belief $P(h)$. If this prior completely captures all of the knowledge that we have about f before we obtain S, then by definition we cannot do better. But in practice, it is often difficult to construct a space $\mathcal{H}$ and assign a prior $P(h)$ that captures our prior knowledge adequately. Indeed, often $\mathcal{H}$ and $P(h)$ are chosen for computational convenience, and they are known to be inadequate. In such cases, the Bayesian committee is not optimal, and other ensemble methods may produce better results. In particular, the Bayesian approach does not address the computational and representational problems in any significant way.

2.2 Manipulating the Training Examples

The second method for constructing ensembles manipulates the training examples to generate multiple hypotheses. The learning algorithm is run several times, each time with a different subset of the training examples. This technique works especially well for *unstable* learning algorithms—algorithms whose output classifier undergoes major changes in response to small changes in the training data. Decision-tree, neural network, and rule learning algorithms are all unstable. Linear regression, nearest neighbor, and linear threshold algorithms are generally very stable.

The most straightforward way of manipulating the training set is called *Bagging*. On each run, Bagging presents the learning algorithm with a training set that consists of a sample of m training examples drawn randomly with replacement from the original training set of m items. Such a training set is called a *bootstrap replicate* of the original training set, and the technique is called *bootstrap aggregation* (from which the term *Bagging* is derived; Breiman, 1996). Each bootstrap replicate contains, on the average, 63.2% of the original training set, with several training examples appearing multiple times.

Another training set sampling method is to construct the training sets by leaving out disjoint subsets of the training data. For example, the training set can be randomly divided into 10 disjoint subsets. Then 10 overlapping training sets can be constructed by dropping out a different one of these 10 subsets. This same procedure is employed to construct training sets for 10-fold cross-validation, so ensembles constructed in this way are sometimes called *cross-validated committees* (Parmanto, Munro, & Doyle, 1996).

The third method for manipulating the training set is illustrated by the ADABOOST algorithm, developed by Freund and Schapire (1995, 1996, 1997, 1998). Like Bagging, ADABOOST manipulates the training examples to generate multiple hypotheses. ADABOOST maintains a set of weights over the training examples. In each iteration ℓ, the learning algorithm is invoked to minimize the weighted error on the training set, and it returns an hypothesis h_ℓ. The weighted error of h_ℓ is computed and applied to update the weights on the training examples. The effect of the change in weights is to place more weight on training examples that were misclassified by h_ℓ and less weight on examples that were correctly classified. In subsequent iterations, therefore, ADABOOST constructs progressively more difficult learning problems.

The final classifier, $h_f(x) = \sum_\ell w_\ell h_\ell(x)$, is constructed by a weighted vote of the individual classifiers. Each classifier is weighted (by w_ℓ) according to its accuracy on the weighted training set that it was trained on.

Recent research (Schapire & Singer, 1998) has shown that ADABOOST can be viewed as a stage-wise algorithm for minimizing a particular error function. To define this error function, suppose that each training example is labeled as $+1$ or -1, corresponding to the positive and negative examples. Then the quantity $m_i = y_i h(x_i)$ is positive if h correctly classifies x_i and negative otherwise. This quantity m_i is called the *margin* of classifier h on the training data. ADABOOST can be seen as trying to minimize

$$\sum_i exp\left(-y_i \sum_\ell w_\ell h_\ell(x_i)\right), \tag{1}$$

which is the negative exponential of the margin of the weighted voted classifier. This can also be viewed as attempting to maximize the margin on the training data.

2.3 Manipulating the Input Features

A third general technique for generating multiple classifiers is to manipulate the set of *input features* available to the learning algorithm. For example, in a project to identify volcanoes on Venus, Cherkauer (1996) trained an ensemble of 32 neural networks. The 32 networks were based on 8 different subsets of the 119 available input features and 4 different network sizes. The input feature subsets were selected (by hand) to group together features that were based on different image processing operations (such as principal component analysis and the fast fourier transform). The resulting ensemble classifier was able to match the performance of human experts in identifying volcanoes. Tumer and Ghosh (1996) applied a similar technique to a sonar dataset with 25 input features. However, they found that deleting even a few of the input features hurt the performance of the individual classifiers so much that the voted ensemble did not perform very well. Obviously, this technique only works when the input features are highly redundant.

2.4 Manipulating the Output Targets

A fourth general technique for constructing a good ensemble of classifiers is to manipulate the y values that are given to the learning algorithm. Dietterich & Bakiri (1995) describe a technique called error-correcting output coding. Suppose that the number of classes, K, is large. Then new learning problems can be constructed by randomly partioning the K classes into two subsets A_ℓ and B_ℓ. The input data can then be re-labeled so that any of the original classes in set A_ℓ are given the derived label 0 and the original classes in set B_ℓ are given the derived label 1. This relabeled data is then given to the learning algorithm, which constructs a classifier h_ℓ. By repeating this process L times (generating different subsets A_ℓ and B_ℓ), we obtain an ensemble of L classifiers $h_1, \ldots, h_L$.

Now given a new data point $\mathbf{x}$, how should we classify it? The answer is to have each h_ℓ classify $\mathbf{x}$. If $h_\ell(\mathbf{x}) = 0$, then each class in A_ℓ receives a vote. If $h_\ell(\mathbf{x}) = 1$, then each class in B_ℓ receives a vote. After each of the L classifiers has voted, the class with the highest number of votes is selected as the prediction of the ensemble.

An equivalent way of thinking about this method is that each class j is encoded as an L-bit codeword C_j, where bit ℓ is 1 if and only if $j \in B_\ell$. The ℓ-th learned classifier attempts to predict bit ℓ of these codewords. When the L classifiers are applied to classify a new point $\mathbf{x}$, their predictions are combined into an L-bit string. We then choose the class j whose codeword C_j is closest (in Hamming distance) to the L-bit output string. Methods for designing good error-correcting codes can be applied to choose the codewords C_j (or equivalently, subsets A_ℓ and B_ℓ).

Dietterich and Bakiri report that this technique improves the performance of both the C4.5 decision tree algorithm and the backpropagation neural network algorithm on a variety of difficult classification problems. Recently, Schapire

(1997) has shown how ADABOOST can be combined with error-correcting output coding to yield an excellent ensemble classification method that he calls ADABOOST.OC. The performance of the method is superior to the ECOC method (and to Bagging), but essentially the same as another (quite complex) algorithm, called ADABOOST.M2. Hence, the main advantage of ADABOOST.OC is implementation simplicity: It can work with any learning algorithm for solving 2-class problems.

Ricci and Aha (1997) applied a method that combines error-correcting output coding with feature selection. When learning each classifier, h_ℓ, they apply feature selection techniques to choose the best features for learning that classifier. They obtained improvements in 7 out of 10 tasks with this approach.

2.5 Injecting Randomness

The last general purpose method for generating ensembles of classifiers is to inject randomness into the learning algorithm. In the backpropagation algorithm for training neural networks, the initial weights of the network are set randomly. If the algorithm is applied to the same training examples but with different initial weights, the resulting classifier can be quite different (Kolen & Pollack, 1991).

While this is perhaps the most common way of generating ensembles of neural networks, manipulating the training set may be more effective. A study by Parmanto, Munro, and Doyle (1996) compared this technique to Bagging and to 10-fold cross-validated committees. They found that cross-validated committees worked best, Bagging second best, and multiple random initial weights third best on one synthetic data set and two medical diagnosis data sets.

For the C4.5 decision tree algorithm, it is also easy to inject randomness (Kwok & Carter, 1990; Dietterich, 2000). The key decision of C4.5 is to choose a feature to test at each internal node in the decision tree. At each internal node, C4.5 applies a criterion known as the information gain ratio to rank-order the various possible feature tests. It then chooses the top-ranked feature-value test. For discrete-valued features with V values, the decision tree splits the data into V subsets, depending on the value of the chosen feature. For real-valued features, the decision tree splits the data into 2 subsets, depending on whether the value of the chosen feature is above or below a chosen threshold. Dietterich (2000) implemented a variant of C4.5 that chooses randomly (with equal probability) among the top 20 best tests. Figure 3 compares the performance of a single run of C4.5 to ensembles of 200 classifiers over 33 different data sets. For each data set, a point is plotted. If that point lies below the diagonal line, then the ensemble has lower error rate than C4.5. We can see that nearly all of the points lie below the line. A statistical analysis shows that the randomized trees do statistically significantly better than a single decision tree on 14 of the data sets and statistically the same in the remaining 19 data sets.

Ali & Pazzani (1996) injected randomness into the FOIL algorithm for learning Prolog-style rules. FOIL works somewhat like C4.5 in that it ranks possible conditions to add to a rule using an information-gain criterion. Ali and Pazzani

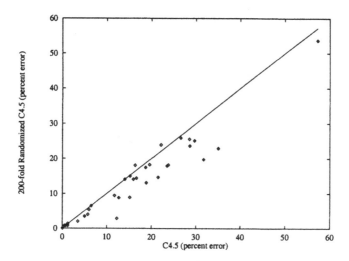

Fig. 3. Comparison of the error rate of C4.5 to an ensemble of 200 decision trees constructed by injecting randomness into C4.5 and then taking a uniform vote.

computed all candidate conditions that scored within 80% of the top-ranked candidate, and then applied a weighted random choice algorithm to choose among them. They compared ensembles of 11 classifiers to a single run of FOIL and found statistically significant improvements in 15 out of 29 tasks and statistically significant loss of performance in only one task. They obtained similar results using 11-fold cross-validation to construct the training sets.

Raviv and Intrator (1996) combine bootstrap sampling of the training data with injecting noise into the input features for the learning algorithm. To train each member of an ensemble of neural networks, they draw training examples with replacement from the original training data. The x values of each training example are perturbed by adding Gaussian noise to the input features. They report large improvements in a synthetic benchmark task and a medical diagnosis task.

Finally, note that Markov chain Monte Carlo methods for constructing Bayesian ensembles also work by injecting randomness into the learning process. However, instead of taking a uniform vote, as we did with the randomized decision trees, each hypothesis receives a vote proportional to its posterior probability.

3 Comparing Different Ensemble Methods

Several experimental studies have been performed to compare ensemble methods. The largest of these are the studies by Bauer and Kohavi (1999) and by Dietterich (2000). Table 1 summarizes the results of Dietterich's study. The table shows that ADABOOST often gives the best results. Bagging and randomized trees give similar performance, although randomization is able to do better in some cases than Bagging on very large data sets.

Table 1. All pairwise combinations of the four ensemble methods. Each cell contains the number of wins, losses, and ties between the algorithm in that row and the algorithm in that column.

	C4.5	AdaBoost C4.5	Bagged C4.5
Random C4.5	14 – 0 – 19	1 – 7 – 25	6 – 3 – 24
Bagged C4.5	11 – 0 – 22	1 – 8 – 24	
AdaBoost C4.5	17 – 0 – 16		

Most of the data sets in this study had little or no noise. When 20% artificial classification noise was added to the 9 domains where Bagging and AdaBoost gave different performance, the results shifted radically as shown in Table 2. Under these conditions, AdaBoost overfits the data badly while Bagging is shown to work very well in the presence of noise. Randomized trees did not do very well.

Table 2. All pairwise combinations of C4.5, AdaBoosted C4.5, Bagged C4.5, and Randomized C4.5 on 9 domains with 20% synthetic class label noise. Each cell contains the number of wins, losses, and ties between the algorithm in that row and the algorithm in that column.

	C4.5	AdaBoost C4.5	Bagged C4.5
Random C4.5	5 – 2 – 2	5 – 0 – 4	0 – 2 – 7
Bagged C4.5	7 – 0 – 2	6 – 0 – 3	
AdaBoost C4.5	3 – 6 – 0		

The key to understanding these results is to return again to the three shortcomings of existing learning algorithms: statistical support, computation, and representation. For the decision-tree algorithm C4.5, all three of these problems can arise. Decision trees essentially partition the input feature space into rectangular regions whose sides are perpendicular to the coordinate axes. Each rectangular region corresponds to one leaf node of the tree.

If the true function f can be represented by a small decision tree, then C4.5 will work well without any ensemble. If the true function can be correctly represented by a large decision tree, then C4.5 will need a very large training data set in order to find a good fit, and the statistical problem will arise.

The computational problem arises because finding the best (i.e., smallest) decision tree consistent with the training data is computationally intractable, so C4.5 makes a series of decisions greedily. If one of these decisions is made incorrectly, then the training data will be incorrectly partitioned, and all subsequent decisions are likely to be affected. Hence, C4.5 is highly unstable, and small changes in the training set can produce large changes in the resulting decision tree.

The representational problem arises because of the use of rectangular partitions of the input space. If the true decision boundaries are not orthogonal to the coordinate axes, then C4.5 requires a tree of infinite size to represent those boundaries correctly. Interestingly, a voted combination of small decision trees is equivalent to a much larger single tree, and hence, an ensemble method can construct a good approximation to a diagonal decision boundary using several small trees. Figure 4 shows an example of this. On the left side of the figure are plotted three decision boundaries constructed by three decision trees, each of which uses 5 internal nodes. On the right is the boundary that results from a simple majority vote of these trees. It is equivalent to a single tree with 13 internal nodes, and it is much more accurate than any one of the three individual trees.

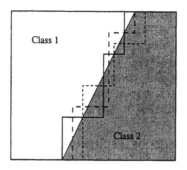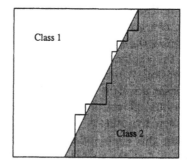

Fig. 4. The left figure shows the true diagonal decision boundary and three staircase approximations to it (of the kind that are created by decision tree algorithms). The right figure shows the voted decision boundary, which is a much better approximation to the diagonal boundary.

Now let us consider the three algorithms: ADABOOST, Bagging, and Randomized trees. Bagging and Randomization both construct each decision tree independently of the others. Bagging accomplishes this by manipulating the input data, and Randomization directly alters the choices of C4.5. These methods are acting somewhat like Bayesian voting; they are sampling from the space of all possible hypotheses with a bias toward hypotheses that give good accuracy on the training data. Consequently, their main effect will be to address the statistical problem and, to a lesser extent, the computational problem. But they do not directly attempt to overcome the representational problem.

In contrast, ADABOOST constructs each new decision tree to eliminate "residual" errors that have not been properly handled by the weighted vote of the previously-constructed trees. ADABOOST is directly trying to optimize the weighted vote. Hence, it is making a direct assault on the representational problem. Directly optimizing an ensemble can increase the risk of overfitting, because the space of ensembles is usually much larger than the hypothesis space of the original algorithm.

This explanation is consistent with the experimental results given above. In low-noise cases, ADABOOST gives good performance, because it is able to optimize the ensemble without overfitting. However, in high-noise cases, ADABOOST puts a large amount of weight on the mislabeled examples, and this leads it to overfit very badly. Bagging and Randomization do well in both the noisy and noise-free cases, because they are focusing on the statistical problem, and noise increases this statistical problem.

Finally, we can understand that in very large datasets, Randomization can be expected to do better than Bagging because bootstrap replicates of a large training set are very similar to the training set itself, and hence, the learned decision tree will not be very diverse. Randomization creates diversity under all conditions, but at the risk of generating low-quality decision trees.

Despite the plausibility of this explanation, there is still one important open question concerning ADABOOST. Given that ADABOOST aggressively attempts to maximize the margins on the training set, why doesn't it overfit more often? Part of the explanation may lie in the "stage-wise" nature of ADABOOST. In each iteration, it reweights the training examples, constructs a new hypothesis, and chooses a weight w_ℓ for that hypothesis. It never "backs up" and modifies the previous choices of hypotheses or weights that it has made to compensate for this new hypothesis.

To test this explanation, I conducted a series of simple experiments on synthetic data. Let the true classifier f be a simple decision rule that tests just one feature (feature 0) and assigns the example to class $+1$ if the feature is 1, and to class -1 if the feature is 0. Now construct training (and testing) examples by generating feature vectors of length 100 at random as follows. Generate feature 0 (the important feature) at random. Then generate each of the other features randomly to agree with feature 0 with probability 0.8 and to disagree otherwise. Assign labels to each training example according to the true function f, but with 10% random classification noise. This creates a difficult learning problem for simple decision rules of this kind (decision stumps), because all 100 features are correlated with the class. Still, a large ensemble should be able to do well on this problem by voting separate decision stumps for each feature.

I constructed a version of ADABOOST that works more aggressively than standard ADABOOST. After every new hypothesis h_ℓ is constructed and its weight assigned, my version performs a gradient descent search to minimize the negative exponential margin (equation 1). Hence, this algorithm reconsiders the weights of all of the learned hypotheses after each new hypothesis is added. Then it reweights the training examples to reflect the revised hypothesis weights.

Figure 5 shows the results when training on a training set of size 20. The plot confirms our explanation. The Aggressive ADABOOST initially has much higher error rates on the test set than Standard ADABOOST. It then gradually improves. Meanwhile, Standard ADABOOST initially obtains excellent performance on the test set, but then it overfits as more and more classifiers are added to the ensemble. In the limit, both ensembles should have the same representational properties, because they are both minimizing the same function (equation 1). But we can see that the exceptionally good performance of Standard ADABOOST on this problem is due to the stage-wise optimization process, which is slow to fit the data.

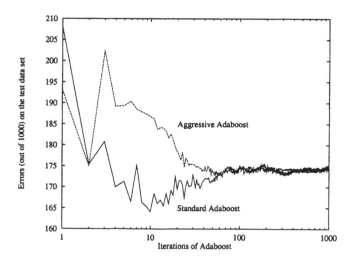

Fig. 5. Aggressive ADABOOST exhibits much worse performance than Standard AD-ABOOST on a challenging synthetic problem

4   Conclusions

Ensembles are well-established as a method for obtaining highly accurate classifiers by combining less accurate ones. This paper has provided a brief survey of methods for constructing ensembles and reviewed the three fundamental reasons why ensemble methods are able to out-perform any single classifier within the ensemble. The paper has also provided some experimental results to elucidate one of the reasons why ADABOOST performs so well.

One open question not discussed in this paper concerns the interaction between ADABOOST and the properties of the underlying learning algorithm. Most of the learning algorithms that have been combined with ADABOOST have been algorithms of a global character (i.e., algorithms that learn a relatively low-dimensional decision boundary). It would be interesting to see whether local algorithms (such as radial basis functions and nearest neighbor methods) can be profitably combined via ADABOOST to yield interesting new learning algorithms.

Bibliography

Ali, K. M., & Pazzani, M. J. (1996). Error reduction through learning multiple descriptions. *Machine Learning, 24*(3), 173–202.

Bauer, E., & Kohavi, R. (1999). An empirical comparison of voting classification algorithms: Bagging, boosting, and variants. *Machine Learning, 36*(1/2), 105–139.

Blum, A., & Rivest, R. L. (1988). Training a 3-node neural network is NP-Complete (Extended abstract). In *Proceedings of the 1988 Workshop on Computational Learning Theory*, pp. 9–18 San Francisco, CA. Morgan Kaufmann.

Breiman, L. (1996). Bagging predictors. *Machine Learning, 24*(2), 123–140.

Cherkauer, K. J. (1996). Human expert-level performance on a scientific image analysis task by a system using combined artificial neural networks. In Chan, P. (Ed.), *Working Notes of the AAAI Workshop on Integrating Multiple Learned Models*, pp. 15–21. Available from http://www.cs.fit.edu/~imlm/.

Dietterich, T. G. (2000). An experimental comparison of three methods for constructing ensembles of decision trees: Bagging, boosting, and randomization. *Machine Learning*.

Dietterich, T. G., & Bakiri, G. (1995). Solving multiclass learning problems via error-correcting output codes. *Journal of Artificial Intelligence Research, 2*, 263–286.

Freund, Y., & Schapire, R. E. (1995). A decision-theoretic generalization of on-line learning and an application to boosting. Tech. rep., AT&T Bell Laboratories, Murray Hill, NJ.

Freund, Y., & Schapire, R. E. (1996). Experiments with a new boosting algorithm. In *Proc. 13th International Conference on Machine Learning*, pp. 148–146. Morgan Kaufmann.

Hansen, L., & Salamon, P. (1990). Neural network ensembles. *IEEE Trans. Pattern Analysis and Machine Intell., 12*, 993–1001.

Hornik, K., Stinchcombe, M., & White, H. (1990). Universal approximation of an unknown mapping and its derivatives using multilayer feedforward networks. *Neural Networks, 3*, 551–560.

Hyafil, L., & Rivest, R. L. (1976). Constructing optimal binary decision trees is NP-Complete. *Information Processing Letters, 5*(1), 15–17.

Kolen, J. F., & Pollack, J. B. (1991). Back propagation is sensitive to initial conditions. In *Advances in Neural Information Processing Systems*, Vol. 3, pp. 860–867 San Francisco, CA. Morgan Kaufmann.

Kwok, S. W., & Carter, C. (1990). Multiple decision trees. In Schachter, R. D., Levitt, T. S., Kannal, L. N., & Lemmer, J. F. (Eds.), *Uncertainty in Artificial Intelligence 4*, pp. 327–335. Elsevier Science, Amsterdam.

Neal, R. (1993). Probabilistic inference using Markov chain Monte Carlo methods. Tech. rep. CRG-TR-93-1, Department of Computer Science, University of Toronto, Toronto, CA.

Parmanto, B., Munro, P. W., & Doyle, H. R. (1996). Improving committee diagnosis with resampling techniques. In Touretzky, D. S., Mozer, M. C., & Hesselmo, M. E. (Eds.), *Advances in Neural Information Processing Systems*, Vol. 8, pp. 882–888 Cambridge, MA. MIT Press.

Raviv, Y., & Intrator, N. (1996). Bootstrapping with noise: An effective regularization technique. *Connection Science, 8*(3–4), 355–372.

Ricci, F., & Aha, D. W. (1997). Extending local learners with error-correcting output codes. Tech. rep., Naval Center for Applied Research in Artificial Intelligence, Washington, D.C.

Schapire, R. E. (1997). Using output codes to boost multiclass learning problems. In *Proceedings of the Fourteenth International Conference on Machine Learning*, pp. 313–321 San Francisco, CA. Morgan Kaufmann.

Schapire, R. E., Freund, Y., Bartlett, P., & Lee, W. S. (1997). Boosting the margin: A new explanation for the effectiveness of voting methods. In Fisher, D. (Ed.), *Machine Learning: Proceedings of the Fourteenth International Conference*. Morgan Kaufmann.

Schapire, R. E., & Singer, Y. (1998). Improved boosting algorithms using confidence-rated predictions. In *Proc. 11th Annu. Conf. on Comput. Learning Theory*, pp. 80–91. ACM Press, New York, NY.

Tumer, K., & Ghosh, J. (1996). Error correlation and error reduction in ensemble classifiers. *Connection Science, 8*(3–4), 385–404.

Experiments with Classifier Combining Rules

Robert P.W. Duin, David M.J. Tax

Pattern Recognition Group, Department of Applied Physics
Delft University of Technology, The Netherlands[1]

Abstract. A large experiment on combining classifiers is reported and discussed. It includes, both, the combination of different classifiers on the same feature set and the combination of classifiers on different feature sets. Various fixed and trained combining rules are used. It is shown that there is no overall winning combining rule and that bad classifiers as well as bad feature sets may contain valuable information for performance improvement by combining rules. Best performance is achieved by combining both, different feature sets and different classifiers.

1 Introduction

It has become clear that for more complicated data sets the traditional set of classifiers can be improved by various types of combining rules. Often none of the basic set of traditional classifiers, ranging from Bayes-normal to Decision Trees, Neural Networks and Support Vector Classifiers (see section 3) is powerful enough to distinguish the pattern classes optimally as they are represented by the given feature sets. Different classifiers may be desired for different features, or may reveal different possibilities for separating the data. The outputs of the input classifiers can be regarded as a mapping to an intermediate space. A combining classifier applied on this space then makes a final decision for the class of a new object.

Three large groups of combining classifiers will be distinguished here as follows:

- *Parallel combining* of classifiers computed for different feature sets. This may be especially useful if the objects are represented by different feature sets, when they are described in different physical domains (e.g. sound and vision) or when they are processed by different types of analysis (e.g. moments and frequencies).
  The original set of features may also be split into subsets in order to reduce the dimensionality and hopefully the accuracy of a single classifier. Parallel classifiers are often, but not necessarily, of the same type.

- *Stacked combining* of different classifiers computed for the same feature space. Stacked classifiers may be of a different nature, e.g. the combination of a neural network, a nearest neighbour classifier and a parametric decision rule.

1. *Author's address:* Department of Applied Physics, Delft University of Technology, Lorentzweg 1, 2628CJ Delft, The Netherlands,
Tel: +31 (15) 278 6143. *Fax:* +31 (15) 278 6740.
E-mail: duin@ph.tn.tudelft.nl. *WWW:* http://www.ph.tn.tudelft.nl/~duin.

J. Kittler and F. Roli (Eds.): MCS 2000, LNCS 1857, pp. 16–29, 2000.
© Springer-Verlag Berlin Heidelberg 2000

- Combining weak classifiers. In this case large sets of simple classifiers are trained (e.g. based on decision trees or the nearest mean rule) on modified versions of the original dataset. Three heavily studied modifications are bootstrapping (bagging), reweighting the data (boosting) and using random subspaces.

For all cases the question arises how the input classifiers should be combined. Various possibilities exist, based on fixed rules like maximum selection, product and majority voting. In addition one may also train a classifier, treating the classifier outputs in the intermediate space as feature values for the output classifier. An important condition is that the outputs of the input classifiers are scaled in one way or another such that they constitute the intermediate space in some homogeneous way.

In this paper we illustrate some issues of combining on a large example. This example has partially been published before [8] in the context of a review on the entire field of statistical pattern recognition. Here additional details will be given, together with a more extensive analysis that, due to lack of space, could not be presented in the original paper. In the next sections the data, the input classifiers and the output classifiers will be presented. Next the results are discussed and analysed. We like to emphasize that it is not our purpose to classify the given dataset optimally, in one way or another. It is merely our aim to illustrate various combining possibilities and analyse the effects on the performance. Leading questions in this analysis will be: when are which combining rules useful? How does this depend on the dataset? How do the input classifiers have to be configured? What is the influence of the combining rule on the final result?

2   The data set

The experiments are done on a data set which consists of six different feature sets for the same set of objects. It contains 2000 handwritten numerals extracted from a set of Dutch utility maps. For each of the ten classes'0', ... ,'9' a set of 200 objects is available. In all experiments we assumed that the 10 classes have equal class probabilities $P_j = 0.1, j = 1, ..., 10$. Each of the classes is split in a fixed set of 100 objects for learning and 100 for testing. Because of computational limitations, we use a fixed subset of only 50 objects per class for training. The six feature sets are:

- Fourier: 76 Fourier coefficients of the character shapes.
- Profiles: 216 profile correlations.
- KL-coef: 64 Karhunen-Loève coefficients.
- Pixel: 240 pixel averages in 2 x 3 windows.
- Zernike: 47 Zernike moments.
- Morph: 6 morphological features.

A slightly different version of this data set has been used in [9]. The presently used data is publicly available under the name 'mfeat' in the Machine Learning Repository [11].

All characters are originally sampled in a 30*48 binary image. The features are all computed from these images and are therefore not strictly independent. In figure 1 the performance for the Fisher classifier is shown for the first 9 principal directions in the Fisher map (i.e. the subspace that maximizes the between scatter of the classes over the averaged within scatter). In figure 2 the 2-dimensional Fisher maps are shown. It is

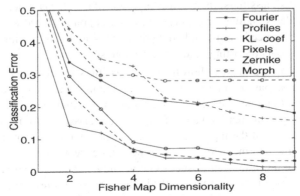

Fig. 1 The Fisher classification error for the six feature
sets optimally projected on low-dimensional subspaces.

hoped these mappings find the most separating directions in the data, and thus reveal
the clusters in the data. Each class is labelled in these figures by one unique marker in
all datasets. In the Morph dataset the features have discrete values. One class can be separated but for other classes (e.g. one with the white circular label) the discrete feature
deteriorates the cluster characteristics. In most feature sets nice clusters can be distinguished. The scaling of the features is comparable over all feature sets. This is caused
by the fact that as a part of the Fisher mapping the data is prewithened to unit variance.

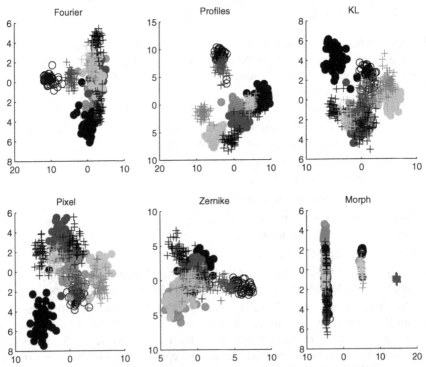

Fig. 2 Scatter plots of all six datasets, mapped on the 2-dimensional Fisher map

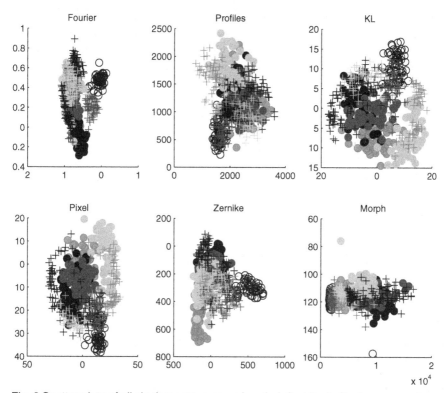

Fig. 3 Scatter plots of all six datasets, mapped on their first 2 principal components

In figure 3 scatter plots of the first two principal components (PCA) of the six datasets are shown. Note the differences in scaling for the various feature sets, which is preserved in these mappings. The PCA plots are focused on the data distributions as a whole, while the Fisher mapping emphasizes the class differences. Although it is not possible to extract quantitative features from these plots, they show that the data sets have quite distinct class distributions.

3   The classifiers

For this experiment we used a set of off-the-shelf classifiers taken from our Matlab toolbox PRTools [12]. They were not optimized for the particular application. In this way they illustrate well the differences between these classifiers, and, moreover, it serves better the aim to study the effects of combining classifiers of various performances. As argued in the introduction, it is important to make the outputs of the classifiers comparable. We use estimates for the posterior probabilities or confidences. This is a number $p_j(x)$, bounded between 0 and 1 computed for test objects x for each of the c classes the classifiers are trained on. These numbers are normalized such that:

$$\sum_{j}^{c} p_j(x) = 1 \tag{4}$$

We will now shortly discuss the set of basic classifiers.

Bayes-normal-2: This is the Bayes rule assuming normal distributions. For each class a separate covariance matrix is estimated, yielding quadratic decision boundaries. Because of the size of the training set (50 objects per class) and the large set of features, regularization is necessary. This was done by estimating the covariance matrix C for the scatter matrix S by

$$C = (1 - \alpha - \beta)S + \alpha \text{diag}(S) + \frac{\beta}{n}\sum \text{diag}(S) \tag{5}$$

in which n is the dimensionality of the feature space. We used $\alpha = \beta = 10^{-6}$. Posterior probabilities are computed from the estimated class densities $f_j(x)$:

$$p_j(x) = \frac{P_j f_j(x)}{\sum_i P_i f_i(x)} \tag{6}$$

Bayes-normal-1: This rule is similar to Bayes-normal-2, except that all classes are assumed to have the same covariance matrix. The decision boundaries are thereby linear.

Nearest Mean: Objects are assigned to the class of the nearest mean. Posterior probabilities are estimated using a sigmoid function over the distance. This is optimized over the training set using the maximum likelihood rule [10].

Nearest Neighbour (1-NN): Objects are assigned to the class of the nearest object in the training set. Posterior probabilities are estimated by comparing the nearest neighbour distances for all classes [10].

k-Nearest Neighbour (k-NN): Objects are assigned to the class having the majority in the k nearest neighbours in the training set. For $k > 2$ posterior probabilities are estimated using the class frequencies in the set of k neighbours. For $k = 1$, see the 1-NN rule. The value of k is optimized for the training set using a leave-one-out error estimation.

Parzen Classifier: Class densities are estimated using Gaussian kernels for each training object. The kernel width is optimized for the training set using a leave-one-out error estimation. Posterior probabilities are computed according to (6).

Fisher's Linear Discriminant (FLD): We computed a FLD between each of the 10 classes and all other classes. For each of these classifiers posterior probabilities are computed using a sigmoid over the distance to the discriminant. These sigmoids are optimized separately over the training set using the maximum likelihood rule [3]. Test objects are assigned to the class with the highest posterior probability. For two-class problems, this classifier is almost equivalent (except for the way posterior probabilities are computed) to Bayes-normal-1. For multi-class problems these rules are essentially different.

Decision Tree: Our algorithm computes a binary decision tree on the multi-class dataset. Thresholds are set such that the impurity is minimized in each step [1]. Early pruning is used in order avoid overtraining [2]. Posterior probabilities are estimated by the class frequencies of the training set in each end node.

Artificial Neural Network with 20 hidden units (ANN-20): This is a standard feedforward network with one hidden layer of 20 neurons and sigmoid transfer functions.

The network is trained by the back-propagation rule using the Matlab Neural Network toolbox [13]. The 10 output values are normalized and used as posterior probabilities.

Artificial Neural Network with 50 hidden units (ANN-50): The same algorithm as above, but now using 50 neurons in the hidden layer.

Support Vector Classifier with linear kernel (SVC-1): This is the standard SVC using a linear inner product kernel [3]. The computation of the multi-class classifier as well as the posterior probabilities is similar to the procedure described above for the FLD.

Support Vector Classifier with quadratic kernel (SVC-2): In this case the squares of the inner products are used as a kernel, resulting in quadratic decision boundaries.

4 The combining rules

Once a set of posterior probabilities $\{p_{ij}(x), i = 1,m; j = 1,c\}$ for m classifiers and c classes is computed for test object x, they have to be combined into a new set $q_j(x)$ that can be used, by maximum selection, for the final classification. We distinguish two sets of rules, fixed combiners and trained combiners.

4.1 Fixed combining rules

Fixed combiners are heavily studied in the literature on combining classifiers, e.g. see [4], [5] and [6]. The new confidence $q_j(x)$ for class j is now computed by:

$$q_j'(x) = \text{rule}_i(p_{ij}(x)) \tag{7}$$

$$q_j(x) = \frac{q_j'(x)}{\sum_j q_j'(x)} \tag{8}$$

The following combiners are used for rule in (7): **Maximum, Median, Mean, Minimum, Product.** Note that the final classification is made by

$$\omega(x) = \arg\max_j(q_j(x)) \tag{9}$$

The Maximum rule selects the classifier producing the highest estimated confidence, which seems to be noise sensitive. In contrast, the Minimum rule selects by (9) the classifier having the least objection. Median and Mean average the posterior probability estimates thereby reducing estimation errors. This is good, of course, if the individual classifiers are estimating the same quantity. This probably will not hold for some of the classifiers discussed in section 3.

A popular way of combining classifiers is **Majority**: count the votes for each class over the input classifiers and select the majority class. This fits in the above framework if this rule is substituted in (7):

$$q_j'(x) = \sum_i I(\arg\max_i(p_{ij}(x)) = i) \tag{10}$$

in which $I()$ is the indicator function: $I(y) = 1$ if y is true and $I(y) = 0$ otherwise.

4.2   Trained combining rules

Instead of using fixed combination rules, one can also train an arbitrary classifier using the $m \times c$ values of $p_{ij}(x)$ (for all i and all j) as features in the intermediate space. The following classifiers are trained as an output classifier, using the same training set as we used for the input classifiers, see section 3: **Bayes-normal-2**, **Bayes-normal-1**, **Nearest Mean** and **1-NN**.

It is point of discussion whether it is wise to use the posterior probabilities directly for building the intermediate feature space. The classes may be far from normally distributed. It might therefore be advantageous to apply some nonlinear rescaling. The use of the Nearest Mean classifier on the posterior probabilities is almost equivalent to the procedure of fuzzy template matching as investigated by Kuncheva et. al. [7].

5   The experiment

In table 1 the obtained test errors x 1000 are listed. The top-left section of this table lists the results for all 12 individual classifiers for all feature sets combined and for the 6 feature sets individually. The combined result is only occasionally somewhat better than the best individual result. The is caused by the high dimensionality of the combined set (649) as well as by differences in scaling of the features. The best results for each feature set separately (column) by an individual classifier are underlined. For instance, an error of 0.037 is obtained, among others, by the 1-NN rule for the Pixels dataset. Because the entire test set contains 10 x 100 = 1000 objects the number 37 is in fact the number of erroneously classified test objects. Due to the finite test set this error estimate has a standard deviation of $\sqrt{0.037 \times (1 - 0.037)/1000} = 0.006$, which is not insignificant. All error estimates, however, are made by the same test set and are thereby not independent.

The bottom-left section of the table deals with the stacked combining rules applied on all 12 input classifiers for each feature set separately. Again, all best results for each feature set are underlined. It appears that the Majority rule frequently scores a best result. In addition all combined results that are better than the best individual classifier are printed in bold. For instance, for the Zernike feature set, the best individual classifier is Bayes-normal-1 (0.180). Combining all classifiers using the Median rule, however, improves this result (0.174). This combination rule is thereby useful.

In the entire right half of the table the results of parallel combining are shown. Combining rules are applied on the 6 results for a single classification rule (e.g. Bayes-normal-2), obtaining an error of 0.068 for the Product rule. The results of the combined set of all 649 features (first column) are not used here. The best results over the 10 combining rules for each classifier are underlined. For instance, the Median rule yields the best combining result (0.028) of all combiners of the Bayes-normal-2 input classifiers. Again all combining results that are better than the results for individual classifiers (now compared over all feature sets) are printed in bold. All these combined classifiers are also better than those the same input classifier trained by the entire feature set. E.g., the Parzen classifier trained on all features simultaneously yields an error of 0.036 (which is better than the best individual feature set result obtained by Parzen of 0.037).

Table 1: Summary of experimental results (error x 1000)[a]

	Classifiers	All (649)	Fourier (76)	Profiles (216)	KL-coef (64)	Pixels (240)	Zernike (47)	Morph (6)	Maximum	Median	Mean	Minimum	Product	Majority	Bayes-normal-2	Bayes-normal-1	Nearest Mean	1-NN
						Feature Set					**Fixed Combiners**					**Trained Combiners**		
Basic Classifiers	Bayes-normal-2	52	257	58	128	62	212	310	200	**28**	63	84	63	68	701	799	67	**50**
	Bayes-normal-1	183	213	34	57	99	180	291	52	37	34	44	31	51	75	99	39	42
	Nearest Mean	87	224	181	99	96	278	540	540	62	45	80	46	75	124	20	103	46
	1-NN	36	192	90	44	37	197	570	569	26	17	35	17	40	46	29	113	30
	k-NN	36	189	92	44	37	193	510	192	54	60	82	42	51	97	27	36	26
	Parzen	36	171	79	37	37	185	521	37	29	32	29	27	51	36	37	31	31
	Fisher	408	248	47	82	153	210	282	39	32	33	65	52	57	48	45	35	36
	Dec. Tree	480	454	403	400	549	598	329	275	134	113	262	110	218	283	104	102	108
	ANN-20	896	900	46	146	852	900	328	900	177	784	900	900	327	45	27	26	21
	ANN-50	900	245	130	823	810	265	717	692	244	290	805	807	163	42	31	55	33
	SVC-1	500	246	66	61	77	294	848	123	108	59	190	101	47	74	69	60	58
	SVC-2	96	212	51	40	60	193	811	40	36	37	42	38	38	40	40	40	40
Fixed Combiners	Maximum	105	747	42	39	44	839	436	39	22	21	53	20	76	33	27	19	19
	Median	34	190	43	36	45	174	287	50	23	25	39	25	50	195	58	19	50
	Mean	53	190	35	45	56	176	285	34	20	21	37	20	46	57	34	20	19
	Minimum	315	790	137	109	200	737	652	138	165	135	131	135	160	58	71	72	56
	Product	215	294	131	44	82	401	412	86	234	86	84	86	568	47	860	851	685
	Majority	33	175	35	32	37	169	318	34	23	20	122	20	48	198	27	21	20
Trained Combiners	Bayes-normal-2	104	273	49	44	99	195	289	244	17	115	133	115	28	822	897	129	64
	Bayes-normal-1	60	427	51	40	53	190	294	160	24	41	49	41	26	107	656	56	63
	Nearest Mean	32	198	37	46	73	181	266	133	20	19	36	19	51	79	42	15	18
	1-NN	33	186	38	41	72	170	328	212	18	18	38	18	41	49	36	19	18

a. ©IEEE

Several combiners of these Parzen classifiers, however, yield even better results, e.g. 0.027 by the Product rule. This shows that combining of classifiers trained on subsets of the feature space can be better than using the entire space directly.

6   Analysis

Our analysis will be focused on the combining of classifiers. The performances of the individual classifiers as shown in the top left section of table 1, however, constitute the basis of this comparison. These classifiers are not optimized to the data sets at hand, but are used in their default configuration. Many classifiers would have performed better if the data would have been rescaled or if other than default parameter values would have been used. Especially the disappointing performances of the Decision Tree (most likely by the way of pruning) and some of the neural networks suffer from this. It is interesting to note that the use of the combined feature sets yields for some classifiers a result better than by using each of the feature sets individually (Bayes-normal-2, Nearest Mean, 1-NN, k-NN) and for other classifiers a result worse than by using each of the feature sets individually (Fisher, ANN-50, SVC-1).

The first thing to notice from table 1 is that combining the results of one classifier on different feature sets is far more effective than combining the results of different classifiers on one feature set. Clearly the combination of independent information from the different feature sets is more useful than the different approaches of the classifiers on the same data. This is also visible in the performances of the different combining rules. For combining the results of classifiers on independent feature sets the product combination rule is expected to work very well. Kittler [4] showed that a product combination rule especially improves the estimate of the posterior probability when posterior probabilities with independent errors are combined. Unfortunately this product rule is sensitive to badly estimated posterior probabilities. One erroneous probability estimation of $p = 0$ overrules all other (perhaps more sensible) estimates. On the other hand for combining posterior probabilities with highly correlated errors, the product combination rule will not improve the final estimate. Instead a more robust mean, median rule or even a majority vote rule is expected to work better. These rules are not very sensitive to very poor estimates.

The results of combining the feature sets show that the product rule gives good results. The product combination of the Bayes-normal-1, 1-NN and Parzen results gives (one of) the best performances over all combination rules. The posterior probabilities of these classifiers on these feature sets appear to have independent errors. The combination results for classifiers trained on the same feature set reflect the fact that here the errors are very correlated. From the fixed combination rules only the majority vote and the mean/median combination improve the classification performance. The product rule never exceeds the best performance obtained by the best individual classifier.

When the different classifiers from one feature set are combined, performance is only improved in case of the Zernike and KL feature sets. For the other feature sets the combining performances are worse than the best individual classifier. For the Morph feature set all combining rules fail except for the Nearest Mean rule which is slightly better than the best individual performance. The maximum, product and especially the minimum rule perform very poorly in combining the different classifiers. These rules are extra sensitive to poorly estimated posterior probabilities, and suffer therefore by the poor performance of the Decision Trees and ANNs.

The Bayes-normal-1 and Bayes-normal-2 combinations probably suffer from the fact that they are trained on the (normalized) posterior probabilities of the first level classifiers. The distributions in the new 120 dimensional space (12 classifiers times 10 classes) are bounded in an unit hypercube, between 0 and 1. Moreover many of these estimated probabilities are 1 or 0 such that most objects are in the corners of the cube. The model of a normal distribution is therefore violated. Remapping the probability to a distance (e.g. by the inverse sigmoid) might remedy the situation.

The best overall performance is obtained by combining both, all classifiers and all feature sets. Although combining the classifiers trained on one feature set does not improve classification performance very much (only the majority and mean combining rules give improvement), combining again over all feature sets show the best performances. Both the product and the median rules work well and give the best overall performances, in the order of 2% error. Only the results obtained by the minimum and product combination is very poor. These outputs are too contaminated by bad posterior probability estimates. Finally the trained combination rules on the results of the fixed combinations of the different classifiers work very well, while trained combiners on the trained Bayes-normal combination of the classifiers seems to be overtrained. Combining the very simple classifier Nearest Mean with a Nearest Mean gives the overall lowest error of 1.5%. To obtain this performance, all classifiers have to be trained on all feature sets. Good performance can already be obtained when an 1-NN classifier is trained on all feature sets and the results are combined by mean or product rule. This gives an error of 1.7%, slightly but not significantly worse than the best 1.5% error.

Combining the estimates of the Parzen classification consistently gives good results, for almost all combining rules. The Parzen density estimation is expected to give reasonable estimates for the posterior probabilities, and is therefore very suitable to be combined by the fixed combining rules. The 1-NN classifier on the other hand gives very rough posterior probability estimates. The fact that these probabilities are estimated in independent feature spaces, cause independent estimation errors, which is corrected very well by the combination rules. Only the maximum combination rule still suffers from the poor density estimates in case of the 1-NN classifiers, while for the Parzen classifiers performance of the maximum rule is very acceptable. In some situations the combining rules are not able to improve anything in the classification. For instance all fixed combination rules perform worse on the ANN combination than the best individual classifier. Also combining SVC-1 and Bayes-normal-2 by fixed combining rules hardly give any performance improvements. For other situations all combination rules improve results, for instance the combination of the Decision Trees. Individual trees perform very poorly, but combining significantly improves them (although performance is still worse than most of the other combination performances). Performances tend to improve when the results of the Decision Trees, Nearest Mean, 1-NN and Parzen classifier are combined.

It is interesting to remark that, similar to the Parzen classifier, all results of the combined Decision Trees, although on a low performance level, improve those of the separate trees. Obviously the posterior probabilities, estimated in the cells of the Decision Trees can be combined well in almost any way. This may be related to the successes reported in combining large sets of weak classifiers often based on Decision Trees.

The trained combination rules work very well for combining classifiers which are not primarily constructed to give posterior probabilities, for instance the ANN, Nearest Mean and SVC. This can also be observed in the combinations of the maximum, minimum and mean combination of the different classifiers. Especially for the minimum rule the trained combination can in some way 'invert' the minimum label to find good classification performance.

Table 2: Combining classifiers for good feature sets only (error x 1000)

	Feature Set			Fixed Combiner						Trained Combiner			
	Profiles (216)	KL-coef (64)	Pixels (240)	Maximum	Median	Mean	Minimum	Product	Majority	Bayes-normal-2	Bayes-normal-1	Nearest Mean	1-NN
Bayes-normal-2	58	128	62	60	59	**48**	64	**47**	55	889	897	51	59
Bayes-normal-1	34	57	99	75	51	64	74	75	46	103	99	86	93
Nearest Mean	181	99	96	165	96	**91**	102	**91**	98	**92**	**47**	179	**75**
1-NN	90	44	37	80	**36**	**36**	**33**	**36**	37	61	65	70	37
k-NN	92	44	37	92	**37**	66	41	66	38	67	66	90	72
Parzen	79	37	37	39	**34**	**36**	40	39	**33**	46	37	**36**	37

From the left upper part in table 1 it is clear that the data in the Profiles, KL-coefficients and Pixel feature sets is better clustered and easier to classify than the Fourier, Zernike and Morph features. Therefore one might expect that for these datasets the posterior probabilities are estimated well. In table 2 six classifiers are trained on only the good feature sets and then combined. In all cases the performances of the combination rules are significantly lower than the individual best classifier. On the other hand, the results are worse than the combination of all six original feature sets. This indicates that although the individual classification performances on the 'difficult' datasets are poor, they still contain valuable information for the combination rules.

Surprisingly the best performance is now obtained by applying the minimum rule on the 1-NN outputs or the majority vote on the Parzen outputs. Only in one case the product combination rule is best: in the combination of the Bayes-normal-2. There is no combining rule which gives consistently good results. The overall performance improvement is far less than in the case of the combination of the six feature sets.

It appears to be important to have independent estimation errors. The different feature sets describe independent characteristics of the original objects. Within the feature sets the features have a common, comparable meaning but between the sets the features are hardly comparable (see also the differences in the PCA scatter plots in figure 3). The classifiers which are used in this experiment, do not use prior knowledge about the distribution in the feature sets. When all features of the six feature sets are redistributed into six new sets, again the classifiers can be trained and combined. The results are shown in table 3. The first notable fact is that the performances of the individual classifiers over the different feature sets are far more comparable. This indicates that the distribution characteristics of the sets do not differ very much. Furthermore the Bayes-normal-1 works very well in all feature sets. This indicates that data described with the large set of (mostly) independent features (more than 100) tends to become normally distributed.

Table 3: Randomized feature sets (error x 1000)

	Feature Sets						Fixed Combiner						Trained Combiner			
	Set 1(108)	Set 2(108)	Set 3(108)	Set4(108)	Set 5(108)	Set 6(109)	Maximum	Median	Mean	Minimum	Product	Majority	Bayes-normal-2	Bayes-normal-1	Nearest Mean	1-NN
Bayes-normal-2	104	134	83	123	110	122	**55**	**57**	**55**	97	**57**	56	897	608	57	62
Bayes-normal-1	26	35	25	49	44	30	28	19	**18**	24	19	**18**	82	**18**	**18**	19
Nearest Mean	164	181	109	142	149	163	117	**92**	**89**	124	**89**	99	396	**46**	158	63
1-NN	87	93	69	86	101	83	**67**	**34**	**31**	40	**31**	42	50	57	48	34
k-NN	83	93	68	86	94	83	**59**	**38**	46	43	45	40	133	50	47	56
Parzen	75	83	65	74	95	76	**37**	**31**	**31**	37	**31**	40	119	67	**31**	**31**

The results of combining these six new random sets, are comparable with the old, well defined feature sets. Results of combining 1-NN and Parzen are again good, but also combining k-NN and Bayes-normal-1 works well. Combining the Bayes-normal-1 classifiers works very well and even gives similar results as the best combining rules on the original feature sets. This may be interesting as this method is fast, in training as well as in testing. This good performance of combining classifiers trained on randomly selected feature sets corresponds with the use of random subspaces in combining weak classifiers. The results of the 1-NN and Parzen combinations are quite acceptable, but are not as good as in the original feature sets. Probably these classifiers suffer from the fact that distances within one feature set are not very well defined (by the differences in scale in the original feature sets, which are now mixed). The combined performance is therefore not much better than the 1-NN and Parzen on the combined feature set with 649 features (left column in table 1).

So we can conclude that here, instead of carefully distinguishing the six separate feature sets, we can train Bayes-normal-1 on random (disjunct) subsets of all features and combine the results using (almost) any combining rule. This gives comparable results as combining the results from the 1-NN on the original feature sets with a mean or product rule.

Table 4: Combining the best classifiers (error x 1000)

	Fixed Combiner						Trained Combiner			
	Maximum	Median	Mean	Minimum	Product	Majority	Bayes-normal-2	Bayes-normal-1	Nearest Mean	1-NN
The best classifier for each feature set	37	<u>24</u>	29	28	26	40	44	52	31	28

Finally in table 4 the best individual classifiers are selected and combined (for the Pixel feature set the Parzen classifier is chosen). All combining rules perform very good, although the best performance does not match the best results in the original combination of the 1-NN classifier. This results might even be somewhat biased, because the best classifiers are selected by their performance on the independent test set. The best performance is reached using the median combination, while the product combination is also very good. The Bayes-normal-1 combination rule now shows the worst performance, although it is still very acceptable. Combining the best classifiers seems to cause overall good performance for all rules, but it might remove some of the independent errors in the intermediate space, such that somewhat less classification errors can be corrected.

7   Conclusions

It should be emphasized that our analysis is based on a single experiment for a single dataset. Conclusions will thereby at most point in a possible direction. They can be summarized as follows:

- Combining classifiers trained on different feature sets is very useful, especially when in these feature set probabilities are well estimated by the classifier. Combining different classifiers trained on the same classifier on the other hand may also improve, but is generally far less useful.
- There is no overall winning combining rule. Mean, median, majority in case of correlated errors, product for independent errors perform roughly as expected, but others may be good as well.
- The divide and conquer strategy works well: the independent use of separate feature sets works well. Difficult datasets should not be thrown away: they contain important information! The use of randomly selected feature sets appears to give very good results in our example, especially for the Bayes-normal-1 classifier.
- The Nearest Mean and the Nearest Neighbour classifiers appear to be very useful and stable when used as combiner.

In retrospection, our experiments may be extended as follows:

- A rescaling of all feature sets to unit variance, which might improve the performance of a number of classifiers.
- Remapping the posterior probabilities to distances for the trained combiners.
- Combining results of combination rules on the different feature-sets (instead of the different classifiers).

8   Acknowledgement

This work is supported by the Foundation for Applied Sciences (STW) and the Dutch Organization for Scientific Research (NWO). The authors thank the IEEE for the permission to reprint table 1, which appears here in an extended version, and which is published before in [8].

9   References

[1]   L. Breiman, J.H. Friedman, R.A. Olshen, and C.J. Stone, *Classification and regression trees*, Wadsworth, California, 1984.

[2]   J. R. Quinlan, Simplifying decision trees, *International Journal of Man-Machine Studies*, vol. 27, 1987, 221--234.

[3]   V.N. Vapnik, *Statistical Learning Theory*, John Wiley & Sons, New York, 1998.

[4]   J. Kittler, M. Hatef, R.P.W. Duin, and J. Matas, On Combining Classifiers, *IEEE Transactions on Pattern Analysis and Machine Intelligence*, vol. 20, no. 3, 1998, 226-239.

[5]   L. Xu, A. Krzyzak, and C.Y. Suen, Methods of combining multiple classifiers and their application to handwriting recognition, *IEEE Trans. SMC*, vol. 22, 1992, 418--435.

[6]   R.E. Schapire, The strenght of weak learnability, *Machine Learning*, vol. 5, pp. 197-227, 1990.

[7]   L.I. Kuncheva, J.C. Bezdek, and R.P.W. Duin, Decision Templates for Multiple Classifier Fusion: An Experimental Comparison, *Pattern Recognition*, 2000, in press.

[8]   A.K. Jain, R.P.W. Duin, and J. Mao, Statistical Pattern Recognition: A Review, *IEEE Transactions on Pattern Analysis and Machine Intelligence*, vol. 22, no. 1, 2000, 4-37.

[9]   M. van Breukelen, R.P.W. Duin, D.M.J. Tax, and J.E. den Hartog, Handwritten digit recognition by combined classifiers, *Kybernetika*, vol. 34, no. 4, 1998, 381-386.

[10]   R.P.W. Duin and D.M.J. Tax, Classifier conditional posterior probabilities, in: A. Amin, D. Dori, P. Pudil, H. Freeman (eds.), *Advances in Pattern Recognition*, Lecture Notes in Computer Science, vol. 1451, Springer, Berlin, 1998, 611-619.

[11]   Machine Learning Repository, UCI, //www.ics.uci.edu/~mlearn/MLRepository.html

[12]   R.P.W. Duin, PRTools 3.0, *A Matlab Toolbox for Pattern Recognition*, Delft University of Technology, 2000.

[13]   H. Demuth and M. Beale, *Neural Network TOOLBOX for use with Matlab*, version 3 Mathworks, Natick, MA, USA, 1998.

The "Test and Select" Approach to Ensemble Combination*

Amanda J.C. Sharkey, Noel E. Sharkey, Uwe Gerecke, and G.O. Chandroth **

Department of Computer Science,
University of Sheffield, UK

Abstract. The performance of neural nets can be improved through the use of ensembles of redundant nets. In this paper, some of the available methods of ensemble creation are reviewed and the "test and select" methodolology for ensemble creation is considered. This approach involves testing potential ensemble combinations on a validation set, and selecting the best performing ensemble on this basis, which is then tested on a final test set. The application of this methodology, and of ensembles in general, is explored further in two case studies. The first case study is of fault diagnosis in a diesel engine, and relies on ensembles of nets trained from three different data sources. The second case study is of robot localisation, using an evidence-shifting method based on the output of trained SOMs. In both studies, improved results are obtained as a result of combining nets to form ensembles.

For every complex problem, there is a solution that is simple, neat, and wrong. Henry Louis Mencken (1880-1956).

1   Introduction

There is a growing realisation that combinations of classifiers can be more effective than single classifiers. Why rely on the best single classifier, when a more reliable and accurate result can be obtained from a combination of several? This essentially is the reasoning behind the idea of multiple classifier systems, and it is an idea that is relevant both to neural computing, and to the wider machine learning community.

In this paper, we are primarily concerned with the development of multi-net systems [1], i.e. combinations of Artificial Neural Nets (ANNs). We shall focus on ensemble combinations of neural nets; providing an overview of methods for

---

* We would like to thank the EPSRC Grant No.GR/K84257 for funding this research.
** G.O.Chandroth is now at Lloyds Register, but his contribution to this paper was made whilst he was at University of Sheffield

J. Kittler and F. Roli (Eds.): MCS 2000, LNCS 1857, pp. 30–44, 2000.

ensemble creation, outlining the test and select approach to to ensemble creation, and illustrating its application in two case studies. However, although our focus is on combining ANNs, it should not be forgotten that the advantages of ensemble combining are not restricted to the area of neural computing, but can be gained when other unstable predictors, such as decision trees, are combined.

Our concern is with ensemble, as distinct from modular combinations. The term *ensemble*, or the less frequent *committee*, is used to refer to combining of a set of redundant nets. In an *ensemble*, the component nets are redundant in that they each provide a solution to the same task. In other words, although better results might be achieved by an ensemble, any one of the individual members of the ensemble could be used on its own to provide a solution to the task. By contrast, under a *modular* approach, a task is decomposed into a number of subtasks, and the complete task solution requires the contribution of all the several modules (even though individual inputs may be dealt with by only one of the modules).

When deciding whether a combination represents an ensemble or modular combination, the notion of redundancy provides a guide. If the several classifers are essentially performing the same task, they represent an ensemble. If, on the other hand, they are responsible for distinct components of the task, their combination is modular in nature. Similarly, the way in which they are combined is important. If the mechanism by which they are combined is one that makes use of all the outputs in some form, (whether by averaging, or voting), the combination is likely to be an ensemble one. Thus Adaboost (see below) [2] is an ensemble approach, in that all of the component members are implicated in the final output, and there is no mechanism that switches control to the most appropriate component. On the other hand, if combining relies on some form of switching mechanism, whereby for each input, the output is taken from the most relevant component, or even the most relevant blend of modules, (as in mixtures of experts, [3]) the combination is likely to be a modular one.

Although our present concern is with ensemble combinations rather than modular ones, that does not imply that the topic of modular combinations is not an interesting one. Often greater performance improvements can be obtained from decomposing a task into modular components, than can be obtained from ensemble combinations (see [4] for an example). The two forms, ensembles and modules, are also not mutually exclusive; as shown in [5] and [4], it is quite possible to create a system that consists of both modules and ensembles, where each module is itself replaced by an ensemble of redundant solutions to that task component. Similarly, the component members of an ensemble combination could themselves be made up of different modular solutions to the problem [6].

We shall turn now to a review of some of the many methods of ensemble˙ creation that have been proposed. This review will be followed by the consideration of the test and select approach to ensemble creation, and an illustration of its application in two case studies; first in the domain of fault diagnosis of a diesel engine, and second in the domain of robot localisation.

2   Methods of Ensemble Creation

What methods can be used for ensemble creation? There is little doubt that ensemble combining usually works, in that there are many demonstrations of the improved results that can be obtained from an ensemble combination over the performance of single nets (see [7] and [8] for reviews). But what are the best methods for constructing an ensemble, and are there some that are more likely to produce good results than others?

In fact, many different methods for ensemble construction have been proposed. A simple method relies on training neural nets from different starting points, or different initial conditions [9]. Another set of methods involves varying the topology or number of hidden units, or the algorithm involved [10]. A further set of ensemble creating techniques rely on varying the data in some way. Methods of varying the data include; sampling, use of different data sources, use of different preprocessing methods, distortion, and adaptive resampling. We shall examine these in more detail below.

Probably the most well-known sampling approach is that exemplified by bagging. The bagging algorithm [11], relies on varying the data, through the bootstrap sampling procedure. New training sets are created by sampling with replacement from a pool of examples; the result being a set of training sets that are different samples taken from a central training pool. When predictors are grown, or trained on these examples, and then combined by voting, they often outperform a single predictor trained on the entire training pool. A related method is to train nets, or predictors, on disjoint samples of a large training pool, i.e. sampling *without* replacement [12], or alternatively, using different cross-validation leave out sets [13].

The use of different data sources for training ensemble members is sometimes possible under circumstances in which data are available from more than one sensor. If the quality of data from each sensor is such that it is sufficient for the classification task (as opposed to poorer quality data where some form of sensor fusion is required before classification becomes possible), then an ensemble can be created from nets each trained on data from a separate sensor (see for instance [14], and the first case study described below). A related approach is to subject the data to different forms of preprocessing; for example, in [16], when three different preprocessing methods (domain expertise, principle component analysis, and wavelet decomposition) were applied to vibration data from an engine, and the resulting nets were combined to form effective ensembles. A similar method was explored by Tumer and Ghosh [17], when they applied different pruning methods, leaving out different input features, to create ensemble members.

There are also a number of related methods, to which the collective term "distortion" could be applied. First there are methods in which ensemble members are created by distorting the inputs or the outputs in the training set in some way. Dietterich and Bakiri [18] describe the application of error-correcting output codes to ensemble creation; finding it resulted in effective ensembles when applied to either C4.5 and backpropagation algorithms. Breiman [19] showed that perturbing the outputs, either by output smearing, or by output flipping, resulted in new training sets that formed effective ensembles. Raviv and Intrator [20] describe a process of noise injection, in which variable amounts of noise are added to the inputs in order to create ensemble members (although they used noise injection together with bootstrap resampling and weight regularisation). And a method termed 'non-linear transformations' [21] has been used to distort, or transform, the inputs in the training set. Such transformations can be accomplished in two ways (i) passing the inputs through an untrained neural net (i.e. a set of random weights), taking the resulting outputs as a new version of the inputs, and training those, or (ii) training the inputs on a new function, for example autoassociation, and taking the resulting hidden unit representations as new versions of the inputs. The new versions of the inputs are then trained in a further net on the required classification. A related approach can be found in [22], where a set of classifiers for combination are grown by training on the same primary task, but with different auxillary tasks.

A final, and currently popular method, for creating ensembles is that of Adaboost [2]. Training using Adaboost proceeds in a number of rounds; in the first round, all examples in a pool of training items have an equal chance of being included in the training set. In the next training round, the predictor developed following training on the first training set is tested on all the items in the pool of training items, and the probability of selecting items is altered for those that are misclassified (or if training examples can be weighted, the weight for those examples is increased). In the next round, the items that were misclassified by the predictor developed in the first round have a greater probability of being included in the next training set. The process continues for the specified number of rounds. Ensembles created through Adaboost have been shown to produce good results when compared to Bagging on a number of data sets ([23]). Breiman suggests that bagging, and some of the methods described above as "distortion" (namely randomising the construction of predictors, and randomising the outputs) are essentially "cut from the same cloth", and that there is something fundamentally different about the adaptive resampling involved in Adaboost, and similar algorithms he terms "arcing" algorithms (**A**daptive **R**eweighting and **C**ombining). Recently, Schapire et al [24] have offered an explanation of Adaboost in terms of margins, demonstrating experimentally that Adaboost produced higher margins between training examples and decision boundaries than bagging.

Although, or perhaps because, many methods of ensemble creation have been proposed, there is as yet no clear picture of which method is best. This is in part because only a limited number of comparisons have been attempted (and several of those have concentrated on comparing Adaboost to bagging). Clearly, further comparisons will be conducted and a clearer picture will emerge. For instance, an understanding of ensemble combining is likely to be improved by future empirical assessments of the circumstances under which particular methods are appropriate (see for example, the finding by Quinlan [25] that Adaboost performs badly in domains with noisy training data).

3   A "Test and Select" Methodology for Ensemble Creation

What makes an ensemble combination work? Explanations of the effect of ensemble combining have been couched in terms of the variance and bias components of the ensemble error [26], [27]; and it can be shown that ensembles provide a means of reducing the variance, or dependence on the data of a set of nets. Another way to think about the behaviour of ensembles is in terms of the number of coincident failures made by the component nets. If the component nets in an ensemble made no coincident errors when tested for generalisation, the result would be 100% generalisation. Each individual error made by a component net on an input would be compensated for by a correct output made by the other nets. The same result would be obtained if errors made by one net were compensated for by a majority of correct responses by the other nets. What is required then is a set of nets, each of which are accurate, but which, when they make errors, make different errors. In other words, a set of nets that are both accurate and *diverse*.

Clearly ensemble combination requires some diversity amongst its component members: there would be no advantage to including nets in an ensemble that were exact replicates, and showed the same patterns of generalisation. What is also needed for good performance is that the nets should each be fairly accurate. The chance of finding a set of nets that show no, or few, coincident errors, is made much simpler, if the nets make very few errors in the first place. For example, it is easier to achieve a set of nets that make no coincident errors, if the nets in question each only make one error. If each net made an error on a third of the training set, the chances of coincident failure would increase.

In order to find out how many coincident errors are made by a set of nets in an ensemble, it is necessary to test them on a test set. Testing the performance of an ensemble provides an indication of the coincident errors, since, where voting is used, a correct output will only be obtained when a majority of the nets produce the correct output. From this idea, it is a short step to adopting this as a methodology. Why not identify and select a good ensemble on the basis of its performance on a test set? Such testing would actually require two test sets; one, a validation set, would be used to identify an ensemble that performed well, and a second test set, would be used to test the performance of the selected ensemble. This way, the final test set would not have been contaminated by any involvement in the selection process (such involvement would result in an artificially inflated estimate of the ensemble's performance). Under the "test and select" methodology, a number of different ensemble combinations could be tested on a validation set, and on the basis of this the best performing ensemble could be identified, and its performance assessed on a final test set.

The proposed "test and select" methodology relies on the idea of selection in ensemble creation. Rather than including all available nets in an ensemble, different selections are tried and compared. Although not usually explicitly discussed in the context of bagging or Adaboost, the notion of selection of ensemble members has been raised in a number of papers. Perrone and Cooper [9] suggested a heuristic selection method whereby the population of trained nets are ordered in terms of increasing mean squared error, and an ensemble is created by including those with lowest mean squared error. The process can be further refined by constructing ensembles and then only adding a new net if adding it results in a lower mean squared error for that ensemble. Partridge and Yates [10] compare the effectiveness of three selection methods, but obtained the best ensemble results from a heuristic picking method; a method similar, but not identical, to that of Perrone and Cooper [9]. Hashem ([29] points out the effect of "harmful collinearity" on the performance of ensembles, and compares two different selection algorithms. Opitz and Shavlik [28] present a method which uses genetic algorithms to actively search for ensemble members which are both accurate and diverse. All of these methods rely on testing the performance of ensembles, although not all of them use the two test sets advocated here.

The machine learning community currently makes little use of the notion of selection; their aim is usually that of identifying an algorithm that creates effective ensembles, applying it, and presenting the results. However, two points can be made with respect to this way of going about things. First, it is quite likely that an approach based on testing and selection will outperform such a method. And second, even the application of an algorithm apparently without selection may implicitly involve testing; for example, testing may be used to determine the appropriate number of bootstrap replicates, or the number of rounds of Adaboost. If testing is being used implicitly, why not make it explicit, and test in order to identify the best performing ensemble? Once an algorithm has been identified that always outperforms such a testing strategy, the need for such testing will become obsolete.

The notion of a test methodology for ensemble construction, is a practical one, particularly while the jury is still deliberating over its decision about which is the best ensemble creation method. In some applications, a fixed set of nets may be available for ensemble creation. Alternatively, a pool of nets could be created by a variety of methods, (i.e. varying the initial conditions, varying the algorithm, sampling, preprocessing, use of different sources of data etc.). Then, having picked a target ensemble size, a search could be made of the possible combinations of an ensemble of size x, and the best performing ensemble selected. Depending on the size of the pool of nets, this search could be exhaustive, (see the robot localisation case study), or some other selection algorithm might be adopted, for instance testing x ensemble combinations (see engine fault diagnosis case study).

In order to see how this "test and select" methodology might work in practice, we shall examine two case studies in which it is applied.

4   Case Study: Fault Diagnosis of a Diesel Engine

In this first case study, ensemble combining was explored in the context of fault diagnosis of a diesel engine. This issue has been previously explored in this context (e.g. [16] [12] [4]), although the focus here is on the test and select methodology. Data was obtained by physically introducing (at different times) four common faults in a 4-stroke twin cylinder diesel engine. The four faults were (i) leaking air inlet, (ii) leaking exhaust valve, (iii) partial blockage of one in four injector nozzle holes, and (iv) injector dribble or leak. Data was collected under each faulty condition, as well as during normal operation. Data corresponding to in cylinder pressure, and to engine vibration were collected; in-cylinder pressure by means of a pressure transducer sensor, and vibration by means of an accelerometer attached to the outside of the cylinder. Further details of the data acquisition process are available [16].

The appropriate fault classification was indicated in the data by pairing the input measurements (whether pressure, vibration or both) with a $1 of n$ output encoding, indicating whether the input corresponded to one of the four possible faults, or to normal operation. Three sets of data were constructed, corresponding to different inputs. The first consisted of 12,000 examples, where a 50 element input vector was based on a selection of inputs from the pressure sensor. These inputs were chosen, on the basis of domain knowledge, from those collected during the combustion phase of each engine cycle. The second data set also consisted of 12,000 examples, and was based on data collected by means of a vibration sensor. It similarly consisted of a 50 element input vector. The third set, termed pressureANDvibration, was created by appending each vibration input vector to the corresponding pressure input vector to create a new 100 element input vector.

The three data sets, Pressure, Vibration, and PressureANDVibration were each subdivided into a training set of 7500 examples, a validation set of 1500 examples, and a final test set of 3000 examples. In all cases the same engine cycle was represented in the three types of data set, with the result that the test sets were equivalent (i.e. each test set example in the Pressure, the Vibration, and the PressureANDVibration data sets corresponded to the same engine cycle, and hence contained the same output classification despite the difference in inputs).

For the present study, a set of 45 nets were trained using backpropagation, and standard multi-layer perceptrons. First, for each data set, five nets were trained using different numbers of hidden units (HUs). Then, a further five nets were trained, for each data set, from different random initial conditions (RICs), using the number of hidden units which had resulted in the best generalisation performance for that data set. And finally, five bootstrap replicates of the original training set were trained, each from the starting point of different initial conditions, but using the same number of hidden units as in the RIC nets. The performance of each of these 45 nets, following training, is shown in Table 1.

Inspection of Table 1 shows that the best single net (marked by **) of the total 45 trained was one based on the PressureANDVibration data set, and that this net got 94.9% of the validation set correct. It would be expected that this performance could be improved upon through the use of ensembles. But which method might be expected to yield the best results? The "test and select" methodology facilitates the comparison of different methods of ensemble construction.

Table 1. Generalisation performances on validation test set

Data Source	HUs	RICs	Bootstrap
Pressure	88.00%	88.10%	85.50%
Pressure	86.93%	88.70%	85.60%
Pressure	88.93%	90.10%	85.30%
Pressure	87.87%	89.00%	85.50%
Pressure	89.53%	89.50%	86.60%
Vibration	88.40%	89.27%	87.00%
Vibration	88.20%	91.53%	88.00%
Vibration	89.13%	89.20%	87.90%
Vibration	90.60%	89.87%	86.90%
Vibration	89.87%	88.73%	86.00%
PressureANDVibration	92.80%	94.40%	92.80%
PressureANDVibration	93.50%	94.30%	93.50%
PressureANDVibration	92.90%	94.30%	92.90%
PressureANDVibration	93.20%	94.10%	93.20%
PressureANDVibration	93.30%	94.90%**	93.30%

A number of ensembles were constructed in which the component nets were all based on nets trained on the same type of data set. In each case the outputs of the ensemble members were combined by means of a simple majority vote. Under each data type (Pressure, Vibration, and PressureANDVibration) five nets had been trained, (i) using different numbers of hidden units, (ii) varying the random initial conditions, and (iii) using different bootstrap replicates. A comparison of the effectiveness of these different methods was possible; the results can be seen in Table 2. Table 2 shows the generalisation results of ensembles that either contained all five of the nets in each category, or that were the best ensemble of three nets, based on an exhaustive search of the 10 possible combinations in each case.

It can be seen in Table 2 that the best ensemble result to be achieved was 96.4%. This was achieved both by combining all 5 nets created from different random initial conditions, and by selecting the best combination of three nets. This represents an improvement over 94.9% generalisation performance of the best single net. The best ensemble performance was achieved by nets based on the combined PressureANDVibration data; generally nets trained on this data set did better. Two further points can be made on the basis of these results. First, there is no evidence here that including all 5 nets in an ensemble resulted in better generalisation performance; as is apparent from a comparison of the corresponding cells in the top and bottom of the table, sometimes better results were obtained from an ensemble of 3 nets, and sometimes from an ensemble of all 5 nets. The second point is that, interestingly, there is no evidence here of better results being obtained as a result of combining a number of bootstrap replicates; in fact performance of ensembles based on combinations of bootstrap replicates

Table 2. Differently constructed ensembles

Ensemble of all five nets			
Data Source	Initial Conditions	Architecture	Bootstrap sample
Pressure	90.81%	91%	87.74%
Vibration	89.51%	93.20%	90.70%
PressureandVibration	96.4%*	95.40%	93.80%
Best ensemble of three nets			
Data Source	Initial Conditions	Architecture	Bootstrap sample
Pressure	91.07%	90.80%	88.13%
Vibration	92.73%	93.27%	90.47%
PressureandVibration	96.4%**	95.67%	93.60%

is generally poorer (reading from left to right in Table 2, combining bootstrap replicates always fares worse than combining nets differing in initial conditions or hidden units, with only one exception). It is clearly not the case that all applications of bagging will result in better performance. Of course, it is likely that combining a larger number of bootstrap replicates would result in better results for the bagging approach. Nonetheless, the point remains that the test and select methodology makes it possible to find the best performing ensemble from a set of alternatives; in this case a combination of three PressureANDVibration nets, trained from the starting point of different random initial conditions. And it was not clear *a priori* that combining nets trained from different RICs would lead to a better ensemble result.

Although the results shown in Table 2 illustrate how it is possible to compare different methods of ensemble construction, it is still possible that the best ensemble result there (96.4%) could be improved upon. However, an exhaustive search of all the possible sized ensemble combinations of 45 nets was not feasible. A solution to this problem, adopted here, is to randomly generate a specified number of combinations, and to choose the best combination from amongst them.

First, 100 random combinations of ensembles of three nets were assembled, and tested on the validation set. As can be seen in Table 3, the averaged performance of these random combinations, chosen with no constraints from amonst the 45 nets, was 89.65%. What method for ensemble generation might be expected to outperform a random choice of ensemble members? Since the generalisation pattern of a net is primarily determined by the data on which it is trained, it seems likely that combining nets based on different sources of data would result in better ensembles than random choices. Accordingly, a further 100 ensembles were generated with the constraint that each of the three nets in every ensemble should be based on a different data source. Inspection of the first column, second row, of Table 2 (94.06%) shows that these combinations do seem to do better on average, both than the random choice with no constraints, and than a further 100 ensembles, randomly generated but for the constraint that in

Table 3. 100 ensemble combinations of three nets

Constraints	Average	Best
None	89.65%	96.53%
One from each sensor	94.06%	96.40%
All from same sensor	91.62%	95.80%

each case all three nets are based on the same type of data. On average then, it would appear that these results suggest that a better result will be obtained by constructing ensembles in which the component nets are based on different types of data.

However, as well as considering which method of generated ensembles is likely to produce better results on average, it is also possible to examine the results of the ensemble experiments, and to identify the ensemble which performs best. When this is done, (see the second column of results in Table 2), it turns out that the best performing ensemble (96.53%) is to be found amongst the 100 ensembles randomly generated with no constraints. This particular ensemble consisted of two PressureANDVibration nets and a Pressure net (with generalisation performances of 94.30%, 93.20% and 88% respectively). As a result of adopting the test and select methodology, an effective ensemble was arrived at through serendipity: one that was unlikely to have been created by design. This ensemble does better on the validation set than any of the others created in the course of the study, even though it was created by means of a generation method (random with no constraints) that on average appears to be less effective than creating ensembles from nets trained on different sources of data.

Having identified the ensemble that performs best on the validation set, the final step is to test its performance on the reserved test set. This ensemble generalised to 95.37% of the 3000 examples in the final test set. This result can be compared to the 93.6% generalisation performance of the best single net on the same final test set, and clearly represents an improvement.

5   Case Study: Robot Localisation

We have provided one illustration of the application of the test and select methodology in the domain of engine fault diagnosis. In this second case study we shall briefly examine its application in another domain (robot localisation), with a different kind of neural net (Self-organising Maps, or SOMs).

In an earlier paper, Gerecke and Sharkey [30] presented a method for localising a "lost robot". The lost robot problem is one in which a robot is switched off and moved to a new location, which it has to identify when it is switched on again. To do this, the robot must match its current sensory information against its knowledge of the operating environment. The method adopted to solve this problem was designed to provide a fast and approximate ("quick and dirty" to use their term) method of localisation, in contrast to other more computationally costly approaches.

Further details can be found in [30], but an overview of the method for robot localisation is provided here. It makes use of a self-organising map (SOM). The basic principle of a SOM is to map the input space R^n onto a regular two-dimensional array of nodes, where each node has a reference vector $\mathbf{m_i} \in R^n$ associated with it. The inputs $m \in R^n$ are compared with the $\mathbf{m_i}$ and the closest vector in Euclidean distance (i.e. the most active) is defined as the winning node in a *winner-takes-all* strategy. After training, the output space of the SOM defines neighbourhoods of input similarity, i.e. similar inputs are mapped onto the same output category. This self-organised grouping is exploited for localisation.

Each SOM was trained on sensor data collected at random positions as the robot traverses the operating environment. Similar inputs will be grouped together. These can be equated with specific locations in the operating environment by the following procedure. Specific reference locations in the operating environment are chosen, in this case, at equidistant grid points, 10 inches apart, distributed throughout the space. Readings, or sensor vectors, are taken at each of these locations. Each vector is presented to the previously trained SOM in turn, and the winning output node recorded. That output node is then associated (or labelled) with the corresponding reference location. Were it not for the problem of perceptual aliasing (see below), following training and labelling of the SOM, the input vector of a "lost robot" could be mapped by the SOM onto the appropriate output category, which in turn would identify its reference location.

However, perceptual aliasing complicates the process. Perceptual aliasing arises because similar sensor readings can be taken from different regions of the environment. Thus, for example, the sensor readings from a robot facing four different grid corners in a symmetrical room are likely to be similar, and therefore would be clustered together. As a result each of the output nodes of the SOM may be associated with a number of candidate reference locations. An evidence-shifting approach was used to solve this problem; the reference location for a set of sensor readings was disambiguated by accumulating evidence following a move. The shortlist of reference locations provided by the SOM is reduced by iteratively moving the robot a short distance, and updating the evidence for each of the candidate reference locations, until only one reference location is compatible with the evidence.

Gerecke and Sharkey [30] present results based on a realistic simulation of a Nomad200 mobile robot. Following training of a SOM on random points, and the application of the evidence shifting method, the correct location of the robot was identified 92% of the time in a localisation test of 500 randomly chosen test points within the environment. This result was based on a radius of uncertainity of 20 in. They concluded that the result supported the utility of the method, and suggested that it might be improved by combining SOM results in ensembles. A preliminary report of that extension is provided here.

Table 4. Combining localisation SOMs

Size of ensemble	No. combinations	Best ensemble	Average ensemble
3	165	95.2%	92.98
5	462	96.4%	94.62
7	330	96.8%	95.46
9	55	96.8%	95.89
11	1	96%	N/A

Considerable experimentation with SOM architectures and learning parameters was carried out before choosing the SOM used in the earlier study; it is therefore possible to look at the improvement that could be gained from combining localisation decisions based on different SOMs, in an ensemble. In total, 11 SOMs were considered. These SOMs differed in some of the following attributes; size, learning steps, learning rates, neighbourhood, and initialisation. The application of the evidence shifting method to the outputs of different SOMs leads to different hypotheses about the location of the robot. In order to form an ensemble output, these different hypotheses were combined by means of voting.

A series of tests were then performed to identify the best performing ensemble. Five ensemble sizes were considered, 3 net, 5 net, 7 net, 9 net and 11 net ensembles. For each size, an exhaustive search of all the possible combinations of the 11 nets was performed. The results of the best ensembles, and the averaged results, are shown in Table 4.

From Table 4, it is first of all apparent that ensemble combining did result in improved performance over the 92% achieved by the best single estimate. Beyond that it is evident that the best ensemble results on the validation set were achieved by a combination of either 7 or 9 nets. On the basis of these results, the best performing ensemble of 9 nets was selected. When that ensemble was tested on the reserved test set of 500 random locations in the environment, it showed a generalisation performance of 97.8%. This compares well to the performance of the best single' net, which when tested on this further test set generalised correctly to 91.2% of the cases.

This second case study provides a further illustration of the test and select methodology. This study involves the combination of localisation decisions, based on the output of different SOMs. The domain of application then is quite different to that of engine fault diagnosis. In addition, in the present case, the small number of nets made exhaustive testing of all ensembles of a specific size possible. This contrasts to the approaches taken to testing in the previous case study in which exhaustive testing was not feasible. Again, it was possible to examine the results of different ensemble experiments, and to select the best combination from the available examples.

6   Conclusions

In the course of this paper, a number of different methods for ensemble construction have been outlined and considered. Some comparisons of the relative effectiveness can be found in the literature, and whilst there is some progress here, there is still no general agreement about which methods are the most appropriate for which problems. Whilst there is still a lack of clarity about the best methods to adopt for particular applications, the "test and select" methodology advocated here provides a useful approach. Under a test and select approach, a number of possible ensemble combinations are tested on a validation set, and the best one selected. This is then tested on a final test set that has not been implicated in the selection. Two ways of applying the methodology were considered; first, where the pool of nets for ensemble combination is small, exhaustive testing of all possible ensemble combinations may be possible. Alternatively, when the pool is larger and exhaustive testing not feasible, a specific number of ensemble combinations could be generated and tested. This second approach makes it possible to see whether on average one method of ensemble creation outperforms another. However, whichever method is applied, it is still possible to search through the ensemble results, and to select the ensemble that performs best on the validation set.

In a sense, the "test and select" methodology merely makes explicit a technique that is commonly used. Several approaches implicitly, or even explicitly, rely on testing the performance of ensembles, and selection. However, the emphasis here on the need for a separate validation set should guard against the overestimation of ensemble performance that would result if both selection, and assessment, were based on the same test set. The methodology can be used to compare different methods of ensemble construction, and to examine the circumstances under which they are most effective. In addition, another important advantage of the methodology, as can be seen in the two case studies, is that it opens the possibility of the accidental (serendipitous) discovery of a more effective ensemble than those created by design.

References

[1] Sharkey, A.J.C. (1999) Combining Artificial Neural Nets: Ensemble and Modular Multi-Net Systems. London, Springer-Verlag.

[2] Freund, Y and Schapire, R. (1996) Experiments with a new boosting algorithm. In Proceedings of the Thirteenth International Conference on Machine Learning, pp149-156, Morgan Kaufmann.

[3] Jacobs, R.A. (1995) Methods for combining experts' probability assessments. Neural Computation, 7, 867-888.

[4] Sharkey, A.J.C., Chandroth, G.O, and Sharkey, N.E. (in press) A Multi-Net System for the Fault Diagnosis of a Diesel Engine. Neural Computing and Applications.

[5] Sharkey, A.J.C., Sharkey, N.E., and Cross, S.S. (1998) Adapting an Ensemble Approach for the Diagnosis of Breast Cancer. In Proceedings of ICANN 98, Springer-Verlag, pp 281-286.

[6] Sharkey, A.J.C. (1999) Multi-net Systems. In (Ed) Amanda Sharkey, Combining Artificial Neural Nets: Ensemble and Modular Multi-Net Systems. London, Springer-Verlag, pp1-25.

[7] Sharkey, A.J.C. (1996) On combining artificial neural nets. Connection Science: Special Issue on Combining Artificial Neural Nets, Ensemble Approaches, 8 (3/4) 299-314.

[8] Dieterich, T.G. (1997) Machine learning research: Four current directions. AI Magazine, 18(4), 97-136.

[9] Perrone, M.P. and Cooper, L.N. (1993) When networks disagree: Ensemble methods for hybrid neural networks. In R.J. Mammone, editor, Neural Networks for Speech and Image Processing, Chapter 10, Chapman-Hall.

[10] Partridge, D., and Yates, W.B. (1996) Engineering multiversion neural-net systems. Neural Computation, 8(4), 869-893.

[11] Breiman, L. (1996) Bagging Predictors. Machine Learning, 24, 123-140.

[12] Sharkey, A.J.C., Sharkey, N.E. and Chandroth, G.O. (1996) Diverse Neural Net solutions to a Fault Diagnosis Problem . Neural Computing and Applications, 4, 218-227.

[13] Parmanto, B., Munro, P.W. and Doyle, H.R. (1996) Reducing variance of committee prediction with resampling techniques. Connection Science, 8, 3/4, 405-416.

[14] Sharkey, A.J.C., Chandroth, G.O. and Sharkey, N.E. (2000) Acoustic Emission, Cylinder Pressure and Vibration: A Multisensor Approach to Robust Fault Diagnosis. In Proceedings of IJCNN2000, Como, Italy, July.

[15] Chandroth, G.O, Sharkey, A.J.C., and Sharkey, N.E. (1999) Vibration signatures, wavelets and principal components in diesel engine diagnostics. In Proceedings of ODRA '99: Third International Conference on Marine Technology, 1999.

[16] Chandroth, G.O. (2000) Diagnositic classifier ensembles: enforcing diversity for reliability in the combination. PhD Dissertation, University of Sheffield.

[17] Tumer, K. and Ghosh, J. (1996) Error correlation and error reduction in ensemble classifiers. Connection Science, 8, 3/4, 385-404.

[18] Dieterich, T.G. and Bakiri, G. (1995) Solving multiclass learning problems via error-correcting output codes. Journal of Artificial Intelligence Research, 2, 263-286.

[19] Breiman, L. (1998) Randomising outputs to increase prediction accuracy, Technical Report 518, Statistic Department, University of California.

[20] Raviv, Y. and Intrator, N. (1996) Bootstrapping with noise: an effective regularization technique. Connection Science, 8, 3/4, 355-372.

[21] Sharkey, A.J.C. and Sharkey, N.E. (1997) Combining Diverse Neural Nets, Knowledge Engineering Review, 12, 3, 1-17.

[22] Parmanto, B., Munro, P.W. and Doyle, H.R. (1994) Neural Network classifier for hepatoma detection. In Proceedings of the World Congress on Neural Networks, Vol 1, Mahway, NJ. Lawrence Erlbaum Associates.

[23] Breiman, L. (1999) Combining predictors. In A.J.C. Sharkey (Ed) Combining Artificial Neural Nets: Ensemble and Modular Multi-net Systems. London, Springer-Verlag, pp 31-50.

[24] Schapire, R., Freund, Y., Bartlett, P. and Lee, W. (1997) Boosting the margin: A new explanation for the effectiveness of voting methods. The Annals of Statistics, 26(5): 1651-1686.

[25] Quinlan, J.R. (1996) Bagging, boosting and C4.5. In Proceedings of the Thirteenth National Conference on Artificial Intelligence, pp725-730 Cambridge, MA. AAAI Press/MIT Press.

[26] Krogh, A., and Vedelsby, J. (1995) Neural network ensembles, cross validation, and active learning. In G.Tesauro, D. Touretzky, and T.Leen (Eds) Advances in Neural Information Processing Systems, 7, 231-238, Cambridge, MA, MIT Press.

[27] Geman, S., Bienenstock, E., Doursat, R. (1992) Neural networks and the bias/variance dilemma. Neural Computation,4, pp1-58.

[28] Opitz, D.W. and Shavlik, J.W. (1996) Actively searching for an effective neural network ensemble. Connection Science, 8, 3/4, 337-353.

[29] Hashem, S. (1996) Effects of collinearity on combining neural networks. Connection Science, 8, 3/4, 315-336.

[30] Gerecke, U., and Sharkey, N.E. (1999) Quick and dirty localisation for a lost robot. In Proceedings of IEEE international conference on Computational Intelligence for Robotics and Automation (CIRA-99), Monterey, CA.

A Survey of Sequential Combination of Word Recognizers in Handwritten Phrase Recognition at CEDAR

Sargur Srihari

Center of Excellence for Document Analysis and Recognition (CEDAR)
State University of New York at Buffalo

Abstract. Several methods for classifier combination have been explored at CEDAR. A sequential method for combining word recognizers in handwritten phrase recognition is revisited. The approach is to take phrase images as concatenations of the constituent words and submit them to multiple recognizers. An improvement of this method takes advantage of the spacing between words in a phrase. We describe the improvements to the overall system as a consequence of the second approach.

1 Introduction

Over the years, a number of classifier combination methods have been developed at our laboratory [1],[2],[3],[4]. These have been devised for character/digit recognition as well as for word and phrase recognition. This paper is an overview of two approaches to the task of phrase recognition, where a sequential combination approach is used. The first concatenates word images ignoring gaps, and the second does use word gaps to advantage.

2 Phrase Recognition Combination

A phrase consists of a sequence of words, such as, for the purposes of this paper, a street name, that appear in a postal address. The Phrase Recognition Combinator (PRC) will be used for phrase recognition. As described in [3], [5], the input to the system is a set of phrase images with associated lexicons. Given a phrase image and corresponding phrase lexicon PRC produces one of two possible outputs.

- Reject the image.
- Accept the image and return as output the recognized phrase.

The goal of the system is to maximize accept rate while keeping error rate and the average processing cost per call within acceptable limits, where these rates are computed over the entire set.

J. Kittler and F. Roli (Eds.): MCS 2000, LNCS 1857, pp. 45–51, 2000.

Two kinds of error may occur. *Classification Error* occurs when an incorrect phrase is selected as the top choice even when the true phrase is present in the lexicon. *Lexicon Hole Error* occurs when the true phrase is missing from the lexicon to begin with. Lexicon holes in a handwritten address interpretation system may result from incorrect location and/or incorrect recognition of the street number or the ZIP Code (or both) or from incomplete databases. The goal is to minimize the frequency of occurrence of either types of errors among the cases accepted.

2.1   Word Classifiers

Two handwritten word classifiers WMR and CMR were developed at CEDAR [6],[7]. As input, each of them uses a binary image and an ASCII lexicon; a confidence for each lexicon entry is computed a confidence and ranked by decreasing confidence. The confidences generated are *absolute*, *i.e.*, the confidence assigned to a particular lexicon entry depends only on the image and its ASCII contents and not on other entries in the lexicon.

WMR (Word Model Recognizer) [6] is a fast, lexicon-driven, analytical classifier that analyzes on the chain-coded description of the phrase image. After slant normalization and smoothing, the image is *over-segmented* at likely character segmentation points. The resulting segments are grouped, and the extracted features matched against letters in each lexicon entry using dynamic programming, and a graph is obtained. However, instead of passing on combination of segments to a generic OCR (as is done in CMR described next) lexicon is brought into play early in the process. A combination of adjacent segments (up to a maximum of 4) are compared by a dynamic programming approach to only those character choices which are possible at the position in the word being considered. The approach can be viewed as a process of accounting for all the segments generated by a given lexicon entry. Lexicon entries are ordered according to the "goodness" of match.

CMR (Character Model Recognizer) [7] uses a different approach. It attempts to isolate and recognize each character in the word using a character segmentation/recognition strategy. Correlations between local and distant pairs of strokes are analyzed. First, a word is segmented at potential character boundaries. Neighboring segments (up to 4) are then grouped together and sent to a OCR which uses a feature set of Gradient, Structural, and Concavity (GSC) features. The possible choices of characters with the respective confidence values is returned by the OCR.

The segmentation points are viewed as nodes of a graph and the corresponding character choices. Finding the word which best matches a lexicon entry is transformed into a search problem. Each path in the graph has an associated cost based on character choice confidences. Character strings obtained from the various paths (ordered by their costs) is matched with the lexicon entries to finally obtain the word recognition choices.

CMR is computationally more intense than WMR. The two recognizers are sufficiently orthogonal in approach as well as in the features used that they are useful in a combination strategy.

Training and test data sets were obtained from mail piece images captured by a postal sorter (MLOCR). Each set consists of street name images and the corresponding expanded lexicons, e.g., abbreviations and suffixes, as determined by the system.

The performance of WMR and CMR are 78% correct rate for both, and the error rates are 2.5% and 6%, respectively.

2.2   Combination Design

To improve overall speed, an important consideration during the design was that a decision ACCEPT or REJECT be reached as early as possible during the processing of an image. This observation argues for a hierarchical strategy for calling classifiers: the slower CMR is called if and only if a decision cannot be made based on the results of WMR. Similarly an attempt to combine classifier decisions is undertaken if and only if a decision cannot be made solely on the results of CMR. The simpler approach of calling both classifiers and combining their ranks or scores using parallel combination schemes proves computationally expensive because of the requirement that both classifiers be called for every image. In addition, parallel combination schemes are generally designed for correction of errors by reordering lexicon entries. The majority of errors in the present scenario is lexicon holes and hence cannot be corrected by reordering, and they can at best be rejected.

Lexicon Reduction WMR is correct more than 99% of the time when the top five choices are taken on a lexicon of size 10. Hence, CMR can be called with the reduced lexicon (5) instead of the complete lexicon.

Lexicon reduction increases efficiency and improves system performance. The improvement results from enhanced recognition performance of the second-stage classifier CMR since it deals with fewer confusion possibilities. Such improvements in recognition performance resulting from serial classifier combination have been empirically demonstrated elsewhere [3].

For the PRC, $n = 5$, $k = 2$ was chosen as a compromise between increased accept and error rates, where n is the size of the original lexicon, and k is the size of the reduced lexicon [5].

The error rate of the PRC on the postal test set is under 2%, and the CMR call rate is close to one-third.

Decision Combination The combination strategy is to sequentially cascade WMR and CMR. Images that either are not rejected or accepted with high confidence are passed to CMR. There are three issues:

1. Acceptance decision of the PRC can be based on the individual confidences returned by the classifiers WMR and CMR.
2. When the classifiers agree on the top choice, then it can be accepted with a high confidence, irrespective of the individual confidences. However, if the lexicon has a hole, this strategy is flawed.
3. When lexicons are small and classifiers are few, it may happen that all classifiers vote for the same entry, and all are in error. The confidences of the top choices must also be considered in the decision whether to accept or reject the image. The individual probabilities of correctness are combined using logistic regression, giving the probability that the common top choice is correct when WMR and CMR agree.

Thresholds Primary among WMR rejects are errors from lexicon holes. Although it is true that the rejects would also contain a small number of images correctly classified by WMR (albeit with low confidence) and some classification errors which may in theory be recovered by CMR, [3],[5] suggest that WMR rejects are best rejected as early as possible since there is no way to recover the truth in these cases (by CMR or by any other means). We also found that in practice, when WMR confidence is low, the probability that CMR correctly classified the image with a high confidence was negligible. Thus, there is little accomplished in terms of performance by *not* rejecting such cases. On the other hand, the reduction in calls to CMR by rejecting at this stage are considerable.

As noted in [3],[5], there are two opposing guidelines for selecting a threshold for WMR rejects: (i) the proportion of errors among the rejects should be high, and (ii) the number of rejects is related inversely to the number of calls to CMR. The threshold is chosen empirically.

The accept threshold for CMR is selected as the point at which the CMR error rate declines to zero. The reject threshold is selected so that the rejects are replete with errors. In this case, the benefit of rejecting larger numbers is not as great since the classifier combination is not an intensive operation. In addition, rejecting fewer correctly classified cases gives the combination a chance to recover these cases. Therefore, rejection is fairly conservative.

The two classifiers may agree on the top choice and still be wrong. A conservative threshold is computed using the individual confidences of the recognizers to reject cases where both recognizers may agree but still be in error.

3   Use of Word Gaps in Improving the System

In the second approach, we treat phrases as a group of words, as opposed to treating them as a single word with no spaces [6]. This has brought some improvement to the overall recognition rates.

The number of characters in an image segment is estimated by counting the number of times the distance between prime primitives is larger than the spatial period of estimated prime frequency. We skip the prime primitives whose distance to the previous neighbor is equal or less than prime period from left to right. But the accuracy of the estimated number strongly depends on the writing style because of flourishes and non-uniform character size or spacing.

3.1   Hypothesis Generation

If a candidate of word gap is significantly large than others, then we can be certain that the gap is a valid word break. As another restriction, if anchors are selected among candidate of word breaks, the matching complexity can be lower.

For the purpose of additional restriction to generate hypotheses, word break point candidates are categorized into two groups: *hard word point* and *soft word point*. The gap confidence is used for the classification. The combination of image segments crossing hard word points is not allowed as hypotheses.

To explain the generation of hypotheses, let us assume that the inputs are images in the application of street name recognition. To overcome missing or incorrect prefix and suffix, each lexicon entry is expanded in all conceivable ways. Also, we assume all additional information can be attached at the end of the street name.

All possible combination of image segments and lexeme are generated within the restriction of class of word break and boundary of estimated number of characters.

Lexemes which are out of range of the number of characters in the image segment are not attempted to be matched.

After generating lexeme hypotheses, phrase (lexicon) hypotheses are generated as a sequence of lexeme hypotheses index. A phrase can have multiple hypotheses sharing common lexeme hypotheses.

3.2   Hypothesis Verification

Because the hypotheses consist of word segments and a subset of possible lexemes, a lexicon driven word recognizer is preferred for hypotheses verification rather than character based word recognizer.

Dynamic programming based matching through character segments and character array of lexicons is used to find the best match between a word image and lexicon.

Since the average of an individual character's matching score is used in the word recognition confidence value, mismatches between characters and character segments are compensated by other good matches. Therefore, a longer string has a better chance of matching.

Finally the best match between the entire group of image segments has an advantage over individual lexeme based matching in hypothesis verification. Each possible group of image segments is submitted to word recognizers with eligible subsets of phrase strings. The word recognition scores are retained as the hypotheses confidence.

3.3 Experiment

The phrase recognition method described is applied to street name recognition. The street name images are collected from live mail pieces and the raw lexicons are obtained from postal databases. Since the testing set comes from live mail pieces, the sizes of lexicons are not fixed; they range from 1 to 100. In the test sets, 9% of images have additional unwanted segments such as apartment numbers in the input image.

The word segmentation algorithm misses actual word segmentation point in about 2% of all images, maintaining a perfect word segmentation in 48% and over segmentation points in 31% of images.

The recognition performance of phrase mode recognition is compared to that of word mode recognition, described in Section 2. The word mode recognition is a simplistic approach where a street name image is treated as a single word by ignoring word spacing.

Phrase mode recognition achieves higher correct ratio maintaining lower or same error rate. When applied to the handwritten address interpretation system, the phrase mode method achieves a 4% increase in finalization (assigning the ZIP + 4 Code). In the first method, all image components that follow the street number are treated as a single word, thereby merging apartment classifier numbers with the street name when the lexicon does not have the apartment information.

4   Conclusions and Future Directions

We have described two designs for a multi-classifier word recognition engine for a real-time phrase recognition application. The salient characteristics of the design are the use of logistic regression and agreement for evidence combination and lexicon reduction for improved throughput as well as performance.

A theory of combining several word recognizers in both sequential and parallel combination is being worked on at CEDAR and will be presented at this symposium.

Acknowledgement

The work described has had many contributions to it at CEDAR, principally Sriganesh Madhvanath, Evelyn Kleinberg, Jaehwa Park, and Venu Govindaraju.

References

1. T.-K. Ho, Theory of Multiple Classifier Systems and Its Application to Visual Word Recognition, PhD Dissertation, Department of Computer Science, SUNY at Buffalo, 1991.

2. D.-S. Lee, A Theory of Classifier Combinations: The Neural Network Approach, PhD Dissertation, Department of Computer Science, SUNY at Buffalo, 1995.
3. S. Madhvanath, Holistic Techniques for Handwritten Word Recognition Engines, PhD Dissertation, Department of Computer Science, SUNY at Buffalo, 1996.
4. J. Park, Hierarchical Character Recognition and Its Use in Word/Phrase Recognition, PhD Dissertation, Department of Electrical Engineering, SUNY at Buffalo, 2000.
5. S. Madhvanath and E. Kleinberg and V. Govindaraju, Empirical Design of a Multi-Classifier Thresholding/Control Strategy for Recognition of Handwritten Street Names, International Journal of Pattern Recognition and Artificial Intelligence, 11(6), 933-946, 1996.
6. G. Kim, Recognition of Offline Handwritten Words and Its Extension to Phrase Recognition, PhD Dissertation, Department of Computer Science, 1996.
7. J.T. Favata, Recognition of Handwritten Words UsingMulti-level Generate-and- Test, PhD Dissertation, Department of Computer Science, 1992.

Multiple Classifier Combination Methodologies for Different Output Levels

Ching Y. Suen[1] and Louisa Lam[1,2]

[1]Centre for Pattern Recognition and Machine Intelligence
Concordia University
1455 de Maisonneuve Blvd. West, Montréal, Québec H3G 1M8, Canada

[2]Department of Mathematics
Hong Kong Institute of Education
10 Lo Ping Road, Tai Po, Hong Kong

Abstract. In the past decade, many researchers have employed various methodologies to combine decisions of multiple classifiers in order to order to improve recognition results. In this article, we will examine the main combination methods that have been developed for different levels of classifier outputs - abstract level, ranked list of classes, and measurements. At the same time, various issues, results, and applications of these methods will also be considered, and these will illustrate the diversity and scope of this research area.

1 Introduction

About a decade ago, researchers initiated many methods to combine the decisions of several classifiers in order to produce accurate recognition results. This approach almost immediately produced promising results as shown in some early work in this area [7, 34, 39]. From this beginning, research in this domain has increased and grown tremendously, partly as a result of the coincident advances in the technology itself. These technological developments include the production of very fast and low cost computers that have made many complex algorithms practicable, among which are many pattern recognition algorithms.

The combination of multiple classifiers can be considered as a generic pattern recognition problem in which the input consists of the results of the individual classifiers, and the output is the combined decision. For this purpose, many developed classification techniques can be applied; in fact, classification techniques such as neural networks [28, 33, 41] and polynomial classifiers [5, 6] have served to combine the results of multiple classifiers.

In this paper, we will examine methodologies for classifier combination that have been developed so far. This discussion will be organized according to the types of output that can be produced by the individual classifiers: abstract level or single class output, ranked list of classes, and measurement level outputs. In the course of the discussion, results will be presented, and it will also be shown that combinations of classifiers have been applied to a wide range of applications.

J. Kittler and F. Roli (Eds.): MCS 2000, LNCS 1857, pp. 52–66, 2000.

2   Combinations of Abstract Level Outputs

In general, the methods that can be used to combine multiple classifier decisions depend on the types of information produced by the individual classifiers. Sometimes, combination methods utilizing all types of information may be used in one classification problem, as is the case for determining the layout of documents by combining results obtained through commercial OCR devices [27].

This section considers combination methods that can be applied when each classifier (also called an *expert*) e outputs a unique label or class for each input pattern. While such outputs are not very informative, this kind of output can be considered the most general, since all other types of outputs can be easily converted to this one. For these abstract-level classifiers, combination methods that have been proposed consist of majority vote [10, 17, 42], weighted majority vote [31], Bayesian formulation [42], a Dempster-Shafer theory of evidence [34], the Behavior-Knowledge Space method [14], and a dependency-based framework for optimal approximation of the product probability distribution [18–20]. All these methods have been applied to the OCR problem.

2.1   Voting Methods

Among the combination methods for abstract-level classifiers, majority vote is the simplest to implement, since it requires no prior training, and it has been used as early as 1974 [38]. The use of this method is especially appropriate in situations where other quantifiable forms of output cannot be easily obtained from individual classifiers, or where the use of other accurate combination methods may be too complex. Obvious examples of the former are some structural classifiers. For the latter, it may be very demanding to design sophisticated combination methods for up to 20,000 weak classifiers [17]. We can also consider the problem of differentiating the language used in printed documents [32]. To differentiate between Asian and Latin scripts (which is then a binary problem), the language category of each text-line can be determined from majority vote of its features, after which the category of each page is decided by majority vote of the text-lines. The results have been found to be 98.1% and 99.6% correct on standard and fine resolution images respectively. This combination method has also been found to be highly effective in determining the language category of documents in more languages in [29], when majority votes of 2 and 3 long text-lines have been used to determine the language category of a document page. The results are shown in Table 1.

From this process of simple majority vote in which the decision of each classifier carries equal weight, various refinements can be made. This can be done by assigning different weights to each classifier to optimize the performance of the combined classifier on the training set, or a Bayesian formulation that takes into consideration the performance of each classifier on each class of patterns.

For the first refinement, weights can be generated by a genetic algorithm and assigned to the vote of each classifier to determine the optimal values for an objective function. This function can incorporate conditions on the recognition and error rates; for example, it can be the function $F = Recognition - \beta \times Error$, where β can take on different values. Obviously, the value of β varies with the accuracy or reliability desired for a particular application, and higher values of β imply higher costs would be imposed on errors. Maximizing this function F is equivalent to minimizing the precision index $Rejection + (\beta + 1) \times Error$. This approach has been implemented [31], and it has been found that the genetic algorithm is effective in detecting redundant and weak classifiers (by assigning low weights to them). The results are presented in Table 2.

Table 1. Results of Language Category Determination [29]

# Text-lines used	# Samples	Recognition(%)	Error(%)	Rejection(%)
1	524	97.52	2.48	0.00
2	524	97.71	0.00	2.29
3	523	99.62	0.38	0.00

2.2 Bayesian Combination Rule

The genetic algorithm implemented assigns a weight to the vote of each classifier, and this weight would be applied to all patterns regardless of the decision made by the expert. Another method of determining the weights is through the Bayesian decision rule, which takes into consideration the performance of each expert on the training samples of each class. In particular, the confusion matrix C of each classifier on a training set of data would be used as indications of its performance. For a problem with M possible classes plus the reject option, C is an $M \times (M + 1)$ matrix in which the entry C_{ij} denotes the number of patterns with actual class i that is assigned class j by the classifier when $j \leq M$, and when $j = M + 1$, it represents the number of patterns that are rejected.

From the matrix C, we can obtain the total number of samples belonging to class i as the row sum $\sum_{j=1}^{M+1} C_{ij}$, while the column sum $\sum_{i=1}^{M} C_{ij}$ represents the total number of samples that are assigned class j by this expert. When there are K experts, there would be K confusion matrices $C^{(k)}$, $1 \leq k \leq K$. Consequently, the conditional probability that a pattern x actually belongs to class i, given that expert k assigns it to class j, can be estimated as

$$P(x \in C_i \mid e_k(x) = j) = \frac{C_{ij}^{(k)}}{\sum_{i=1}^{M} C_{ij}^{(k)}}, \tag{1}$$

and this term can represent the degree of accuracy when expert k assigns class i to a sample.

For any pattern x such that the classification results by the K experts are $e_k(x) = j_k$ for $1 \leq k \leq K$, we can define a belief value that x belongs to class i as

$$bel(i) = P(x \in C_i \mid e_1(x) = j_1, ..., e_K(x) = j_K). \tag{2}$$

By applying the Bayes' formula and assuming independence of the expert decisions [42], $bel(i)$ can be approximated by

$$bel(i) \doteq \frac{\prod_{k=1}^{K} P(x \in C_i \mid e_k(x) = j_k)}{\sum_{i=1}^{M} \prod_{k=1}^{K} P(x \in C_i \mid e_k(x) = j_k)} \tag{3}$$

for $1 \leq i \leq M$.

For any input pattern x, we can assign x to class j if $bel(j) > bel(i)$ for all $i \neq j$ and $bel(j) > \alpha$ for a threshold α. Otherwise x is rejected, and it is also rejected if $e_k(x) = M + 1$ for all k (i.e., if x is rejected by all classifiers). The results obtained from this method depend on the value of α chosen. As α increases, so does the degree of certainty expected of the decision; therefore the error rate would decrease, but the recognition rate would be also lower.

The methods of majority vote, weighted majority vote, and Bayesian formulation were applied to combine the results of seven classifiers on handwritten digits. The combinations were trained on 13272 samples and tested on 8752 samples, and the results are shown in Table 2.

Table 2. Performance of Classifiers on Handwritten Numerals

	Training Set		Test Set	
Expert	Recognition	Error	Recognition	Error
e1	82.791	3.187	84.004	3.005
e2	91.132	1.982	92.207	1.874
e3	93.264	1.575	93.864	1.165
e4	87.176	1.831	88.425	1.714
e5	94.929	0.799	95.007	0.857
e6	95.999	0.821	96.023	0.697
e7	93.716	5.327	95.212	4.273
Combination				
Majority vote	96.233	0.196	96.778	0.160
Bayesian	98.162	0.218	97.784	0.571
Genetic alg.	96.903	0.151	97.075	0.228

For the results shown, the value of α used in the Bayesian method was chosen to maximize the value of the same objective function F. These results indicate the following:

(i) The training set probably contains more difficult samples and is not completely representative, which means algorithms highly fitted to the training set may not generalize well.
(ii) This training set of 13272 samples is insufficient to establish accurate values of the belief function for the Bayesian method. This problem is especially serious due to the product form of $bel(i)$.

(iii) Despite its simplicity, majority vote still remains a reliable means of combining results from abstract level classifiers. This is true especially when the reliability factor is considered ($reliability = \frac{correct}{1-rejection}$).

2.3   Other Abstract Level Combination Methods

For the Bayesian method described above, the calculation of the belief function assumes conditional independence of the expert decisions in order to obtain

$$
\begin{aligned}
&P(x \in C_i, e_1(x) = j_1, ..., e_K(x) = j_K) \\
&= P(e_1(x) = j_1, ..., e_K(x) = j_K \mid x \in C_i)P(x \in C_i) \\
&= P(x \in C_i)\prod_{k=1}^{K} P(e_k(x) = j_k \mid x \in C_i),
\end{aligned}
\tag{4}
$$

and in this way the difficulty of calculating the $(K + 1)st$ order probability distribution had been reduced.

The Behavior-Knowledge Space (BKS) method [14], which can be considered to be a refinement of the Bayesian method, does not assume conditional independence, and it establishes this high order probability distribution from the frequencies of occurrence in the training set. This implies the need for estimating M^{K+1} probabilities when M classes and K classifiers are involved, and a huge volume of training data would be required. It is therefore not surprising that 4000 samples of handwritten digits had been found to be deficient for combining 4 to 6 experts by this method [18–20].

These last references also do not assume independence, and they approximate a high order probability distributions with a product of low order distributions by using a dependency-directed approach. Then classifiers are combined by Bayesian rules through the approximate distributions. These methods reduce the storage needs of the BKS method, but the computational costs are not negligible. The new algorithms have been trained and tested on 4000 and 2000 samples of handwritten digits respectively, and they do produce results superior to those of the BKS method. However, it is not clear that these results are definitely better than those obtained from simple majority vote when the reliability factor is important [19]. To establish their superiority, perhaps it would be desirable to train and test these methods on larger data sets.

The recognition results of these combination methods are summarized in Table 3, in which CIAB denotes the Conditional Independence Based Bayesian method, while ΔFODB and ΔSODB represent respectively the First and Second Order Dependency-Based methods proposed in [19]. The numbers in parentheses denote rejection rates.

2.4   Observations on Combining Abstract Level Outputs

For a group of abstract level classifiers each of which outputs only a class label for each input pattern, the means of obtaining a combined decision is bound to be limited to some sort of voting scheme, with or without taking prior performance into consideration.

When prior performance is not considered, simple majority vote is used. By nature of its simplicity, its requirements (of time and memory) are negligible. It has the further advantage that theoretical analyses can be made of this method, so that certain facets of its behavior can be deduced. For example, we can confidently predict that an even number $2n$ of classifiers would produce more reliable combined recognition results than can be obtained by adding another classifier, or by eliminating one of the classifiers. This conclusion is valid whether the classifiers are independent or not. For this and other properties of this method, the reader is referred to [30].

Table 3. Combinations of Classifiers by a Dependency-based Framework

Combination	Five classifiers
Voting	97.20 (1.35), 97.50 (1.05), 97.40 (1.60), 97.35 (1.50), 96.55 (2.25), 96.55 (2.40)
BKS	91.15 (8.30), 91.75 (8.00), 92.90 (6.75), 92.20 (7.40), 92.00 (7.35), 90.90 (8.35)
CIAB	96.55 (0.00), 97.10 (0.00), 97.35 (0.00), 97.35 (0.00), 97.55 (0.00), 97.20 (0.00)
ΔFODB	97.65 (0.00), 97.70 (0.00), 98.25 (0.00), 97.80 (0.00), 97.65 (0.00), 97.65 (0.00)
ΔSODB	97.75 (0.00), 97.90 (0.00), 97.90 (0.00), 98.05 (0.00), 97.60 (0.00), 97.90 (0.00)
Combination	Six classifiers
Voting	97.60 (1.10)
BKS	89.55 (10.25)
CIAB	97.60 (0.00)
ΔFODB	98.00 (0.00)
ΔSODB	98.05 (0.00)

Recently, an experimental study has been conducted to evaluate the results of simple majority vote and Dempster-Shafer combination method in relation to the degree of correlation among the experts [15]. This work assumes that all classifiers have the same recognition rate and no rejections. For a group A of experts, the *Similarity Index* ρ_A is defined to be the average pairwise correlation among the experts of A. For each value of ρ_A, 10 sets of experts (having different numbers of experts and different recognition rates) have been considered and tested over 100 simulated data items. The results are given of the combined recognition rate as a function of ρ_A for the various groups. One main finding of this work is that majority vote achieves higher reliability than the Dempster-Shafer method, while the second combination method usually has higher recognition rates.

The incorporation of prior performance into the combined decision can assume different forms. In [4], the accuracy of expert k assigning class i to a sample, viz. $P(x \in C_i \mid e_k(x) = j)$ can be used to break ties when decisions of two experts are combined. For the majority vote of two classifiers (which is actually agreement), the recognition rate cannot exceed that of the lower performing classifier, and any tie breaking procedure will certainly increase the recognition rate, even though this may involve a trade-off in reliability. In general, this tie-breaking procedure will increase the recognition rate when even numbers of classifiers are combined. However, it would not be useful in improving recognition rates when odd numbers of experts are combined, because it is highly unlikely that the quantities would be large enough to change the results of simple majority vote in these cases.

As we refine this voting process through increasingly specific knowledge acquisition and modeling, we consider (in that order) weighted majority vote, Bayesian formulation, and the BKS method. The demands on memory also increase in that order, until we arrive at the exponential requirements of the BKS method. More importantly, these methods also impose heavy demands on the quality and size of the training set. Highly specific modeling requires large volumes of representative data; otherwise overfitting may occur, and the generalization capability would diminish. In an effort to reduce the requirements of the BKS method, statistical approaches have been used to approximate a high order probability distribution with a product of lower order distributions [18–20], and that is the current state of the art on this aspect of the subject.

3   Combinations of Ranked Lists

Some classifiers can output a list of possible classes with rankings attached to them. These rankings can be simply an order, or they can be represented by confidence values or distances, which are considered to be measurement level outputs. These measurements represent the most informative outputs that can be provided by classifiers, and the methods for combining these outputs also have the greatest variety. In this section, we consider combinations of only the rankings.

Rankings can be the preferable parameters for use in combination because there may be a lack of consistency in the measurements produced by different classifiers. Advantages of using rankings have been described in detail in [11]. Compared to majority vote, combinations of rankings are suitable for pattern recognition problems with many classes, so that the correct class may not appear as the class designated by a classifier, but the occurrence of a class near the top of the list should be significant. For this reason, ranked lists are used more often in word recognition problems with a sizeable lexicon (as opposed to the set of digits).

Borda counts have been used to determine the ranking of a group of experts [11]. This method is equivalent to majority vote in that it requires no training and is very simple to compute. As with majority vote, it does not take into consideration the different abilities of the individual classifiers. However, unlike majority vote, this method is not supported by theoretical underpinnings; on the contrary, the outcomes of using Borda counts are well known to depend on the scale of numbers assigned to the choices.

In order to account for different levels of performance, the Borda count can be modified by the assignment of weights to the rank scores produced by each classifier to denote the relative importance of the ranking made by each classifier. This procedure involves a training process, and it can be considered to be analogous to weighted majority vote. Using this method, the *log-odds* or *logit* is approximated by a linear combination of the rank scores output by the classifiers as

$$\frac{\log \pi(\mathbf{x})}{1 - \pi(\mathbf{x})} = \alpha + \beta_1 x_1 + \beta_2 x_2 + \ldots + \beta_K x_K, \tag{5}$$

where $\mathbf{x} = (x_1, x_2, \ldots, x_K)$ is the vector of rank scores assigned by the K experts, and α, β_1, β_2, $\ldots$, β_K are model parameters that can be determined from the training set. In [11], the parameters are estimated by linear regression analysis for four classifiers in a word recognition problem. For a fingerprint verification system [16] in which three matching algorithms are used, the parameters are estimated to minimize the Type I Error at each level of Type II Error by numerical algorithms.

As a further refinement in the use of rank scores, the distribution of rankings produced by the classifiers can be used to denote the quality of the input pattern. For example, a high degree of agreement among the top choices can indicate an easily recognizable pattern. In the training process, the training set can be partitioned according to this state of agreement and a regression model estimated separately for each subset of the partition. In the test stage, an input pattern can be mapped to an appropriate partition by the state of agreement among classifier outputs, and the corresponding regression model applied to produce the recognition result. This dynamic selection approach was implemented in [11], and it was found to have the highest performance among all combination methods for the top three choices. The results of these methods are summarized in Table 4.

Table 4. Word Recognition Results [11]

Combination	% Correct in Top N Choices				
	N = 1	2	3	5	10
Borda count	87.4	95.8	97.2	98.2	99.0
Linear regression	90.7	96.2	97.5	98.5	99.0
Dynamic selection	93.9	97.2	97.9	98.3	99.0

Another method in which rank scores can be used in the combination of classifiers is by a serial architecture, in which the rankings assigned by one recognizer can be used to reduce the number of target classes for subsequent classification(s) by other recognizers. This approach has been implemented in [9], for processing the legal amount written on bank cheques. For each word to be processed, a KNN wholistic word recognizer is used to reduce the lexicon size from about

30 classes down to 10, from which an HMM recognizer determines the target classes. This combination has produced a 2% increase in recognition rate of the top choice, as shown in Table 5.

From the two preceding sets of results, it can be noted that the effectiveness of a combination method may be best seen in the results of the top choice (rather than the top N choices for $N > 1$). Perhaps this exemplifies the *Law of Diminishing Returns* - when classifiers have higher levels of performance (as is the case when more choices are included), it becomes much more difficult to improve on their performance.

In general, rank scores have been used less often for combination purposes, probably because few classifiers are devoted to producing only rank scores for output. If measurements are produced for output, these would provide a potentially richer source of information on the data than the resultant rank scores derived from them, and there are more ways of combining these measurements to advantage. Even when the measurements produced by different classifiers may not be consistent in magnitude, various normalization procedures and functions have been devised to make these measurements more comparable. On the other hand, classifiers that do not provide output information in the form of confidence values or distances would have difficulty ranking the classes in an effective manner. Perhaps for these reasons, less research has been published on this aspect of the subject.

Table 5. Recognition Results of French Legal Amount Words [9]

		% Correct in Top N Choices		
Classifier	N = 1	2	5	10
KNN	78.3	91.8	98.9	99.9
HMM	84.7	92.9	97.9	99.4
KNN + HMM	86.7	94.6	98.7	99.9

4   Combinations of Measurement Level Outputs

In recent years, much attention has been devoted to the development of classifiers that can output confidence values or distance measures for each input sample, for each target class. This includes in particular the many neural network classifiers that have been designed and implemented for various pattern recognition tasks. These measurements can denote the likelihood of a sample belonging to a class, and also provide information relative to other classes. These numerical measurements can be transformed through various functions to yield new representations. With this potentially rich source of information available, it is natural for combination strategies to make use of these measurements experimentally, and many such combination strategies have been developed. These will be discussed in this section. As in the consideration of other kinds of outputs, we will begin with methods that do not require prior training.

4.1   Basic Combination Operators

When there are K classifiers each producing M measurements (one for each of M classes) for each sample pattern, the simplest means of combining them to obtain a decision are the *Max, Min, Sum,* and *Median* rules. The *Ave* rule is equivalent to the *Sum* rule.

These rules have often been used to combine recognition results. For example, in [2] three neural networks using different feature sets have been trained and tested on the NIST SD3 database, with very high recognition rates of 99.3%, 99.14%, and 99.21%. A recognition rate of 99.59% was achieved when the confidence values of the classifiers were combined using the *Sum* operator.

The *Min, Ave* and *Bayes* rules have been used in [13] to combine confidence outputs of operators from isolated digit classification. Pairwise combinations of four digit recognizers (two hardware- and two software-based) were made. The *Bayes* operator considers the confidences as probabilities and combines them using Bayes' Rule. If C_A and C_B represent the confidences assigned to a given character by recognizers A and B, then the combined confidence is given by

$$C_{AB} = \frac{C_A C_B}{C_A C_B + \frac{(1-C_A)(1-C_B)}{M-1}}, \tag{6}$$

where M is the number of classes. Among the operators used, the authors have found the *Ave* operator to be the most robust against peculiarities of individual classifiers. A similar result has been observed in a sensitivity analysis conducted in [24], where the *Sum* rule is shown to be most resilient to estimation errors. This work also reports on an experimental comparison of various combination schemes, for four classifiers applied to the recognition of the database of handwritten digits in the CEDAR CDROM. The results are shown in Table 6.

Table 6. Results on Handwritten Digits in the CEDAR Database [24]

Individual classifier	Recognition rate %
Structural	90.85
Gaussian	93.93
Neural Net	93.20
HMM	94.77
Combining rule	Recognition rate %
Majority vote	97.76
Sum	98.05
Max	93.93
Min	86.00
Product	84.69
Median	98.19

Another experiment was conducted to investigate these basic combination rules by simulation [1]. Tests were conducted for a single point in the *a posteriori* space one at a time, and this point has a fixed value. For each such point, experts' estimates are considered to be this posterior probability plus noise. Noise can be added by uniform or Gaussian noise generators at different levels. The simulated outputs of experts are combined using the different rules, and the combined results noted for different kinds and levels of noise. In general, it was found that the combinations (especially *Sum* and *Median*) produced better results than the single expert. However, the single expert may be preferable over the *Product*, *Min* and *Max* operators under Gaussian noise with high standard deviations. This conclusion also supports the findings of [13] and [24].

A common theoretical framework for these combination rules has been established in [22–26]. These works establish that when multiple experts use different representations, the calculation of the *a posteriori* probability for the combined decision can be simplified with certain assumptions to result in the basic combination rules mentioned in this section. The *Product* and *Min* rules can be obtained by assuming the classifiers to be conditionally statistically independent. The *Sum*, *Max*, *Median* and Majority Vote rules can follow from the additional assumption that the *a posteriori* probabilities computed by the respective classifiers will not deviate significantly from the prior probabilities. While these assumptions may appear to be strong (especially the latter one), the conditional independence assumption is often made for ease of computation. As indicated already, the basic combination rules are often used, and have been found to be effective in improving classification results. The theoretical derivation given in the works cited here represents one possible avenue of providing a theoretical basis for them.

4.2   Weighted Operators on Measurement Level Outputs

The basic operators discussed in the last section are the most immediate means of combining measurement level outputs from individual classifiers, and they do not require prior training. It is logical to broaden the combination methodologies and include information on prior performances of the individual classifiers to obtain better informed combined decisions.

As is the case with combinations of outputs at other levels, one natural extension would be the introduction of weights to the outputs of classifiers. These weights should be indicative of the performance of each classifier, and they have been introduced through various means. In [21], the outputs of two classifiers (an HMM and a multi-layer perceptron) are assigned weights of 1 and 2 simply according to their performance ranking, with the better performer assigned the weight of 2. The weights are then used either as factors (LCA method) or as exponents of the outputs (weighted multiplication). The weighted outputs for each class are summed for the LCA method and multiplied together for the second method, after which the combined decision is obtained by the *Max* rule. This method is applied to the recognition of the words and abbreviations used to represent the month on handwritten bank cheques, with the results shown in Table 7.

Other means of assigning weights to measurements consist of using linear regression to approximate *log odds* as discussed in the section on ranked lists. This approach had been used for pairwise combinations in [13] for the recognition of isolated digits, and in [28] for the recognition of digits and words. Several interesting observations have been made in these articles. The former work stated that none of the combination operators had shown a clear advantage over the others, and that by far the best predictor of the outcome of a pairwise combination was the performance of the individual classifiers. It is reasonable to suppose that this statement would apply to combinations of small numbers of classifiers. When larger numbers of classifiers are involved, the contributions of each classifier to the combination may be less clear, and the interaction between classifiers would assume more significance. For this consideration, it is worth noting [28] that redundant classifiers can be detected in the process of determining the weights when four classifiers are combined using the *log-linear* rule for the combination of candidate lists [8]. When the number of classifiers should be reduced for practical implementation, this can become a useful process.

Table 7. Recognition Results of Month Words [21]

Classifier	N =	1	2	3	4	5
		% Correct in Top N Choices				
HMM		76.6	86.2	90.4	93.4	95.3
MLP		80.0	90.5	94.0	95.5	96.9
Combination						
Voting		84.1	92.2	95.3	96.9	98.3
LCA		84.9	92.8	95.4	97.0	98.2
Multiplication		87.3	94.1	96.3	97.0	97.7

4.3   Other Combinations of Measurement Level Outputs

In the Introduction section of this article, it has been stated that the combination of multiple classifiers can be considered as a generic pattern recognition problem in which the input consists of the results of the individual classifiers, and the output is the combined decision. The combination operator also functions as a classifier in this respect; conversely, standard classification techniques can be made to function as combinators. This is clearly evident in the use of neural networks for combining the confidence values of classifiers to produce, in turn, new confidence values. This method has been widely applied to different recognition problems.

For example, this method had been used in [33] for handwritten digits, [28] for words, and [41] for the classification of documents. This last article reports on a content-based text categorization of printed German business letters into pre-defined message types such as order, invoice, etc. using a combination of two classifiers by a neural network.

The use of neural networks for combination usually increases significantly the need for a large amount of representative data, as this is necessary for training the network so that it will generalize well. When we add to this the need for data with which to train the individual classifiers, the requirement increases steeply.

As a further example of other combination methods, a fuzzy integral has been implemented to combine three neural network classifiers for recognition of bacteria [40]. As pattern recognition methodologies develop, it can safely be predicted that combination strategies will be developed in conjunction.

5   Concluding Remarks

In this article, we have described methods for combining the decisions of classifiers for different types of outputs. The combination methods can be applied by various architectures [3, 12, 35–37]. For each type of output, combination methods have been developed from simple operations requiring no prior training, to complex and highly tailored methods that can produce higher recognition rates. However, these better recognition rates may be accompanied by higher costs in terms of computation requirements, quantity of training data, and difficulty of theoretical analysis.

Acknowledgements

This research was supported by the Natural Sciences and Engineering Research Council of Canada, the National Networks of Centres of Excellence program of Canada, and the FCAR program of the Ministry of Education of the province of Québec.

References

1. F. M. Alkoot and J. Kittler. Experimental evaluation of expert fusion strategies. *Pattern Recognition Letters*, 20:1352–1369, 1999.
2. A. S. Atukorale and P. N. Suganthan. Combining classifiers based on confidence values. In *Proc. Fifth Int. Conf. on Document Analysis and Recognition*, pages 37–40, Bangalore, India, Sept. 1999.
3. Y.-C. Chim, A. A. Kassim, and Y. Ibrahim. Dual classifier system for handprinted alphanumeric character recognition. *Pattern Analysis and Applications*, 1:155–162, 1998.
4. L. P. Cordella, P. Foggia, C. Sansone, F. Tortorella, and M. Veneto. Reliability parameters to improve combination strategies in multi-expert systems. *Pattern Analysis and Applications*, 2:205–214, 1999.
5. J. Franke. Statistical combination of multiple classifier adapted on image parts. In *Proc. 1st European Meeting on Postal Technology (JET POSTE)*, pages 566–572, Nantes, France, 1993.
6. J. Franke and M. Oberlander. Writing style detection by statistical combination of classifiers in form reader applications. In *Proc. 2nd Int. Conf. on Document Analysis and Recognition*, pages 581–584, Tsukuba, Japan, Oct. 1993.

7. P. D. Gader, D. Hepp, B. Forrester, and T. Peurach. Pipelined systems for recognition of handwritten digits in USPS ZIP codes. In *Proc. U. S. Postal Service Advanced Technology Conf.*, pages 539–548, 1990.

8. N. Gorski. Practical combination of multiple classifiers. In *Proc. Fifth Int. Workshop on Frontiers in Handwriting Recognition*, pages 115–118, Colchester, UK, Sept. 1996.

9. D. Guillevic and C. Y. Suen. HMM-KNN word recognition engine for bank cheque processing. In *Proc. 14th ICPR*, pages II: 1526–1529, Brisbane, Australia, August 1998.

10. T. K. Ho. The random subspace method for constructing decision forests. *IEEE Trans. PAMI*, 20(8):832–844, 1998.

11. T. K. Ho, J. J. Hull, and S. N. Srihari. Decision combination in multiple classifier systems. *IEEE Trans. PAMI*, 16:66–75, 1994.

12. T.K. Ho. Adaptive coordination of multiple classifiers. In J.J. Hull and S.L. Taylor, editors, *Document Analysis Systems II*, pages 371–384. World Scientific, 1998.

13. G.F. Houle, D.B. Aragon, R.W. Smith, M. Shridhar, and D. Kimura. A multi-layered corroboration-based check reader. In J.J. Hull and S.L. Taylor, editors, *Document Analysis Systems II*, pages 495–546. World Scientific, 1998.

14. Y. S. Huang and C. Y. Suen. Combination of multiple experts for the recognition of unconstrained handwritten numerals. *IEEE Trans. Pattern Anal. Mach. Intell.*, 17:90–94, 1995.

15. S. Impedovo and A. Salzo. Evaluation of combination methods. In *Proc. Fifth Int. Conf. on Document Analysis and Recognition*, pages 394–397, Bangalore, India, Sept. 1999.

16. A. K. Jain, S. Prabhakar, and S. Chen. Combining multiple matches for a high security fingerprint verification system. *Pattern Recognition Letters*, 20:1371–1379, 1999.

17. C. Ji and S. Ma. Combinations of weak classifiers. *IEEE Trans. Neural Networks*, 8(1):32–42, 1997.

18. H.-J. Kang, K. Kim, and J. H. Kim. Optimal approximation of discrete probability distribution with kth-order dependency and its application to combining multiple classifiers. *Pattern Recognition Letters*, 18:515–523, 1997.

19. H.-J. Kang and S.-W. Lee. Combining classifiers based on minimization of a Bayes error rate. In *Proc. Fifth Int. Conf. on Document Analysis and Recognition*, pages 398–401, Bangalore, India, Sept. 1999.

20. H.-J. Kang and S.-W. Lee. A dependency-based framework of combining multiple experts for the recognition of unconstrained handwritten numerals. In *Proc. 1999 IEEE Computer Society Conf. on Computer Vision and Pattern Recognition*, pages 124–129, Fort Collins, Colorado, USA, June 1999.

21. J. H. Kim, K. K. Kim, C. P. Nadal, and C. Y. Suen. A methodology of combining HMM and MLP classifiers for cursive word recognition. In *Proc. 15th Int. Conf. on Pattern Recognition*, Barcelona, Spain, Sept. 2000. To appear.

22. J. Kittler. Improving recognition rates by classifier combination. In *Fifth Int. Workshop on Frontiers in Handwriting Recognition*, pages 81–101, Colchester, UK, Sept. 1996.

23. J. Kittler. Combining classifiers: a theoretical framework. *Pattern Analysis and Applications*, 1:18–27, 1998.

24. J. Kittler. On combining classifiers. *IEEE Trans. PAMI*, 20(3):226–239, 1998.

25. J. Kittler. Pattern classification: fusion of information. In *Proc. Int. Conf. on Advances in Pattern Recognition*, pages 13–22, Plymouth, UK, November 1998.

26. J. Kittler, M. Hatef, and R.P.W. Duin. Combining classifiers. In *Proc. 13th Int. Conf. on Pattern Recognition*, pages II: 897–901, Vienna, Austria, August 1996.

27. S. Klink and T. Jager. *MergeLayouts* - overcoming faulty segmentations by a comprehensive voting of commercial OCR devices. In *Proc. Fifth Int. Conf. on Document Analysis and Recognition*, pages 386–389, Bangalore, India, Sept. 1999.

28. S. Knerr, O. Baret, D. Price, J.C. Simon, V. Anisimov, and N. Gorski. The A2iA recognition system for handwritten checks. In *Proc. IAPR Workshop on Document Analysis Systems*, pages 431–494, Malvern, Penn., USA, October 1996.

29. L. Lam, J. Ding, and C. Y. Suen. Differentiating between Oriental and European scripts by statistical features. *Int. J. Pattern Recogn. and Artificial Intell.*, 12(1):63–79, 1998.

30. L. Lam and C. Y. Suen. Application of majority voting to pattern recognition: an analysis of its behavior and performance. *IEEE Trans. Systems, Man, and Cybernetics*, 27(5):553–568, 1997.

31. L. Lam and C.Y. Suen. Optimal combinations of pattern classifiers. *Pattern Recognition Letters*, 16:945–954, 1995.

32. D.-S. Lee, C. R. Nohl, and H. S. Baird. Language identification in complex, un-oriented, and degraded document images. In *Proc. IAPR Workshop on Document Analysis Systems*, pages 76–98, Malvern, Penn., USA, October 1996.

33. D.S. Lee and S.N. Srihari. Handprinted digit recognition: A comparison of algorithms. In *Pre-Proc. 3rd Int. Workshop on Frontiers in Handwriting Recognition*, pages 153–162, Buffalo, USA, May 1993.

34. E. Mandler and J. Schuermann. Combining the classification results of independent classifiers based on the Dempster/Shafer theory of evidenc. In E.S. Geselma and L.N. Kanal, editors, *Pattern Recognition and Artificial Intelligence*, pages 381–393. North Holland, Amsterdam, 1988.

35. R.K. Powalka, N. Sherkat, and R.J. Whitrow. Multiple recognizer combination topologies. In M.L. Simner, C.G. Leedham, and A.J.W.M. Thomasson, editors, *Handwriting and Drawing Research : Basic and Applied Issues*, pages 329–342. IOS Press, 1996.

36. A.F.R. Rahman and M.C. Fairhurst. An evaluation of multi-expert configurations for the recognition of handwritten numerals. *Pattern Recognition*, 31(9):1255–1273, 1998.

37. F.R. Rahman and M. C. Fairhurst. Serial combination of multiple experts: a unified evaluation. *Pattern Analysis and Applications*, 2:292–311, 1999.

38. A. A. Spanjersberg. Combination of different systems for the recognition of handwritten digits. In *Proc. 2nd Int. Joint Conf. on Pattern Recognition*, pages 208–209, Copenhagen, Aug. 1974.

39. C.Y. Suen, C. Nadal, T.A. Mai, R. Legault, and L. Lam. Recognition of totally unconstrained handwritten numerals based on the concept of multiple experts. In *Proc. Int. Workshop on Frontiers in Handwriting Recognition*, pages 131–143, Montréal, Canada, April 1990.

40. D. Wang, J. M. Keller, C.A. Carson, K.K. McAdoo-Edwards, and C. W. Bailey. Use of fuzzy-logic-inspired features to improve bacterial recognition through classifier fusion. *IEEE Trans. SMC*, 28B(4):583–591, 1998.

41. C. Wenzel, S. Baumann, and T. Jager. Advances in document classification by voting of competitive approaches. In *Document Analysis Systems II*, pages 385–405. World Scientific, 1998.

42. L. Xu, A. Krzyzak, and C. Y. Suen. Methods of combining multiple classifiers and their application to handwritten numeral recognition. *IEEE Trans. Systems, Man, and Cybernetics*, 22:418–435, 1992.

A Mathematically Rigorous Foundation for Supervised Learning [*]

Eugene M. Kleinberg

Department of Mathematics, The State University of New York, Buffalo NY 14214.
kleinbrg@math.buffalo.edu

Abstract. This paper consists of two parts, one theoretical, and one experimental. And while its primary focus is the development of a mathematically rigorous, theoretical foundation for the field of supervised learning, including a discussion of what constitutes a "solvable pattern recognition problem", it will also provide some algorithmic detail for implementing the general classification method derived from the theory, a method based on classifier combination, and will discuss experimental results comparing its performance to other well-known methods on standard benchmark problems from the U.C. Irvine, and Statlog, collections. The practical consequences of this work are consistent with the mathematical predictions. Comparing our experimental results on 24 standard benchmark problems taken from the U.C. Irvine, and Statlog, collections, with those reported in the literature for other well-known methods, our method placed 1st on 19 problems, 2nd on 2 others, 4th on another, and 5th on the remaining 2.

Keywords: machine learning, pattern recognition, classification algorithms, stochastic discrimination, SD, boosting.

1 Introduction

We are about to develop the ideas behind a particular approach to solving problems in supervised learning. The method derived from this approach is very general, and algorithmic implementations have produced results which, in most observed cases, are superior to those produced by any other method of which we are aware. And while this should certainly be an important consideration for interest here, we feel that it is the underlying mathematical theory, and the implications of this theory providing a perspective underlying existing work in the field in general, as well as a basis for future work, which merits the greatest attention. As one example of this, we might note that the mathematics we are about to develop provides a complete theoretical explanation for the experimentally observed success of the method of boosting, including the ability of boosting to generalize to unseen data; and, based on this theoretical understanding, provides a clear direction for improvement for future boosting algorithms (see [7,8]).

---

[*] This work uses software copyrighted by K Square Inc

J. Kittler and F. Roli (Eds.): MCS 2000, LNCS 1857, pp. 67–76, 2000.
© Springer-Verlag Berlin Heidelberg 2000

Although we will not present explicit pseudo-code for an algorithmic implementation of our method, we will provide a description sufficient for creating such an implementation. As motivation for the mathematics which will be presented in later sections of this paper, we begin with a discussion of experimental results, comparing our particular algorithmic implementation of the method, henceforth referred to as *SDK*, to other well-know pattern recognition methods. Our use of the word "motivation" here is somewhat nonstandard. It is our hope that readers will find the experimental results for SDK sufficiently promising that they are motivated to thoroughly read the mathematical theory which follows, and use their understanding of it to create their own, hopefully superior, implementations.

Detail concerning our implementation, SDK, can be found in [7]. However, we feel that it might be useful, at this time, to point out the following: SDK operates by first (pseudo) randomly sampling (with replacement) from a space of *subsets* of the feature space underlying a given problem, and then combining these subsets to form a final classifier. There are many ways to contrast this approach with other classification methods, but perhaps the most striking deals with the perspective from which one attacks the problem of establishing theoretical bounds on classifier performance. For when proving theorems concerning the accuracy of classifiers built using SDK, we initially consider probabilities *with respect to the sample space of **subsets** of the given feature space*, rather than with respect to the feature space itself. It is only by appealing to something know as the *duality lemma* (see [6]), that one can translate these accuracy estimates into standard error rates over the feature space.

2   Experimental Results

The Datasets We worked with datasets from two major sites containing sets of standardized problems in machine learning, the repository at the University of California at Irvine, and the repository (of Statlog problems) at the University of Porto in Portugal.

We carried out experiments with 17 datasets from the Irvine collection, datasets which seemed to be the most popular appearing in the recent literature dealing with comparative studies of pattern recognition methods. The sets we used were, Australian credit (henceforth abbreviated "crx"), Pima diabetes (dia), glass (gls), Cleveland heart (hrt), hepatitis (hep), ionosphere (ion), iris (iri), labor (lab), letter (let), satimage (sat), segment (seg), sonar (son), soybean-large (soy), splice (spl), vehicle (veh), vote (vot), and Wisconsin breast cancer (wsc). In [3], Freund and Schapire report on experimental results they derived for these problems using 9 different classification methods, namely, three underlying "weak learning algorithms" FindAttrTest (henceforth denoted, "FIA"), FindDecRule (FID), and Quinlan's C4.5 (C45) (see [10]), the boosted ([3]) versions of these algorithms, denoted ABO, DBO, and 5BO, respectively, and the bagged ([1]) versions, denoted ABA, DBA, and 5BA, respectively. Our learning runs on these datasets used the same study methodologies (either 10-fold cross validation, or training/test set, depending on the dataset) as used by Freund and Schapire, with the sole change (due to time constraints) of running two of the training/test problems (letter and splice) only once, using the default seed of 1 in each case.

Of the 10 Statlog sets publicly available from Porto, we eliminated two from consideration (heart and German credit) since they involved nontrivial cost matrices, something SDK is not designed to deal with, and eliminated a third (shuttle) since it was extremely underrepresented in some classes (class seven contained 2 test points out of a sample containing 58,000 training and test examples). On the remaining 7 sets, we carried out training runs using the same study methodologies (either a cross validation, or a training/test set, depending on the dataset) as [9].

The Results We compare our results on the Irvine problems with those reported in [3] in Figures 1 and 2. The table shows error rates for each method on each problem, with the *italicized* entry in each row belonging to the method which produced the lowest error rate. And in the graph, we produce for each method, a bar ranging from the best rank to the worst rank for that method across all problems, and place a left tic at the method's average rank, and a right tic at the method's mode. The methods are listed in order of average rank, and we superimpose a line graph showing these average ranks.

In Figures 3 and 4, we basically do the same thing, as we compare our results on the Statlog datasets from Porto with those reported in [9]. (Note the row/column switch in the table.)

Note that the data in Figures 1 and 3 shows that SDK was the best performing method in 14 of the 17 U.C. Irvine experiments, and in 5 of the 7 Statlog experiments.

3   The Theory

The Prototypical Problem Our first goal is to try to formalize from a foundational mathematical point of view the notion of "building classifiers based on the study of training data". We assume we are at a point in the process where data has already passed through an initial feature extraction stage and that there exists a fixed positive integer n such that the objects among which we are interested in discriminating have all been reduced to numeric records of length n. Conforming to standard practice, we refer to the subspace of Euclidean n-space in which these records reside as the "feature space" of the problem.

The prototypical supervised learning problem in pattern recognition asks one to build a classifier from "representative" examples. From a mathematical perspective, what does "representative" mean here? Clearly, it would be impossible to proceed with any rigorous development of the theory underlying supervised learning without first answering this question.

	FIA	ABO	ABA	FID	DBO	DBA	C45	5BO	5BA	SDK
crx	14.5	14.4	14.5	14.5	13.5	14.5	15.8	13.8	13.6	*12.4*
dia	26.1	*24.4*	26.1	27.8	25.3	26.4	28.4	25.7	*24.4*	25.5
gls	51.5	51.1	50.9	49.7	48.5	47.2	31.7	22.7	25.7	*20.3*
hrt	27.8	18.8	22.4	27.4	19.7	20.3	26.6	21.7	20.9	*17.4*
hep	19.7	18.6	16.8	21.6	18.0	20.1	21.2	16.3	17.5	*16.2*
ion	17.8	8.5	17.3	10.3	6.6	9.3	8.9	*5.8*	6.2	6.2
iri	35.2	4.7	28.4	38.3	4.3	18.8	5.9	5.0	5.0	*4.2*
lab	25.1	8.8	19.1	24.0	7.3	14.6	15.8	13.1	11.3	*6.1*
let	92.9	92.9	91.9	92.3	91.8	91.8	13.8	*3.3*	6.8	*3.3*
sat	58.3	58.3	58.3	57.6	56.5	56.7	14.8	8.9	10.6	*8.7*
seg	75.8	75.8	54.5	73.7	53.3	54.3	3.6	*1.4*	2.7	1.9
son	25.9	16.5	25.9	31.4	15.2	26.1	28.9	19.0	24.3	*10.6*
soy	64.8	64.5	59.0	73.6	73.6	73.6	13.3	6.8	12.2	*5.9*
spl	37.0	9.2	35.6	29.5	8.0	29.5	5.8	*4.9*	5.2	*4.9*
veh	64.3	64.4	57.6	61.3	61.2	61.0	29.9	22.6	26.1	*22.1*
vot	4.4	3.7	4.4	4.0	4.4	4.4	*3.5*	5.1	3.6	*3.5*
wsc	8.4	4.4	6.7	8.1	4.1	5.3	5.0	3.3	3.2	*2.6*

Fig 1. Experimental Results - Error Rates on Irvine Problems

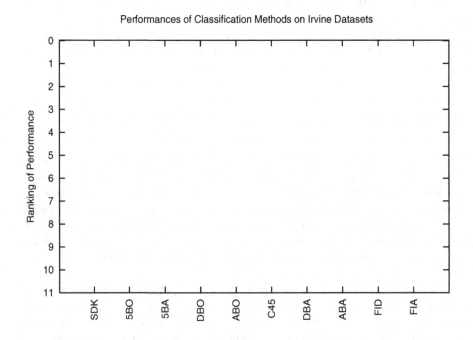

Fig 2. Relative Performance Ranks - Irvine Problems

	crx	dia	dna	let	sat	seg	veh
Ac2	0.181	0.276	0.245	0.245	0.157	0.031	0.296
Alloc80	0.201	0.301	0.064	0.064	0.132	0.030	0.173
BackProp	0.154	0.248	0.327	0.327	0.139	0.054	0.207
BayTree	0.171	0.271	0.124	0.124	0.147	0.033	0.271
Bayes	0.151	0.262	0.529	0.529	0.287	0.265	0.558
C4.5	0.155	0.270	0.132	0.132	0.150	0.040	0.266
Cal5	0.131	0.250	0.253	0.253	0.151	0.062	0.279
Cart	0.145	0.255	NA	NA	0.138	0.040	0.235
Castle	0.148	0.258	0.245	0.245	0.194	0.112	0.505
Cn2	0.204	0.289	0.115	0.115	0.150	0.043	0.314
Default	0.440	0.350	0.960	0.960	0.769	0.760	0.750
Dipol92	0.141	0.224	0.176	0.176	0.111	0.039	0.151

	crx	dia	dna	let	sat	seg	veh
Discrim	0.141	0.225	0.302	0.302	0.171	0.116	0.216
IndCart	0.152	0.271	0.130	0.130	0.138	0.045	0.298
Itrule	0.137	0.245	0.594	0.594	NA	0.455	0.324
KNN	0.181	0.324	0.068	0.068	0.094	0.077	0.275
Kohonen	NA	0.273	0.252	0.252	0.179	0.067	0.340
LVQ	0.197	0.272	0.079	0.079	0.105	0.046	0.287
LogDisc	0.141	0.223	0.234	0.234	0.163	0.109	0.192
NewId	0.181	0.289	0.128	0.128	0.150	0.034	0.298
QuaDisc	0.207	0.262	0.113	0.113	0.155	0.157	0.150
Radial	0.145	0.243	0.233	0.233	0.121	0.069	0.307
SDK	0.126	0.233	0.033	0.038	0.0865	0.021	0.201
Smart	0.158	0.232	0.295	0.295	0.159	0.052	0.217

Fig 3. Experimental Results - Error Rates on Statlog Problems

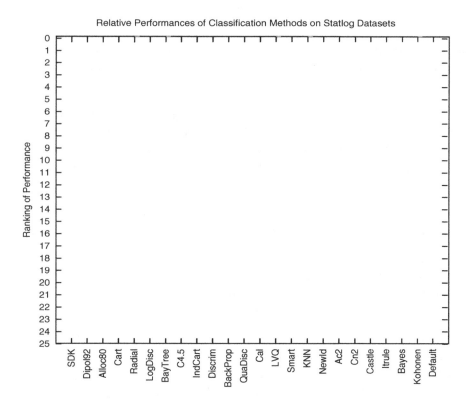

Fig 4. Relative Performance Ranks - Statlog Problems

In practice, a set A is usually viewed as being representative of a set B if it is spatially distributed throughout the region of the feature space occupied by B. This is a simple, pragmatic, derivative thesis which tends to work to greater or lesser extents based on the specifics of any particular problem being considered. But it is not really what one means by the notion "representative". Most people would agree that, from a more fundamental perspective, the intuition is that a set A is representative of a set B if given any classifier C, the error rate of C (for its task of recognition) when measured on members of A is equal to, or at least close to, its error rate when measured on members of B. Another way to express this intuition in a more operational, but less precise, way is to simply say that a set A is representative of a set B if any classifier C built using A generalizes to B.

Needless to say this description has serious flaws. For if C were the classifier which simply cataloged the points in A, and then classified any (new) point based on whether or not it sat in this list, then the error rate of that classifier when measured on A would be 0, yet, assuming A were substantially smaller than B, would be substantially larger than 0 when measured on B.

Thus the notion "A is representative of B" must be dependent on both the sets A and B, *and on some expectation concerning the nature of the classifier itself.* In other words, the notion "representative" can never be an absolute; when one is given a particular pattern recognition problem through a training set of examples which are declared to be "representative", the understanding *must* be that the examples are "representative" only so long as possible classifiers derived as solutions to the problem are restricted to satisfy certain additional requirements.

In most practical applications, there is an implicit assumption that if training sets are sufficiently densely distributed throughout class regions in the feature space, then by seeking classifiers which are restricted to carve out sufficiently "thick" subsets of the feature, such training sets are "representative". In effect, the assumption is one of spatial proximity of like points between training and test sets.

However, given our desire for generality, we feel that there is a far more elegant, and natural, way to formalize the notion "representative". We will simply define what it means, given some collection **M** of subsets of the feature space, (intuitively, the building blocks of allowed, possible classifiers) for a subset A of the feature space to be **M**-representative of another subset B of the feature space. In this way, although we can encompass the usual proximity-based approach as a special case, we don't require any topological relationship between training and test sets, and as such allow for a number of interesting alternative possibilities. Most important we feel that this definition constitutes the minimal requirement for "representativeness".

The underlying idea is very simple. In order for a set A to be **M**-representative of a set B, it must be impossible to tell the difference between points in A and points in B using the expressive power inherent in the sets of **M**. There is a slight irony here. In pattern recognition one tries to find a solution which must succeed in discriminating between points of different classes, yet one which must simultaneously fail to discriminate between training and test subsets of a given class.

It is this "indiscernibility" between training and test sets modulo the expressive power of sets in **M** which serves as the basis for our development here.

Indiscernibility and Representativeness Let n be a fixed positive integer, and assume that our feature space F is some fixed, finite subset of Euclidean n-space. Since F is finite we can consider it to be a measure space under the counting measure μ.

Let us denote by $\mathbf{F}$, the power set of F, that is, the collection of all subsets of F.

Definition 1. *For a given collection $\mathbf{M}$ of subsets of F, we define a binary relation $\sim_{\mathbf{M}}$ on the collection of nonempty subsets of F as follows: for any sets A and B contained in F, $A \sim_{\mathbf{M}} B$ iff for every M in $\mathbf{M}$, $Pr(M|A) = Pr(M|B)$*

(Viewing F as a sample space, $Pr(M|A)$ denotes the probability of M given A.)

Having $A \sim_{\mathbf{M}} B$ would certainly appear to be a necessary condition for B being $\mathbf{M}$-indiscernible from A. But it is easy to construct examples showing that it is not sufficient, that is, examples where $A \sim_{\mathbf{M}} B$ for distinct sets A and B, yet $\mathbf{M}$ contains information capable of showing $A \neq B$.

In order to have true $\mathbf{M}$-indiscernibility, it must be the case that any "profile" of A which can be deduced using information from $\mathbf{M}$ is identical with a similarly deduced "profile" of B. Thus consider the following function $f_{\mathbf{M},x,A}$, defined for any subset $\mathbf{M}$ of $\mathbf{F}$, any nonempty subset A of F, and any real x for which there exist M in $\mathbf{M}$ such that $Pr(M|A) = x$, which maps A into the reals: given any member q of A,

$$f_{\mathbf{M},x,A}(q) = Pr_{\mathbf{M}}(q \in M | Pr(M|A) = x).$$

(Since we will be dealing with several different probability spaces in what follows, there might be times when confusion could arise as to just which space we are taking probabilities with respect to. At times of such potential ambiguity, we will use Pr_T to denote probabilities taken with respect to the space T.)

In some sense, the random variable $f_{\mathbf{M},x,A}$ defines a profile of the coverage of points in A by those members M of $\mathbf{M}$ such that $Pr(M|A) = x$. We restrict to those M such that $Pr(M|A) = x$ for the sake of simplicity, for there is often a clear expectation of coverage for such M. For example, if $\mathbf{M}$ were equal to the full power set of F, it is fairly easy to see that for any q in A, $f_{\mathbf{M},x,A}(q) = x$ for any x.

Using this notation, we are now in a position to precisely define the notion of indiscernibility:

Definition 2. *Given sets A and B contained in F, and given a collection $\mathbf{M}$ of subsets of F, we say that A is $\mathbf{M}$-indiscernible from B if*

(a) $A \sim_{\mathbf{M}} B$;
(b) for every x, the random variables $f_{\mathbf{M},x,A}$ and $f_{\mathbf{M},x,B}$ have the same probability mass functions.

Let us now rigorously define the notion "representative". Since, in a typical pattern recognition problem, we are given, for some positive integer m (the number of classes), training subsets TR_1, TR_2, ... TR_m which are supposed to be "representative" of the available sets A_1, A_2, ... , A_m, we wish to define, in general, what it means for a sequence of subsets $\boldsymbol{C} = (C_1, C_2, ...C_m)$ of a feature space F to be **M**-representative of another sequence of subsets $\boldsymbol{D} = (D_1, D_2, ...D_m)$. We start with natural generalizations of concepts given above.

Definition 3. *Given a positive integer m, a sequence $C = (C_1, C_2, ...C_m)$ of subsets of F, and a sequence $x = (x_1, x_2, ...x_m)$ of reals, $\mathbf{M}_{x,C}$ denotes the set of those M in $\mathbf{M}$ such that for each j, $1 \le j \le m$, $Pr(M|C_j) = x_j$.*

Definition 4. *Given any subset $\mathbf{M}$ of $\mathbf{F}$, any positive integer m, any sequence $C = (C_1, C_2, ...C_m)$ of subsets of F, and any sequence $x = (x_1, x_2, ...x_m)$ of reals such that $\mathbf{M}_{x,C}$ is nonempty, for any j, $1 \le j \le m$, $f^j_{\mathbf{M},x,C}$ is the random variable defined on C_j whose value at any q (in C_j) is given by*

$$f^j_{\mathbf{M},x,C}(q) = Pr_{\mathbf{M}}(q \in M | M \in \mathbf{M}_{x,C}).$$

The definition of "representative" is now completely natural.

Definition 5. *Given any subset $\mathbf{M}$ of $\mathbf{F}$, any positive integer m, and any two sequences $\boldsymbol{D} = (D_1, D_2, ...D_m)$ and $\boldsymbol{C} = (C_1, C_2, ...C_m)$ of subsets of F, we say that $\boldsymbol{C}$ is $\mathbf{M}$-representative of $\boldsymbol{D}$ if*

(a) for any j, $1 \le j \le m$, $C_j \subseteq D_j$,
(b) for any j, $1 \le j \le m$, $C_j \sim_\mathbf{M} D_j$,
(c) for any sequence $\boldsymbol{x} = (x_1, x_2, ...x_m)$ of reals, and for any j, $1 \le j \le m$, the random variables $f^j_{\mathbf{M},x,C}$ and $f^j_{\mathbf{M},x,D}$ have the same probability density functions.

Enrichment and Uniformity Simply having an **M**-representative set of training examples could not possibly guarantee one's ability to find a classifier which accurately solved the given problem. For example, if **M** consisted of the single set F, the feature space itself, then given *any* two sequences $\boldsymbol{D} = (D_1, D_2, ...D_m)$ and $\boldsymbol{C} = (C_1, C_2, ...C_m)$ of subsets of F such that for any j, $1 \le j \le m$, $C_j \subseteq D_j$, $\boldsymbol{C}$ is **M**-representative of $\boldsymbol{D}$.

There are actually two, natural requirements a collection **M** must satisfy in order to have any chance of building a reasonable classifier from an **M**-representative set of training examples.

The first of these, called uniformity, whose formal definition will be given shortly, basically requires that the members of **M** uniformly cover all regions of the feature space where training examples are present. This is clearly an essential requirement, for otherwise **M**-representative would really amount to "representative in this region of the feature space but not in this other region". Trivially, since $\{F\}$ uniformly covers F, if **M** were equal to $\{F\}$, **M** would be uniform.

The second requirement, called enrichment, would not be satisfied were **M** equal to $\{F\}$. Here we basically require that the different (training) classes constituting the given problem not be **M**-indiscernible from one another. Again, this requirement, whose formal definition will be given shortly, is both reasonable and essential. For if we created a problem by distributing all points in a sufficiently complex feature space among two classes at random, and then specified training sets by random sampling, the training sets would certainly be $\{F\}$-representative, and $\{F\}$ would be uniform, but the classification problem would (and should), by any reasonable standard, be unsolvable.

Motivated by this discussion, we now present the formal definitions:

Definition 6. *For a given sequence of subsets* $\boldsymbol{C} = (C_1, C_2, ...C_m)$ *of* F, $\mathbf{M}$ *is said to be* $\boldsymbol{C}$-*uniform if for every* j, $1 \leq j \leq m$, *every member* q *of* C_j, *and every sequence* $\boldsymbol{x} = (x_1, x_2, ..., x_m)$ *of real numbers such that* $\mathbf{M}_{x,C}$ *is nonempty,*

$$Pr_{\mathbf{M}}(q \in M | M \in \mathbf{M}_{x,C}) = x_j.$$

While it may not be apparent that this definition formalizes the intuitive description of uniformity given above, in [6] we prove, mathematically, that it does.

Now for the issue of enrichment.

Definition 7. *Given a sequence* $\boldsymbol{C} = (C_1, C_2, ..., C_m)$, *the* $\boldsymbol{C}$-*enrichment degree of* $\mathbf{M}$ *(written* $e(\boldsymbol{C}, \mathbf{M})$*) is defined to be*

$$inf\{|Pr(M|C_i) - Pr(M|C_j)| \ |M \in \mathbf{M}, 1 \leq i \leq m, 1 \leq j \leq m\}.$$

$\mathbf{M}$ *is said to be* $\boldsymbol{C}$-*enriched if* $e(\boldsymbol{C}, \mathbf{M}) > 0$.

This definition clearly does formalize the intuitive description of enrichment given above.

The Solvability Theorem We are now in a position to give the central definition of this paper. In light of the development above, this definition is completely natural, and seems to constitute the minimal condition appropriate to the concept of solvability.

Definition 8. *An m-class problem in supervised learning, presented as two finite sequences* $\boldsymbol{E} = (E_1, E_2, ...E_m)$ *and* $\boldsymbol{T} = (T_1, T_2, ...T_m)$ *of classes in a finite feature space (intuitively, the examples and the training examples, respectively), is said to be* solvable *if there exists a collection* $\mathbf{M}$ *of subsets of the feature space such that* $\boldsymbol{T}$ *is* $\mathbf{M}$-*representative of* $\boldsymbol{E}$, *and such that* $\mathbf{M}$ *is* $\boldsymbol{T}$-*enriched and* $\boldsymbol{T}$-*uniform.*

The following theorem says, in essence, that any solvable problem in supervised learning can actually be solved:

Theorem 1. *There exists an algorithm* $\mathcal{A}$ *with the following property: given any solvable problem,* $\boldsymbol{E}$, $\boldsymbol{T}$, *in supervised learning, if* $\mathbf{M}$ *is a collection of subsets of the feature space such that* $\boldsymbol{T}$ *is* $\mathbf{M}$-*representative of* $\boldsymbol{E}$, *and if* $\mathbf{M}$ *is* $\boldsymbol{T}$-*enriched and* $\boldsymbol{T}$-*uniform, then given any desired upper bound* u *on error rate,* $\mathcal{A}$ *will output, within time proportional to* $1/u$ *and inversely proportional to the square of* $e(\boldsymbol{T}, \mathbf{M})$, *a classifier whose expected error rate on* $\boldsymbol{E}$ *is less than* u.

The algorithm $\mathcal{A}$ builds classifiers by sampling, with replacement, from the set $\mathbf{M}$, and then combining the "weak classifiers" in the resulting sample. We reduce n-class problems to n-many 2-class problems; given a training pair (T_1, T_2) for any such 2-class problem, a sample $\mathbf{S}$ of size t produces the classifier which assigns any given example q to class 1 if

$$\frac{1}{t} \sum_{S \in \mathbf{S}} \frac{\chi_S(q) - Pr(S|T_2)}{Pr(S|T_1) - Pr(S|T_2)} > 0.5$$

(where χ_S is the characteristic function of S). For a rigorous proof of this theorem, and related results, see [5,6,7].

Let us also note that the estimate given in the statement of the theorem for run time of the algorithm $\mathcal{A}$ is intentionally crude, and is provided solely for the purpose of indicating computational feasibility. For more useful statistical estimates, we refer the reader to [2].

4   Conclusions

Our intention in this paper was to examine, from a purely mathematical perspective, fundamental issues in the field of supervised learning; and to then explore the usefulness of such a perspective in practical application. The results we derived show a good deal of promise for the general approach, and our hope is that as new algorithmic implementations are developed, results will improve even further.

References

1. L. Breiman, Bagging Predictors, *Machine Learning*, **24**, 1996, pp. 123-140.
2. D. Chen, Statistical Estimates for Kleinberg's Method of Stochastic Discrimination, Ph.D. Thesis, SUNY/Buffalo, 1998.
3. Y. Freund, R. E. Schapire, Experiments with a New Boosting Algorithm, *Proceedings of the Thirteenth International Conference on Machine Learning*, Bari, Italy, July 3-6, 1996, pp. 148-156.
4. T. K. Ho, Random Decision Forests, *Proc. of the 3rd Int'l Conference on Document Analysis and Recognition*, Montreal, Canada, 1995, pp. 278-282.
5. E. M. Kleinberg, Stochastic Discrimination, *Annals of Mathematics and Artificial Intelligence*, 1990, pp. 207-239.
6. E. M. Kleinberg, An Overtraining-Resistant Stochastic Modeling Method for Pattern Recognition, *Annals of Statistics*, 1996, pp. 2319-2349.
7. E. M. Kleinberg, On the Algorithmic Implementation of Stochastic Discrimination, *IEEE Transactions on Pattern Analysis and Machine Intelligence*, to appear.
8. E. M. Kleinberg, A Note on the Mathematics Underlying Boosting, preprint, to appear.
9. D. Michie, D. Spiegelhalter, C. C. Taylor, *Machine Learning, Neural and Statistical Classification*, Ellis Horwood, 1994.
10. R. Quinlan, *C4.5: Programs for Machine Learning*, Morgan Kaufmann, Oct 1993.

Classifier Combinations: Implementations and Theoretical Issues

Louisa Lam

Department of Mathematics
Hong Kong Institute of Education
10 Lo Ping Road, Tai Po, Hong Kong

Centre for Pattern Recognition and Machine Intelligence
Concordia University
1455 de Maisonneuve Blvd. West, Montréal, Québec H3G 1M8, Canada

Abstract. Much work has been done in the past decade to combine decisions of multiple classifiers in order to obtain improved recognition results. Many methodologies have been designed and implemented for this purpose. This article considers some of the current developments according to the structure of the combination process, and discusses some issues involved in each structure. In addition, theoretical investigations that have been performed in this area are also examined, and some related issues are discussed.

1   Introduction

In the domain of pattern recognition, there has been a very significant movement during the past decade to combine the decisions of classifiers. This trend, which had originated from empirical experimentation due to a practical need for higher recognition performances, has developed widely in methodology and has led to some theoretical considerations. A significant body of literature on the topic has been produced, some of which are included in the references of this article.

In general, combination methods seem to have progressed in different directions recently. As various implementations have been attempted and reported, some researchers have been involved with progressively specialized and task-oriented, tailored methods for solving particular problems. At the same time, there has been interest in the development, understanding and implementation of formal and theoretical issues of various combination processes. This article attempts to broadly categorize various combination structures that have been developed and implemented, and to consider some of the theoretical issues underlying these developments.

2   Categorization of Combination Methods

Combination of multiple classifiers is a fascinating problem that can be considered from many broad perspectives, and combination techniques can be grouped

J. Kittler and F. Roli (Eds.): MCS 2000, LNCS 1857, pp. 77–86, 2000.

and analyzed in different ways. On a theoretical level, one can consider that there are basically two classifier combination scenarios: all classifiers use the same representation of the input pattern, or different representations [12–15]. Examples of the former are classifiers using the same feature set but different classification parameters, or neural networks using the same architecture. In such cases, each classifier can be considered to produce an estimation of the same *a posteriori* class probability. However, for most combination methods reported in the literature, the classifiers make use of different representations in the form of feature vectors or recognition methods.

In terms of implementation, categorization of combination methods can be made by considering the combination topologies or structures employed, as described in [23] and [24]. These topologies can be broadly classified as multiple, conditional, hierarchical, or hybrid.

2.1   Conditional Topology

Under this structure, a primary classifier is first used. When it rejects a pattern due to inability to give a classification, or when the classification is made with low confidence, a secondary classifier is deployed. This structure has the advantage of computational efficiency when the primary classifier is a fast one, as it processes most of the easily recognizable patterns. Then the secondary classifier, which can be more elaborate and time-consuming, is invoked only for more difficult patterns. Examples of this strategy can be found in [2, 19, 26].

In [19], a fast tree classifier was used to classify about 80% of handwritten numerals, while a robust but computationally demanding method of relaxation matching was used to process the rejected samples. The same database was processed for the structure of [26], in which a neural network is the primary recognizer that processes most samples. When the output confidence levels indicate a possible confusion between the top choices, an expert system is invoked to resolve the conflict. This expert system makes use of a knowledge base of the samples belonging to the conflicting classes for its decision. In [2], two classifiers use different sets of features and the Radial Basis Function network for classification, with one network processing the samples rejected by the other, and vice versa. Experimental results of this last reference indicate that the performance of the primary classifier plays a more prominent role in the combined results, which is reasonable since the primary classifier processes most of the patterns.

For this topology, an interesting question is the following: if computational resources required of the two classifiers is not a matter of consequence, then should the classifier of better performance be the primary one? This is worth considering, because while the primary classifier processes most of the patterns, the more difficult ones are left to the other, which would imply some trade-off between the recognition and error rates is involved in the decision for such cases. This aspect of the problem may be worth further exploration.

When more than two classifiers are available, more configurations exist for the conditional topology. Suppose we have three classifiers A, B, and C, with computational speeds in the same order, classifier A being the fastest. Then it is possible to apply them conditionally in the following orders:

- Classifier A, then B, followed by C, with rejects of each classifier processed by the next;
- Classifier A and B in parallel first. The samples on which they agree would have the common class as its label, and C is used to classify the rest. The decision of C can be further combined with those of A and B by majority vote. Doing this would produce a more reliable combined classifier, because agreement of two classifiers does produce lower error rates [20].

When the number of available classifiers increases, more different configurations are possible, and one can also exploit the results proved in [20] that majority vote of odd numbers of classifiers produce higher recognition rates than even numbers, while the latter would have lower error rates.

A different perspective on this structure is provided in [8], in which the dynamic selection of classifiers is considered. If it were possible to select a classifier for the input pattern based on some parameters of the pattern or its extracted features, then one can use the least expensive classifier that can achieve a desired level of accuracy. However, the estimation of such parameters is not an easy task unless a large collection of samples are derived from the same source, in which case one may form some conclusions on the image quality. Otherwise the dynamic selection of classifiers requires an appropriate mapping of a pattern to a classifier, which may be more difficult than the classification task itself.

2.2   Hierarchical (Serial) Topology

Using this topology, classifiers are applied in succession, with each classifier producing a reduced set of possible classes for each pattern, so that the individual classifiers or experts can become increasingly focused. Through this process, a complicated problem is progressively reduced to simpler ones. An example of this approach is shown in [25], which presents a comprehensive discussion of the concept, considerations, and implementations of serial combinations of multiple experts, with detailed experimental results and analyses. Its implementation involves four experts, and each expert is used to reduce the set of classes for the next one. The experts are deployed in the order of decreasing error rates, so that the expert with the highest error rate is applied first. The individual and combined results on 3 databases of alphanumerics are given (two of the sets consist of handwritten characters, while the other is machine printed). Detailed discussions are also presented of the relation of performance to the size of the subset of classes output by the previous expert. In particular, the experimental results show that the performance of an expert improves when the number of classes output by the preceding expert decreases.

This approach has also been implemented in [5], which presents a serial application of two recognizers for the processing of the legal amount on bank cheques. For this problem, a lexicon of about 30 words is involved. A wholistic K nearest neighbor classifier is used to output the top 10 classes for each word, after which an HMM classifier is applied to the reduced lexicon.

Naturally, an important consideration must be that the true class of a pattern must be among the subset produced by the preceding expert if the subsequent classification is to be correct. Therefore a theoretical question must follow as to whether there exists requirements on the performance of the experts (especially when deployed in the reverse order according to performance) if class reduction is to improve performance.

When individual classifiers output a ranked list of classes for each pattern, two methods of class set reduction have been proposed by [7] to determine the intersection of large neighborhoods and the union of small neighborhoods. These methods have the effect of determining minimum numbers of classes that should be passed to the next classifier if the training set is to be correctly classified. The minimum number can then be applied in the testing process.

2.3   Hybrid Topology

Since certain recognition approaches may perform better on particular types of patterns, this information could be used to select the recognizer(s) to run in a multiple classifier system when certain features or parameters of the pattern have been extracted. Such an approach is discussed in [23], in which the choice between the application of wholistic and segmentation-based word recognizers is based on the estimated length of the word to be processed. Longer words are classified by the wholistic recognizer as they contain more word-shape information, while a segmentation-based approach would be less effective on longer words due to the need to correctly segment and recognize more characters in such cases.

Other strategies to coordinate and combine classifiers are proposed in [8] that may be adaptive to image quality, probability of confusion between classes, agreement of decisions by selected classifiers, or a mix of these factors. While direct estimation of image quality is difficult, selection strategies driven by reliability or classifier agreement (obtained from results on a training set) can be easily used. Using the last strategy, the sample space can be partitioned according to the reliability of agreement among the classifiers on the training set; based on the agreement obtained on a test pattern, an appropriate classifier (or classifiers) can be selected to provide the identity of the pattern.

This partition of the pattern space according to classifier agreement has been applied to one extremity in the Behavior-Knowledge Space (BKS) method [10], where this agreement actually provides the classification. Under this method, the training data is partitioned into cells, each cell being defined by the complete set of classes output by the classifiers. When a test pattern is processed, the set of classes assigned by the recognizers is determined, so the pattern can be mapped to the appropriate cell. Then it is assigned to the class having the highest probability of being in that cell (according to the training set). This method requires a very fine partition of the training set into a large number of cells ($(m + 1)^k$ cells each containing $m + 2$ items of information for an m-class problem with k classifiers). Consequently, a very sizeable training set would be required to cover the cells to sufficient density for providing reliable statistical data.

2.4   Multiple (Parallel) Topology

For this topology, multiple classifiers first operate in parallel to produce classifications of a pattern, after which the decisions are combined to yield a final decision. This structure has the disadvantage that it incurs additional computational costs, since several classifiers have to be operated first, after which a fusion operation would be performed. However, the operation of individual classifiers can run under parallel hardware architectures. In addition, the individual operation of classifiers allows for development and introduction of new classifiers without requiring major modifications to the fusion process.

Parallel combinations can be implemented using different strategies, and the combination method depends on the types of information produced by the classifiers. This output information can be provided at the abstract level in the form of a class label, as a ranked list of possible classes, or at the measurement level, where the classifier produces a measurement value for each label.

For abstract-level classifiers, where each classifier outputs only a label, he simplest combination method is by majority vote, which requires no prior training [4, 28, 29]. This procedure of assigning equal weights to the decision of each recognizer can be refined by assigning weights according to the overall performance of each classifier on the training set [21]. As a further refinement, different weights in the form of posterior probabilities can be obtained for each class from the confusion matrix of each classifier on the training data. These posterior probabilities are then combined by a product rule under an assumption of independence [30]. Of course, a product rule is particularly vulnerable to a near-zero value in one of the terms forming the product.

For classification problems involving a large number of classes, the probability that a classifier can correctly identify the class of each pattern tends to decrease. For such cases, it becomes important that each classifier should produce a number of choices in the form of a ranked list of classes, because secondary choices may include the true class of a pattern when there is no agreement on the top choices. An example of such a problem would be word recognition with a sizeable lexicon. For such problems, rankings produced by individual classifiers can be used to derive combined decisions by the highest rank, Borda count, logistic regression, and dynamic classifier selection methods [7].

When classifiers return measurements for each class, more information is provided. Whether these measurements are confidence levels or distances, simple operators such as *Max*, *Min*, *Sum*, *Median*, and *Product* can be used to combine the outcomes [9, 13]. Experimental results in [9] show the *Ave* operator to be the most robust against classifier peculiarities. Similarly, [13] finds that the *Sum* operator outperforms the other operators mentioned above, and it shows theoretically that the *Sum* rule is most resilient to estimation errors. Other means of combining measurements output by classifiers include the use of neural networks ([18, 22] for example) and fuzzy integrals [29]. The former approach uses the output from individual classifiers as input for a neural network, and the latter method uses the recognition rates of the classifiers on the training set as densities of the fuzzy measures.

3   Theoretical Issues in Classifier Combinations

Much of the work on classifier combinations has been experimental in nature. Very specialized and domain-specific methods have also been designed. In all these cases, using a combination of classifiers has resulted in (sometimes remarkable) improvements in the recognition results. Alongside these empirical developments, there has been a parallel attempt to establish theoretical frameworks for classifier combinations. The idea of developing such foundations is an attractive one; however, the more specially tailored methods do not lend themselves easily to theoretical analysis. On the other hand, the simplest of combination methods – majority vote, has yielded a significant body of results in this direction because of the clarity of the assumptions and the possibility of applying mathematical analysis. The theoretical foundations and behavior of majority vote have been analyzed in [20]. In this section we will consider some of these results, and conclude with some issues related to other combination topologies.

3.1   Theoretical Aspects of Majority Vote

Majority vote has been a much studied subject among mathematicians and social scientists since its origin in the Condorcet Jury Theorem (CJT) [3], which provided validity to the belief that the judgment of a group is superior to those of individuals, provided the individuals have reasonable competence. If we assume that n independent experts have the same probability p of being correct, then the probability of the majority being correct, denoted by $P_C(n)$, can be computed using the binomial distribution, and CJT states the following:

Theorem (CJT): Suppose n is odd and $n \geq 3$. Then the following are true:
(a) If $p > 0.5$, then $P_C(n)$ is monotonically increasing in n and $P_C(n) \to 1$ as $n \to \infty$.
(b) If $p < 0.5$, then $P_C(n)$ is monotonically decreasing in n and $P_C(n) \to 0$ as $n \to \infty$.
(c) If $p = 0.5$, then $P_C(n) = 0.5$ for all n.

The convergence stipulated in the CJT is actually quite rapid; for example, when $p = 0.75$ (which would be much below the performance of any acceptable classifier today) and $n = 9$, then $P_C(n) > 0.95$. It is notable the CJT has been reflected in some recent literature on the combinations of large numbers of easily generated classifiers (described as stochastic discrimination in [16,17], random decision forests in [6], and "weak" classifiers in [11]). In these articles, the emphasis is on randomly generating a large number of classifiers for combination.

As opposed to highly specialized classifiers, the classifiers under discussion should be computationally cheap and easy to generate by random processes.

The stochastic modeling method in [16, 17] makes use of large numbers of *weak models* which are subsets of the feature space. For each input pattern (represented as a point in the feature space) and each class, a random variable incorporating information from the training set is defined on the set of weak models. An input pattern would be assigned to the class having the maximum average value of the random variable. One fundamental aspect of this method is that it is based on random sampling from the collection of weak models; as the number of sampled weak models increases, recognition rates also increase. This method is resistant to the phenomenon of overtraining because the use of simple, weak models made the process highly generalizable. When 7634 weak models and a training set of size 4997 were used, this method was found to outperform the nearest neighbor classifier and at many times its speed [16].

In [11], weak classifiers are linear classifiers with recognition rates slightly higher than 0.5 on the training set, and they are generated by random selections of hyperplanes. An additional weak classifier's performance is determined mainly on the set of training samples incorrectly classified by the combination of classifiers already selected, and results of combining up to 20,000 such classifiers by majority vote have been found to be comparable to the method of [17] on the NIST database of handwritten digits, with 4.23% error rate. While the results may not be state-of-the-art ([27] reports recognition rates of up to 99.07% for the NIST TD1 database, while [1] presents a 99.59% recognition rate for NIST SD3), this article also establishes a bound for the generalization error of the combined classifier. It establishes a polynomial rate at which the generalization error approaches zero as the number of classifiers increases.

For the decision forests of [6], the decision trees are constructed systematically by pseudorandomly selecting subsets of components of the feature vector, and each sample would be assigned to a terminal node by each tree. The probability that the sample belongs to a particular class ω can be estimated by the fraction of class ω samples over all samples in the training set that are assigned to the terminal node, and the discriminant function is defined by the average posterior probability of each class at the leaves. For fully split trees, the decision is equivalent to a majority vote among the classes decided by the trees. Experimental results of combinations of up to 100 trees on various publicly available datasets are given in this paper.

The research cited above are theoretically interesting because they represent a direction diametrically opposite to the development of highly accurate and specific classifiers. Instead, they rely mainly on the power of numbers as stipulated in the CJT rather than on the performance of individual classifiers. The classifiers can be easily generated, and the combined results are within acceptable bounds; however, space and time complexities should be considerations for this approach.

For combinations of small numbers of classifiers by majority vote, another factor that merits attention would be the trade-off between recognition and error rates. It has been proved theoretically [20] that combinations of even numbers of experts would produce both lower correct and error rates (and higher reject rates) than combinations of odd numbers of experts. Adding one classifier to an even number would increase both the recognition and error rates, while adding this to an odd number would decrease both rates. This is true regardless of whether the experts are independent or not. With the assumption of independence, it has also been proved that addition of two experts to an even number would increase the recognition rate, while the change in the error rate would depend on the performance of the individual experts; on the other hand, the addition of two experts to an odd number would tend to reduce the error rate. Other strategies such as doubling the vote of the best expert while eliminating the weakest one are also considered in the paper cited. The conclusions are theoretically proved to depend on the familiar notion of the odds ratio, and the conclusions have also been seen in experimental results, even when independence of classifiers cannot be guaranteed.

3.2   Independence of Classifiers

In combining classifiers, several terms have often been mentioned as being desirable qualities in classifiers to be combined; among these are orthogonality, complementarity, and independence. Orthogonality is used to denote classifiers' tendency to make different decisions. Since classifiers may have different strengths and weaknesses, combining them is assumed to have a compensatory or complementary effect. However, it must be admitted that these terms lack precise definitions and means of measurement.

Independence is better understood, because of its frequent use in probability theory, and the assumption of independence among the classifiers has allowed for theoretical analysis of the behavior of their combinations. For example, [15] establishes that when multiple experts using different representations, the calculation of the *a posteriori* probability for the combined decision can be simplified with certain assumptions to derive some commonly used methods of classifier combination. The *Product* and *Min* rules can be obtained by assuming the classifiers to be conditionally statistically independent. The *Sum, Max, Median* and Majority Vote rules can follow from the additional assumption that the *a posteriori* probabilities computed by the respective classifiers will not deviate significantly from the prior probabilities. While these assumptions may appear to be strong (especially the latter one), the resulting rules are often used, and have been found to be effective in improving classification results, as has been mentioned in this article.

In general, the qualities of orthogonality, complementarity, and independence need to be better understood, and means to quantify them to be devised. Since the significance of these qualities may depend on the combination methods used, perhaps these could be studied in conjunction with combination methods. (In [9], orthogonality of errors between pairs of classifiers has been found to be a poor predictor of pairwise accuracy for the combination methods used, which is a rather striking conclusion).

4   Concluding Remarks

Combination of classifiers is a rich research area that can be considered from many different perspectives, as it encompasses the areas of feature extraction, classifier methodologies, and the fusion process. In this article, the current trends in classifier combinations have been categorized and considered according to the topologies employed, and some issues related to the various methods have been discussed. It is clear that a profusion of work has been done in this area to develop highly specialized systems for practical applications, using many different methods. At the same time, there is a need for this work to be examined by analysis based on sound foundations. Some work has already been done in this direction, and it is hoped that further investigations can be initiated.

Acknowledgements

This research was supported by the Natural Sciences and Engineering Research Council of Canada and the FCAR program of the Ministry of Education of the province of Quebec. The author is also supported by a conference grant from the Hong Kong Institute of Education.

References

1. A. S. Atukorale and P. N. Suganthan. Combining classifiers based on confidence values. In *Proc. Fifth Int. Conf. on Document Analysis and Recognition*, pages 37–40, Bangalore, India, Sept. 1999.
2. Y.-C. Chim, A. A. Kassim, and Y. Ibrahim. Dual classifier system for handprinted alphanumeric character recognition. *Pattern Analysis and Applications*, 1:155–162, 1998.
3. N. C. de Condorcet. *Essai sur l'application de l'analyse à la probabilité des décisions rendues à la pluralité des voix.* Imprimerie Royale, Paris, 1785.
4. P. D. Gader, D. Hepp, B. Forrester, and T. Peurach. Pipelined systems for recognition of handwritten digits in USPS ZIP codes. In *Proc. U. S. Postal Service Advanced Technology Conf.*, pages 539–548, 1990.
5. D. Guillevic and C. Y. Suen. HMM-KNN word recognition engine for bank cheque processing. In *Proc. 14th ICPR*, pages II: 1526–1529, Brisbane, Australia, August 1998.
6. T. K. Ho. The random subspace method for constructing decision forests. *IEEE Trans. PAMI*, 20(8):832–844, 1998.
7. T. K. Ho, J. J. Hull, and S. N. Srihari. Decision combination in multiple classifier systems. *IEEE Trans. PAMI*, 16:66–75, 1994.
8. T.K. Ho. Adaptive coordination of multiple classifiers. In J.J. Hull and S.L. Taylor, editors, *Document Analysis Systems II*, pages 371–384. World Scientific, 1998.
9. G.F. Houle, D.B. Aragon, R.W. Smith, M. Shridhar, and D. Kimura. A multi-layered corroboration-based check reader. In J.J. Hull and S.L. Taylor, editors, *Document Analysis Systems II*, pages 495–546. World Scientific, 1998.
10. Y. S. Huang and C. Y. Suen. Combination of multiple experts for the recognition of unconstrained handwritten numerals. *IEEE Trans. Pattern Anal. Mach. Intell.*, 17:90–94, 1995.

11. C. Ji and S. Ma. Combinations of weak classifiers. *IEEE Trans. Neural Networks*, 8(1):32–42, 1997.
12. J. Kittler. Combining classifiers: a theoretical framework. *Pattern Analysis and Applications*, 1:18–27, 1998.
13. J. Kittler. On combining classifiers. *IEEE Trans. PAMI*, 20(3):226–239, 1998.
14. J. Kittler. Pattern classification: fusion of information. In *Proc. Int. Conf. on Advances in Pattern Recognition*, pages 13–22, Plymouth, UK, November 1998.
15. J. Kittler, M. Hatef, and R.P.W. Duin. Combining classifiers. In *Proc. 13th Int. Conf. on Pattern Recognition*, pages II: 897–901, Vienna, Austria, August 1996.
16. E. M. Kleinberg. An overtraining-resistant stochastic modeling method for pattern recognition. *Annals of Statistics*, 24(6):2319–2349, 1996.
17. E. M. Kleinberg and T. K. Ho. Pattern recognition by stochastic modelling. In *Pre-Proc. 3rd Int. Workshop on Frontiers in Handwriting Recognition*, pages 175–183, Buffalo, NY, USA, May 1993.
18. S. Knerr, O. Baret, D. Price, J.C. Simon, V. Anisimov, and N. Gorski. The A2iA recognition system for handwritten checks. In *Proc. IAPR Workshop on Document Analysis Systems*, pages 431–494, Malvern, Penn., USA, October 1996.
19. L. Lam and C. Y. Suen. Structural classification and relaxation matching of totally unconstrained handwritten zip-code numbers. *Pattern Recognition*, 21(1):19–31, 1988.
20. L. Lam and C. Y. Suen. Application of majority voting to pattern recognition: an analysis of its behavior and performance. *IEEE Trans. Systems, Man, and Cybernetics*, 27(5):553–568, 1997.
21. L. Lam and C.Y. Suen. Optimal combinations of pattern classifiers. *Pattern Recognition Letters*, 16:945–954, 1995.
22. D.S. Lee and S.N. Srihari. Handprinted digit recognition: A comparison of algorithms. In *Pre-Proc. 3rd Int. Workshop on Frontiers in Handwriting Recognition*, pages 153–162, Buffalo, USA, May 1993.
23. R.K. Powalka, N. Sherkat, and R.J. Whitrow. Multiple recognizer combination topologies. In M.L. Simner, C.G. Leedham, and A.J.W.M. Thomasson, editors, *Handwriting and Drawing Research : Basic and Applied Issues*, pages 329–342. IOS Press, 1996.
24. A.F.R. Rahman and M.C. Fairhurst. An evaluation of multi-expert configurations for the recognition of handwritten numerals. *Pattern Recognition*, 31(9):1255–1273, 1998.
25. F.R. Rahman and M. C. Fairhurst. Serial combination of multiple experts: a unified evaluation. *Pattern Analysis and Applications*, 2:292–311, 1999.
26. N.V.S. Reddy and P. Nagabhushan. A connectionist expert system model for conflict resolution in unconstrained handwritten recognition. *Pattern Recognition Letters*, 19:161–169, 1998.
27. N. W. Strathy. Handwriting recognition for cheque processing. In *Proc. 2nd Int. Conf. on Multimodal Interface*, pages III: 47–50, Hong Kong, Jan. 1999.
28. C.Y. Suen, C. Nadal, R. Legault, T. A. Mai, and L. Lam. Computer recognition of unconstrained handwritten numerals. *Proc. IEEE*, 80:1162–1180, 1992.
29. D. Wang, J. M. Keller, C.A. Carson, K.K. McAdoo-Edwards, and C. W. Bailey. Use of fuzzy-logic-inspired features to improve bacterial recognition through classifier fusion. *IEEE Trans. SMC*, 28B(4):583–591, 1998.
30. L. Xu, A. Krzyzak, and C. Y. Suen. Methods of combining multiple classifiers and their application to handwritten numeral recognition. *IEEE Trans. Systems, Man, and Cybernetics*, 22:418–435, 1992.

Some Results on Weakly Accurate Base Learners for Boosting Regression and Classification

Wenxin Jiang

Northwestern University, Evanston, IL 60208, USA

Abstract. One basic property of the boosting algorithm is its ability to reduce the training error, subject to the critical assumption that the base learners generate 'weak' (or more appropriately, 'weakly accurate') hypotheses that are better that random guessing. We exploit analogies between regression and classification to give a characterization on what base learners generate weak hypotheses, by introducing a geometric concept called the angular span for the base hypothesis space. The exponential convergence rates of boosting algorithms are shown to be bounded below by essentially the angular spans. Sufficient conditions for nonzero angular span are also given and validated for a wide class of regression and classification systems.

1 Introduction

Boosting, as a very useful tool for constructing multiple classifier systems, has become increasingly popular during the past decade [Schapire (1990), Freund and Schapire (1997)]. One basic theoretical property of boosting is its ability to reduce the training error, or roughly speaking that it boosts a weak learner to be strong. How this works is relatively well understood, subject to the major assumption of a weak base learner, that the hypotheses generated by the base learner in boosting are 'weak', or are capable of beating a random guesser for a finite amount [see Schapire (1999)].

Our goal is to investigate this assumption based on an analogy of boosting in least squares regression. We will see that the weak learner assumption does not always hold, and that it does hold for a large class of base hypothesis spaces. For this purpose we introduce a geometric concept called the angular span for the base hypothesis space. We show that the weak learner is implied by a nonzero angular span, which also gives a bound on the exponential convergence rate of boosting. This concept is later adapted to the case of classification where the boosting method originated, and provides a similar characterization of the weak learner. In this formalism we also provide primitive conditions and examples of the base hypothesis space that accommodates a weak learner, for both regression and classification.

It is noted that, for classification problems, the conditions under which a weak edge needed by boosting algorithms can always be achieved were explored by Freund (1995), as well as Goldmann, Hastad and Razborov (1992). See

J. Kittler and F. Roli (Eds.): MCS 2000, LNCS 1857, pp. 87–96, 2000.
© Springer-Verlag Berlin Heidelberg 2000

also Freund and Schapire (1996) and especially Breiman (1997a,b). As a referee pointed out, the difference between these works and the current paper is that in these other works, the infemum in the definition of the classification angular span (Section 4) would not be taken over the example labels. Instead these labels would be fixed. It may be more natural for the labels to be fixed rather than part of the infemum since a boosting algorithm is not permitted to change the example labels. A disadvantage of guarding against all possible labels is that the resulting bound on the convergence rate may be too pessimistic as compared to the actual performance on a particular data set. For example, in the formalism of the current paper, the angular span typically decreases towards zero as the size of the data set increases. The current approach, however, guards against the worst possible data sets, and enables one to relate the assumption of weak hypotheses directly to the richness of the base hypothesis space. Such a treatment also provides an analogous characterization in the case of regression boosting.

The ideas in this paper are related to other work in this area. In particular, we benefited much from Schapire (1999) for the idea of achieving strong learners by recursive applications of weak learners; from Friedman, Hastie and Tibshirani (1999) for the idea of considering boosting as sequential regression; from Mason, Baxter, Bartlett and Frean (1999) for the idea of considering inner product spaces with general cost functions; and from Breiman (1998) who pointed out the limitation of the original formulation of weak PAC-learnability in the context of learning with noisy data.

Below we first provide a description of the set-up of statistical learning with noisy data, and define some relevant concepts and useful results. Then we consider the set-up of boosting or sequential learning, and provide a survey of the main results, from regression to classification. For convenience, we will formulate everything for predictors valued in $[0, 1]$, although everything can be easily extended to more general domains that may be multi-dimensional. More details and proofs are contained in an unpublished technical report (Jiang 2000).

2   Some Useful Concepts

In statistical learning, we are faced with an observed data set $(X_i, Y_i)_1^n$, where X_1^n are *predictors*, which can either be fixed or random, and are valued in $[0, 1]$, take $m(\leq n)$ distinct values $\{x_1^m\}$ with *multiplicity* $\{\nu_1^m\} \in \{1, 2, 3, \ldots\}^m$. The locations of these m distinct values are called the *design points*, with the name borrowed from the context of fixed-predictor regression. We allow the *responses* Y_1^n to be random for potential noises of the data. Sometimes we relabel $(Y_i)_1^n$ to have two indices as $(Y_{jk})_{1,1}^{m,\nu_j}$ or $\{Y_k(x_j)\}_{1,1}^{\nu_j,m}$, to highlight the x-locations. It is noted that in the machine learning literature the Y_i's are usually fixed and the X_i's are random with no multiplicity; while in statistics the Y_i's are invariably random, and the X_i's can be sometimes fixed and chosen by the researcher who collects the data. In this case, as well as in the case of random but discrete X_i's, the concept of multiplicity is useful. We call n and m respectively the sample size and the number of design points. The Y_i's are real for regression problems and are $\{0,1\}$ valued in the classification problem, where a useful transform $Z_i = 2Y_i - 1$ valued in $\{-1,+1\}$ is often used.

In learning, we usually have a *hypothesis space* of real regression functions $\mathcal{H}_r$ or a *hypothesis space* of $\{\pm 1\}$ valued classification functions $\mathcal{H}_c$ to fit the data. A hypothesis space called the *base hypothesis space* or *base system* $H_{r,c}$ can be made more complex by linear combinations of t members as the *t-combined system* or *t-combined hypothesis space* denoted as $\text{lin}^t(H_{r,c})$. Formally, $\text{lin}^t(H) = \{\sum_1^t \alpha_s f_s : (\alpha_s, f_s) \in \Re \times H\}$. A regression space $\mathcal{H}_r$ is said to *induce* a classifier space $\mathcal{H}_c$, if $\mathcal{H}_c = \text{sgn}(\mathcal{H}_r) = \{\text{sgn}(f) : f \in \mathcal{H}_r\}$.

We now introduce a concept for describing the capacity or powerfulness of a hypothesis space $\mathcal{H}_r$, called the *angular span* or *a-span*. [Its relations to some ('smaller') analogs of the VC dimension and the pseudo-dimension are investigated in Jiang (1999).] We first define the angular span for a general set of vectors A in an inner product space with inner product $(\,,\,)_{norm}$ and squared norm $||v||^2 = (v,v)_{norm}$, which is denoted as

$$\text{asp}(A;\ norm) = \inf_{\epsilon \neq 0} \sup_{v \in A} (\epsilon/||\epsilon||,\ v/||v||)^2_{norm},$$

and is a quantity valued in $[0,1]$. The smaller this quantity, the less well distributed the vectors in A. If A spans the vector space then the asp is nonzero. We later will see that the nonzeroness of the a-span is crucial for validating the weak learner assumption for regression problems, and will define a similar quantity for the classification problems. Now consider a regression hypothesis space $\mathcal{H}_r$, and an inner product space associated with a set of distinct points x_1^m with multiplicity ν_1^m, with the inner product defined by $(f,g)_{x_1^m,\nu_1^m} = \sum_1^m \nu_j f(x_j) g(x_j) / \sum_1^m \nu_j$ for $f,g \in \mathcal{H}_r$. The *regression a-span* for $\mathcal{H}_r$ with this particular norm is now defined as

$$\text{asp}(\mathcal{H}_r;\ x_1^m, \nu_1^m) = \inf_{\epsilon \in \Re^m,\ ||\epsilon||=1} \sup_{f \in \mathcal{H}_r} (\epsilon,\ f/||f||)^2_{x_1^m, \nu_1^m},$$

with the obvious extension of the inner product acting on any two m-vectors a_1^m and b_1^m: $(a,b)_{x_1^m,\nu_1^m} = \sum_1^m \nu_j a_j b_j / \sum_1^m \nu_j$, such that for a function f the corresponding m-vector is $f_1^m = f(x_j)_1^m$. By definition the regression a-span has the following monotone properties with respect to the hypothesis space and with respect to the number of design points:

(i). $\mathcal{H}_r \subset \mathcal{H}_r'$ implies that $\text{asp}(\mathcal{H}_r;\ x_1^m, \nu_1^m) \leq \text{asp}(\mathcal{H}_r';\ x_1^m, \nu_1^m)$;

(ii). $\text{asp}(\mathcal{H}_r;\ x_1^{m+1}, \nu_1^{m+1}) \leq \text{asp}(\mathcal{H}_r;\ x_1^m, \nu_1^m)$.

Some examples of the regression a-span are given below, for the case without multiplicity $(\nu_1^m = 1_1^m)$.

1. If the hypothesis is the $(p-1)$th order regression $H = \{\sum_0^{p-1} a_k x^k : a_0^{p-1} \in \Re^p\}$, then $\text{asp}(H;\ x_1^m, 1_1^m) = I\{m \leq p\}$. (I.e., asp=1 if $m \leq p$ and 0 if $m > p$.)

2. If the hypothesis contains m orthonormal basis vectors on x_1^m, i.e., $H = \{\phi_k(\cdot)_1^m : [\phi_k(x_j)]_{1,1}^{m,m}$ is an orthogonal matrix$\}$, then $\text{asp} = 1/m$. This is because, in this case, the asp is the squared cosine of the angle between the major diagonal of an m-dimensional cube and any of its edges.

3. If $H = \{x^k : k = 0, \ldots, m\}$ then $0 < \text{asp} \le 1/m$.
4. If $H = \{\cos(ax) : a \in \Re\}$, $m = 2$ and $x_1^m = (0, 1)$, then the asp is $\cos^2(\pi/4)$ or 0.5.
5. If $H = \{\sin(ax) : a \in \Re\}$, $m = 2$ and $x_1^m = (0, 1)$, then the asp is zero.

The following two lemmas relate the condition of nonzero a-span to more primitive conditions that are easy to validate. The first lemma was proved from the definition of a-span, and the second by constructing a sequence of m functions, which, when evaluated at the design points, produce a sequence of matrices with a nonzero limiting determinant.

Lemma 1 *If, for any set of distinct design points x_1^m, we can find m functions f_1^m from a hypothesis space H_r which produces a nonsingular matrix $[f_k(x_j)]_{1,1}^{m,m}$, then we have $\text{asp}(H_r; x_1^m, \nu_1^m) > 0$ for all possible multiplicities ν_1^m.*

Lemma 2 *Suppose the closure of H_r contains the set of all sign functions. More formally, suppose H_r contains, for any real number a, a sequence of functions $\{f^{(i),a}\}_{i=1}^{\infty}$ such that $f^{(i),a}$ converges to the function $\text{sgn}(x - a)$ at all points $x \ne a$. Then, for any set of distinct design points x_1^m, we can find m functions f_1^m from H_r or m functions f_1^m from $\text{sgn}(H_r)$ which produce a nonsingular matrix $[f_k(x_j)]_{1,1}^{m,m}$.*

Remark 1 The condition of this last lemma is satisfied by many base hypothesis spaces. They include all base systems that contain a family of 'shifted' cumulative distributing functions (cdf) $\{2F\{(\cdot - \mu)/\sigma\} - 1 : \sigma > 0, \mu \in \Re\}$. Examples include the case when F is the logistic cdf, when the q-combined system is the usual neural nets with q (tanh) nodes; the case when F is the normal cdf; the threshold base system with a Heaviside cdf; the base system of mixtures of two experts [Jacobs, Jordan, Nowlan and Hinton (1991)]; and any more complicated base systems that include these base systems as submodels — for example the base system of a neural net, or the base system of a CART tree. By the consequences of the previous lemmas and the later ones, we see that all these base systems accommodate weak learners that can be boosted to be 'strong' at a nonzero exponential rate, which is related to the nonzeroness of the angular span of these base systems.

Now we describe the set up for boosting the least squares regression sequentially.

3 Boosting Regression Base Learners

The *least squares cost function* for f in a regression hypothesis space $\mathcal{H}_r$, with respect to a data set $(X_i, Y_i)_1^n$, is decomposable into two parts, one does not depend on f and the other does:

$$n^{-1} \sum_{i=1}^{n} \{Y_i - f(X_i)\}^2 =$$

$$n^{-1} \sum_{k=1}^{\nu_j} \{Y_k(x_j) - Y_B(x_j)\}^2 + \sum_{j=1}^{m} \left(\frac{\nu_j}{\sum_{k=1}^{m} \nu_k} \right) \{Y_B(x_j) - f(x_j)\}^2,$$

where $Y_B(x_j) = \nu_j^{-1} \sum_{k=1}^{\nu_j} Y_k(x_j)$, the sample average at the design point x_j. We use subscript B since it is analogous to the optimal Bayes solution in the classification context. It is then obvious that the least squares approach effectively minimizes the second part, which is called the *reducible error*, and conveniently written as $||Y_B - f||^2_{x_1^m, \nu_1^m}$ — we will suppress the subscripts of the norm or inner product here.

We now consider a hypothesis space H_r to be the base hypothesis space, and first build onto it by attaching a coefficient: $\alpha f \in \Re \times H_r$, and then later sequentially adding up such terms to form $\sum_1^t \alpha_s f_s \in \text{lin}^t(H_r)$. A *base learner* or *base learning algorithm* is defined to be an algorithm which is capable of mapping any 'compressed' data [such as $Y_B(x_j)_1^m$] to $\Re \times H_r$, which can be written as $\hat{\alpha}\hat{f} : \Re^m \mapsto \Re \times H_r$. When the fit is obtained by the least squares procedure, it is typically assumed that $\hat{\alpha}\hat{f} = \arg\min_{\alpha f \in \Re \times H_r} ||Y_B - \alpha f||^2$ achieves the infemum of the objective function. We slightly relax this assumption and allow an approximate fit, by introducing a concept called the *tolerance* (level) of $\hat{\alpha}\hat{f}$, denoted as

$$\text{tol}(\hat{\alpha}\hat{f}) = \sup_{\epsilon \in \Re^m,\ \epsilon \neq 0} (||\epsilon - \hat{\alpha}\hat{f}_\epsilon||^2/||\epsilon||^2 - \inf_{\alpha f \in \Re \times H_r} ||\epsilon - \alpha f||^2/||\epsilon||^2).$$

(This tolerance level is relative to the best cost function achievable in $\Re \times H_r$; the smaller the tolerance the higher the precision. The typical approaches assume $\text{tol} = 0$ and that the minimizations are fully completed.)

Now we introduce the concept of weak learner similar to Schapire (1999). A base learner $\hat{\alpha}\hat{f}$ is δ-*weak* ($\delta > 0$), with respect to the set of design points x_1^m with multiplicities ν_1^m, if

$$\sup_{\epsilon \in \Re^m,\ \epsilon \neq 0} ||\epsilon - \hat{\alpha}\hat{f}_\epsilon||^2/||\epsilon||^2 \leq 1 - \delta.$$

Our definition of weak learner differs slightly from that of Schapire in that we restrict the base learner to handle a specific set of x_1^m and ν_1^m. This is sufficient for us later to prove the strong learner result. A *strong learner* related to a hypothesis space $\mathcal{H}_r$ is here defined to be a sequence of *learners* $\hat{F}_t : \Re^m \mapsto \mathcal{H}_r, t = 1, 2, \ldots$, such that $\lim_{t \to \infty} \sup_{\epsilon \in \Re^m,\ \epsilon \neq 0} ||\epsilon - (\hat{F}_t)_\epsilon||^2/||\epsilon||^2 = 0$. (We sometimes also use $\hat{F}_t$ to denote the hypothesis in $\mathcal{H}_r$ that is chosen by the learning algorithm, which should be clear from the context.)

The following sequential algorithm, from Friedman (1999), is an analog to the boosting in the regression context, and we will show that it provides a strong learner given that the weak learner assumption holds.

Algorithm Boost.Reg:
1. Let $\hat{F}_0 = 0$.
2. For all $t = 1, 2, \ldots$:

a. Let $\hat{\alpha}_t \hat{f}_t = \hat{\alpha}\hat{f}|_{\epsilon_{t-1}}$ be a base hypothesis chosen by a base learner minimizing a cost function $||\epsilon_{t-1} - \alpha f||^2$ over $\Re \times H_r$, with perhaps a nonzero tolerance, where $\epsilon_{t-1} = Y_B - \hat{F}_{t-1}$.

b. Let $\hat{F}_t = \hat{F}_{t-1} + \hat{\alpha}_t \hat{f}_t$.

The following lemma is similar to Schapire (1999) and says that the assumption of weak base learner implies a strong combined learner, with an exponential convergence rate.

Lemma 3 *If the base learner $\hat{\alpha}\hat{f}$ used in Step 2a of Boost.Reg is δ-weak, then for any nonzero Y_B, $||Y_B - \hat{F}_t||^2/||Y_B||^2 \leq (1 - \delta)^t \leq e^{-\delta t}$.*

The next lemma says that if the angular span of the base hypothesis space is nonzero, then it is always possible to make the weak learner assumption hold, by using a base learning algorithm that is precise enough in minimizing the least squares objective function.

Lemma 4 *Suppose $\mathrm{asp}(H_r) > \mathrm{tol}(\hat{\alpha}\hat{f}) \geq 0$. Then $\hat{\alpha}\hat{f}: \Re^m \mapsto \Re \times H_r$ is δ-weak with $\delta = \mathrm{asp}(H_r) - \mathrm{tol}(\hat{\alpha}\hat{f}) > 0$.*

In fact the critical condition of a nonzero a-span for the base system is in some sense also necessary for weak learners to exist.

Proposition 1 *Consider any specified set of design points x_1^m with multiplicities ν_1^m. A base learner $\hat{\alpha}\hat{f}$ valued in $\Re \times H_r$ can be made δ-weak for some positive δ, by using a sufficiently small tolerance, if and only the base hypothesis space H_r has a nonzero a-span.*

These results were proved by applying the definitions of the a-span and the tolerance.

Remark 2   a. The critical condition $\mathrm{asp}(H_r) > 0$, and consequently the weak learner assumption, does not always hold. A trivial example is that the linear regression base system for 3 design points has zero a-span. However, more primitive conditions given in the previous section show that a large class of base systems do have nonzero a-spans.

b. It may not be reasonable to define a δ-weak learner uniformly for arbitrary number of design points, since our previous examples show that the a-spans of the base hypothesis spaces often decrease towards zero as m increases.

These lemmas immediately lead to the following proposition:

Proposition 2 *Suppose the base hypothesis space H_r and the base learning algorithm $\hat{\alpha}\hat{f}$ satisfies $\mathrm{asp}(H_r) > \mathrm{tol}(\hat{\alpha}\hat{f}) \geq 0$. Then the reducible training error $||Y_B - \hat{F}_t||^2$ of the sequential hypothesis $\hat{F}_t$ in $\mathrm{lin}^t(H_r)$ obtained from Boost.Reg satisfies, for all t,*

$$||Y_B - \hat{F}_t||^2 \leq ||Y_B||^2 \exp[-t\{\mathrm{asp}(H_r) - \mathrm{tol}(\hat{\alpha}\hat{f})\}].$$

This result was used in Jiang (1999) to partially understand the overfitting behavior of Boost.Reg, in the large time (t) limit.

4   Angular Span for Classification

The response Y_i's are $\{0,1\}$ valued in the classification problem, where a useful transform $Z_i = 2Y_i - 1$ valued in $\{-1,+1\}$ is often used. A hypothesis space $\mathcal{H}_c$ is a set of functions $f : [0,1] \mapsto \{\pm 1\}$. It can often be induced by a regression space $\mathcal{H}_r$ by $\mathcal{H}_c = \text{sgn}(\mathcal{H}_r)$. For measuring the capacity of $\mathcal{H}_c$, we define the *classification angular span* related to a set of design points x_1^m (it does not depend on the multiplicities). Denoting $P^m = \{w_1^m : w_j \geq 0, \sum_1^m w_j = 1\}$, we define

$$\text{asp}_c(\mathcal{H}_c; x_1^m) = \inf_{w_1^m \in P^m, z_1^m \in \{\pm 1\}^m} \sup_{f \in \mathcal{H}_c} \left| \sum_{j=1}^m w_j z_j f(x_j) \right|.$$

This quantity obviously lies in $[0,1]$, as the regression a-span. It also has similar monotone properties: (i). $\mathcal{H}_c \subset \mathcal{H}_c'$ implies that $\text{asp}_c(\mathcal{H}_c; x_1^m) \leq \text{asp}_c(\mathcal{H}_c'; x_1^m)$; (ii). $\text{asp}_c(\mathcal{H}_c; x_1^{m+1}) \leq \text{asp}_c(\mathcal{H}_c; x_1^m)$. On the other hand, unlike the regression a-span, the classification a-span no longer has the 'angular' interpretation.

Some simple examples are:

6. For the hypothesis space of delta-functions [Schapire et al. (1998)] $\mathcal{H}_c = \{s \cdot \delta_a : s \in \{\pm 1\}, a \in \Re\}$, where $\delta_a(x) = 2I\{x = a\} - 1$, we have $3/m \geq \text{asp}_c(\mathcal{H}_c) \geq 1/m$ for any set of m design points;
7. For the hypothesis space of threshold-functions $\mathcal{H}_c = \{s \cdot \text{sgn}_a : s \in \{\pm 1\}, a \in \Re\}$, where $\text{sgn}_a(x) = 2I\{x \geq a\} - 1$, we have $2/m \geq \text{asp}_c(\mathcal{H}_c) \geq 1/m$ for any set of m design points.
8. Suppose $x_1^m = \{0,1\}$, $\mathcal{H}_c = \{\text{sgn}[\cos\{a(x-1/2)\}] : a \in \Re\}$. Then $\text{asp}_c(\mathcal{H}_c) = 0$, which is easily proved by applying the definition and taking $w_1^m = \{1/2, 1/2\}$ and $z_1^m = \{-1, 1\}$.

The following lemma has been useful for obtaining upper bounds for the classification a-span, which follows again from the definition.

Lemma 5 *(Sign Change.) Suppose all the hypotheses in $\mathcal{H}_c$ change signs K times or less. More formally, let $\mathcal{K}_f$ be the number of connected components of the positive support $\{x : f(x) = 1\}$, plus the number of connected components of the negative support $\{x : f(x) = -1\}$, and suppose that $\sup_{f \in \mathcal{H}_c} \mathcal{K}_f \leq K$. Then we have $\text{asp}_c(\mathcal{H}_c : x_1^m) \leq K/m$ for any set of (distinct) design points x_1^m.*

Sufficient conditions for $\text{asp}_c > 0$ are summarized in the following lemmas which are analogous to the ones in the regression case.

Lemma 6 *Suppose $\mathcal{H}_c = \text{sgn}(\mathcal{H}_r)$ and there exist $f_1^m \in \mathcal{H}_r$ such that the matrix $[f_k(x_j)]_{1,1}^{m,m}$ is non-singular, then $\text{asp}_c(\mathcal{H}_c; x_1^m) > 0$.*

By Lemma 2, we therefore also have

Proposition 3 *$\mathcal{H}_c = \text{sgn}(\mathcal{H}_r)$ and $\mathcal{H}_r$ can approximate any sign function (see Lemma 2) imply that $\text{asp}_c(\mathcal{H}_c; x_1^m) > 0$ for any set of (distinct) design points x_1^m.*

(That is, the classification a-span is nonzero if the base classifier space H_c is induced by a regression space H_r which can approximate any sign function.)

Now we show that, like the regression case, a nonzero a-span of the classification base system H_c implies that the (reducible) training error can be made arbitrarily small by applying the base learners sequentially, and that the usual assumption of weak learner is reasonable. We now introduce the set-up.

5   Boosting Classification Base Learners

Let $S = (X_i, Y_i)_1^n$ $(Y_i \in \{0, 1\})$ be the observed data, with a set of design points x_1^m and multiplicities ν_1^m. Let $Y_{pred}(\cdot) \in H_c$ be a prediction based on the observed data, also taking values from $\{0, 1\}$. Then the *training error* can be conveniently denoted as $P_S\{Y \neq Y_{pred}(X)\}$ where (X, Y) is a pair of random variables following the sample distribution of the observed data S. Like the training error in the regression case, the training error also contains a reducible part and a part that is not reducible. Denote $Y_B(\cdot)$ to be any $\{0, 1\}$-valued function such that $Y_B(x_j) = I\{\nu_j^{-1} \sum_{k=1}^{\nu_j} Y_k(x_j) \geq 1/2\}$ (the majority prediction or the Bayes prediction). Specifically, we have

$$P_S\{Y \neq Y_B(X)\} \leq P_S\{Y \neq Y_{pred}(X)\}$$
$$\leq P_S\{Y \neq Y_B(X)\} + P_S\{Y_{pred}(X) \neq Y_B(X)\}.$$

The second part is the *reducible training error*: $P_S\{Y_{pred}(X) \neq Y_B(X)\} = \sum_{j=1}^m \pi_j I\{Y_{pred}(x_j) \neq Y_B(x_j)\}$ where $\pi_j = \nu_j / \sum_{k=1}^m \nu_k$.

Suppose the corresponding sign-valued prediction $Z_{pred} = 2Y_{pred} - 1$ is induced by a real hypothesis: $Z_{pred} = \text{sgn} \circ F$ for some $F \in H_r$, and denote $Z_B = 2Y_B - 1$. Then we have the following inequality

$$P_S\{Y_{pred}(X) \neq Y_B(X)\} \leq D(F) \equiv \sum_{j=1}^m \pi_j e^{-F(x_j)Z_B(x_j)}.$$

This upper bound $D(F)$ is the cost function used by boosting. The hypothesis space H_r of the F's is the space of linear combinations of t base hypotheses: $H_r = \text{lin}^t(H_c)$ at round t. Put in a form that is parallel to the Boost.Reg algorithm, the boosting algorithm of classification, Boost.Cl, is the following:

Algorithm Boost.Cl:
1. Set $\hat{F}_0 = 0$, $Y_{pred,0} = (1 + \text{sgn} \circ \hat{F}_0)/2$.
2. For $t = 1, 2, \ldots$:
   a. Find some $(\alpha, f) = (\hat{\alpha}_t, \hat{f}_t) \in \Re \times H_c$ which exactly or approximately minimizes $D(\hat{F}_{t-1} + \alpha f)/D(\hat{F}_{t-1})$.
   b. Set $\hat{F}_t = \hat{F}_{t-1} + \hat{\alpha}_t \hat{f}_t$, $Y_{pred,t} = (1 + \text{sgn} \circ \hat{F}_t)/2$.

Proposition 4 *Suppose that* tol^2 *is a nonnegative number such that*

$$\{D(\hat{F}_{t-1} + \hat{\alpha}_t \hat{f}_t)/D(\hat{F}_{t-1})\}^2 - \inf_{(\alpha, f) \in \Re \times H_c} \{D(\hat{F}_{t-1} + \alpha f)/D(\hat{F}_{t-1})\}^2 \leq tol^2$$

for all t in Step 2a of Boost.Cl. Suppose $asp^2 = \{\text{asp}_c(H_c)\}^2$. Then we have, for all t, the following bound for the reducible training error:

$$P_S\{Y_{pred,t}(X) \neq Y_B(X)\} \leq (1 - asp^2 + tol^2)^{t/2} \leq e^{-t(asp^2 - tol^2)/2}.$$

The proof is similar to the classical derivation of AdaBoost [such as in Schapire (1999)].

Remark 3 It is noted that in the original AdaBoost, the Step 2a of Boost.Cl first performs a complete minimization with respect to α. In this context 2a is reduced to maximizing $(\hat{\epsilon}_t - 1/2)^2$ where $\hat{\epsilon} = \sum_{j=1}^{m} w_j^{(t)} I\{Z_B(x_j) \neq \hat{f}_t(x_j)\}$. The δ-weak learner approach assumes that $|\hat{\epsilon}_t - 1/2| \geq \delta$ for all t for some positive δ. Our approach shows that this quantity δ can be taken as $(1/2)\sqrt{asp^2 - tol^2}$, and can be made positive if the angular span of the base hypothesis space is nonzero, by achieving a relatively precise optimization in Step 2a. A 'necessary and sufficient' result relating the notion of weak learner and a nonzero a-span is also available (Jiang 2000), similar to Proposition 1 in the regression case. Even if the a-span is not always nonzero (see Example 8), the previous lemmas show that many common base hypothesis spaces H_c do have nonzero a-span; namely when $H_c = \text{sgn}(H_r)$ and H_r can approximate the family of sign functions. This to a large extent validates the usual assumption that the base learner generates weak hypotheses in boosting so that the training error decreases exponentially fast [see Schapire (1999)].

6   Conclusions

This paper investigates some theoretical properties of a regression boosting algorithm [Friedman (1999), Friedman et al. (1999)] and shows that it has similar properties to classification boosting. The concepts and methodology used in that context, by analogy, turn out to also be applicable to the original boosting methods for classification, which allow us to further our understanding of the well-known weak learner assumption. This approach also provides bounds of predictive error that are tight in the limit of large time (the rounds of boosting), for fixed or discrete random predictors in Jiang (1999).

Acknowledgments
    As a new researcher in this field, I am very grateful to a referee who pointed out existing works in this area and provided a comprision, and to all referees for their valuable comments and suggestions.

References

BREIMAN, L. (1998). Arcing classifiers. *The Annals of Statistics*, **26** 801-849.
BREIMAN, L. (1997a). Prediction games and arcing classifiers. *Technical Report 504, Statistics Department, University of California at Berkeley, 1997.*

BREIMAN, L. (1997b). Arcing the edge. *Technical Report 486, Statistics Department, University of California at Berkeley, 1997.*

FREUND, Y. (1995). Boosting a weak learning algorithm by majority. *Information and Computation,* **121** 256-285.

FREUND, Y. AND SCHAPIRE, R. E. (1996). Game theory, on-line prediction and boosting. *Proceedings of the Ninth Annual Conference on Computational Learning Theory,* 325-332.

FREUND, Y. AND SCHAPIRE, R. E. (1997). A decision-theoretic generalization of on-line learning and an application to boosting. *Journal of Computer and System Sciences,* **55** 119-139.

FRIEDMAN, J. H. (1999). Greedy function approximation: a gradient boosting machine. *Technical Report, Department of Statistics, Stanford University.*

FRIEDMAN, J., HASTIE, T. AND TIBSHIRANI, R. (1999). Additive logistic regression: a statistical view of boosting. *Technical Report, Department of Statistics, Stanford University.*

GOLDMANN, M., HASTAD, J., AND RAZBOROV, A. (1992). Majority gates vs. general weighted threshold gates. *Computational Complexity,* **2** 277-300.

JACOBS, R. A., JORDAN, M. I., NOWLAN, S. J., AND HINTON, G. E. (1991). Adaptive mixtures of local experts. *Neural Comp.* **3** 79-87.

JIANG, W. (1999). Large time behavior of boosting algorithms for regression and classification. *Technical Report, Department of Statistics, Northwestern University.*

JIANG, W. (2000). On weak base learners for boosting regression and classification. *Technical Report, Department of Statistics, Northwestern University.*

MASON, L., BAXTER, J., BARTLETT, P. AND FREAN, M. Boosting algorithms as gradient descent in function space. *Technical Report, Department of Systems Engineering, Australian National University.*

SCHAPIRE, R. E. (1990). The strength of weak learnability. *Machine Learning,* **5** 197-227.

SCHAPIRE, R. E. (1999). Theoretical views of boosting. *Computational Learning Theory: Fourth European Conference, EuroCOLT'99,* 1-10.

SCHAPIRE, R. E., FREUND, Y., BARTLETT, P. AND LEE, W. S. (1998). Boosting the margin: A new explanation for the effectiveness of voting methods. *The Annals of Statistics,* **26** 1651-1686.

Complexity of Classification Problems and Comparative Advantages of Combined Classifiers

Tin Kam Ho

Bell Laboratories, Lucent Technologies
700 Mountain Avenue, 2C425, Murray Hill, NJ 07974, USA
tkh@bell-labs.com

Abstract. We studied several measures of the complexity of classification problems and related them to the comparative advantages of two methods for creating multiple classifier systems. Using decision trees as prototypical classifiers and bootstrapping and subspace projection as classifier generation methods, we studied a collection of 437 two-class problems from public databases. We observed strong correlations between classifier accuracies, a measure of class boundary length, and a measure of class manifold thickness. Also, the bootstrapping method appears to be better when subsamples yield more variable boundary measures and the subspace method excels when many features contribute evenly to the discrimination.

1 Introduction

Since the early 1990's many methods have been developed for classifier combination. These methods are results of two parallel lines of study: (1) assume a given, fixed set of carefully designed and highly specialized classifiers, attempt to find an *optimal combination* of their decisions; and (2) assume a fixed decision combination function, *generate* a set of mutually complementary, generic classifiers that can be combined to achieve optimal accuracy. We refer to combination strategies of the first kind as *decision optimization* methods and the second kind as *coverage optimization* methods.

Theoretical claims of optimality for single or combined classifiers are often dependent on an assumption of infinite sample size. In practice, limits in training data often mean that models and heuristics are needed to generalize decisions to unseen samples. Practical systems use specialized classifiers to include domain-specific heuristics in different ways, and their cooperation is thus desirable to provide a more balanced coverage of the domain. Such a balance is explicitly sought after in coverage optimization methods, though a heuristic choice is still needed to specify a family of component classifiers, such as specific kinds of kernels or trees. In either case, sparse training samples and the biases of the heuristics often leave the optimality goals unfulfilled.

Just like with a single classifier, when a combined system performs at suboptimal accuracy, the reasons are often unclear. Theoretically[4] and empirically, there is a general understanding that different types of data require different

J. Kittler and F. Roli (Eds.): MCS 2000, LNCS 1857, pp. 97–106, 2000.

kinds of classifiers. Similar arguments can be made for combined systems. However, we believe that it is possible and desirable to make more explicit the nature of such a dependency on data characteristics. A recent attempt is a step in this direction [20].

Deeper investigation of methods for creating multiple classifiers and their behavior points back to many fundamental questions in pattern recognition. Competence of classifiers is closely related to the sufficiency of the chosen features and metrics for separating the classes. Generalization ability and independence of classifiers also closely resemble similar properties of individual features. This suggests that studies of behavior of combined classifiers will benefit from a better understanding of the nature of difficulties of a recognition problem. In this paper we attempt to characterize such difficulties and their effects on classifier behavior.

2   Sources of Error of a Classification Problem

We begin with a brief analysis of the sources of error of a classification problem. We isolate these sources for convenience of discussion, though we understand that real world problems often include difficulties from more than one sources. For simplicity we assume that each problem is on discrimination of two classes. Multiclass problems are reduced to dichotomies, and we note that it is not trivial to recombine such pairwise decisions to a final decision. We assume that a problem is defined with a given set of samples described as points in a vector (feature) space, and each point is labeled with a class from a given set.

Class ambiguity.   Some problems are known to have nonzero Bayes error [9]. That is, samples of two different classes may have identical feature values. This can happen regardless of the shape of the class boundary and feature space dimensionality. While certain problems may be intrinsically ambiguous, others may be so because of poor feature selection. The ambiguity is intrinsic if the given features are complete for reconstruction of the patterns. Otherwise, it is possible that the ambiguity can be removed by redefining the features. The Bayes error is a measure of difficulty in this aspect and it sets a lower bound on the achievable error rate.

Imperfectly modeled boundary complexity.   Some problems have a long, geometrically or topologically complicated (Bayes) optimal decision boundary. These problems are complex by Kolmogorov's notion (the boundary needs a long description or a long algorithm to reproduce, possibly including an enumeration of all points of each class) [14]. An example is a set of randomly located points arbitrarily labeled as one of two classes. Classifiers need to have a matching capacity to model the boundary, otherwise error will occur. This is independent of sampling density, class ambiguity, and feature space dimensionality.

Small sample effect and feature space dimensionality.   The danger of having a small training set is that it may not reflect the full complexity of the underlying problem, so from the available samples the problem appears deceptively simple. This happens easily in a high dimensional space where the class boundary can vary with a larger degree of freedom. The representativeness of a training set is related to the generalization ability of classifiers, which is a focus of study in Vapnik's statistical learning theory [22] and is also discussed in Kleinberg's arguments on M-representativeness [12], Berlind's hierarchy of indiscernibility [2], and Raudys' and Jain's practical considerations [18]. It is also discussed in many studies of error rate estimation [6] [11] [21].

Imperfect accuracy of classifiers may be due to a combination of these reasons. Attempts to improve classifiers have to deal with each of them in some way. Among these, class ambiguity is either a nature of the problem or requires additional discriminatory features, and little can be done using classifiers after feature extraction. On the other hand, most classifiers are designed with the goal of finding a good decision boundary. So in this paper we will focus on the boundary complexity. Our discussion is to be qualified in the context of statistical estimation, as sample size constrains what can be learned about either class ambiguity or boundary complexity of a given problem.

3   Measures of Problem Complexity

Practical classification problems involve geometrical characteristics of the classes in the feature space coupled with probabilistic events in the sampling processes. Some theoretical studies focus on distribution-free or purely combinatorical arguments without taking into account the geometrical aspects of the problems. This may lead to unnecessarily weak results. Most classifier designs are based on simple geometrical heuristics such as proximity, convexity, and globally or locally linear boundaries. We believe that such elementary geometrical properties of the data distributions are of central importance in pattern recognition, so we emphasize these in this study.

We consider a number of measures proposed in the literature for characterizing geometrical complexity. These measures give empirical estimates of the *apparent* complexity of a problem, which may or may not be close to the true complexity depending on the sparsity of training data.

Certain practical problems possess a structure or regularity so that there exists a transformation with which samples can be mapped to a new space where class discrimination becomes easier. The existence of such a transformation is not always obvious for an arbitrary problem (i.e., Kolmogorov complexity is not effectively computable[15]), so our discussion of problem complexity will be simplified by refering to a fixed, given feature space.

Length of Class Boundary

To measure the length of the boundary between two classes, we consider a method proposed by Friedman and Rafsky [5]. Given a metric, a minimum spanning tree (MST) is constructed that connects all sample points regardless of class. Thus some edges will connect points belonging to two different classes. The length of boundary is then given as a count of such edges (Figure 1(a)). With n points there are $n - 1$ edges in the MST, so the count can be simply normalized as a percentage of n.

This measure is sensitive to both the separability of the classes and the clustering properties of the points of each class. A linearly separable problem with wide margins (relative to the intra-class distances) may have only one edge going across the classes. But another linearly separable problem may have many such edges if the points of the same class happen to be farther apart than they are from those of the other class. On the other hand, a problem with a complicated nonlinear class boundary may still have only one boundary-crossing edge as long as the points are dense and close within each class.

Space Covering by ϵ-Neighborhoods

The local clustering properties of a point set can be described by an ϵ-neighborhood pretopology [13]. Here we consider a reflexive and symmetrical binary relation $\mathcal{R}$ of two points x and y in a set F. $\mathcal{R}$ is defined by $x\mathcal{R}y \Leftrightarrow d(x, y) < \epsilon$, where $d(x, y)$ is a given metric and ϵ is a given nonzero constant. Define $\Gamma(x) = \{y \in F | y\mathcal{R}x\}$ to be the $\epsilon - neighborhood$ of x, an adherence mapping ad from the power set $\mathcal{P}(F)$ to $\mathcal{P}(F)$ is such that

$$
\begin{cases}
ad(\phi) = & \phi \\
ad(\{x\}) = \{x\} \cup \Gamma(x) \\
ad(A) = & \bigcup_{x \in A} ad(\{x\}) \qquad \forall A \subseteq F.
\end{cases}
$$

Adherence subsets can be grown from a singleton $\{x\}$: $\{x\} = ad^0(\{x\})$, $ad(\{x\}) = ad^1(\{x\})$, ..., $ad(ad^n(\{x\})) = ad^{n+1}(\{x\})$, where j is called the *adhesion order* in $ad^j(\{x\})$. From a point of each class one can grow successive adherence subsets to the highest order n such that $ad^n(\{x\})$ includes only points of the same class but $ad^{n+1}(\{x\})$ includes points of other classes.

We keep for each point only the highest order n adherence subset such that all elements of $ad^n(\{x\})$ are within the class of x, and eliminate any adherence subsets that are strictly included in others. Using the ϵ-neighborhoods with Euclidean distance as d, each retained adherence subset associated with a point is the largest hypersphere that contains it and no points from other classes, in units of the chosen ϵ (Figure 1(b)). In our experiments we used $\epsilon = 0.55\delta$ where δ is the distance between two closest points of opposite classes. We chose 0.55 arbitrarily just so that it is larger than 0.5 and the lowest adhesion order is always zero, occurring at the points closest to the class boundary.

A list of such ϵ-neighborhoods needed to cover the two classes is a composite description of the shape of the classes. The count and order of the retained adherence subsets show the extent to which the points are clustered in hyperspheres or distributed in thinner structures. In a problem where each point is closer to points of the other class than points of its own class, each adherence subset is retained and is of a low order. We normalize the count by the total number of points.

Feature Efficiency

With a high dimensional problem we are concerned about how the discriminatory information is distributed across the features. Here we consider a measure

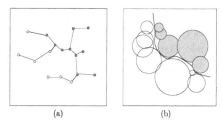

Fig. 1. (a) A minimum spanning tree where the thicker edges connect two classes. (b) Retained adherence subsets for two classes near the boundary.

of efficiency of individual features that describes how much each feature contributes to the separation of the two classes [10].

We consider a local continuity heuristic such that all points of the same class may have values of each feature falling between the maximum and minimum of that class. If there is an overlap in the feature values of two classes, we consider the classes ambiguous in that region along that dimension. Given that, a problem is easy (i.e. linearly separable) if there exists one feature dimension where the ranges of values spanned by each class do not overlap. For other problems that are globally unambiguous, one may progressively remove the ambiguity between the two classes by separating only those points that lie outside the overlapping region in each chosen dimension.

We define the *individual feature efficiency* to be the fraction of all remaining points separable by that feature. *Maximum feature efficiency* is the maximum individual feature efficiency computed using the entire point set. In this procedure we consider only separating hyperplanes perpendicular to the feature axes, i.e., joint effects of the features are not accounted for.

4   Classifiers and Their Combination

Accuracies of decision optimization methods are limited by the given set of classifiers, which makes it difficult to discuss the effects of data characteristics on their behavior. Therefore we focus our study on the coverage optimization methods. Two typical methods of this category construct a collection of classifiers systematically by varying either the training samples or the features used. These are respectively represented by the bootstrapping (or *bagging*) method [3] and the random subspace method [7][8]. In bagging, subsets of the training points are independently and randomly selected with replacement according to a uniform probability distribution. A classifier is constructed using each selected subset. In the random subspace method, in each pass all training points are projected onto a randomly chosen coordinate subspace in which a classifier is derived. Both methods are known to work well using decision trees as component classifiers, and the combined classifier is called a *decision forest*.

A decision forest is the most general form of classifiers since it allows both serial (at different levels of the tree) and parallel (with different trees) combinations of arbitrary discriminators. Decisions at the internal nodes can be simple splits on a single feature or any other linear or nonlinear discriminators. Other classifiers are special cases of decision forests.

In this study the decision trees use oblique hyperplanes to split the data at each internal node [16]. The hyperplanes are derived using a simplified Fisher's method [7], i.e., by looking for the error minimizing hyperplane perpendicular to a line connecting the centroids of two classes. Assuming no class ambiguity, the tree can always be fully split, and trees constructed this way are usually small.

5   The Collection of Problems

We investigated these complexity measures and classifiers' behavior using two collections of problems. The first consists of 14 datasets from the UC-Irvine Machine Learning Depository, selected from those containing at least 500 points and no missing values: *abalone, car, german, kr-vs-kp, letter, lrs, nursery, pima, segmentation, splice, tic-tac-toe, vehicle, wdbc, and yeast*. Categorical features were all numerically coded. With each dataset, we took every pair of classes to be a problem. Of the 844 two-class problems, 452 were found to be linearly separable[1]. We used the remaining 392 problems in this study. The second collection consists of 10,000 handwritten digit images from the NIST special database 3. There are 1000 images for each of the 10 digits, and we took each pair of digits as an individual problem. Each image is represented as gray levels in [-8,8] in 28×28 pixels, so the feature space has 784 dimensions. Despite the dimensionality, all these 45 problems were found to be linearly separable – recall that this is an apparent complexity from limited samples.

6   Results and Discussions

Figure 2 shows some pairwise scatter plots of the complexity and accuracy measures. The measures we studied include:

1. error rate of the 1-nearest-neighbor classifier using Euclidean distance, estimated by the leave-one-out method;
2. error rate of the decision tree classifier, estimated by two-fold cross validation with 10 random splits;
3. error rate of the subsampling decision forests using 100 trees, estimated by two-fold cross validation with 10 random splits;
4. error rate of the subspace decision forests using 100 trees, estimated by two-fold cross validation with 10 random splits;
5. percent improvement of subsampling decision forests over single trees (reduction in error rate normalized by the single tree error rate);
6. percent improvement of subspace decision forests over single trees (reduction in error rate normalized by the single tree error rate);
7. percent points on boundary estimated by the MST method;
8. percent points with associated adherence subsets retained; and
9. maximum (individual) feature efficiency.

Figure 2 (a)-(d) plot the error rates of 1NN, decision tree, subsampling forests and subspace forests against % points on boundary estimated by the MST method. In each plot we see a strong positive correlation and an almost linear relationship, which suggests that % points on boundary is a good indicator of problem difficulty. This measure seems to set an accuracy limit on both the individual and combined classifiers. Say, if over 50% of the points are on boundary, none of the classifiers can get to lower than 20% error rate. So no matter how much gain we may have by combining multiple classifiers of this kind and in these ways, we should not expect them to get beyond this intrinsic limit determined by the data. Though, a few off-diagonal points in each plot suggest that accuracy is affected by some other factors as well.

Figure 2 (e)-(h) plot the same error rates against % points with associated adherence subsets retained. In these plots, we see that problems with few adherence subsets retained are easier for each classifier. All those problems with a high error rate have close to 100% points retaining their own highest order adherence subset, though the converse is not necessarily true. This suggests that difficult problems tend to have classes forming long and thin structures along the class boundary. Combining with the plots in Figure 2 (a)-(d), we can see that those thin structures may still be dense enough that few points are closer to the opposite class than other members of their own (those problems have many retained adherence subsets but very few points on cross-boundary edges of the MST). The classifiers perform well on such cases.

Figure 2 (i)(j) plot the % improvement (reduction in error rate) of the decision forests over the single tree classifiers against the maximum feature efficiency. We observe (in (j)) that the subspace method tends to have larger improvement for those problems when the maximum feature efficiency is lower (an indication that the contribution to discrimination is more evenly distributed across the feature dimensions). Plot (i) shows that the subsampling method is better for some cases with higher maximum feature efficiency, but for other such cases it can also be worse than the single tree classifier. Notice that these improvement measures are normalized by the error rate of the single tree classifier, so that a large percentage (either positive or negative) may happen when the single tree error rate is small. Plot (k) shows that for most cases that have thicker classes (less retained adherence subsets), the subsampling method does not offer a substantial advantage (say, over 20%) and may even be worse. Interestingly, for the same cases, though the subspace method also yields only minor improvements, it does not perform worse than the single tree classifier (plot (l)). Both (k) and (l) show that the combined systems offer significant improvements when the classes are thin, despite that those cases are hard for a single tree classifier ((g) and (h)).

Figure 2 (m)-(p) compare the single classifiers and combined classifiers against one another. In (m) we see that the two classifiers 1NN and decision tree differ by much for some cases (off diagonal points). In (n) we compare the subsampling method vs. the subspace method in terms of improvement over single trees, and we observe two off diagonal clusters suggesting that both types of cases exist for which one method is substantially better than the other. In (o) we notice that for many cases when 1NN does not perform well, the subsampling method can yield an improved classifier. Compared to (p) we see that for those cases subsampling are also better than the subspace method. These correspond to the lower cluster in (n).

Finally, we calculate the standard deviation in the boundary measure as we take subsamples or subspace projections of the training set, and examine their correlation with the advantages of the decision forests. These are shown in Figure 2 (q)-(t). In (r) we see that the subspace method is good essentially when the boundary characteristics are similar in different subsamples (small standard deviation). For the more variable cases the subsampling method is preferable (q). When the subspace variation is small, there are more cases for which the subspace method yields over 40% improvement ((s) and (t)).

7   Conclusions

We presented some empirical observations of the relationship between classifier and combined classifier accuracies and several measures of problem complexity. We conclude that there exist obvious dependences of classifiers' behavior on those data characteristics. Such dependences may serve as a guide for the expectation and direction of future efforts for optimizing classifiers and their combinations.

Our main observations are:

– there exist complementary advantages between nearest neighbor and decision tree classifiers, as well as between subsampling and subspace methods for generating multiple classifiers;
– intrinsic characteristics of the data set a limit on achievable accuracy of either single or combined classifiers that are based on these simple geometrical models;
– classes with long boundaries or thin structures are harder for all these classifiers;
– when the discrimination power is dispersed across many features, the subspace method yields better improvement over single classifiers of the same type; and
– when the sample is very sparse so that subsamples yield more variable characteristics, the subsampling method yields better improvements.

We used the number of training samples to normalize many measures. In most of these problems the sample size is determined by convenience or resource limitations rather than by a rigorous sampling rule. As a result, the sampling density may be very different across different problems, which may introduce a hidden source of variance.

While we have not tried to exclude problems with any special characteristics, this collection is nevertheless small and may not be representative. It will be interesting if future studies turn up exceptions to the rules observed from this collection. Future work will also need to answer methodological questions such as what is a reasonable collection of problems to study along these lines, and to what extent can we generalize these conclusions.

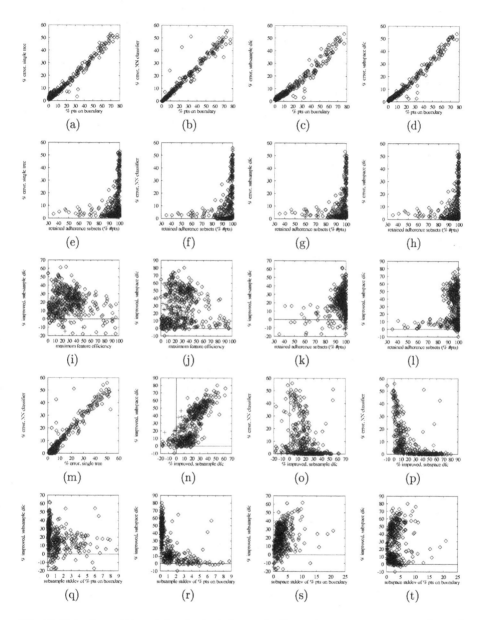

Fig. 2. Pairwise scatter plots of selected complexity and accuracy measures. In each plot, diamonds mark the 392 UCI problems and crosses mark the 45 NIST problems.

References

1. Basu, M., Ho, T.K., The learning behavior of single neuron classifiers on linearly separable or nonseparable input, *Proc. of the 1999 Int'l Joint Conf. on Neural Networks*, Washington, DC, July 1999.
2. Berlind, R., *An Alternative Method of Stochastic Discrimination with Applications to Pattern Recognition*, Doctoral Dissertation, Dept. of Mathematics, SUNY at Buffalo, 1994.
3. Breiman, L., Bagging predictors, *Machine Learning*, **24**, 1996, 123-140.
4. Devroye, L., Any discrimination rule can have an arbitrarily bad probability of error for finite sample size, *IEEE Trans. on PAMI*, **4**, 2, March 1982, 154-157.
5. Friedman, J.H., Rafsky, L.C., Multivariate generalizations of the Wald-Wolfowitz and Smirnov two-sample tests, *Annals of Statistics*, **7**, 4, 1979, 697-717.
6. Fukunaga, K., Kessell, D.L., Estimation of classification error, *IEEE Trans. on Computers*, **20**, 12, December 1971, 1521-1527.
7. Ho, T.K., Random decision forests, *Proc. of the 3rd Int'l Conf. on Document Analysis and Recognition*, Montreal, August 14-18, 1995, 278-282.
8. Ho, T.K., The random subspace method for constructing decision forests, *IEEE Trans. on PAMI*, **20**, 8, August 1998, 832-844.
9. Ho, T.K., Baird, H.S., Large-scale simulation studies in image pattern recognition, *IEEE Trans. on PAMI*, **19**, 10, October 1997, 1067-1079.
10. Ho, T.K., Baird, H.S., Pattern classification with compact distribution maps, *Computer Vision and Image Understanding*, **70**, 1, April 1998, 101-110.
11. Kittler, J., Devijver, P.A., Statistical properties of error estimators in performance assessment of recognition systems, *IEEE Trans. on PAMI*, **4**, 2, March 1982, 215-220.
12. Kleinberg, E.M., An overtraining-resistant stochastic modeling method for pattern recognition, *Annals of Statistics*, **4**, 6, December 1996, 2319-2349.
13. Lebourgeois, F., Emptoz, H., Pretopological approach for supervised learning, *Proc. of the 13th Int'l Conf. on Pattern Recognition*, Vienna, 1996, 256–260.
14. Li, M., Vitanyi, P., *An Introduction to Kolmogorov Complexity and Its Applications*, Springer-Verlag, 1993.
15. Maciejowski, J.M., Model discrimination using an algorithmic information criterion, *Automatica*, **15**, 1979, 579-593.
16. Murthy, S., Kasif, S., Salzberg, S., A System for Induction of Oblique Decision Trees, *J. of Artificial Intelligence Research*, **2**, 1, 1994, 1-32.
17. Raudys, S., On dimensionality, sample size, and classification error of nonparametric linear classification algorithms, *IEEE Trans. on PAMI*, **19**, 6, June 1997, 667-671.
18. Raudys, S., Jain, A.K., Small sample size effects in statistical pattern recognition: Recommendations for practitioners, *IEEE Trans. on PAMI*, **13**, 3, 1991, 252-264.
19. Raudys, S., Pikelis, V., On dimensionality, sample size, classification error, and complexity of classification algorithm in pattern recognition, *IEEE Trans. on PAMI*, **2**, 3, May 1980, 242-252.
20. Sohn, S.Y., Meta analysis of classification algorithms for pattern recognition, *IEEE Trans. on PAMI*, **21**, 11, 1999, 1137-1144.
21. Toussaint, G.T., Bibliography on estimation of misclassification, *IEEE Trans. on Information Theory*, **20**, 4, July 1974, 472-479.
22. Vapnik, V., *Statistical Learning Theory*, John Wiley & Sons, 1998.

Effectiveness of Error Correcting Output Codes in Multiclass Learning Problems

Francesco Masulli[1,2] and Giorgio Valentini[1,2]

[1] Istituto Nazionale per la Fisica della Materia
via Dodecaneso 33, 16146 Genova, Italy
[2] DISI - Dipartimento di Informatica e Scienze dell'Informazione
Università di Genova
via Dodecaneso 35, 16146 Genova, Italy
{masulli, valenti}@disi.unige.it

Abstract. In the framework of decomposition methods for multiclass classification problems, error correcting output codes (ECOC) can be fruitfully used as codewords for coding classes in order to enhance the generalization capability of learning machines. The effectiveness of error correcting output codes depends mainly on the independence of codeword bits and on the accuracy by which each dichotomy is learned. Separated and non-linear dichotomizers can improve the independence among computed codeword bits, thus fully exploiting the error recovering capabilities of ECOC. In the experimentation presented in this paper we compare ECOC decomposition methods implemented through monolithic multi-layer perceptrons and sets of linear and non-linear independent dichotomizers. The most effectiveness of ECOC decomposition scheme is obtained by *Parallel Non-linear Dichotomizers* (*PND*), a learning machine based on decomposition of polychotomies into dichotomies, using non linear independent dichotomizers.

1 Introduction

Error correcting output codes (ECOC) [3] can be used in the framework of decomposition methods for multiclass classification problems to enhance the generalization capability of learning machines.

In [5,6], Dietterich and Bakiri applied ECOC to multiclass learning problems. Their work demonstrated that ECOC can be useful used not only in digital transmission problems [12], but also can improve the performances of generalization of classification methods based on distributed output codes [20]. In fact, using *codewords* for coding classes leads to classifiers with error recovering abilities. The learning machines they proposed are multi-layer perceptrons (MLP) [19] or decision trees [10] using error correcting output codes and with implicit dichotomizers learning in a way dependent on the others. We will call classifiers of this kind as *monolithic classifiers.*

In this paper we outline that on one hand the approach based on monolithic classifiers reduces the accuracy of the dichotomizers, and on the other hand

J. Kittler and F. Roli (Eds.): MCS 2000, LNCS 1857, pp. 107–116, 2000.

the dependency among codeword bits limits the effectiveness of error correcting output codes [18]. On the contrary, we show that the correlation among codeword bits can be lowered using separated and independent learning machines. In fact, the error recovering capabilities of ECOC can be used in the framework of the decomposition of polychotomies into dichotomies, associating each codeword bit to a separated dichotomizer and coming back to the original multiclassification problem in the reconstruction stage [15,13]. However, in real applications, the decomposition of a polychotomy gives rise to complex dichotomies that in turn need complex dichotomizers. Moreover, decompositions based on error correcting output codes can sometimes produce very complex dichotomies.

For these reasons, in this paper we propose to implement decomposition schemes generated via error correcting output codes using *Parallel Non-linear Dichotomizers (PND)* model [21,14] that is a learning machine based on decomposition of polychotomies into dichotomies making use of dichotomizers non-linear and independent on each other. In this way we can combine the error recovering capabilities of ECOC codes with a high accurate dichotomizers.

In the next section we introduce the application of ECOC to polychotomy problems. In Sect.s 3 and 4, an experimental comparison of monolithic and decomposition based classifiers is reported and discussed. Conclusions are given in Sect. 5.

2   ECOC for Multiclass Learning Problems

In classification problems based on decomposition methods[1], usually we code classes trough binary strings, or codewords. ECOC coding methods can improve performances of the classification system, as they can recover errors produced by the classification system [3].

Let be a K classes polychotomy(or *K-polychotomy*) $\mathcal{P} : \mathbf{X} \rightarrow \{C_1, \ldots, C_k\}$, where $\mathbf{X}$ is the multidimensional space of attributes and $C_1, \ldots, C_k$ are the labels of the classes. The decomposition of the K-polychotomy generates a set of L dichotomizers $f_1, \ldots, f_L$. Each dichotomizer f_i subdivides the input patterns in two complementary superclasses $\mathcal{C}_i^+$ and $\mathcal{C}_i^-$, each of them grouping one or more classes of the K-polychotomy. Let be also a *decomposition matrix* $D = [d_{ik}]$ of dimension $L \times K$ represents the decomposition, connecting classes $C_1, \ldots, C_k$ to the superclasses $\mathcal{C}_i^+$ and $\mathcal{C}_i^-$ identified by each dichotomizer. An element of D is defined as:

$$d_{ik} = \begin{cases} +1 \text{ if } C_k \subseteq \mathcal{C}_i^+ \\ -1 \text{ if } C_k \subseteq \mathcal{C}_i^- \end{cases}$$

When a polychotomy is decomposed into dichotomies, the task of each dichotomizer $f_i : \mathbf{X} \rightarrow \{-1, 1\}$ consists in labeling some classes with $+1$ and others with -1. Each dichotomizer f_i is trained to associate patterns belonging to class C_k with values d_{ik} of the decomposition matrix D. In the decomposition matrix,

---

[1] A more detailed discussion of decomposition methods for classification is presented in [13].

rows correspond to dichotomizers tasks and columns to classes. In this way, each class is univocally determined by its specific codeword. Using ECOC codes as codewords we can achieve a so-called ECOC decomposition (Fig. 1).

$$
\begin{pmatrix}
+1 & +1 & +1 & -1 \\
+1 & +1 & -1 & +1 \\
+1 & +1 & -1 & -1 \\
+1 & -1 & +1 & +1 \\
+1 & -1 & +1 & -1 \\
+1 & -1 & -1 & +1 \\
+1 & -1 & -1 & -1
\end{pmatrix}
$$

Fig. 1. ECOC decomposition matrix for a 4 classes classification problem.

After the a-priori decomposition, the dichotomizers f_i are trained to associate patterns belonging to class C_k with values d_{ik} of the decomposition matrix D, their outputs are used to reconstruct the polychotomy in order to determine the class $C_i \in \{C_1, \ldots, C_k\}$ of the input patterns, using a suitable measure of similarity. The polychotomizer then chooses the class whose codeword is the *nearest* to that computed by the set of dichotomizers:

$$
class_{out} = \arg \max_{1 \leq i \leq K} Sim(F, c_i) \tag{1}
$$

where $class_{out}$ is the class computed by the polychotomizer, c_i is the codeword of class C_i, the vector F is the codeword computed by the set of dichotomizers, and $Sim(x, y)$ is a general similarity measure between two vectors x and y, e.g. Hamming distance or L_1 or L_2 norm distances for dichotomizers with are continuous outputs.

It is worth noting that classifiers based on decomposition methods and classifiers based on ensemble averaging methods [17,9] share the idea of using a set of learning machines acting on the same input and recombining their outputs in order to make decisions; the main difference lies in the fact that in classifiers based on decomposition methods the task of each learning machine is specific and different from that of the others.

There are two main approaches to the design of a classifier using ECOC codes:

- The first codes directly the outputs of a monolithic classifier, such us a MLP, using ECOC [5,6].

– The second is based on the usage of ECOC in the framework of decomposition of polychotomies into dichotomies, and leads to the distribution of the learning task among separated and independent dichotomizers. In this case, we call the resulting learning machines *Parallel Linear Dichotomizers* (*PLD*) if the dichotomizers used for implementing the dichotomies are linear (as in [1]), or *Parallel Non-linear Dichotomizers* (*PND*) if the dichotomizers are non-linear [21,14].

Parallel Non-linear Dichotomizers (*PND*) are multiclassifiers based on the decomposition of polychotomies into dichotomies, using dichotomizers solving their classification tasks independently from each other [21,14]. Each dichotomizer is implemented by a separate *non-linear* learning machine, and learns a different and specific dichotomic task using a training set common to all the dichotomizers. In the reconstruction stage a L_1 norm or another similarity measure between codewords is used to predict classes of unlabeled patterns.

Parallel Linear Dichotomizers (*PLD*) are also multiclassifiers based on decomposition of polychotomies into dichotomies, but each dichotomizer is implemented by a separate *linear* learning machine (see, e.g., [1]).

Error correcting codes are effective if errors induced by channel noise on single code bits are independent. In [18], Peterson showed that if errors on different code bits are correlated, the effectiveness of error correcting code is reduced. Moreover, if a decomposition matrix contains very similar rows (dichotomies), each error of an assigned dichotomizer will be likely to appear in the most correlated dichotomizers, thus reducing the effectiveness of ECOC.

Monolithic ECOC classifiers implemented on MLPs show an higher correlation among codeword bits compared with classifiers implemented using parallel dichotomizers. In fact, outputs of monolithic ECOC classifiers share the same hidden layer of the MLP, while *PND* dichotomizers, implemented with a separated MLP for each codeword bit, have their own layer of hidden units, specialized for a specific dichotomic task.

Moreover, concerning decomposition methods implemented as PLD [1], we point out that this approach reduces the correlation among codeword bits, but error recovering capabilities induced by ECOC are counter-balanced by higher error rates of linear dichotomizers.

In next section, we will experimentally test the following hypotheses about the effectiveness of ECOC:

Hypothesis 1 *Error correcting output codes are more effective for PND classifiers rather than monolithic MLP classifiers.*

Hypothesis 2 *In PLD error recovering induced by ECOC is counter-balanced by the higher error rate of the dichotomizers.*

Table 1. Data sets general features. The data sets *glass, letter* and *optdigits* data sets are from the *UCI repository* [16].

Data set	Number of attributes	Number of classes	Number of training samples	Number of testing samples
p6	3	6	1200	1200
p9	5	9	1800	5-fold cross-val
glass	9	6	214	10-fold cross-val
letter	16	26	16000	4000
optdigits	64	10	3823	1797

3   Experimental Results

In order to verify the hypotheses stated above, we have compared classification performances of *Parallel Non-linear Dichotomizers* (*PND*), *Parallel Linear Dichotomizers* (*PLD*) and monolithic classifiers implemented by MLP, using both ECOC and one-per-class (OPC)[2] decomposition methods.

PND are implemented by a set of multi-layer perceptrons with a single hidden layer, acting as dichotomizers, and *PLD* are implemented by a set of single layer perceptrons.

Monolithic MLP are built using a single hidden layer and sigmoidal activation functions, both in hidden and output neurons. The number of neurons of the hidden layer amounts roughly from ten to one hundred according to the complexity of the data set to be learned.

The programs used in our experiments have been developed using *NEUR-Objects* [22], a C++ library for neural networks development. We have used different data sets, both real and synthetic, as shown in Tab. 1. The data sets *p6* and *p9*, are synthetic and composed by normal distributed clusters associated. *p6* contains 6 class with connected regions, while the regions of the 9 classes of *p9* are not connected. *glass, letter* and *optdigits* data sets are from the *UCI repository* [16].

In the experimentation we used resampling methods, using a single pair of training and testing data set or the *k-fold cross validation* [4]. In particular the first (an simpler) form has been used for the data sets *p6, letter, optdigits,* and cross validation for the data sets *p9* and *glass*. For testing the significance of differences in performances of two different classification systems applied to the same data set, we have used *Mc Nemar's* test [8] and the *k-fold cross validated paired t test* [7].

---

[2] In One-Per-Class (OPC) decomposition scheme (see, e.g., [2]), each dichotomizer f_i have to separate a single class from all the others. As a consequence, if we have K classes, we will use K dichotomizers.

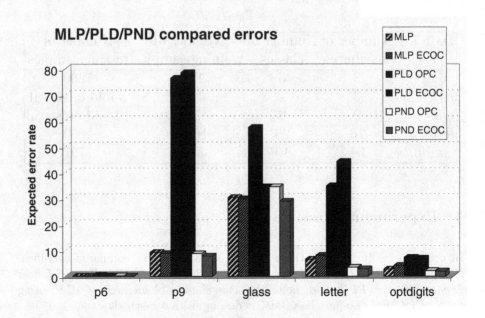

Fig. 2. Comparisons of classification expected error estimates over different data sets.

Fig. 2, shows the comparison the performances in classification of MLP, PLD and PND over the considered data sets.

Concerning monolithic MLP standard (OPC) and ECOC MLP, over data sets *p6*, *p9* and *glass* does not exist statistically significant difference between, but over *letter* and *optdigits* standard MLP performs better. In other words, *ECOC MLP monolithic classifiers do not outperform standard MLP*. This result is in contrast with Dietterich and Bakiri's thesis [6] stating that ECOC MLP outperform standard MLP. Note that, however, Dietterich and Bakiri themselves, in the experimentation over the same data set *letter* we have used, obtains better performances for standard MLP.

Concerning *PLD*, over data sets *p6*, *p9*, and *optdigits* there is no significant statistical difference among OPC and ECOC decomposition, while over *glass* *PLD* ECOC outperforms all other types of polychotomizers, but with *letter* *PLD* OPC achieve better results.

Considering *PND*, for data sets *p6* and *optdigits* no significant differences among OPC and ECOC *PND* can be noticed. Over the *p9* data set, ECOC shows expected errors significantly smaller than OPC. Expected errors over *glass* and *letter* data sets are significantly smaller for ECOC compared with OPC. So we can see that *ECOC PND show expected error rates significantly lower than OPC PND*.

We can remark that, on the whole, expected errors are significantly smaller for *PND* compared with direct monolithic MLP classifiers and *PLD*. Moreover, *PLD* shows higher errors over all data sets, and in particular it fails over *p9* that is an hard non-linearly separable synthetic data set.

We have seen that ECOC MLP classifiers do not outperform standard MLP; moreover ECOC *PND* show expected error rates significantly lower than OPC *PND*. Also, ECOC *PND* largely outperform ECOC *PLD*. It follows that *Error correcting output codes are more effective for PND classifiers rather than direct MLP and PLD classifiers*. Then hypotheses 1 and 2 have been validated by the shown experiments.

4   Discussion

In [11], on the basis of geometrical arguments, it has been shown that, using ECOC codes, decision boundaries among classes are learned several times, and however at least a number of times equal to the minimal Hamming distance among codeword of the classes, while standard classifiers learn decision boundaries only two times. In this way ECOC classifiers can recover errors made by some dichotomizers. Moreover, in [5,11] it has been stated that ECOC classifiers should be preferred to directs standard classifiers, as they reduce error bias and variance more than standard classifiers and present experimental results confirming these hypotheses, with the exception of some cases over complex data sets (such us *letter* from UCI repository) where standard MLP classifiers perform better than ECOC MLP.

Our experimentation has pointed out that not always ECOC MLP outperform standard MLP classifiers, while we found a significant difference between ECOC and OPC *PND* performances (fig. 2).

ECOC codes have been originally used to recover errors in serial transmission of messages coded as bits sequences [3], supposing that channel noise induces errors in random and not correlated positions of the sequence. On the contrary, in a classification problem, each codeword bit corresponds to a particular dichotomy, and then similar dichotomizers can induce correlations among codeword bits. As shown by Peterson [18], the effectiveness of error correcting output codes decreases, if the errors on different codeword bits are correlated. ECOC algorithms used to recover errors in serial data transmission do not care about any correlations among codeword bits, and then a transformation of these algorithms for classification problems must at least provide for a control to avoid the generation of identical dichotomizers. More specifically, effectiveness of ECOC codes applied to classification systems depends mainly on the following elements:

1. Error recovering capabilities of ECOC codes.
2. Codeword bits correlation.
3. Accuracy of dichotomizers.

Error recovering capabilities of ECOC codes depends on the minimal Hamming distance among codeword of classes, and it is a property of the ECOC algorithm used. Accuracy of dichotomizers depends on the difficulty of the dichotomization problems (for example if the dichotomy is linearly separable or not). Accuracy depends also on the structure and properties of the dichotomizer and on the cardinality of the data set: A dichotomizer with too parameters with respect to the data set size will be subjected to overfitting and an high error variance. Correlation among computed ECOC codeword bits is less for *PND* compared to MLP classifiers: in *PND* each codeword bit is learned and computed by its own MLP, specialized for its particular dichotomy, while in monolithic classifiers each codeword bit is learned and computed by linear combinations of hidden layer outputs pertaining to one and only shared multi-layer perceptron. Hence, inter-dependence among MLP ECOC outputs lowers the effectiveness of ECOC codes for this kind of classifiers. Moreover, we point out that a "blind" ECOC decomposition can in some cases generate complex dichotomies, counter-balancing error recovering capabilities of error correcting output codes, especially if dichotomizers are too simple for their dichotomization task (with respect to the data set cardinality), as in the case of *PLD*. *PND*, instead, join independence of dichotomizers (low correlation among codeword bits) with a good accuracy of their non linear dichotomizers. These conditions are both necessary for the effectiveness of ECOC codes in complex classification tasks.

5   Conclusions

Decomposition methods for multiclass classification problems constitute a powerful framework to improve generalization capabilities of a large set of learning machines. Moreover, a successful technique to improve generalization capabilities of classification systems is based on Error correcting output codes (ECOC) [5, 6].

Our experimental results show that ECOC is more effective if used in the framework of decomposition of polychotomies into dichotomies, especially if non linear dichotomizers, such us multi-layer perceptrons implementing *Parallel Non-linear Dichotomizers* [21,14] are used for the individual and separated learning of each codeword bit coding a class. Moreover, monolithic classifiers does not fully exploit the potentialities of error correcting output codes, because of the correlation among codeword bits, while *Parallel Linear Dichotomizers* (see, e.g., [1]), even though implementing non linear classifiers starting from linear ones, do not show good performances in case of complex problems, due to the linearity of their dichotomizers.

Effectiveness of error correcting output codes depends on codeword bits correlation, dichotomizers structure, properties and accuracy, and on the complexity of the multiclass learning problem.

On the basis of the experimental results and theoretical arguments reported in this paper we can claim that the most effectiveness of ECOC decomposition scheme can be obtained with *PND*, a learning machine based on decomposition of polychotomies into dichotomies, that are in turn solved using non linear independent classifiers implemented by MLP.

Acknowledgments

This work was partially supported by INFM, Università of Genova, Madess II CNR. We thank Eddy Mayoraz for his suggestions and helpful discussions.

References

1. E. Alpaydin and E. Mayoraz. Combining linear dichotomizers to construct nonlinear polychotomizers. Technical report, IDIAP-RR 98-05 - Dalle Molle Institute for Perceptual Artificial Intelligence, Martigny (Switzerland) 1998. ftp://ftp.idiap.ch/pub/reports/1998/rr98-05.ps.gz.
2. R. Anand, G. Mehrotra, C.K. Mohan and S. Ranka. Efficient classification for multiclass problems using modular neural networks. *IEEE Transactions on Neural Networks*, 6:117–124, 1995.
3. R.C. Bose and D.K. Ray-Chauduri. On a class of error correcting binary group codes. *Information and Control*, (3):68–79, 1960.
4. V. N. Cherkassky and F. Mulier. *Learning from data: Concepts, Theory and Methods*. Wiley & Sons, New York, 1998.
5. T. Dietterich and G. Bakiri. Error - correcting output codes: A general method for improving multiclass inductive learning programs. In *Proceedings of AAAI-91*, pages 572–577. AAAI Press / MIT Press, 1991.
6. T. Dietterich and G. Bakiri. Solving multiclass learning problems via error-correcting output codes. *Journal of Artificial Intelligence Research*, (2):263–286, 1995.
7. T.G. Dietterich. Approximate statistical test for comparing supervised classification learning algorithms. *Neural Computation*, 7 (10):1895–1924, 1998.
8. B.S. Everitt. *The analysis of contingency tables*. Chapman and Hall, London, 1977.
9. S. Hashem. Optimal linear combinations of neural networks. *Neural Computation*, 10:599–614, 1997.
10. J.R. Quinlan. *C4.5 Programs for Machine Learning*. Morgan Kauffman, 1993.
11. E. Kong and T. Dietterich. Error - correcting output coding correct bias and variance. In *The XII International Conference on Machine Learning*, pages 313–321, San Francisco, CA, 1995. Morgan Kauffman.
12. S. Lin and D.J.Jr. Costello. *Error Control Coding: Fundamentals and Applications*. Prentice-Hall, Englewood Cliffs, 1983.
13. F. Masulli and G. Valentini. Comparing decomposition methods for classification. In *KES'2000, Fourth International Conference on Knowledge-Based Intelligent Engineering Systems & Allied Technologies*, Brighton, England. (in press).
14. F. Masulli and G. Valentini. Parallel Non linear Dichotomizers. In *IJCNN2000, The IEEE-INNS-ENNS International Joint Conference on Neural Networks*, Como, Italy. (in press).
15. E. Mayoraz and M. Moreira. On the decomposition of polychotomies into dichotomies. In *The XIV International Conference on Machine Learning*, pages 219–226, Nashville, TN, July 1997.

16. C.J. Merz and P.M. Murphy. UCI repository of machine learning databases, 1998. www.ics.uci.edu/mlearn/MLRepository.html.
17. M.P. Perrone and L.N. Cooper. When networks disagree: ensemble methods for hybrid neural networks. In Mammone R.J., editor, *Artificial Neural Networks for Speech and Vision*, pages 126–142. Chapman & Hall, London, 1993.
18. W.W. Peterson and E.J. Jr. Weldon. *Error correcting codes*. MIT Press, Cambridge, MA, 1972.
19. D.E. Rumelhart , G.E. Hinton and R.J. Williams. Learning internal reperesentations by error propagation. In Rumelhart D.E., McClelland J.L., editor, *Parallel Distributed Processing: Explorations in the Microstructure of Conition*, volume 1, chapter 8. MIT Press, Cambridge, MA, 1986.
20. T. J. Sejnowski and C. R. Rosenberg. Parallel networks that learn to pronounce english text. *Journal of Artificial Intelligence Research*, (1):145–168, 1987.
21. G. Valentini. Metodi scompositivi per la classificazione. Master's thesis, Dipartimento di Informatica e Scienze Informazione - Università di Genova, Genova, Italy, 1999.
22. G. Valentini and F. Masulli. NEURObjects, a set of library classes for neural networks development. In *Proceedings of the third International ICSC Symposia on Intelligent Industrial Automation (IIA'99) and Soft Computing (SOCO'99)*, pages 184–190, Millet, Canada, 1999. ICSC Academic Press.

Combining Fisher Linear Discriminants for Dissimilarity Representations

Elżbieta Pękalska, Marina Skurichina, and Robert P.W. Duin

Pattern Recognition Group, Department of Applied Physics,
Faculty of Applied Sciences, Delft University of Technology,
Lorentzweg 1, 2628 CJ Delft, The Netherlands

Abstract Investigating a data set of the critical size makes a classification task difficult. Studying dissimilarity data refers to such a problem, since the number of samples equals their dimensionality. In such a case, a simple classifier is expected to generalize better than the complex one. Earlier experiments [9,3] confirm that in fact linear decision rules perform reasonably well on dissimilarity representations.
For the Pseudo-Fisher linear discriminant the situation considered is the most inconvenient since the generalization error approaches its maximum when the size of a learning set equals the dimensionality [10]. However, some improvement is still possible. Combined classifiers may handle this problem better when a more powerful decision rule is found. In this paper, the usefulness of bagging and boosting of the Fisher linear discriminant for dissimilarity data is discussed and a new method based on random subspaces is proposed. This technique yields only a single linear pattern recognizer in the end and still significantly improves the accuracy.

1 Introduction

A difficult classification task arises when the training samples are far from being sufficient for representing the real distribution (the curse of dimensionality [8]). Simple decision rules, as linear classifiers, are expected to give lower generalization errors in such cases, since less parameters are to be estimated.

We are interested in applications in which the data is initially represented by a $n \times n$ dissimilarity matrix, e.g. all distances between a set of curves to be used for shape recognition. Our goal is to solve the recognition problem by a linear classifier, i.e. a linear combination of dissimilarities computed between the testing and training objects. In this representation the dimensionality k equals the number of samples: $k = n$ and one has to deal with the critical sample size problem. The Fisher linear discriminant (FLD) fails in such a case [9,3], since the estimated covariance matrix becomes singular.

The Pseudo-Fisher linear discriminant (PFLD) makes use of the pseudo-inverse, instead. However, $n = k$ reflects the worst situation for this classifier. It has been derived [10] and observed in reality [11] that the PFLD learning curve (generalization error as a function of training set size) is characterized by a peaking behavior exactly for this point (Figure 1), which is of our interest. However, some improvement is possible, either by using less objects or less features.

J. Kittler and F. Roli (Eds.): MCS 2000, LNCS 1857, pp. 117–126, 2000.
© Springer-Verlag Berlin Heidelberg 2000

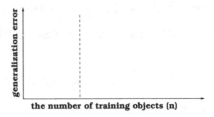

Figure 1. A typical learning curve for the (Pseudo)-Fisher linear discriminant.

Recently, the idea of combining (weak) classifiers has gained more attention. Combining simple pattern recognizers introduces some flexibility and can result in a more powerful decision rule in the end. A number of successful methods in this field exists. In this paper, we concentrate on boosting [4], bagging [1] and the random subspace method (RSM) [6,7] applied to dissimilarity data.

The paper is organized as follows. Section 2 gives some insight into dissimilarity-based pattern recognition. Boosting and bagging of the FLDs for distance data are discussed in section 3. A new technique operating in random subspaces is proposed in section 4. The simulation study on one artificial and two real datasets, alongside with the experimental set-up, is described in section 5. The results are discussed in section 6 and the conclusions are summarized in section 7.

2   The FLD for Dissimilarity-Based Pattern Recognition

In the traditional approach to learning from objects classifiers are constructed in a feature space. Dissimilarity-based pattern recognition offers alternative ways for building classifiers on dissimilarity (distance) representations. This can be especially of use, when the original data consist of a large set of attributes. In some cases it may be also easier or more natural to formulate a dissimilarity measure between objects than explicitly the features. Such measures differ according to various datasets or applications. For classification purposes, it is assumed that distances between two different objects are positive and zero otherwise.

A straightforward way of dealing with such a problem is based on relations between objects, which leads to the rank-based methods, e.g. the nearest neighbor rule. Another possibility is to treat distances as a description of a specific feature space, where each dimension corresponds to an object. This does not essentially change the classical feature-based approach, although a special case is considered: $n = k$ and each value expresses the magnitude of dissimilarity between two objects. In general, any arbitrary classifier operating on features can be used. In the learning process, the pattern recognizers are built on the $n \times n$ distance matrix. The p test objects are classified by using their distances to the n training samples (the test data consists of $p \times n$ dissimilarities).

Our earlier experiments [9] show that the feature-based classifiers operating on dissimilarity data often outperform the rank-based ones. Linear classifiers are of interest because of their simplicity. Distances are often built as a sum of many values and, under general conditions, they are approximately normally distributed. Therefore, a normal-based classifier seems to be a reasonable one. Its simplest representative is the linear decision rule, assuming the same covariance matrix for all classes. For 2 equally probable classes it is given by [5]:

$$f(\boldsymbol{x}) = [\boldsymbol{x} - \frac{1}{2}(\overline{\boldsymbol{x}}_{(1)} + \overline{\boldsymbol{x}}_{(2)})]^T S^{-1} (\overline{\boldsymbol{x}}_{(1)} - \overline{\boldsymbol{x}}_{(2)}) = \boldsymbol{w}^T \boldsymbol{x} + w_0,$$

where: $\boldsymbol{w} = S^{-1} (\overline{\boldsymbol{x}}_{(1)} - \overline{\boldsymbol{x}}_{(2)})$ and $w_0 = -\frac{1}{2} (\overline{\boldsymbol{x}}_{(1)} + \overline{\boldsymbol{x}}_{(2)})^T \boldsymbol{w}$. This is equivalent to the FLD, obtained by maximizing the ratio of between-scatter to within-scatter (Fisher criterion [5]). Therefore, we refer to this function as to the FLD.

However, the rank r of the estimated covariance matrix S is smaller than n and its inverse cannot be found. The PFLD, using a pseudo-inverse operation, is proposed instead. The pseudo-inverse relies on the singular value decomposition of the matrix S and it becomes the inverse of S in the subspace spanned by the eigenvectors corresponding to r non-zero eigenvalues. The classifier is found in this subspace and to which it is orthogonal in the remaining $n - r$ directions.

A linear classifier can be also found by using the support vector approach [2]. However, in such a sparse distance space most of the objects become support vectors which means that the classifier is based on a high number of learning samples. This is not optimal, since the training relies on solving a difficult quadratic programming problem and the obtained result yields nearly no redundancy.

3   Boosting and Bagging for the PFLD

Boosting [4] is a method designed for combining weak classifiers, which are obtained sequentially during training by using the weighted objects. At each step the incorrectly classified objects from the previous step are emphasized with larger weights. Such (misclassified) samples tend to lie close to the class boundary, so they play a major role in building a classifier, indirectly approximating the support vectors [2]. However, when the learning set is not large enough, nearly all training objects are correctly classified. As a result, not much variation in weights is introduced, which makes all constructed classifiers alike. Consequently, very little can be gained by their combination [12]. Therefore, boosting seems not to be an appropriate method for our distance representations, where $n = k$.

Studying the PFLD learning curve (Figure 1) two possible approaches can improve the situation, when $n = k$. The first one tries to reduce the number of objects (going to the left side of the peak), while the second - the number of features (going to the right side of the peak, by shifting the curve to the left). The first idea can be put into practice by bagging and the second - by combing classifiers in random subspaces.

Bagging [1] is based on bootstrapping and aggregating, i.e. on generating multiple versions of a classifier and obtaining an aggregated (combined) decision rule. Using bootstrap replicates relates to unstable classifiers, for which a small change in the learning set causes a large change in their performance. Combining classifiers and emphasizing those which give better results, may finally lead to substantial gains in accuracy. Many rules exist for combining linear classifiers, such as average (weighted) majority vote or by applying some operation (mean, product etc) on posterior probabilities of the combined classifiers.

Because of bootstrap characteristics, bagging may be of use in our case. In the training process the number of different objects is reduced, and we are practically placed in a situation in which dimensionality is larger then the number of samples (left side of the peak in Figure 1). This potentially enables us to construct a set of better performing classifiers and a more powerful decision rule in the end.

4   The FLD in Random Subspaces

It is known that multiple-tree and nearest neighbor classifiers combined in random subspaces [6,7] can gain a high accuracy. They outperform the single classifier constructed in the original space. The RSM, as an indeterministic approach, is based on a stochastic process in which a number of features is randomly selected. A classifier is then constructed in a subspace defined by those features. Proceeding in this way, a high-dimensional space can be exploited more effectively. The individual classifiers are built in subspaces, in which they are better defined. They are able to generalize well, although they do not have the full discrimination power. This stochastic process introduces some independence between classifiers and by combining them a better performance may be achieved.

This approach seems to be suitable for our problem, since it can profit from the high-dimensional data by exploring the possibilities in subspaces, thus it does not suffer from the curse of dimensionality [8]. Hopefully, the chosen dimensionality will turn out to be small so that the classifiers can be built in a cheap way. However, this issue has to be discussed and verified in practice. Another question refers to the number of subspaces needed to get a high accuracy.

Our proposal is to combine the FLDs in this stochastic way. Since the PFLD achieves its worst accuracy for $n = k$, the RSM may improve the performance in this case. The individual classifiers are built in subspaces of the fixed dimensionality and combined by averaging their coefficients, which yields only one linear classifier in the end. This is the advantage over combining rules based on posterior probabilities of the classifiers, where all of them should be stored for this purpose. Our RSM algorithm, called PF-RSM1, is briefly presented below:

```
K - the pre-defined number of selected features
for i=1 to N (the pre-defined number of combined classifiers) do
  Select randomly K features: f_{i_{p(1)}}, ..., f_{i_{p(K)}};
  Build the FLD in a subspace obtaining the coef.: w_{i_{p(1)}}, ..., w_{i_{p(K)}}, w_{i_0};
  Set to zero all coefficients of the ignored dimensions;
end
Determine the final decision rule with the coefficients: w_1, ..., w_n, w_0
by averaging the coefficients of all classifiers (including the
introduced zeros), i.e. w_0 = 1/N ∑_{i=1}^{N} w_{i_0} and w_j = 1/N ∑_{i=1}^{N} w_{ij}, j = 1, ..., n;
```

A slightly different version of this algorithm, namely PF-RSM2, is considered by using a validation set for the FLD trained in a subspace. This set is used to determine a scaling factor for the FLD's coefficients. The scaling is done in such a way that the classified objects represent as well as possible posterior probabilities on the validation set. This does not influence the decision boundary itself.

In the proposed way of combining classifiers, although they are designed in subspaces, they are finally treated in the original space. This is achieved by setting the coefficients of the ignored dimensions to zero. Therefore, the final combination procedure (averaging) addresses them in the original, high-dimensional distance space. By doing this, the most preferable directions in the original space are emphasized and by including more and more classifiers all coefficients of the final decision rule become more accurate. It seems to be also possible to combine the classifiers explicitly in subspaces, which is an interesting concept for further research.

5   Datasets and Experiments

One artificial and two real datasets are used in our experimental study. The first set consists of 200-dimensional correlated Gaussian data [11]. There are two classes, each represented by 100 samples.

The second set is derived from NIST database [13] and consists of 2000 16×16 images of digits evenly distributed over 10 classes. In our simulations a 2-class problem was considered, for digits 3 and 5, to which we refer as to Digit35.

Vibration was measured with 5 sensors mounted on a submersible pump operating in one normal and 3 abnormal states [14]. The data consists of the wavelet decomposition of the power spectrum. For each sensor the 100 coefficients with the largest variances were considered. A 2-class problem was studied here to which we refer as to Pump2. It is described by 500 features and 450 samples equally distributed over 2 classes: bearing failure and loose foundation.

The squared Euclidean distance was considered for our experiments. For each dataset, the dissimilarity representation was computed, which became then our starting point for a recognition problem. Only the 2-class situations were investigated, since for binary problems the linear classifier is uniquely defined and our aim is to illustrate the potential of combination such simple pattern recognizers. This dissimilarity measure was chosen as an example, since our goal is not to optimize the classification error for the given data with respect to the distance measure used, but rather present what may be gained by combining single decisions for such problems.

Table 1. Characteristics of the datasets used in experiments.

	Gaussian	Digit35	Pump2
Original dimensionality	200	256	500
Number of samples for TR/TE	100 / 100	100 / 300	150 / 300
Distance representation for TR	100×100	100×100	150×150
Distance representation for TE (no valid. set)	100×100	300×100	300×150
Distance representation for TE (a valid. set)	66×100	266×100	250×150

A simulation study was done for boosting, bagging and the RSM. All the experiments were run 25 times. For the artificial dataset, 25 different sets were randomly drawn from the multi-normal distribution according to the specified parameters. For the real datasets, they were randomly split into the training and testing sets 25 times, each time taking care that prior probabilities for two classes remain equal. Table 1 shows characteristics of the explored sets.

6   Discussion

Boosting (see [12]) performs poorly on the investigated datasets. It does not improve accuracy of the single PFLD at all. In each run all objects are equally weighted, so the final decision rule is based on multiple identical discriminants. Therefore no boosting results are present in Figure 2.

Boosting relies on the weighted majority vote, the RSM is based on the average, therefore the bagging experiment is conducted for both cases. In Figure 2, for clarity only, the error bar of bagging based on the average of 250 classifiers is plotted. For all datasets, the generalization errors reached by this combination rule and the weighted majority vote are very similar. The differences are however larger, when the number of combined classifiers is small, in disfavor of the weighted majority. Bagging seems to work well for the datasets under study; the accuracy is improved considerably by about $60\% - 65\%$, which is a beneficial achievement over the PFLD result. The details are shown in Table 2.

Table 2. The averaged generalization error and standard deviation (in %) for bagging.

No. of	Gaussian		Digit35		Pump	
PFLD	Average	Majority	Average	Majority	Average	Majority
5	14.36 (0.67)	14.88 (0.63)	6.43 (0.29)	6.59 (0.25)	8.64 (0.34)	8.92 (0.40)
10	13.68 (0.69)	14.28 (0.66)	5.71 (0.26)	6.05 (0.26)	8.19 (0.38)	9.09 (0.38)
50	13.44 (0.73)	13.88 (0.77)	5.36 (0.24)	5.41 (0.24)	7.87 (0.39)	7.88 (0.38)
100	13.64 (0.74)	13.72 (0.77)	5.37 (0.24)	5.47 (0.24)	7.61 (0.38)	7.67 (0.34)
250	13.32 (0.75)	13.68 (0.80)	5.31 (0.21)	5.24 (0.20)	7.71 (0.37)	7.73 (0.37)

The RSM, as our proposal, is more thoroughly investigated. The dependency on the number of combined classifiers is studied and the dimensionality of the subspaces, as well. The results of our experiments are presented in Figure 2. The left/right pictures represent the situation either without or with a validation set. Its role is to scale the coefficients of the FLD found in a subspace so that the classified objects can represent as well as possible posterior probabilities. The number of samples used for a validation set was about 1/3 of the training set. It seems to be enough for determination of one scaling factor.

In our experiments, the RSM seems to work very well, accomplishing in its best case about $90\% - 110\%$ improvement over the PFLD result in the original space, competing the bagging achievements. The curves of the generalization error versus the subspace dimensionality indicate that in fact a small number of selected dimensions gives good results. This is essential, since in a low-dimensional

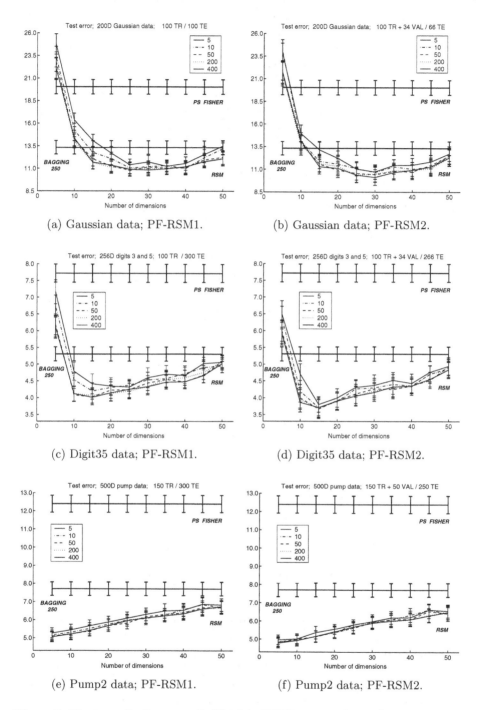

(a) Gaussian data; PF-RSM1.

(b) Gaussian data; PF-RSM2.

(c) Digit35 data; PF-RSM1.

(d) Digit35 data; PF-RSM2.

(e) Pump2 data; PF-RSM1.

(f) Pump2 data; PF-RSM2.

Figure 2. The generalization error (in %) of the PFLD compared to its bagging version and to the RSM. The legend refers to the number of the FLDs combined.

space, the FLD can be determined in a computationally cheaper way. The subspace dimensionality deviates around $7\% - 15\%$ of all features. The best result is observed for the Pump2 case (see Figure 2(e)-(f)), when the gain in accuracy is more than twice for 5 dimensions.

One notices also that already 5 or 10 combined FLDs decrease the generalization error substantially. Considering, e.g. the Digit35 data, it can be seen from Figure 2(c)-(d), that very small error is achieved in case of 5 combined classifiers for 15-dimensional subspaces. It gives us not more than 75 dimensions needed in total. For the Pump2 data (Figure 2(e)-(f)) this is even better, since the performance is improved already for 5-dimensional subspaces. So, the method makes use of not more than 25 features in the end. This is an important observation, suggesting that in practice a part of information may be skipped (especially of interest for large distance data), while gaining a high accuracy.

Table 3. The averaged error (in %) for the RSM with different combining rules.

No of.	Gaussian					
dim.	Average	Min	Mean	Median	Max	Product
5	22.08	18.04	22.60	25.12	18.04	22.08
10	14.36	13.12	14.44	14.56	13.12	14.36
15	11.68	12.36	11.64	11.80	12.36	11.68
20	11.36	11.40	11.56	11.36	11.40	11.36
35	10.96	12.28	10.84	10.96	12.28	11.08
50	12.08	15.36	11.92	11.94	15.36	14.60
	Digit35					
5	6.11	4.76	6.45	6.71	4.76	6.08
10	4.12	4.81	4.21	4.28	4.81	4.61
15	4.01	6.00	3.97	3.99	6.00	5.47
20	4.15	6.16	3.95	3.97	6.16	6.12
35	4.52	7.12	4.41	4.37	7.12	7.04
50	5.03	7.04	5.01	4.99	7.04	7.04
	Pump2					
5	5.05	5.29	5.05	5.00	5.29	5.05
10	5.21	5.48	5.21	5.16	5.48	5.21
15	5.41	5.72	5.43	5.41	5.72	5.41
20	5.68	6.00	5.65	5.61	6.00	5.69
35	6.23	6.64	6.21	6.17	6.64	6.53
50	6.70	8.60	6.64	6.60	8.60	8.37

With the growing number of subspace dimensions the generalization error first decreases, reaches its minimum and then starts to increase. The rule of thumb says that the classifiers generalize well when the number of training objects is e.g. 5-10 times larger than the number of features. Therefore, the increase of generalization error with the dimensionality larger then 5 (the Pump2 data), 15 (the Digit35 data) or $25 - 30$ (the Gaussian data) is not surprising. When the number of features k slowly approaches the number of objects n ($k \rightarrow n$), the FLD is going in the direction of the PFLD. It is then characterized by worse performance (we are somewhat to the left of the peak in Figure 1), and their combination yields a worse decision rule, as well. Using a validation set seems to improve the results slightly, however one hoped that adjusting the FLD's coefficients would give much better improvement. It is possible, however, that another way of scaling may gain that.

One could argue whether other combing rules are not significantly better than our average-based RSM. Therefore, some of them were also studied. The comparison is presented in Table 3. As it can be noticed, the error obtained by average is very close to that one obtained by the mean rule and similar to that one gained by the median rule. This proves our point that averaging is useful, also especially it is computationally more efficient and yields only one classifier.

7   Conclusions

Studying distance representations may become useful when the data is characterized by many features or when experts cannot define the right attributes, but they are able to provide a dissimilarity measure, instead. The classical approach to such data is the rank-based one, namely the (condensed) nearest neighbor rule. We argue [3,9] that the feature-based approach, in which linear classifiers are built in the distance space can be more beneficial. However, in such a case one deals with the critical training size problem, since the number of training objects equals their dimensionality. Therefore, the usefulness of boosting, bagging and the RSM of the FLDs for dissimilarity representations has been investigated here. The novelty of our approach is that we concentrate on distance data, which is specific because of its $n \times n$ training size and because of its nature, i.e. relative information on objects and the structure being given in the data values.

It is also important to emphasize here that the combined classifiers can be advantageous when the generalization error of the single PFLD is higher than the overlap between classes. When it approaches the Bayes error, not much improvement may be gained. As an example, the squared Euclidean distance was studied as a measure of dissimilarity. Our goal is to investigate what may be achieved by combining single decisions for distance data. From our experiments the following conclusions can be drawn:

Firstly, boosting is not advantageous for our problem. It does not improve accuracy of the the single PFLD at all. No variation in weights is introduced during the training and the final decision rule is built from multiple identical discriminants. As suggested in [12], boosting is useful for large learning sizes.

Secondly, bagging, based either on the average or on the majority vote, improves the PFLD performance for all datasets studied. The achievement is about $60\% - 65\%$, which is a considerable value. By using bootstrap replicates, the number of different samples is reduced, so bagging deals practically with the situation when $n < k$. We are then placed on the left side of the peak of the PFLD learning curve (see Figure (1)).

Finally, we have proposed to combine the FLDs in random subspaces. Our technique yields a single linear classifier and gives the best improvement in accuracy, which is about 100% for our datasets. The method constructs the FLDs in randomly selected subspaces of a fixed dimensionality and combines them by averaging their coefficients in the end. The experiments show that the best results are reached when a validation set was used and when the number of chosen dimensions deviates between 4% (The Pump2 data) and 30% (the Digit35 data) of all features. It allows for building classifiers in a cheap way. Even for a small number of combined classifiers, e.g. 5 or 10, the generalization error decreases substantially. This suggests that in practice some dimensions can be skipped, which is important for high-dimensional data.

8   Acknowledgments

This work was partly supported by the Foundation for Computer Science Research in The Netherlands (SION) and the Dutch Organization for Scientific Research (NWO).

References

1. L. Breiman. Bagging predictors. *Machine Learning*, 24(2):123–140, 1996.
2. C. Cortes and V. Vapnik. Support-vector networks. *Machine Learning*, 20:273–297, 1995.
3. R. P. W. Duin, E. Pękalska, and D. de Ridder. Relational discriminant analysis. *Pattern Recognition Letters*, 20(11-13):1175–1181, 1999.
4. Y. Freund and R. E. Schapire. Experiments with a new boosting algorithm. In *Machine Learning: Proc. of the 13th International Conference*, pages 148–156, 1996.
5. K. Fukunaga. *Introduction to Statistical Pattern Recognition*. Acad. Press, 1990.
6. T. K. Ho. Nearest neighbours in random subspaces. In *Proceedings of the Second International Workshop on Statistical Techniques in Pattern Recognition*, pages 640–648, Sydney (Australia), 1998.
7. T. K. Ho. The random subspace method for constructing decision forest. *IEEE Transactions on Pattern Analysis and Machine Intelligence*, 20(8):832–844, 1998.
8. A. K. Jain and B. Chandrasekaran. Dimensionality and sample size considerations in pattern recognition practice. In P. R. Krishnaiah and L. N. Kanal, editors, *Handbook of Statistics*, volume 2, pages 835–855. North-Holland, Amsterdam, 1987.
9. E. Pękalska and R. P. W. Duin. Classifiers for dissimilarity-based pattern recognition. In *ICPR*, Barcelona (Spain), 2000, accepted.
10. S. Raudys and R. P. W. Duin. On expected classification error of the Fisher linear classifier with pseudo-inverse covariance matrix. *Pattern Recognition Letters*, 19(5-6), 1998.
11. M. Skurichina and R. P. W. Duin. Bagging for linear classifiers. *Pattern Recognition*, 31(7):909–930, 1998.
12. M. Skurichina and R. P. W. Duin. Boosting in linear discriminant analysis. In *First International Workshop on Multiple Classifier Systems*, Cagliari (Italy), 2000.
13. C.L. Wilson and M.D. Garris. Handprinted character database 3. Technical report, National Institute of Standards and Technology, February 1992.
14. A. Ypma, D. M. J. Tax, and R. P. W. Duin. Robust machine fault detection with independent component analysis and support vector data description. In *IEEE International Workshop on Neural Networks for Signal Processing*, pages 67–76, Wisconsin (USA), 1999.

A Learning Method of Feature Selection for Rough Classification

Katsuhiko Takahashi and Atsushi Sato

NEC Corporation, Kawasaki, Kanagawa 216-8555, Japan
{katuhiko, asato}@ccm.cl.nec.co.jp

Abstract. In this paper, we present a new method of learning a feature selection dictionary for rough classification. In the learning stage, both the n-dimensional learning vectors and the n-dimensional reference vectors are transformed into an $m(<n)$-dimensional learning vector and the m-dimensional reference vector, respectively, using a current feature selection dictionary. The feature selection dictionary is then successively modified for each learning vector so as to decrease the distance between the learning vector and the m-dimensional reference vector corresponding to the correct category. Furthermore, the feature selection dictionary is modified for each learning vector so as to increase the distance between the learning vector and the m-dimensional reference vector that is the nearest incorrect reference vector of the learning vector. The experimental results showed that our method's processing time is 9 times faster than that without rough classification, even if the recognition rates are the same.

1 Introduction

The number of dimensional features that statistical character recognition methods usually use is in the tens or much higher. As a result, if there are many categories to be recognized, processing time increases significantly. For example, the Japanese language uses more than three thousand characters. In order to cope with this processing-time problem, a reduction in the dimensionality is often utilized [1]-[3]. The recognition rate of methods using low-dimensional features, however, tends to be worse compared with the methods that use the original features because of loss of information. Therefore, a hierarchical scheme, which consists of rough classification with lower-dimensional features and fine classification with the original features, is an effective way of both maintaining the recognition rate and reducing processing time. Rough classification utilizes efficient m-dimensional features that are transformed from the original $(m < n)$ n-dimensional features and chooses candidate vectors based on the distance between the m-dimensional input vector and the m-dimensional reference vectors. Fine classification is carried out only on these candidates. There are several ways to obtain the m-dimensional features. Linear or non-linear principal component analysis [5] [6] and independent component analysis (ICA) [7]-[9] are unsupervised techniques to generate the feature selection dictionary, which is utilized

J. Kittler and F. Roli (Eds.): MCS 2000, LNCS 1857, pp. 127–136, 2000.

to transform the n-dimensional features into the m-dimensional features. Although these techniques give the most suitable feature axes for representing the whole pattern distribution, they do not always give the best features for classification. Another techniques for feature extraction is a supervised technique like canonical discriminant analysis. Canonical discriminant analysis, however, has a disadvantage in that it assumes a normal Gaussian pattern distribution. Moreover, it cannot extract more feature axes than the number of categories.

In this paper, we present a new supervised learning method of a feature selection dictionary for rough classification. In the learning stage, both the n-dimensional learning vectors and the n-dimensional reference vectors are transformed into an m-dimensional learning vector and the m-dimensional reference vector, respectively, using a current feature selection dictionary. The feature selection dictionary is then successively modified for each learning vector so as to decrease the distance between the learning vector and the m-dimensional reference vector corresponding to the correct category. Furthermore, the feature selection dictionary is modified for each learning vector so as to increase the distance between the learning vector and the m-dimensional reference vector that is the nearest incorrect reference vector of the learning vector. This modification increases the probability that the reference vector corresponding to the correct category will be contained in the candidates. Therefore, the performance of rough classification will be improved as well.

Section 2 presents the structure of the recognition system assumed in this paper. Section 3 describes the learning method for creating the feature selection dictionary. The results of a character recognition experiment are given in section 4 and discussed in section 5. Section 6 is a brief conclusion.

2   Structure of the Recognition System

We assume a recognition system structure like that in Fig. 1. The original features, which are extracted from the input pattern, are represented by an n-dimensional vector. N-dimensional reference vectors for fine classification are constructed by generalized learning vector quantization (GLVQ)[4] in advance. The rough classification unit maps both the n-dimensional input vector and the n-dimensional reference vectors into an m $(< n)$ -dimensional space, and outputs the candidate vectors that are the closest to the m-dimensional input vector. The fine classification unit calculates the distances between the n-dimensional input vector and the n-dimensional reference vectors that correspond to the candidate vectors. Therefore, the recognition rate of the system depends on the quality of the feature selection dictionary. The feature selection dictionary, which can choose the correct reference vectors as candidate vectors, is required to avoid any reduction in recognition rate. The method given in this paper makes it possible to generate such a good feature selection dictionary.

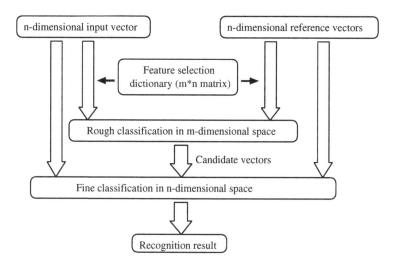

Fig. 1. Structure of the recognition system

3   Learning Method for Generating the Feature Selection Dictionary

Figure 2 shows the flowchart of the learning process. In step A, the feature selection dictionary is revised for each learning pattern. The learning process is finished when this revision has been performed a given number of times. This is the key step of our method. The details of step A are given in the following subsection.

3.1   Proposed Method 1

Let X be the n-dimensional original feature vector, Z be the feature selection dictionary ($m * n$ matrix), Y be the m-dimensional vector transformed from the feature vector X using the dictionary Z, P_i be the i-th n-demensional reference vector, and R_i be the i-th m-dimensional reference vector corresponding to the vector P_i. The distance, d, between the m-dimensional learning vector Y and the m-dimensional reference vector R_i is defined as square of the Euclidean distance,

$$d = \| Y - R_i \| = \| Z(X - P_i) \|^2 . \tag{1}$$

Step A modifies the feature selection dictionary so as to decrease the distance between the m-dimensional learning vector and the m-dimensional reference vector R_{c1} corresponding to the correct category, and it increases the distance between the learning vector and the m-dimensional reference vector R_{c2} that is the nearest incorrect reference vector of the learning vector. If the recognition dictionary has several reference vectors for each category, the reference vector R_{c1} is one which corresponds to the correct category and is the nearest to the

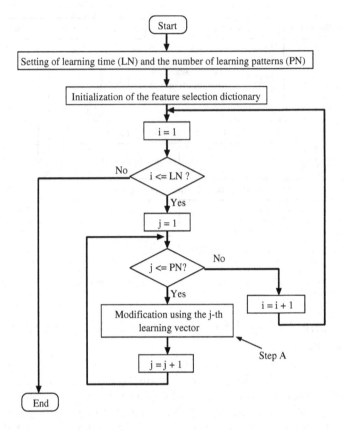

Fig. 2. Flowchart of learning process

learning vector. In other words, the modification makes the distance d_1 smaller and the distance d_2 bigger, which are given by

$$d_1 = \parallel Y - R_{c1} \parallel = \parallel Z(X - P_{c1}) \parallel^2, \quad d_2 = \parallel Y - R_{c2} \parallel = \parallel Z(X - P_{c2}) \parallel^2. \quad (2)$$

By this modification, the distance between the reference vector corresponding to the correct category and the m-dimensional learning vector becomes relatively close. Therefore, the reference vector, which corresponds to the correct category, is more likely to be chosen as a candidate vector. The gradient of the distance, d, in the m-dimensional feature space is given by

$$\frac{\partial d}{\partial Z} = 2Z(X - P_i)(X - P_i)^T. \quad (3)$$

Therefore, the feature selection dictionary should be changed along the negative gradient direction in order to decrease the distance d_1 and changed along the positive gradient direction in order to increase the distance d_2. This results in the following equations:

$$Z \longleftarrow Z - \rho_1(t)\frac{\partial d_1}{\partial Z} = Z - \rho_1(t) \cdot 2Z(X - P_{c1})(X - P_{c1})^T, \quad (4)$$

$$Z \longleftarrow Z + \rho_2(t)\frac{\partial d_2}{\partial Z} = Z + \rho_2(t) \cdot 2Z(X - P_{c2})(X - P_{c2})^T, \tag{5}$$

where $\rho_1(t)$ and $\rho_2(t)$ are time-depending functions of positive values. In the following section, we define these parameters as follows:

$$\rho_1(t) = \frac{\varepsilon d_2 l'(\frac{d_2-d_1}{d_1+d_2}t)}{d_1 + d_2}, \quad \rho_2(t) = \frac{\varepsilon d_1 l'(\frac{d_2-d_1}{d_1+d_2}t)}{d_1 + d_2}, \tag{6}$$

where ε denotes a positive learning coefficient, t denotes learning time and $l(\cdot)$ denotes a sigmoid function. The definition of $\rho_1(t)$ and $\rho_2(t)$ is based on consideration presented in [4]. As these equations can be applied to the feature selection dictionary at the same time, we finally obtain the equation,

$$Z \longleftarrow Z - \frac{\varepsilon l'(\frac{d_2-d_1}{d_1+d_2}t)}{d_1 + d_2} \cdot 2Z\{d_2(X-P_{c1})(X-P_{c1})^T - d_1(X-P_{c2})(X-P_{c2})^T\}. \tag{7}$$

3.2   Proposed Method 2

Method 1 uses the correct m-dimensional reference vector R_{c1} that is the closest vector of the m-dimensional learning vector Y. The n-dimensional reference vector corresponding to this R_{c1} is not always the closest vector to the n-dimensional learning vector. So, instead of using R_{c1}, we can choose the vector $R_{c1'}$ that corresponds to the correct category and whose corresponding n-dimensional reference vector $P_{c1'}$ is the closest to the n-dimensional learning vector X. The feature selection dictionary is then modified so as to decrease the distance between $R_{c1'}$ and the m-dimensional learning vector Y. If the distance between $R_{c1'}$ and Y is denoted by $d_{1'}$, we obtain,

$$Z \longleftarrow Z - \frac{\varepsilon l'(\frac{d_2-d_{1'}}{d_{1'}+d_2}t)}{d_{1'} + d_2} \cdot 2Z\{d_2(X - P_{c1'})(X - P_{c1'})^T - d_{1'}(X - P_{c2})(X - P_{c2})^T\}. \tag{8}$$

4   Experiments

We applied our methods to a character recognition problem to test its effectiveness. The characters to be recognized were alpha-numeric and KATAKANA characters. The total number of categories was 82. Each learning data and test data included about 90 thousand patterns (Fig. 3). The dimensionality of the original features was 400 (n=400). 1-NN classification method was utilized for fine classification and its reference vectors were generated by using GLVQ. Each category had 10 reference vectors, so the total number of reference vectors was 820. The initial values of the feature selection dictionary were defined by using the principal component analysis technique. In the following experiments, unless an explicit definition is given, the number of candidate vectors is 10 and the learning coefficient is 10^{-3}.

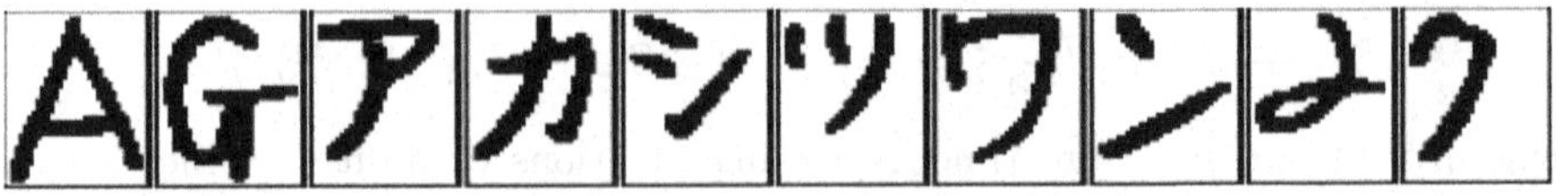

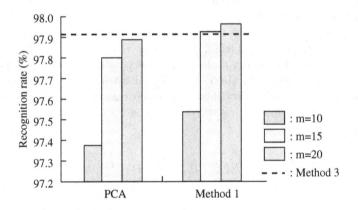

Fig. 3. Sample patterns to be recognized

4.1   Recognition Rate and Recognition Speed

Method 1 was utilized in this experiment. The dimensionality m for rough classification was set at 10, 15 and 20. The recognition rates of a method whose feature selection dictionary for rough classification was constructed by principal component analysis (PCA) and that of the method without rough classification (method 3) were evaluated for comparison. Figure 4 shows the results. The recognition rate of the proposed method was higher than those of the PCA methods in all cases. Moreover, the recognition rate of the method 1 slightly exceeded the recognition rate of method 3, when more than 15 features were utilized for rough classification.

Fig. 4. Comparison of recognition rate

Figure 5 shows the recognition speed of method 1 and method 3. In this case, the dimensionality of rough classification was 15. The values in this figure are the processing times for one pattern (using a 100 MHz CPU). The time for feature extraction and for feature selection was included. This figure shows us that the proposed method reduced processing time to one-ninth that of method 3.

4.2   Comparison of Method 1 and Method 2

The results of this comparison are shown in Fig. 6. The horizontal axis is the learning time and the vertical axis is the recognition rate estimated by using the

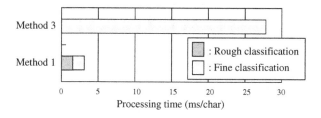

Fig. 5. Processing time

feature selection dictionary obtained in each learning time. This figure shows that the recognition rate of both methods declined at once. The recognition rates then gradually increased until they exceeded that of method 3. Although the recognition rates of methods 1 and 2 are almost the same, the recognition rate of method 2 exceeded the recognition rate of the method 3 faster than method 1.

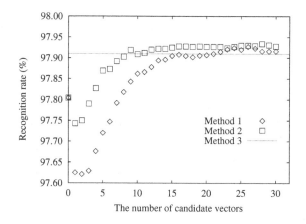

Fig. 6. Comparison of the method 1 and 2

4.3 Relationship between the Number of Candidates and the Recognition Rate

Method 1 was used, and the number of candidates was 5, 8, 10, 15 and 20 in this experiment. The dimensionality of the features for rough classification was set at 15 and 20, and the learning coefficient was set at 10^{-2} and 10^{-3}. Figure 7 shows that if the number of candidates was more than 10, the recognition rate exceeded that of method 3. Moreover, the recognition rate was the highest when the number of candidates was 10. If 15 or 20 candidates were chosen, the recognition rate slightly decreased.

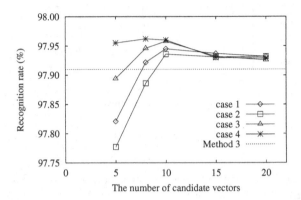

Fig. 7. Relation between the recognition rate and the number of candidate vectors (case1:m=15,$\varepsilon=10^{-2}$, case2:m=15,$\varepsilon=10^{-3}$, case3:m=20,$\varepsilon=10^{-2}$, case4:m=20,$\varepsilon=10^{-3}$)

5 Discussion

If the number of features for rough classification exceeds 15 and the number of candidates are exceeds 10, the proposed methods can achieve a recognition rate that is slightly higher than that of method 3. Moreover, the recognition speed of the methods 1 and 2 are 9 times faster than that of method 3. We also got the following interesting result. Intuitively, we can expect that the recognition rate of the system with rough classification should be worse than that of the system without rough classification. However, the experimental result was counter to this expectation. In this section, we shall discuss this point.

The fine classification based on the 1-NN classifier uses the Euclidean distance measure. This measure is suitable when data for each category has a spherical Gaussian distribution in the n-dimensional feature space. However, real data do not have such a distribution. If the number of reference vectors is not enough, this difference may cause misclassification. Since the feature selection operation gives different weights to each feature value, the m-dimensional feature space might be more suitable for the Euclidean distance measure than the original n-dimensional feature space. In other words, the variance of data distribution in the n-dimensional feature space may be normalized by linear transformation in the feature selection. This may be the reason why the recognition rate increases slightly by incorporating the feature selection.

To consider the difference in the recognition rate from another point of view, we focus on the rank (in candidate selection) of the reference vector V that is the nearest to the n-dimensional feature vector X. If the m-dimensional reference vector corresponding to V is selected as one of candidate vectors, the recognition result corresponds the category of this vector. First, we divided the test patterns into two groups. Group A consists of patterns in which the fine classification unit without the rough classification classifies correctly. Group B consists of other patterns. For each of these patterns, we extracted the nearest vector V to the input vector from among all reference vectors in the n-dimensional feature space. The rank of V in the rough classification was then calculated. The result is shown in Fig. 8. It shows that a V in group A is much more likely to be in a higher rank than those of group B. Therefore, if the number of candidates is about 10, almost all V of group A are selected as candidate vectors with high accuracy, and some of the V of group B are not selected as candidate vectors. Therefore, in this situation, the recognition rate of the proposed method is slightly higher than that of method 3. If the number of the candidates is more than 15, the recognition rate of the proposed method approaches the recognition rate of method 3.

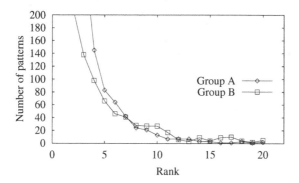

Fig. 8. Rank of V in the rough classification

6   Conclusion

The presented learning method for creation of the feature selection dictionary for rough classification has been proven to be effective for character recognition. The experimental results showed that our method's processing time is 9 times faster than that without rough classification, even if the recognition rates are the same. In addition, we showed that the recognition rate does not increase as the number of candidate increases and that the optimal number of candidate is about 10.

References

1. Bishop, C.M.: Neural Networks for Pattern Recognition. Oxford University Press (1995)
2. Wakabayashi, T., Tsuruoka, S., Kimura, F., Miyake, Y.: A Study on Feature Selection for Small Class Classification Problems. Trans. of the IEICE, Vol.J80-D-II, No.1 (1997) 73-80 (in Japanese)

3. Kawamura, A., Nitta, T.: Feature-Extraction-Based Character Recognition Using Minimum Classification Error Training. Trans. of the IEICE, Vol.J81-D-II, No.12 (1998) 2749-2756 (in Japanese)
4. Sato, A., Yamada, K.: A formulation of learning vector quantization using a new misclassification measure. Proc. of the Fourteenth ICPR (1998) 322-325
5. Jain, A. K., Duin, R. P. W., Mao, J.: Statistical pattern recognition : A Review Trans. on PAMI, Vol.22, No.1 (2000) 4-37
6. Lerner, B., Guterman, H., Aladjem, M., Dinstein, I.: A comparative study of neural network based feature extration paradigms. Pattern Recognition Letters 20 (1999) 7-14
7. Jutten, C., Herault, J.: Blind separation of sources, Part I : An adaptive algorithm based on neuromimetic architecture. Signal Processing 24 (1991) 1-10
8. Bell, A. J., Sejnowski, T. J.: An information-maxmization approach to blind separation and blind deconvolution. Neural Computation, Vol.7 (1995) 1129-1159
9. Cardoso, J. F.: Blind signal separation : Statistical principles. Proc. of the IEEE, Vol.86, No. 10 (1998) 2009-2025 Signal Processing 24 (1991) 1-10

Analysis of a Fusion Method
for Combining Marginal Classifiers

Mark D. Happel and Peter Bock

Department of Computer Science, The George Washington University, Washington, DC 20052, USA
{mhappel, pbock}@seas.gwu.edu

Abstract. The use of multiple features by a classifier often leads to a reduced probability of error, but the design of an optimal Bayesian classifier for multiple features is dependent on the estimation of multidimensional joint probability density functions and therefore requires a design sample size that, in general, increases exponentially with the number of dimensions. The classification method described in this paper makes decisions by combining the decisions made by multiple Bayesian classifiers using an additional classifier that estimates the joint probability densities of the *decision space* rather than the joint probability densities of the *feature space*. A proof is presented for the restricted case of two classes and two features; showing that the method always demonstrates a probability of error that is less than or equal to the probability of error of the marginal classifier with the lowest probability of error.

1. Background

Given a set of objects and their corresponding *feature vectors* $X = [\chi_1\, \chi_2\, ...\, \chi_d]^T$ in *feature space* Π, one of the fundamental problems of pattern classification is to define a function (a *classifier*) $\Psi: \Pi \rightarrow \Delta$ that can assign an appropriate *class label* ω_i to any given X in the feature space. The assignment itself is called a *classification decision* $\delta \in \Delta$, and the set of all possible decisions is the *decision space* Δ. In a Bayesian classifier, the classification decision is made based on the *a posteriori* probabilities that the input is a member of a given class given the input. For a given input X, the *a posteriori* probability for class ω_i, $p(\omega_i \mid X)$, can be calculated using Bayes' rule:

$$p(\omega_i \mid X) = \frac{p(X \mid \omega_i) P(\omega_i)}{\sum_i p(X \mid \omega_i) P(\omega_i)} \tag{1}$$

The Bayesian decision rule selects the class label which corresponds to the maximum *a posteriori* probability. The class-conditional probability density function $p(X \mid \omega_i)$ is often referred to as the *likelihood function* [5], and the likelihood function weighted by the *a priori* probability $P(\omega_i)$ is referred to here as the *weighted likelihood*. Since the sum of the weighted likelihoods (the denominator in the

J. Kittler and F. Roli (Eds.): MCS 2000, LNCS 1857, pp. 137-146, 2000.
© Springer-Verlag Berlin Heidelberg 2000

equation above) is positive and common to all of the *a posteriori* probabilities, it can be factored out and the comparison made of the weighted likelihoods instead:

$$\delta = \omega_i \text{ such that } p(\mathbf{X}\mid\omega_i)P(\omega_i) > p(\mathbf{X}\mid\omega_j)P(\omega_j) \text{ for all } i \neq j \qquad (2)$$

If the probability of error attained by a Bayesian classifier is unacceptably high for the requirements of a given problem, two or more features can be used simultaneously to form multivariate joint probability density functions. By using two or more features, the multivariate classifier is often able to achieve a significantly better classification performance than a comparable univariate classifier.

The Bayesian classifier is optimal in the sense that it has the lowest possible probability of error ε_β for a given set of probability density functions [6]. If the classes' density functions are not known, then they must be estimated from sample data. However, the estimation of multivariate density functions in high-dimensional spaces is nontrivial, and may require an unrealistically large design sample size to attain a sufficiently accurate estimate. This "curse of dimensionality" [1] leads to an interesting paradox: as the number of dimensions increases, the theoretical performance of the Bayesian classifier improves but the practical problems involved in implementing such a classifier also increase, resulting in a decline in the actual classification performance beyond a certain threshold dimensionality [6]. Consequently, for situations in which the optimal Bayesian classifier performance is insufficient for d dimensions, it may not be possible in practice to attain better classification performance using $d+1$ dimensions, even though the theoretical Bayesian performance should increase.

From the preceding discussion, it is apparent that a method for obtaining an improvement in the classification performance for the d-dimensional Bayesian classifier without requiring the estimation of $d+1$ dimensional density functions would prove useful. It is intuitively appealing to imagine combining several, lower-dimensional Bayesian classifiers in such a way as to provide a lower error rate than any one of them alone can achieve, and perhaps even to approach the error rate attainable with a higher-dimensional classifier.

Current strategies for obtaining group decisions can be divided into two broad categories: dynamic classifier selection and classifier fusion [12]. Dynamic classifier selection (DCS) strategies attempt to predict or identify, for a given input, the best decision out of the set of decisions made by the individual classifiers. In contrast, classifier fusion algorithms define a function $\xi: \Delta \to \Delta$ that can be used to calculate a decision based on the simultaneous decisions of all of the individual classifiers. Classifier fusion methods include majority voting [9], weighted majority voting, averaged Bayesian decisions [13], naive Bayesian classifiers [2, 10], Dempster-Shafer approaches [3, 11], and stacking strategies [4]. Stacking strategies differ from other classifier fusion strategies in that the fusion function $\xi: \Delta \to \Delta$ is not defined *a priori* but is instead learned by a "combining classifier" [4]. The combining classifier Ψ^* receives as input the classification decisions of m member classifiers $\Psi_i(\mathbf{X})$ and computes a final classification decision δ^*:

$$\delta^* = \Psi^* \left[\Psi_1(\mathbf{X}), \Psi_2(\mathbf{X}), \cdots, \Psi_m(\mathbf{X})\right] \qquad (3)$$

In this paper, a stacking method is proposed as a means of combining marginal decisions into a single, "pseudo-multivariate" decision.

2.   Proposed Method

The method proposed here is to use the marginal decisions as features, thereby forming a *decision vector*. An additional Bayesian classifier, called a *supervisory classifier*, can then be used to classify the vector of marginal decisions and generate a combined classification decision. The supervisory classifier makes its classification decision based on estimates of the joint probability densities of the decision space rather than the joint probability densities of the feature space.

A block diagram of this architecture is shown in Figure 1. The example shown uses a feature vector $X = [\chi_1 \ \chi_2]^T$ that consists of only two features. Like the marginal classifiers Ψ_1 and Ψ_2, the supervisory classifier Ψ_H is a Bayesian classifier, allowing the sytem to be implemented from a common building block. Feature χ_1 is a random variable with the class-conditional probability density function $p(\chi_1 \mid \omega_i)$. Likewise, feature χ_2 is a random variable with the class-conditional probability density function $p(\chi_2 \mid \omega_i)$. An optimal Bayesian bivariate classifier $\Psi_B(\chi_1,\chi_2)$ would generate a decision δ_B based on the bivariate class-conditional probability density function $p(\chi_1,\chi_2 \mid \omega_i)$ and the *a priori* probability $P(\omega_i)$ using Equation 2. This requires the bivariate density functions to be known beforehand or to be estimated using sample data.

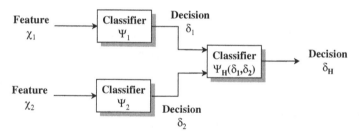

Fig. 1. A Stacking Architecture for Combining Marginal Classification Decisions

However, in this case the intention is to avoid the need to estimate the bivariate density functions. The proposed method accomplishes this by first generating classification decisions δ_1 and δ_2 based on the univariate (marginal) density functions. Classifiers Ψ_1 and Ψ_2 can be viewed as performing a nonlinear transformation of features χ_1 and χ_2 from the feature space Π to the decision space Δ. This mapping will generally be many-to-one, as there are generally far fewer classes defined for a given problem than there are values for the defined features, resulting in considerable compression from feature space to decision space.

The second step in the proposed method is to combine the decisions δ_1 and δ_2 by means of a supervisory classifier, Ψ_H, which uses decisions δ_1 and δ_2 as features. In order to use the Bayesian decision rule, classifier Ψ_H needs the bivariate class-conditional probability density function $p(\delta_1,\delta_2 \mid \omega_i)$, which can be estimated using the same design sample used to estimate $p(\chi_1 \mid \omega_i)$ and $p(\chi_2 \mid \omega_i)$. Since the decision space is a discrete space with relatively few entries (as compared to the number of feature values in feature space), $p(\delta_1,\delta_2 \mid \omega_i)$ can be estimated using a much smaller sample size than can $p(\chi_1,\chi_2 \mid \omega_i)$. Note that the supervisory classifier can "override" the decisions of the marginal classifiers, choosing a different class from any of the marginal decisions. This *override property* is a key factor in the superiority of the proposed method to voting methods. Further information on the operation of the method and the utility of the override property may be found in [7, 8].

3. Properties of the Proposed Method

To better understand the behavior of the proposed method, research to date has focused on the simplest case: a problem requiring the classification of patterns into one of two classes (Grey or 'G' and Black or 'B') based on the values of two features. The proposed method divides the feature space into multiple *partitions* based on the locations of the decision surfaces determined by the marginal classifiers. It then generates classification decisions for each partition by choosing the maximum class-conditional probability (i.e., the class with the largest volume under its weighted likelihood within the partition). The marginal classification decisions, partitions, and partition classification decisions are shown in Figure 2.

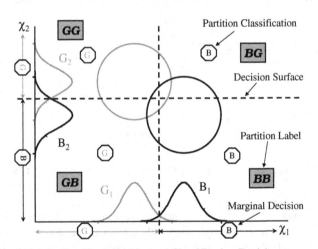

Fig. 2. Classifier Partitions and Classification Decisions

One of the goals of the preliminary research effort was to determine the properties of the proposed method without requiring assumptions regarding the parametric forms of the complete or marginal likelihoods to be made. Consequently, it was found to be advantageous to graphically represent the partitions and the associated marginal and partition classifications, without explicitly representing the likelihoods themselves. A *partition plot* for the example in Figure 2 is shown in Figure 3.

By examining all of the possible partition arrangements, it is possible to determine upper and lower bounds on the probability of error ε_H of the proposed method as applied to a 2 class and 2 feature case without making assumptions as to the form or parameters of the likelihoods. Several lemmas that are helpful for establishing these bounds are proved below. It is also important to note that the magnitude of the hypervolume under a portion of the complete density function is equal to the magnitude of the associated hypervolume under the corresponding marginal density function [8]. The first lemma will be used to discard some of the possible candidate classification arrangements due to the inconsistency between the partition classifications and the corresponding marginal classification.

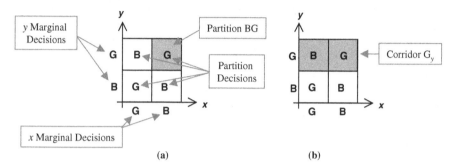

Fig. 3. Partition plots for the analysis. Note that marginal decisions are shown along the respective axes, while the partition decisions are shown within each partition. Therefore, in (a) the shaded partition BG (i.e., $\delta_x = B$ and $\delta_y = G$) has been classified as G. All of the partitions that correspond to a given marginal decision form a *corridor*, shown as a shaded region in (b).

Lemma 1:   Suppose that all of the partitions θ_k in a given corridor c of the decision space are assigned the same class label ω_i. Then the class label assigned to the corresponding decision region by the corresponding marginal classifier will be ω_i.

Proof: The assignment of label ω_i to all of the partitions θ_k in the corridor implies that, within each of these partitions, the volume under the $p(X|\omega_i)P(\omega_i)$ surface is greater than the volume under any other classes' surface:

$$\int_{\theta_k} p(X|\omega_i)P(\omega_i)\,dX \; > \; \int_{\theta_k} p(X|\omega_j)P(\omega_j)\,dX ; \quad 1 \geq j \geq N, i \neq j. \tag{4}$$

Likewise, it follows that the corridor's ω_i volume, composed of the sum of the ω_i volumes within each partition in the corridor, will also be the largest class-conditional volume within the corridor:

$$\int_c p(X|\omega_i)P(\omega_i)\,dX \; > \; \int_c p(X|\omega_j)P(\omega_j)\,dX ; \quad 1 \geq j \geq N, i \neq j. \tag{5}$$

As noted above, the volume under the complete weighted likelihood within a corridor is equal to the volume (or area, if one-dimensional) under the corresponding marginal weighted likelihood. Consequently,

$$\int p(X|\omega_i)P(\omega_i)\,dX \;>\; \int p(X|\omega_j)P(\omega_j)\,dX;\quad 1\geq j\geq N,\, i\neq j. \tag{6}$$

and the classification decision, in accordance with the Bayesian decision rule will be ω_i. *QED.*

As a result of Lemma 1, ten of the candidate classification arrangements can be discarded, since they contain corridors with partitions that share classification labels that are not the same as the label of the corresponding marginal classification region. The six remaining candidate classification arrangements, shown in Figure 4, are all valid arrangements.

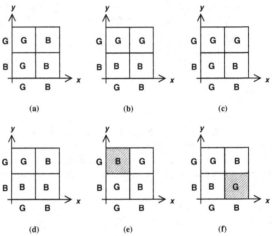

Fig. 4. Legal Arrangements of Partition Classifications. The shaded partitions in arrangements (e) and (f) represent decision overrides.

Lemma 2:   Suppose that, for every corridor associated with a given marginal classifier x, the partitions within a given corridor are assigned the same class label. Then the probability of error ε_H for the proposed method is equal to the probability of error ε_x of the associated marginal classifier.

Proof: Refer to Figure 4(a). Let R_ω represent the region classified as class ω by the marginal classifier, and let C_ω represent the associated corridor. The probability of error for a given classifier is equal to the sum of the probabilities of the less likely classes (i.e., all of the classes except the most likely one). Consequently, the probability of error for the x marginal classifier in Figure 4(a) is given by:

$$\varepsilon_x = \int_{R_G} p(x|\omega_B)\,P(\omega_B)\,dx \;+\; \int_{R_B} p(x|\omega_G)\,P(\omega_G)\,dx \tag{7}$$

and the probability of error for the proposed method in Figure 8 is given by:

$$\varepsilon_H = \iint_{C_G} p(x, y \mid \omega_B) \, P(\omega_B) \, dx \, dy \;\; + \;\; \iint_{C_B} p(x, y \mid \omega_G) \, P(\omega_G) \, dx \, dy \tag{8}$$

The volume under the complete weighted likelihood for each class within a given corridor is equal to the volume (or area, in this case) under the marginal weighted likelihood for the same class.

$$\int_{R_{\omega_j}} p(x \mid \omega_i) \, P(\omega_i) \, dx \;\; = \;\; \iint_{C_{\omega_j}} p(x, y \mid \omega_i) \, P(\omega_i) \, dx \, dy \; ; \quad i \neq j \tag{9}$$

Consequently, it is apparent by substituting terms that $\varepsilon_x = \varepsilon_H$. In addition, it can be shown [8] that the probability of error ε_x of the associated marginal classifier will be lass than or equal to the probability of error ε_y of the other marginal classifier. *QED.*

The next lemma concerns two of the remaining four arrangements. In these arrangements, three of the four partitions share a common class label, as shown in the examples in Figures 4(c) and 4(d). It can be shown that these arrangements result in a probability of error ε_H that is equal to or less than the smaller probability of error of the two marginal classifiers.

Lemma 3:   Suppose that the proposed method is used to discriminate between two-dimensional patterns belonging to two classes with arbitrary joint probability density functions, and that three of the four possible partitions are assigned the same class label. Then the probability of error for the proposed method ε_H is less than the smaller probability of error of the associated marginal classifiers.

Proof: Refer to Figure 4(d). Let ε_i, $1 \le i \le 4$, represent the contribution of marginal region R_i to the marginal classifier's probability of error (*i.e.*, the volume under the weighted likelihood of the unchosen class in that region). Let I_p represent the volume under the weighted likelihood curve for class I within partition P (i.e., B_{GB} would refer to the volume under the weighted likelihood for class B in partition GB). By Lemma 2, the marginal probabilities of error ε_x and ε_y can be related to the volumes within the partitions and hence to the probability of error of the proposed method:

$$\varepsilon_x = \left(B_{GB} + B_{GG} \right) + \left(G_{BB} + G_{BG} \right) \tag{10}$$

$$\varepsilon_y = \left(B_{GG} + B_{BG} \right) + \left(G_{GB} + G_{BB} \right) \tag{11}$$

$$\varepsilon_H = B_{GG} + G_{GB} + G_{BG} + G_{BB} \tag{12}$$

The proposed classifier, which selects the largest volume within a partition, classified partition GB as B and partition BG as B. This implies that

$$G_{GB} \le B_{GB} \quad \text{and} \quad G_{BG} \le B_{BG} \tag{13}$$

Assume that $\varepsilon_x \le \varepsilon_H$. This implies that

$$B_{GB} + B_{GG} + G_{BB} + G_{BG} \quad \leq \quad B_{GG} + G_{GB} + G_{BG} + G_{BB} \tag{14}$$

Eliminating common terms yields

$$B_{GB} \leq G_{GB} \tag{15}$$

which contradicts equation 13. Therefore, $\varepsilon_x > \varepsilon_H$. Similarly, assume that $\varepsilon_y \leq \varepsilon_H$. This implies that

$$B_{GG} + B_{BG} + G_{GB} + G_{BB} \quad \leq \quad B_{GG} + G_{GB} + G_{BG} + G_{BB} \tag{16}$$

Eliminating common terms yields

$$B_{BG} \leq G_{BG} \tag{17}$$

which also contradicts Equation 13. Therefore, $\varepsilon_y > \varepsilon_H$. Since $\varepsilon_H < \varepsilon_x$ and $\varepsilon_H < \varepsilon_y$, ε_H is less than the smaller of ε_x and ε_y. A similar argument can be used to show that similar contradictions also result when partition BB is the sole partition classified as B. QED.

The final lemma concerns the two remaining arrangements, Figures 4(e) and 4(f), which share the property of having a partition that has been classified differently than either of the corresponding marginal regions. As discussed previously, this amounts to having the supervisory classifier "override" all of the decisions made by the marginal classifiers, choosing a class that was not selected by either of the marginal classifiers.

Lemma 4:   Suppose that the proposed method is used to discriminate between two-dimensional patterns belonging to two classes with arbitrary joint probability density functions, and that a partition is assigned a class label that is different than the label assigned to either of the two corresponding marginal classification regions. Then the probability of error for the proposed method ε_H is less than the smaller probability of error of the associated marginal classifiers.

Proof: This proof will be performed in a manner similar to that of Lemma 3. Assume that the partition and marginal region classifications are given by Figure 4(f). Let ε_i, $1 \leq i \leq 4$, represent the contribution of marginal region R_i to the marginal classifier's probability of error (i.e., the volume under the weighted likelihood of the unchosen class in that region). Let I_p represent the volume under the weighted likelihood curve for class I within partition P. The marginal probabilities of error ε_x and ε_y can be related to the volumes within the partitions and hence to the probability of error of the proposed classifier:

$$\varepsilon_x = (B_{GB} + B_{GG}) + (G_{BB} + G_{BG}) \tag{18}$$

$$\varepsilon_y = (B_{GG} + B_{BG}) + (G_{GB} + G_{BB}) \tag{19}$$

$$\varepsilon_H = B_{GG} + G_{GB} + G_{BG} + B_{BB} \tag{20}$$

The proposed classifier, which selects the largest volume within a partition, classified partition GB as B, partition BB as G, and partition BG as B. This implies that

$$G_{GB} \leq B_{GB} , \ G_{BG} \leq B_{BG} , \text{ and } B_{BB} \leq G_{BB} \tag{21}$$

Assume that $\varepsilon_x \leq \varepsilon_H$. This implies that

$$B_{GB} + B_{GG} + G_{BB} + G_{BG} \ \leq \ B_{GG} + G_{GB} + G_{BG} + B_{BB} \tag{22}$$

Eliminating common terms yields

$$B_{GB} + G_{BB} \leq G_{GB} + B_{BB} \tag{23}$$

Since the volumes are all positive quantities, this contradicts Equation 21. Therefore, $\varepsilon_x > \varepsilon_H$. Similarly, assume that $\varepsilon_y \leq \varepsilon_H$. This implies that

$$B_{GG} + B_{BG} + G_{GB} + G_{BB} \leq B_{GG} + G_{GB} + G_{BG} + B_{BB} \tag{24}$$

Eliminating common terms yields

$$B_{BG} + G_{BB} \leq G_{BG} + B_{BB} \tag{25}$$

Since the volumes are all positive quantities, this contradicts Equation 21. Therefore, $\varepsilon_y > \varepsilon_H$. Since $\varepsilon_H < \varepsilon_x$ and $\varepsilon_H < \varepsilon_y$, ε_H is less than the smaller of ε_x and ε_y. A similar argument can be used to show that similar contradictions also result when partition GG is classified as B. *QED.*

By using the lemmas that were proven in the previous section, it is possible to construct a proof for Theorem 1.

Theorem 1:   Suppose that two features x and y are used to discriminate between patterns belonging to two classes M and B for which the class-conditional bivariate probability density functions are known. Then $\varepsilon_\beta \leq \varepsilon_H \leq \min(\varepsilon_x, \varepsilon_y)$.

Proof: For a two class and two feature scenario, there are 16 candidate arrangements of partition classifications. In accordance with Lemma 1, ten of those arrangements are inconsistent with the properties of any arbitrary likelihood function and can therefore never occur. This leaves the six arrangements shown in Figure 4. In accordance with Lemma 2 through 4, these arrangements yield the following probability of error ε_H:

$$\varepsilon_H \leq \min(\varepsilon_x, \varepsilon_y) \tag{26}$$

The Bayesian classifier is optimal in the sense that it has the lowest possible probability of error ε_β for a given set of probability density functions. Therefore,

$$\varepsilon_\beta \leq \varepsilon_H \leq \min(\varepsilon_x, \varepsilon_y) \tag{27}$$

QED.

4.   Conclusions

The use of multiple features by a classifier often leads to a reduced probability of error, but the design of an optimal Bayesian classifier for multiple features requires a design sample size that, in general, increases exponentially with the number of dimensions. This project explores a method of combining the classification decisions of multiple classifiers, each utilizing a different subset of the set of features, into a single decision. The current research has focused on the restricted problem of classifying two classes given two features. It has been proven that, for this restricted problem, the method always demonstrates a probability of error that is greater than or equal to the probability of error of the optimal joint Bayesian classifier and less than or equal to the probability of error of the marginal classifier with the lowest probability of error.

References

1. Bellman, R., 1961. *Adaptive Control Processes: A Guided Tour.* New Jersey: Princeton University Press.
2. Bloch, I., January 1996.   "Information Combination Operators for Data Fusion: A Comparative Review With Classification" in *IEEE Transactions on Systems, Man and Cybernetics, Part A,* vol. 26, no. 1, pp. 52 -67.
3. Buede, D., and P. Girardi, 1997.   „A Target Identification Comparison of Bayesian and Dempster-Shafer Multisensor Fusion" in *IEEE Transactions on Systems, Man, and Cybernetics - Part A: Systems and Humans,* Vol. 27, No. 5, pp. 569-577.
4. Dietterich, T., 1997.   „Machine Learning Research: Four Current Directions" in *AI Magazine,* Winter 1997, pp. 97-136.
5. Duda, R., and P. Hart, 1973.   *Pattern Classification and Scene Analysis.* New York: John Wiley & Sons, Inc.
6. Fukunaga, K., 1990.   *Introduction to Statistical Pattern Recognition_*(2nd ed.).   Boston: Academic Press, Inc.
7. Happel, M., and P. Bock, 2000.   "Overriding the Experts: A Stacking Method For Combining Marginal Classifiers" in Proceedings of the 13th International FLAIRS Conference. Menlo Park, CA: AAAI Press, forthcoming.
8. Happel, M., 1999. *A Fusion Method for Combining Marginal Classification Decisions using an Override-Capable Classifier* (unpublished dissertation proposal). Washington, DC: The George Washington University.
9. Lam, L., and C. Suen, 1997.   „Application of Majority Voting to Pattern Recognition: An Analysis of Its Behavior and Performance" in *IEEE Transactions on Systems, Man, and Cybernetics - Part A: Systems and Humans,* Vol. 27, No. 5, pp. 553-568.
10. Mitchell, T, 1997.   *Machine Learning.* Boston: McGraw-Hill.
11. Shafer, G., 1976.   *A Mathematical Theory of Evidence.* Princeton, NJ: Princeton University Press.
12. Woods, K., W. Kegelmeyer Jr., and K. Bowyer, 1997.   „Combination of Multiple Classifiers using Local Accuracy Estimates" in *IEEE Transactions on Pattern Analysis and Machine Intelligence,* vol. 19, no. 4, pp. 405-410.
13. Xu, L., A. Krzylak, and C. Suen, 1992.   „Methods of Combining Multiple Classifiers and Their Applications to Handwriting Recognition" in *IEEE Transactions on Systems, Man, and Cybernetics,* vol. 22, no. 3, pp. 418-435.

A hybrid projection based and radial basis function architecture[*]

Shimon Cohen   Nathan Intrator

Computer Science Department
Tel-Aviv University
www.math.tau.ac.il/~nin

Abstract. A hybrid architecture that includes Radial Basis Functions (RBF) and projection based hidden units is introduced together with a simple gradient based training algorithm. Classification and regression results are demonstrated on various data sets and compared with several variants of RBF networks. In particular, best classification results are achieved on the vowel classification data [1].

1   Introduction

The duality between projection-based approximation and radial kernel methods has been explored theoretically [2]. it was shown that a function can be decomposed into mutually exclusive parts, the radial part and the ridge (projection based) part and that the two parts are mutually exclusive. It is difficult however, to separate the radial portion of a function from its projection based portion before they are estimated, and sequential methods which attempt to first find the radial part and then proceed with a projection based approximation are likely to get stuck in non-optimal local minima.

Earlier approaches to kernel based estimation were based on Volterra and Wiener kernels [17, 19] but they failed to produce a practical optimization algorithm that can compete with MLPs or RBFs. The relevant statistical framework is Generalized Additive Models (GAM) [6, 7]. In that framework, the hidden units (the components of the additive model)

---

[*] This work was partially supported by the Israeli Ministry of Science and by the Israel Academy of Sciences and Humanities — Center of Excellence Program. Part of this work was done while N. I. was affiliated with the Institute for Brain and Neural Systems at Brown University and supported in part by ONR grants N00014-98-1-0663 and N00014-99-1-0009.

J. Kittler and F. Roli (Eds.): MCS 2000, LNCS 1857, pp. 147–156, 2000.

have some parametric form, usually polynomial, which is estimated from the data. While this model has nice statistical properties [18], the additional degrees of freedom, require strong regularization to avoid over-fitting.

Higher order networks have at least a quadratic terms in addition to the linear term of the projections [9] as a special case of GAM. While they present a powerful extension of MLPs, and can form local or global features, they do so at the cost of squaring the number of input weights to the the hidden nodes. Flake has suggested an architecture similar to GAM where each hidden unit has a parametric activation function which can change from a projection based to a radial function in a continuous way [4]. This architecture uses a squared activation function, thus called Squared MLP (SMLP) and only doubles the number of free parameters. The use of B-Splines was also suggested in this context [8] with the argument that such network can combine properties of global and local receptive fields. These networks are more general than the proposed model. In high dimensional problems, a network that is too general has more free parameters and is more likely to over-fit the data. We shall compare the proposed model to the current state of the art in performance on the data set that we use to show that our proposed model does not suffer from such over-fitting problem.

It achieved very good results on some data sets and was only outperformed by our proposed architecture (see below).

This paper introduces a simple extension to both MLP and RBF networks by combining RBF and Perceptron units in the same hidden layer. Unlike the previously described methods, this does not increase the number of parameters in the model, at the cost of predetermining the number of RBF and Perceptron units in the network. The new hybrid architecture, which we call Perceptron Radial Basis Net (PRBFN), automatically finds the relevant functional parts from the data concurrently, thus avoiding possible local minima the result from sequential methods. It leads to superior results on data sets on which radial basis function have so far produced best results, in particular the vowel classification data [1] where current best results are obtained.

2   The hybrid RBF/FF architecture and training

For simplicity, we shall consider a single hidden layer architecture, since the extension to a multi-layer net is simple. In the hybrid architecture, some hidden units are of radial functions and the others are of projection type. All the hidden units are connected via a set of weights to the output layer which can be linear, for regression problems, or non-linear for classification problems.

Figure 1 presents the proposed hybrid architecture. There is a set of weights connecting the hidden units to the output units and a set of weights for the hidden units, which is in case of the perceptron units the projecting vectors, and the RBF centers for the RBF units.

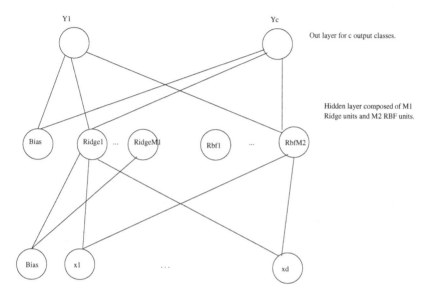

Fig. 1. PRBF hybrid neural network with M hidden units, M1 RBFs and M2 Perceptrons and M = M1 + M2.

There are several steps in estimating parameters to the hybrid architecture; First, the number of cluster centers is determined from the data and the number of RBF hidden units is chosen accordingly. Each RBF units is assigned to one of the cluster centers. The clustering can be done by a k-means procedure [3]. A discussion about the benefits of more recent approaches to clustering is beyond the scope of this paper. Unlike Orr [11], we assume that the clusters are symmetric, although each cluster may have a different radius. This is done in order to reduce the number of free parameters, while it is likely that in data-sets where Orr's method outperforms other RBF methods (see results on Friedman's data below), this assumption is not valid. The weights for the hidden projection based units can be set randomly using a certain weight distribution. The second layer of weights can then be found using a pseudo-inverse of the activity matrix or via a least mean square procedure.

The last step in the parameter estimation is to refine the weights of the hybrid network via some form of gradient descent minimization on the full architecture.

2.1   Gradient based parameter optimization

We start by deriving the gradient of the full architecture. The output of a radial basis unit is given by:

$$\phi(x, w_i) = \exp^{\frac{-(x-w_i)^2}{2r_i^2}} .$$

The output of a projection based unit is given by:

$$a_j = g(\sum_i (w_{ji} \cdot z_i)),$$

Where z is the output of the previous layer or the input to the hidden layer and w is the weight vector associated with this unit. The transfer function g is monotone and smooth such as sigmoidal. It is linear in the case of regression. The total error is given by the sum of the errors for each pattern:

$$E = \sum_{n=1}^{N} E^n .$$

The error on K outputs for the n'th pattern is given by:

$$E^n = \frac{1}{2} \sum_{k=1}^{K} (y_k^n - t_k^n)^2,$$

where t_k^n and y_k^n are the target value and output value for the n'th pattern of the k'th output respectively. The partial derivatives of the error function with respect to the output weights is given by:

$$\frac{\partial E^n}{\partial w_{kj}} = g'(a_k)(y_k^n - t_k^n)z_i.$$

where z_i is the output of the previous layer and $g'(a_k)$ is the derivative of the transfer function at the linear value a_k.

The error term δ for the radial hidden units is given by:

$$\delta_k^n = (y_k^n - t_k^n)g'(a_k),$$

and for the projection hidden units by:

$$\delta_j^n = g'(a_j) \sum_{k=1}^{K} \delta_k^n w_{kj}.$$

Using this notation, the partial derivatives of the error function with respect to first layer of weights (from the patterns to Ridge units) is given by:

$$\frac{\partial E^n}{\partial w_{ji}} = \delta_j^n x_i^n.$$

The partial derivatives of the error function with respect to the centers of the RBFs is given by:

$$\frac{\partial E^n}{\partial m_j} = \sum_{k=1}^{K} \delta_k^n w_{kj} \frac{(x^n - m_j)}{r_j^2} \phi(x^n, w_j).$$

The partial derivatives of the error function with respect to the radii is given by:

$$\frac{\partial E^n}{\partial r_j} = \sum_{k=1}^{K} \delta_k^n w_{kj} \frac{\| x^n - m_j \|^2}{r_j^3} \phi(x^n, w_j).$$

A momentum term can be added to the gradient, however it was not found to be useful with the hybrid gradient. A Levenberg Marquardt updating rule was found to be very useful for updating the weights, the centers and the radii. It is given by

$$w_{new} = w_{old} - (Z^T Z + \lambda I)^{-1} Z^T w_{old},$$

where the matrix Z is given by:

$$(Z)_{ni} = \frac{\partial y^n}{\partial w_i}.$$

3   Eliminating un-needed RBF units

It is likely that after the clustering algorithm, some cluster centers do not represent real clusters which could be approximated by an RBF, thus such cluster centers should be eliminated with the hope that the projection based units will be more useful in approximating the function in those regions. We have used several criteria for eliminating such clusters.

Size of a cluster

We discard clusters whose size in terms of number of patterns is too small, or the size in terms of scatter is too large. Given a certain threshold a, we consider only clusters which satisfy $(N/k \geq a)$ where N is the total number of patterns and k is the number of clusters.

The scatter of cluster i is given by:

$$J_i = \frac{1}{N_i} \sum_{k=1}^{N_i} (\| X_k - M_i \|)^2$$

We discard clusters for which $J_i \geq a$ for a certain threshold a. This criterion however is not very effective for non-radial clusters. In that case the Mahalanobis distance should be used.

Spectrum criteria

Clusters with a large difference between highest to lowest eigen values indicate that some directions have little variation which can be attributed to noise only. Such clusters should be projected on the more meaningful directions. At this point, we discard such clusters, and leave the approximation in this region to the MLP.

4   Experimental results

This section describes regression and classification results of several variants of RBF and the proposed PRBFN architecture on several data sets. The results which are only given for the test data are an average over 10 runs and include the standard deviation. We start with a comparison on four simulated regression data sets that were used by Orr to asses the performance of RBF. The results are summarized in Table 1.

The first data set is a 1D sine wave [11].

$$y = \sin(12x),$$

with $x \in [0, 1]$. A Gaussian noise was added to the outputs with a standard deviation of $\sigma = 0.1$. 10 sets of 50 train and 50 test patterns randomly sampled from the data with the additive noise were used.

The second data-set is a 2D sine wave,

$$y = 0. \sin(x_1/4) \sin(x_2/2),$$

with 200 training patterns sampled at random from an input range $x_1 \in$ [0, 10] and $x_2 \in [-5, 5]$. The clean data was corrupted by additive Gaussian noise with $\sigma = 0.1$. The test set contains 400 noiseless samples arranged as a 20 by 20 grid pattern, covering the same input ranges. Orr measured the error as the total squared error over the 400 samples. We report the error as simply the MSE on the test set.

The third data set [10, 12] is based on a one dimensional Hermite polynomial

$$y = (1 + (x + 2x^2)e^{-x^2}.$$

100 input values are sampled randomly between $-4 < x < 4$, and Gaussian noise of standard deviation $\sigma = .1$ was added to the output.

The fourth data-set is a simulated alternating current circuit with four input dimensions (resistance R, frequency ω, inductance L and capacitance C and one output impedance $Z = \sqrt{R^2 + (\omega L - 1/\omega C)^2}$. Each training set contained 200 points sampled at random from a certain region [13, for further details]. Again, additive noise was added to the outputs. The experimental design is the same as the one used by Friedman in the evaluation of MARS [5]. Friedman's results include a division by the variance of the test set targets. We do not make this division and report the MSE on the test set. Orr's regression trees method [13] outperforms the other methods on this data set.

	MacKay	1D Sine	2D Sine	Friedman
Rbf-Orr	1.7e-3±0	1.2e-3±0	7.4e-3±6e − 3	7.0±0.1
Rbf-Matlab	2.1e-3±9.5e − 5	8.0e-4±6.0e − 3	8.3e-3±5e − 4	10.9±0.4
Rbf-Bishop	1.8e-2±9.7e − 6	1.7e-2±1.5e − 5	4.9e-3±1.4e − 3	11.7±0.7
PRBFN	1.5e-3±9.1e − 4	1.1e-3±2.0e − 4	6.8e-3±1.8e − 4	10.6±0.6

Table 1. Comparison of Mean squared error results on two data sets (see [13] for details). Results on the test set are given for several variants of RBF networks which were used also by Orr to asses RBFs. MSE Results of an average over 10 runs including standard deviation are presented.

4.1   Classification

We have used several data sets to compare the classification performance of the proposed methods to other RBF networks. The sonar data set attempts to distinguish between a mine and a rock. It was used by Gorman and Sejnowski [14] in their study of the classification of sonar signals using neural networks. The data has 60 continuous inputs and one binary output for the two classes. It is divided into 104 training patterns and 104 test patterns. The task is to train a network to discriminate between sonar signals that are reflected from a metal cylinder and those that are reflected from a similar shaped rock. There are no results for Bishop's algorithm as we were not able to get it to reduce the output error. Gorman and Sejnowski report on results with feed-forward architectures [16] using 12 hidden units. They achieved 84.7% correct classification on the test data. This result outperforms the results obtained by the different RBF methods, and is only surpassed by the proposed hybrid RBF/FF network.

The Deterding vowel recognition data [1, 4] is a widely studied benchmark. This problem may be more indicative of the type of problems that a real neural network could be faced with. The data consists of auditory features of steady state vowels spoken by British English speakers. There are 528 training patterns and 462 test patterns. Each pattern consists of 10 features and it belongs to one of 11 classes that correspond to the spoken vowel. The speakers are of both genders. The best score so far was reported by Flake using his SMLP units. His average best score was 60.6% [4] and was achieved with 44 hidden units. Our algorithm achieved 65.7% correct classification with only 19 hidden units. As far as we know, it is the best result that was achieved on this data set.

The seismic1 and seismic2 data sets are two different representations of seismic data. The data sets include waveforms from two types of explosions and the task is to distinguish between the two types. This data was used a "Learning" course in the last two years for performance evaluation of many different classifiers[1]. one of these two classes. The dimensionality of seismic1 is 352 representing 32 time frames of 11 frequency bands, and the dimensionality of seismic2 patterns is 242 representing 22 time frames of 11 frequency bands. Principal Component Analysis (PCA) was used to reduce the data representation into 12 dimensions. Both data-sets have 65 training patterns and 19 test patterns which were chosen to be the most difficult for the desired discrimination.

Table 2 summarizes the percent correct classification results on the different data sets for the different RBF classifiers and the proposed hybrid architecture. As in the regression case, the STD is also given however, on the seismic data, due to the use of a single test set (as we wanted to see the performance on this particular data set only) the STD is often

---

[1] For details see http://www.math.tau.ac.il~nin/learn98,9

zero as only a single classification of the data was obtained in all 10 runs.

Algorithm	Sonar	Vowel	Seismic1	Seismic2
RBF-Orr	71.7±0.5	–	63±0	79±0
RBF-Matlab	82.3±2.4	51.6±2.9	73±4	81±3
RBF-Bishop	–	48.4±2.4	60±4	77±5
PRBFN	87.1±3.3	65.7±1.9	89±0	85±3

Table 2. Percent classification results of different RBF variants on four data sets.

5 Discussion

The general ideas of a hybrid architecture is not new and is covered in the theory of generalized additive models [7]. The novelty of the proposed architecture and training algorithm is the simplicity of training, and the fact that the number of model parameters is not increased. The draw back compared with more flexible methods is that the number of RBFs and ridge functions have to be pre-determined.

In the extensively studied vowel data set, our proposed hybrid architecture achieved average results which are superior to the best known results [15]. Moreover, this result was achieved with a smaller number of hidden units suggesting that the internal representation found by the hybrid architecture is richer and generalizes better. The proposed method also outperformed a feed-forward architecture and RBF architectures on the sonar data [14]. This architecture is thus a viable alternative to the use of either projection based or radial basis functions. It shares the good convergence properties of both, and with a good parameter estimation procedure it is expected to outperform either on difficult tasks.

References

1. D. H. Deterding. *Speaker Normalisation for Automatic Speech Recognition*. PhD thesis, University of Cambridge, 1989.
2. D. L. Donoho and I. M. Johnstone. Projection-based approximation and a duality with kernel methods. *Annals of Statistics*, 17:58–106, 1989.
3. R. O. Duda and P. E. Hart. *Pattern Classification and Scene Analysis*. John Wiley, New York, 1973.
4. G. W. Flake. Square unit augmented, radially extended, multilayer percpetrons. In G. B. Orr and K. Müller, editors, *Neural Networks: Tricks of the Trade*, pages 145–163. Springer, 1998.

5. J. H. Friedman. Mutltivariate adaptive regression splines. *The Annals of Statistics*, 19:1–141, 1991.

6. T. Hastie and R. Tibshirani. Generalized additive models. *Statistical Science*, 1:297–318, 1986.

7. T. Hastie and R. Tibshirani. *Generalized Additive Models*. Chapman and Hall, London, 1990.

8. S. Lane, D. Handelman, J. Gelfand, and M. Flax. Function approximation using multi-layered neural networks and b-spline receptive fields. In R. P. Lippmann, J. E. Moody, and D. S. Touretzky, editors, *Advances in Neural Information Processing Systems*, volume 3, pages 684–693, San Mateo, CA, 1991. Morgan Kaufmann.

9. Y. C. Lee, G. Doolen, H. H. Chen, G. Z.Sun, T. Maxwell, H.Y. Lee, and C. L. Giles. Machine learning using higher order correlation networks. *Physica D,*, 22:276–306, 1986.

10. D. J. C. MacKay. Bayesian interpolation. *Neural Computation*, 4(3):415–447, 1992.

11. M. J. Orr. Introduction to Radial Basis Function networks. Technical report, 1996. http://www.anc.ed.ac.uk/~mjo/rbf.html.

12. M. J. Orr. Recent advances in Radial Basis Function networks. Technical report www.anc.ed.ac.uk/~mjo/papers/recad.ps.gz, 1999.

13. M. J. Orr, J. Hallman, K. Takezawa, A. Murray, S. Ninomiya, M. Oide, and T. Leonard. Combining regression trees and radial basis functions. Division of informatics, Edinburgh University, 1999. Submitted to IJNS.

14. Gorman R. P. and Sejnowski T. J. Analysis of hidden units in a layered network trained to classify sonar targets. *Neural Network*, pages 75–89, 1988. Vol. 1.

15. A. J. Robinson. *Dynamic Error Propogation Networks*. PhD thesis, University of Cambridge, 1989.

16. D. E. Rumelhart, G. E. Hinton, and R. J. Williams. Learning internal representations by error propagation. In D. E. Rumelhart and J. L. McClelland, editors, *Parallel Distributed Processing*, volume 1, pages 318–362. MIT Press, Cambridge, MA, 1986.

17. M. Schetzen. *The Volterra and Wiener Theories Of Nonlinear Systems*. John Wiley and Sons, New York, 1980.

18. C. J. Stone. The dimensionality reduction principle for generalized additive models. *The Annals of Statistics*, 14:590–606, 1986.

19. V. Volterra. *Theory of Functional and of Integro-differential Equations*. Dover, 1959.

Combining Multiple Classifiers
in Probabilistic Neural Networks

Jiří Grim[1], Josef Kittler[2], Pavel Pudil[1], and Petr Somol[1]

[1] Institute of Information Theory and Automation,
P.O.BOX 18, CZ-18208 Prague 8, Czech Republic,
grim@utia.cas.cz, pudil@utia.cas.cz, somol@utia.cas.cz
[2] School of Electronic Engineering, Information Technology and Mathematics,
University of Surrey, Guildford GU2 5XH, United Kingdom

Abstract. We first summarize main features of a new probabilistic approach to neural networks recently developed in a series of papers in the framework of statistical pattern recognition. We consider a simplifying binary approximation of the output variables and, in order to prevent the arising information loss, we propose to combine multiple solutions. However, instead of combining different a posteriori probabilities, we make a parallel use of the binary output vectors to compute the standard Bayesian classifier.

1 Introduction

The probabilistic approach to neural networks is closely related to statistical pattern recognition. The fundamental idea of probabilistic neural networks (PNN) is to approximate the class-conditional distributions by finite mixtures and to identify the components of mixtures with neurons (cf. e.g. [15,16,9,6]). In the present paper we first summarize the basic principles of PNN. In order to prevent information loss in multilayer feed-forward PNN we consider a special type of classifier fusion. The standard approach to improve recognition accuracy and generalization performance of practical solutions, widely used both in statistical pattern recognition [10,11] and neural network ensembles [1,7,8,12,13] is to combine the outputs (e.g. a posteriori probabilities of classes, decisions) produced by different classifiers. In the present paper we propose an alternative utilization of multiple classifiers which derives from the output representation adopted. Instead of applying various rules to different a posteriori probabilities of classes or output node excitations we make parallel use of multiple solutions by composing the corresponding binary subvectors.

The parallel use of multiple solutions in the form of a joint binary output vector opens new possibilities to utilize the underlying decision information. The

---

[0] Supported by the Grant of the Academy of Sciences No. A2075703, by the Grant of the Czech Ministry of Education No. VS 96063 and partially by the Complex research project of the Academy of Sciences No. K1075601 of the Czech Republic

J. Kittler and F. Roli (Eds.): MCS 2000, LNCS 1857, pp. 157–166, 2000.

advocated representation is not unlike the feature coding method of Sung and Poggio [17]. However it differs in two key elements: in the use of structurally optimized class modeling, and in node output normalization. The proposed approach also treats the classifier design and classifier combination in a unified manner. Moreover, it is underpinned theoretically.

The paper is organized as follows. In the next section the basic probabilistic neural network model adopted is described. We introduce the information preserving transform which reduces the statistical complexity of the feature coding. The proposed probabilistic neural network model with structural optimization capability is introduced in Section 3, followed by the discussion of binary approximation of output variables in Section 4. Section 5 proposes the novel classifier fusion method. The effectiveness of the complete design methodology is demonstrated in Section 6 on a character recognition problem. Section 7 draws the paper to conclusion.

2   Probabilistic Neural Networks

Considering the probabilistic approach to neural networks we assume that there is a finite set of mutually exclusive classes $\Omega = \{\omega_1, \omega_2, \ldots, \omega_K\}$ and some N-dimensional observations $\boldsymbol{x} = (x_1, x_2, \ldots, x_N)$ from a space $\mathcal{X}$ occur randomly according to the a priori probabilities $p(\omega)$ and the class-conditional probability distributions $P(\boldsymbol{x}|\omega)$. [1] In the following let $\boldsymbol{x} \in \mathcal{X}$ be N-dimensional vector of binary variables

$$\boldsymbol{x} = (x_1, x_2, \ldots, x_N) \in \mathcal{X}, \quad x_n \in \{0, 1\}, \quad \mathcal{X} = \{0, 1\}^N. \tag{1}$$

All statistical information about the set of classes Ω given some observation $\boldsymbol{x} \in \mathcal{X}$ is expressed by the Bayes formula for a posteriori probabilities

$$p(\omega|\boldsymbol{x}) = \frac{P(\boldsymbol{x}|\omega)p(\omega)}{P(\boldsymbol{x})}, \quad \omega \in \Omega, \quad P(\boldsymbol{x}) = \sum_{\omega \in \Omega} P(\boldsymbol{x}|\omega)p(\omega) \tag{2}$$

where $P(\boldsymbol{x})$ is the unconditional joint probability distribution of $\boldsymbol{x}$. Note that the a posteriori probabilities $p(\omega|\boldsymbol{x}), \omega \in \Omega$ are easily used to compute a unique decision, if necessary. In view of Eq. (2) the solution of the above statistical decision problem $\{\mathcal{X}, P(\cdot|\omega)p(\omega), \omega \in \Omega\}$ is available, if the probabilistic description of classes is known. With the concept of probabilistic neural networks on mind we assume that the conditional distributions $P(\boldsymbol{x}|\omega)$ can be approximated by finite mixtures of the form

$$P(\boldsymbol{x}|\omega) = \sum_{m \in \mathcal{M}_\omega} F(\boldsymbol{x}|m, \omega)f(m|\omega), \quad \boldsymbol{x} \in \mathcal{X}, \quad \sum_{m \in \mathcal{M}_\omega} f(m|\omega) = 1, \quad \omega \in \Omega \tag{3}$$

where $f(m|\omega) \geq 0$ are some conditional probabilistic weights, $F(\boldsymbol{x}|m, \omega)$ the component distributions and $\mathcal{M}_\omega$ is the index set. An important feature of PNN

---

[1] In this paper we use capital letters to distinguish multivariate probability distributions from the univariate ones.

is the possibility to estimate the parameters of mixtures (3) from data by means of EM algorithm (cf. [14,2,6]).

For the sake of simple notation we introduce a consecutive indexing of components. We denote $\mathcal{M}_{\omega_k}$ the index set of the class $\omega_k \in \Omega, (k = 1, \ldots, K)$:

$$\mathcal{M}_{\omega_k} = \{M_{\omega_{k-1}} + 1, M_{\omega_{k-1}} + 2, \ldots, M_{\omega_k}\}, \quad M_{\omega_{k-1}} < M_{\omega_k}, \quad M_{\omega_0} = 0, \quad (4)$$

i.e. the number of components of the mixture $P(\boldsymbol{x}|\omega_k)$ is $|\mathcal{M}_{\omega_k}| = (M_{\omega_k} - M_{\omega_{k-1}})$. In this way the component index m uniquely identifies the class $\omega \in \Omega$ and therefore the parameter ω can be partly omitted in Eq. (3). By using substitution

$$P(\boldsymbol{x}|\omega)p(\omega) = \sum_{m \in \mathcal{M}_\omega} F(\boldsymbol{x}|m)f(m), \quad f(m) = f(m|\omega)p(\omega) \qquad (5)$$

we can express the joint probability distribution $P(\boldsymbol{x})$ in the form

$$P(\boldsymbol{x}) = \sum_{m \in \mathcal{M}} F(\boldsymbol{x}|m)f(m), \quad \boldsymbol{x} \in \mathcal{X}, \quad \mathcal{M} = \cup_{\omega \in \Omega} \mathcal{M}_\omega, \quad M = |\mathcal{M}|. \qquad (6)$$

As it can be seen, the set of component distributions $F(\boldsymbol{x}|m)$ naturally introduces an additional "descriptive" decision problem $\{\mathcal{X}, F(\cdot|m)f(m), m \in \mathcal{M}\}$ with a priori probabilities $f(m)$ whereby each component in the mixture (6) may correspond e.g. to an elementary situation on the input [3]. Given an observation $\boldsymbol{x} \in \mathcal{X}$, the a posteriori probabilities of components

$$f(m|\boldsymbol{x}) = \frac{F(\boldsymbol{x}|m)f(m)}{P(\boldsymbol{x})}, \quad m \in \mathcal{M}, \quad \boldsymbol{x} \in \mathcal{X} \qquad (7)$$

may be interpreted as a measure of presence of different elementary situations on input.

The basic idea of PNN is to view the component distributions $F(\boldsymbol{x}|m)$ as formal neurons, i.e. the functioning of a neuron is determined by the parameters of the corresponding component $F(\boldsymbol{x}|m)$. In multilayer neural networks each neuron of a given layer realizes a coordinate function of a vector transform $\boldsymbol{T}$ mapping the input space $\mathcal{X}$ into the space of output variables $\mathcal{Y}$. We denote

$$\boldsymbol{T} : \mathcal{X} \to \mathcal{Y}, \quad \mathcal{Y} \subset R^M, \quad \boldsymbol{y} = \boldsymbol{T}(\boldsymbol{x}) = (T_1(\boldsymbol{x}), T_2(\boldsymbol{x}), \ldots, T_M(\boldsymbol{x})) \in \mathcal{Y}. \quad (8)$$

It has been shown (cf. [3,18]) that the transform defined by Eqs.

$$y_m = T_m(\boldsymbol{x}) = \log f(m|\boldsymbol{x}), \quad \boldsymbol{x} \in \mathcal{X}, \quad m \in \mathcal{M} \qquad (9)$$

is information preserving and minimizes the entropy of the output space $\mathcal{Y}$.

Note that given input vector $\boldsymbol{x} \in \mathcal{X}$, the decision information is fully expressed by the a posteriori distribution $f(m|\boldsymbol{x})$. As the information preserving transform (8), (9) actually "unifies" the points $\boldsymbol{x} \in \mathcal{X}$ with identical posterior distributions $f(m|\boldsymbol{x})$, the arising partition of the input space $\mathcal{X}$ doesn't cause any information loss. Simultaneously, this partition of the input space is the "simplest" one [3,18]. The principle of information preserving transform can be used for sequential design of multilayer neural networks by transforming the descriptive decision problem along with the training data and by using the estimation procedures repeatedly (cf. [3]).

3   Subspace Approach

A typical feature of multilayer neural networks is the possibility to connect any particular neuron with arbitrary subset of nodes of input layer. Unfortunately, in probabilistic neural networks this structural freedom is not compatible with a statistically correct Bayesian decision-making. Because of the norming condition all the neurons must be connected with all the input variables and, in this sense, the biologically unnatural complete interconnection property of probabilistic neural networks is enforced by the very basic paradigm of probabilistic description.

As proposed in an earlier paper [4] the undesirable complete interconnection of PNN can be avoided by using special type of mixtures including binary structural parameters. Making substitution

$$F(\boldsymbol{x}|m) = F(\boldsymbol{x}|0)G(\boldsymbol{x}|m, \phi_m),$$

we introduce a modified mixture of distributions

$$P(\boldsymbol{x}|\omega) = \sum_{m \in \mathcal{M}_\omega} F(\boldsymbol{x}|0)G(\boldsymbol{x}|m, \phi_m)f(m|\omega) \tag{10}$$

where

$$F(\boldsymbol{x}|0) = \prod_{n \in \mathcal{N}} \theta_{n0}^{x_n}(1 - \theta_{n0})^{1-x_n}, \quad \mathcal{N} = \{1, 2, \dots, N\} \tag{11}$$

is a nonzero "background" probability distribution common to all classes $\omega \in \Omega$. The background distribution is usually defined as a product of marginals, i.e. $\theta_{n0} = \mathcal{P}\{x_n = 1\}$. The component functions $G(\boldsymbol{x}|m, \phi_m)$ include additional binary structural parameters $\phi_{mn} \in \{0, 1\}$:

$$G(\boldsymbol{x}|m, \phi_m) = \prod_{n \in \mathcal{N}} \left[\left(\frac{\theta_{nm}}{\theta_{n0}}\right)^{x_n} \left(\frac{1 - \theta_{nm}}{1 - \theta_{n0}}\right)^{1-x_n} \right]^{\phi_{mn}}. \tag{12}$$

The main motivation for the structural model (10) becomes clear in the Bayes formula since the background distribution $F(\boldsymbol{x}|0)$ can be cancelled and we can write

$$p(\omega|\boldsymbol{x}) = \frac{\sum_{m \in \mathcal{M}_\omega} G(\boldsymbol{x}|m, \phi_m)f(m)}{\sum_{j \in \mathcal{M}} G(\boldsymbol{x}|j, \phi_j)f(j)}. \tag{13}$$

It can be seen that the a posteriori probability $p(\omega|\boldsymbol{x})$ is proportional to the weighted sum of the component functions $G(\boldsymbol{x}|m, \phi_m)$ and, for the sake of Bayesian decision-making, we may consider only the respective subsets of variables defined by $\phi_{mn} = 1$. The formula (13) is actually dimension-independent because, by means of structural parameters ϕ_{mn}, the EM algorithm automatically chooses only some component-specific subsets of informative variables from the original N-dimensional input vector $\boldsymbol{x}$ (cf. [4,6]).

4   Binary Approximation

It is an important aspect of the structural model (10) that the background distribution can be cancelled in the formula (7) for the a posteriori component weights

$$f(m|\boldsymbol{x}) = \frac{G(\boldsymbol{x}|m, \phi_m)f(m)}{\sum_{j \in \mathcal{M}} G(\boldsymbol{x}|j, \phi_j)f(j)}, \quad m \in \mathcal{M}. \tag{14}$$

Let us recall that in the information-preserving transform (9) the output of a neuron is defined as logarithm of the a posteriori weight (14). The binary approximation of the information preserving transform discussed in this section (cf. [5]) makes the norming term in the coordinate functions irrelevant and therefore the input subspaces ("receptive fields") of neurons could correspond to the respective subsets of variables specified by the structural parameters.

It is well known practical experience that with increasing dimensionality the multivariate component distributions $F(\boldsymbol{x}|m)$ of mixtures tend to have only small "overlap" and, consequently, the a posteriori weights $f(m|\boldsymbol{x})$ tend to have only two extreme values, namely 0 and 1. For example, estimating multivariate Bernoulli mixtures in a 1024-dimensional binary cube [6] we obtained repeatedly maximal values of the a posteriori weights $f(m|\boldsymbol{x})$ about 0.99 on average.

Motivated by practical arguments we shall consider the binary approximation of the coordinate functions as proposed in the paper [5]. We assume only small overlap of the components of the mixture $P(\boldsymbol{x})$ and define the binary coordinate functions as follows

$$y_m = T_m(\boldsymbol{x}) = \begin{cases} 1, m = \mu(\boldsymbol{x}) \\ 0, m \neq \mu(\boldsymbol{x}) \end{cases}, \quad \boldsymbol{x} \in \mathcal{X}, \quad m \in \mathcal{M}. \tag{15}$$

whereby $\mu(\boldsymbol{x})$ identifies the highest a posteriori probability $f(m|\boldsymbol{x})$. We define the function $\mu(\boldsymbol{x})$ by Eq.

$$\mu(\boldsymbol{x}) = \min\{\arg \max_{m \in \mathcal{M}} \{\log[G(\boldsymbol{x}|m)f(m)]\}\} \tag{16}$$

which doesn't contain the norming term occurring in the formula (14). As it has been shown (cf. [5]) the arising information loss caused by the considered binary approximation is bounded by the approximation error in certain sense.

5   Parallel Use of Multiple Classifiers

There are several arguments to combine classifiers in PNN. Let us recall first that we could improve the recognition accuracy which may be impaired by the binary approximation of neuron outputs or by the imperfectly estimated mixtures. There is also a computational aspect. The EM algorithm as an optimization procedure is known to converge to a possibly local maximum of the log-likelihood function and therefore it is starting-point dependent. A standard method to improve the quality of the estimated mixture is to repeat the computation with sufficiently many different initial values. In this way we obtain multiple solutions of the optimization problem as a natural by-product.

From the point of view of combining classifiers it occurs useful that, in our case, multiple solutions obtained by EM algorithm may be expected to be essentially different since the underlying multivariate Bernoulli mixtures are known to be unidentifiable. More generally, any finite mixture of product components

$$P(\boldsymbol{x}) = \sum_{m \in \mathcal{M}} f(m) F(\boldsymbol{x}|m), \quad F(\boldsymbol{x}|m) = \prod_{n \in \mathcal{N}} f_n(x_n|m), \quad x_n \in X_n \qquad (17)$$

where $f_n(x_n|m)$ are univariate discrete distributions cannot be uniquely identified from independent observations of the corresponding random vector. In other words, any distribution of the form (17) can be equivalently expressed in many different ways. In particular, note that any nontrivial univariate discrete distribution $f_n(x_n|m)$, $(f_n(x_n|m) < 1$ for all $x_n \in X_n)$ can be expressed as a weighted average of two (or more) distributions in infinitely many ways, e.g.

$$f_k(x_n|m) = \alpha f'_k(x_n|m) + (1 - \alpha) f''_k(x_n|m), \quad) < \alpha < 1, \quad f'_k \neq f''_k. \qquad (18)$$

By means of the substitution (18) we can express the component $f(m)F(\boldsymbol{x}|m)$ as a sum of two different components

$$f(m)F(\boldsymbol{x}|m) = \alpha f(m)F'(\boldsymbol{x}|m) + (1 - \alpha) f(m) F''(\boldsymbol{x}|m) \qquad (19)$$

and therefore, after substituting (19) in (17), we obtain a formally different mixture.

Let us recall finally that the binary approximation of the information preserving transform yields a vector of binary output variables. The dimension of this vector is equal to the total number of components $M = |\mathcal{M}|$ whereby, for any input vector $\boldsymbol{x} \in \mathcal{X}$, only one of the variables is equal to 1 and all the others are zero. This fact can be expressed by Eq.

$$\boldsymbol{y} = \boldsymbol{T}(\boldsymbol{x}) = (\delta(1, \mu(\boldsymbol{x})), \delta(2, \mu(\boldsymbol{x})), \ldots, \delta(M, \mu(\boldsymbol{x}))), \quad \boldsymbol{x} \in \mathcal{X} \qquad (20)$$

In the case of parallel use of multiple solutions the number of nonzero output variables is equal to the number of the solutions involved and the resulting neural network model is more realistic from the biological point of view.

6   Numerical Example

The numeral database of Concordia University in Montreal, Canada has been chosen to demonstrate the performance of PNN (cf. [6]) as it is widely used for benchmarking of pattern recognition algorithms. The totally unconstrained handwritten numerals were collected from so called "dead-letter" envelopes by the U.S. Postal Service at different locations in the United States. They are digitized in bilevel on a 64x224 grid of 0.153 mm square raster fields. The numerals show great variability in style and size. For this reason they are usually size-normalized in the published experiments. As a rule the authors follow the suggestion of the original documentation to use 4000 specified numerals for training of classifiers (400 per class) and 2000 numerals (200 per class) for independent testing.

Table 1. Recognition of numerals from the database of Concordia University, Montreal. Classification accuracy (class-conditional and global) of 8 independent randomly initialized solutions as verified by independent test set of 2000 numerals (extended by 25 shifts). The second column contains the number of components M and the next column the total number of parameters r involved by the respective solutions. The following 10 columns represent recognition accuracy of the classes "0", "1", ..., "9" respectively and the last column contains the global (mean) accuracy.

Class:	(M)	(r)	0	1	2	3	4	5	6	7	8	9	Mean
Sol. 1	151	39673	0.920	0.855	0.945	0.810	0.815	0.825	0.935	0.895	0.850	0.905	0.8755
Sol. 2	186	71558	0.810	0.810	0.920	0.820	0.830	0.805	0.930	0.895	0.840	0.900	0.8560
Sol. 3	203	59997	0.925	0.860	0.955	0.825	0.875	0.845	0.955	0.860	0.895	0.900	0.8895
Sol. 4	183	60003	0.935	0.905	0.935	0.820	0.835	0.825	0.960	0.850	0.905	0.910	0.8880
Sol. 5	185	58102	0.940	0.900	0.910	0.830	0.875	0.815	0.945	0.880	0.905	0.875	0.8875
Sol. 6	118	35001	0.885	0.905	0.895	0.810	0.865	0.780	0.950	0.865	0.845	0.870	0.8670
Sol. 7	160	46413	0.905	0.855	0.940	0.795	0.825	0.805	0.935	0.805	0.860	0.900	0.8625
Sol. 8	157	54835	0.900	0.865	0.925	0.820	0.845	0.870	0.940	0.855	0.905	0.910	0.8835

In our recent paper [6] the training- and testing sets were also used as proposed in documentation. In the preprocessing phase all the numerals were normalized to the size 32x32 in a simple way, by periodically deleting or doubling the rows and/or columns. No special feature extraction method was used, however, in order to decrease positional dependences, the training data set was extended by 5 horizontal and 5 vertical shifts with the resulting number of 100000, (= 5x5x4000) training numerals. The same procedure was applied to independent test sets whereby the maximum a posteriori probability obtained for different shifts of a given input vector x was used to define its final classification (cf. Tab.1). This idea can be viewed as an analogy of the well known microscopic movements of human eye observing a fixed object.

The class-conditional distributions were approximated in the original 1024-dimensional space by the structural distribution mixtures (10), i.e. in the form

$$P(x|\omega) = F(x|0) \sum_{m \in \mathcal{M}_\omega} f(m|\omega) \prod_{n \in \mathcal{N}} \left[\left(\frac{\theta_{nm}}{\theta_{n0}} \right)^{x_n} \left(\frac{1 - \theta_{nm}}{1 - \theta_{n0}} \right)^{1-x_n} \right]^{\phi_{mn}} . \quad (21)$$

The parameters $f(m|\omega)$, θ_{mn} and ϕ_{mn} were computed by means of the EM algorithm. The class-conditional distributions were estimated in 8 independent randomly initialized computational experiments. In all experiments (Sol.1 - Sol.8) we obtained recognition accuracy between 85% and 89%, as shown in Table 1.

In repeated computations the EM algorithm was started randomly with identical number of components $|\mathcal{M}_\omega| = 35$. However, the number of components was spontaneously suppressed in the course of EM iterations. The total number of nonzero parameters ϕ_{mn} was set in different experiments to different values between 2000 and 7000 for each conditional distribution $P(x|\omega)$ with their initial position chosen randomly. In the course of iterations we observed a clear tendency to accumulate the specific parameters θ_{mn} at a small number of significant components. The EM iteration process repeatedly resulted in a small number of components (10 - 20) each with a relatively high number of component specific parameters (300 - 500). By displaying the location of the chosen specific parameters at the raster we could see that the components roughly correspond to different variants of the respective numeral in the database.

All the 8 solutions of Tab. 1 were used to transform the training data sets and the independent test sets by Eq. (20). The resulting vector of 1343 binary variables consists of 8 subvectors of the form (20) and of the dimension M (cf. Tab.1). The estimation procedures were applied to the transformed data sets again with the results shown in Table 2.

Table 2. Transformed problem of recognition of numerals from the database of Concordia University, Montreal. Classification accuracy achieved on the transformed data sets of the dimension $d = 1343$ in 9 independent randomly initialized solutions and verified by independent test set. The second and third columns contain the number of components M and the total number of parameters r respectively. The following 10 columns represent recognition accuracy of the classes "0", "1", ..., "9" respectively and the last column contains the global (mean) accuracy.

Class:	(M)	(r)	0	1	2	3	4	5	6	7	8	9	Mean
Sol. 1	446	10017	0.930	0.950	0.970	0.860	0.895	0.890	0.955	0.915	0.930	0.895	0.9190
Sol. 2	183	2002	0.930	0.930	0.950	0.840	0.900	0.875	0.965	0.920	0.925	0.890	0.9125
Sol. 3	50	10046	0.940	0.920	0.965	0.840	0.900	0.880	0.970	0.890	0.920	0.930	0.9155
Sol. 4	50	19986	0.925	0.920	0.965	0.885	0.915	0.865	0.975	0.925	0.915	0.925	0.9215
Sol. 5	10	10008	0.955	0.925	0.965	0.895	0.915	0.875	0.965	0.910	0.925	0.930	0.9260
Sol. 6	10	3036	0.950	0.920	0.965	0.900	0.920	0.880	0.965	0.915	0.920	0.925	0.9260
Sol. 7	10	302	0.940	0.860	0.965	0.880	0.875	0.710	0.960	0.875	0.845	0.855	0.8765
Sol. 8	20	10021	0.940	0.930	0.950	0.880	0.915	0.870	0.965	0.905	0.920	0.910	0.9185
Sol. 9	10	13430	0.930	0.935	0.965	0.890	0.910	0.865	0.965	0.905	0.920	0.945	0.9230

Lacking any a priori knowledge about the properties of the transformed data we varied both the number of components ($|\mathcal{M}_\omega| : 1 - 50$) and the number of independent parameters ($r : 300 - 14000$). As it can be seen there are only small differences between the recognition accuracy obtained in different experiments (cf. Tab.2) except for the solution 7 where the chosen number of independent parameters ($r = 302$) seems to be insufficient. It appears that the transformed variables y_m are nearly independent since the best results were obtained under assumption of conditional independence, i.e. with $\mathcal{M}_\omega = 1$ for each class $\omega \in \Omega$. This conclusion corresponds well with the expected statistical simplicity of the transformed variables.

7 Concluding Remarks

Let us remark first that, to our best knowledge, in literature there is no similar statistically correct subspace approach to Bayesian decision-making which would be directly applicable to the input space. Recall that in our case the a posteriori probabilities of classes $p(\omega|\boldsymbol{x})$ (cf. (13) may be computed from different subsets of input variables without any preprocessing of the data vectors $\boldsymbol{x} \in \mathcal{X}$. In literature the subspace representation of classes is usually considered at the level of extracted features.

The main motivation of our paper was the statistically correct design and neurophysiological plausibility of the proposed neural network model. Nevertheless, the achieved recognition accuracy is not much worse than in the best published experiments. Table 3 (cf. [6]) shows some classification results relating to the same data. For the sake of comparison we confined ourselves to formally identical experiments only with the recommended training- and test sets. Also, to keep the comparison simple, we ignored the reject option considered by several authors. As it appears, in the published papers the numerals were size-normalized and, unlike our solutions, transformed to a relatively small number of highly informative features. Thus, Kim & Lee and Cho used so called Kirsch masks to compute directional features. Hwang & Bang extracted features called "peripheral directional contributivity", Lam & Suen and Legault & Suen used structural approaches to extract features. It is well known that the feature extraction methods often make use of some informal a priori knowledge which may essentially improve the final recognition quality. On the other hand, our "featureless" classification method is more universally applicable.

Table 3. Comparison of published results on recognition of numerals from the database of Concordia University, Montreal. Only experiments using the recommended training- and test sets are included. (For detailed references see [6].)

Author	year	accuracy	Author	year	accuracy
Lam & Suen	(1988)	0.9310	Legault & Suen	(1989)	0.9390
Krzyzak et al.	(1990)	0.8640	Krzyzak et al.	(1990)	0.9485
Mai & Suen	(1990)	0.9295	Nadal & Suen	(1990)	0.8605
Suen et al.	(1990)	0.9305	Kim & Lee	(1994)	0.9540
Kim & Lee	(1994)	0.9585	Lee	(1995)	0.9780
Hwang & Bang	(1996)	0.9785	Cho	(1997)	0.9605

References

1. Cho S.B., Kim J.H., (1995): Multiple network fusion using fuzzy logic, IEEE Transactions on Neural Networks, vol. 6, no. 2, pp. 497-501.

2. Dempster, A.P., Laird, N.M., & Rubin, D.B., (1977): Maximum likelihood from incomplete data via the EM algorithm. *Journal of the Royal Stat. Soc.*, **B 39**, pp. 1-38.

3. Grim, J., (1996b): Design of multilayer neural networks by information preserving transforms. In: E. Pessa, M.P. Penna, A. Montesanto (Eds.), *Proceedings of the Third European Congress on System Science* (pp. 977-982), Roma: Edizzioni Kappa.

4. Grim J. (1999b): Information approach to structural optimization of probabilistic neural networks. In *Proceedings of 4th System Science European Congress*, L. Ferrer et al. (Eds.), (pp. 527-540), Valencia: Sociedad Espanola de Sistemas Generales, 1999.

5. Grim J. & Pudil P., (1998): On virtually binary nature of probabilistic neural networks. In: *Advances in Pattern Recognition*, (Proceedings of the IAPR International Workshops SSPR'98 and SPR'98), Sydney, August 11 - 13, 1998), A. Amin, D. Dori, P. Pudil, H. Freeman (Eds.), (pp. 765 - 774), Springer: New York, Berlin, 1998.

6. Grim J., Pudil P., Somol P. (1999a): Recognition of handwritten numerals by structural probabilistic neural networks. (To be presented at the *Int. Symp. on Neural Computation, Berlin, 2000*).

7. Hansen L.K., Salamon P., (1990): Neural network ensembles, IEEE Transactions on Pattern Analysis and Machine Intelligence, vol. 12, no. 10, pp. 993- 1001.

8. Hashem A., Schmeiser B., (1995): Improving model accuracy using optimal linear combinations of trained neural networks, IEEE Transactions on Neural Networks, vol. 6, no. 3, 792-794.

9. Haykin, S., (1993): *Neural Networks: a comprehensive foundation.* San Mateo CA: Morgan Kaufman.

10. Kittler J., (1998): Combining classifiers: A theoretical framework. Pattern Analysis and Applications, 1:18–27.

11. Kittler J., Duin R.P.W., Hatef M., Matas J., (1998): On combining classifiers. IEEE Transactions on Pattern Analysis and Machine Intelligence, 20:226–239, 3.

12. Krogh A., Vedelsby J., (1995): Neural network ensembles, cross validation, and active learning, in: Advances in neural information processing systems 7, ed. G. Tesauro, D.S. Touretzky, T.K. Leen, MIT Press, Cambridge MA.

13. Rogova G., (1994): Combining the results of several neural network classifiers, Neural Networks, vol. 7, no. 5, 777-781.

14. Schlesinger, M.I., (1968): Relation between learning and self-learning in pattern recognition. (in Russian), *Kibernetika*, (Kiev), No. 2, pp. 81-88.

15. Specht, D.F., (1988): Probabilistic neural networks for classification, mapping or associative memory. In: *Proceeding of the IEEE International Conference on Neural Networks, July 1988*, Vol. I, (pp. 525-532).

16. Streit, L.R., & Luginbuhl, T.E., (1994): Maximum likelihood training of probabilistic neural networks. *IEEE Trans. on Neural Networks*, **5**, pp. 764-783.

17. Sung K., Poggio T., (1994): Example-based learning for view-based human face detection, Technical Report: AI Memo 1521, AI Lab, MIT, Boston, MA.

18. Vajda I. & Grim J., (1998): About the maximum information and maximum likelihood principles in neural networks. *Kybernetika*, Vol. 34, No. 4, pp. 485-494.

Supervised Classifier Combination through Generalized Additive Multi-model

Claudio Conversano[1], Roberta Siciliano[1], and Francesco Mola[2]

[1] Dipartimento di Matematica e Statistica, Universitá di Napoli Federico II,
Via Cintia, Monte S. Angelo, I-80126 Napoli, Italia
conversan@dms.unina.it, roberta@unina.it
http://www.dms.unina.it
[2] Dipartimento di Economia, Universitá di Cagliari,
Viale Frá Ignazio, I-09100 Cagliari, Italia
mola@unica.it
http://www.unica.it

Abstract. [1] In the framework of supervised classification and prediction modeling, this paper introduces a methodology based on a general formulation of *combined model integration* in order to improve the fit to the data. Despite of Generalized Additive Models (GAM) our approach combines not only and not necessarily estimations derived from smoothing functions, but also those provided by either parametric or nonparametric models. Because of the multiple classifier combination we have named this general class of models as Generalized Additive Multi-Models (GAM-M). The estimation procedure iterates the *inner algorithm* - which is a variant of the backfitting algorithm - and *the outer algorithm* - which is a standard local scoring algorithm - until convergence. The performances of GAM-M approach with respect to alternative approaches are shown in some applications using real data sets. The stability of the model estimates is evaluated by means of bootstrap and cross-validation. As a result, our methodology improves the goodness-of-fit of the model to the data providing also stable estimates.

1 Introduction

Classification and prediction problems are one of the main area of interest for statisticians. These are solved using various procedures based on different kinds of statistical models. In the literature, a distinction is made between *non-supervised* and *supervised* classification. The first concerns *cluster analysis* procedures, aimed to detect the presence of groups of objects in a given data set and, consequently, to verify if these groups exist and which are the objects belonging to them. In the second the groups are defined *a-priori*, and the aim is to formulate reliable rules able to assign some new object(s) to the most appropriate group(s).

---

[1] Research was supported by MURST funds 1999 (prot. 9913182289).

J. Kittler and F. Roli (Eds.): MCS 2000, LNCS 1857, pp. 167–176, 2000.

The supervised classification will be focused in this paper by considering prediction rules based on regression type models. In section 2 we briefly describe the main approaches, considering in particular semi-parametric models named Generalized Additive Models (GAM) introduced by Hastie and Tibshirani [9] and a non parametric approach given by Classification And Regression Trees of Breiman et al. [3]. In section 3 we present a new methodology yielding to the so-called Generalized Additive Multi-Models (GAM-M) which can be understood as a combination of classification/prediction procedures. This approach aims to calibrate the estimation provided by parametric, non-parametric and semi-parametric models. We describe the estimation procedure and some properties of GAM-M in section 4. Section 5 is dedicated to the benchmarking of GAM-M approach compared to alternative approaches. As a result, we find that our methodology improves always the goodness-of-fit. Finally, we also evaluate the stability of the estimates coming from the proposed model considering bootstrap and v-fold cross-validation.

2   Semi-parametric and Non-parametric Approaches

In the framework of regression analysis we focalize our attention on two main approaches: semi-parametric GAM models and non-parametric classification and regression trees. Both approaches are suitable for any type of dependence analysis where the response variable, which can be of numerical or categorical type, is explained by numerical and/or categorical predictors.

The *Generalized Additive Models (GAM)* introduced by Hastie and Tibshirani [9] are based on the sum of d non-parametric functions of the d predictors of $\mathbf{X}$ (plus an intercept term). In addition, they allow for a known link function, $G(\cdot)$, belonging to the exponential family that relates the sum of functions $f(\cdot)$ to the dependent variable Y, yielding to the following formulation:

$$E(Y|\mathbf{X}) = G\{\alpha + \sum_{j=1}^{d} f_j(X_j)\} \tag{1}$$

where $E(Y|\mathbf{X})$ denotes the usual expectation of the dependent variable given the set of predictors and $E\{f_j(X_j)\} = 0$ for each j. These models aim to examine the effects of covariates one at a time, conditioned on the presence of the other covariates. GAM are an example of semi-parametric models, because they consist of a parametric and a non-parametric component. The response variable might depend on some covariates in a parametric (e.g. linear) fashion and on an additional (or several) covariate(s), not full-filling a parametric assumption(s).

The functions f_j in (1) are smoothing functions (in the sense of having small derivatives), so fitting the model provides a *smoothing* of the data. An estimate of the function f_j is named *smoother*. A *scatterplot smoother* of a set of observations $(x_1, y_1), \ldots, (x_n, y_n)$ can be thought of as an estimate of $E(Y|\mathbf{X} = \mathbf{x}_i)$. A variety of smoothers have been proposed in literature. A trivial example is based on the definition of bins for some $\mathbf{x}_i$ in terms of nearest neighbors, so that the fitted values are the means of Y in each bin. Such a smoother is called *moving average smother*. *Running line smoother* incorporate trends detectable in the individual neighborhoods using simple ordinary least squares linear regression lines within each neighborhood. In *locally-weighted running lines smoother* (Cleveland, [4]), the data used in constructing running line smoothers can be weighted to reflect the distances from x_0 of the points used in determining least squares estimation. Moreover, *smoothing splines* (Silvermann, [15]), which usually are cubic polynomials, represent the fit as a piecewice polynomials.

In GAM models, the estimation is provided by the *backfitting* algorithm, an iterative procedure based on the use of partial residuals. Given an initial value of the estimates, backfitting works by (non-parametrically) regressing each predictor (in turn) on the residuals of the previous iterations, until convergence is reached. In the case of a non-trivial link function, instead of using Y in the backfitting algorithm, we have to use a transformation of Y, which is essentially the inverse of the link function applied to Y. After every iteration of the backfitting algorithm, the link function relates the sum of estimated functions $\hat{f}_j(\cdot)$ to the dependent variable. In this case backfitting is the inner algorithm, and the outer algorithm is called *local scoring*.

A recent proposal of Yee [16] allows for the extension of the GAM models to the multivariate case when dealing with a multivariate response variable. This extension yields to the vector GAM models (VGAM).

An alternative and totally non-parametric approach to supervised classification and prediction problems is provided by tree-structured methods. The milestone in this field is the *CART (Classification And Regression Trees)* methodology of Breiman et al. [3]. Basically, a binary tree is grown by a recursive partitioning procedure of N cases of into two subgroups which are internally the most homogeneous and externally the most heterogeneous according to a given splitting criterion. A tree-based model has been formalized by Friedman [8] as follows

$$E(Y|\mathbf{X}) = \sum_{l=1}^{L} a_l B_l(\mathbf{X}) \tag{2}$$

In this framework, the $B_l(\mathbf{X})$s are basis functions defined on the hyper-rectangles which are derived from the tree fitting algorithm with L being the number of terminal nodes of the tree and the a_ls being the coefficients that are estimated by the mean response value in each terminal node.

As a matter of fact, CART consists of two procedures: the splitting procedure to grow the maximal tree which terminal nodes include very few cases, and the pruning procedure to reduce the size of the tree defining a sequence of pruned trees. A suitable selection criterion is defined to choose one of the pruned trees as decision tree to classify new cases of unknown response. Usually, a distinction is made between a training sample for splitting and pruning and a test sample for selecting the tree.

Tree-based models can be very useful for providing an easy interpretation of the dependence relationships among variables and at the same time they can be considered as decision rules to classify/predict new cases. The choice of splitting criteria is crucial to grow exploratory trees, whereas the selection of the decision rule is very important to define honest-size trees with a reasonable good performance in classifying new cases. With respect to the different aim alternative procedures need to be considered [13] [12]. Tree-structured models could be also considered when the response variable is multivariate [14].

3   Generalized Additive Multi-model

Equation (1) is the starting point for our definition of a general formulation of *combined model integration*. Despite of GAM, our methodology combines, not only and not necessarily estimations derived from smoothing functions, but also those provided by either parametric or non-parametric models, *one for each predictor*. The result is an alternative and even more general class of models that we name *Generalized Additive Multi-Model (GAM-M)*. We define a set of available models $(M_1, \ldots, M_K)$ that are suitable for fitting the relation of the dependent variable Y on a given predictor X_j. This set might include not only smoothing functions but also tree-based models, linear model, etc. The idea is to associate just one model to each predictor and to combine the estimations obtained from different types of models in an additive manner by means of a variant of the backfitting algorithm.

To this purpose, we introduce the following generalization of (1):

$$E[Y|\mathbf{X}] = G\left(\alpha + \sum_{j=1}^{d}\sum_{i=1}^{K} \delta_{ij} f_{ij}(X_j|\theta_{ij})\right) \tag{3}$$

where

- the f_{ij} denotes the i-th model assigned to the j-th predictor;
- the θ_{ij} is a vector of parameters of the i-th model fitted to the j-the predictor;
- the δ_{ij} is a dummy variable such that $\sum_i \delta_{ij} = 1$.

By definition only one model is assigned to each predictor and thus the additive part of the model consists of the sum of just d terms.

Some trivial cases of (3) are the following. We can obtain the *linear regression model* when $K = 1$, $G(\cdot)$ is an identity function and $f_j(X_j|\beta_j) = X_j\beta_j$, so that

$$E[Y|\mathbf{X}] = \alpha + \sum_{j=1}^{d} X_j\beta_j \tag{4}$$

Similarly, we can derive the *logistic regression model* when $K = 1$, $G(\cdot)$ is a logistic function and $f_j(X_j|\beta_j) = X_j\beta_j$ so that

$$E[Y|\mathbf{X}] = \frac{exp(\alpha + \sum_{j=1}^{d} X_j\beta_j)}{1 + exp(\alpha + \sum_{j=1}^{d} X_j\beta_j)} \tag{5}$$

In the particular case that the set of models includes only smoothing functions the GAM-M becomes equivalent to the GAM model so that the equation (3) merely reformulates the GAM model (1). In this case, if the link function $G(\cdot)$ is an identity function then we obtain the additive model.

Our formulation has the advantage to show that a given set of K smoothing functions needs to be fixed a-priori when dealing with a lot of predictors. In practice, the same smoother type could be applied to different predictors through the dummy variable whereas only one smoother is assigned to each predictor.

As a matter of fact, the GAM-M model definition allows for applying an even more general approach, that consists in combining not only smoothing functions but also tree-based models, parametric as well as semi-parametric models. This combination becomes feasible by means of a suitable estimation procedure based on a variant of the backfitting algorithm as well as a local scoring algorithm to take account of the link function.

In case of an additive model, if the model (3) is correct, then for any j we obtain:

$$E\left(Y - \alpha - \sum_{j \neq s} \sum_i \delta_{is} f_{is}(X_s|\theta_{is})\right) = f_{i^*j}(X_j|\theta_{i^*j}) \tag{6}$$

where i^* indicates the most suitable model for the predictor X_j such that $E\{f_{i^*j}(X_j|\theta_{i^*j})\} = 0$ for each j. The variant of the backfitting algorithm will be basically structured in two steps: in the first, we find the most suitable model M_{i^*} for each predictor, and, in the second, we consider an iterative algorithm for computing all the $f_{i^*s}(X_s|\theta_{i^*s})$. When readjusting the estimates provided by the current model we remove the effects of all the other variables from the dependent variable before fitting another model to the partial residual against the current predictor.

The proposed approach could also take account of the predictor transformation of the type $g(X_j)$ for a fixed $g(\cdot)$ function estimated with the data. This yields to the following formulation of GAM-M model:

$$E[Y|\mathbf{X}] = G\left(\alpha + \sum_{j=1}^d \sum_{i=1}^K \delta_{ij} f_{ij}(g(X_j)|\theta_{ij})\right) \tag{7}$$

By the equation (7) we might take account of different types of integration between non-parametric and semi-parametric approaches. As an example, tree-based criteria can be used to identify some optimal bin-widths for the smoothing function which fits the relation of the dependent variable against each predictor ([5] [11] [7]). As a matter of fact, a tree-based model can be understood as a regressogram so that it could be used as a function $g(X_j)$ for each j [1].

4   The Estimation Procedure

In this section we describe the estimation procedure for GAM-M (3) which generalizes the procedure used in GAM modeling based on the backfitting algorithm.

Basically, this consists of two algorithms, the *inner algorithm* for the additive part of the model combination (AM-M algorithm) and the *outer algorithm* for the suitable transformation through the exponential link function (GAM-M algorithm). Obviously, if the $G(\cdot)$ is an identity function then we can just consider the AM-M algorithm. A detailed description of the algorithms implemented in $S+$ can be found in Conversano [6].

The set of available models which includes also smoothing functions to be tried out are fixed depending on the type of variables. Among the smoothing functions we could choose the estimation through either the smoothing spline S or the local regression LO based on locally-weighted running lines smoothers. As parametric models we can consider the linear regression for numerical response (*Linear*) and the linear discriminant analysis for categorical response (*LDA*) [10]. As nonparametric models or tree-based models (*Tree*) we can fix either the regression tree for numerical response or the classification tree for categorical response. All these models will be considered in the applications presented in section 5.

The Additive Multi-Model (AM-M) algorithm is described in Table 1. Step 1 of the algorithm assigns either a model or a smoother to each predictor, step 2 set some assignments and step 3 fits iteratively the model to the current partial residuals until convergence (step 4). It can be noticed that at each iteration r we fit d models, one for each predictor, obtaining the estimates $\hat{f}_{i*j}(\mathbf{x}_j|\hat{\theta}_{i*j})$ that update the previous ones. The estimation is obtained by regressing the current partial residuals $e_j^{(r)}$, once the effect of all other predictors is removed from the dependent variable, against the current predictor X_j for each j. We have denoted by $\mathbf{x}_j$ the n-vector of observations of the predictor X_j and by $\mathbf{y}$ the n-vector of observations of the dependent variable.

When the response variable is categorical we specify a function $G(\cdot)$ within the family of exponential functions such as for example the logistic function. In table 2 we describe the GAM-M algorithm for this case.

This consists of an outer loop and an inner loop: the former considers the inverse of the link function in order to define a transformation of the dependent variable and a system of weights for the covariates; the latter is the AM-M algorithm which allows to update the additive component of the model.

5   The Benchmarking of GAM-M Approach

In this section, we present the results of two applications on real data sets, comparing our GAM-M model with other approaches. First, we dispose of a data set coming from SPSS library concerning a sample of 474 employers. The aim is to predict the actual salary (Y) with respect to the initial salary (X_1), number of working months in previous employment (X_2), number of working months during the actual employment (X_3), and education level (X_4). The second data set is a survey of Bank of Italy of 1995 concerning the *Italian Household Budgets*. The response variable (dichotomous) is the use of an electronic card for highways payment. Our aim is to estimate the probability of using such card on the basis of

Table 1. The AM-M algorithm

1. For each $j - th$ predictor fit the models $M_1, \ldots, M_K$ and choose the best model M_{i^*} that minimize the residual deviance. Fix $\delta_{i^* j} = 1$ and $\delta_{ij} = 0$ for $i \neq i^*$.

2. *Initialize.* Put iteration counter $r = 0$.
   Set the following assignments: $\hat{f}_{i^* j}^{(0)} = 0$ for each j.
   Center the predictors $\mathbf{X}$ and the response variable $\mathbf{y}$, and save the means.

3. *Update.* Put iteration counter $r = r + 1$.
   Set the following assignments: $\hat{f}_{i^* j}^{(r)} = \hat{f}_{i^* j}^{(r-1)}$ for each j.
   For $j = 1, \ldots, d$ fit the model $f_{i^* j}^{(r)}$ to the residuals:
   $e_j{}^{(r)} = \{\mathbf{y} - \sum_{s \neq j} \sum_i \delta_{is} \hat{f}_{is}^{(r)}(\mathbf{x}_s | \hat{\theta}_{is})\}$
   against the predictor X_j yielding to $\hat{f}_{i^* j}^{(r)}(\mathbf{x}_j | \hat{\theta}_{ij})$.
   Update $\hat{f}_{i^* j}^{(r)}(\mathbf{x}_j | \hat{\theta}_{ij})$.

4. *Verify.* Cycle step 3 until convergence of the MSE of predictions.

Table 2. The GAM-M algorithm

1. For each $j - th$ predictor fit the models $M_1, \ldots, M_K$ and choose the best model M_{i^*} that minimize the residual deviance. Fix $\delta_{i^* j} = 1$ and $\delta_{ij} = 0$ for $i \neq i^*$.

2. *Initialize*
   $$\hat{f}_{i^* j}(\mathbf{x}_j | \hat{\theta}_{i^* j}) = 0 \qquad \text{for each } j \qquad \hat{\alpha} = \text{logit}(\bar{y})$$
   $$r = 0$$

3. *Update*
   $$\hat{G}^{(r)}(\mathbf{x}_j) = \hat{\alpha} + \sum_{j=1}^d \hat{f}_{i^* j}^{(r)}(\mathbf{x}_j | \hat{\theta}_{i^* j})$$
   $$\hat{p} = \text{logit}^{-1}(\hat{G}^{(r)}(\mathbf{x}_j)) = \frac{\exp(\hat{G}^{(r)}(\mathbf{x}_j))}{[1+\exp(\hat{G}^{(r)}(\mathbf{x}_j))]}$$
   $$z = \hat{G}^{(r)}(\mathbf{x}_j) + \frac{(y-\hat{p})}{[\hat{p}(1-\hat{p})]}$$
   $$w = \hat{p}(1 - \hat{p})$$
   $$r = r + 1$$

   Update $\hat{f}_{i^* j}(\mathbf{x}_j | \hat{\theta}_{i^* j})$ applying the AM-M algorithm to the transformed response variable $\mathbf{z}$ on the basis of the covariates $\mathbf{X}$ using weights $\mathbf{w}$.

4. Verify convergence through the log-likelihood criterion:
   $$D(\mathbf{y}, \hat{\mathbf{p}}) = -2 \sum [y_n \ln \hat{p}_n + (1 - y_n) \ln(1 - \hat{p}_n)]$$

four predictors, namely Age (X_1), Income (X_2), Personal Consumption (X_3) and Real Estate/Income ratio (X_4). We compared the goodness of fit in each iteration when applying both GAM-M and GAM approaches. For GAM-M methodology we consider the models $\{LO, S, Tree, Linear\}$ for the first data set and the models $\{LO, S, Tree, LDA\}$ for the second data set. The results are respectively summarized in Table 3 by means of the Mean Square Error (MSE) and in Table 4 by means of the Log-Likelihood Statistic $D(\mathbf{y}, \hat{\mathbf{p}})$. We also indicate for each iteration r the dimensionality of the vector of parameters θ fitted in each model in GAM-M approach and the dimensionality of the vector of parameters ν fitted in each smoothing function in GAM approach. In both cases, it is clear that

Table 3. Goodness of fit comparison at each iteration between GAM-M and GAM for the *Employers* data set

r	Model	$dim(\theta)$	MSE$_{(AM-M)}$	Smoothing function	$dim(\nu)$	MSE$_{(GAM)}$
1	$LO(X_4)$	4	1046.880	$LO(X_4)$	4	540.804
1	$LO(X_1)$	5	773.024	$LO(X_1)$	5	511.143
1	$Tree(X_3)$	5	739.357	$S(X_3)$	3	480.850
1	$Tree(X_2)$	11	671.318	$S(X_2)$	3	458.256
2	$LO(X_4)$	4	607.328	$LO(X_4)$	4	456.183
2	$LO(X_1)$	5	564.212	$LO(X_1)$	5	456.050
2	$Tree(X_3)$	11	540.668	$S(X_3)$	3	455.769
2	$Tree(X_2)$	6	542.002	$S(X_2)$	3	455.020
3	$LO(X_3)$	4	497.491	$LO(X_3)$	4	454.930
3	$LO(X_1)$	5	479.133	$LO(X_1)$	5	454.933
3	$Tree(X_3)$	6	471.378	$S(X_3)$	3	454.945
3	$Tree(X_2)$	9	433.209	$S(X_2)$	3	454.851
4	$LO(X_3)$	4	419.872	$LO(X_3)$	4	454.854
4	$LO(X_1)$	5	411.140	$LO(X_1)$	5	454.854
4	$Tree(X_3)$	6	408.195	$S(X_3)$	3	454.849
4	$Tree(X_2)$	7	390.099	$S(X_2)$	3	454.831

we reduce considerably the MSE and the log-likelihood statistic in our GAM-M approach with respect to the classical GAM.

In order to evaluate the stability of the estimates coming from the GAM-M approach we could perform bootstrap and cross-validation. Table 5 shows the results for the first data set. In particular, we considered 100 bootstrap samples of four different sizes $n = 50, 100, 150, 200$ on which we applied the linear model, the regression tree, the GAM model, the proposed GAM-M model. Moreover, we also considered a 10-fold cross-validation on the data set. For each model estimates we calculated the standard deviation of the MSE within the 100 bootstrap samples of a given size as a measure of *internal stability*, and within the 10 cross-validated

Table 4. Goodness of fit comparison at each iteration between GAM-M and GAM for the *Bank of Italy* data set

r	Model	$dim(\theta)$	$D(\mathbf{y},\hat{\mathbf{p}})_{(GAM-M)}$	Smoothing function	$dim(\nu)$	$D(\mathbf{y},\hat{\mathbf{p}})_{(GAM)}$
1	$Tree(X_1)$	3	435.13	$S(X_1)$	4	389.00
1	$LDA(X_2)$	1	390.41	$Linear(X_2)$	1	330.73
1	$LO(X_3)$	6	320.45	$LO(X_3)$	6	291.87
1	$S(X_4)$	8	278.20	$S(X_4)$	8	283.64
2	$Tree(X_1)$	5	235.87	$S(X_1)$	4	254.98
2	$LDA(X_2)$	1	223.76	$Linear(X_2)$	1	250.65
2	$LO(X_3)$	6	201.27	$LO(X_3)$	6	227.02
2	$S(X_4)$	8	188.20	$S(X_4)$	8	222.13
3	$Tree(X_1)$	7	165.87	$S(X_1)$	4	212.94
3	$LDA(X_2)$	1	157.76	$Linear(X_2)$	1	212.25
3	$LO(X_3)$	6	152.27	$LO(X_3)$	6	212.22

samples as a measure of *external stability*. The results confirm that the proposed GAM-M methodology provides more stable estimates.

Table 5. Bootstrap and 10-fold Cross-Validation estimates for the standard deviation of the MSE in the *Employers* data set

Model	Bootstrap Estimate				10-fold Cross Validation Estimate
	$n = 50$	$n = 100$	$n = 150$	$n = 200$	
Linear Regression	20.646	16.618	13.528	11.157	13.965
Regression Tree	25.935	18.726	14.956	13.232	12.967
GAM	18.231	13.543	10.998	9.837	11.012
GAM-M	14.275	9.285	7.384	6.188	10.492

6   Concluding Remarks

The proposed GAM-M approach is useful not only to improve the quality of the estimation coming from different models, but also to identify the more appropriate model for each variable. Moreover it removes for each predictor the observations not influencing the estimation provided by a certain model by assigning their residuals to the other models. As a result, our methodology might prevent from an incorrect choice of the model and is particularly suitable for complex data sets. The proposed approach is totally different from the methods based on the use of some combination of functions and/or variables, such as the bagging procedure of Breiman [2]. These procedures work with models which are previously defined, whereas our procedure adapts simultaneously the estimations coming from different models in the successive iterations, allowing at the same time for the possibility to consider interactions between terms in the model.

References

1. Antoch, J., Mola, F.: Parsimonious regressograms for generalized additive models. In N.C. Lauro (Ed.): *Sviluppi Metodologici Applicativi dell'Inferenza Computazionale nell'Analisi Multidimensionale dei Dati*, (1996), Rocco Curto, Napoli, 46–59.
2. Breiman, L.: Bagging Predictors. *Machine Learning, 26*, (1996), 46–59.
3. Breiman, L., Friedman, J.H., Olshen, R.A. and Stone, C.J.: *Classification and Regression Trees*, Belmont C.A. Wadsworth, (1984).
4. Cleveland, W. S.: Robust locally weighted regression and smoothing scatterplots, *Journal of the American Statistical Association*, **74**, (1979), 829-836.
5. Conversano, C.: A Regression Tree Procedure for Smoothing in Generalized Additive Models. In M. Huskova et al. (eds.): *Prague Stochastics'98 Abstracts*, 13-14, Union of Czech Mathematicians and Physicists, (1998).
6. Conversano, C.: *Semiparametric Models for Supervised Classification and Prediction. Some Proposals for Model Integration and Estimation Procedures* (in Italian), Ph.D Thesis in Computational Statistics and Data Analysis, Università di Napoli Federico II, (2000).
7. Conversano, C., Siciliano, R.: *Modelling MIB30 Index Volatility: Regression Tree Criteria for Smoothing and Variable Selection in Generalized Additive Models*, submitted.
8. Friedman, J.H.: Multivariate Adaptive Regression Splines. *The Annals of Statistics*, **23**, (1991), 1–149.
9. Hastie, T.J., and Tibshirani, R.J.: *Generalized Additive Models*. Chapman and Hall, London, (1990).
10. Mardia, K.V., Kent, J.T., Bibby, J.M.: *Multivariate Analysis*. Academic Press, London, (1995).
11. Mola, F.: Selection of Cut Points in Generalized Additive Models. In: *Classification and Data Analysis: Theory and Application*, Springer Verlag, Berlin, (1998), 121–128.
12. Mola, F., Siciliano, R.: A Fast Splitting Procedure for Classification Trees, *Statistics and Computing*, 7, (1997), 208-216.
13. Siciliano, R.: Exploratory versus Decision Trees, in R. Payne, P. Green (Eds.): *Proceedings in Computational Statistics: COMPSTAT '98*, Physica-Verlag, Heidelberg (D), (1998), 113-124.
14. Siciliano, R., Mola, F: Multivariate Data Analysis through Classification and Regression Trees, *Computational Statistics and Data Analysis*, 32, Elsevier Science, (2000), 285-301.
15. Silvermann B. W.: Some aspects of the spline smoothing approach to nonparametric regression curve fitting, *Journal of the Royal Statistical Society*, **B 47**, (1985) 1-52.
16. Yee, T.W., Wild, C.J.: Vector generalized additive models, *Journal of Royal Statistical Society*, **B 58**, (1996), 481-493.

Dynamic Classifier Selection

Giorgio Giacinto and Fabio Roli*

Dept. of Electrical and Electronic Eng., Univ. of Cagliari, Piazza d'Armi, 09123, Italy
Phone +39 070 6755874 Fax +39 070 6755900
e-mails {giacinto,roli}@diee.unica.it

Abstract. At present, the usual operation mechanism of multiple classifier systems is the combination of classifier outputs. Recently, some researchers have pointed out the potentialities of "dynamic classifier selection" as an alternative operation mechanism. However, such potentialities have been motivated so far by experimental results and qualitative arguments. This paper is aimed to provide a theoretical framework for dynamic classifier selection and to define the assumptions under which it can be expected to improve the accuracy of the individual classifiers. To this end, dynamic classifier selection is placed in the general framework of statistical decision theory and it is shown that, under some assumptions, the optimal Bayes classifier can be obtained by selecting non-optimal classifiers. Two classifier selection methods that derive from the proposed framework are described. The experimental results obtained in the classification of remote-sensing images and comparisons among different combination methods are reported.

1. Introduction

In the fields of machine learning, neural networks, and pattern recognition, the "fusion" of multiple classifiers (also called "experts" or "learners") has been proposed as an approach to the development of high performance classification systems [1-10]. Typically, classifiers are combined by voting rules, statistical techniques, belief functions, Dempster-Shafer evidence theory, and other fusion schemes [1]. Suen et al. proposed a classification of combination methods according to the types of outputs have produced by the individual classifiers [1,11]. Other researchers have proposed alternative schemes for classifying combination methods [8].

Theoretical and experimental results reported in the literature have clearly shown that classifier fusion is effective if the individual classifiers are "accurate" and "diverse", that is, if they exhibit low error rates (at least lower than 50%) and if they make different errors [8,12,13]. In particular, it has been shown that the combination of "weak" classifiers making independent errors can offer dramatic improvements in performance [13]. Accordingly, error independence among individual classifiers is commonly regarded as a requirement for effective classifier fusion, even though a

---

* Corresponding Author: Tel. +39 070 6755874 Fax +39 070 6755900

J. Kittler and F. Roli (Eds.): MCS 2000, LNCS 1857, pp. 177-189, 2000.

recent paper has clearly pointed out that "negatively" dependent classifiers are better than independent classifiers [14]. In our opinion, the impact of the accuracy-diversity trade-off on classifier fusion remains to be investigated in detail.

Unfortunately, the reported experimental and theoretical results have pointed out that the creation of accurate and diverse classifiers is a very difficult task [15-18]. In real applications, the most likely situation is to have reasonably accurate but "positively" dependent classifiers (i.e., classifiers that make many identical errors). Typically, classifiers make identical errors on difficult patterns.

On the other hand, it can be verified experimentally that it is easier to design a classifier ensemble, where on considering each pattern, at least one classifier can classify it correctly, while the remaining classifiers could make the same error [19-21]. Accordingly, the authors and other researchers have proposed an alternative approach to classifier combination, based on the concept of "dynamic classifier selection" (DCS) [3,19-21]. DCS is based on the definition of a "function" that for each pattern selects the classifier that is more likely to classify it correctly. So far the potentialities of DCS have been motivated by experimental results and qualitative arguments. To the best of the authors' knowledge, no previous work has dealt with understanding how and why DCS can produce improved classification results. Accordingly, this paper is aimed to provide a theoretical framework for DCS. In particular, we have placed DCS in the general framework of statistical decision theory, and defined the assumptions under which the optimal Bayes classifier can be obtained through the dynamic selection of non-optimal classifiers (Section 2). Afterwards, two classifier selection methods that derive from the proposed framework are described (Section 3). The experimental results and comparisons are reported in Section 4. The conclusions are drawn in Section 5.

2. A Bayesian Framework for Dynamic Classifier Selection

2.1 Basic Concepts

Let us consider a pattern classification task for M data classes ω_i, i = 1,..,M. Each pattern is characterised by a feature vector $\mathbf{X}$. A pattern classifier can be represented by a set of M "discriminant" functions $d_i(\mathbf{X})$, $i=1,..,M$. The classifier assigns a pattern $\mathbf{X}$ to the class ω_i if $d_i(\mathbf{X}) > 0$. Therefore, such functions subdivide the feature space into M decision regions, R_i, i=1,..,M, such that $\forall \mathbf{X} \in R_i\ d_i(\mathbf{X}) > 0$. The locus of the points satisfying the equation $d_i(\mathbf{X}) = 0$ represents a decision "boundary" for the class ω_i. According to Bayes theory, the "optimal" decision regions are defined to maximise the probability of correct classification. The classifier maximising this probability is named "optimal Bayes classifier". In the following, we indicate the discriminant functions and decision regions related to the optimal Bayes classifier with the terms $d_i^B(\mathbf{X})$ and R_i^B, respectively.

2.2 The Theoretical Framework

Let us consider a multiple classifier system (MCS) made up of K different classifiers. Each classifier C_j, $j = 1,..,K$ is represented by a set of discriminant functions $d_i^j(\mathbf{X})$, $i = 1,..,M$ that subdivide the feature space into M decision regions R_i^j.

Definition 1: Optimal and Non-optimal Decision Regions

Without loosing generality, each decision region R_i^j can be considered subdivided into the regions $R_{i+}^j = R_i^j \cap R_i^B$ and $R_{i-}^j = R_i^j - R_{i+}^j$. Accordingly, $R_i^j = R_{i+}^j \cup R_{i-}^j$. The decisions made by each classifier C_j are equal to those of the optimal Bayes classifier within R_{i+}^j. Non-optimal decisions are made within R_{i-}^j.

Definition 2: Feature-space Partitioning Generated by an MCS

The decision boundaries of the K classifiers can be represented by the equations $d_i^j(\mathbf{X}) = 0$, $i = 1,..,M$, $j=1,..,K$. The union of such boundaries subdivide the feature space into "parts" P_l, $l=1,..,L$. These parts can be formally defined by introducing "discriminant" functions $b_l(\mathbf{X})$ such that $\forall \mathbf{X} \in P_l$, $b_l(\mathbf{X}) > 0$ and $\forall \mathbf{X} \notin P_l$, $b_l(\mathbf{X}) < 0$. In particular, we define each part by the following equations:

$$\forall \mathbf{X} : b_l(\mathbf{X}) = 0 \implies \sum_{j=1}^{K}\sum_{i=1}^{M} \beta_i^j(\mathbf{X}) d_i^j(\mathbf{X}) = 0 \tag{1}$$

$$\forall \mathbf{X} : b_l(\mathbf{X}) > 0 \implies \forall i,j \ \ d_i^j(\mathbf{X}) \neq 0 \tag{2}$$

where the terms $\beta_i^j(\mathbf{X})$ represent binary functions $\beta_i^j(\mathbf{X}) = \{0,1\}$ that satisfy the condition $\sum_{j=1}^{K}\sum_{i=1}^{M} \beta_i^j(\mathbf{X}) = 1$. Equation 1 formally states that the boundary of each part P_l is defined by the union of "pieces" of the decision boundaries of the K classifiers. Accordingly, the boundary $b_l(\mathbf{X}) = 0$ is regarded as a sum of pieces of classifier boundaries. Each piece is identified by an appropriate function $\beta_i^j(\mathbf{X})$. Equation 2 states that no classifier boundary can be contained within a part P_l. As illustrated by the following example (Figure 2), this means that we are considering the smallest parts generated by the union of classifier boundaries, and consequently each region R_i^j can be obtained by the union of a certain number of parts P_l, i.e., $\forall i,j \ R_i^j = \bigcup_{l \in A_i^j} P_l$, $A_i^j \subset \{1,...,L\}$. It is also easy to see that equation 2 implies that the proposition $\forall l, j \ \exists i : P_l \subseteq R_i^j$ is true. Otherwise, it would be false to say that no classifier boundary is contained within a part. Based on the above definitions, the partition P generated by an MCS is defined by the following equations:

$$P = \bigcup_{l=1}^{L} P_l = \bigcup_{i=1}^{M} R_i^j \quad j = 1,..,K \tag{3}$$

$$P_m \cap P_n = \varnothing, \ m \neq n \tag{4}$$

In order to illustrate the above concepts, let us consider an MCS made up of two classifiers C_1 and C_2, and a simple two-dimensional classification task with three data classes. Figures 1(a) and 1(b) show the decision regions R_i^j of the two classifiers.

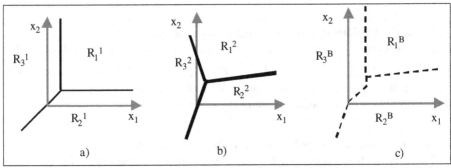

Fig. 1. Example of a two-dimensional classification task with three data classes: a) boundaries of the decision regions of classifier C_1; b) boundaries of the decision regions of classifier C_2; c) boundaries of the optimal Bayes decision regions.

Linear decision boundaries have been assumed for the sake of simplicity. Figure 1(c) shows the optimal Bayes decision regions R_i^B hypothesised for this classification task. Figure 2 shows the partitioning of the feature space generated by the MCS. It is worth noticing that, according to the above definition, the seven parts forming this partition do not contain decision boundaries, and consequently, they are the smallest parts identified by the union of classifier boundaries.

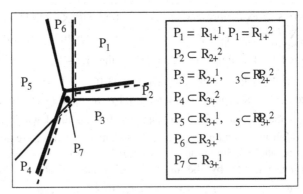

$P_1 = R_{1+}^1, \ P_1 = R_{1+}^2$

$P_2 \subset R_{2+}^2$

$P_3 = R_{2+}^1, \ _3 \subset R_{2+}^2$

$P_4 \subset R_{3+}^2$

$P_5 \subset R_{3+}^1, \ _5 \subset R_{3+}^2$

$P_6 \subset R_{3+}^1$

$P_7 \subset R_{3+}^1$

Fig. 2. Feature-space partitioning generated by two classifiers in Figures 1.a and 1.b.

Theorem about the Bayesian optimality of DCS

Let us assume that the following two conditions are satisfied:

Hypothesis 1: Decision region complementarity

$$R_i^B = \bigcup_{j=1}^{K} R_{i+}^j \qquad i = 1,..,M$$

Hypothesis 2: Decision boundary complementarity

$$\forall \mathbf{X} : d_i^B(\mathbf{X}) = 0 \;\Rightarrow\; \sum_{j=1}^{K} \alpha_j(\mathbf{X}) d_i^j(\mathbf{X}) = 0$$

where the terms $\alpha_j(\mathbf{X})$ are binary functions $\alpha_j(\mathbf{X}) = \{0,1\}$ that satisfy the condition

$$\sum_{i=1}^{K} \alpha_j(\mathbf{X}) = 1;$$

then, we can prove that the following proposition is true:

$$\forall l \; \exists ij : \; P_l \subseteq R_{i+}^j$$

Hypothesis 1 assumes that the optimal Bayes decision regions R_i^B can be "restored" by joining the optimal classifier regions R_{i+}^j. Hypothesis 2 assumes that the optimal decision boundaries $d_i^B(\mathbf{X}) = 0$ coincide piecewise with the boundaries $d_i^j(\mathbf{X}) = 0$ of the K classifiers. Therefore, the optimal boundaries can be restored by a sum of "pieces" of classifier boundaries. (Each piece is identified by an appropriate function $\alpha_j(\mathbf{X})$). Accordingly, a reasonable degree of complementarity among K classifiers is hypothesised. In particular, classifiers should make optimal Bayes decisions in different parts of the feature space. It is worth noting that it is reasonable to assume that classifier ensembles that satisfy Hypothesis 1 also satisfy Hypothesis 2, since the complementarity of the decision regions should also imply the complementarity of the decision boundaries.

Under the two above hypotheses, the theorem shows the Bayesian optimality of DCS by proving that all parts P_l are contained in regions R_{i+}^j. In other words, we prove that in each part there is at least one classifier C_j that makes optimal Bayes decisions. Accordingly, the optimal Bayes classifier can be obtained by selecting one classifier for each part.

Proof

We know from the definition of feature-space partitioning that $\forall i,j \; R_i^j = \bigcup_{l \in A_i^j} P_l \quad A_i^j \subset \{1,...,L\}$.

Hypothesis 2 allows to extend this conclusion to the regions R_{i+}^j by writing the following equation:

$$\forall i, j \; R_{i+}^j = \bigcup_{l \in A_{i+}^j} P_l \quad A_{i+}^j \subset \{1,...,L\} \tag{5}$$

since optimal decision boundaries coincide piecewise with classifier boundaries. It is worth noticing that equation 5 "partially" proves the theorem, since it shows that some parts P_l are contained within the regions R_{i+}^j. Formally speaking, it shows that $\exists l : \exists ij : P_l \subseteq R_{i+}^j$. This can be seen by observing that $\forall ij\ A_{i+}^j \subset \{1,...,L\}$, i.e. A_{i+}^j is a subset of the set P that contains all the parts P_l, $l = 1,...,L$. However, to prove the theorem, we must show that all the parts are contained in the regions R_{i+}^j, i.e. that the following equation holds[1]:

$$\bigcup_{i=1}^{M}\bigcup_{j=1}^{K}R_{i+}^j = \bigcup_{l \in A_+}P_l = P \quad A_+ = \bigcup_{i=1}^{M}\bigcup_{j=1}^{K}A_{i+}^j \tag{6}$$

According to equation 5 and Hypothesis 1, the following can be written:

$$\forall i\ \ R_i^B = \bigcup_{j=1}^{K}R_{i+}^j = \bigcup_{l \in A_{i+}}P_l \quad A_{i+} = \bigcup_{j=1}^{K}A_{i+}^j \tag{7}$$

In addition, we know that the union of the optimal regions R_i^B "covers" the entire partitioning P:

$$\bigcup_{i=1}^{M}R_i^B = \bigcup_{l=1}^{L}P_l = P \tag{8}$$

Accordingly, equation 6 and consequently the theorem are proved.

An Example

Let us again consider the classification task described in Figures 1 and 2. From an analysis of these figures it can be seen that Hypothesis 1 of the theorem is satisfied. As an example, it is easy to check that $R_1^B = R_{1+}^1$ (It is worth noticing that since the number of optimal classifier regions to be used to restore the Bayesian regions R_i^B depends on the data class, this number can be smaller than K). Figure 2 clearly shows that Hypothesis 2 is also satisfied, since the optimal decision boundaries coincide piecewise with the classifier boundaries. Accordingly, the legend in Figure 2 shows that the theorem holds, i.e., all the parts P_l, $l=1,..,7$ are contained in regions R_{i+}^j.

3. Methods for Dynamic Classifier Selection

3.1 Selection by Classifier Local Accuracy

The framework described in Section 2 does not deal with methods for classifier selection, since this topic is beyond its scope. Its objective is simply to show the

---

[1] In equation 6, it is worth noticing that $A_+ = \bigcup_{i=1}^{M}\bigcup_{j=1}^{K}A_{i+}^j = \{1,...,L\}$

hypotheses under which the optimal Bayes classifier can be obtained by selecting non-optimal classifiers. However, it is easy to see that a simple classifier selection method derives naturally from the framework. According to the above theorem, in each part P_l, there is at least one classifier that makes optimal Bayes decisions. The classification accuracy of this classifier is certainly higher than that of other classifiers in the part. Consequently, for each part P_l, the accuracy of the K classifiers can be estimated using validation data belonging to the part, and the classifier with the maximum accuracy value can be selected. However, according to the framework, this optimal selection method needs an exact knowledge of the classifier decision boundaries. Such a hypothesis is satisfied for simple classification tasks. In general, we can try to estimate the classifier decision boundaries by analysing the decisions taken by classifiers for a large set of patterns. Unfortunately, there are real classification tasks, characterised by high dimensional feature spaces and small training sets, where such an estimate of classifier boundaries is too expensive or unfeasible. However, it is quite easy to see that, for each test pattern belonging to a part P_l, the classifier accuracy required by the optimal selection method can be estimated using a local region of the feature space defined in terms of the k-nearest neighbours of such a test pattern. (k-nearest neighbours belonging to a validation set). This is the so-called "classifier local accuracy" (CLA) previously introduced by the authors and other researchers [19,20]. It is worth noting that, for each test pattern, the optimal neighbourhood is the part P_l containing the pattern. (Unfortunately, the definition of the optimal neighbourhood requires the knowledge of classifier decision boundaries). In practice, for each part P_l, CLA is a good estimate of classifier accuracy if the neighbourhood of the test pattern is strictly contained in the part, and if it contains a sufficient number of validation patterns. Therefore, good estimates of classifier accuracy can be obtained for test patterns quite far from the parts' boundaries.

To sum up, the basic idea of our selection methods is to estimate the accuracy of each classifier in a local region of the feature space surrounding an unknown test pattern, and then to select the classifier with the highest value of this CLA to classify the test pattern. In the following, two methods for estimating CLA, and a classifier selection algorithm using one or the other are described.

3.2 An a priori Selection Method

For each unknown test pattern X*, let us consider a local region of the feature space defined in terms of the k-nearest neighbours in the validation data. Validation data are extracted from the training set and are not used for classifier training. These data are classified after the training phase, in order to estimate local classifier accuracy. It is easy to see that CLA can be estimated as the ratio between the number of patterns in the neighbourhood that were correctly classified by the classifier C_j, and the number of patterns forming the neighbourhood of X* [19,20]. As in the k-nearest neighbour classifier, the appropriate size of the neighbourhood is decided by trial and error. If the classifier outputs can be regarded as estimates of the a posteriori probabilities, we propose to take these probabilities into account in order to improve the estimation of the above CLA. Given a pattern $\mathbf{X} \in \omega_i$, i = 1,..,M, belonging to the neighbourhood of X^*, the $\hat{P}_j(\omega_i | \mathbf{X})$ provided by the classifier C_j can be regarded as a measure of the classifier accuracy for the validation pattern X. Moreover, in order to handle the "uncertainty" in defining the appropriate neighbourhood size, the a posteriori probabilities can been "weighted" by a term $W_n = 1/ d_n$, where d_n is the Euclidean distance of the neighbouring pattern X_n from the test pattern X^*. Therefore, we propose to estimate CLA as follows:

$$CLA_j(\mathbf{X}^*) = \frac{\sum_{n=1}^{N} \hat{P}_j(\omega_i | \mathbf{X}_n \in \omega_i) \cdot W_n}{\sum_{n=1}^{N} W_n} \quad j = 1,..,K \ \ i = 1,..,M \tag{9}$$

where N is the number of validation patterns contained in the neighbourhood of the test pattern X^*.

Finally, let us point out that, according to equation (9), CLA is computed "a priori", that is, without knowing the class assigned by the classifier C_j to the test pattern X^*.

3.3 An a posteriori Selection Method

Let us assume that the data class ω_i assigned by the classifier C_j to the test pattern X^* is known. We indicate this by $C_j(X^*) = \omega_i$. Such an assumption simply implies that the test pattern is classified by all the classifiers C_j before performing the selection. (This is why the method is named "a posteriori"). In this case, it is easy to see that CLA can be estimated as the fraction of correctly classified neighbouring patterns assigned to class ω_i by the classifier C_j. As in the a priori method, if the classifiers provide estimates of the class posterior probabilities, CLA can be estimated by computing the probability that the test pattern X^* is correctly assigned to class ω_i by the classifier C_j. According to the Bayes theorem, this probability can be estimated as follows:

$$\hat{P}\left(\mathbf{X}^* \in \omega_i | C_j\left(\mathbf{X}^*\right) = \omega_i\right) = \frac{\hat{P}\left(C_j(\mathbf{X}^*) = \omega_i | \mathbf{X}^* \in \omega_i\right)\hat{P}(\omega_i)}{\sum_{m=1}^{M} \hat{P}\left(C_j(\mathbf{X}^*) = \omega_i | \mathbf{X}^* \in \omega_m\right)\hat{P}(\omega_m)} \quad j = 1,..,K \tag{10}$$

where $\hat{P}(C_j(\mathbf{X}^*) = \omega_i | \mathbf{X}^* \in \omega_i)$ is the probability that the classifier C_j classifies the patterns belonging to class ω_i correctly. This probability can be estimated by averaging the posterior probabilities $\hat{P}_j(\omega_i | \mathbf{X}_n \in \omega_i)$ on the "neighbouring" patterns X_n belonging to the class ω_i.

The prior probabilities $\hat{P}(\omega_i)$ can be estimated as the fraction of neighbouring patterns that belong to class ω_i. Therefore, CLA can be estimated as follows:

$$CLA_j(\mathbf{X}^*) = \frac{\sum_{\mathbf{X}_n \in \omega_i} \hat{P}_j(\omega_i \mid \mathbf{X}_n) \cdot W_n}{\sum_{m=1}^{M} \sum_{\mathbf{X}_n \in \omega_m} \hat{P}_j(\omega_i \mid \mathbf{X}_n) \cdot W_n} \tag{11}$$

where, as in equation (9), the terms W_n take into account the distances of the neighbouring patterns from the test pattern.

3.4 A DCS Algorithm

In the following, a dynamic classifier selection algorithm using either of the two above methods for estimating CLA is described.

Input parameters: test pattern X*, classification labels of validation data, size of neighbourhood, rejection threshold value, and selection threshold value

Output: classification of test pattern X*

STEP 1: If all the classifiers assign X* to the same data class, then the pattern is assigned to this class

STEP 2: Compute $CLA_j(\mathbf{X}^*)$, $j = 1,...,K$

STEP 3: *If* $CLA_j(\mathbf{X}^*) <$ rejection-threshold *then* disregard classifier C_j

STEP 4: Identify the classifier C_m exhibiting the maximum value of $CLA_j(\mathbf{X}^*)$

STEP 5: For each classifier C_j, compute the following differences
$$d_j = \left[CLA_m(\mathbf{X}^*) - CLA_j(\mathbf{X}^*)\right]$$

STEP 6: *If* $\forall j, j \neq m, d_j >$ selection-threshold *then* Select Classifier C_m
else Select randomly one of the classifiers for which $d_j <$ selection-threshold

Step 3 is aimed at excluding from the selection process the classifiers that exhibit CLA values smaller than the given rejection threshold. Step 5 computes the differences d_l in order to evaluate the "reliability" of the selection of the classifier C_m. If all the differences are higher than the given selection threshold, then it is reasonably "reliable" that classifier C_m should correctly classify the test pattern X*. Otherwise, a random selection is performed among the classifiers for which $d_j <$ selection-threshold. Alternatively, random selection can be substituted by the combination of these classifiers.

4. Experimental Results

The used data set consists of a set of multisensor remote-sensing images related to an agricultural area near the village of Feltwell (UK). For our experiments, we selected 10,944 pixels belonging to five agricultural classes (i.e., sugar beets, stubble, bare soil, potatoes, and carrots) and randomly subdivided them into a training set (5,124 pixels), a validation set (582 pixels), and a test set (5,238 pixels). Each pixel was characterised by a fifteen-element "feature vector" containing brightness values in six optical bands and over nine radar channels. More details about the selected data set can be found in [22,23].

A classifier ensemble made up of the following four classifiers has been defined, i.e., three multilayer perceptron (MLP) neural networks with different architectures (see Table 1), and one k-nearest neighbour (k-nn) classifier. All the networks had respectively fifteen input units and five output units as the number of input features and data classes. With regard to the k-nn classifier, a "k" parameter value of twenty-one was used. Table 1 shows the classification accuracy provided by the four classifiers on the test set in terms of percentage classification accuracy and Kappa coefficient values.

Table 1. Percentage accuracy and Kappa coefficient values provided by the four classifiers. For each MLP network, the number of neurons per layer is given in brackets. The value of the "k" parameter used for the k-nn classifier is also given in brackets.

Classifier	% Accuracy	Kappa value
MLP neural network (15-30-15-5)	86.66	0.82
MLP neural network (15-7-7-5)	84.86	0.80
MLP neural network (15-15-5)	89.39	0.86
k-nn (k=21)	89.84	0.87

Table 2 shows the performances of the "a priori" and "a posteriori" selection methods, and that of the combination method based on the majority-voting rule. For the sake of comparison, the performances of the best individual classifier and the "oracle" are also shown. The "oracle" is the ideal selector that always chooses the classifier, if any, with the correct classification. Table 3 shows the values of the Zeta statistics related to the statistical significance of the differences in accuracy between our selection methods, the majority combination method, and the best individual classifier. Such differences are very significant, apart from the difference related to the a priori selection and the majority rule. (We recall that they exhibit degrees of significance higher than 95%, if the Zeta Statistics values are larger than 1.96, while the degrees of significance are higher than 99%, if the Zeta Statistics values exceed 2.58).

Table 2. Percentage accuracy and Kappa coefficient values of the two proposed DCS methods. For the sake of comparison, the performance of the majority rule, that of the best classifier, and that of the "oracle" are also shown. Obviously the Kappa coefficient value of the oracle could not be computed.

Classification Algorithm	% Accuracy	Kappa value
Best classifier	89.84	0.87
Oracle	94.01	-
A priori selection	92.23	0.90
A posteriori selection	93.22	0.91
Majority Rule	88.86	0.89

Concerning the size of the "neighbourhood" used for the classifier local accuracy estimates, we ran experiments with values ranging from one to fifty-one using the Euclidean distance metric. This neighbourhood was defined with respect to validation data. It is worth noticing that the accuracy of the DCS methods shown in Table 2 are the maximum accuracy, obtained by varying the size of the "neighbourhood" within the considered range. The DCS methods always outperformed the best classifier in the ensemble, thus suggesting that dynamic classifier selection is an effective approach for improving individual classifier accuracy. The accuracy provided by DCS was also better than that provided by the combination using the majority-voting rule. In our opinion this result shows that the assumption required by DCS is easier to satisfy than the error-diversity assumption required by the majority combination method. Finally, it should be pointed out that, in these experiments, the performances of our selection methods are reasonably close to those of the "oracle".

Table 3. Values of the Zeta statistics related to the statistical significance of the differences in accuracy between our selection methods, the majority combination method, and the best individual classifier.

Zeta Statistics	Best Classifier	Majority Rule
A priori selection	4.27	0.98
A posteriori selection	6.35	3.02

5. Conclusions

So far experimental results and qualitative arguments have motivated dynamic classifier selection. To the best of our knowledge, no previous work has dealt with understanding how and why DCS can produce improved classification results. In this paper, we started investigating this problem. We proposed a Bayesian framework for dynamic classifier selection, and defined the assumptions under which the optimal Bayes classifier can be obtained through the dynamic selection of non-optimal classifiers. Two classifier selection methods that derive from this framework have been described. Reported performances from the classification of remote-sensing images were better than those provided by the combination using the majority-voting rule. It is worth noting that the proposed framework also provides a theoretical basis for the classifier selection methods proposed by Woods et al. [20].

Among other things, our future work should investigate in greater detail the extent to which the hypotheses made in the framework can be satisfied in real applications. In addition, the impact of the data-set size on the proposed framework validity should also be studied. It is worth noting that we are currently developing other classifier selection methods [24].

Finally, it should be pointed out that dynamic selection is also used in the so-called "modular" approaches to the combination of neural networks [8]. Modular-combination methods focus on "task decomposition" and try to exploit specialist capabilities of individual nets by dynamic selection [25]. Differently, this paper deals with the so-called "ensemble combination" that is aimed to exploit the "complementarity" of the individual classifiers with respect to the entire classification task [8].

Acknowledgements

This work was supported by the Italian Space Agency, within the framework of the project "Metodologie innovative di integrazione, gestione, analisi di dati da sensori spaziali per l'osservazione della idrosfera, dei fenomeni di precipitazione e del suolo".

References

[1] Xu, L., Krzyzak A., and Suen C.Y., Methods for combining multiple classifiers and their applications to handwriting recognition, IEEE Trans. on Systems, Man, and Cyb. 22 (1992) 418-435.

[2] Lam, L. and Suen C.Y., Application of Majority Voting to Pattern Recognition: An Analysis of Its Behavior and Performance, IEEE Trans. on Systems, Man and Cybernetics-Part A 27 (1997) 553-568.

[3] Ho, T.K., Hull, J.J., and Srihari S.N., "Decision combination in multiple classifiers systems", IEEE Trans. on Pattern Analysis and Machine Intelligence, Vol.16, No.1, Jan. 1994, pp. 66-75.

[4] Battiti, R. and Colla A.M., Democracy in neural Nets: Voting Schemes for Classification, Neural Networks 7 (1994) 691-707.

[5] Kittler, J. , Hatef M., Duin R.P.W. and Matas J., On Combining Classifiers, IEEE Trans. on Pattern Analysis and Machine Intelligence 20 (1998) 226-239.

[6] Huang, Y.S. and Suen C.Y., A method of combining multiple experts for the recognition of unconstrained handwritten numerals, IEEE Trans. on Pattern Analysis and Machine Intelligence 17 (1995) 90-94.

[7] Wolpert, D.H., Stacked generalisation, Neural Networks 5 (1992) 241-259.

[8] Sharkey, A., Multi-Net Systems, Combining Artificial Neural Nets, Ensemble and Modular Multi-Net Systems, Springer-Verlag, 1999, pp. 1-27

[9]Breiman, L., Bagging Predictors, Machine Learning, 24(2), 1996, pp. 123-140

[10] Dietterich, T.G., An experimental comparison of three methods for constructing ensembles of decisions trees: Bagging, boosting, and randomization, Machine Learning, 2000, in press

[11]Suen C.Y., and Lam L., Multiple classifier combination methodologies for different output levels, Proc. of the First International Workshop on Multiple Classifier Systems (MCS2000), June 21-23 2000, Cagliari, Italy, Springer-Verlag Ed., in press

[12]Tumer K., and Ghosh J., Linear and order statistics combiners for pattern classification, Combining Artificial Neural Nets, Ensemble and Modular Multi-Net Systems, Springer-Verlag, 1999, pp. 127-157

[13] Hansen, L. K. and Salamon P., Neural network ensembles, IEEE Transactions on Pattern Analysis and Machine Intelligence 12 (1990) 993-1001.

[14]Kucheva L.I. et al., Is independence good for combining classifiers?, Proc. of ICPR2000, 15th Int. Conference on Pattern Recognition, Barcelona, Spain, September 3-8, 2000, in press

[15] Giacinto G., and Roli F., Design of effective neural network ensembles for image classification purposes, Image and Vision Computing Journal, 2000, in press

[16]Sharkey A., Sharkey N.E., Gerecke U., Chandroth G.O., The "test and select" approach to ensemble combination, Proc. of the First International Workshop on Multiple Classifier Systems (MCS2000), June 21-23 2000, Cagliari, Italy, Springer-Verlag Ed., in press

[17] Partridge, D. and Yates W.B., Engineering multiversion neural-net systems, Neural Computation 8 (1996) 869-893.

[18] Opitz, D.W. and Shavlik J.W., Actively searching for an effective neural network ensemble, Connection Science 8 (1996) 337-353.

[19] Giacinto, G., and Roli, F., "Adaptive Selection of Image Classifiers". Proc. of the 9th Int. Conference on Image Analysis and Processing, Lecture Notes in Computer Science 1310, Springer Verlag Ed., 1997, pp.38-45.

[20] Woods, K., Kegelmeyer, W.P., and Bowyer, K.: "Combination of multiple classifiers using local accuracyestimates". IEEE Trans. on Pattern Analysis and Machine Intelligence, 1997, 19(4), pp. 405-410.

[21] G. Giacinto, F. Roli, and G. Fumera, Selection of image classifiers, Electronics Letters, vol. 36, no. 05, 2nd March 2000, pp. 420-422

[22] Roli F., Multisensor image recognition by neural networks with understandable behaviour International Journal of Pattern Recognition and Artificial Intelligence 10 (1996) 887-917.

[23] Giacinto G, Roli F., Bruzzone L, Combination of neural and statistical algorithms for supervised classification of remote-sensing images, Pattern Recognition Letters, May 2000, vol. 21, no. 5, pp. 385-397

[24] G. Giacinto, F. Roli, and G. Fumera, Selection of Classifiers based on Multiple Classifier Behaviour, Proc. of the Joint international workshops on Syntactical and Structural Pattern Recognition & Statistical Pattern Recognition, Alicante, Spain, August 30 - September 1, 2000, in press

[25] R. A. Jacobs, M.I. Jordan, S.J. Nowlan and G.E. Hinton, "Adaptive Mixtures of Local Experts", *Neural computation* 3, 1995, 79-87

Boosting in Linear Discriminant Analysis

Marina Skurichina and Robert P.W.Duin

Pattern Recognition Group, Department of Applied Physics, Faculty of Applied Sciences,
Delft University of Technology, P.O. Box 5046, 2600GA Delft, The Netherlands
Phone: +(31) 15 2783538, FAX: +(31) 15 2786740
{marina, duin}@ph.tn.tudelft.nl

Abstract. In recent years, together with bagging [5] and the random subspace method [15], boosting [6] became one of the most popular combining techniques that allows us to improve a weak classifier. Usually, boosting is applied to Decision Trees (DT's). In this paper, we study boosting in Linear Discriminant Analysis (LDA). Simulation studies, carried out for one artificial data set and two real data sets, show that boosting might be useful in LDA for large training sample sizes while bagging is useful for critical training sample sizes [11]. In this paper, in contrast to a common opinion, we demonstrate that the usefulness of boosting does not depend on the instability of a classifier.

1 Introduction

When data are highly dimensional, having small training sample sizes compared to the data dimensionality, it may be difficult to construct a good single classification rule. Usually, a classifier, constructed on small training sets is biased and has a large variance. Consequently, such a classifier may have a poor performance [1]. In order to improve a weak classifier by stabilizing its decision, a number of techniques could be used, for instance, regularization [2] or noise injection [3].

Another approach is to construct many weak classifiers instead of a single one and combine them in some way into a powerful decision rule. Recently a number of such combining techniques have been developed. The most popular ones are bagging [5], boosting [6] and the random subspace method [15]. In bagging, one samples the training set, generating random independent bootstrap replicates [4], constructs the classifier on each of these and aggregates them by a simple majority vote in the final decision rule. In boosting, classifiers are constructed on weighted versions of the training set, which are dependent on previous classification results. Initially, all objects have equal weights, and the first classifier is constructed on this data set. Then, weights are changed according to the performance of the classifier. Erroneously classified objects get larger weights and the next classifier is boosted on the reweighted training set. In this way a sequence of training sets and classifiers is obtained, which are then combined by a simple majority vote or by a weighted majority vote in the final decision. In the random subspace method classifiers are constructed in random subspaces of the data feature space. Then, only classifiers with the zero classification error on the training set are combined by simple majority vote in the final decision rule.

Usually, bagging, boosting and the random subspace method are applied to DT's [7],[8],[9],[10],[15], where they often produce an ensemble of classifiers, which is superior to a single classification rule. However, these techniques may also perform

J. Kittler and F. Roli (Eds.): MCS 2000, LNCS 1857, pp. 190–199, 2000.
© Springer-Verlag Berlin Heidelberg 2000

well for other classification rules, than DT's. For instance, it was shown that bagging and boosting may be useful for perceptrons (see, e.g. [16]). It was demonstrated that bagging may be beneficial in LDA for small and critical training sample sizes (when the number of training objects is comparable with data dimensionality) [11]. Our initial study [17] has shown that also boosting may be advantageous in LDA.

In this paper we intend to study the usefulness of boosting for linear classifiers and in particular to investigate its relation with the instability of classifiers. We consider the nearest mean classifier [12], the Fisher Linear Discriminant function (FLD) [12] and the regularized FLD [2]. This choice is made in order to observe many different classifiers with a dissimilar instability and, by that, to establish whether the usefulness of boosting depends on the classifier instability or on other classifier peculiarities. The chosen classification rules and their instability are discussed in section 4. One artificial data set and two real data sets representing the 2-class problem are used in our simulation study. They are described in section 3, but first a short description of the boosting algorithm is given in section 2. Simulation results on the performance of boosting in LDA are discussed in section 5. Conclusions are summarized in section 6.

2   The Boosting Algorithm

Boosting, proposed by Freund and Schapire [6], is a technique to combine weak classifiers, having a poor performance, in a strong classification rule with a better performance. As it was already mentioned before, in boosting, classifiers and training sets are obtained sequentially, in a strictly deterministic way. At each step, training data are reweighted in such way that incorrectly classified objects get larger weights in a new modified training set. By that, one actually maximizes margins between training objects. It suggests the connection between boosting and Vapnik's Support Vector Classifier (SVC) [7],[13], as objects obtaining large weights may be the same as the support objects. Boosting is organized by us in the following way.

1. Repeat for $b=1,2,...,B$.

a)   Construct   the   classifier $C^b(X*)$ on   the   weighted   version $X* = (w_1^b X_1, w_2^b X_2, ..., w_n^b X_n)$ of training data set $X = (X_1, X_2, ..., X_n)$, using weights w_i^b, $i=1,...,n$ ($w_i^b = 1$ for $b=1$).

b)   Compute   probability   estimates   of   the   error $err_b = \frac{1}{n}\sum_{i=1}^{n} w_i^b \xi_i^b$, $\xi_i^b = \begin{cases} 0, if \ X_i \ is \ classified \ correctly \\ 1, otherwise \end{cases}$, and $c_b = \frac{1}{2}\log\left(\frac{1-err_b}{err_b}\right)$.

c) If $0 < err_b < 0.5$, set $w_i^{b+1} = w_i^b \exp(-c_b \xi_i^b)$, $i=1,...,n$, and renormalize so that $\sum_{i=1}^{n} w_i^{b+1} = n$. Otherwise, set all weights $w_i^b = 1$, $i=1,...,n$, and restart.

2. Combine classifiers $C^b(X*)$ by the weighted majority vote with weights c_b to a final decision rule.

3   Data

One artificial data set and two real data sets are used for our experimental study. The first set is a 30-dimensional *correlated Gaussian data* set (*Data I*) constituted by two classes with equal covariance matrices. Each class consists of 500 vectors. The mean of the first class is zero for all features. The mean of the second class is equal to 3 for the first two features and equal to 0 for all other features. The common covariance matrix is a diagonal matrix with a variance of 40 for the second feature and a unit variance for all other features. The intrinsic class overlap (Bayes error) is 0.064. This data set is rotated using a 30×30 rotation matrix which is $\begin{bmatrix} 1 & -1 \\ 1 & 1 \end{bmatrix}$ for the first two features and the identity matrix for all other features.

Two real data sets are taken from the UCI Repository [14]. The first is the 34-dimensional *ionosphere* data set (*Data II*) with 225 and 126 objects belonging to the first and the second data class, respectively. The second is the 8-dimensional *diabetes* data set (*Data III*) consisting of 500 and 268 objects from the first and the second data class, respectively. These two data sets were also used in [8], when studying bagging and boosting for decision trees. The diabetes data set was also used when bagging and boosting were studied for LDA [8].

Training sets with 3 to 400, with 3 to 100 and with 3 to 200 objects per class are chosen randomly from a total set for the data I, II and III, respectively. The remaining data are used for testing. All experiments are repeated 50 times for independent training sets. In all figures the averaged results over 50 repetitions are presented. The standard deviations of the mean generalization errors for single and boosted linear classifiers are of the similar order for each data set. When increasing the training sample size, they are decreasing approximately from 0.015 to 0.004, from 0.014 to 0.007 and from 0.018 to 0.004 for the data I, II and III, respectively. When the mean generalization error of the boosted regularized FLD shows a peaking behaviour on the ionosphere data set (see Fig. 4), its standard deviation is about 0.03.

4   The Performance and the Instability of Linear Classifiers

In order to study a large group of linear classifiers and their instability, let us consider regularized classifiers in LDA.

The *Regularized Fisher Linear Discriminant* function (RFLD) [2] is defined as

$$g_{RFLD}(x) = \left[x - \frac{1}{2}(\overline{X}^{(1)} + \overline{X}^{(2)}) \right]' (S + \lambda I)^{-1} (\overline{X}^{(1)} - \overline{X}^{(2)}) ,$$

where the ridge estimate $S + \lambda I$ is used instead of the mean class covariance matrix S. One can see, that the RFLD represents a large family of linear classifiers (see Fig. 1). When $\lambda = 0$, one obtains the *Fisher Linear Discriminant* function (FLD) [12]

$$g_{FLD}(x) = \left[x - \frac{1}{2}(\overline{X}^{(1)} + \overline{X}^{(2)}) \right]' S^{-1} (\overline{X}^{(1)} - \overline{X}^{(2)}).$$

When $\lambda \to \infty$, the information concerning covariances between features is lost. Then, the classifier approaches the *Nearest Mean Classifier* (NMC) [12]

$$g_{NMC}(x) = \left[x - \frac{1}{2}(\overline{X}^{(1)} + \overline{X}^{(2)}) \right]' (\overline{X}^{(1)} - \overline{X}^{(2)}) ,$$

and the probability of misclassification may appreciably increase. Small values of the regularization parameter λ may stabilize the decision and improve the classifier performance. However, for very small λ, the effect of regularization will be neglible. In this case the RFLD performs similar to the *Pseudo Fisher Linear Discriminant* (PFLD) [12], having a high classification error around the critical training sample sizes, when the number of training objects is comparable to the data dimensionality.

In order to understand better, when boosting can be beneficial, it is useful to consider the instability of a classifier [11]. The classifier instability is measured by us by calculating the changes in classification of a training set caused by the bootstrap replicate of the original learning data set. Repeating this procedure several times on the training set (we did it 25 times) and averaging the results, an estimate of the classifier instability is obtained. The mean instability of linear classifiers (on 50 independent training sets) defined in this way is presented in Fig. 2. One can see that the instability of the classifier decreases when the training sample size increases. The instability and the performance of a classifier are correlated: more stable classifiers perform better than less stable ones. In this example, however, the performance of the NMC does not

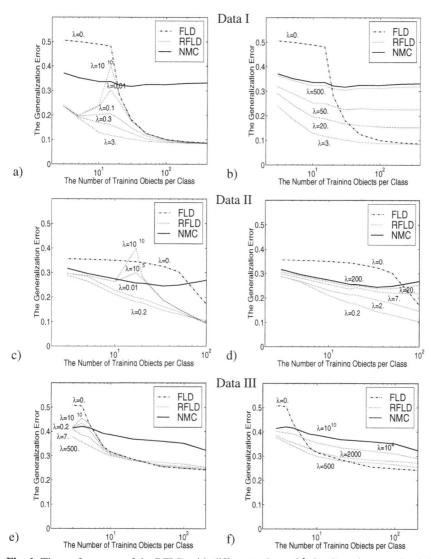

Fig. 1. The performance of the RFLD with different values of λ for Gaussian correlated data. (Data I) (a,b), for ionosphere data set (Data II) (c,d) and for diabetes data set (Data III) (e,f)

depend on the training sample size. In contrast to other classifiers, it remains a weak classifier for large training sample sizes, while its stability increases. Theory of boosting is developed for weak classifiers and large training sample sizes. Therefore, one may expect that boosting may be beneficial for the NMC.

5   Boosting for Linear Classifiers

Let us now consider the performance of boosting in LDA on the example of the NMC, the FLD and the RFLD with different values of regularization parameter λ.

The NMC. Boosting is useful for the NMC (see Fig. 3f, Fig. 4f and Fig. 5f). Especially it performs nicely for the Gaussian correlated data set, reducing the general-

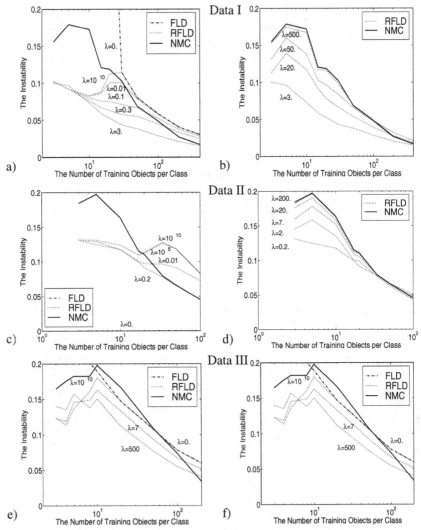

Fig. 2. The instability of the RFLD with different values of λ for Gaussian correlated data (Data I) (a,b), for ionosphere data set (Data II) (c,d) and for diabetes data set (Data III) (e,f)

ization error of a single NMC more than twice. In boosting, wrongly classified objects get larger weights. Mainly, they are objects on the border between classes. Therefore, boosting performs best for large training sample sizes, when the border between data classes becomes more informative. In this case, boosting the NMC performs similar to the linear SVC [13]. However, when the training sample size is large, the NMC is stable. It puts us on the observation that, in contrast to bagging, the usefulness of boosting may not depend directly on the stability of the classifier. It depends on the "quality" of the erroreously classified objects (usually, around the border between data classes) and on the ability of the classifier (its complexity) to distinguish them correctly.

The FLD. Simulation results (see Fig. 3a, Fig. 4a, Fig. 5a) show that boosting is

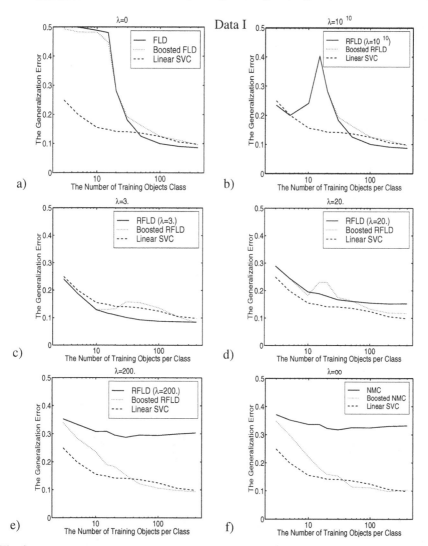

Fig. 3. The performance of the boosting (B=250) for linear classifiers on *Gaussian correlated* data (Data I). Boosting becomes useful, when increasing regularization and the RFLD becomes similar to the NMC

completely useless for the FLD. The performance and the stability of the FLD depends on the training sample size. For small training sample sizes, the classifier is very unstable and has a poor performance, as sample estimates of means have a large bias and a sample estimate of a common covariance matrix is singular or nearly singular. When increasing the training sample size, the sample estimates are less biased, and the classifier becomes more stable and performs better. In boosting, objects on the border between data classes get larger weights. By that, the number of actually used training objects decreases. When the training sample size is smaller than the data dimensionality, all or almost all objects lie on the border. Therefore, almost all training objects are

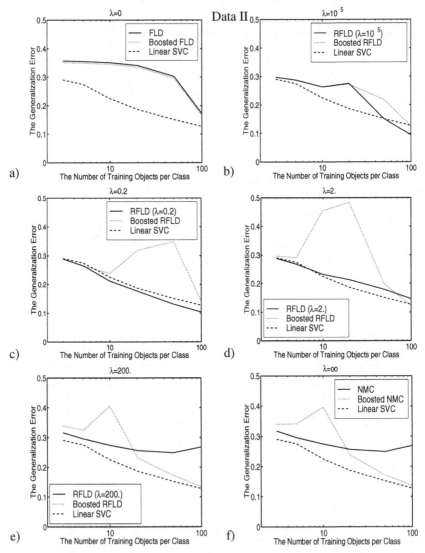

Fig. 4. The performance of boosting ($B=250$) for linear classifiers on *ionosphere* data (Data II). Boosting becomes useful, when increasing regularization and the RFLD becomes similar to the NMC

used at each step of the boosting algorithm. One gets many similar classifiers that per-form badly. Combining such classifiers does not improve the FLD. When the training sample size increases, the FLD performs better. In this case, boosting may perform similar to a single FLD (if the number of objects on the border is sufficiently large to construct a good FLD) or may worsen the situation (if the number of actually used training objects at each step of boosting is not sufficiently large to define a good FLD).

The PFLD. Boosting the PFLD, which is similar to the RFLD with a very small value of the regularization parameter λ, is also useless (see Fig. 3b, Fig. 4b, Fig. 5b). For the training sample sizes larger than the data dimensionality the PFLD, maximiz-

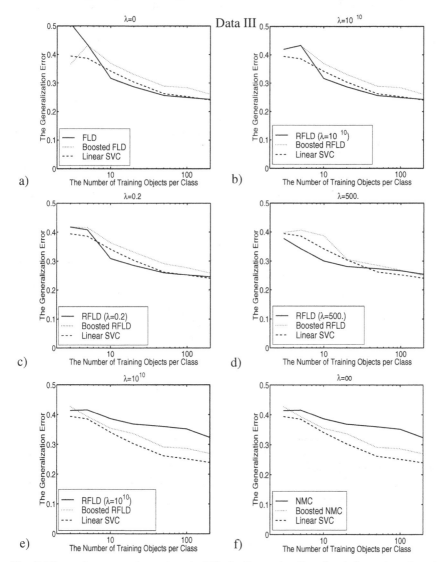

Fig. 5. The performance of boosting ($B=250$) for linear classifiers for *diabetes* data (Data III). Boosting becomes useful, when increasing regularization and the RFLD becomes similar to the NMC

ing the distance to all given samples, is equivalent to the FLD. For the training sample sizes smaller than the data dimensionality, however, the PFLD finds a linear subspace, which covers all the data samples. On this plane the PFLD estimates the data means and the covariance matrix, and builds a linear discriminant perpendicular to this subspace in all other directions for which no samples are given. Therefore, for these training sample sizes, the apparent error (the classification error on the training set) of the PFLD is always zero. Thus boosting is completely useless for the PFLD.

The RFLD. Considering the RFLD with different values of the regularization parameter λ, one can see that boosting is also not beneficial for these classifiers with exception of the RFLD with very large values of λ, which performs similar to the NMC. For small training sample sizes, when all or almost all training objects have similar weights at each step of the boosting algorithm, the modified training set is similar the original one, and the boosted RFLD performs similar to the original RFLD. For critical training sample sizes, the boosted RFLD may perform worse or even much worse (having a high peak of the generalization error) than the original RFLD. This is caused by two reasons. The first is that the modified training sets used in boosting usually contain less training objects than the original training set. Smaller training sets give more biased sample estimates of classes means and the covariance matrix than larger training sets. Therefore, the RFLD constructed on the smaller training set usually has a worse performance. An ensemble of the worse quality classifiers constructed on the smaller training sets may perform worse than the single classifier constructed on the larger training set. The second reason is that the objects on the border between data classes (which are getting larger weights in the boosting algorithm) have often other distribution than the original training set. Therefore, on such modified training set, the RFLD with certain value of the regularization parameter λ may perform differently than the same RFLD on the original training set. Regularization may not be sufficient, causing the generalization error peak similar to the RFLD with very small values of λ. However, on large training sample sizes, boosting may be beneficial for the RFLD, if the single RFLD performs worse than a linear support vector classifier. As a rule, it is the RFLD with very large values of λ. Thus, boosting is useful only for the RFLD with large values of the regularization parameter λ and for large training sample sizes.

6   Conclusions

Summarizing simulation results presented in the previous section, we can conclude the following:

Boosting may be useful in LDA for classifiers that perform poor on large training sample sizes. Such classifiers are the Nearest Mean Classifier and the Regularized Fisher's Linear Discriminant with large values of the regularization parameter λ, which approximates the NMC.

Boosting is useful only for large training sample sizes, if the objects on the border give a better representation of the distribution of the data classes than the original data classes distribution and the classifier is able (by its complexity) to distinguish them well.

It was shown theoretically and experimentally for DT's [7] that boosting increases the margins of the training objects. By that, boosting is similar to the maximum margin classifiers [13], based on the number of support vectors. In this paper, we have experimentally shown, that boosted linear classifiers may achieve the performance of the linear support vector classifier when training sample sizes are large compared with the data dimensionality.

As boosting is useful only for large training sample sizes, when classifiers are usually stable, the performance of boosting does not depend on the instability of the classifier.

The success of boosting depends on many factors including the training sample size, the choice of a weak classifier (the DT, the FLD, the NMC or other), the exact way how the training set is modified, the choice of the combining rule [17] and, finally, the data distribution. By that, it becomes quite difficult to establish universal criteria predicting the usefulness of boosting. Obviously, this question needs more investigation in future.

Acknowledgment

This work is supported by the Foundation for Applied Sciences (STW) and the Dutch Organization for Scientific Research (NWO).

References

1. Jain, A.K., Chandrasekaran, B.: Dimensionality and Sample Size Considerations in Pattern Recognition Practice. In: Krishnaiah, P.R., Kanal, L.N. (eds.): Handbook of Statistics, Vol. 2. North-Holland, Amsterdam (1987) 835-855
2. Friedman, J.H.: Regularized Discriminant Analysis. JASA **84** (1989) 165-175
3. An, G.: The Effects of Adding Noise During Backpropagation Training on a Generalization Performance. Neural Computation **8** (1996) 643-674
4. Efron, B., Tibshirani, R.: An Introduction to the Bootstrap. Chapman and Hall, New York (1993)
5. Breiman, L.: Bagging predictors. Machine Learning Journal **24**(2) (1996) 123-140
6. Freund, Y., Schapire, R.E.: Experiments with a New Boosting Algorithm. In: Machine Learning: Proceedings of the Thirteenth International Conference (1996) 148-156
7. Schapire, R.E., Freund, Y., Bartlett, P., Lee, W.: Boosting the Margin: A New Explanation for the Effectiveness of Voting Methods. The Annals of Statistics **26**(5) (1998) 1651-1686
8. Breiman, L.: Arcing Classifiers. Annals of Statistics, **26**(3) (1998) 801-849
9. Friedman, J., Hastie, T., Tibshirani, R.: Additive Logistic Regression: a Statistical View of Boosting. Technical Report (1999)
10. Dietterich, T.G.: An Experimental Comparison of Three Methods for Constructing Ensembles of Decision Trees: Bagging, Boosting, and Randomization. Machine Learning, to appear
11. Skurichina, M., Duin, R.P.W.: Bagging for Linear Classifiers. Pattern Recognition **31**(7) (1998) 909-930
12. Fukunaga, K.: Introduction to Statistical Pattern Recognition. Academic Press (1990) 400-407
13. Cortes, C., Vapnik, V.: Support-Vector Networks. Machine Learning **20** (1995) 273-297
14. Blake, C.L. & Merz, C.J. (1998). UCI Repository of machine learning databases [http://www.ics.uci.edu/~mlearn/MLRepository.html]. Irvine, CA: University of California, Department of Information and Computer Science
15. Ho, T.K.: The Random Subspace Method for Constructing Decision Forests. IEEE Transactions on Pattern Analysis and Machine Intelligence **20**(8) (1998) 832-844
16. Avnimelech, R., Intrator, N.: Boosted Mixture of Experts: An Ensemble Learning Scheme. Neural Computation **11** (1999) 483-497
17. Skurichina, M., Duin, R.P.W.: The Role of Combining Rules in Bagging and Boosting. Submitted to S+SSPR 2000, Alicante, Spain

Different Ways of Weakening Decision Trees and Their Impact on Classification Accuracy of DT Combination

Patrice Latinne[1], Olivier Debeir[2], and Christine Decaestecker[3]

[1] IRIDIA Laboratory, Université Libre de Bruxelles,
50, avenue Franklin Roosevelt cp 196/06
B-1050 Brussels, Belgium
platinne@ulb.ac.be
http://www.ulb.ac.be/polytech/march
[2] Information and Decision Systems, Université Libre de Bruxelles
50, avenue Franklin Roosevelt cp 165/57
B-1050 Brussels, Belgium
odebeir@ulb.ac.be
[3] Laboratory of Histopathology , Université Libre de Bruxelles,
808, route de Lennik cp 620
B-1070 Brussels, Belgium
cdecaes@ulb.ac.be

Abstract. Recent classifier combination frameworks have proposed several ways of weakening a learning set and have shown that these weakening methods improve prediction accuracy. In the present paper we focus on learning set sampling (Breiman's bagging) and random feature subset selections (Bay's Multiple Feature Subsets). We present a combination scheme labeled 'Bagfs', in which new learning sets are generated on the basis of both bootstrap replicates and selected feature subsets. The performances of the three methods (Bagging, MFS and Bagfs) are assessed by means of a decision-tree inducer (C4.5) and a majority voting rule. In addition, we also study whether the way in which weak classifiers are created has a significant influence on the performance of their combination. To answer this question, we undertook the strict application of the Cochran Q test. This test enabled us to compare the three weakening methods together on a given database, and to conclude whether or not these methods differ significantly. We also used the McNemar test to compare algorithms pair by pair. The first results, obtained on 14 conventional databases, show that on average, Bagfs exhibits the best agreement between prediction and supervision. The Cochran Q test indicated that the weak classifiers so created significantly influenced combination performance in the case of at least 4 of the 14 databases analyzed.

J. Kittler and F. Roli (Eds.): MCS 2000, LNCS 1857, pp. 200–209, 2000.
© Springer-Verlag Berlin Heidelberg 2000

1   Introduction

Many theoretical and experimental studies have shown that a multiple classifier system is an effective technique for reducing prediction errors [9,10,11,20,19].

These studies identify mainly three elements that characterize a set of classifiers:

- The representation of the input (what each individual classifier receives by way of input).
- The architecture of the individual classifiers (algorithms and parametrization).
- The way to cause these classifiers to take a decision together.

It can be assumed that a combination method is efficient if each individual classifier makes errors 'in a different way', so that it can be expected that most of the classifiers can correct the mistakes that an individual one does [1,19]. The term 'weak classifiers' refers to classifiers whose capacity has been reduced in some way so as to increase their prediction diversity. Either their internal architecture is simple (e.g., they use mono-layer perceptrons instead of more sophisticated neural networks), or they are prevented from using all the information available. Since each classifier sees different sections of the learning set, the error correlation among them is reduced. It has been shown that the majority vote is the best strategy if the errors among the classifiers are not correlated. Moreover, in real applications, the majority vote also appears to be as efficient as more sophisticated decision rules [2,13].

One method of generating a diverse set of classifiers is to upset some aspect of the training input of which the classifier is rather *unstable*. In the present paper, we study two distinct ways to create such weakened classifiers; i.e. learning set resampling (using the 'Bagging' approach [5]), and random feature subset selection (using 'MFS', a Multiple Feature Subsets approach [3]). Other recent and similar techniques are not discussed here but are also based on modifications to the training and/or the feature set [7,8,12,21].

Bagging is a popular solution for classification problems and consists of building bootstrap replicates of an original data set and of using these to run a learning algorithm. Ross Quinlan [15] has validated the bagging method with C4.5 decision-trees. Once the classifiers have been independently induced from the data (decision tree building), their predictions, made on an independent testing case, are combined with a majority vote rule. Breiman [5] argues that the main reason why bagging works is the *instability* of the chosen learning algorithm (i.e. decision trees or neural networks) with respect to the variations in the learning set introduced by bootstrapping.

MFS consists of training a given number of classifiers (R), with each having as its input a given proportion of features (k) picked *randomly* from the original set of f features with or without replacement. So, like bagging with training patterns, MFS attempts to use classifier instability (this time, with respect to feature selection) to generate a set of classifiers with uncorrelated errors [3].

2 Methods

In order to take qualitative advantages of both techniques (bagging and MFS), we investigated their association in the same architecture we labeled 'Bagfs'. For this purpose, we generated B bootstrap replicates of the learning set. In each replicate we independently sampled R subsets of f' features, randomly selected from amongst the f initial ones without replacement. We denoted $k = f'/f$ as the proportion of features in these R subsets. The proposed architecture thus has three parameters, k, B and R, to be set.

More generally, given L as a learning set (N cases described by f features), B bootstrap replicates $\{Bag_i\,; i = 1, ..., B\}$ are created. For each replicate Bag_i, R subsets $\{Fs_j\,; j = 1, ..., R\}$ of f' randomly chosen features (without replacement) are generated. This gives rise to $B * R$ new learning sets $\{Bag_i Fs_j\,; i = 1, ..., B, j = 1, ..., R\}$ to which the base learning algorithm is applied. This process generates $B * R$ decision trees. Let us suppose that we have to make predictions on T, an independent testing set (N' new cases described by the same features). For each pattern $x_n \in T$, for which the true class, c_n, is known ($n = 1, ..., N'$), the series of outputs of the $B * R$ decision trees are computed $\{\varphi_{ij}(x_n); i = 1, ..., B; j = 1, ..., R\}$ (i.e. the series of classes is predicted by the different trees). From this series our approach, Bagfs, computes the majority class (1) for all the $B * R$ predictions.

$$Majority\{\varphi_{ij}(x_n);\ i = 1, ..., B;\ j = 1, ..., R\} = \tilde{c}_n \qquad (1)$$

We were able to evaluate the prediction accuracy of Bagfs by comparing the estimated classes $\tilde{c}_n$ with the true ones c_n, $n = 1, ..., N'$, .

We tested the different algorithms (Bagging, MFS and Bagfs) with respect to Ross Quinlan's decision-tree inducer $C4.5$ *Release 8* [14] with its default values and its pruning method (All the decision trees were pruned).

3 Material

We applied bagging, MFS and Bagfs to 14 databases (see Table 1). 12 of these were downloaded from the UCI Machine Learning repository [4], i.e. iris, wine, glass, ionosphere, BUPA liver disorders, segmentation, new thyroid gland, waveform, satimage, Wisconsin breast-cancer , car evaluation and Pima Indian diabetes. We also included Ringnorm and Twonorm, two other databases used by Breiman in [6]. Wisconsin Breast-cancer and car evaluation are purely symbolic databases, while all the others are wholly continuous.

4 Experimental Design

In the present paper we investigate the interest of using different ways to weaken a learning set to create diverse decision-trees: learning set bootstrapping and multiple feature selections. This is illustrated by the three methods described

above, namely bagging, MFS and Bagfs. The comparisons were made with the
same number of classifiers. Firstly, we compared Bagfs ($B = 7$ and $R = 7$, labeled
Bag_7fs_7) to bagging with $B = 49$ (labeled Bag_{49}) and MFS with $R = 49$
(labeled MFS_{49}). We then built Bagfs with $B = 49$ and $R = 7$ using the
same 49 bootstrap replicates as Bag_{49}. Once again, we compared this latter
architecture to bagging with $B = 343$ (49*7) and MFS with $R = 343$. A stratified
3-fold cross-validation was performed for each experiment and database. For the
smallest databases (fewer than 2000 examples), 10 replications of the 3-fold
cross-validation were also performed to validate our estimates. Evaluations and
comparisons were made on the basis of the same learning and testing set resulting
from each stratified 3-fold cross-validation.

The degree-of-agreement coefficient (κ) was computed between the test pattern predictions and the corresponding true classes (supervision). κ was proposed
by Rosenfield and al. [16]. It represents an efficient accuracy measurement that
estimates the level of agreement (θ_1) after any chance agreement (θ_2) has been
discarded (see also Siegel et al. [18] and Rosner [17]):

$$\kappa = \frac{\theta_1 - \theta_2}{1 - \theta_2}$$

$\kappa = 1$ if the prediction agrees perfectly with the supervision, $\kappa = 0$ if this
agreement is obtained by chance, and $\kappa < 0$ if it is worse than that obtained by
chance.

In this paper, we use the Cochran Q test (see Siegel et al. [18]). This non-
parametric test provides an exact and strict method for testing whether k algorithms *differ significantly among themselves*. Furthermore, this test helped us
prove that the way in which the classifiers are weakened either has or does not
have a significant impact on the overall performance of the combination using
a majority vote. Given a testing set with N cases, let G_j be the number of
cases well-classified by algorithm j ($j = 1, \ldots, k$). L_i is the total number of algorithms that correctly classify the example i ($i = 1, \ldots, N$). If the null hypothesis
H_0 is true, i.e. if there is no difference between the algorithms' predictions, the
following statistic, Q, will be distributed approximately as χ^2 with $df = k - 1$:

$$Q = \frac{k(k-1) \sum_{j=1}^{k}(G_j - \overline{G})^2}{k \sum_{i=1}^{N} L_i - \sum_{i=1}^{N} L_i^2}$$

So, hypothesis H_0 is rejected if the value of Q is so great that the probability
associated with its occurrence when H_0 is true is equal to or less than the level
of significance ($\alpha = 1\%$). This means that the good prediction rate of at least
one algorithm differs significantly from the others.

We also compared the results given by the Cochran Q test with the results obtained with the McNemar non-parametric test. This latter, of which the Cochran

Q test is an extension, enabled us to compare the algorithms pair by pair. Given the two algorithms A and B, this test compared the number of cases misclassified by A, but not by B, with the number of cases misclassified by B, but not by A [18,17]. These non-parametric tests, Cochran and McNemar, are preferred to parametric ones (such as the commonly used t-test) because no assumption is required and they are independent of any evaluation measurement (error rate, degree of agreement kappa,...).

5   Results and Discussion

Table 1. Performance in term of κ degree-of-agreement estimates

Data Set	Training Set Size	# Feat.	# Class	Bagfs 7 × 7	MFS 49	Bag 49	Bagfs 49 × 7	MFS 343	Bag 343	k_{opt}	(f'/f)
glass	214	9	6	.653	.640	.640	.661	.653	.638	0.4	(4/9)
iris *	150	4	3	.918	.911	.914	.922	.911	.915	0.4	(2/4)
ionosphere	351	34	2	.851	.844	.813	.858	.850	.816	0.4	(13/34)
liver disorders	345	6	2	.359	.254	.378	.400	.243	.386	0.7	(5/6)
new-thyroid	215	5	3	.886	.843	.871	.873	.851	.872	0.3	(2/5)
breast-cancer-w	699	9	2	.922	.920	.879	.928	.926	.882	0.2	(2/9)
wine	178	13	3	.969	.972	.923	.980	.975	.933	0.3	(4/13)
segmentation *	210	18	7	.881	.862	.888	.896	.868	.890	0.6	(11/18)
car	1728	6	4	.805	.784	.817	.816	.783	.815	1	(6/6)
diabetes	768	8	2	.439	.413	.449	.450	.412	.461	0.7	(6/8)
ringnorm *	7400	20	2	.950	.948	.901	.965	.954	.909	0.4	(8/20)
twonorm *	7400	20	2	.936	.926	.926	.945	.940	.938	0.5	(10/20)
satimage	6435	36	6	.888	.890	.876	.892	.895	.880	0.5	(18/36)
waveform *	5000	21	3	.759	.758	.752	.784	.763	.761	0.5	(11/21)
Mean				**.801**	**.783**	**.787**	**.812**	**.787**	**.792**		

Table 1 shows the results of the estimated accuracy based on the degree of agreement, κ. The last two columns represent the proportions of selected features (k_{opt}) and the corresponding number of features. k_{opt} is the effective proportion of features obtained by maximizing κ when performing a 10-fold stratified cross-validation on each learning set of the global 3-fold cross-validation. We used this nested cross-validation process to keep one testing set independent of the data used for the training and tuning of the internal parameter, k. This nested cross-validation was applied to Bagfs and MFS, and for each database we identified the same k_{opt} value for these two algorithms (i.e. the k_{opt} value reported in Table 1).

The results in Table 1 show that Bagfs was a competitive method when used on these 14 databases. These results also point to the low level of improvement obtained by increasing the number of classifiers 7 times, from 49 to 343, for both the bagging and the MFS.

Table 2 for the 49-classifier architectures and Table 3 for the 343-classifier architectures summarize the results of a drastic comparison of all algorithms with respect to the Cochran Q and McNemar test statistics when they were performed on the 14 databases.

This comparison is drastic in the sense that, for the small databases (i.e. $N < 2000$), we performed 10 replications of the 3-fold cross-validations and concluded that if the Cochran H_0 hypothesis is rejected on 6 replications or more, then at least one algorithm will be significantly different from the others. For the large databases we performed only one test on the total set of predictions resulting from one 3-fold cross-validation. This strict procedure was the same for the McNemar rejection decision. In Tables 2 and 3 we report the sum of each total number of cases well-classified by each method (denoted G_j, in section 4) for each replication of the 3-fold cross-validation, for which H_0 was rejected.

Table 1 also shows the usefulness of the nested cross-validation process for determining k_{opt} values. Indeed, when k_{opt} is larger than 0.5 (in the case of 4 different databases), Bag_7Fs_7 systematically exhibits lower results than bagging (Bag_{49}). This both indicates that the MFS layer included in Bagfs is not useful, and agrees with the fact that a large number of features is required for better performance. Furthermore, in this case ($k_{opt} > 0.5$), MFS_{49} systematically shows a low level of accuracy, so confirming its minor usefulness.

Table 2. the Cochran and McNemar tests used to compare algorithms combining 49 classifiers: A zero value means that the hypothesis that the models are identical is not rejected; a bold value designates a database for which the models differ significantly with respect to our experimental design (A=Bag_{49}, B=MFS_{49} and C=Bag_7Fs_7). See details in the text.

Data Set	A	B	C	Cochran rejection	McNemar A/B	A/C	B/C
glass	0	0	0	0	-	-	-
Iris	0	0	0	0	-	-	-
ionosphere	633	657	656	2	-	-	-
liver disorders	729	652	722	3	A	-	-
new-thyroid	0	0	0	0	-	-	-
breast-cancer-w	5282	5399	5398	**8**	B	C	-
wine	492	521	521	3	-	-	-
segmentation	189	177	188	1	-	-	-
car	7929	7770	7884	5	A	-	C
diabetes	0	0	0	0	-	-	-
ringnorm	7033	7208	7214	**1**	B	C	-
twonorm	7125	7127	7164	**1**	-	C	C
satimage	5790	5863	5852	**1**	B	C	-
waveform	0	0	0	0	-	-	-

Table 3. The Cochran and McNemar tests used to compare algorithms combining 343 classifiers. A zero value means that the hypothesis that the models are identical is not rejected; a bold value designates a database for which the models differ significantly with respect to our experimental design (A=Bag_{343}, B=MFS_{343} and C=$Bag_{49}Fs_7$). See details in the text.

Data Set	A	B	C	Cochran rejection	McNemar A/B	A/C	B/C
glass	150	167	166	1	-	-	-
Iris	0	0	0	0	-	-	-
ionosphere	638	653	659	2	-	-	-
liver disorders	2205	1985	2227	**9**	A	-	C
new-thyroid	0	0	0	0	-	-	-
breast-cancer-w	5950	6078	6089	**9**	B	C	-
wine	668	700	703	4	-	-	-
segmentation	387	368	386	2	-	-	-
car	14233	13992	14240	**9**	A	-	C
diabetes	1174	1126	1175	2	-	-	-
ringnorm	7063	7229	7271	**1**	B	C	C
twonorm	0	0	0	0	-	C	-
satimage	5811	5888	5875	**1**	B	C	-
waveform	4205	4210	4279	**1**	-	C	C

Concluding this discussion, a method of selecting one of the compared algorithms is:

- If $k_{opt} > 0.5$, then MFS is not an appropriate way of weakening a classifier and should not be used.
- If $k_{opt} \leq 0.5$, then both bagging and MFS are adequate methods for improving classification accuracy with C4.5.

Moreover, whatever the k_{opt} may be, the Bagfs method has never featured significantly lower performance than any other. This model even performs significantly better than bagging and MFS on at least 4 databases (See McNemar test results). Furthermore, increasing the number of classifiers (from 49 to 343) seems more beneficial to Bagfs rather than the other two methods.

Why Bagfs works better can be explained by observing the influence on the global accuracy estimates of the induced diversity and error decorrelation between all the classifiers. Dietterich [7] recently used the κ index as a measurement of the 'diversity' between two classifier predictions. In this case, the κ index was computed on a confusion table based on the predictions made by the two classifiers.

We used a similar approach here, having κ as a measurement of accuracy and diversity. The results, obtained on the 14 databases, all lead to the same overall observations. To obtain an effective weak multiple classifier system, we expect to have a scatter plot where the dots are in the high diversity and low individual accuracy region. Figure 1 illustrates four representative diagrams for which the

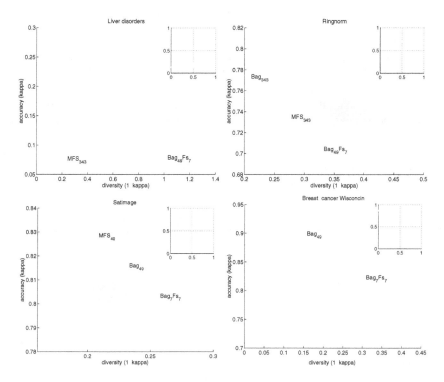

Fig. 1. Kappa - Kappa diagrams on four databases where the algorithms are significantly different with respect to the Cochran Q test. On the upper and right region is represented the same diagram showing the trade-off between diversity and accuracy on the same scale.

compared algorithms are significantly different with respect to Cochran test (See Tables 2 and 3). Each dot in Fig. 1 corresponds to a pair of classifiers included in the different combination schemes. Each possible pair is characterized by both the kappa index computed on the predictions of these two classifiers ($1 - \kappa$ is reported on the x coordinate as a measurement of the diversity of these classifiers) and the kappa index of agreement between prediction and supervision averaged over the two classifiers (reported on the y coordinate as a measurement of the accuracy of these classifiers). These figures show that individual Bagfs classifiers always exhibit a greater degree of diversity than bagging and MFS, and also a lower level of accuracy (each individual classifier is *weaker* on average).

6   Conclusion

This paper compares three methods: Breiman's bagging, Bay's MFS and a novel approach, labeled 'Bagfs', that mixes the first two, for generating multiple learning sets with C4.5 decision trees and the majority voting rule. Our aim is the strict application of a statistical method, the Cochran Q test, to investigate the significant differences between these ways of weakening decision trees and their impact on classification accuracy. The experimental results obtained on 14 conventional databases showed that these three models differed significantly on at least 4 databases with respect to the Cochran Q test. Furthermore, using the McNemar test of significance, we also showed that Bagfs never performed worse, and on at least 4 databases, even performed better than the other models combining the same number of classifiers. We use several representative databases where the models are significantly different with respect to the Cochran test to illustrate that individual Bagfs classifiers have a higher level of diversity and a lower level of accuracy than the other models. So, if the optimal proportion of selected features is not too large, Bagfs is able to exhibit the highest level of diversity between its components, and thus offers the highest degree of accuracy. This last conclusion also emphasizes the possible significant impact of associating two or more ways of weakening a classifier (bagging and MFS in this paper) to create diverse decision trees.

Acknowledgements

Patrice Latinne and Olivier Debeir are supported by a grant under an ARC (Action de Recherche Concertée) programme of the Communauté Française de Belgique. Christine Decaestecker is a Research Associate with the 'F.N.R.S' (Belgian National Scientific Research Fund).

References

1. Ali and Pazzani. Error reduction through learning multiple descriptions. *Machine Learning*, 24:173–202, 1996.
2. R. Battiti and A.M. Colla. Democracy in neural nets : voting schemes for classification. *Neural Networks*, 7(4):691–708, 1995.
3. Stephen D. Bay. Nearest neighbor classification from multiple feature subsets. In *Proceedings of the International Conference on Machine Learning*, Madison, Wisc., 1998. Morgan Kaufmann Publishers.
4. C. Blake, E. Keogh, and C.J. Merz. Uci repository of machine learning databases. [http://www.ics.uci.edu/ mlearn/MLRepository.html]. Irvine, CA: University of California, Department of Information and Computer Science, 1998.
5. Leo Breiman. Bagging predictors. *Machine Learning*, 24, 1996.
6. Leo Breiman. Bias, variance and arcing classifiers. Technical report, Statistics department. University of California, 1996.
7. Thomas G. Dietterich. An experimental comparison of three methods for constructing ensembles of decision trees : bagging, boosting and randomization. *Machine Learning*, pages 1–22, 1999.
8. Ioav Freund and Robert E. Schapire. Experiments with a new boosting algorithm. In *In Prod. of the 13th International Conference on Machine Learning*, pages 146–148. Morgan Kaufmann, 1996.

9. T.K Ho, Jonathan J. Hull, and Sargur N. Srihari. Decision combination in multiple classifier systems. *IEEE Transactions on Pattern Analysis and Machine Intelligence*, 16(1):66–75, 1994.
10. Y. S. Huang and Ching Y. Suen. A method of combining multiple experts for the recognition of unconstrained handwritten numerals. *IEEE Transactions on Pattern Analysis and Machine Intelligence*, 17(1), 1995.
11. Joseph Kittler. Combining classifiers : a theoretical framework. *Pattern Analysis and Applic.*, 1:18–27, 1998.
12. Ron Kohavi and Clayton Kunz. Option decision trees with majority votes. In *Proceedings of the Fourtheeth International Conference on Machine Learning*, pages 161–169, San Francisco, CA, 1997. Morgan Kaufmann.
13. Louisa Lam and Ching Y. Suen. Application of majority voting to pattern recognition : an analysis of its behavior and performance. *IEEE tr. on systems, man and cybernetics*, 27(5), 1997.
14. J.R. Quinlan. *C4.5 : Programs For Machine Learning*. Morgan Kaufmann Publishers, San Mateo, California, 1993.
15. J.R. Quinlan. Bagging, boosting, and c4.5. In *Proceedings of the Thirteenth National Conference on Artificial Intelligence*, pages 725–730, 1996.
16. G.H. Rosenfield and K. Fitzpatrick-Lins. A coefficient of agreement as a measure of thematic classification accuracy. *Photogrammetric Engineering and Remote Sensing*, 52(2):223–227, February 1986.
17. Bernard Rosner. *Fundamentals of Biostatistics*. Duxbury Press (ITP), Belmont, CA, USA, 4th edition, 1995.
18. S. Siegel and N.J. Castellan. *Nonparametric Statistics for the behavioral sciences*. McGraw-Hill, second edition, 1988.
19. K. Tumer and J. Ghosh. Classifier combining : analytical results and implications. In *Proceedings of the National Conference on Artificial Intelligence*, Portland, OR, 1996.
20. L. Xu, A. Krzyzak, and Ching Y. Suen. Methods of combining multiple classifiers and their applications to handwriting recogntion. *IEEE tr. on systems, man and cybernetics*, 22(3):418–435, 1992.
21. Zijian Zheng. Generating classifier committees by stochastically selecting both attributes and training examples. In *Proceedings of the 5th Pacific Rim International Conferences on Artificial Intelligence (PRICAI'98)*, pages 12–23. Berlin: Springer-Verlag, 1998.

Applying Boosting to Similarity Literals for Time Series Classification

Juan J. Rodríguez Diez and Carlos J. Alonso González

Departamento de Informática
Grupo de Sistemas Inteligentes
Universidad de Valladolid, Spain
{juanjo,calonso}@infor.uva.es

Abstract. A supervised classification method for temporal series, even multivariate, is presented. It is based on boosting very simple classifiers, which consists only of one literal. The proposed predicates are based in similarity functions (i.e., euclidean and dynamic time warping) between time series.

The experimental validation of the method has been done using different datasets, some of them obtained from the UCI repositories. The results are very competitive with the reported in previous works. Moreover, their comprehensibility is better than in other approaches with similar results, since the classifiers are formed by a weighted sequence of literals.

1 Introduction

Multivariate time series classification is useful in domains such as biomedical signals [12], continuous systems diagnosis [2] and data mining in temporal databases [5]. This problem can be tackled extracting features of the series, through some kind of preprocessing, and using some conventional machine learning method. Nevertheless, this approach has several drawbacks [11], these techniques are usually *ad hoc* and domain specific, there are several heuristics applicable to temporal domains that are difficult to capture by a preprocess and the obtained descriptions using these features can be hard to understand. The design of specific machine learning methods for the induction of temporal series classifiers allows the construction of more comprehensible classifiers in a more efficient way.

In multivariate time series classification, each example is composed by several time series. Each time series is an attribute of the examples, and normally they are called variables, because they are attributes that vary with time. We propose a simple, although effective, technique for temporal series classification based on boosting [18] literals relative to the results of similarity function between time series.

The rest of the paper is organised as follows. The base classifiers are described in section 2. Boosting these classifiers is explained in section 3. Section 4 presents the experimental validation. Finally, section 5 concludes.

J. Kittler and F. Roli (Eds.): MCS 2000, LNCS 1857, pp. 210–219, 2000.
© Springer-Verlag Berlin Heidelberg 2000

2   Similarity-Based Classifiers

Several machine learning methods, such as instance-based learning, are based on
the use of distances, similarity functions, between examples. Nevertheless, the
distance between examples can also be used, as new attributes of each example, in inductive methods such as decision trees and rule inducers. In our case,
multivariate time series, we use predicates with the following form:

$$<distance>\_le(\text{ Example, Reference, Variable, Value })$$

which is true if the $<distance>$, for one Variable of the examples, between the
Example considered and another Reference example is less or equal (_le) than
$<Value>$.

The predicate euclidean_le uses the *euclidean* distance. It is defined, for two
univariate series s and t as: $\sqrt{\sum_{i=1}^{n}(s_i - t_i)^2}$. Its execution time is $O(n)$

2.1   Dynamic Time Warping

Dynamic Time Warping (DTW) aligns a time series to another reference series
in a way that a distance function is minimized, using a dynamic programming
algorithm [5]. If the two series have n points, the execution time is $O(n^2)$. The
predicate dtw_le uses the minimized value obtained from the DTW as a similarity
function between the two series.

2.2   Selection of Literals

Given a collection of examples, the best literal must be selected according to
some criterion. If there are e examples, v variables in each example and $d(n)$ is
the time necessary for calculating the distance between two series with n points
(n for the euclidean distance, n^2 for DTW), the best literal for a given reference
example can be calculated in $O(ve\,d(n) + ve\lg e)$. The time for calculating the
distance between the reference to the rest of examples is $O(ev\,d(n))$. The time
necessary for ordering the distances to the reference example and selecting the
best value according to the criterion is $O(ve\lg e)$. If r reference examples are
considered then the necessary time is $O(rve(d(n) + \lg e))$.

3   Boosting

At present, an active research topic is the use of *ensembles* of classifiers. They are
built by generating and combining base classifiers, with the aim of improving the
accuracy with respect to the base classifiers. One of the most popular methods
for creating ensembles is boosting [18], a family of methods, AdaBoost being the
most representative example. They work assigning a weight to each example.
Initially, all the examples have the same weight. In each iteration a base classifier
is constructed, according to the distribution of weights. Afterwards, the weights

Table 1. Example of classifier. It corresponds to the class upward of the control charts dataset. It shows the literal, the number and total weight of the covered examples and the error and weight of the individual classifier. The number of positive and negative examples in the training set are 80 and 420, respectively.

literal	examples $\oplus$	examples $\ominus$	weights $\oplus$	weights $\ominus$	literal error	literal weight
euclid_le(E, upward_90, x, 52.027)	35	7	0.073	0.015	0.108	1.054
euclid_le(E, upward_77, x, 107.494)	80	80	0.474	0.153	0.153	0.857
euclid_le(E, upward_30, x, 43.538)	24	4	0.101	0.015	0.193	0.714
not euclid_le(E, downward_42, x, 179.359)	29	49	0.337	0.116	0.303	0.417
euclid_le(E, upward_30, x, 67.343)	75	62	0.506	0.246	0.289	0.450
not euclid_le(E, increasing_89, x, 45.122)	74	354	0.401	0.190	0.220	0.633
not euclid_le(E, increasing_8, x, 50.418)	75	328	0.309	0.221	0.238	0.583
euclid_le(E, upward_26, x, 52.977)	10	2	0.071	0.008	0.174	0.777
euclid_le(E, upward_100, x, 68.076)	71	50	0.480	0.156	0.195	0.710
not euclid_le(E, increasing_70, x, 51.274)	61	325	0.294	0.152	0.257	0.532

are readjusted according to the result of the example in the base classifier. The final result is obtained combining the weighted votes of the base classifiers.

Inspired by the good results of works using ensembles of very simple classifiers [9], sometimes named *stumps*, we have opted for base classifiers consisting only of one literal. Table 1 shows one of these classifier. The reasons for using so simple base classifiers are:

- Ease of implementation. In fact, it is simpler to implement a boosting algorithm than a decision tree or rule inducer. A first approximation to the induction of rules for time series classification is described in [15].
- Comprehensibility. It is easier to understand a sequence of weighted literals than a sequence of weighted decision trees or rules.

The criterion used for selecting the best literal is to select the one with less error, relative to the weights. In each iteration r reference examples are randomly selected (it is possible to use only positive reference examples or positive and negative). If i is the number of iterations in boosting, the worst number of reference examples considered is $\min(ir, e)$. Hence, the execution time for the boosting process is $O(\min(ir, e)ve\,d(n) + irve\lg e)$.

Multiclass problems. The simpler AdaBoost algorithm is defined for binary classifications problems [18], although there are extensions for multiclass problems [19]. In our case the base classifiers are also binary (only one literal) and it excludes some techniques for handling multiclass problems. We have used a simple approximation: the problem is reduced to several binary classification problems, as many as classes, which decide if an example is, or is not, of the corresponding class. Every binary problem is solved independently using boosting.

Table 2. Characteristics of the datasets

Dataset	Classes	Examples	Points
CBF	3	798	128
Control charts	6	600	60
Waveform	3	900	21
Wave + noise	3	900	40

The advantages of using boosting for binary problems are that it is always possible to find a literal with an error less or equal than 0.5, necessary for the boosting algorithm, since the problem is binary, and that the results are more comprehensible because they are organised by classes.

To classify a new example, it is evaluated by all the binary classifiers. If only one of them classifies it as positive, then the example is assigned to the corresponding class. If the situation is not so idyllic, we can consider that the multiclass classifier is not able to handle this example. This is a very pessimistic attitude. In the experiments, the classification error obtained with this point of view is named *maximum error*.

When using boosting in a binary problem, the result is positive or negative depending of the sign of the sum of the results of the individual classifiers, conveniently weighted. In a multiclass problem, if we have conflicts among several of the binary classifiers we use these sums of weights, normalised to $[-1, 1]$, to select the winner. In the experiments, the error obtained with this method is called *combined error*.

4   Experimental Validation

4.1   Datasets

The characteristics of the datasets are sumarised in table 2. The main criterion for selecting them has been that the number of examples available were big enough, to ensure that the results were reliable.

Waveform. This dataset was introduced by [7]. The purpouse is to distinguish between three classes, defined by the evaluation in $1, 2 \ldots 21$, of the following functions:

$$x_1(i) = uh_1(i) + (1 - u)h_2(i) + \epsilon(i)$$
$$x_2(i) = uh_1(i) + (1 - u)h_3(i) + \epsilon(i)$$
$$x_3(i) = uh_2(i) + (1 - u)h_3(i) + \epsilon(i)$$

where $h_1(i) = \max(6 - |i - 7|, 0)$, $h_2(i) = h_1(i - 8)$, $h_3(i) = h_1(i - 4)$, u is a uniform aleatory variable in $(0, 1)$ and $\epsilon(t)$ follows a standard normal distribution.

We use the version from the UCI ML Repository [6]. In the experiments the first 300 examples of each class were used, the total number of examples available in the dataset is 5000.

Wave + Noise. This dataset is generated in the same way than the previous one, but 19 points are added at the end of each example, with mean 0 and variance 1. Again, we used the first 300 examples of each class of the corresponding dataset from the UCI ML Repository.

Cylinder, Bell and Funnel (CBF). This is an artificial problem, introduced by Saito [16]. The learning task is to distinguish between these three classes: cylinder (c), bell (b) or funnel (f). Examples are generated using the following functions:

$$c(t) = (6 + \eta) \cdot \chi_{[a,b]}(t) + \epsilon(t)$$
$$b(t) = (6 + \eta) \cdot \chi_{[a,b]}(t) \cdot (t - a)/(b - a) + \epsilon(t) \qquad \chi_{[a,b]} = \begin{cases} 0 \text{ if } t < a \vee t > b \\ 1 \text{ if } a \leq t \leq b \end{cases}$$
$$f(t) = (6 + \eta) \cdot \chi_{[a,b]}(t) \cdot (b - t)/(b - a) + \epsilon(t)$$

η and $\epsilon(t)$ are obtained from a standard normal distribution $N(0, 1)$, a is an integer obtained from a uniform distribution in $[16, 32]$ and $b-a$ is another integer obtained from another uniform distribution in $[32, 96]$. For ease of comparison with previous results, 266 examples of each class were generated.

Control Charts. In this dataset there are six different classes of control charts, synthetically generated by the process in [1]. Each time series is of length n, and is defined by $y(t)$, with $1 \leq t \leq n$:

1. Normal: $y(t) = m + s\,r(t)$. Where $m = 30$, $s = 2$ and $r(t)$ is a random number in $[-3, 3]$.
2. Cyclic: $y(t) = m + s\,r(t) + a\sin(2\pi t/T)$. a and T are in $[10, 15]$.
3. Increasing: $y(t) = m + s\,r(t) + gt$. g is in $[0.2, 0.5]$.
4. Decreasing: $y(t) = m + s\,r(t) - gt$.
5. Upward: $y(t) = m + s\,r(t) + x\,k(t)$. x is in $[7.5, 20]$ and $k(t) = 0$ before time t_0 and 1 after this time. t_0 is in $[n/3, 2n/3]$.
6. Downward: $y(t) = m + s\,r(t) - x\,k(t)$.

The data used was obtained from the UCI KDD Archive [4]. It contains 100 examples of each class, with 60 points in each example.

4.2   Results

The experiments were performed using 50 iterations in boosting and with 20 reference examples (10 positive, 10 negative) in each iteration. Three settings were used for each dataset: using the euclidean distance, DTW and using the two literals. The results for each dataset and setting were obtained using five five-fold stratified cross-validation. Table 3 and figure 1 resume the results. The table also shows the standard deviation for the 50 iterations: σ_{25} is the standard

Table 3. Experimental results. For each dataset and distance, the first column shows the maximum error and the second one the combined error, both in percentage. In boldface, the best result. The standard deviation, for the 50 iterations, is shown in the rows σ_5 and σ_{25}.

	Iter.	Wave		Wave + Noise		CBF		Control	
Euclidean	1	41.20	27.73	41.29	30.27	33.43	22.50	39.83	22.20
	5	33.13	17.71	36.96	19.38	19.74	10.35	17.30	5.77
	10	27.33	14.91	31.53	16.93	15.09	7.77	10.47	3.17
	15	25.13	14.73	28.91	15.96	12.20	6.44	8.13	2.10
	20	23.78	14.33	27.93	15.49	10.83	6.11	5.80	1.80
	25	23.15	14.04	27.11	15.22	9.88	5.46	4.53	1.57
	30	22.60	13.98	26.82	15.33	8.75	4.71	3.90	1.60
	35	22.51	13.87	25.78	**15.02**	8.25	4.56	3.57	1.40
	40	21.76	13.67	25.44	15.20	7.57	4.46	**2.73**	1.27
	45	21.82	13.51	25.29	15.93	7.17	4.31	2.83	1.27
	50	**21.31**	**13.44**	**24.93**	15.13	**6.72**	**4.11**	2.80	**1.17**
	σ_5	0.69	0.47	1.19	0.72	0.36	0.26	0.38	0.12
	σ_{25}	2.95	2.23	2.93	2.77	1.77	1.80	1.68	1.23
DTW	1	39.67	28.58	44.31	31.51	20.73	12.90	18.17	15.97
	5	39.20	23.29	40.64	24.64	5.69	2.46	6.93	1.50
	10	35.49	21.33	37.04	21.93	3.63	1.33	3.97	0.73
	15	33.67	20.09	35.60	20.71	2.35	0.93	2.77	0.63
	20	31.98	19.64	34.00	20.29	1.78	0.65	2.13	0.60
	25	30.91	19.13	32.69	19.07	1.58	0.63	2.00	0.63
	30	30.31	18.76	32.47	19.20	1.45	0.60	1.73	0.67
	35	29.93	18.07	31.71	19.02	1.23	0.45	1.60	0.57
	40	28.89	18.04	31.27	19.16	1.10	0.43	1.53	**0.53**
	45	28.53	18.07	30.60	**18.64**	**0.93**	0.43	1.43	**0.53**
	50	**28.22**	**17.73**	**30.31**	18.78	0.98	**0.40**	1.27	0.53
	σ_5	0.48	0.91	1.22	1.33	0.11	0.16	0.38	0.08
	σ_{25}	3.42	2.34	2.91	2.72	0.81	0.54	1.02	0.76
Euclidean + DTW	1	38.00	27.22	40.78	29.22	20.48	13.14	17.17	15.07
	5	32.11	17.62	36.16	18.91	5.74	2.25	6.26	1.93
	10	27.78	14.98	31.38	17.24	3.30	1.10	4.20	1.07
	15	26.29	14.56	28.69	15.76	1.85	0.80	3.13	0.83
	20	25.27	13.93	27.62	15.60	1.55	0.60	2.73	0.73
	25	24.69	14.04	26.87	15.47	1.15	0.55	1.97	0.73
	30	24.78	14.00	26.29	15.44	1.00	0.42	1.80	0.80
	35	23.29	13.96	25.67	15.58	0.88	0.42	1.83	**0.67**
	40	23.24	**13.76**	25.02	15.31	0.83	0.40	1.70	0.70
	45	23.09	14.11	24.93	15.18	0.70	**0.35**	**1.53**	0.70
	50	**22.78**	13.98	**24.76**	15.07	**0.68**	0.40	1.60	0.73
	σ_5	0.59	0.73	0.63	1.26	0.17	0.10	0.54	0.33
	σ_{25}	3.10	2.67	2.96	2.35	0.62	0.47	1.34	1.03

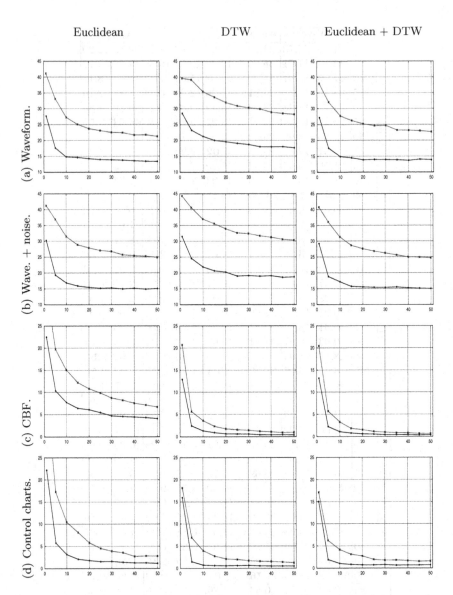

Fig. 1. Graphs of the results for the different datasets. For each graph, the maximum and combined errors are plotted.

deviation of the 25 executions, and σ_5 is the standard deviation of the 5 means obtained from each cross validation.

Globally, we can highlight the good evolution of the errors for each dataset with the number of iterations in the boosting process. In most of the cases the best values are in the last iteration, and in the rest of the cases the results for the last iteration are not far from the results for the best iteration. Another remarkable point is the differences between the different settings. In the first two cases the euclidean performs much better than DTW, and in the last two cases the situation is the opposite. The simultaneous use of the two literals gives results that are always nearer to the best case using only one literal than to the worst case.

Waveform. In this case, the results are much better using euclidean than using DTW, since in the definition of the dataset all the randomness is in the vertical axis, and none in the horizontal axis.

The best previously published result, to our knowledge, for this dataset is an error of 15.90 [16], using 100 training examples and 1000 test examples, although the results reported after averaging 10 times gives a result of 16.16 [17]. The error of an optimal Bayes classifier on this dataset is approximately of 14 [7].

Since our results using the euclidean distance (with or without DTW) are better than the optimal Bayes classifier, the experiments were repeated, using only the euclidean distance, in a more difficult setting. First, all the available examples (5000) were used, instead of selecting the first 300 of each class (several works, see below, use 300 examples in total). Again, five five-fold stratified cross-validaton was used, but with the difference that 1 fold was used for learning and 4 for validation, instead of using 4 for learning and 1 for validation. The results with this setting were 23.00 for the maximum error (σ_5: 0.35, σ_{25}: 0.87) and 14.86 for the combined error (σ_5: 0.19, σ_{25}; 0.53).

This dataset is frequently used for testing classifiers. It has also been tested with boosting (and other methods of combining classifiers), over the raw data, in different works [14, 10, 20, 8]. The best results we know for this dataset of other authors is an error of 15.21 [8] These results were obtained using base classifiers, trees, much more complex than out base classifiers (similarity literals).

Wave + Noise. Again, the results of the euclidean are better than the results of DTW. The best result achieved for the combined error is 15.02 using the euclidean distance in the iteration 35, although the best value using the two literals, 15.07 is very close. Again, the error of an optimal Bayes classifier on this dataset is of 14. This dataset was tested with bagging, boosting and variants over MC4 (similar to C4.5) [3], using 1000 examples for training and 4000 for test, and 25 iterations. Although their results are in graphs, it seems that their best error is approximately 17.5.

Cylinder, bell and funnel. The best result, to our knowledge, previously published, with this dataset is an error of 1.9 [11], using 10 fold cross validation.

From the iteration 10, the results using DTW (with or without euclidean), shown in table 3 are better than this result, and from the iteration 15 the results are smaller than 1. Moreover, even the maximum error is always under 1.8 from the iteration 20. In this dataset DTW greatly improves the classifier, which could be expected due to the temporal displacement shown by examples of the same class.

Control charts. The best result is obtained using only DTW, in the iteration 40 . . . 50, with an error of 0.53. From the iteration 10, all the values are less than 0.75. The unique results we know with this dataset are for similarity queries [1], and not for supervised classification. To check if this dataset was trivial, we tested it with C4.5 [13], over the raw data, obtaining an averaged error of 8.6 (using also five five-fold cross validation).

5   Conclusions and Future Work

A temporal series classification system has been presented. It is based on boosting very simple classifiers. The individual classifiers are formed only by one literal. The predicates used are based on the similarity between two examples. Two similarity functions has been used: euclidean and DTW, obtaining very different results. Nevertheless, no one is better than the other for all the considered datasets. The simultaneous use of the two kinds of predicates gives results nearly as good as using only the most adequate predicate for the dataset.

The results obtained, for accuracy, for each dataset are better than any other results known by the authors. Without significance tests we cannot conclude than out method is better than others for these datasets. The reasons for not doing so are that, unfortunately, there are not standard reference methods for time series classification and that the existent methods are not publicly available.

Acknowledgements

This work has been supported by the CYCIT project TAP 99–0344.

To the maintainers of the ML [6] and KDD [4] UCI Repositories. To David Aha for donating the *Wave* dataset and to Robert J. Alcock for donating the *Control Charts* dataset.

References

[1] Robert J. Alcock and Yannis Manolopoulos. Time-series similarity queries employing a feature-based approach. In 7th *Hellenic Conference on Informatics*, Ioannina, Greece, 1999.

[2] Carlos J. Alonso González and Juan J. Rodríguez Diez. A graphical rule language for continuous dynamic systems. In Masoud Mohammadian, editor, *Computational Intelligence for Modelling, Control and Automation.*, volume 55 of *Concurrent Systems Engineering Series*, pages 482–487, Amsterdam, Netherlands, 1999. IOS Press.

[3] Eric Bauer and Ron Kohavi. An empirical comparison of voting classification algorithms: Bagging, boosting and variants. *Machine Learning*, 36(1/2):105–139, 1999.

[4] Stephen D. Bay. The UCI KDD archive, 1999. http://kdd.ics.uci.edu/.

[5] D.J. Berndt and J. Clifford. Finding patterns in time series: a dynamic programming approach. In U.M. Fayyad, G. Piatetsky-Shapiro, P. Smyth, and R. Uthurusamy, editors, *Advances in Knowledge Discovery and Data Mining*, pages 229–248. AAAI Press /MIT Press, 1996.

[6] C.L. Blake and C.J. Merz. UCI repository of machine learning databases, 1998. http://www.ics.uci.edu/$\sim$mlearn/MLRepository.html.

[7] L. Breiman, J.H. Friedman, A. Olshen, and C.J. Stone. *Classification and Regression Trees*. Chapman & Hall, New York, 1993. Previously published by Wadsworth & Brooks/Cole in 1984.

[8] Thomas G. Dietterich. An experimental comparison of three methods for constructing ensembles of decision trees: bagging, boosting, and randomization. *Machine Learning*, 1999.

[9] Y. Freund and R. Schapire. Experiments with a new boosting algorithm. In *13th International Conference om Machine Learning (ICML-96)*, pages 148–156, Bari, Italy, 1996.

[10] Michael Harries. Boosting a strong learner: Evidence against the minimum margin. In Ivan Bratko and Saso Dzeroski, editors, *16th International Conference of Machine Learning (ICML-99)*. Morgan Kaufmann, 1999.

[11] Mohammed Waleed Kadous. Learning comprehensible descriptions of multivariate time series. In Ivan Bratko and Saso Dzeroski, editors, *Proceedings of the 16th International Conference of Machine Learning (ICML-99)*. Morgan Kaufmann, 1999.

[12] M. Kubat, I. Koprinska, and G. Pfurtscheller. Learning to classify biomedical signals. In R.S. Michalski, I. Bratko, and M. Kubat, editors, *Machine Learning and Data Mining*, pages 409–428. John Wiley & Sons, 1998.

[13] J.Ross Quinlan. *C4.5: programs for machine learning*. Machine Learning. Morgan Kaufmann, San Mateo, California, 1993.

[14] J.Ross Quinlan. Boosting, bagging, and C4.5. In *13th National Conference on Artificial Inteligence (AAAI'96)*, pages 725–730. AAAI Press, 1996.

[15] Juan J. Rodríguez Diez and Carlos J. Alonso González. Time series classification through clauses restricted to literals on intervals. In Ana M. García Serrano, Ramón Rizo, Serafín Moral, and Francisco Toledo, editors, *8th Conference of the Spanish Association for Artificial Intelligence (CAEPIA'99)*, pages 125–132, Murcia, Spain, November 1999. In spanish.

[16] Naoki Saito. *Local Feature Extraction and Its Applications Using a Library of Bases*. PhD thesis, Department of Mathematics, Yale University, 1994.

[17] Naoki Saito and Ronald R. Coifman. Local discriminant bases and their applications. *J.Mathematical Imaging and Vision*, 5(4):337–358, 1995.

[18] Robert E. Schapire. A brief introduction to boosting. In Thomas Dean, editor, *16th International Joint Conference on Artificial Intelligence (IJCAI-99)*, pages 1401–1406. Morgan Kaufmann, 1999.

[19] Robert E. Schapire and Yoram Singer. Improved boosting algorithms using confidence-rated predictions. In *11th Annual Conference on Computational Learning Theory (COLT-98)*, pages 80–91. ACM, 1998.

[20] Geoffrey I. Webb. MultiBoosting: A technique for combining boosting and wagging. *Machine learning*, 1999. In press.

Boosting of Tree-Based Classifiers
for Predictive Risk Modeling in GIS

Cesare Furlanello and Stefano Merler

ITC-irst,
38050 Trento, Italy
{furlan, merler}@itc.it
http://pan.itc.it:8008

Abstract. Boosting of tree-based classifiers has been interfaced to the Geographical Information System (GIS) GRASS to create predictive classification models from digital maps. On a risk management problem in landscape ecology, the performance of the boosted tree model is better than either with a single classifier or with bagging. This results in an improved digital map of the risk of human exposure to tick-borne diseases in Trentino (Italian Alps) given sampling on 388 sites and the use of several overlaying georeferenced data bases. Margin distributions are compared for bagging and boosting. Boosting is confirmed to give the most accurate model on two additional and independent test sets of reported cases of bites on humans and of infestation measured on roe deer. An interesting feature of combining classification models within a GIS is the visualization through maps of the single elements of the combination: each boosting step map focuses on different details of data distribution. In this problem, the best performance is obtained without controlling tree sizes, which indicates that there is a strong interaction between input variables.

1 Introduction

This paper introduces boosting of tree-based classifiers for predictive classification within a Geographical Information System (GIS). Firstly we have integrated bagging and now boosting within a GIS to develop accurate risk assessment models based on digital maps. The procedure is applied to determine the risk of human exposure to the tick *Ixodes ricinus*, the chief vector of Lyme disease and of other serious tick-borne illnesses in Europe. In this problem, the target function is the association between habitat patterns of environmental variables and the presence of *I. ricinus* as measured in sampling sites. We modeled this function with decision trees: either a single tree, bagging [1] or boosting were applied. For boosting we used the Adaboost algorithm [2], implemented as suggested in [3]. As the real spatial distribution of *I. ricinus* is currently unknown, predictive errors have been estimated using a bootstrap procedure. Bagging and boosting showed remarkable improvement in predictive accuracy, with error on training

J. Kittler and F. Roli (Eds.): MCS 2000, LNCS 1857, pp. 220–229, 2000.

data going rapidly to zero with boosting only, and an overall improved performance for boosting. Moreover, we have obtained results which are very similar to [4] in the analysis of the margin distributions for bagging and boosting.

The integration of the models within a GIS has allowed further analysis that will be also discussed in this paper.

Firstly, it has been possible to test the different models over two additional independent sets of georeferenced data about tick bites. Again, the boosted tree model produced the most accurate results.

Secondly, developing the model as a GIS function offered the chance of visualizing the intermediate steps of the two procedures via the use of maps. In bagging the intermediate maps can be seen as alternative realizations of the risk function, while the boosting steps show different focusing on habitat configuration.

Finally, we have investigated the effect of a truncation strategy based on a maximum number of terminal nodes for the base classifiers. The best results were found for fully grown (maximal trees), indicating the need for higher order interaction between the predictor features in this problem, as suggested by the simulation studies in [5].

2   Predictive Models and GIS for Tick Risk Assessment

GIS studies typically aim to upscale prediction (i.e. generalizing) to a landscape of millions of territory cells starting from a sample of a few hundreds sites for the response variable. A reasonable mesoscale model of Trentino (the Autonomous Province of Trento, a region of $6\,200\ km^2$ in the Italian Alps), is described at the cell resolution of 50×50 meters by almost 2.5 million cells. The digital elevation model (DEM) of the same area is actually available at the 10 meter resolution. Thus, it is easy to realize that building classification models on georeferenced data naturally leads to significant problems from a machine learning point of view. Moreover, providing the ground measures is often costly and not repeatable in ecological problems, which makes it difficult to sacrifice training material for validation and test data. It is clear that there is a need for non overfitting models with good generalization properties. Furthermore, data extracted from a GIS are usually described by heterogeneous variables: the ground measures of the response variable at a site is associated, through its geographic reference, to a vector of variables from the thematic raster maps available in the GIS (e.g. elevation, vegetation type, class of exposure, main geology). Tree-based classifiers are appropriate for summarizing large multivariate data sets described by a mix of numerical and categorical attributes. Trees may have a high discriminative power, but they are potentially prone to overfitting. Therefore, the need for model selection and now for model combination methods that may minimize the out-of-sample error.

The first computational model for tick-risk assessment in Trentino was based on a single decision tree and 100 sampling sites [6]. In order to control overfitting, the optimal model was selected according to the bootstrap 632+ rule, a

Table 1. Description of Model Variables

Name	Description
presence	discrete (2 classes)
elevation	numeric (in m, min: 200, av: 957, max: 1900)
soil substratum	discrete (5 classes)
exposure	discrete (9 classes)
deer density	numeric (in head/100ha, min:0. av. 5, max:38)
percfu-i	numeric (in %: for $i = 1 \ldots 8$)
perced-j	numeric (for %: for $j = 1 \ldots 6$)

Table 2. List of data bases

Code	Description
z96A:	1996 data, not infested sites
z96P:	1996 data, infested sites
hc:	1996 human cases
rd0:	1994 data: not infested deer
rd1:	1994 data: 1-10 ticks found on deer
rd2:	1994 data: 10+ ticks found on deer

refinement of the bootstrap method for assigning measures of accuracy to classification error estimates [7,8]. Predictive accuracy (estimated by an external cross-validation loop) of the 632+ tree was better than using standard tree selection methods or a linear discriminant procedure. On the extended survey data set of 388 sampling sites (204 presence, 184 absence) the results were confirmed, and a remarkable improvement was subsequently obtained by applying bagging as an aggregation of 100 tree models obtained from bootstrap data replicates [9]. Site locations were georeferenced and incorporated into the unified GIS and database management system. GIS software was developed with GRASS technology[1]. Software routines have been constructed to produce an interface between GRASS and the S-PLUS computational statistical system, thus yielding a flexible environment for landscape epidemiology [10].

The risk exposure to tick bites has been initially modeled as a binary presence/absence output in terms of a multivariate description of the sampling site habitat (the response variable and the 18 predictor variables are listed in Table 1, including 14 variables for vegetation description). Two independent control data bases were also considered in this study: 562 roe bucks were harvested during the first 2 weeks of September 1994 and subsequently checked for adult ticks (infestation was discretized in terms of three classes); an additional control data

---

[1] GRASS: Geographic Resources Analysis Support System, originally by the USA Center for Environmental Research Laboratory)

base hc of georeferenced 98 human cases of tick bites in 1996 was also included in the study. A summary of the available data is reported in Table 2.

3   Methods

3.1   Base Learner and Definition of the Error Estimate

We adopted the rpart[2] recursive partitioning method, as the base learning algorithm, after modification of its C language version in order to implement the bagging, Adaboost and a specific error estimate. To compare the different aggregation algorithms, errors were estimated by bootstrap: at each step, a sample of the same cardinality of the original data was extracted with replacement according to the empirical distribution. The extracted data, possibly including several repeated examples, constituted the current bootstrap learning set and it was used for training a model according to bagging or boosting prescriptions. Due to the replacement process, about .368 of the original data was held out and considered as a test set for the trained model. The procedure was repeated 50 times and then the error distribution was considered in order to obtain a prediction error estimate as well as the confidence bands.

3.2   Boosting

The boosting algorithm considered in this paper is the basic Adaboost [2] in the implementation discussed in [3]. Given a training data set $L = \{(x_i, y_i)\}_{i=1,\ldots,N}$, where the x_i are input vectors (numerical, categorical or mixed) and the y_i are class labels taking values -1 or 1, the discrete Adaboost classification model is defined as the sign of an incremental linear combination of classifiers, each one trained on weighted bootstrap samples of the training data, increasing the weights for the samples currently misclassified:

$$F(x) = sign(\sum_{i=1}^{M} c_m f_m(x; L_m)).$$

At the first step, L_1 is a sample with replacement of L, every instance having probability $p(i) = 1/N$ (empirical distribution), and $f_1(\cdot; L_1)$ is the classification model trained on L_1. At the m-th step, the error of the model f_{m-1} is computed over the training data L:

$$e_{m-1} = \sum_{i=1}^{N} d(i)p(i),$$

where $d(i) = 1$ if the i-th case is misclassified, otherwise zero. The weight of the model f_{m-1} is set to

---

[2] The rpart library for recursive partitioning has been implemented by Therry Thernau and Beth Atkinson of Mayo Clinic.

$$c_{m-1} = log((1 - e_{m-1})/e_{m-1})$$

and the probabilities of the instances are updated according to the following rule:

$$p(i) \leftarrow p(i) \, exp \, (c_{m-1}d(i)), \quad i = 1, ..., N$$

normalized such that $\sum_{i=1}^{N} p(i) = 1$.

The basic idea of this algorithm is to give higher weights to the models with low prediction error over the training set L, whilst simultaneously increasing the probabilities of the misclassified cases to enter in the learning set currently available to a new instance of the base classifier. To avoid negative or undefined weights, if $e_m \geq 0.5$ or $e_m = 0$, the probability for each instance is reset to $1/N$ and procedure is restarted.

The bootstrap-based technique for predictive model error estimate described has been used in this paper as an external loop to the Adaboost procedure, but it may also be considered as a stopping rule by analyzing the distribution of the error at the current step.

3.3   Experiment Design

As stated in the introduction, the goals of the experiment were (1) a comparison between single tree, bagging and boosting to select the best learning algorithm and (2) an indication of the degree of regularization (pruning, or better stopping) to apply to the base classifiers to control their sizes. The tree size is in fact a metaparameter of the recursive partitioning methods which is apparently inherited by bagging and boosting. One way to ignore this metaparameter is working with stumps (i.e. trees with only one split) which were found to be very effective in [5]. Stumps have low computational cost and one could think of exchanging more boosting steps with a reduced tree size. However, our first experiments with bagging for tick-risk assessments favoured an aggregation of maximal trees as remarked in paragraph 2.4.1 of [3]. The use of maximal trees is more computationally expensive, but it is still a viable solution to avoid size selection. From these goals, the following main experiments were performed and evaluated with the bootstrap generic procedure (50 replicates) described in Subsection 3.1:

1. single tree
2. *boosting*: up to 200 maximal trees
3. *boosting*: up to 200 trees, with stopping rule min 50 cases per node
4. *boosting*: up to 200 trees, with stopping rule min 10 cases per node
5. *bagging*: up to 200 maximal trees.

The results were also evaluated by analyzing the margin distribution. In this binary decision problem, the margin for bagging or boosting is the the vote for the correct class minus the vote for the wrong one. Margin maximization has been proposed in [4] as a key property of boosting algorithms, although, counterexamples have been developed in which direct margin maximization does

Table 3. Summary of results

Algorithm	Control	50M	100M	200M
single tree	cv	29.8	–	–
bagging	MAX:	26.1	25.6	25.5
boosting	min 10:	30.8	29.5	28.2
boosting	min 50:	28.2	27.8	27.2
boosting	MAX:	27.0	24.9	24.5

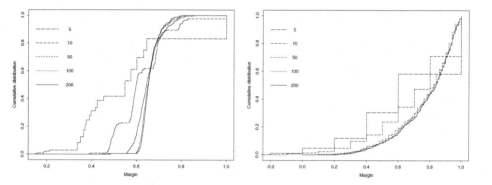

Fig. 1. Comparison of boosting (left) and bagging (right) margin distributions

not imply an improvement of generalization error (see for instance [3]). For binary outputs -1 and 1, good classification algorithms should push most of their margin distributions over 0.5.

4   Results

The natural baseline value for the experiments is the bootstrap error estimate 29.8%, which is for a single tree (Experiment 1). For each bootstrap replicate we used standard cross-validation to select the optimal tree size. Results for Experiments 1–5 are collected in Table 3.

A comparison of margins distributions for Experiment 2 (boosting with maximal trees) and Experiment 5 (bagging with maximal trees) is displayed in Fig. 1. In this configuration boosting (on the left) is clearly more aggressive with low margins than bagging (on the right), even at the price of lowering very high margins. After 100 boosting steps (i.e. 100 combined models), the classification margin is greater than 0.6 for the whole training set, whilst with bagging even with 200 models 10 % of the margin distribution is still below 0.5. However, with bagging there are margins close to 1, which correspond to the cases that are always correctly classified.

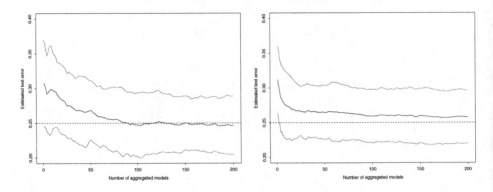

Fig. 2. Comparison of boosting (left) and bagging (right) error estimates, with 95% confidence band

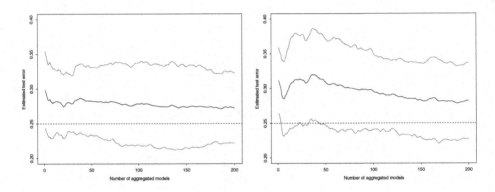

Fig. 3. Comparison of error estimates for boosting with min 50 (left) and min 10 (right) cases for terminal nodes, with 95% confidence band

A comparison of the error estimates for increasing number of steps (i.e. models) for Experiment 2 (boosting with maximal trees) and Experiment 5 (bagging with maximal trees) is displayed in Fig. 2: 95% confidence bands are added to each plot. The same plots are reproduced for Experiment 3 (boosting which stops at 50 cases per node) and Experiment 4 (boosting which stops at 10 cases per node) in Fig. 3.

Boosting with maximal trees resulted in the most accurate model. However any of the combined models improved the accuracy of the single tree model. It is worth noting from Table 3 and Figures 2 and 3 that boosting with trees of moderate sizes is less accurate than both boosting and bagging with maximal trees: the result indicates a strong interaction between input variables in this risk assessment problem [5]. Note also that the response variable (presence or absence of *I. ricinus* is not affected by noise; as discussed in [11], this remark

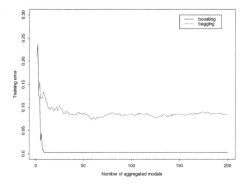

Fig. 4. Comparison of errors on training set

may explain the advantage of boosting over bagging in this task. A comparison of the different trends in training error is reported in Fig. 4 for boosting and bagging (both with maximal trees). Training error reaches zero after 9 iterations for boosting, whilst it oscillates between 7.4% and 8.7% for bagging after 35 iterations. The digital maps corresponding to the first nine boosting iterations are displayed in Fig. 5. The final results of the boosting procedure is shown in Fig. 6: the risk map has been computed at $50 \times 50 \ m^2$ cell resolution, in a window of $116 \times 97 \ km^2$.

5 Conclusions

The risk map presented in this paper represents an advancement towards landscape epidemiology of tick-borne diseases. A summary of results is given in Table 4: for each data set described in Sect. 2, Table 2, the proportion of data correctly classified by the boosting risk map is reported. Good accuracy is obtained also on the independent test sets, demonstrating that the risk map can be used by public agencies as a basis for effective vaccination in endemic areas and for tick-management strategies to prevent human cases of tick-borne diseases (Lyme

Table 4. Summary of results

Data Set	Accuracy (%)
z96P	80.8
z96A	89.3
hc	79.3
rd0	66.4
rd1	64.6
rd2	82.8

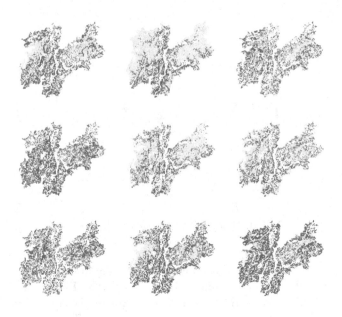

Fig. 5. GIS representation of the final boosting sequence (first 9 terms)

Borreliosis and TBE). The GIS data available in Trentino are of sufficient quality for supporting model development. Overall, good generalization without overfitting has been obtained by the integration of boosting within the GIS methodology. Model combination by boosting is now a mature methodology in this applicative domain.

Acknowledgments

The authors wish to thank Claudio Chemini and Annapaola Rizzoli (Center of Alpine Ecology) for active collaboration and illuminating discussions, and Josi Rosenfeld for useful comments. We also thank the Statistics, Forest, and Wildlife Management Services of the Autonomous Province of Trento for making available their GIS data, and the GSC group of ITC for precious support with software and hardware resources. The Center of Preventive Medicine of Trentino kindly provided data about the human cases data base.

References

1. Breiman, L.: Bagging Predictors. Machine Learning. **24(2)** (1996) 123–140
2. Freund, Y., and Schapire R.: Experiments with a new boosting algorithm. In: Machine Learning: Proceedings of the Thirteenth International Conference (1996) 148–156

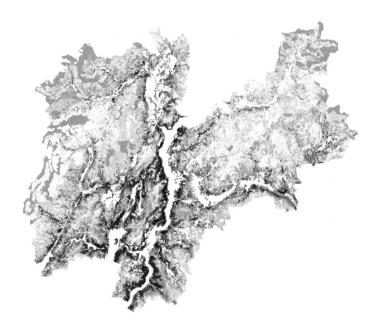

Fig. 6. The boosting risk map. Darker grey levels indicate higher risk of exposure to tick bites

3. Breiman, L.: Combining predictors. In: Sharkey, A., (ed.): Combining Artificial Neural Nets: Ensemble and Modular Multi-Net Systems. Springer-Verlag, London (1999) 31–50
4. Schapire, R., Freund, Y., Bartlett, P., and Lee W.: Boosting the margin: a new explanation for the effectiveness of voting methods. The Annals of Statistics **26(5)** (1998) 1651–1686
5. Friedman, J., Hastie, T., and Tibshirani R.: Additive logistic regression: a statistical view of boosting. Technical report, Stanford University, (1999)
6. Merler, S., Furlanello, C., Chemini, C., and Nicolini, G.: Classification tree methods for analysis of mesoscale distribution of ixodes ricinus (acari: ixodidae) in Trentino, Italian Alps. Journal of Medical Entomology **33(6)** (1996) 888–893
7. Efron, B., and Tibshirani, R.: Cross-validation and the bootstrap: estimating the error rate of a prediction rule. Technical report, Standford University, (1995)
8. Merler, S., and Furlanello, C.: Selection of tree-based classifiers with the bootstrap 632+ rule. Biometrical Journal **39(2)** (1997) 1–14
9. Furlanello, C., Merler, S., Rizzoli, A., Chemini, C., and Genchi, C.: Bagging as a predictive method for landscape epidemiology of Lyme disease. Giornale Italiano di Cardiologia **29(5)** (1999) 143–147
10. Furlanello, C., Merler, S., and Chemini, C.: Tree-based classifiers and GIS for biological risk forecasting. In: Morabito, F., (ed.): Advanced in Intelligent Systems. IOS Press, Amsterdam (1997) 316–323
11. Dietterich, T.G: An Experimental Comparison of Three Methods for Constructing Ensembles of Decision Trees: Bagging, Boosting, and Randomization. Machine Learning (1999) (to appear).

A New Evaluation Method for Expert Combination in Multi-expert System Designing

S. Impedovo and A. Salzo

Dipartimento di Informatica - Università degli Studi di Bari- Via E. Orabona 4 - 70126 Bari- Italy

Abstract. In this paper a new evaluation method for expert combination is presented. It takes into account the correlation among experts, their number and their recognition rate. An extended investigation on Majority Vote, Bayesian, Behaviour Knowledge Space and Dempster-Shafer method for abstract-level classifiers is presented. The two-way analysis of variance test and the Scheffè post-hoc comparison have been used to investigate on the factors that influence the recognition rate of the multi-expert system and to collect useful information for the multi-expert system designing.

1   Introduction

As it is well known, the multi-expert systems have been recently used to improve the results obtained to solve several pattern recognition problems. In a multi-expert system the final decision is obtained by combining the outputs of several classifiers. Up to now many combination techniques have been proposed; they essentially depend on the information that the classifiers provide [1]. Some of them use combination rules based on voting principle [2], others use rules based on the bayesian theory [1], on belief functions and Dempster-Shafer theory of evidence [1], [3], on fuzzy rules [4], on Behaviour Knowledge Space [5], and so on. Combination methods based both on classifiers independence [1] and dependence assumption [6] have also been proposed. Furthermore, a theoretical framework for combining classifiers has been recently developed and it has been shown how many existing combination schemes can be considered as a special cases of compound classification where all the representations are used jointly to make a decision [7].

In spite of the great number of combination methods proposed, the problem of why a combination method gives good performance under specific conditions has not been sufficiently investigated. To solve the problem, some approaches focus the attention on classifier selection rather than on the classifier combination [8]. Some "selection-based multi-classifier systems" have been recently proposed; they are based on the idea that a dynamic classifier selector chooses the most appropriate classifier for each input pattern [9]. However, the solution of the problem requires the integration of classifier selection with an accurate analysis of combination methods performance. Generally this one was carried out on heuristic basis by considering specific set of classifiers and database. But these approaches are not general and they do not allow to

J. Kittler and F. Roli (Eds.): MCS 2000, LNCS 1857, pp. 230-239, 2000.

infer information on combination methods performances when different sets of classifiers or different databases are used [10].

In order to design a powerful multi-expert system, a systematic evaluation of combination methods must be carried out. In this paper an extended investigation about a new methodology for the evaluation of combination methods for abstract-level classifiers recently proposed [11], [12] is carried on to evaluate the performance of four combination methods: the Majority Vote method [1], [13], the Bayesian method [1], the Behaviour Knowledge Space method [5] and the Dempster-Shafer method [1]. This methodology is based on the definition of an estimator of classifiers correlation called "similarity index". By mean of the two-way analysis of variance test [14], [12] and the Scheffè post-hoc comparison [15], the effects of the choice of combination method, of the similarity index, of the number of classifiers combined and of their recognition rates on the recognition rate of the multi-expert system have been studied. The multi-expert systems have been applied to the problem of numeral recognition.

In Section 2, the methodology for the evaluation of combination method is reported and the four combination methods are briefly described in Section 3. The experimental results are presented and discussed in Section 4 and finally the conclusions are reported in Section 5.

2   Evaluation of Combination Methods

In the process of classifiers combination, each classifier A_i, $i=1,...,K$ decides the membership of the input pattern p_t to the m pattern classes ω_1, ω_2,..., ω_m. Let $A_i(p_t)$ be the response of the i-th classifier when the pattern p_t is processed; the combination method E provides the final response by combining the responses of the individual classifiers.

The methodology used to evaluate the efficiency of a combination method for *abstract-level* classifiers is based on the assumption that no rejection is allowed at the level of individual classifier i.e. $R_i+S_i=100\%$, being R_i and S_i respectively the recognition and substitution rate of A_i, $i=1,2,...,K$. A suitable parameter, called *Similarity Index*, is used to estimate stochastic correlation of a set of classifiers by measuring the agreement among their outputs.

Let $A=\{A_i /i=1,2,...,K\}$ be a set of classifiers and $P=\{p_t|t=1,2,...,N\}$ a set of patterns. The *Similarity Index* of set A is defined as:

$$\rho_A = \left(\sum_{\substack{i,j=1,...K \\ i<j}} \rho_{A_i,A_j} \right) \bigg/ \binom{K}{2} \tag{1}$$

where:

$$\rho_{A_i,A_j} = \frac{1}{N} \sum_{t=1}^{N} F(A_i(p_t), A_j(p_t)) \tag{2}$$

$$F(A_i(p_t), A_j(p_t)) = \begin{cases} 1 & \text{if } A_i(p_t) = A_j(p_t) \\ 0 & \text{otherwise} \end{cases}$$

From the above definition, it results that $\rho_A \in [0,1]$. Specifically, it is possible to prove by induction on the number of classifiers K that ρ_A ranges from ρ_{min} to 1 where ρ_{min} is defined as:

$$\rho_{min} = \left(k'R' + \binom{k'}{2} \right) \Big/ \binom{K}{2} \qquad \text{if } k' \geq 2 \tag{3}$$

$$\rho_{min} = R' \Big/ \binom{K}{2} \qquad \text{if } k' = 1$$

$$\rho_{min} = 0 \qquad \text{if } k' = 0$$

$$k' = \lfloor KR \rfloor, \quad R' = KR - \lfloor KR \rfloor$$

In order to analyse in a systematic way the performances of the combination methods, an automatic procedure has been used. It simulates the responses of sets of classifiers, having a similarity index spanning within the entire range of possible values.

3   Combination Methods

Four combination methods for abstract-level classifiers have been used in this paper: the Majority Vote (MV) method, the Behavior Knowledge Space (BKS) method, the Dempster Shafer (DS) method and the Bayesian method with the Independence assumption (BI). A brief description of each combination method is reported below.

3.1   Majority Vote (MV)

The MV method combines the classifier outputs by using a decision rule based on the voting principle; for an unknown pattern p_t, the MV method assigns to each semantic class ω_i a score $V(\omega_i)$ equal to the number of classifiers which select the class ω_i. Successively, the following decision rule is used:

$$MV(p_t) = \begin{cases} \omega_i & \text{if } V(\omega_i) = \max_1 = \max_{j=1,\dots,m} V(\omega_j) \text{ and } \max_1 - \max_2 > 0 \\ Reject & \text{otherwise} \end{cases}$$

where $\max_2 = \max_{\substack{j \neq i \\ j=1,\dots,m}} V(\omega_j)$ and $p_t \in P$.

3.2   Dempster Shafer (DS)

The DS method combines the output of different classifiers by using their recognition and substitution rates as a priori knowledge.

In the first phase for each input pattern p_t the classifiers that output the same class label are collected into equivalent classifiers B_k where k=1,...,K' and K' $\leq$ K. For those classifiers A_j that don't produce the same output class, the equivalent classifiers B_k still remain equal to A_j.

In the second phase the new recognition and substitution rates for the B_k classifier are computed and used for the estimation of the belief of the correct output $Bel(\omega_j)$ and the belief of the wrong output $Bel(\neg\omega_j)$. The DS method finally uses the following decision rule:

$$DS(p_t) = \begin{cases} j & d_j = \max_{i=1,...,m} d_i > \alpha \\ Reject & otherwise \end{cases}$$

where $d_i = Bel(\omega_i) - Bel(\neg\omega_i)$ and $\alpha=0.5$.

3.3   Bayesian Method with Independence Assumption (BI)

By supposing the classifiers independence, the BI method assigns to each semantic class ω_i a value $Bel(i)$ which is computed on the basis of the conditional probabilities $P(p_t \in \omega_i \mid A_k(p_t) = j_k)$ $k = 1,...,K$ $i = 1,...,m$ which   denote   the probability that the input pattern p_t belongs to ω_i when the output of the k-th classifier is $A_k(p_t) = j_k$. These probabilities are computed by mean of the confusion matrix of the K classifiers [1]. The BI finally uses the following decision rule:

$$BI(p_t) = \begin{cases} j & if \quad Bel(j) = \max_{i=1,...,m} Bel(i) \geq \alpha \\ Reject & otherwise \end{cases}$$

where $\alpha=0.5$.

3.4   Behavior-Knowledge Space (BKS) Method

The BKS method operates in two phases: the learning and the test phase. In the learning phase, it uses the outputs of the K classifiers to fill a K-dimensional space. Each K-tuple of classifier answers identifies a point, called "focal unit" (FU), in the BKS space. Each focal unit contains the following information:
a) the total number of incoming samples T_{FU} ;
b) the best representative class of the focal unit $R_{FU} \in \{\omega_1, \omega_2, ..., \omega_m\}$;
c) the number of incoming samples $n(j)$ belonging to each semantic class ω_j $j = 1,...,m$.

In the test phase, the K-tuple of classifier answers is used to select a focal unit in the BKS and then the final decision, on an unknown pattern p_t, is taken by analyzing the information contained within the selected focal unit.

Since the efficiency of the BKS method depends on the representative degree of the BKS, in this paper a BKS method cooperating with the Bayesian one has been used for the test [5] and the following decision rule has been adopted:

$$BKS(p_t) = \begin{cases} R_{FU} & \text{if } (T_{FU} > 0 \text{ and } \dfrac{n(R_{FU})}{T_{FU}} \geq \lambda) \\ j & \text{if } (T_{FU} > 0 \text{ and } \dfrac{n(R_{FU})}{T_{FU}} < \lambda) \text{ and } (Bel(j) = \max_{i=1,..,m} Bel(i) \geq \beta) \\ Reject & \text{Otherwise} \end{cases}$$

where $\lambda = 0.5$, $\beta = 0.5$ and $Bel(j)$ is the belief value which represents the degree that the input p_t belongs to class j and which is computed by mean of the confusion matrix of the K classifiers [1].

4   Experimental Results

In this paper, sets of K=2,3,4,5,6,7 classifiers each having a recognition rate R=75%,80%,85%,90%,95% have been considered. For sake of simplicity, it has been assumed that the classifiers have the same recognition rate i.e. $R_i=R$, for $i=1,2...K$. They were grouped into 30 different groups S_i i=1...30. For each group, and so for each value of (K, R), different sets of classifiers were simulated, each having a similarity index ρ spanning within the range of variability $[\rho_{min}, 1]$. Table 1 shows the ρ_{min} values considered. A suitable procedure is used to control the similarity index value during the simulation process.

Table 1. ρ_{min} values

ρ_{min} Classifier number K	Classifier Recognition Rate R				
	R = 75%	R = 80%	R = 85%	R = 90%	R = 95%
K = 2	0.5	0.6	0.7	0.8	0.9
K = 3	0.5	0.6	0.7	0.8	0.9
K = 4	0.5	0.6	0.7	0.8	0.9
K = 5	0.52	0.6	0.7	0.8	0.9
K = 6	0.53	0.61	0.7	0.8	0.9
K = 7	0.54	0.62	0.71	0.8	0.9

For each value of ρ, r = 10 sets of classifiers were considered for the test and each set was tested over N=100 simulated input data. Furthermore, p = 15 sets of classifiers were used for the learning phase of BKS method.

Table 2 lists the mean recognition rates obtained by MV, DS, BI and BKS methods for each group S_i i=1...30.

In order to analyze the dependencies of the recognition rate of combination methods when ρ (similarity index), K (number of classifiers) and R (classifiers recognition rate) change, the two-way analysis of variance ("anova") test [12], [14] has been used. More specifically, three different tests have been carried out, each one having a significance level $\alpha = 0.01$.

Table 2. Mean Recognition Rate of combination methods for each group S_i i=1,..,30

Groups S_i i=1,...,30	MV	DS	BI	BKS
K=2 R=75%	62,75	75,46	87,30	87,43
K=3 R=75%	81,73	81,62	89,17	87,04
K=4 R=75%	76,70	82,39	90,61	86,30
K=5 R=75%	82,83	82,31	90,93	85,92
K=6 R=75%	79,23	83,20	91,46	84,67
K=7 R=75%	82,62	82,56	91,52	86,12
K= 2 R=80%	70,24	80,83	90,01	89,93
K= 3 R=80%	85,20	84,95	91,73	90,06
K= 4 R=80%	81,23	85,75	92,47	88,62
K= 5 R=80%	86,46	86,55	93,01	88,74
K= 6 R=80%	83,53	86,32	93,63	90,19
K= 7 R=80%	86,42	86,40	93,62	89,63
K= 2 R=85%	77,74	85,38	92,52	92,40
K= 3 R=85%	88,91	88,56	93,72	92,54
K= 4 R=85%	86,06	89,51	94,55	91,29
K= 5 R=85%	89,66	89,82	95,20	92,14
K= 6 R=85%	87,99	89,67	95,31	92,90
K= 7 R=85%	89,95	89,71	95,48	93,18
K= 2 R=90%	85,24	90,78	95,18	94,94
K= 3 R=90%	92,54	92,65	95,98	94,74
K= 4 R=90%	90,62	92,83	94,18	96,68
K= 5 R=90%	92,95	92,77	96,90	94,11
K= 6 R=90%	92,14	93,43	96,83	94,08
K= 7 R=90%	93,38	93,35	97,14	93,54
K= 2 R=95%	92,73	95,00	97,70	97,44
K= 3 R=95%	96,35	96,23	98,05	97,49
K= 4 R=95%	95,46	96,59	98,31	96,55
K= 5 R=95%	96,57	96,64	98,55	97,39
K= 6 R=95%	96,22	96,74	98,52	97,94
K= 7 R=95%	96,60	96,35	98,66	97,52

4.1   First Test

The first test analyzes the variability of combination methods performance within each group S_i i=1...30. For a fixed value of K and R, it checks whether the recognition rate of a multi-classifier system depends or not on the correlation among the classifiers considered and on the combination method used. The first "anova" test checks the validity of the following null hypotheses:

1. The variability of the performance of the multi-classifier system doesn't depend on the choice of the combination method.
2. The variability of the performance of the multi-classifier system doesn't depend on the correlation among classifiers.
3. There are no interaction effects between the choice of the combination method and the classifier correlation.

The results of the "anova" test show that the null hypotheses can be rejected for all groups S_i.

The "anova" test is generally used to determine if a significant difference exists between groups of samples. But in order to identify where the difference is located, a further post-hoc test should be performed. In this paper the Scheffè post-hoc comparison [15] has been used to investigate these differences.

Table 3 show the results of Scheffè post-hoc comparison for (K=2 R=95%). The cells marked with "*SIGNIF*" evidence the groups for which the mean recognition rates of the multi-expert system are significantly different, while the white cells identify not significant groups. Finally, the gray cells identify not useful or already done comparisons.

Table 3. Results of Scheffè post-hoc comparison on similarity index

K=2 R=95		Similarity index										
Mean Recognition Rate %	Simil. index	0,9	0,91	0,92	0,93	0,94	0,95	0,96	0,97	0,98	0,99	1
96,25	0,9							SIGNIF	SIGNIF	SIGNIF	SIGNIF	SIGNIF
96,3	0,91							SIGNIF	SIGNIF	SIGNIF	SIGNIF	SIGNIF
96	0,92									SIGNIF	SIGNIF	SIGNIF
96,15	0,93								SIGNIF	SIGNIF		SIGNIF
95,825	0,94											SIGNIF
95,925	0,95									SIGNIF		SIGNIF
95,5	0,96											
95,5	0,97											
95,175	0,98											
95,25	0,99											
95	1											

Table 4. Results of Scheffè post-hoc comparison on combination method

		Combination Method			
	K=2 R=95	MV	DS	BI	BKS
Combination Methods	MV		SIGNIF	SIGNIF	SIGNIF
	DS			SIGNIF	SIGNIF
	BI				
	BKS				

Table 3 shows, for instance, that, when K=2 classifiers with individual recognition rate R=95% and similarity index $0.9 \leq \rho \leq 0.95$ are combined, multi-expert systems having, on the average, the same recognition rate can be designed. This means that, if a set of classifiers having a similarity index $\rho=0.9$ is combined, in order to obtain a significant change in the recognition rate of the multi-expert system, sets of classifiers having $\rho=0.96, 0.97, 0.98, 0.99, 1$ should be considered. However, since the performance of the multi-expert system decrease when the similarity index ρ increases (see Table 3), then the choice of $\rho=0.9$ is the most suitable.

Let's consider now the effect of combination method choice. The test shows that the performance of the multi-expert system change when different combination methods are chosen, with the only exception of BI and BKS methods that are on the average equal (Table 4). Furthermore, as Table 2 shows, they are the best combination methods for the case considered.

Obviously, similar consideration can be derived by applying the post-hoc test to the other groups S_i i=1,...,30 considered in the experiment.

4.2   Second Test

The second test analyzes the variability of combination methods performance when the cardinality of classifiers set grows. For a fixed value of R (classifiers recognition rate), it checks whether the recognition rate of the multi-classifier system depends or not on the combination method used and on the number of classifiers combined (K). The null hypotheses of this test are:

1. The variability of the performance of the multi-classifier system doesn't depend on the choice of the combination method.
2. The variability of the performance of the multi-classifier system doesn't depend on the number of classifiers combined.
3. There are no interaction effects between the choice of the combination method and the number of classifiers combined.

The result of "anova" test allows the rejection of the null hypotheses for all cases considered (R=75%,80%,85%,90%,95%). The Scheffè post-hoc comparison has been also used to identify the values of K and the combination method that caused the rejection of the null hypotheses.

Table 5 summarizes the results of the post-hoc comparison when classifiers having an individual recognition rate R=75% are considered.

Table 5. a)Results of Scheffè post-hoc comparison on classifier number K when R=75%. b)Results of Scheffè post-hoc comparison on combination method for R=75%,80%,85%,90%,95%.

R=75%	K=2	K=3	K=4	K=5	K=6	K=7
K=2		SIGNIF	SIGNIF	SIGNIF	SIGNIF	SIGNIF
K=3						
K=4						SIGNIF
K=5						
K=6						SIGNIF
K=7						

a)

R=75%	MV	DS	BI	BKS
MV		SIGNIF	SIGNIF	SIGNIF
DS			SIGNIF	SIGNIF
BI				SIGNIF
BKS				

b)

Table 5a) shows that the multi-expert system having K=3 classifiers differs only from that having K=2 classifiers. This means that for R=75% if a greater number of classifiers is combined the performance of the multi-expert system don't significantly change. Conversely, the last one is strongly affected by the choice of the combination method (see Table 5b) not only for the case at the hand but also for all cases considered in the experiment (R=75%,80%,85%,90%,95%). More specifically, BI method is, on the average, the best combination method (Table 6).

Table 6. Mean recognition rates of the combination methods (evaluated for K=2,3,4,5,6,7)

	MV	DS	BI	BKS
R=75	76,39	80,15	89,50	85,26
R=80	80,85	83,92	91,52	88,45
R=85	85,69	87,9	93,97	91,72
R=90	90,51	92,07	96,21	93,75
R=95	95,24	95,87	98,13	97,16

4.3   Third Test

Finally, the third test analyzes the variability of combination methods performance when classifiers having different recognition rate are combined. For a fixed value of K (number of classifiers combined), it checks whether the recognition rate of the multi-classifier system depends on the type of combination method used and on the recognition rate of the classifiers combined (R). The null hypotheses of this test are:

1. The variability of the performance of the multi-classifier system doesn't depend on the choice of the combination method.
2. The variability of the performance of the multi-classifier system doesn't depend on the classifier recognition rate.
3. There are no interaction effects between the choice of the combination method and the classifier recognition rate.

The "anova" test suggests the rejection of the three null hypotheses for all cases considered (K=2,3,4,5,6,7) and the Scheffè post-hoc comparison has been used to identify the values of R and the combination method that caused the rejection of the null hypotheses. Table 7 and Table 8 summarize the overall results of the post-hoc comparison.

Table 7. Third test: Scheffè post-hoc comparison results on recognition rate R

K=2 K=3 K=4 K=5 K=6 K=7	R=75	R=80	R=85	R=90	R=95
R=75		SIGNIF	SIGNIF	SIGNIF	SIGNIF
R=80			SIGNIF	SIGNIF	SIGNIF
R=85				SIGNIF	SIGNIF
R=90					SIGNIF
R=95					

Table 8. Third test: Scheffè post-hoc comparison results on combination method

K=2	MV	DS	BI	BKS
MV		SIGNIF	SIGNIF	SIGNIF
DS			SIGNIF	SIGNIF
BI				
BKS				

K=3 K=5 K=7	MV	DS	BI	BKS
MV			SIGNIF	SIGNIF
DS			SIGNIF	SIGNIF
BI				SIGNIF
BKS				

K=4 K=6	MV	DS	BI	BKS
MV		SIGNIF	SIGNIF	SIGNIF
DS			SIGNIF	SIGNIF
BI				SIGNIF
BKS				

The individual recognition rate of the classifiers strongly affects the performance of the multi-expert system for every K=2,3,4,5,6,7 (Table 7). On the other hand, the choice of the combination method also affects the recognition rate of the system but in different way depending to the number of classifiers combined. For instance, when odd values of K (K=3,5,7) are chosen, the MV and DS methods have the same recognition rate while they are significantly different if an even value of K is used (K=2,4,6) (Table 8). Conversely, for K=2, BI and BKS methods have the same recognition rate.

5   Conclusions

In this paper an extended investigation about a new methodology for the evaluation of combination methods for abstract-level classifiers has been presented. Four combination methods have been considered: the MV method, the BI method, the BKS method and the DS method. The new methodology is based on the definition of an estimator of classifiers correlation called "similarity index". The effects of selection of combination method, of the similarity index, of the number of classifiers combined and of their recognition rates on the recognition rate of the multi-expert system have been studied by mean of the two-way analysis of variance test. Furthermore the

Scheffè post-hoc comparison has provided very useful information that can assist the multi-expert system designers not only in avoiding the choice of less significant cases but also in the selection of the best combination method for the specific set of classifiers.

References

1. L. Xu, A. Krzyzak, C. Y-Suen, "Methods of Combining Multiple Classifiers and Their Applications to Handwriting Recognition", IEEE Transaction on Systems, Man and Cybernetics, Vol. 22, N. 3, 1992, pp. 418-435.
2. F. Kimura, M. Shridhar, "Handwritten Numeral Recognition Based on Multiple Algorithm", Pattern Recognition, vol. 24 no.10, 1991, pp. 969-983.
3. E. Mandler and J. Schuermann, "Combining the Classification Results of independent classifiers based on the Dempster/Shafer theory of evidence", in Pattern Recognition and Artificial Intelligence, Eds. E.S. Gelsema and L.N. Kanal, North Holland, Amsterdam, 1988, pp. 381-393.
4. S.B. Cho, J.H. Kim, "Combining Multiple Neural Networks by Fuzzy Integral for Robust Classification", IEEE Trans. Systems, Man and Cybernetics, vol. 25, no.2, 1995, pp.380-384.
5. Y.S. Huang and C.Y. Suen, "A Method of Combining Multiple Experts for the Recognition of Unconstrained Handwritten Numerals". IEEE Trans. On Pattern Analysis and Machine Intelligence, vol. 17, no.1, 1995, pp.90-94.
6. H.J. Kang, S.W. Lee, "Combining Classifiers Based on Minimization of a Bayes Error Rate", Proc. of Fifth International Conference on Document Analysis and Recognition (ICDAR99), Bangalore, India, 20-22 Sept. 1999, pp. 398-401.
7. J.Kittler, M. Hatef, R. P.W. Duin, J. Matas, "On Combining Classifiers", IEEE on Pattern Analysis and Machine Intelligence, vol.20 No.3, March 1998, pp.226-239.
8. N.Srihari et al, "Decision combination in multiple classifier systems", IEEE on Pattern Analysis and Machine Intelligence, vol.16 No.1, Jan. 1994, pp.66-75.
9. G. Giacinto, F. Roli, "Methods for Dynamic Classifier Selection", Proc. of 10th Intern. Conference on Image Analysis and Processing ICIAP'99, Venice, Italy, Sept. 27-29,1999, pp. 659-664.
10. J. Kittler, "Improving Recognition rates by classifier combination: A Theoretical Framework", Progress in Handwriting Recognition, edited by A.C.Downton and S. Impedovo, World Scientific Publishing Co. Pte. Ltd., Singapore, 1997, pp. 231-247.
11. G. Dimauro, S. Impedovo, G. Pirlo, A. Salzo, "Multiple Experts: a new methodology for the evaluation of the combination processes", Progress in Handwriting Recognition, edited by A.C. Downton and S. Impedovo, World Scientific Publishing Co. Pte. Ltd., Singapore, pp. 329-335.
12. S. Impedovo, A. Salzo, "Evaluation of Combination Methods", Proc. of Fifth International Conference on Document Analysis and Recognition (ICDAR99), Bangalore, India, 20-22 Sept. 1999, pp. 394-397.
13. C.Y. Suen, C. Nadal, R. Legault, T.A. Mai, L. Lam, "Computer Recognition of unconstrained hand-written Numerals", Proc. IEEE, Vol. 80, N. 7, 1992, pp. 1162-1180
14. E. Kreyszig, "Introductory Mathematical Statistics- Principle and Methods-", John Wiley & Sons Publ., New York, 1970, pp. 262-284.
15. H. Scheffè, "A method for judging all contrasts in the analysis of variance", Biometrika, 40, 1953, pp.87-104.

Diversity between Neural Networks and Decision Trees for Building Multiple Classifier Systems

Wenjia Wang, Phillis Jones, and Derek Partridge

Department of Computer Science, University of Exeter,
Exeter, EX4 4PT, UK. Email: w.wang@ex.ac.uk

Abstract: A multiple classifier system can only improve the performance when the members in the system are diverse from each other. Combining some methodologically different techniques is considered a constructive way to expand the diversity. This paper investigates the diversity between the two different data mining techniques, neural networks and automatically induced decision trees. Input decimation through salient feature selection is also explored in the paper in the hope of acquiring further diversity. Among various diversities defined, the coincident failure diversity (CFD) appears to be an effective measure of useful diversity among classifiers in a multiple classifier system when the majority voting decision strategy is applied. A real-world medical classification problem is presented as an application of the techniques. The constructed multiple classifier systems are evaluated with a number of statistical measures in terms of reliability and generalisation. The results indicate that combined MCSs of the nets and trees trained with the selected features have higher diversity and produce better classification results.

1 Introduction

The technique that combines the trained neural networks to create an ensemble, an equivalent multiple version system in conventional software engineering, has been explored by many researchers [Hansen et al 1990, Krogh et al 1995, Gedeon 1997, Partridge et al 1997, Wang et al 1998] to solve various problems and appeared to be beneficial in some applications. The basic process of the technique is to produce many versions of the classifier or predictor for a specific problem and combine them in a variety of structures. However, the studies in both traditional software engineering [Eckhardt et al 1985, Littlewood & Miller 1989] and modern inductive programming [Partridge et al 1996] have shown that the multiple version systems even developed 'independently' of each other are likely to fail dependently. The key for success is whether the classifiers in a system are diverse enough from each other, or in other words, that the individual classifiers have a minimum of failures in common. If one classifier makes a mistake then the others should not be likely to make the same mistake. Nevertheless, a high level of diversity is not forthcoming by simply integrating N classifiers to form a multi-classifier system. Particularly, in the case of combining neural networks it is not easy to achieve high level diversity between the trained neural nets by just manipulating initial conditions, architecture and learning parameters due to the methodological similarity of supervised training algorithms. The study carried out by [Partridge et al. 1996] found that the gain on diversity by these

J. Kittler and F. Roli (Eds.): MCS 2000, LNCS 1857, pp. 240-249, 2000.

strategies is limited. In terms of diversity generated, the strategies they studied were ranked in the following order with the most diverse strategy first: type of neural nets > training sets > architecture of nets >= initial conditions. The ranking again confirmed the hypothesis established by [Eckhardt et al 1985 and Littlewood & Miller 1989] which states that classifiers implemented by different methodologies may produce higher level diversity than other variations. Neural networks and decision trees are different learning methods and therefore a combination of them is potential to achieve diverse and better systems. In addition, employing the technique of input decimation and data partitions could provide further improvement on diversity, which can be justified by the way neural nets are developed. Neural nets are trained to learn from the data provided so they are data-dependent. Different data set may represent different dominant knowledge of the problem. The success of the Boosting technique [Freund & Schapire 1996] is one example, in which the classifiers are forced to learn different knowledge in a data set by adding some weight to "hard" patterns.

This paper will describe the technique of input decimation by selecting salient features for developing classifiers, and the methodology of combining neural networks and decision trees to construct a multiple classifier system. Then it presents some measures of diversity and reliability for a system. These are followed by the results of applying these techniques to a real-world problem, i.e. the osteoporosis disease classification.

2 Input Decimation with Selection of Salient Features

Partridge et al (1996) have explored various possible strategies to improve diversity between the neural nets. Their results indicate that using different data subsets could generate more diversity than manipulating the other parameters, e.g. initial conditions (weights, learning rate) and structure of nets. Tuner & Oza (1999) tried to use different subsets of input features in various sizes to train nets and reported the improvement on the performance of multiple classifier systems they subsequently built. However, in the latter study they selected the features according to correlation coefficient of features to the corresponding output class. Our research [Wang, et al 1998] found that selecting features with such a method usually produces poor results except for some simple, linear problems. We developed some other techniques for identifying the salience of input features and the comparative study [Wang, Jones & Partridge 1999] indicates that our techniques performed better for complicated, noise real-world problems.

- Identification of salient input features

A number of techniques we investigated for identifying salience of input features are developed based primarily on neural network technology. Two of them are our own proposed methods, i.e. neural net clamping and the decision tree heuristic algorithm. The other two methods are input-impact analysis [Tchaban et al 1998] and the linear correlation analysis which is used as a base line. The details of investigation can be found in [Wang, Jones and Partridge 1999].

- Input decimation

The features are ranked in accordance with their value of salience, i.e. the impact ratio in the clamping results or significant score with decision tree heuristic. The larger are the value the more salient the features. Then different numbers of salient input features can be selected from the top of ranks to form subsets of features for training classifiers.

- Data partitioning

Each dimensionality-reduced data set (including the original data set) will be partitioned at random into two subsets at a ratio of about 70:30, i.e. a training-validation set and a test set. Then the training-validation set is further partitioned into two sub-subsets: Q_t and Q_v, i.e. a real training set ($Q_t = 40\%$, say) and a validation set ($Q_v=30\%$). The latter partition is carried out N times to create N training sets and their corresponding validation sets. This strategy is different from the Bagging in that the sampling is controlled by a specific rule [Wang and Partridge 1998] to meet a specific overlap rate between the subsets. This rate could be altered from 0 (no overlap, i.e. disjoint) to 1 (completely overlap) in order to purposely examine diversity created by the data partitions.

3 Multi-classifier System (MCS)

3.1 Multi-classifier Systems of Neural Networks

The technique of a multiple classifier system of neural nets has been widely used in various applications. However, a multiple classifier system does not always produce better performance because the members in such a system, i.e. the trained neural nets are highly correlated and tend to make the same mistakes simultaneously. So much attention and effort have been put into finding methods that could create diversity between nets.

This study focused on investigating constructing multiple classifier systems with the multi-layer perceptrons neural nets trained by using different subsets of input features (even initial weights and number of hidden units are also varied). Only multi-layer perceptrons are utilised here primarily because they are the most popularly used type of neural nets in the constructions of multiple classifier systems. The procedure we used for building a multiple net system is below. For each input decimated data set:

   (i) Partitioning the data set with the procedure described in the earlier section.
   (ii) Training and validating neural nets with the training and validation data sets respectively. (Three nets designed with 3 different number of hidden nodes were trained with each training set using different initial conditions. Thus a cube of 27 nets in total were produced and placed in a pool as the candidates of classifiers.)
   (iii) Constructing multiple net systems by randomly selecting the nets from the candidate pool.
   (iv) Estimating the diversity and assessing the performance with the test data set.

3.2 Multiple Classifier Systems of Decision Trees

A decision tree is a representation of a decision generating procedure induced from the contents of a given data set. Induction of a decision tree is a symbolic, supervised learning process using information theory, which is methodologically different from the learning of neural networks. We use the C5.0 decision tree induction software package (as a black box) -- the lasted development from ID3 [Quinlan 1986], to generate the member candidates of trees. Moreover, a heuristic algorithm is developed based on the trees induced to determine the salience of input features for input decimation.

The procedure for building a multiple tree system is the same as the one for building multiple net systems except that the candidates are the decision trees induced by varying pruning levels.

3.3 Hybrid Multiple Classifier Systems

With two different candidates of classifiers, i.e. neural nets and decision trees, available, it is now possible to combine them to construct hybrid multiple classifier systems. A specific mechanism was designed to build a combined MCS, in which the number of classifiers from each type is controlled by a given ratio. For an N classifier system, m of N classifiers must come from a designated candidate type pool and the remaining (N-m) from another. For instance, if m is the number of trees in an MCS, altering m from 0 to N, we can obtain a set of hybrid systems that composed of different numbers of trees (from 0 to N) and a complement number of nets (from N to 0). In fact, when m=0, the hybrid systems become the multiple classifier systems purely composed of neural nets. On the other hand, when m=N, the systems are the pure multiple tree systems. In this way, the previous two types of multiple classifier systems are just two special cases of hybrid systems.

3.4 Decision Fusion Strategies

For the multi-classifier systems of neural nets two decision strategies, i.e. *averaging* and *majority-voting*, can be employed to determine the system output because the outputs of individual members (nets) are continuous. For the systems of decision trees, voting or winner-takes-all strategies appear appropriate because the outputs of trees are categorical.

4 Diversity Measures and Performance Assessment

Littlewood & Miller defined some measures in terms of probability of simultaneous classifier failure, such as, $E(\Theta)$ — the probability that a randomly selected classifier, Θ, from N classifiers fails on a randomly selected input, $E(\Theta^2)$ — the probability of two classifiers selected at random from N classifiers will both fail on a random input, and variance $Var(\Theta)=E(\Theta^2)- E(\Theta)^2$. These quantities were derived on assumption of infinite sets of classifiers and inputs, and intend to measure independence of failure. In reality, both the numbers of classifiers and input instances are likely to be very small. Therefore, Partridge et al (1997) have defined some other measures for those situations. Notations:

        M = the number of test patterns,

        N = number of classifiers in system A, (usually, N set to an odd number)

        k_n = the number of patterns that fail on exactly n classifiers in A

The probability p_n that exactly n classifiers fail on a randomly selected test pattern x is defined as:

$$p_n = \frac{k_n}{M} \qquad n = 1,2,...,N \tag{1}$$

4.1 Reliability Measures

The following are some probabilities usually defined as reliability measures.
- The probability that a randomly selected classifier in A fails on a randomly selected input:

$p(1) = P(one\,randomly\,chosen\,classifier\,fails\,on\,x)$

$\quad = \sum\limits_{n=1}^{N} P(exactly\,n\,classifiers\,fail\,on\,x\,and\,the\,chosen\,classifier\,is\,one\,of\,the\,failures)$

$\quad = \sum\limits_{n=1}^{N} P(chosen\,classifier\,fails\,|\,exactly\,n\,classifiers\,fail\,)*P(exactly\,n\,classifiers\,fails)$

$\quad = \sum\limits_{n=1}^{N} \dfrac{n}{N}*p_n \tag{2}$

Similarly,
- The probability that two classifiers selected from A at random (without replacement) both fail on a randomly selected input:

$$P(2different\,classifiers\,in\,A\,fail) = \sum\limits_{n=1}^{N} \frac{n(n-1)}{N^2} p_n \tag{3}$$

- In general, the probability that r randomly chosen classifiers fail on a randomly

$p(r) = P(r\,randomly\,chosen\,classifiers\,fail)$

$\quad = \sum\limits_{n=1}^{N} \dfrac{n}{N}*\dfrac{(n-1)}{(N-1)}*...\dfrac{(n-r+1)}{(N-r+1)}*p_n \qquad \forall\ r = 2,3,...,N \tag{4}$

chosen input can be formulated as:

In addition, the probabilities, e.g. p(1 out of 2 correct), that 1 out of 2 randomly selected classifiers produces correct answer, p(2 out of 3 correct), etc, have also been used for measuring the reliability of a system.

4.2 Coincident Failure Diversity (CFD)

The essence of developing multiple classifier systems is to reduce chance that members in a system make mistakes coincidentally. Therefore, a diversity that measures coincident failures of N members on the same input can be estimated by the following equation.

$$CFD \equiv \begin{cases} \dfrac{1}{1-P_0} \sum\limits_{n=1}^{N} \dfrac{N-n}{N-1} P_n, & if\ P_0 < 1 \\ 0, & if\ P_0 = 1 \end{cases} \tag{5}$$

CFD $\in$ [0, 1]. CFD = 0 indicates either all failures are the same for all classifiers—hence no diversity; or there is no test failure at all, i.e. all classifiers are perfect and identical—hence no diversity (no need for diversity if a perfect classifier is produced). CFD=1 when all test failures are unique to one classifier, i.e. p_1 =1.

The probability that the majority of the classifiers, $(N+1)/2$, in A produce the correct answer for a randomly chosen input:

$$p(maj) = 1 - \sum P(minority\ of\ classifiers\ in\ A\ fail) = 1 - \sum_{n=(N+1)/2}^{N} p_n = \sum_{n=0}^{(N-1)/2} p_n \qquad (6)$$

4.3 Assessment of Classification Accuracy

The classification accuracy of a multi-classifier system can be measured by the generalisation. However, this measure has a serious drawback, i.e. its value does not really indicate the true performance of a classifier when a test data set is unbalanced.

For dichotomy classification problems the Receiver Operation Characteristic (ROC) curve is an effective measure of performance. It can avoid the above drawback by showing the sensitivity and specificity of classification for two classes over a complete domain of decision thresholds. The sensitivity and (1-specificity) at a specific threshold value or/and the area under the curve are usually quoted as indicators of performance.

5 Application to Osteoporosis Problem

We have applied our techniques to a number of real-world problems after tested them on some artificial problems. Here we present the results of one of those real-world problems, i.e. osteoporosis disease classification (prediction).

5.1 Osteoporosis Problem

Osteoporosis is a disease that causes bones to become porous and to break easily. Identification of the most salient risk factors for the disease and the use of these risk factors for predicting the disease development will be very helpful for medical profession. We have collected the data on 719 cases from regional hospitals. The data contains 31 risk factors identified initially by the medical field experts as relevant to the disease. The outcome is a diagnosis decision, i.e. osteoporotic or non-osteoporotic, based on the T-test score from the ultrasound scanners. It is essentially a classification problem and therefore taken as application of our techniques. 519 patterns randomly sampled out of 719 are partitioned to a training set (319) and a validation set (200). The remaining 200 patterns are kept for testing. The sampling is repeated N (in this case, N=9) times.

5.2 Results from the MCS of Nets

Table 1 is a sample of the evaluation results produced by our multi-version system program for one of 9-classifier systems of neural nets.

Block (a) shows the individual performance of 9 classifiers. Generalisation, sensitivity and specificity are obtained when the threshold = 0.5. The average generalisation is 0.74. Block (b) shows the coincident failures of 9 classifiers in this system. Each row tells that k_n patterns failed exactly n classifiers, e.g. in row 3, 16 test patterns failed on exactly 2 classifiers of 9, and the probability p_2 is 0.08.

The last block (c) summarises the system performance defined in the earlier sections. It can be seen that the generalisation, is improved by 3% when *majority-voting* strategy, *G(voting)*, is employed, compared with that of the *averaging* strategy, *G(averaging)*. The magnitude of improvement is not significant because the Coincident Failure Diversity (CFD) among its 9 members is not high, only around 0.40.

Table 2 summarises the evaluation results of multiple classifier systems which were built by respectively picking the classifiers from 4 pools of the nets trained with the top 5, 10, 15 and 20 salient features selected from original 31 features. The mix MCSs were also built by choosing 9 nets randomly from all 4 pools.

Table 1. System Assessments

(a) Individual performance

classifier	gen.	sensitivity	specificity
1	0.765	0.516	0.853
2	0.740	0.438	0.882
3	0.760	0.500	0.875
4	0.740	0.438	0.882
5	0.765	0.516	0.882
6	0.760	0.516	0.875
7	0.705	0.531	0.787
8	0.725	0.422	0.868
9	0.700	0.516	0.787

(b) Classifier coincident failures

n	k_n	p_n
0/9	121	0.605
1/9	4	0.020
2/9	16	0.080
3/9	2	0.010
4/9	11	0.055
5/9	4	0.020
6/9	6	0.030
7/9	3	0.015
8/9	4	0.020
9/9	29	0.145

(c) System performance

$E(\Theta)= 0.2533$, $E(\Theta^2)= 0.2056$,
$Var(\Theta)= 0.1413$,   **CFD= 0.4035**
p(2 different both fail)= 0.1996
P(1 out of 2 correct) = 0.8050
P(1 out of 3 correct) = 0.8250
P(2 out of 3 correct) = 0.7549
P(1 out of 9 correct) = 0.8550
G(averaging)   **= 0.7400**
G(voting)   **= 0.7700**

It should be noted that all numbers quoted in the Table are the average value over 27 experiments, i.e. 27 MCSs, and their standard deviations (s.d.). *G(mean)* is the mean value of individual classifiers in the MCS.

Table 2 The evaluations of the multiple classifier systems of neural nets

features selected	G(mean)		G(averaging)		G(voting)		CFD	
	average	s.d.	average	s.d.	average	s.d.	average	s.d.
5	0.715	0.003	0.716	0.003	0.725	0.003	0.223	0.070
10	0.732	0.005	0.772	0.008	0.777	0.006	0.465	0.036
15	0.734	0.004	0.752	0.003	0.757	0.008	0.455	0.010
20	0.700	0.003	0.702	0.003	0.712	0.003	0.345	0.074
mix-all	0.721	0.008	0.744	0.008	0.768	0.009	0.476	0.053

The results can be concluded as follows:

- The diversity CFD in the intra-category MCSs is considerably small (0.18 < CFD <0.35), which is already expected, varying as the number of features used for nets' training and the ranking method.
- The inter-category MCSs have larger CFD, which leads to some extent of improvement compared to the mean of the MCSs with *majority-voting* strategy applied.
- The generalisation obtained by the *majority-voting* strategy in MCSs in any category is only marginally better than that of MCSs with the *averaging* strategy, which suggest that these decision strategies behaved similar in this circumstance.
- The mixed MCSs do increase the diversities (0.40<CFD<0.51) but the generalisations of majority-voting are not increased proportionally because of lower *mean* generalisation over all the individual nets.
- The MCSs constructed with the nets from some specific groups (e.g. nets trained with 10-salient-feature data set) produce the best performance.

5.3 Results from MCSs of the Decision Trees

Table 3 summarises the results of evaluations on the MCSs that were only composed of the decision trees induced with all 31 input features (i.e. no input decimation) in the data by setting the pruning confidence level to 10%, 25%(the default level) and 50%.

It is obvious that the diversity CFD increases as the pruning level rises and the difference between the generalisations obtained by the *majority-voting* and *mean* also increases. The

Table 3. Performance of the tree's MCSs

pruning level(%)	worst tree	best tree	G(mean)	G(voting)	CFD
10	0.680	0.755	0.726	0.750	0.490
25	0.650	0.745	0.709	0.740	0.592
50	0.655	0.735	0.692	0.740	0.629

generalisations by *majority-voting* are about 2.4-4.8% higher than the mean value of members in those systems. The systems yield generalisation almost as good as that of the best individual classifiers in the systems even though the overall generalisation still remains almost the same.

Table 4 summarises the evaluation results for the multi-classifier systems that were constructed with the trees induced by using the selected features. The results indicate (i) the multi-classifier systems built with the trees trained by the 10 selected features out-performed the others; (ii) All the tree's MCSs have relatively higher CFD. The mixed MCSs yield the highest CFD (0.614). In general,

Table 4. Tree MCSs with input decimation

features chosen	worst tree	best tree	G(mean)	G(voting)	CFD
10	0.710	0.785	0.748	0.780	0.574
15	0.685	0.750	0.720	0.750	0.557
20	0.660	0.750	0.715	0.745	0.592
mix-all	0.660	0.765	0.723	0.771	0.614

- Multi-classifier systems of the decision trees have higher CFD diversity (than those of the neural nets), but
- The generalisation performance is no better (or worse) than the MCSs of the nets.
- Trees are much quicker to develop.

5.4 Results of Hybrid MCSs

The results from the hybrid systems are depicted in Figure 1. With *majority-voting* strategy applied, the MCSs built purely with the neural nets ($m=0$, i.e. nets=9, trees=0) have relatively lower diversity (CFD= 0.445 on average) but a little bit higher generalisation, *G(voting)*=0.783, and the highest *G(average)* because of higher individual performance of the trained nets. On the other end, the MCSs built purely with the decision trees ($m=9$) have higher diversity (CFD=0.543 on average) but slightly lower generalisation *G(voting)*=0.781, and much

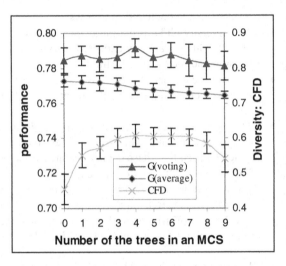

Figure 1 Diversity and generalisation performance of the hybrid multiple classifier

lower *G(average)*. By introducing a certain number of the diverse trees to the nets-dominated MCS, CFD is increased, which means that nets and decision trees have learned different knowledge embedded in the data set and that they are diverse. Hence, the generalisation with the *majority-voting* strategy is then improved (nearly 3% when $m=4$). Nevertheless, when the number of trees in the MCS is further increased ($m>=5$), the *voting*-performance of the MCSs on average deteriorates because the diversity decreases, but magnitude of reduction on the performance is very small. The middle line in the figure shows the average generalisation of the hybrid systems achieved by using *averaging* decision strategy. It shows that as the number of the trees in the MCSs increases, the *averaging*-performance of the MCSs deteriorates because of lower performance of the decision trees.

6 Conclusions

This paper investigated the diversity between trained neural nets and the automatically induced decision trees and the methodology of combining these types of classifiers to create hybrid multiple classifier systems. The evaluation results presented in this paper have shown that the classifiers trained with the data sets after input feature decimation are more diverse and performed better than those trained without feature selection. Higher performance achieved by the neural nets (or trees) trained with less salient features means that input decimation by ranking salient features was very successful not only in reducing the dimensions of the data set but also in improving the accuracy of classification. With a higher diversity the system is more reliable and produces consistent performance when tested with different data sets. However, the diversity between the trained neural nets is still not high enough to improve the performance significantly. The trees we induced appeared more diverse but have lower individual generalisation.

The multiple classifier systems constructed with the classifiers selected only from the same candidate pool (either trained neural nets or induced decision trees) can improve generalisation performance to a relatively small extent due to lower diversity within members of the pool when majority-voting strategy is applied. Combining neural nets and decision trees does create further diversity and consequently improve the accuracy of classification under the condition that the system is constructed with a majority of good nets and a minority of diverse-trees.

Acknowledgements

This research was funded by the EPSRC, UK, under grant number GR/K78607, and is now supported under grant GR/M75143.

References

Eckhardt, D. et al. (1985): A theoretical basis for the analysis of multiversion software subject to coincident errors. *IEEE Trans. Software Eng.* SE-11, pp1511-1517.

Freund, Y. & Schapire R.E. (1996): Experiments with a new boosting algorithm, in L. Saitta, ed., Machine Learning: Proceedings of the 13th national conference, Morgan Kaufmann. pp148-156.

Gedeon, T. (1997): Data mining of inputs: analysis magnitude and functional measures. *Int. J. of Neural Networks*. 8, pp209-218.

Hansen, L. et al. (1990): Neural network ensembles. IEEE Trans. *Patterns Analysis and Machine Intelligence*, vol. 12 pp993-1001.

Krogh, K. & Vedelsby, J. (1995): Neural network ensembles, cross-validation and active learning. In G. Tesauro, D.S Touretzky, and T.K. Leen, eds, *Advances in Neural Information Processing System*. vol.7. pp231-238, MIT press.

Littlewood, B. & Miller, D. (1989): Conceptual modelling of coincident failures in multiversion software. *IEEE Trans. Software Eng.* vol. 15, no. 12, pp1596-1614.

Partridge, D. et al. (1996): Engineering multiversion neural-net systems. *Neural Computation*, vol. 8, pp869-893.

Partridge, D. & Krzanowski, W. (1997): Software diversity: practical statistics for its measurement and exploitation. *Information and Software Technology*, vol. 39, pp707-717.

Quinlan, J. R. (1986): Induction of decision trees. *Machine Learning*, 1, pp81-106.

Tchaban, T., Taylor, M J, & Griffin, J.P. (1998): Establishing impacts of the inputs in a feedforward network, *Neural Computing \& Applications*, 7, pp309-317.

Tuner, K. & Oza, N. (1999): Decimated input ensembles for improved generalisation. Proceedings of IJCNN1999, Washington DC, October, 1999.

Wang, W. & Partridge, D. (1998): Multiversion neural network systems. Proceedings of neural networks and their applications, NEURAP'98, Marseilles, France, 1998, p351-357.

Wang, W., Jones, P. & Partridge, D. (1998): Ranking pattern recognition features for neural networks. in S. Singh, ed. *Advances in Patterns Recognition*, Springer, pp232-241.

Wang, W., Jones, P. & Partridge, D. (1999): Assessing the impact of input features in a feedforward network. *Neural Computing and Applications*. in press.

Self-Organizing Decomposition of Functions

N. Griffith[1] and D. Partridge[2]

[1] Department of Computer Science
University of Limerick, Ireland
[2] Department of Computer Science
University of Exeter, Exeter EX4 4PT, UK

Abstract. This paper discusses some of the issues raised by various approaches to decomposing functions and modular networks, and it offers a unified framework for multiple classifier (MC) systems in general. It argues that as yet there is no general approach to this problem although several approaches provide solutions to situations in which parametric labelling of a function allows the task facing classifying networks to be simplified. An MC connectionist system consisting of networks that process sub-spaces within a function based upon the similarity of patterns within its input domain is proposed and evaluated in the context of previous approaches to modular networks, and in the broader context of MC systems more generally. This simple *automatic* partitioning scheme is investigated using several different problems, and is shown to be effective. The degree to which the sub-spaces are specialized on a predictable subset of the overall function is assessed, and their performance is compared with equivalent single-network, and undivided multiversion systems. Statistical measures of 'diversity' previously used to assess voting MC systems are shown to apply to the measurement of the the degree of specialization or bias within groups of sub-space nets as well as provide a useful indicator across the range of MC systems. By successively increasing the overlap between sub-space partitions we show a transition from experts subnets, through voting version sets to optimal single classifiers. Finally, a unified framework for MC systems is presented.

1 Multiple Classifier Systems — A Farrago of Options

Approaches to Multiple classifier (MC) systems fall into two broad camps – although the distinction is not always clear-cut.

- "ensembles" - where a set of networks trained over different initial conditions combine their solutions either by way of *voting* for a decision (e.g., Partridge and Yates, 1996), or by *summing* their outputs (e.g., Drucker et al., 1994); a variety names are used for such ensembles, e.g., 'diverse' ensembles (used

J. Kittler and F. Roli (Eds.): MCS 2000, LNCS 1857, pp. 250–259, 2000.

below), committees, and multiversion systems; all ensembles attempt to optimize a result by exploiting in some way the "average" result across a set of approximations to the target function.

- "experts" - where a function is divided into sub-spaces that are processed by different "expert" networks. Each expert's task is simpler and their generalization is expected to improve over a single network because dividing up the function avoids undesirable cross-talk between regions within it - irrespective of how representative a training sample is. Subfunctions may be *ex machina* quite distinct conceptually, e.g. the *what* and *where* vision tasks (Jacobs, Jordan and Barto, 1991).

In this paper we focus on the "experts" approach and on beginning to unify the variety of options. First we will review two prominent techniques that use sets of simpler "expert" functions or sub-functions.

The first technique is the "boosting algorithm" (Schapire, 1990; Drucker, Schapire and Simard, 1993). In this scheme three networks are trained successively on sets of patterns filtered by the previously trained ones (the first is unfiltered). In a subsequent paper (in Perrone, 1993), a modified boosting algorithm was proposed: the second and third networks are trained on filtered subsets of the training set for the first network, rather than on filtered additional training sets. Bauer and Kohavi (1998) survey and empirically assess recent developments, such as Adaboost.

The second prominent technique is the modular architecture first reported by Jacobs et.al. (Jacobs, Jordan and Barto, 1991) and in (Jacobs, Jordan, Nowlan and Hinton 1991; Jacobs and Jordan 1991; Nowlan and Hinton, 1991). This architecture demonstrated that in certain situations there are clear gains to be made in generalization performance over 'equivalent' single MLPs. An important feature of the modular architecture is that the decomposition is to some extent learned. Task-specific knowledge identified *ex machina* with groups of patterns, e.g. the sex of a speaker (Nowlan and Hinton 1991), is used to label the patterns being classified. These labels are not part of the task being learned, e.g. vowel identity, but are used to train a gate network that determines which one of a set of "experts" will process each pattern. This system was further explored in (Jordan and Jacobs, 1994; Jacobs, 1997) to allow the system to perform both tasks simultaneously.

The modular architecture is demonstrably successful when learning what resources to allocate to a particular task - *when the basis on which that task should be subdivided is identified for it*. Where there is no *ex machina* division of the input domain into feature sets to be classified and features to be used to drive the gate networks the architecture needs to learn two things:

1. Which parts of the input domain description to use as inputs to the experts and which to use as inputs to the gates.
2. Which regions (i.e. categorical divisions) of the output domain are to be attended to by each gate network.

One route to a general solution is to group the inputs on the basis of their similarities. This requires no prior knowledge of the function. This approach will arbitrarily divide the function up according to the similarities between patterns in the input domain.

2   Automatic Decomposition

Subdivision of the task is performed by using a Kohonen Feature Map (KFM) (Kohonen 1989) to 'partition' the data. Construction of the set of network sub-spaces is a two-step procedure:

- the training data for the complete task is presented to a KFM in order to divide the data into groups whose input descriptions are similar.
- the data in each group is used to train a sub-space network — an expert subnet.

The final system, the sub-space-net system, is organized as a set of sub-spaces (e.g. each a trained multilayer perceptron (MLP)) preceded by the KFM, where each sub-space MLP receives its input from one category of the KFM. A new input is then fed through the KFM and into the particular sub-space associated with the category to which this input is assigned. The chosen sub-space computes with this input and the system output is simply the output of this particular sub-space as illustrated in Figure 1.

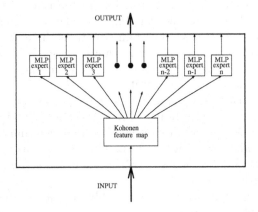

Fig. 1. A multiversion system of n sub-spaces

3   Measuring Diversity

In neural computing, averaging across the ensemble versions is the favoured decision strategy — i.e. summing the outputs of the individual versions and returning the average as the ensemble output. Bishop (1995) presents an analysis of this technique which he calls "committees" of networks. He shows that the sum-of-squares error (in fact, any convex error function) in the committee performance may be as little as $1/N$ times the average error of the N constituent versions. This optimal improvement will be realized when version errors are uncorrelated and have a zero mean. So, in effect, this property defines ensemble diversity with respect to the summing decision strategy.

Software engineers have also explored ensemble approaches which they call "multiversion" systems. In this context, voting is the preferred decision strategy and the coincidence of errors between two or more versions is taken as the basis for ensemble diversity (e.g. Littlewood and Miller, 1989). Such diversity is arguably a reflection of the bias associated with the network function and may be used to support a majority vote across a set of versions.

A first measure of this diversity developed and explored (in Partridge, 1996), GD, is defined as follows:

$$GD = 1 - \frac{p(2)}{p(1)}$$

where $p(1)$ is the probability that a randomly chosen version will fail on a random test, and $p(2)$ is the probability that two randomly chosen versions will *both* fail on a random test.

This measure has a value of 1.0 for a maximally diverse set, because when every test failure is unique to one version $p(2) = 0$. It has a minimum value of 0.0 for a minimally diverse set, because if every error is repeated in every version $p(1) = p(2)$. A subsequent enhancement of this diversity measure has been proposed, coincident-failure diversity (CFD) by Partridge and Krzanowski (1997).

These diversity measures (developed for use with voting ensemble systems) can also be used to assess the degree of 'specialized expertise' (i.e. variance) obtained in a sub-space system. If we have a 'perfect' set of non-overlapping sub-spaces, then any test will be correctly computed by just the appropriate sub-space and incorrectly computed by the other sub-spaces. If there are N sub-space nets in the system, then the probability that exactly $N - 1$ sub-space nets will fail on a random test will be 1.0, i.e. $p_{N-1} = 1.0$. Hence, all other p_n values (i.e. $n = 0, 1, 2, \ldots, N - 2$ and $n = N$) will be zero. In this case. both GD and CFD collapse to $1/(N - 1)$.

These diversity measures thus give us a first indicator that spans the MC spectrum. If $GD \longrightarrow 1.0$ then treat the MC system as a voting ensemble; if $GD \longrightarrow 1/(N-1)$ then treat the system as expert sub-spaces; and if $GD \longrightarrow 0.0$ then select the best version and use that alone (the same argument holds for CFD).

4   Experimental Tasks

1. *LIC1*: If $d((x_1, y_1), (x_2, y_2))$ is the Euclidean distance between two co-ordinate points $(x_1, y_1) and (x_2, y_2)$ then,

$$LIC1 = \begin{cases} \textbf{true } if \ \ d((x_1, y_1), (x_2, y_2)) > LENGTH \\ \textbf{false } otherwise \end{cases}$$

   where x_1, y_1, x_2, y_2 and LENGTH are all real valued in the range (0,1) to six decimal places.

2. *LIC4*: This is a more complex boolean function involving the area of a triangle defined by three x-y co-ordinate points. If $\triangle$ is the area of the triangle defined by the three co-ordinate points (x_1, y_1), (x_2, y_2) and (x_3, y_3) then,

$$LIC4 = \begin{cases} \textbf{true } if \ \ \triangle > AREA \\ \textbf{false } otherwise \end{cases}$$

   where $x_1, y_1, x_2, y_2, x_3, y_3$ and AREA are all real valued in the interval (0,1) to six decimal places.

3. *OCR*: a data-defined problem; the database that defines it is publicly available (aha@ics.uci.edu) and consists of 20,000 uppercase letter images that have each been transformed into 16 numeric feature values (each feature is an integer in the range 0 to 15). The original images are derived from a variety of different fonts and were randomly distorted before the feature vectors were calculated, (Frey and Slate, 1991, give full details and performance statistics of a recognition system).

   This previous study used the first 16,000 image vectors (of the randomized 20,000) for training purposes and the final 4000 as the test set. We do likewise (the OCR16 systems). In addition we have run simulations using three random selections of 9,000 from the first 16,000 vectors as the training sets (the OCR9 systems). The two LIC tasks were trained and tested on (different) random sets of 1000 patterns.

5   Experimental Detail

All the networks used were MLPs containing a single layer of hidden units. All training and test sets of patterns were randomly selected (or generated).

After random initialization of the weights (in range -0.5 to 0.5), all MLPs were trained with the standard backpropagation algorithm with momentum (Rumelhart, Hinton and Williams, 1986). The training regime for each of the three problems was identical. For each function a "cube" of networks was produced by varying 3 parameters. These were 3 counts of Hidden Units, 3 seeds to generate the initial states of the network weights, and 3 seeds to either generate the data points input (LIC1 and LIC4) or to select at random 9,000 from the first 16,000 training patterns for the OCR9 sets.

To develop the sub-space system the training sets were partitioned using a two-dimensional KFM, with a three by three output surface (nine partitions) - a number consistent with other studies we have undertaken on MC systems, and having the advantage of being reasonable in terms of computational resources. There were thus 243 ($3 \times 3 \times 3 \times 9$) nets trained for LIC1, LIC4 and OCR9 and 81 ($3 \times 3 \times 9$) were trained for OCR16. The same process of partitioning was carried out for test sets using the same KFM weights.

The techniques for developing MC systems (for voting or averaging) have been fully explained and demonstrated elsewhere (e.g. Partridge and Yates, 1996). Such a MC system is composed of a set of nets each differently trained on problem data. The differences may be generated by varying the initial weight set, the number of hidden units, the composition of the training set or even the network type used (e.g. MLP or Radial Basis Function network).

6   Results

Each OCR system is assessed using either a thresholding criterion, (9T & 16T), in which a version is correct only if the target output is the only output greater than 0.5; and a maximum strategy, (9M & 16M), in which a version is correct if the target output unit contains the maximum value (of the 26 outputs), irrespective of its absolute value.

Table 1 compares the sub-space results (*exp as exp* column) with those arising from misusing sub-spaces as non-specialist nets (using an averaging and a majority-voting decision strategy)as well as both a diverse set of undivided versions used as a majority-voting system and a single network (both of these latter two systems were trained on the same resources as the sub-space networks). All the reported results are averages over 'cubes' of networks (described earlier).

Comparisons, over a range of different parameters, indicates that, for LIC1, sub-space systems perform consistently better (a 25% reduction in residual error) than diverse voting ensembles.

Table 1. Summary results of sub-space-net systems and diverse multiversion systems.

Data set	exp as exp	exp as nonexp averaging	voting	GD	div ensemble 'best'5 or 3	GD	single net
LIC1	98.8	78.6	89.6	0.65	98.4	0.62	99.3
LIC4	98.3	61.6	51.2	0.28	96.2	0.75	96.9
OCR9T	90.6	27.7	18.8	0.27	90.6	0.46	89.1
OCR9M	95.0	34.4	18.2	0.34	95.4	0.49	94.5
OCR16T	92.7	27.2	7.5	0.27	91.5	0.54	90.9
OCR16M	96.1	35.4	21.2	0.35	96.1	0.58	95.6

For LIC4 the strategy of using a sub-space system yields a 2% performance improvement over the best diverse ensemble system. The diverse multiversion system, for LIC4 in Table 1, was composed of five networks selected from a larger pool (see Partridge and Yates, 1996, for full details).

The OCR diverse ensemble results are for populations of the 3 best performing nets. The performance of the misused OCR sub-spaces is very low (column *exp as nonexp*) — not much better than random guessing among 16 alternatives. On OCR, the performance of the sub-spaces as experts and that of diverse ensembles of nets is largely equivalent.

The results shown above are for sub-space systems in which each sub-space is disjoint: each training pattern occurs in exactly one sub-space training set. However, it is instructive to consider successive relaxations of this constraint such that any given training pattern may occur in n sub-space training sets (where $n = 1, 2, 3, \ldots, N$). To illustrate and investigate this idea, the distances measured between a pattern and the KFM node weights were used to rank the similarity between a node and a pattern. This allows a pattern to be associated with more than one node. The sub-spaces overlap to various degrees with each other, e.g. in an m3 system each sub-space encompasses patterns for which a node was the 1st., 2nd., and 3rd. most 'similar'.

Table 2 summarizes the results for sub-spaces with varying degrees of overlapping membership when used as experts (i.e., to compute only inputs that fall within their own sub-space of 'expertise'). The second (double) column is again when the sub-space nets are (mis)treated as diverse ensembles using averaging and majority voting, respectively, as the decision strategies.

Table 2. Summary of performance for overlapping sub-space systems and diverse multiversion systems (OCR16M).

overlap n	exp as exp	exp as nonexp		GD	CFD
sub-spaces, mn		averaging	voting		
m1	**95.9**	36.0	22.0	0.35	0.40
m3	95.0	69.8	79.0	0.61	0.71
m5	94.3	76.9	91.7	0.71	0.83
m7	94.2	86.1	**95.3**	0.74	0.90
m9	94.0	94.0	94.0	0.00	0.00

7   Discussion

In Table 2, the best performance results are set in bold type: 95.9% for an expert subnet system, and 95.3% for a majority voting ensemble. However, these two, seemingly very different approaches to MC systems, were constructed using the same sub-space blurring procedure. For the first result, $n = 1$, and for the second, $n = 7$. They are two systems selected from a continuum, and they both perform very well when appropriately treated as very different kinds of MC systems. Finally, notice that the diversity measures indicate the optimum points in the series of MC systems at which to apply the very different decision procedures to obtain the best results. For the m1 system (i.e. no overlap) GD

at 0.35 approaches the 'expert' optimum of $1/(9-1) = 0.125$, whereas for the m7 system the GD of 0.74 approaches the maximum of 1.0.

It seems unlikely that decomposing a function will deliver an actual saving in resources over a single net. For example, this seems to be the case for the modular gate architecture. From what can be approximated from published figures, the modular gate architecture uses more weights over all its experts and gate network than a single network alone - between 1.5 and 4 times as many[1].

The simulations described in this paper have been designed to look at the utility of automatically subdividing the data sets for both well-specified and data-defined functions using self-organizing techniques. Such an approach avoids the requirement for *ex machina* information and does not require inordinate amounts of training data.

The diversity indicators, GD and CFD, are the first example of a unifying feature within the farrago of apparently unconnected approaches to MC systems — they link voting ensembles and the sub-space systems. A further link was revealed and illustrated by blurring sub-spaces.

As a first point of departure for a unified framework for the full range of MC systems, consider the illustration in Figure 2. It shows a hierarchical taxonomy of MC options, with the names of the options at the nodes and the criteria for classification on the arcs. It also shows the main cross connections developed and illustrated in this paper.

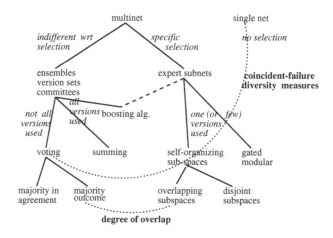

Fig. 2. A hierarchical taxonomy of MC systems with two unifying 'features'

---

[1] This estimate is on the basis that even if a resource is relatively unused, if it is required for the architecture to function successfully it has been included as a system resource

8   Conclusions

The question of how it may be possible to adequately decompose functions using automatic decomposition remains open. While the automatic decomposition process explored in this paper appears to be as effective as training nets on non-partitioned pattern sets and combining these in a voting ensembles for particular network resource levels. Where the input domain is not differentiated apart from the identity of the classes that are the subject of training then splitting the input domain up can be seen to have a negative effect. That is to say - for a given set of resources - when subdivided nets are compared to undivided nets then the undivided nets may perform better.

The diversity of a MC system is usefully defined as that property of the component subsystems which can be exploited to produce an overall system error that is less than the error of any component subsystem. Diversity is thus not a property solely dependent upon the set of MC subsystems. It must be considered in relation to a decision strategy — e.g. majority voting, summing, or subnet selection.

What is required is an efficient means to probe the available networks in order to establish which of the many (if any) MC approaches will deliver an optimal system within the specific constraints and requirements of the particular task. This implies that some unifying framework exists and contains measurable features that span the full range of possibilities. We have presented and illustrated the use of one such probe — a coincident-failure diversity measure. Others will be needed.

Acknowledgements

This research was in part supported by a grant (no. GR/H85427) from the EPSRC/DTI Safety-Critical Systems Programme, and subsequently by an EPSRC grant (no. GR/K78607). Current support from the EPSRC (grant no. GR/M75143) is gratefully acknowledged.

References

1. Bauer, E. and Kohavi, R., 1998, An empirical comparison of voting classification algorithms: bagging, boosting, and variants, *Machine Learning*, vol. 13, pp. 1-38.
2. Bishop, C.M. 1995, *Neural Networks for Pattern Recognition*, Oxford University Press, Oxford.
3. Drucker, H., Schapire, R. and Simard, P., 1993, Improving performance in neural networks using a boosting algorithm, *Advances in Neural Information Processing Systems 5*, 42-49.
4. Drucker, H. et.al., 1994, Boosting and other ensemble methods, *Neural Computation* vol. 6, no. 6, pp. 1289-1301.
5. Frey, P. and Slate, D., 1991, Letter recognition using holland-style adaptive classifiers. *Machine Learning*, vol. 6, pp. 161-182.

6. Geman, S., Bienenstock, E. and Doursat, R. 1992, Neural networks and the bias/variance dilemma. Neural Computation, vol. 4, no. 1, pp. 1-58.

7. Jacobs, R. A., Jordan, M. I, Barto, A. G., 1991, Task decomposition through competition in a modular connectionist architecture: the what and where vision tasks, *Cognitive Science*, vol. 15, pp. 219-250.

8. Jacobs, R. A., Jordan, M. I., Nowlan, S.J. & Hinton, G.E., 1991, Adaptive Mixtures of Local experts, *Neural Computation*, vol. 3, pp. 79-87.

9. Jacobs, R. A., and Jordan, M. I., 1991, A Competitive Modular Connectionist Architecture, *Advances in Neural Information Processing Systems 3*, R. P. Lippman, J. Moody and D. S. Touretzky (Eds.), 767-773.

10. Jacobs, R. A., 1997, Bias/Variance analyses of mixtures-of-experts architectures *Neural Computation*, vol. 9, pp. 369-383.

11. Jordan, M. I., and Jacobs, R.A., 1994, Hierarchical Mixtures of experts and the EM Algorithm, *Neural Computation*, vol. 6, pp. 181-214.

12. Kohonen, T., 1989, *Self-organization and Associative Memory*, Springer Verlag, Berlin.

13. Littlewood, B., and Miller, D. R., Conceptual modelling of coincident failures in multiversion software engineering, 1986, *IEEE Trans. on Software Engineering*, vol. 15, no. 12, pp. 1596-1614.

14. Nowlan, S. J., and Hinton, G. E., 1991, Evaluation of Adaptive Mixtures of Competing Experts, *Advances in Neural Information Processing Systems 3*, R. P. Lippman, J. Moody and D. S. Touretzky (Eds.), 774-780.

15. Partridge, D., 1996, Network Generalization Differences Quantified, *Neural Networks*, vol. 9, no. 2, pp. 263-271.

16. Partridge, D., and Griffith, N., 1995, Strategies for Improving Neural Net Generalisation, *Neural Computing & Applications*, vol. 3, pp. 27-37.

17. Partridge, D., and Krzanowski, W., 1997, Software Diversity: practical statistics for its measurement and exploitation, *Information and Software Technology*, vol. 39, pp. 707-717.

18. Partridge, D., and Yates, W. B., 1996, Engineering Multiversion Neural-Net Systems, *Neural Computation*, vol. 8, no. 4, pp. 869-893.

19. Partridge, D. and Yates, W. B., 1997, Data-defined Problems and Multiversion Neural-net Systems, *Journal of Intelligent Systems*, vol. 7, nos. 1-2, pp. 19-32.

20. Perrone, M.(Ed), 1993, Pulling it all together: methods for combining neural networks, ONR Tech. Rep. 69, Institute for Brain and Neural Systems, Brown University (*mpp@brown.edu*).

21. Rumelhart, D.E and Hinton, G.E. and Williams, R.J., 1986, Learning internal representations by error propagation., In *Parallel Distributed Processing: Explorations in the Microstructure of Cognition, Vol. 1:Foundations*, (Eds.) D.E Rumelhart and J.L. McClelland, MIT Press, Cambridge, MA:.

22. Schapire, R., 1990, The strength of weak learnability. *Machine Learning*, vol. 5, no. 2, pp. 197-227.

Classifier Instability and Partitioning

Terry Windeatt

Centre for Vision, Speech and Signal Proc., School of EE, IT & Maths,
University of Surrey, Guildford, Surrey, United Kingdom GU2 5XH
t.windeatt@surrey.ac.uk

Abstract. Various methods exist for reducing correlation between classifiers in a multiple classifier framework. The expectation is that the composite classifier will exhibit improved performance and/or be simpler to automate compared with a single classifier. In this paper we investigate how generalisation is affected by varying complexity of unstable base classifiers, implemented as identical single hidden layer MLP networks with fixed parameters. A technique that uses recursive partitioning for selectively perturbing the training set is also introduced, and shown to improve performance and reduce sensitivity to base classifier complexity. Benchmark experiments include artificial and real data with optimal error rates greater than eighteen percent.

1   Introduction

The idea of combining multiple classifiers is based on the observation that achieving optimal performance in combination is not necessarily consistent with obtaining the best performance for a single classifier. However certain conditions need to be satisfied to realise the performance improvement, in particular that the constituent (base) classifiers be not too highly correlated, as discussed in [1]. Various techniques have been devised to reduce correlation between classifiers before combining, including: (i) reducing dimension of training set to give different feature sets, (ii) incorporating different types of base classifier, (iii) designing base classifiers with different parameters for same type of classifier, (iv) resampling training set so each classifier is specialised on different subset, and (v) coding multi-class binary outputs to create complementary two-class problems. In this paper, we investigate how base classifier complexity affects generalisation in a framework that incorportes correlation reduction technique (iv), which uses different training sets. In addition, we introduce a recursive partitioning technique that uses a measure of inconsistency of classification to extract a maximally separable subset and to identify inconsistently classified patterns. We investigate the effect on combined classifier performance of leaving out inconsistently classified patterns from base classifier training sets.

Training on subsets appears to work well for unstable classifiers, such as neural networks and decision trees, in which a small perturbation in the training set may lead to a significant change in constructed classifier. Effective methods based on perturbing the training set prior to combining, include Bagging and Boosting. Training set perturbation methods were generally developed with classification trees as base classifiers, and do not necessarily improve performance with neural network base classifiers, since random weight initialisation provides its own perturbation.

J. Kittler and F. Roli (Eds.): MCS 2000, LNCS 1857, pp. 260-269, 2000.

2   Correlation Measure

The partitioning method proposed here is based on a spectral representation of 2-class target vector with respect to individual binary classifier decisions. The transformation of binary data may be carried out using a variety of matrices that differ only in row ordering. For example, the Hadamard transform T^n with entries $\in \{-1,+1\}$ is a complete orthogonal square matrix that can be expressed as a recursive structure:.

$$T^n = \begin{bmatrix} T^{n-1} & T^{n-1} \\ T^{n-1} & -T^{n-1} \end{bmatrix}. \tag{1}$$

The Walsh and Rademacher-Walsh transform matrices have similar row entries but use a different ordering of the 2^n functions that collectively constitute the closed set. The inverse for all these three orderings exists, but since our functions may be incompletely specified, noisy and contradictory we are interested in information content, and concentrate on spectral coefficients rather than computation of the inverse. We can therefore use any spectral ordering, and choose any binary coding instead of $\{+1,-1\}$. Representing the transform by $T^n Y = S$, where Y is the target vector and if $X = (x_1, x_2... x_n)$, the subscript notation and corresponding meaning for coefficients up to third order is given in [2] as follows:

s_0	correlation between $f(X)$ and constant	
$s_i \; i=1...n$	correlation between $f(X)$ and x_i	(2)
$s_{ij} \; i,j = 1...n, \; i \neq j$	correlation between $f(X)$ and $x_i \oplus x_j$	
$s_{ijk} \; i,j,k = 1...n, \; i \neq j \neq k$	correlation between $f(X)$ and $x_j \oplus x_k \oplus x_k$	

Interestingly, first order coefficients s_i in (2) provide a unique identifier if the function is linearly separable (Chow parameters), and although there is no known mathematical relationship between these parameters and weight/threshold values of a single perceptron, implementation tables exist for $n \leq 7$.

3   Extracting Separable Subsets

A constructive approach, similar to the Sequential Learning (SL) algorithm [3], is selected to partition the training data (for a review of constructive methods for binary data see [4]). The principle behind SL is to identify and remove a maximally separable subset of patterns at each partitioning step. It relies on finding a half-space consistent with all patterns of one class and a maximal subset of the other class - an NP-hard problem [5]. Various ways of approximating the algorithm can be found in the literature [6], and we select an approach based upon applying a necessary check for separability from threshold logic theory.

By assigning one of two classes to each base classifier and repeating b times, each training pattern may be regarded as a vertex in the b-dimensional binary hypercube:

$$X_m = (x_{m1}, x_{m2}, ..., x_{mb}) \qquad x_{mj} \text{ and } f(X_m) \in \{0,1\} \tag{3}$$

By comparing vertices in the hypercube, a value is assigned to each binary component x_j in (3) that we call sensitivity (σ) according to the following rule (generalisation of the first stage of logic minimisation originally described in [7]):

$$\text{For all } X_1, X_2 \text{ such that } f(X_1) \neq f(X_2) \tag{4}$$

$$\text{Assign } |\sigma_j| = |x_{1j} - x_{2j}||X_1 \oplus X_2|^{-1}$$

where σ_j is excitatory $= \sigma_j^+$ if $x_{1j} = f(X_1)$

σ_j is inhibitory $= \sigma_j^-$ if $x_{1j} \neq f(X_1)$

$|\sigma_j|$ is therefore inversely proportional to Hamming Distance, and to keep excitatory and inhibitory contributions separate are labelled σ_j^+ and σ_j^-, and summed over all patterns. The existence of $\sum_X \sigma_j^+ > 0$ and $\sum_X \sigma_j^- > 0$ provides evidence that the set of patterns is not 1-monotonic in the jth component and therefore non-separable. A discussion of k-monotonicity as necessary and increasingly sufficient conditions for separability is given in [2] [8]. For a completely specified function and considering nearest neighbours only, summing σ_j^+ and σ_j^- is identical to spectral summation, and $\sum_X \sigma_j^+$ and $\sum_X \sigma_j^-$ give the first order spectral coefficients, decomposed into excitatory and inhibitory contributions. Further details of calculating spectral contributions, with examples using simple Boolean functions can be found in [6].

To identify a maximal separable subset, each pattern is assigned a measure h_{mon1}, representing its contribution to separability, based on the summation of evidence of each component, as follows:

$$h_{mon1} = \sum_{j=1}^{b} \left[signum(\sum_X \sigma_j^+ - \sum_X \sigma_j^-) \left(\frac{\sigma_j^+}{\sum_X \sigma_j^+} - \frac{\sigma_j^-}{\sum_X \sigma_j^-} \right) \right] \tag{5}$$

where $signum()$ ensures that sign of the jth contribution to h is based on the larger of $\sum_X \sigma_j^+$ and $\sum_X \sigma_j^-$.

Figure 1 shows a typical plot of cumulative sum of patterns sorted by h_{mon1}. The peak is used as the threshold to extract each separable subset. For example in Figure 1 (Gaussian), the second extracted subset for class 1 represented by the smaller peak, contains approx. 50 patterns which results from thresholding the larger class 1 peak at approx. 150 patterns. For experiments reported here, four separable subsets (two class 1 and two class 2) are extracted and we refer to the remaining patterns as the inconsistently classified set (ICS). The first two class 1 (or class 2) extracted subsets contain unambiguously correctly and incorrectly classified patterns respectively, and for the two-dimensional artificial data of experiment 3 we were able to observe that patterns in ICS clustered around the Bayes boundary [9].

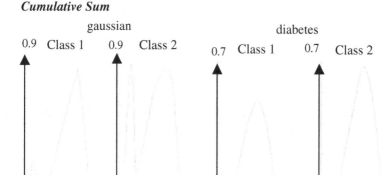

Fig. 1. Cumulative sum h_{mon1} versus number of sorted patterns for two extracted subsets, class 1 and class 2, Gaussian data (*left*) and Diabetes data.

The *ICS* is split into approximately k equal subsets, each subset being left out of a base classifier training set to obtain the new ICS estimate for the next recursion:

$ICS(1) = ICS$ estimate after one recursion using empty ICS (i.e. no patterns left out)

$ICS(m) = ICS$ estimate after one recursion using $ICS(m-1)$, m is recursion number

3   Results

Test and train error rates for varying base classifier complexity are presented for artificial data as well as real problems from Proben1 benchmark datasets (Diabetes, Cancer [10]). In particular the Diabetes data is difficult to improve with methods that perturb the training set, allegedly due to noise [11] [12]. Each experiment is repeated ten times, with a different random 50/50 training/testing split in experiment 1 and 2, and different random seed for train and test pattern generation in experiment 3. The artificial data is useful as a development tool for visualising decision boundaries, but appears much harder to overfit compared with experiment 1 and 2.

All experiments use conventional MLP base classifier with single hidden layer, Levenberg-Marquardt optimisation algorithm and random initial weights. The parameters of the base classifier are fixed, but the number of hidden nodes h and the number of epochs *nepochs* are systematically varied. The classifier is run $b=50$ times with a random subset *(1/k)* of *ICS* left out of the training set of each base classifier. Decisions of b base classifiers are combined by majority vote, which is reported for all experiments. Additionally we calculate a weighted combination of classifier outputs using a single layer perceptron. The orientation weights of the perceptron are fixed at values proportional to $\sum_X \sigma_j^+$ or $\sum_X \sigma_j^-$ defined in (4). Although the spectral counting method described in (4) uses binary decisions to determine orientation weights, the bias weight is learned by gradient descent with real-valued classifier outputs (before decision-taking) applied to perceptron inputs. For the experiments reported here, we found no significant difference in the mean values of the two combiners, so we only report the majority vote.

Experiment 1:   Cancer   50/50 Training/Testing

For the cancer data the base classifier uses a single hidden node, $h = 1$. To quantify performance sensitivity with respect to *nepochs* and k, the following procedure is adopted. For each fixed value of k, *ICS(1)* is first estimated at *nepochs* = 64, and *nepochs* is reduced (log scale) after each recursion using the *ICS* estimate obtained at the previous higher value. Figure 2 (a) (b) show training error rate and test error rate respectively versus *nepochs*, at $k = 2, 3, \infty$. The case $k = \infty$ indicates that no patterns are left out of base classifier training sets, i.e. correlation is reduced by random weight initialisation alone. Figure 2 (c) shows pre-combined and combined train and test error rates versus *nepochs* at $k = 2$. Figure 2 (d) shows pre-combined and combined training and test error rates versus k at *nepochs* = 8. The pre-combined error rates are mean over b base classifiers. Combined rate refers to the majority vote combination. One std error bars are shown for the test rates in (c) (d).

Experiment 2:   Diabetes   50/50 Training/Testing

In the first Diabetes experiment k is fixed, $k = 2$ for $h = 1, 2, 3, 4$. For each fixed value of h, *ICS(1)* is estimated at *nepochs* = 64, and *nepochs* is reduced (log scale) after each recursion using the *ICS* estimate obtained at the previous higher value. Figure 3 (a) (b) show training error rate and test error rate respectively versus *nepochs*, for $h = 4, 3, 2$. Figure 3 (c) shows pre-combined and combined train and test error rates versus *nepochs* at $h = 2$. Figure 3 (d) shows pre-combined and combined train and test error rates versus h at *nepochs* = 8.

In the second Diabetes experiment k, h, *nepochs* are fixed at 2, 2, 8 respectively for each recursion. Figure 4 (a) (b) show training error rate and test error rate respectively versus *number of recursions*. Figure 4 (c) shows pre-combined and combined train and test error rates versus *number of recursions*. Figure 4 (d) shows number of patterns (%) in ICS versus *number of recursions*.

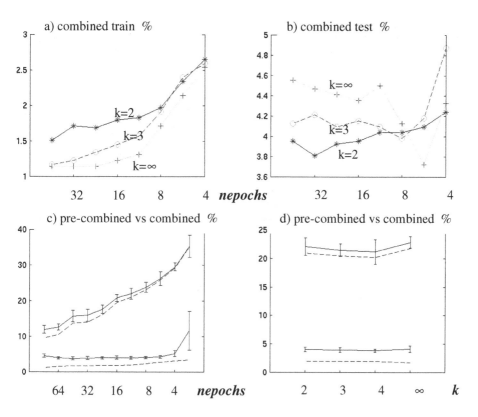

Fig. 2. Error rates cancer data, h = 1 (a) train error rates versus nepochs for k = 2,3, ∞ (b) test error rates versus nepochs for k = 2,3, ∞ (c) train (*dashed*) and test (*solid*) error rates before and after combining versus nepochs, k = 2 (d) train (*dashed*) and test (*solid*) error rates before and after combining versus k, nepochs = 8

Experiment 3:   Gaussian 400 Training & 30,000 Test Patterns Evenly Divided between Class 1 & 2, *Nepochs* **= 50.**

To develop and understand the method of Section 3, we use the two-dimensional overlapping Gaussian data of [13], which has class 1{mean (0,0), variance 1}and class 2{mean (2,0), variance 4}. The Bayes boundary is circular for this problem with Bayes error rate of 18.49%. The advantage of this simple problem is that we can visualise decision boundaries and see how the Bayes boundary is approximated. Typical individual decision boundaries with respect to the circular Bayes boundary are given for a few base classifiers in figure 5, along with the combined decision boundary for ICS(2), *k* = 2, *h* = 3, *nepochs* = 50.

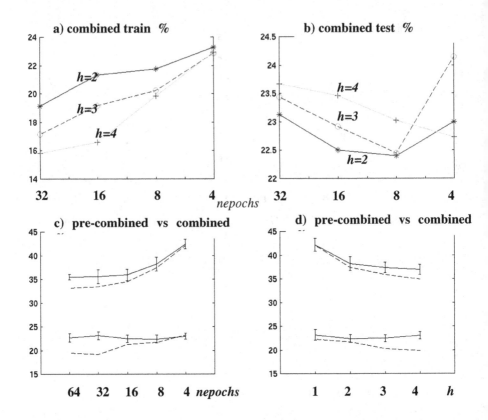

Fig. 3. Error rates Diabetes data, k = 2 (a) train error rates versus nepochs for h = 2, 3, 4 (b) test error rates versus nepochs for h = 2, 3, 4   (c) train (*dashed*) and test (*solid*) error rates before and after combining versus nepochs, h = 2 (d) train (*dashed*) and test (*solid*) error rates before and after combining versus h, nepochs = 8

For the Gaussian data, higher values of h may be used and *nepochs* is fixed at 50. For each fixed value of k, *ICS(1)* is estimated at $h = 10$, and h reduced after each recursion in single node steps, using the *ICS* estimate obtained at the previous higher node. Figure 6 (a) (b) show training error rate and test error rate respectively versus h, for $k = 10, 5, 4$. Figure 6 (c) shows pre-combined and combined train and test error rates versus h at $k = 4$. Figure 6 (d) shows pre-combined and combined train and test error rates versus k at $h = 7$.

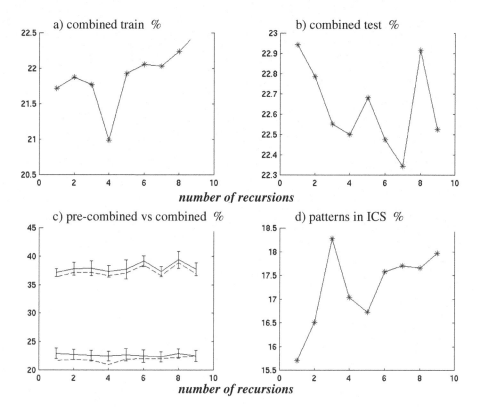

Fig. 4. Error rates Diabetes data, k = 2, h = 2, nepochs = 8 (a) train rates versus number recursions (b) test rates versus number recursions (c) train (dashed) and test (solid) error rates before and after combining versus number recursions (d) number of patterns in ICS (%) versus number recursions.

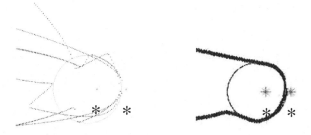

Fig. 5. Individual and combined boundaries, showing circular Bayes and Gaussian centres (*).

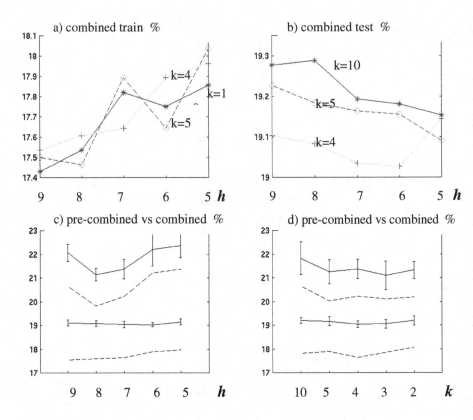

Fig. 6. Error rates Gaussian data, nepochs = 50   (a) train rates versus h for k = 10, 5, 4 (b) test rates versus h for k = 10, 5, 4   (c) train (dashed) and test (solid) error rates before and after combining versus h, k = 4   (d) train (dashed) and test (solid) error rates before and after combining versus k, h = 7.

4   Discussion and Conclusion

Base classifier complexity is varied by reducing h or *nepochs*, while at the same time recursively leaving out a random subset of inconsistently classified patterns from classifier training sets. The number of patterns left out is determined by k, the number of random subsets.

What ever value is chosen for k, including k = ∞, improvement as a result of combining compared with mean base classifier performance is quite dramatic (figure 2 (c) (d), figure 3 (c) (d) and figure 6 (c) (d)). It appears that as k is decreased the neural net base classifier can become more complex, without overfitting. Also as k is decreased, generalisation becomes less sensitive to *nepochs* (Figure 2 (b)) and h (Figure 6(b)), so that the tuning required to achieve similar level of performance should be less difficult.

The experimental results in Section 3 do not include a comparison with Bagging and Boosting for these problems. However the case $k = \infty$ uses perturbation by random weight initialisation and is therefore similar to Bagging. Also for the two benchmark data sets results are reported elsewhere, and in particular performance with Boosting on Diabetes data is shown to be worse than Bagging [12].

In Figure 3 (d) we show the number of patterns in *ICS*, for successive recursions with fixed *h, k, nepochs*. This is related to earlier work [9] which indicated that the stability of the *ICS* estimate may give information on selecting *h, k, nepochs*.

The background behind the proposed approach is similar to the noisy transmission channel concept used in Error-Correcting Output Coding (ECOC), which models the prediction task as a communication problem [14]. ECOC is an example of correlation reduction technique (v) in Section 1, and it should be possible to use ECOC codes to handle the multi-class case.

References

1. K. Tumer and J. Ghosh, Error correlation and error reduction in ensemble classifiers, Connection Science, Special Issue on Combining Artificial Neural Networks: Ensemble Approaches, 8(3-4), pp 385-404, 1996.
2. S. L. Hurst, D.M. Miller and J.C. Muzio, Spectral Techniques in Digital Logic, Academic Press, 1985.
3. M. Marchand, M. Golea and P. Rujan, A convergence theorem for sequential learning in two-layer perceptrons, Europhys. Lett. 11(6), pp 487-492, 1990.
4. M. Muselli, On sequential construction of binary neural networks, IEEE Trans. Neural Networks 6(3), 678-690, 1995.
5. M. Marchand and M. Golea, On learning simple neural concepts: from halfspace intersections to neural decision lists, Network Computation in Neural Systems 4 (1), pp 67-85, 1993.
6. T. Windeatt, R. Tebbs, Spectral technique for hidden layer neural network training, Pattern Recognition Letters, DecemberVol.18, No.8, pp.723-731, 1997.
7. E. J. McCluskey, Minimisation of boolean functions, Bell Syst. Tech. J., Vol 35(5), pp1417-1444, 1956.
8. S. Muroga, Threshold Logic & its Applications, Wiley, 1971.
9. T. Windeatt, Spectral partitioning for boundary estimation, In J.S. Boswell(ed.) Proc. of Int. Joint Conf. Neural Networks, Washington DC, #0733 , July 1999.
10. L. Prechelt, Proben1, Tech Report 21/94, Univ. Karlsruhe, Germany, 1994.
11. G. Ratsch and T. Onoda, Soft margin for Adaboost, Tech Report 021, NeuroCOLT2, Berlin, Aug 1998.
12. J. R. Quinlan, Bagging, Boosting and C4.5, in Proc 14th National Conf. on Artificial Intelligence, pp725-730, MIT press, 1996.
13. P. Yee, Classification requirements involving Backpropagation and RBF networks, Tech Report 249, McMasters Univ, Ontario, 1992.
14. T. G. Dietterich and G. Bakiri, Solving multiclass learning problems via error-correcting output codes, J. of Artificial Intelligence Research 2, pp263-286, 1995.

A Hierarchical Multiclassifier System for Hyperspectral Data Analysis

Shailesh Kumar[1], Joydeep Ghosh[1], and Melba Crawford[2]

[1] Laboratory of Artificial Neural Systems,
Department of Electrical and Computer Engineering,
The University of Texas at Austin, Austin TX-78712, USA.
{skumar, ghosh}@lans.ece.utexas.edu
[2] Center for Space Research,
The University of Texas at Austin, Austin TX-78712, USA.
crawford@csr.utexas.edu

Abstract. Many real world classification problems involve high dimensional inputs and a large number of classes. Feature extraction and modular learning approaches can be used to simplify such problems. In this paper, we introduce a hierarchical multiclassifier paradigm in which a C-class problem is recursively decomposed into $C - 1$ two-class problems. A generalized modular learning framework is used to partition a set of classes into two disjoint groups called meta-classes. The coupled problem of finding a good partition and of searching for a linear feature extractor that best discriminates the resulting two meta-classes are solved simultaneously at each stage of the recursive algorithm. This results in a binary tree whose leaf nodes represent the original C classes. The proposed hierarchical multiclassifier architecture was used to classify 12 types of landcover from 183-dimensional hyperspectral data. The classification accuracy was significantly improved by 4 to 10% relative to other feature extraction and modular learning approaches. Moreover, the class hierarchy that was automatically discovered conformed very well with a human domain expert's opinion, which demonstrates the potential of such a modular learning approach for discovering domain knowledge automatically from data.

1   Introduction

Many real world classification problems are characterized by a large number of inputs and a moderately large number of classes that can be assigned to any input. Two popular simplifications have been considered for such problems: (*i*) *feature extraction*, where the *input space* is projected into a smaller *feature space*, thereby addressing the curse of dimensionality issue, and (*ii*) *modular learning*, where a number of classifiers, each focusing on a specific aspect of the problem, are learned instead of a single classifier. Several methods for feature extraction and modular learning have been proposed in the computational intelligence community [1],[2].

J. Kittler and F. Roli (Eds.): MCS 2000, LNCS 1857, pp. 270–279, 2000.
© Springer-Verlag Berlin Heidelberg 2000

Prediction of landcover type from airborne/spaceborne sensors is an important classification problem in remote sensing. Due to advances in sensor technology, it is now possible to acquire hyperspectral data simultaneously in more than 100 bands, each of which measures the integrated response of a target over a narrow window of the electromagnetic spectrum [3]. The bands are ordered by their wavelengths and spectrally adjacent bands are generally statistically correlated with target dependent groups of bands. Using such high dimensional data for classification of landcover potentially improves discrimination between classes but dramatically increases problems with parameter estimation and storage and management of the extremely large datasets.

In this paper we propose a novel modular learning system comprised of an automatically generated hierarchy of classifiers, each solving a simple two class problem and having its own feature space. The set Ω of C classes is first partitioned into two disjoint subsets referred to as "meta-classes". A linear feature extractor that best discriminates the two meta-classes as well as the class partition itself is learned automatically. The two meta-classes are further partitioned recursively till the resulting meta-classes have only one of the C original classes. The binary tree generated as a result has C leaf nodes, one for each class, and $C-1$ internal nodes, each having a Bayesian classifier and a linear feature extractor. We illustrate the methodology by applying a hierarchical multiclassifier to a twelve class landcover prediction problem where the input space is a 183 band subset of the 224 bands (per pixel), each of 10 nanometer width, acquired by the NASA AVIRIS spectrometer over Kennedy Space Center in Florida. Apart from a significant improvement in classification accuracy, the proposed architecture also provided important domain knowledge that was consistent with a human expert's assessments in terms of the class hierarchy obtained. A significant reduction in the number of features from 183 to only one was obtained as a result of the classifier.

2   Hyperspectral Data

Hyperspectral methods for deriving information about the Earth's resources using airborne or space-based sensors yield information about the electromagnetic fields that are reflected or emitted from the Earth's surface, and in particular, from the spatial, spectral, and temporal variations of those electromagnetic fields [3]. Chemistry-based responses which are the primary basis for discrimination of land cover types in the visible and near infrared portions of the spectrum are determined from data acquired simultaneously in multiple windows of the electromagnetic spectrum. In contrast to airborne and space-based multispectral sensors which acquire data in a few (< 10) broad channels, hyperspectral sensors can now acquire data in hundreds of windows, each less than ten nanometers in width. Because many landcover types have only subtle differences in their characteristic responses, this potentially provides greatly improved characterization of the unique spectral characteristics of each, and therefore increases the classification accuracy required for detailed mapping of species from remotely sensed data. A hyperspectral image is essentially a three dimensional array $I(m, n, s)$, where (m, n) denotes a pixel location in the image and s denotes a spectral band (wavelength range). The value stored at $I(m, n, s)$ is the response (reflectance or emittance) from the pixel (m, n) at a wavelength corresponding to the spectral band s. There are typically 25-200+ spectral bands in typical hyperspectral data sets.

Analysis of hundreds of simultaneous channels of data necessitates the use of either feature selection or extraction algorithms prior to classification. Feature selection algorithms for hyperspectral classification are costly, while feature extraction methods based on KL-transforms, Fisher's discriminant or Bhattacharya distance cannot be used directly in the input space because the covariance matrices required in all these are highly unreliable, given the ratio of the amount of training data to the number of input dimensions. The results are also difficult to analyze in terms of the physical characteristics of the individual classes and are not generalizable to other images.

Lee and Landgrebe [4] proposed methods for *feature extraction based on decision boundaries* for both Bayesian and neural network based classifiers. After learning a classifier in the input space, the data is projected in a direction normal to the decision boundary. Jia and Richards [5],[6] proposed a feature extraction technique based on *segmented principal components transformation* (SPCT) for two class problems. Principal components transform is computed separately for each group of highly correlated bands. Selection of first few bands from each group results in a small number of features. Recently, we developed a best-bases algorithm [7] that extends the local discriminant bases (LDB) approach [8], developed for signal and image classification. The LDB was generalized to project an adjacent group of highly correlated bands onto the Fisher discriminant for each pair of classes in a pairwise classifier framework [9],[10]. For a C class problem, it required $\binom{C}{2}$ pairwise classifiers to be learned. In this paper, we propose an algorithm for partitioning the C class problem into a hierarchy of $C - 1$ two-class problems, each of which seeks to distinguish between two groups of classes or meta-classes. The automatic problem decomposition algorithm and Fisher projection based feature extraction algorithm is presented in the next section.

3   The Hierarchical Multiclassifier Architecture

Different ways of dividing a problem into simpler sub-problems have been investigated by the pattern recognition and computational intelligence communities. Each sub-problem, for example, could focus on a different subset of input features, different parts of the input space (e.g. mixture of experts [11]), or different training samples (e.g. boosting [12], bagging [13]). In [9],[10] we proposed a pairwise classifier architecture in which each sub-problem focuses on discriminating between a pair of classes. To be exhaustive, such an approach requires $\binom{C}{2}$ i.e. $\mathcal{O}(C^2)$ pairwise classifiers for a C class problem and, therefore, could be computationally expensive for problems with a large number of classes.

In this section we describe a new hierarchical multiclassifier architecture that requires only $C-1$ pairwise classifiers arranged as a binary tree with C leaf nodes, one for each class, and $C-1$ internal nodes, each with its own feature space. The root node (indexed 1) of the binary tree represents the original C class problem with its "class-set" $\Omega_1 = \mathbf{\Omega}$. The complete recursive partitioning algorithm is given below. In this algorithm, the two children of an internal node indexed n are indexed $2n$ and $2n+1$, and its class-set is denoted by Ω_n.

BUILDTREE(Ω_n)

1. Partition Ω_n into two: $(\Omega_{2n}, \Omega_{2n+1}) \leftarrow PartitionNode(\Omega_n)$
2. Recurse on each child:
   - if $|\Omega_{2n}| > 1$ then BUILDTREE(Ω_{2n})
   - if $|\Omega_{2n+1}| > 1$ then BUILDTREE(Ω_{2n+1})

The purpose of the PARTITIONNODE function is to find a partition of the set of classes Ω_n into two disjoint subsets such that the discrimination between the two partitions Ω_{2n} and Ω_{2n+1}, also referred to as "meta-classes", is high. It also finds a linear projection of the original D dimensional space into a smaller one dimensional space in which such a discrimination is maximum. The two problems of finding a partition, as well as the feature extractor that maximizes discrimination between the meta-classes obtained as a result of this partition, are coupled. In this paper, we use an approach based on our GENERALIZED ASSOCIATIVE MODULAR LEARNING SYSTEMS (GAMLS) [14] to solve these coupled problems, as described in the next section.

In the GAMLS framework, modularity is introduced through soft association of each training sample with every module. Initially, each sample is almost equally associated with all the modules. The learning phase in GAMLS comprises of two alternate steps: (i) for the current associations, update all the module parameters, and (ii) for the current module parameters, update the associations of all the training samples with each module. Using ideas from deterministic annealing, a temperature parameter is used to slowly converge the associations to hard partitions in order to induce specialization and decoupling among the modules. A growing and pruning mechanism is also proposed for GAMLS that automatically leads to the right number of modules required for the dataset.

The hierarchical multiclassifier architecture proposed in this paper is closely related to the association and specialization ideas of the GAMLS framework. The goal in the multiclassifier architecture is to partition the problem hierarchically in its output (class) space. At each level, the set of classes is partitioned into two meta-classes. Instead of associating a sample with a module, each class is associated with both the meta-classes. The update of these associations and meta-class parameters is done alternately while gradually decreasing the temperature. The complete algorithm is described below.

3.1   Partitioning a Set of Classes

Let Ω be any class-set with $K = |\Omega| \geq 2$ classes that needs to be partitioned into two meta-classes denoted by Ω_α and Ω_β. Association between a class $\omega \in \Omega$

with meta-class Ω_γ, $(\gamma \in \{\alpha, \beta\})$ is interpreted as the posterior probability of ω belonging to Ω_γ and is denoted by $P(\Omega_\gamma|\omega)$.

$$P(\Omega_\alpha|\omega) + P(\Omega_\beta|\omega) = 1, \quad \forall \omega \in \Omega. \tag{1}$$

Let μ_ω and Σ_ω denote the mean vector and covariance matrix, respectively, of any class $\omega \in \Omega$. Let $\mathcal{X}_\omega$ denote the training set comprised of $N_\omega = |\mathcal{X}_\omega|$ examples of class ω. For any given posterior probabilities $\{P(\Omega_\gamma|\omega), \gamma \in \{\alpha, \beta\}\}_{\omega \in \Omega}$, the mean μ_γ and covariance Σ_γ $(\gamma \in \{\alpha, \beta\})$ are given by:

$$\mu_\gamma = \sum_{\omega \in \Omega} P(\omega|\Omega_\gamma)\mu_\omega, \quad \gamma \in \{\alpha, \beta\} \tag{2}$$

$$\Sigma_\gamma = \sum_{\omega \in \Omega} \frac{P(\omega|\Omega_\gamma)}{N_\omega} \left[\sum_{\mathbf{x} \in \mathcal{X}_\omega} (\mathbf{x} - \mu_\gamma)(\mathbf{x} - \mu_\gamma)^T \right], \quad \gamma \in \{\alpha, \beta\}, \tag{3}$$

where by Bayes rule,

$$P(\omega|\Omega_\gamma) = \frac{P(\omega)P(\Omega_\gamma|\omega)}{P(\Omega_\gamma)}, \quad \gamma \in \{\alpha, \beta\}, \tag{4}$$

and the meta-class priors $P(\Omega_\gamma)$ are given by:

$$P(\Omega_\gamma) = \sum_{\omega \in \Omega} P(\omega)P(\Omega_\gamma|\omega), \quad \gamma \in \{\alpha, \beta\}. \tag{5}$$

The class priors $P(\omega) = \frac{N_\omega}{N}$, where $N = \sum_{\omega \in \Omega} N_\omega$.

Equation (3) is $\mathcal{O}(N)$ and can be reduced to $\mathcal{O}(|\Omega|)$ by a simple manipulation leading to:

$$\Sigma_\gamma = \sum_{\omega \in \Omega} P(\omega|\Omega_\gamma) \left[\Sigma_\omega + (\mu_\omega - \mu_\gamma)(\mu_\omega - \mu_\gamma)^T \right], \quad \gamma \in \{\alpha, \beta\} \tag{6}$$

For a c class problem, the Fisher discriminant [15] projects any $D(\geq c - 1)$ dimensional space into a $c - 1$ dimensional space. Here, each internal node is solving a $c = 2$ class problem (discriminating between meta-classes Ω_α and Ω_β) hence the linear feature extractor based on Fisher discriminant projects the D dimensional space into a one dimensional space at each internal node of the multiclassifier tree. This projection is defined in terms of the WITHIN CLASS covariance matrix $\mathbf{W}$ that measures a weighted covariance of the classes and is given by:

$$\mathbf{W} = P(\Omega_\alpha)\Sigma_\alpha + P(\Omega_\beta)\Sigma_\beta, \tag{7}$$

and the BETWEEN CLASS covariance matrix $\mathbf{B}$ given by:

$$\mathbf{B} = (\mu_\alpha - \mu_\beta)(\mu_\alpha - \mu_\beta)^T \tag{8}$$

The Fisher projection $\mathbf{w}$ that maximizes the discriminant

$$\mathcal{J}(\mathbf{w}) = \frac{\mathbf{w}^T \mathbf{B} \mathbf{w}}{\mathbf{w}^T \mathbf{W} \mathbf{w}} \tag{9}$$

is given by:

$$\mathbf{w} = \mathbf{W}^{-1}(\mu_\alpha - \mu_\beta) \tag{10}$$

The partitioning algorithm for any set of classes Ω is:

1. **Initialize:** $P(\Omega_\alpha|\omega_1) = 1$ for some $\omega_1 \in \Omega$ and $P(\Omega_\alpha|\omega) = 0.5, \quad \forall\, \omega \in \Omega - \omega_1$. Temperature $T = T_0$ (user defined parameter).
2. Compute the Fisher projection vector $\mathbf{w}$ using (10).
3. Compute the mean log-likelihood of meta-classes Ω_γ ($\gamma \in \{\alpha, \beta\}$):

$$\mathcal{L}(\Omega_\gamma|\omega) = \frac{1}{N_\omega} \sum_{\mathbf{x} \in \mathcal{X}_\omega} \log p(\mathbf{w}^T\mathbf{x}|\Omega_\gamma), \quad \gamma \in \{\alpha, \beta\}, \quad \forall\, \omega \in \Omega \tag{11}$$

where the pdf of Ω_γ in the one dimensional projected space is modeled as a Gaussian:

$$p(\mathbf{w}^T\mathbf{x}|\Omega_\gamma) = \frac{1}{\sqrt{(2\pi)\mathbf{w}^T\Sigma_\gamma\mathbf{w}}} \exp\left[-\frac{(\mathbf{x}-\mu_\gamma)^T\mathbf{w}^T\mathbf{w}(\mathbf{x}-\mu_\gamma)}{2\mathbf{w}^T\Sigma_\gamma\mathbf{w}}\right], \quad \gamma \in \{\alpha, \beta\} \tag{12}$$

4. Update the meta-class posteriors:

$$P(\Omega_\alpha|\omega) = \frac{\exp(\mathcal{L}(\Omega_\alpha|\omega)/T)}{\exp(\mathcal{L}(\Omega_\alpha|\omega)/T) + \exp(\mathcal{L}(\Omega_\beta|\omega)/T)}, \tag{13}$$

5. Repeat Steps 2 through 4 until the percentage increase in $\mathcal{J}(\mathbf{w})$ (Equation 9) is significant (e.g. 5%).
6. Compute Entropy of meta-class posteriors:

$$\mathcal{H} = \frac{1}{|\Omega|} \sum_{\omega \in \Omega} [P(\Omega_\alpha|\omega) \log_2 P(\Omega_\alpha|\omega) + P(\Omega_\beta|\omega) \log_2 P(\Omega_\beta|\omega)]. \tag{14}$$

7. If $\mathcal{H} < \theta_H$ (user defined threshold) then stop, otherwise:
   - Cool temperature: $T \leftarrow T\theta_T$ ($\theta_T < 1$ is a user defined cooling parameter)
   - Go back to step 2.

Each internal node n of the binary tree contains a projection vector $\mathbf{w}(n)$, and the parameters $(\mu_k, \Sigma_k, k \in \{2n, 2n+1\})$. The Bayesian classifier at node n generates the posterior probabilities $P(\Omega_{2n}|\mathbf{x}, \Omega_n)$ and $P(\Omega_{2n+1}|\mathbf{x}, \Omega_n)$.

3.2 Combining

After learning the hierarchical multiclassifier, a novel example $\mathbf{x}$ can be classified using the following theorem:

Theorem 1: The posterior probability $P(\omega|\mathbf{x})$ of any input $\mathbf{x}$ can be computed by multiplying the posterior probabilities of all the internal classifiers leading to the leaf node containing class ω from the root node, i.e.

$$P(\omega|\mathbf{x}) = \prod_{\ell=0}^{\mathcal{D}(\omega)-1} P(\Omega_{n(\omega)}^{(\ell)}|\mathbf{x}, \Omega_{n(\omega)}^{(\ell+1)}),\tag{15}$$

where $n(\omega)$ is the index of the leaf node containing class ω, $\mathcal{D}(\omega)$ is the depth of $n(\omega)$, $\Omega_n^{(\ell)}$ is the meta-class at the ℓth ancestor of node n such that $\Omega_{n(\omega)}^{(0)} = \{\omega\}$ and $\Omega_{n(\omega)}^{(\mathcal{D}(\omega))} = \Omega_1 =$ root node for any $\omega \in \Omega$.

Proof: The class posteriori $\{P(\omega|\mathbf{x})\}_{\omega \in \Omega}$ and the outputs $P(\Omega_n^{(\ell)}|\mathbf{x}, \Omega_n^{(\ell+1)})$ are related as:

$$P(\Omega_n^{(\ell)}|\mathbf{x}, \Omega_n^{(\ell+1)}) = \frac{\sum_{\rho \in \Omega_n^{(\ell)}} P(\rho|\mathbf{x})}{\sum_{\rho \in \Omega_n^{(\ell+1)}} P(\rho|\mathbf{x})}\tag{16}$$

Using (16) the right hand side of (15) can be written as:

$$\prod_{\ell=0}^{\mathcal{D}(\omega)-1} \left(\frac{\sum_{\rho \in \Omega_{n(\omega)}^{(\ell)}} P(\rho|\mathbf{x})}{\sum_{\rho \in \Omega_{n(\omega)}^{(\ell+1)}} P(\rho|\mathbf{x})} \right)\tag{17}$$

This reduces to

$$\frac{\sum_{\rho \in \Omega_{n(\omega)}^{(0)}} P(\rho|\mathbf{x})}{\sum_{\rho \in \Omega_{n(\omega)}^{(\mathcal{D}(\omega))}} P(\rho|\mathbf{x})}\tag{18}$$

But $\Omega_{n(\omega)}^{(0)} = \{\omega\}$ and $\Omega_{n(\omega)}^{(\mathcal{D}(\omega))} = \Omega_1 = \Omega$, so (18) is reduced to

$$\frac{P(\omega|\mathbf{x})}{\sum_{\rho \in \Omega} P(\rho|\mathbf{x})} = P(\omega|\mathbf{x})\tag{19}$$

since the denominator in (19) sums to 1.

Once the class posterior probabilities $\{P(\omega|\mathbf{x})\}_{\omega \in \Omega}$ are known, the maximum aposteriori probaiblity rule can be used to assign a class label to $\mathbf{x}$:

$$\omega(\mathbf{x}) = \arg \max_{\omega \in \Omega} P(\omega|\mathbf{x})\tag{20}$$

4   Experimental Results

The efficacy of the proposed multiclassifier architecture for hyperspectral data analysis is shown by experiments using a 183 band subset of the 224 bands, each of 10 nanometer width acquired by the NASA AVIRIS spectrometer over Kennedy Space Center in Florida. For classification purposes, 12 landcover types listed in Table 1. There were ≈ 350 examples for each class. These were randomly partitioned into 50% training and 50% test sets for each of the 10 experiments. In all the experiments the tree obtained is shown in Figure 1.

Table 1. 12 classes in AVIRIS hyperspectral dataset

Num	Class Name
Upland Classes	
1	Scrub
2	Willow Swamp
3	Cabbage palm hammock
4	Cabbage oak hammock
5	Slash pine
6	Broad leaf oak/hammock
7	Harwood swamp
Wetland Classes	
8	Graminoid marsh
9	Spartina marsh
10	Cattail marsh
11	Salt marsh
12	Mud flats

The 12 classes were grouped by a human expert based on traditional characterization of vegetation into seven upland and five wetland classes (Table 1). Classes 1, 3, 4, 5, and 6 are all trees which grow in an uplands environment. Classes 2 and 7 are also trees, but the soil is saturated if not inundated. Classes 8-12 are generally characterized as marsh grasses. Here the soils are usually saturated and periodically inundated. Even though willow swamp (class 2) and hardwood swamp (class 7) are actually wetland species, they were designated as members of the uplands group by the expert due to their biomass. In light of these observations, the class partitioning shown in Figure 1 obtained by the proposed multiclassifier architecture from the training data is remarkable as it not only conforms to the expert's opinions but is also able to designate classes 2 and 7 as members of the same group. Using the combining technique described in section 3.2, novel examples from the test set were classified. The overall classification accuracy on the test set averaged over the 10 experiments was found to be **97%**. This was a significant improvement over the 93% classification accuracy obtained by a Bayesian pairwise classifier architecture that uses class pair dependent feature selection and a maximum likelihood classifier for each pair of classes. To compare with a single classifier approach, an MLP with 50 hidden units, 183 inputs and 12 output units was trained until change in training accuracy was insignificant. The test accuracy averaged over 10 experiments was found to be only 74.5%. As compared to other feature extraction methods based on principal component analysis [5] and MNF transforms [16] the classification accuracy of the hierarchical multiclassifier was at least 10% higher.

A significant reduction in the number of features is also obtained by the proposed architecture because each internal node represents a two class classifier using only a one dimensional feature space obtained by projecting the 183 dimensional input space onto a Fisher dimension. As compared to other feature

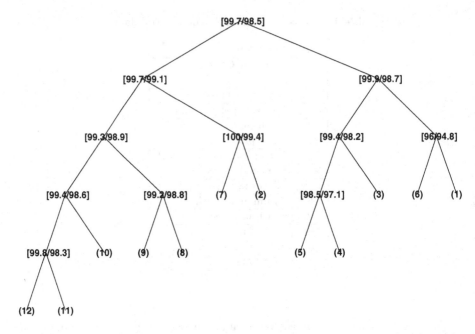

Fig. 1. Multiclassifier binary tree for AVIRIS data: The 12 classes are listed in the table. Each leaf node in the binary tree is labeled with one of the 12 classes it represents. The numbers on an internal node represent the classification accuracy of the two-class classifier at that node on the training data and the test data.

extraction algorithms based on the principal components and feature selection algorithms based on Bhattacharya distance, this reduction in dimensionality was also very significant.

5   Conclusions

A hierarchical multiclassifier architecture was proposed in this paper for the analysis of hyperspectral data. An algorithm using the generalized associative modular learning paradigm was developed for partitioning a set of classes into two groups and simultaneously finding the best feature projection that distinguishes the two groups. The results obtained on a 183 dimensional hyperspectral data for a 12 class problem were significantly better than approaches based on other feature extraction and problem decomposition techniques. Moreover, the automatic decomposition of 12 classes into a binary hierarchy conforms well with the expert's opinion and therefore provides significant domain knowledge about the relationships between different classes.

Acknowledgement

This research was supported in part by ARO contracts DAAD19-99-1-0012, DAAG55-98-1-0230 and DAAG55-98-1-0287, NSF grant ECS-9900353, the Texas Advanced Technology Research Program (CSRA-ATP-009).

References

1. Roderick Murray-Smith and Tor Arne Johansen. *Multiple Model Approaches to Modelling and Control*. Taylor and Francis, UK, 1997.
2. A. Sharkey, editor. *Combining Artificial Neural Nets*. Springer-Verlag, 1999.
3. V. Haertel and D. Landgrebe. On the classification of classes with nearly equal spectral responses in remote sensing hyperspectral image data. *IEEE Transactions on Geoscience and Remote Sensing*, 37(5-2):2374–2386, September 1999.
4. C. Lee and D. A. Landgrebe. Decision boundary feature extraction for neural networks. *IEEE Transactions on Neural Networks*, 8(1):75–83, January 1997.
5. X. Jia and J. A. Richards. Segmented principal components transformation for efficient hyperspectral remote-sensing image display and classification. *IEEE Transactions on Geoscience and Remote Sensing*, 37(1):538–542, January 1999.
6. X. Jia. *Classification techniques for hyperspectral remote sensing image data*. PhD thesis, Univ. College, ADFA, University of New South Wales, Australia, 1996.
7. S. Kumar, J. Ghosh, and M. M. Crawford. Classification of hyperspectral data using best-bases feature extraction algorithms. In *Proc. of SPIE: Applications and Science of Computational Intelligence III, Orlando*, April 2000.
8. N. Saito and Ronald R. Coifman. Local discriminant bases. In *Mathematical Imaging: Wavelet Applications in Signal and Image Processing II, Proc. of SPIE*, volume 2303, pages 2–14, 1994.
9. S. Kumar, M. M. Crawford, and J. Ghosh. A versatile framework for labeling imagery with large number of classes. In *Proceedings of the International Joint Conference on Neural Networks*, Washington, D.C., 1999.
10. M. M. Crawford, S. Kumar, M.R.Ricard, J.C.Gibeaut, and A.Neuenshwander. Fusion of airborne polarimetric and interferometric SAR for classification of coastal environments. *IEEE Transactions on Geoscience and Remote Sensing*, 37(3):1306–1315, May 1999.
11. M.I. Jordan and R.A. Jacobs. Hierarchical mixture of experts and the EM algorithm. *Neural Computation*, 6:181–214, 1994.
12. Yoav Freund and Robert E. Schapire. Experiments with a new boosting algorithm. In *Proceedings of the 13th International Conference on Machine Learning*, pages 148–156. Morgan Kaufmann, 1996.
13. L. Breiman. Bagging predictors. *Machine Learning*, 24(2):123–40, 1996.
14. S. Kumar and J. Ghosh. GAMLS: A generalized framework for associative modular learning systems (invited paper). In *Proceedings of the Applications and Science of Computational Intelligence II*, pages 24–34, Orlando, Florida, 1999.
15. R. A. Fisher. The use of multiple measurements in taxonomic problems. *Annal of Eugenics*, 7:179–188, 1936.
16. A. A. Green, M. Berman, P. Switzer, and M. Craig. A transformation for ordering multispectral data in terms of image quality with implications for noise removal. *IEEE Transactions on Geoscience and Remote Sensing*, 26(1):65–74, 1988.

Consensus Based Classification of Multisource Remote Sensing Data

Jon Atli Benediktsson and Johannes R. Sveinsson

Department of Electrical and Computer Engineering, University of Iceland
Hjardarhagi 2-6, 107 Reykjavik, Iceland.

Abstract. Multisource classification methods based on neural networks, statistical modeling, genetic algorithms, and fuzzy methods are considered. For most of these methods, the individual data sources are at first treated separately and modeled by statistical methods. Then several decision fusion schemes are applied to combine the information from the individual data sources. These schemes include weighted consensus theory where the weights of the individual data sources reflect the reliability of the sources. The weights are optimized in order to improve the combined classification accuracies. The methods are applied in the classification of a multisource data set, and the results compared to accuracies obtained with conventional classification schemes.

1   Introduction

Decision fusion can be defined as the process of fusing information from individual data sources after each data source has undergone a preliminary classification. In this paper a combination of several neural, fuzzy, genetic, and statistical decision fusion schemes will be tested in classification of a multisource remote sensing and geographic data set. Most of the considered decision fusion approaches are based on consensus theory [1].

The need to optimize the classification accuracy of remotely sensed imagery has led to an increasing use of Earth observation data with different characteristics collected from different sources or from a variety of sensors from different parts of the electromagnetic spectrum. Combining multisource data is believed to offer enhanced capabilities for the classification of target surfaces [1,2,3,4].

Several researchers have used neural networks in the classification of multisource remote sensing data sets. Benediktsson *et al.* [5,6] used neural networks for the classification of multisource data and compared their results to statistical techniques. They showed that if the neural networks are trained with representative training samples they can show improvement over statistical methods in terms of overall accuracies. However if the distribution functions of the information classes are known, statistical classification algorithms work very well. On the other hand if data are combined from completely different sources, they are not expected to fit well the statistical model and, therefore, neural networks may be more appropriate.

J. Kittler and F. Roli (Eds.): MCS 2000, LNCS 1857, pp. 280–289, 2000.

The paper is organized as follows. First, consensus theory and its weight selection schemes are discussed in Section 2. In Section 3 parallel consensual neural network is reviewed along with neural network approaches with regularization and pruning. In Section 4 and 5, classification methods based on genetic algorithms and fuzzy methods, respectively, are discussed. Experimental results for a multisource remote sensing and geographic data set are given in Section 6. Finally, conclusions are drawn.

2   Consensus Theory

Consensus theory [1,5,6] involves general procedures with the goal of combining single probability distributions to summarize estimates from multiple experts with the assumption that the experts make decisions based on Bayesian decision theory. The combination formula obtained is called a consensus rule. The consensus rules are used in classification by applying a maximum rule, i.e., the summarized estimate is obtained for all the information classes and the pattern X is assigned to the class with the highest summarized estimate.

Probably the most commonly used consensus rule is the linear opinion pool (LOP) which has the following (group probability) form for the user specified information (land cover) class ω_j if n data sources are used:

$$C_j(X) \; = \; \sum_{i=1}^{n} \lambda_i p(\omega_j | x_i) \tag{1}$$

where $X = [x_1, \ldots, x_n]$ is an input data vector where each x_i is a source-specific pattern which is multidimensional if the data source is multidimensional, $p(\omega_j | x_i)$ is a source-specific posterior probability and λ_i's $(i = 1, \ldots, n)$ are source-specific weights which control the relative influence of the data sources. The weights are associated with the sources in the global membership function to express quantitatively the goodness of each data source [1].

Another consensus rule, the logarithmic opinion pool (LOGP), has been proposed to overcome some of the problems with the LOP. The LOGP can be described by

$$L_j(X) \; = \; \prod_{i=1}^{n} p(\omega_j | x_i)^{\lambda_i} \tag{2}$$

or

$$\log(L_j(X)) \; = \; \sum_{i=1}^{n} \lambda_i \log(p(\omega_j | x_i)). \tag{3}$$

The LOGP differs from the LOP in that it is unimodal and less dispersed. Also, the LOGP treats the data sources independently. Zeros in it are vetos; i.e., if any expert assigns $p(\omega_j | x_i) = 0$, then $L_j(X) = 0$. This dramatic behavior is a drawback if the density functions are not carefully estimated.

2.1 Weight Selection Schemes for Consensus Theory

The weight selection schemes in consensus theory should reflect the goodness of the separate input data sources, i.e., relatively high weights should be given to data sources that contribute to high accuracy. There are at least two potential weight selection schemes [5]. The first scheme is to select the weights such that they weight the individual data sources but not the classes within the sources. Here, reliability measures which rank the data sources according to their goodness can be used as a bases for *heuristic weight selection*. These reliability measures might be, for example, source-specific overall classification accuracy of training data, overall separability or equivocation [1].

The second scheme is to choose the weights such that they not only weight the individual stages but also the classes within the stages. This scheme consists of defining a function f which can be used to optimize classification accuracy with the usual maximum selection rule.

In the case when f is non-linear, a neural network can be used to obtain a mean square estimate of the function, and the consensus theoretic classifiers with equal weights can be considered to preprocess the data for the neural networks. Then, a neural network learns the mapping from the source-specific posteriori probabilities to the information classes. Thus, the neural network is used to optimize the classification capability of the consensus theoretic classifiers [5].

3 The Parallel Consensual Neural Network

Benediktsson *et al.* [6] proposed the parallel consensual neural network (PCNN) as a neural network version of statistical consensus theory. The rationale for the PCNN is that consensus theory has the goal of combining several opinions, and a collection of different neural networks should be more accurate than a single network in classification. It is important to note that neural networks have been shown to approximate posterior probabilities, $p(\omega_j|z_i)$, at the output in the mean square sense [7]. By the use of that property it becomes possible to implement consensus theory with neural networks. The architecture of the PCNN consists of several stages where each stage is a particular neural network, called a stage neural network (SNN). The SNN has the same number of output neurons as the number of data classes and is trained for a fixed number of iterations or until the training procedure converges. The input data to the individual stages are obtained by performing data transformations (DTs) of the original input data. When the training of all the stages has finished, the consensus for the SNNs is computed. The consensus is obtained by taking class-specific weighted averages of the output responses of the SNNs. In neural network processing, it is very important to find the "best" representation of input data. The PCNN attempts to improve its classification accuracy by averaging the SNN responses from several input representations. Using this architecture it can be guaranteed that the PCNNs should do no worse that single stage networks, at least in training [8].

For the DTs, the wavelet packet transformation (WPT) [9] is suggested in [6]. The WPT provides a systematic way for transforming the input data for the PCNN. Each level of the full WPT can be considered to consist of input data for the different SNNs.

The weights selected for the PCNN, LOP, and LOGP can be critical in terms of obtaining the best classification accuracies. Here a neural network can be used to obtain a mean-square estimate of f [6]. If $Y = D$ is the desired output for the whole classification problem, the process can be described by the equation

$$\Lambda_{nlopt} = \arg\min_{\Lambda} \|D - f(X, \Lambda)\|^2 \qquad (4)$$

where Λ corresponds to the weights of the neural network.

The update equation for the weights of the neural network is

$$\Delta\Lambda = \eta \|D - f(X, \Lambda)\| \nabla_{\Lambda} f$$

where η is a learning rate.

Regularization and pruning [9,10] for individual SNNs in the PCNN can also be critical for the overall classification accuracies. Here, a regularization scheme in conjunction with Optimal Brain Damages (OBD) is used in experiments.

4   Genetic Algorithms

Genetic algorithms [12] are inspired by the evolution of populations. In a particular environment, individuals which better fit the environment will be able to survive and hand down chromosomes to their descendants, while less fit individuals will become extinct. The aim of genetic algorithms is to use simple representations to encode complex structures and simple operations to improve these structures. Therefore, genetic algorithms are characterized by their representations and operators. Furthermore, genetic algorithms can find a global minimum under suitable circumstances where neural networks often only reach a local minimum.

The genetic algorithms create populations of individuals and evolve the populations to find good individuals as measured by a fitness function. The individuals can either be represented by a binary string or real values. A fitness function is defined which measures the fitness of each individual. There are two major genetic operators: Mutation and crossover. In mutation each bit in the binary representation is flipped with some small probability The crossover is done by randomly pairing individuals and then randomly choosing a crossover point. Both mutation and crossover have their analogous definitions when real valued representation is used [12].

Genetic algorithms have been used in conjunction with neural networks in the following three schemes:

1. Training a neural network.
2. Pruning a trained neural network.

3. Training and pruning of a neural network.

In this paper, the first two approaches are considered. Binary valued representation is used to prune trained neural networks. For the pruning only one bit is needed for each weight in the network. If a bit becomes 0 a connection in a neural network can be disconnected and consequently the network will be pruned. On the other hand, real valued representation is used here for the training of a neural network. The reason for the use of the real valued representation is the large number of parameters involved in the optimization. For instance, in a PCNN with 6 SNNs, 6 outputs at each SNN, and 6 information classes, there are at least 222 weights that need to be determined in a one layer neural network optimizer. It would be very difficult to solve such a problem using binary strings.

The training of a neural network with a genetic algorithm using crossover and mutation can be very slow. Therefore, a recently proposed extinction and immigration [13] operator is used here. This operator is based on the fact that after several generations, the fittest individuals in a population can become very similar.

5   Approaches Based on Fuzzy Methods

5.1   Fuzzy Integral

The fuzzy integral is a nonlinear functional which is defined with respect to a fuzzy measure, especially the g_λ-fuzzy measure introduced by Sugeno. The following definition of fuzzy integral comes from [14]:

Let $Y = \{y_1, y_2, ..., y_k\}$ be a finite set and $h : \rightarrow [0,1]$ a fuzzy subset of Y. The fuzzy integral over Y of the function h with respect to a fuzzy measure g is defined by

$$h(y) \circ g(\cdot) = \max_{E \subseteq Y} \left[\min \left(\min_{y \in E} h(y), g(E) \right) \right]$$
$$= \max_{\alpha \in [0,1]} [\min(\alpha, g(F_\alpha))]$$

where

$$F_\alpha = \{y | h(y) \geq \alpha\}.$$

Here, $h(y)$ measures the degree to which the concept h is satisfied by y. The term $\min_{y \in E} h(y)$ measures the degree to which the concept h is satisfied by all the elements in E. Moreover, the value $g(E)$ is a measure of the degree to which the subset of object E satisfies the concept measured by g. Then the value obtained from comparing these two quantities in terms of the min operator indicates the degree to which E satisfies both the criteria of the measure g and $\min_{y \in E} h(y)$. Finally, the max operation takes the biggest of these terms. One can interpret the fuzzy integral as finding the maximal grade of agreement between the objective evidence and expectation. In our case h corresponds to the source specific posterior discriminative information and g is a fuzzy measure based on the reliabilities of the data sources. The fuzzy integral is computed for each class. Then the classification is done by taking the maximum overa all classes.

5.2 Fuzzy Associate Memories

In experiments, Fuzzy Associate Memories (FAMs) are also considered but they were proposed by Kosko [15]. The FAMs have similar structure as consensus theoretic approaches but they map a fuzzy set, A, to another fuzzy set, B, where A and B do not need to be of the same dimension. The FAM consists of m rules which are derived from a pre-defined FAM matrix with m elements. Each rule returns a vector B'_i. These vectors are then weighted and added to return the result B. Then defuzzification [15] follows and the classification result is achieved. Here, the FAMs are used as classifiers rather than combiners.

6   Experimental Results

To compare the approaches above, classification was performed on a data set consisting of the following 4 data sources: Landsat MSS data (4 spectral data channels), Elevation data (in 10 m contour intervals, 1 data channel), Slope data (0-90 degrees in 1 degree increments, 1 data channel), and Aspect data (1-180 degrees in 1 degree increments, 1 data channel).

The area used for classification is a mountainous area in Colorado. It has 10 ground-cover classes which are listed in Table 1. One class is water; the others are forest types. It is very difficult to distinguish among the forest types using the Landsat MSS data alone since the forest classes show very similar spectral response. Two thousand and nineteen reference points were available for each class. Approximately 50% of the reference samples were used for training, and the rest were used to test the classification methods.

Table 1. Training and Test Samples for Information Classes in the Experiment on the Colorado Data Set.

Class #	Information Class	Training Size	Test Size
1	Water	301	302
2	Colorado Blue Spruce	56	56
3	Mountane/Subalpine Meadow	43	44
4	Aspen	70	70
5	Ponderosa Pine 1	157	157
6	Ponderosa Pine/Douglas Fir	122	122
7	Engelmann Spruce	147	147
8	Douglas Fir/White Fir	38	38
9	Douglas Fir/Ponderosa Pine/Aspen	25	25
10	Douglas Fir/White Fir/Aspen	49	50
	Total	1008	1011

The overall classification accuracies for the different classification methods are summarized in Tables 2 (training) and 3 (test). From Tables 2 and 3 it can been seen that the LOGP with non-linearly optimized weights outperformed the best single stage neural network classifiers both in terms of training and test accuracies. In contrast, the Conjugate Gradient Backpropagation (CGBP) optimized LOP did not achieve the training and test accuracies of the single stage CGBP neural network with 40 hidden neurons. However, the CGBP optimized

LOP improved significantly (between 15% and 25%) on the LOP result with equal weights in terms of average and overall accuracies of training and test data.

Table 2. Training Accuracies in Percentage for the Classification Methods Applied to the Colorado Data Set.

Method	Average Accuracy	Overall Accuracy
MED	37.8	40.3
LOP (equal weights)	49.3	68.1
LOP (heuristic weights)	55.8	74.2
LOP (optimal linear weights)	66.2	80.3
LOP (optimized with CGBP)	74.6	83.5
LOGP (equal weights)	69.2	79.0
LOGP (heuristic weights)	69.2	80.5
LOGP (optimal linear weights)	65.1	79.7
LOGP (optimized with CGBP)	89.1	91.4
CGBP (0 hidden neurons)	76.1	84.2
CGBP (40 hidden neurons)	95.6	96.3
PCNN (equal weights)		87.1
PCNN (optimal weights)		91.9
Fuzzy Integral	63.7	85.6
FAM	97.2	97.1
Genetic Algorithm (without pruning)	78.5	80.2
Genetic Algorithm (with pruning)	79.1	80.9
Number of Samples		1008

Table 3. Test Accuracies in Percentage for the Relative Classification Methods Applied to the Colorado Data Set.

Method	Average Accuracy	Overall Accuracy
MED	35.5	38.0
LOP (equal weights)	46.5	66.4
LOP (heuristic weights)	54.9	73.4
LOP (optimal linear weights)	66.1	80.2
LOP (optimized with CGBP)	72.9	82.2
LOGP (equal weights)	69.0	78.7
LOGP (heuristic weights)	66.8	79.6
LOGP (optimal linear weights)	64.3	80.0
LOGP (optimized with CGBP)	75.1	82.3
CGBP (0 hidden neurons)	68.6	79.7
CGBP (40 hidden neurons)	67.0	78.4
PCNN (equal weights)		80.7
PCNN (optimal weights)		80.8
Fuzzy Integral	53.7	75.8
FAM	67.0	78.1
Genetic Algorithm (without pruning)	74.3	80.2
Genetic Algorithm (with pruning)	76.1	82.1
Number of Samples		1011

Two versions of the PCNN were used in the experiments, i.e., PCNNs that utilize the equal weighting method, and the optimized linear combination based on a minimum mean-squared error. It can be seen that the PCNN with the optimal weights outperforms the equally weighted PCNN when it comes to training, but the test accuracies for both methods are similar.

The fuzzy integral was only used in conjunction with the LOP and achieved lower classification accuracies than the LOP using optimal linear and non-linear combiners, as can be seen from Tables 2 and 3. The fuzzy integral is somewhat

Table 4. Source-Specific Overall Training and Test Classification Accuracies.

Source	Training Accuracy (%)	Test Accuracy (%)
1	71.5	67.9
2	71.5	67.9
3	41.6	41.3
4	45.4	45.4

sensitive to the selection of the g values for the sources (the accuracies varied around 2% from the results in Tables 2 and 3 in terms of training and test for different g values). The best classification accuracies were achieved using gs based on classification accuracies of the individual data sources. The FAM trained on the original 7 channel data outperformed fuzzy integral method both in overall training and test accuracies (between 11.5% and 2.5%).

Although several methods were used in order to speed up the learning of the genetic algorithms in optimization, the genetic algorithms were extremely slow as it took them several days to achieve comparable results to the CGBP optimization. In contrast, the CGBP results were obtained in only a few hours. However, the genetic algorithms were shown to be very useful for pruning of the CGBP neural networks and the overall test accuracies were improved after pruning but the pruned networks had removed over 25% of the connections in the original networks.

6.1 Consensus Based on Pruning and Regularization

It was investigated how the use of neural network with pruning capabilities [17] performed in the PCNN. Two types of experiments were done:

1. First, each data source was trained by a neural network with pruning capabilities in order to approximate the source-specific posterior probabilities in (1). Then, the consensus from these individual neural networks was computed by the use of a similar type of a network.
2. The whole multisource data set (all seven channels) was trained by a neural network with pruning and regularization capabilities ("No Consensus").

In order to use the consensus approach (in 1.), the overall classification accuracies for the individual sources were assessed (see Table 4) after removing around 50% of the weights in each case.

The results for the combination of source-specific probabilities are shown in Table 5 and compared to the results of an approach which was trained on all seven channels in one stage ("No consensus"). The consensus combination scheme was based on using either pruning or no pruning. In the table it can be seen that pruning helped in the combination, and that the pruned combiner outperformed the neural network trained on the original data in terms of both training and test accuracies. The excellent performance of the pruning combiner, when compared to the no-pruning combiner, is mostly due to two reasons:

Table 5. Combined Overall Training and Test Classification Accuracies.

Method	Pruning?	Training Accuracy (%)	Test Accuracy (%)
Consensus	No	73.9	74.2
Consensus	Yes	87.5	80.0
No Consensus	No	81.1	77.6

1. There was a lot of redundancy in the input to the combiners. (For 4 data sources with 10 information classes there are 36 inputs and 9 outputs.)
2. A huge number of weights was estimated from a very limited number of training samples.

The redundancy at the combination stage of a consensus theoretic classifier can be a serious problem when several data sources are used with many information classes.

7   Conclusions

In this paper, several multisource classification schemes were looked at. The results presented demonstrate that decision fusion methods based on consensus theory can be considered desirable alternatives to conventional classification methods when multisource remote sensing data are classified. The LOGP consensus theoretic classifier was in experiments the best classifier applied in terms of test accuracies. Consensus theoretic classifiers have the potential of being more accurate than conventional multivariate methods in classification of multisource data since a convenient multivariate model is not generally available for such data. Also, consensus theory overcomes two of the problems with the conventional maximum likelihood method. First, using a subset of the data for individual data sources lightens the computational burden of a multivariate statistical classifier. Secondly, a smaller feature set helps in providing better statistics for the individual data sources, when a limited number of training samples is available.

The genetic approach with pruning showed promise in classification of multisource remote sensing and geographic data. The genetic method has the advantage of looking at several possible solutions at once. However, computationally it can be very demanding. The neural network with pruning and regularization is also very promising. The use of hybrid neural/statistical approaches with pruning and regularization is the topic of future research.

Acknowledgements

This research is supported in part by the Icelandic Research Council, and the Research Fund of the University of Iceland. The authors gratefully acknowledge the contribution of Professor Jan Larsen of Denmark's Technical University (DTU), Lyngby, Denmark to this research. The Colorado data set was originally acquired, preprocessed and loaned to us by Dr. Roger Hoffer of Colorado State University. Access to the data set is acknowledged.

References

1. Benediktsson, J.A., Swain, P.H.: Consensus theoretic classification methods. IEEE Transactions on Systems Man and Cybernetics. **22** (1992) 688-704.
2. Kanellopoulos, I., Fierens, F., Wilkinson, G.G.: Combination of parametric and neural classifiers for analysis of multi-sensor Remote Sensing imagery. Neural and Stochastic Methods in Image and Signal Processing III (Edited by Su-Shing Chen), Proceedings SPIE 2304 (1994).
3. Serpico S.B. Roli, F.: Classification of multisensor remote-sensing images by structured neural networks. IEEE Transactions on Geoscience and Remote Sensing. **33**(1995) 562-578.
4. Solberg, A.H.: Contextual Data Fusion Applied to Forest Map Revision. IEEE Transactions on Geoscience and Remote Sensing. **37** (1999) 1234-1243.
5. Benediktsson, J.A. Sveinsson, J.R., Swain, P.H.: Hybrid consensus theoretic classification. IEEE Transactions on Geoscience and Remote Sensing. **35** (1997) 833-843.
6. Benediktsson, J.A., Sveinsson, J.R., Ersoy, O.K., Swain, P.H.: Parallel Consensual Neural Networks. IEEE Transactions on Neural Networks. **8** (1997) 54-65.
7. Ruck, D.W., Rogers, S.K., Kabrisky, M., Oxley, M.E., Suter, B.W.: The multilayer perceptron as an approximation to a Bayes optimal discrimination function. IEEE Transactions on Neural Networks. **1** (1990) 296-298..
8. Mani, G.: Lowering Variance of decisions by using artificial neural network portfolios. Neural Computation. **3** (1991) 484-486.
9. Coifman, R.R., Wickerhauser, M.V.: Entropy-based algorithms for best basis selection. IEEE Transactions on Information Theory **38** (1992) 713-718.
10. Larsen, J., Svarer, C., Nonboe Andersen, L., Hansen, L.K.: Adaptive regularization in neural network modeling. Neural Networks: Tricks of the Trade. Lecture Notes in Computer Science **1524**. Springer-Verlag, Berlin (1998) 113-132.
11. Nonboe Andersen, L., Larsen, J., Hansen, L.K., Hintz-Madsen, M.: Adaptive regularization of neural classifiers. Proceedings of the IEEE Workshop on Neural Networks for Signal Processing VII. IEEE Press, Piscataway (1997).
12. Michalewicz Z.: Genetic Algorithms + Data Structures = Evolution Programs, Third, Revised and Extended and Edition, Springer-Verlag, New York (1995).
13. Yao, L., Seathers, W.A.: Nonlinear parameter estimation via the genetic algorithm. IEEE Transactions on Signal Processing **42**(1994) 927-935.
14. Cho, S-B, Kim, J.H.: Multiple network fusion using fuzzy logic. IEEE Transactions on Neural Networks **6** (1995) 497-501.
15. Kosko, B.: Neural Networks and Fuzzy Systems, A Dynamical Systems Approach to Machine Intelligence. Prentice Hall, Englewood Cliffs, N.J. (1992).
16. Richards, J.A., Jia, X.: Remote Sensing Digital Image Analysis, An Introduction. Third, Revised and Enlarged Edition. Springer-Verlag, Berlin (1999).
17. Benediktsson, J.A., Benediktsson K. Hybrid consensus theoretic classification with pruning and regularization, Proceedings of the 1999 International Geoscience and Remote Sensing Symposium (IGARSS '99). Hamburg, Germany (1999) 2486-2488.

Combining Parametric and Nonparametric Classifiers for an Unsupervised Updating of Land-Cover Maps

Lorenzo Bruzzone[1], Roberto Cossu[1], and Diego Fernández Prieto[2]

[1] DICA - University of Trento, Via Mesiano, 77,
I-38050, Trento, Italy
{lorenzo.bruzzone, roberto.cossu}@ing.unitn.it
[2] DIBE - University of Genoa, Via Opera Pia, 11 A,
I-16145, Genova, Italy
prieto@dibe.unige.it

Abstract. In this paper, the problem of unsupervised retraining of supervised classifiers for the analysis of multitemporal remote-sensing images is considered. In particular, two techniques are proposed for the unsupervised updating of the parameters of the maximum-likelihood and the radial basis function neural-network classifiers, on the basis of the distribution of a new image to be classified. Given the complexity inherent with the task of unsupervised retraining, the resulting classifiers are intrinsically less reliable and accurate than the corresponding supervised approaches, especially for complex data sets. In order to overcome this drawback, we propose to use methodologies for the combination of different classifiers to increase the accuracy and the reliability of unsupervised retraining classifiers. This allows one to obtain in an unsupervised way classification performances close to the ones of supervised approaches.

1   Introduction

In the past few years, supervised classification techniques have proven effective tools for the automatic generation of land-cover maps of extended geographical areas [1]-[5]. The capabilities of such techniques and the frequent availability of remote-sensing images, acquired periodically in many regions of the world by space-borne sensors, make it possible to develop monitoring systems aimed at mapping the land-cover classes that characterize specific geographical areas on a regular basis. From an operational point of view, the implementation of a system of this type requires the availability of a suitable training set (and hence of ground-truth information) for each new image to be categorized. However, the collection of a reliable ground truth is usually an expensive task in terms of time and economic cost. Consequently, in many cases, it is not possible to rely on training data as frequently as required to ensure an efficient monitoring of the site considered.

Recently, the authors faced this problem by proposing a combined supervised and unsupervised classification approach able to produce accurate land-cover maps even for images for which ground-truth information is not available [6]. This approach allows the unsupervised updating of parameters of a classifier on the basis of the distribution of the new image to be classified. Although the above-mentioned method

J. Kittler and F. Roli (Eds.): MCS 2000, LNCS 1857, pp. 290-299, 2000.
© Springer-Verlag Berlin Heidelberg 2000

was presented in the context of a maximum-likelihood (ML) classifier, it can be also applied to other classifiers (in this paper we will also consider radial basis function neural-network classifiers). However, given the complexity inherent with the task of unsupervised retraining, the resulting classifiers are intrinsically less reliable and accurate than the corresponding supervised approaches, especially for complex data sets. Consequently, it seems interesting to consider the above-mentioned approach in the context of combination of classifiers, in order to increase the accuracy and the reliability of the classification system devoted to monitoring the considered area.

In the past few years, significant efforts have been devoted to the development of effective techniques for combining different types of classifiers in order to exploit the complementary information that they provide [7]-[9]. However, even if the multiple-classifier approach has been extensively used in many application domains (e.g., character recognition [10]-[11]), little work has been done for applying these techniques in the context of remote-sensing problems [12]-[13]. Among these few works, it is worth mentioning the *Consensus Theory* proposed by Benediktsson [3], [12]. Such a theory allows one to integrate different classifiers by taking into account the overall and the class-by-class reliabilities of each classification algorithm.

In this paper, we propose to apply multiple classifiers to monitoring systems aimed at classifying multitemporal remote-sensing images. In particular, the combination of ensembles of classifiers able to perform unsupervised retraining is considered as a tool for increasing the accuracy and the reliability of the results obtained by a single classifier. The proposed system is based on two different unsupervised retraining classifiers: a parametric maximum-likelihood (ML) classifier [14] and nonparametric radial basis function (RBF) neural networks [5]. Both techniques allow the existing "knowledge" of the classifier (i.e., the classifier's parameters obtained by supervised learning on a first image, for which a training set is assumed available) to be updated in a unsupervised way, on the basis of the distribution of the new image to be classified. Classical approaches to classifier combination are adopted.

2   General Formulation of the Problem

We face this problem by focusing on an important group of real-world applications in which the considered test sites can be assumed to be characterized by fixed sets of land-cover classes: only the spatial distributions of such land-covers are supposed to vary over time. Examples of such applications include studies on forestry, territorial management, and natural-resource monitoring on a national or even continental scale [15]-[17].

Let $X_1 = \left\{ x_1^1, x_2^1, ..., x_{I \times J}^1 \right\}$ denote a multispectral image of dimensions $I \times J$ acquired in the area under analysis at the time t_1, x_j^1 being the feature vector associated with the j-th pixel of the image. Let $\Omega = \{ \omega_1, \omega_2, ..., \omega_C \}$ be the set of C land-cover classes that characterize the geographical area considered at t_1. Let X_1 be a multivariate random variable that represents the pixel values (i.e., the feature vector values) in $\mathbf{X}_1$. Finally, let us assume that a reliable training set $\mathbf{T}_1$ is available at t_1.

In the context of the Bayes decision theory, the decision rule adopted for classifying a generic pixel x_j^1 [14] can be expressed as:

$$x_j^1 \in \omega_k, \quad \text{if} \quad \omega_k = \arg\max_{\omega_i \in \Omega}\left\{\hat{P}_1\left(\omega_i / x_j^1\right)\right\}, \tag{1}$$

where $\hat{P}_1\left(\omega_i / x_j^1\right)$ is the estimate of the posterior probability of the class ω_i given the pixel x_j^1. According to (1), the classification of the image X_1 requires the estimation of the posterior probability $P_1(\omega_i / X_1)$ for each class $\omega_i \in \Omega$. Such estimates can be obtained by using classical parametric (e.g., maximum-likelihood) or non-parametric (e.g., neural networks, k-nn) supervised classification techniques, which exploit the information that is present in the considered training set T_1 [14]. In all the cases, the estimation of $P_1(\omega_i / X_1)$ for each class $\omega_i \in \Omega$ involves the computation of a parameter vector ϑ_1, which represents the knowledge of the classifier concerning the class distributions in the features space. The number and nature of the vector components will be different depending on the specific classifier used.

Let us now assume that, at the time t_2, a new land-cover map of the study area is required. Let $X_2 = \left\{x_1^2, x_2^2, ..., x_{I \times J}^2\right\}$ be a new image acquired at t_2 in the study area, which is assumed to be characterized by the same set of land-cover classes $\Omega = \{\omega_1, \omega_2, ..., \omega_C\}$. Let us also assume that at t_2 the corresponding training set is not available. This prevents the generation of the required land-cover map as the training of the classifier cannot be performed. At the same time, it is not possible to apply the classifier trained on the image X_1 to the image X_2 because, in general, the estimates of statistical class parameters at t_1 do not provide accurate approximations for the same terms at t_2. This is due to several factors (e.g., differences in the atmospheric and light conditions at the image-acquisition dates, sensor nonlinearities, different levels of soil moisture, etc.) that alter the spectral signatures of land-cover classes in different images and consequently the distributions of such classes in the feature space.

In this context, we propose two different unsupervised retraining approaches to overcome the above-mentioned problem: the former is a parametric approach, based on the ML classifier; the latter consists of a non-parametric technique based on RBF neural networks. Both techniques allow the parameter vectors ϑ_1^p (corresponding to the parametric approach) and ϑ_1^n (corresponding to the nonparametric approach), which are obtained by supervised learning on the first image X_1, to be updated in a unsupervised way, on the basis of the distribution $p(X_2)$ of the new image X_2 to be classified. However, the intrinsic complexity of unsupervised retraining procedures may lead to less reliable and accurate classifiers than the corresponding supervised ones, especially for complex data sets. In this context, we propose the use of a multiple-classifier approach to integrate the complementary information provided by ensembles composed of the parametric and the nonparametric classifiers considered.

In the proposed multiple-classifier approach, at the time t_1, N different classifiers are trained by using the information contained in the training set available $\mathbf{T}_1$. In particular, a classical parametric ML classifier [14] and N-1 different configurations of the nonparametric RBF neural networks [5] are used. As a result, a parameter vector ϑ_1^p, corresponding to the parametric approach, and N-1 parameter vectors ϑ_{1i}^n, $i=1,...,N$-1, corresponding to the nonparametric RBF approach, are derived. Such vectors represent the "knowledge" of the classifiers concerning the current image $\mathbf{X}_1$. Then, at time t_2, the considered classifiers are retrained in an unsupervised way by using the information contained in the distribution $p(X_2)$ of the new image $\mathbf{X}_2$. At the end of the unsupervised retraining phase, a new vector parameter is obtained for each of the N classifiers used. At this point, the classification results of the considered ensemble of classifiers are combined by using a classical multiple-classifier approach in order to improve the results provided by the single unsupervised classifiers.

3   The Proposed Unsupervised Retrainig Techniques

The main idea of the proposed unsupervised retraining techniques is that the first approximate estimates of the parameter values that characterize the classes considered at the time t_2 can be obtained by exploiting classifier's parameters estimated at the time t_1 by supervised learning. Then such rough estimates are improved on the basis of the distribution $p(X_2)$ of the new image X_2. In the following, a detailed description of the proposed unsupervised retraining techniques is given.

3.1 The Proposed Retraining Technique for an ML Classifier

In the case of an ML classifier, the parameters vector that represents the "knowledge" of the classifier present in the new image X_2 can be described as $\vartheta_2^p = \left[\theta_2^1, P_2(\omega_1), \theta_2^2, P_2(\omega_2), ..., \theta_2^C, P_2(\omega_C) \right]$, where θ_2^i is the vector of parameters that characterizes the density function $p_2(X_2 / \omega_i)$ (e.g., the mean vector and the covariance matrix of ω_i in the Gaussian case). For each class $\omega_i \in \Omega$, the initial values of both the prior probability $P_2^0(\omega_i)$ and the conditional density function $p_2^0(X_2 / \omega_i)$ can be approximated by the value computed in the supervised training phase at t_1. Then, such estimates can be improved by exploiting the information associated with the distribution $p_2(X_2)$ of the new image X_2. In particular, the proposed method is based on the observation that the statistical distribution of the pixel values in X_2 can be described by the mixed-density distribution:

$$p_2(X_2) = \sum_{i=1}^{C} P_2(\omega_i) p_2(X_2 / \omega_i) , \qquad (2)$$

where the mixing parameters and the component densities are the *a priori* probabilities and the conditional density functions of classes, respectively. In this context, the retraining of the ML classifier at the time t_2 becomes a mixture density estimation problem, which can be solved by using the EM algorithm [18]-[20] as described in [6]. The estimates obtained for each class $\omega_i \in \Omega$ at convergence are the new parameters of the ML classifier at the time t_2.

3.2 The Proposed Unsupervised Retraining Technique for RBF Neural-Network Classifiers

The proposed nonparametric classifier is based on a Gaussian RBF neural network that consists of three layers: an input layer, a hidden layer, and an output layer. The input layer relies on as many neurons as input features. Input neurons just propagate input features to the next layer. Each one of the K neurons in the hidden layer is associated with a Gaussian kernel function. The output layer is composed of as many neurons as classes to be recognized. Each output neuron computes a simple weighted summation over the responses of the hidden neurons for a given input pattern (we refer the reader to [5] for more details on RBF neural-network classifiers).

In the context of RBF classifiers, the conditional densities of equation (2) can be written as a sum of contributes due to the K kernel functions φ_k of the neural network [21]:

$$p_2(X_2) = \sum_{i=1}^{C} P_2(\omega_i) p_2(X_2 / \omega_i) = \sum_{k=1}^{K} P_2(\varphi_k) p_2(X_2 / \varphi_k) , \tag{3}$$

where the mixing parameters and the component densities are the *a priori* probabilities and the conditional density functions of the kernels. Equation (3) can be rewritten as:

$$p_2(X_2) = \sum_{i=1}^{C} \sum_{k=1}^{K} P_2(\varphi_k) \cdot P_2(\omega_i / \varphi_k) \cdot p_2(X_2 / \varphi_k) , \tag{4}$$

where the mixing parameter $P_2(\omega_i / \varphi_k)$ is the conditional probability that the kernel φ_k belongs to class ω_i. In this formulation, kernels are not deterministically owned by classes and so the formulation can be considered as a generalization of a standard mixture model [21]. The value of the weight w_{ij} that connects the jth hidden unit to the ith output node, can be computed as:

$$w_{ij} = P(\omega_i / \varphi_j) \cdot P(\varphi_j) . \tag{5}$$

Therefore, as for the ML classifier, the retraining of the RBF classifier at time t_2 becomes a density estimation problem, which can be solved by using the EM algorithm [21].

4   Strategies for the Combination of Classifiers

We propose the use of different combination strategies to integrate the complementary information provided by an ensemble of the parametric and nonparametric classifiers described in the previous section. The use of such strategies for combining the decisions provided by each single classifier can lead to a more robust behavior in terms of accuracy and reliability of the final classification system.

Let us assume that a set of N classifiers (one unsupervised retraining ML classifier and N-1 unsupervised retraining RBF classifiers with different architectures) are retrained on the X_2 image in order to update the corresponding classifiers parameters by using the procedures described in Section 3. In this context, several strategies for combining the decisions of the different classifiers may be adopted [22], [9]. We will focus on three wide spread combination strategies: the *Majority Voting Principle* [22], the *Bayesian Combination Strategy* [9] and the *Maximum Posterior Probability Strategy*. It is worth noting that the use of these simple and unsupervised combination strategies is mandatory in our case because a training set is not available at t_2, and therefore more complex approaches cannot be adopted.

The *Majority Voting Principle* faces the combination problem by considering the results of each single classifier in terms of the class labels assigned to the patterns. A given input pattern receives, therefore, N classification labels from the multiple-classifier system, each label corresponding to one of the C classes considered. The combination method is based on the interpretation of the classification label resulting from each classifier as a "vote" for one of the C land-cover classes. The data class that receives a larger number of votes than a prefixed threshold is taken as the class of the input pattern. Generally, the decision rule is a "majority" rule (i.e., the decision threshold is equal to $N/2+1$), even if more conservatives strategies can be chosen.

The second method considered, the *Bayesian Combination Strategy*, is based on the observation that for a given pixel x_j^2 in the image X_2 the N classifiers considered provide an estimate of the posterior probability $P_2\left(\omega_i / x_j^2\right)$ for each class $\omega_i \in \Omega$. Therefore, a possible strategy for combining these classifiers consists in the computation of the average posterior probabilities, i.e.,

$$P_2^{ave}\left(\omega_i / x_j^2\right) = \frac{\sum_{k=1}^{N} \hat{P}_2^k\left(\omega_i / x_j^2\right)}{N} \tag{6}$$

where $\hat{P}_2^k\left(\omega_i / x_j^2\right)$ is the estimate of the *a-posteriori* probability $P_2\left(\omega_i / x_j^2\right)$ provided by the *k-th* classifier. The classification is then carried out according to the Bayes rule by selecting the land-cover class associated with the maximum average probability.

The third method considered (i.e. the *Maximum Posterior Probability Strategy*) is based on the same observation of the previous method. However, in this case, the strategy for combining classifiers consists in a winner-takes-all approach: the data class that has the larger posterior probability among all classifiers is taken as the class of the input pattern.

5 Experimental Results

In order to assess the effectiveness of the proposed approach, different experiments were carried out on a data set made up of two multispectral images acquired by the Thematic Mapper (TM) multispectral sensor of the Landsat 5 satellite. The selected test site was a section (380×373 pixels) of a scene showing the area of Cagliari on the Island of Sardinia, Italy. The two images used in the experiments were acquired in September 1995 (t_1) and July 1996 (t_2). Figure 1 shows channels 2 of both images.

The available ground truth was used to derive a training set and a test set for each image. Five land-cover classes (i.e., urban area, forest, pasture, water, bare soil), which characterize the test site at the above-mentioned dates, were considered. To carry out the experiments, we assumed that only the training set associated with the image acquired in September 1995 was available. It is worth noting that the images were acquired in different periods of the year. Therefore, the unsupervised retraining problem turned out to be rather complex.

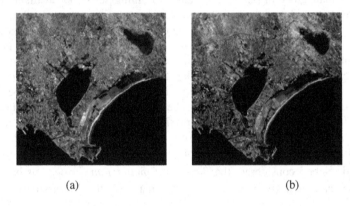

(a)   (b)

Figure 1. Band 2 of the Landsat-5 TM images utilized for the experiments: (a) image acquired in September 1995; (b) image acquired in July 1996.

An ML and two RBF classifiers (one with 150 hidden neurons, i.e. RBF1, the other with 200 hidden neurons, i.e. RBF2) were trained in a supervised way on the September 1995 image to estimate the parameters that characterize the density functions of the classes at the time t_1. For the ML classifier, the assumption of Gaussian distributions was made for the density functions of the classes (this was a reasonable assumption, as we considered TM images). In order to exploit the non-parametric characteristic of the two RBF neural classifiers, they were trained using not only the 6 available bands but also 4 texture features based on the Gray-Level Co-occurence matrix (i.e. sum variance, correlation, entropy and difference entropy) [23]. After training, the effectiveness of the classifiers were evaluated on the test sets for both images. On the one hand, as expected, the classifiers provided high classification accuracy (e.g., 92.81% for the ML classifier) for the test set related to the September 1995 image. On the other hand, they exhibited very poor performances for the July 1996 test set. In particular, the overall classification accuracy provided by the ML classifier for the July test set was equal to 35.91%, which cannot be considered an acceptable result. Also the accuracies exhibited by the two RBF neural classifiers considered are not very high.

Table 1. Classification accuracy exhibited by the considered classifiers before the unsupervised retraining.

Classification technique	Classification accuracy (%)	
	Test set (September 1995)	Test set (July 1996)
ML	92.81	35.91
RBF1	85.69	77.94
RBF2	90.44	81.09

At this point, the considered classifiers were retrained on the t_2 image (July 1996) by using the proposed unsupervised retraining techniques. At the end of the retraining process, the three classifiers were combined by using the strategies described in Section 4. In order to evaluate the accuracy of the resulting classification system, it was applied to the July 1996 test set. The results obtained are given in Tables 2 and 3. By a comparisons of these two tables with Table 1, one can see that the classification accuracies provided by the considered ensemble of unsupervised retraining classifiers for the July test set are sharply higher than the ones exhibited by the single classifiers trained on the September 1995 image.

Table 2. Classification accuracy on July 1996 test set after the unsupervised retraining.

Classification technique	Classification accuracy (%) (July 1996 test set)
ML	94.94
RBF1	95.66
RBF2	95.47

Table 3. Classification accuracy for the July 1996 test set after the application of the considered combination strategies.

Combination strategy		
Majority rule	Bayesian combination	Maximum a posteriori probability
96.41%	96.52%	96.12%

6 Discussion and Conclusions

In this paper, the problem of unsupervised retraining of classifiers for the analysis of multitemporal remote-sensing images has been addressed by considering a multiple-classifier approach. The proposed approach allows the generation of accurate land-cover maps of a specific study area also from images for which a reliable ground truth (hence a suitable training set) is not available. This is made possible by an unsupervised updating of the parameters of an ensemble of parametric and nonparametric classifiers on the basis of the new image to be classified. In particular, an ML parametric classifier and RBF neural network non-parametric classifiers have been considered. However, given the complexity inherent with the task of unsupervised retraining, the resulting classifiers are intrinsically less reliable and accurate than the corresponding supervised approaches, especially for complex data sets. Therefore, it is important to use methodologies for the combination of classifiers in order to increase the reliability and the accuracy of single unsupervised retraining classifiers.

Experiments carried out on a multitemporal data set confirmed the validity of the proposed retraining algorithms and of the adopted combination strategy. In particular, they pointed out that the proposed system is a reliable tool for attaining high classification accuracies also for images for which a training set is not available.

The presented method is based on the assumption that the estimates of the classifier parameters derived from a supervised training on a previous image of the considered area can represent rough estimates of the class distributions in the new image to be categorized. Then the EM algorithm is applied in order to improve such estimates iteratively on the basis of the global density function of the new image. It is worth noting that when the initial estimates are very different from the true ones (e.g., when the considered image has been acquired under atmospheric or light conditions very different from the ones in the image exploited for the supervised initial training of the classifier), the EM algorithm may lead to inaccurate final values for all classifiers considered in the ensemble. Therefore, in order to overcome this problem, we strongly recommend the application of a suitable pre-processing phase aimed at reducing the differences between images due to the above-mentioned factors.

References

1. Richards. J. A.: Remote sensing digital image analysis, 2nd edn. Springer-Verlag, New York (1993).
2. Benediktsson, J. A., Swain, P. H., Ersoy, O. K.: Neural networks approaches versus statistical methods in classification of multisource remote sensing data. IEEE Transactions on Geoscience and Remote Sensing, **28** (1990) 540-552.
3. Benediktsson, J. A., Swain, P. H.: Consensus theoretic classification methods. IEEE Transactions on Systems, Man and Cybernetics, **22** (1992) 688-704.
4. Bruzzone, L., Fernàndez Prieto, D., Serpico, S. B.: A neural statistical approach to multitemporal and multisource remote-sensing image classification. IEEE Transactions on Geoscienec and remote Sensing **37** (1999) 1350-1359.

5. Bruzzone, L., Fernàndez Prieto, D.: A technique for the selection of kernel-function parameters in RBF neural networks for classification of remote-sensing images. IEEE Transactions on Geoscience and Remote-Sensing **37** (1999) 1179-1184.

6. Bruzzone, L., Fernàndez Prieto, D.: An Unsupervised Re-training of a Maximum-Likelihood Classifier by Using the Expectation-Maximization Algorithm. Proc. of the Conference on Image and Signal Processing for Remote Sensing V (EUROPTO'99), Florence, Italy, (1999) 20-24.

7. Kittler, J., Hojjatoleslami, A., Windeatt, T.: Strategies for combining classifiers employing shared and distinct pattern representations, Pattern Recognition Letters **18** (1997) 1373-1377.

8. Louisa Lam, Ching Y. Suen.: Optimal combinations of pattern classifiers. Pattern Recognition Letter **16** (1995) 945-954.

9. Kittler, J., Hatef, M., Duin, R.P.W., Mates, J.: On combining classifiers. IEEE Transactions on pattern Analysis and machine Inteligence **20** (1998) 126-239.

10. Bajaj, R., Chaudhury, S.: Signature verification using multiple neural classifiers. Pattern Recognition **30** (1997) 1-7.

11. Lin, X., Ding, X., Chen, M., Zhang, R., Wu, Y.: Adaptive confidence transform based classifiers combination for chinese character recognition. Pattern Recognition Letters, **19** (1998) 975-988.

12. Benediktsson, J. A., Sveinsson, J. R., Ersoy, O. K., Swain, P. H.: Parallel consensual neural Networks. IEEE Transactions on Neural Networks **8** (1997) 54-64.

13. Giacinto, G., Roli, F., Bruzzone, L.: Combination of neural and statistical algorithms for supervised classification of remote-sensing images. Pattern Recognition Letters, **21** (2000), in press.

14. Tou, J.T., Gonzalez R.C.: Pattern recognition principles. Addison, Reading, MA (1974).

15. Maselli, F., Gilabert, M. A., Conese, C.: Integration of high and low resolution NDVI data for monitoring vegetation in mediterranean environments. Remote Sensing of Environment, **63** (1998) 208-218.

16. Grignetti, A., Salvatori, R., Casacchia R., Manes, F.: Mediterranean vegetation analysis by multi-temporal satellite sensor data. International Journal of Remote Sensing, **18** (1997) 1307-1318.

17. Friedl, M.A., Brodley C. E., Strahler, A. H.: Maximizing land cover accuracies produced by decision trees at continental to global scales. IEEE Transactions on Geoscience and Remote-Sensing **37** (1999) 969-977.

18. Dempster, A. P., Laird, N.M., Rubin, D.B.: Maximum likelihood from incomplete data via the EM algorithm. Journal of Royal Statistic. Soc. **39** (1977) 1-38.

19. Shahshahani B.M., Landgrebe, D.: The effect of unlabeled samples in reducing the small sample size problem and mitigating the Hughes phenomenon. IEEE Transactions on Geoscience and Remote-Sensing. **32** (1994) 1087-1095.

20. Moon, T.K.: The Expectation-Maximization algorithm. Signal Processing Magazine. **13** (1996) 47-60.

21. Miller, D. J., Hasan S. U.: Combined Learning and Use for a Mixture Model Equivalent to the RBF Classifier. Neural Computation. **10** (1998) 281-293.

22. Lam, L., Suen, C. Y.: Application of majority voting to pattern recognition: An analysis of its behavior and performance. IEEE Transactions on System, man and Cybernetics **27** (1997) 553-568.

23. Haralick R. M., Shanmugan K., and Dinstein I.: Textural features for image classification. IEEE Transactions on System, man and Cybernetics **3** (1993) 610-621.

A Multiple Self-Organizing Map Scheme for Remote Sensing Classification

Weijian Wan and Donald Fraser

School of Electrical Engineering, University College, The University of New South Wales, Australian Defence Force Academy, Canberra, ACT 2600, Australia.
weijianw@agrecon.canberra.edu.au, d-fraser@adfa.edu.au

Abstract. This paper presents a multiple classifier scheme, known as Multiple Self-Organizing Maps (MSOM), for remote sensing classification problems. Based on the Kohonen SOM, multiple maps are fused, in either unsupervised, supervised or hybrid manners, so as to explore discrimination information from the data itself. The MSOM has the capability to extract and represent high-order statistics of high dimensional data from disparate sources in a nonparametric, vector-quantization fashion. The computation cost is linear in relation to the dimensionality and the operation complexity is simple and equivalent to a minimum-distance classifier. Thus, MSOM is very suitable for remote sensing applications under various data and design-sample conditions. We also demonstrate that the MSOM can be used for hyperspectral data clustering and joint spatio-temporal classification.

1   Introduction

Satellite and computer technology is producing ever richer, more accurate and timely data about the Earth at a high definition scale and in all spectral, spatial and temporal forms. The result is that the discrimination capability of data for classification purposes has continuously improved. In the new century, the greatest challenge from a remote sensing perspective is to find an automatic, efficient and flexible way to maximally extract and exploit useful information from all available data sources to produce more accurate, timely and versatile results for applications. Multiple classifier systems may provide an adequate solution.

Several major problems exist in the current design of classifiers for (compound) modeling of complex data in remote sensing. These include: a) high dimensionality; b) complexity of data statistics from disparate sources; c) training samples and d) sophistication of modeling requirements. The essential issue is the automatic extraction and efficient representation of high-order statistics of high dimensional data of disparate sources. A desirable "industry-strength" solution should: a) have a capability of maximally exploring the discrimination information from data itself; b) be able to represent high-order statistics at the feature level; c) be simple in computation and in the operation that enables handling of feature and decision fusions for joint modeling requirements. Also, it should be versatile, able to deal with all kinds of design-sample situations and should maximally explore all possible discrimination information from both labeled and unlabeled samples. With all of the above in mind, we have developed a multiple classifier scheme, known as Multiple Self-Organizing Maps (MSOM).

In the following section, we describe the MSOM methodology and analyze its advantages for classification problems. In Section 3, we present experimental results with simulated and real remote sensing data to demonstrate the effectiveness of our method.

J. Kittler and F. Roli (Eds.): MCS 2000, LNCS 1857, pp. 300–309, 2000.

2   Methodology: MSOM

An emerging solution to difficult pattern recognition tasks is the multiple classifier system (MCS). The study of neural networks provides one of the most promising building blocks in the construction of MCS. The best-known neural network module is the multi-layer perceptron, which has been applied to remote sensing with other statistical and decision-fusion techniques (e.g., [1]-[2]). The other mainstream module is the self-organizing neural network ([3]-[4]), which is probably the most biologically plausible model from brain-net studies. In fact, the neural model that appears to most closely resemble the brain cortex spatial organization is the self-organizing map (SOM) of Kohonen ([3]). In engineering, the SOM is regarded as a vector quantization method for space approximation and tessellation, which can be used to faithfully approximate statistical distributions in a nonparametric, model-free fashion. The SOM learning is also efficient and effective, suitable for high dimensional processing. Thus, in both statistical and computational terms SOM is a promising scheme for sophisticated applications.

However, although a single map can generate an overall data coverage, it is difficult to use the formed map to produce a meaningful and sensible clustering or classification result (e.g., Fig.2b). This is because the single map lacks an inherent partition mechanism to uncover and distinguish salient statistical structures for clustering or classification. To overcome this problem, we introduced a concept of multiple maps ([5], [6]), in which several, smaller maps are used and fused in various ways to explicitly represent class or cluster regions for their statistical distributions. Through the use of "multiple maps" to deliberately specialize the representation of clusters or classes, not only can each region be approximated very well due to the map elasticity, but also the region borders can be dealt with to achieve an "optimal" compromise between the classes. The MSOM allows high-order statistics of classes to be extracted and represented, in both overall generalization and local specialization terms. Based on the above idea, we have developed the MSOM into a powerful design framework for remote sensing classification, where all kinds of sample situations can be handled and all sorts of data dependencies over the hyperspectral, multisources, spatial and temporal domains as well as between input and output domains can be maximally explored ([6]-[7]).

2.1   MSOM Models

We have developed four basic MSOM models and one extended model, indicating ways to fuse multiple maps for different purposes. Fig. 1 depicts the schematic architectures of these, being a) supervised MSOM (sMSOM); b) unsupervised MSOM (uMSOM); c) two feedforward mapping MSOMs (fMSOM); d) augmented MSOM (aMSOM), and e) joint MSOM (jMSOM). Fig. 2 illustrates formation results of various basic models on a simulated data set for comparison.

The MSOM models are natural extensions of the original Kohonen SOM (also inspired by the Hecht-Nielsen CPN), where the fundamental change is that the single map is replaced by multiple maps. We treat the CPN (Outstar module of Grossberg, too) as a hierarchical mapping or labeling extension to the flat architecture of SOM. There are two CPNs, one is feedforward and the other is augmented (denoted as fCPN and aCPN, respectively). The strength of the SOM structure is that it generalizes and specializes discrete samples in a continuous approximation fashion. Whereas, the MSOM approach allows the multiple maps to generalize the class-oriented regions from discrete samples and specialize at the region boundaries at the same time.

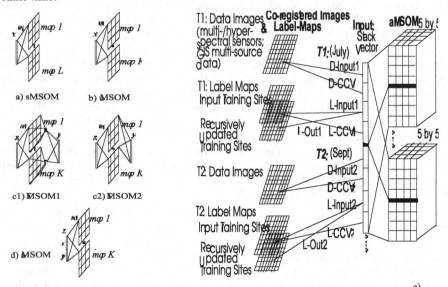

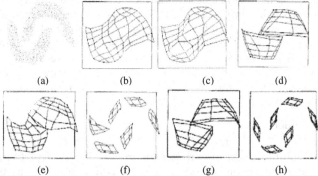

Fig. 1. Architectures: a) sMSOM; b) uMSOM; c) fMSOM: c1) fMSOM1 and c2) fMSOM2; d) aMSOM. Here, x is input and y are desired output vectors. z is augmented vector, (x, y). e) jMSOM. Input: pixel data and label vectors plus their respective CCVs (e.g., D- and L-Input, D- and L-CCV) in 2 time slots, T1 and T2. Output: label images in 2 time slots (i.e., L-Out).

Fig. 2. SOM/MSOM comparison: a) test data distribution, b) SOM, c) LVQ/SOM; d) uMSOM: 2 maps, e) uMSOM: 2 maps, f) uMSOM: 6 maps, g) aMSOM: 2 maps, h) aMSOM: 6 maps.

sMSOM and uMSOM. Both sMSOM (Fig.1a) and uMSOM (Fig.1b) have a one-layer, flat architecture, similar to SOM, with multiple maps. The difference is that one is supervised and the other is unsupervised. The former deploys multiple maps to approximate class distributions that need to be specified by adequate class-designated samples. In this sense sMSOM is largely reliant on labeled samples to discriminate classes. Whereas, the latter uses only unlabeled samples and has an inherent partition mechanism to discover statistically sensible structures from the data, where the multiple maps are formed together to partition the data space, ideally in a non-overlapping manner, for clustering purposes (Fig.2d).

Further, LVQ (Kohonen's Learning Vector Quantization) can be applied to minimize the classification or clustering errors. In the case of sMSOM classification errors are corrected if a wrong sub-map wins the competition with respect to a specific sample. Whereas, with uMSOM, clustering errors are corrected if the winning units do not belong to the sub-map of the majority winners in the competition.

fMSOM and aMSOM. Inspired by Hecht-Nielsen CPNs (both feedforward and augmented), feedforward MSOM (fMSOM, Fig.1c) and augmented MSOM (aMSOM, Fig.1d) are two labeling architectures for hybrid classification based on the uMSOM. fMSOM has a two-layer architecture that implements a two-step, feedforward association/mapping for uMSOM. The first is the normal uMSOM formation for clustering and the second is the association and labeling of clusters for classification. Because of two levels of representation of cluster structures at both the sub-map and unit levels by uMSOM, there are two fMSOMs for the purposes of mapping. The first one (fMSOM1) implements the mapping at the sub-map level and the second (fMSOM2) implements the mapping at the unit level. If the class structures are not too complex (e.g., not too fragmented within one class and relatively separable between classes), a formed uMSOM requires far fewer labeled samples to label the cluster structures (i.e., with sub-maps) corresponding to the class structures (label vectors). In this case, fMSOM1 should be used to implement the cluster-map and class-label association. Otherwise, fMSOM2 can be used to implement the more complex cluster-class associations at a more detailed, cluster-unit level. With the labeling structure, classification errors can be identified after the initial formation of the uMSOM layer. Again, the LVQ algorithm can be applied to refine the uMSOM formation, particularly at the class-borders, to minimize errors.

Another labeling scheme is called aMSOM, which has a one-layer, flat architecture, similar to uMSOM, that associates both the input, X, and output, Y, vectors in an augmented manner (forming the vector Z). In this way, aMSOM is able to simultaneously explore the cluster structures from both input and output vectors and, at the same time, associate the input and output vectors for cluster-to-class mappings. aMSOM is a truly hybrid scheme that can fully explore the clustering information and the class-mapping information from both the input and output sources in a mutual conditioned manner.

Among the basic MSOMs, aMSOM is the most advanced model, not only because of its capacity for joint modeling of both input and output data but also its capability to flexibly manipulate the augmented vectors. Depending on the availability of samples, it can take any part of the augmented vector (e.g., Z, X, Y or any part of them) to process either at training or in production. For example, aMSOM can process input X or any part of it with known missing features (which should be nullified if the corresponding Y is not available). Whenever, Y is available then the association between (X, Y) can be learned. Obviously with the simultaneous representation of multiple features in a joint vector form, a close association and mutual conditioning between all sources and features (including input-output) will occur after a repeated presentation of cross-linked, even partial samples.

In addition, the joint vector can be expanded to include all sorts of data or labeling attributes, where sequential expansion and training is possible, where the new fields are subsequently trained in a successive manner with the already formed fields. Sometimes, progressive training is also useful, where the model begins to learn with some carefully selected, representative samples for areas or classes of interest and then moves to generalize in other areas or classes. In a word, aMSOM is a versatile scheme for practical applications.

jMSOM. We have extended the aMSOM to joint MSOM (jMSOM) for remote sensing applications. Fig.1e depicts the architecture of jMSOM as a feature fusion and spatio-temporal classification model. The joint vector has been extended to enclose all sorts of spectral, spatial and temporal, as well as geographical data sources and their respective label vectors.

Because of the simultaneous presence of all features, jMSOM is able to exploit all data source dependencies between the various sources and within sources, over both spatio-temporal and input-output domains, in a mutual conditioned manner. Not only is it able to form a compound, statistical model of class-conditional distributions of all features for classification, but also due to the flexibility of aMSOM we can operate and manipulate the input and output domains, temporally and spatially, to exploit the full potential of the data and samples. For example, temporal data and partially labeled samples, if these are available, are used to form the respective domains. The multiple temporal mappings are formed simultaneously through the strong correlation within temporal data itself and between data and labels. The same effects occur over all the fused data sources. All the data dependencies within and between the spectral and hyperspectral domain, the spatial and temporal domain, the geographic sources, and between the input and output can be explored.

In addition, we can manipulate the output results over its spatial and temporal domains in an iterative manner. For example, after an initial training we output the classification results into a separate, label image and recursively use and update that image, spatially and temporally, to refine the formation of the jMSOM layer. This generates a desirable, spatial and temporal relaxation effect in a statistical sense on the final classification result since it lets the MSOM achieve a compromise in minimizing the approximation errors at both the scene-overall and local pixel-neighborhood levels.

Furthermore, in the spatial domain we introduce a so-called contextual co-occurrence vector (referred to as CCV) that measures the spatial frequencies of the feature values over a local image extent (e.g., a 3x3 neighborhood). A label CCV is formed by coding the label co-occurrence frequencies over the 3x3 context. For spectral data features, we use a separate front-end uMSOM (preferably using a uMSOM of multiple, connected rings of a 1D topology) to process the whole scene of multi-dimensions first and then use the formed 1D uMSOM to produce the cluster-labels over the local context as the data CCV features. In the temporal domain, as we already mentioned, the jMSOM is able to learn from any temporally labeled samples to associate the temporal features over both data and label domains. At the classification stage, we can use any temporal features, separately or jointly, to produce desired temporal outputs over the time slots. We will further demonstrate the jMSOM with a real bitemporal data set.

2.2 Learning Equations

MSOM training is a competitive learning process that uses the simplest, Euclidean merit, i.e.,

$$\| z(t) - m_{w,k}(t) \| = \min_{\forall i} \{ \| z(t) - m_{i,k}(t) \| \} \tag{1}$$

to learn from samples, z. In most of cases, we select K winners, $N_K = \{w_k\}$, in which w_k is the kth winner ($w = w_1$). We use z to represent a joint input and output vector,

(x, y), however, in the different processing contexts, z can be x, y, or any part of x or y. The term $m_{i,j}$ is a weight vector at the ith unit of the jth sub-map. The following SOM equation increases the matching by decreasing the distance between x and $m_{i,j}$ as well as its neighbors,

$$m_{i,j}(t+1) = m_{i,j}(t) + \alpha(t)\{z(t) - m_{i,j}(t)\}, \quad i \in M_j \tag{2}$$

in a neighborhood, around w, over a grid-like topology of 2D (or 1D). The neighborhood is chosen with a size beginning large to avoid the stuck-vector problem and decreasing with t to a small size. The learning rate, α, also decreases. The MSOM learning has a relaxation effect to maintain and organize the sub-maps and their units into a topological order that fit and partition the sample feature space in self-discovered clusters over every dimension. This provides the representation and discrimination capacity for high dimensional and complex data.

To effectively fuse and coordinate the multiple maps, we introduce a secondary learning using the same formula with a lower rate (e.g., one half of α). It is invoked if the other winners (e.g., second and third) fall into a different sub-map from that of the first winner, w,

$$m_{i,j}(t+1) = m_{i,j}(t) + 0.5\alpha(t)\{z(t) - m_{i,j}(t)\}, \quad i \in N_K - \{w\} \wedge C_i \neq C_w. \tag{3}$$

Here, N_K forms a secondary, K-nearest neighborhood of w and C_i and C_w are the cluster-map labels of unit i and w. In a similar way to the ordering of units by Eq. 2, the above equation has a self-organizing effect on the ordering and coordination of topological adjacent sub-maps through the localized specialization of the cross-border units. This improves the generalization and specialization capability of MSOMs over the map borders, to allow a smooth distinction between sub-maps.

2.3   Optimality Analysis

We use the sMSOM as an example to analyze the Bayes optimality of the MSOM scheme. Let $M_S = M_1 \cup ... \cup M_L$ denote a super map of an sMSOM, a union of sub-maps M_j, each of which consists of a grid of topologically linked, prototypic units. Let $F_S : X \rightarrow Y_S = Y_1 \cup ... \cup Y_L$ denote a corresponding partition of X into Y_S, a union of sub-spaces Y_j as class regions. Let us define a class-region indicator function with respect to Y_i,

$$I_i(x) = \begin{cases} 1 & \text{if } x(\omega_i) \in Y_i, x \text{ with label } \omega_i \text{ occurs in } Y_i, \\ 0 & \text{if } x(\omega_i) \notin Y_i, x \text{ with } \omega_i \text{ does not occur in } Y_i. \end{cases}$$

We also define a classification figure-of-merit function with point probability $p(x)$,

$$\Delta\big(r(M_S)\big) = \sum_{i=1, \forall x}^{L} \big[r(M_i(x)) - I_i(x)\big]^2 p(x),$$

to set a sub-space specific merit between M_i and Y_i. With respect to x, $r(M_i)$ is an actual class-map output from M_S by the minimum-distance rule and I_i is a desired sub-space output Y_i (label ω_i) to which x belongs. To a given M_S, we need to find an estimate, $r(M_S)$, with the "best" probability that minimises the above SSE (sum squared errors). Taking the extremality, we have

$$\Delta\big(r\big(M_S\big)\big)\big|_{r=r^*} = \sum_{i=1,\ \forall x}^{L} r^*\big(M_i(x)\big)p(x) - \sum_{i=1,\ \forall x}^{L} I_i(x)p(x) = 0,$$

which is equivalent to $\displaystyle\sum_{i=1,\ \forall x}^{L} r^*\big(M_i(x)\big)p(x) = \sum_{i=1,\ \forall x}^{L} I_i(x)p(x).$

With respect to a specific ω_i, for any x we then obtain the result $\sum_{\forall x} r^*\big(M_i(x)\big)p(x) = p(Y_i\,|\,x),$ which implies that $E\big\{r^*\big(M_i(x)\big)\big\} = p(Y_i\,|\,x)\,(= p(\omega_i\,|\,x)).$ The last equation means that the mean of best estimates of each formed sub-map M_i approximates the Bayes probabilities of each ω_i in the minimisation of SSE sense. The left side (ie, $E\big\{r^*\big(M_i(x)\big)\big\}$) indicates a mean approximation process that minimises the distance between a sub-map M_i and a region Y_i (notably, the sMSOM and LVQ algorithms realize an iterative version of such a mean error minimization process), while the right side indicates an estimation process that maximises class Bayes probabilities, $p(\omega_i\,|\,x)$. Also on the left the final decision uses the k-NP rule on minimum-distance while on the right the decision uses the Bayes rule on maximum probability in solving class overlappings.

From the last equation, we have established an explicit relationship between minimization of class-region specific squared error between M_i and Y_i (in which M_i maintains and approximates a class distribution function $f(x\,|\,\omega_i)$) and estimation of Bayes probabilities $p(\omega_i\,|\,x)$. If we assume the equiprobability, i.e., $p(\omega_i) = p(\omega_j)$, $i \neq j$, then with the Bayes rule to a given sample x' we have $\omega = \omega_i: p(x'\,|\,\omega_i) \geq p(x'\,|\,\omega_j)$, $\forall j$. In practice, this means that, with the use of "class-maps" for representation and approximation of class $f(x\,|\,\omega_i)$, the distance-minimization process on $f(x\,|\,\omega_i)$ resembles a probability-maximization process of Bayes learning on $p(x\,|\,\omega_i)$. At classification, in the same way as the maximum-likelihood method, sMSOM uses the minimum-distance rule in replacement of the maximum-probability rule for Bayes decisions. Class prior probabilities $p(\omega_i)$ can also be used, of course. The elastic map form for representation of class statistical distributions by sMSOM can faithfully approximate complex class structures. In this sense, the MSOM is a statistically sustainable MSC scheme that is able to explore the meaningful regularities from data in complex, noisy and hyperdimensional environments.

Thus, subject to training samples and proper training, we have demonstrated the empirical Bayes optimality of sMSOM for supervised classification. A similar analysis is applicable to all other MSOMs, either unsupervised or hybrid. The main reason is the use of multiple maps to effectively represent cluster or class structures. Our experiments on many data sets (e.g., Fig. 2) demonstrate and strongly support our analysis for MSOMs.

3   Experiments

We have generated several simulated data sets and used many real data sets to demonstrate the performance of various MSOMs and usefulness of MSOM for practical applications. Examples with a simulated set are shown in Fig. 2, where best results were obtained with aMSOM and six maps, with 0.3% errors (Fig. 2h).

3.1   Hyperspectral Data Clustering

We obtained a subset of a Jasper-Ridge AVIRIS scene with image size of 256 by 256. We chose to use only 152 of the original 224 bands after removal of some superfluous, water absorption, and noisy channels, etc. There are high correlations between adjacent bands and between band segments over the spectral domain. Automatic exploitation of these natural correlations can be of great help in discriminating ground classes at more precise levels. We implemented a uMSOM (using 4 maps with 3x3 units) to test the unsupervised clustering capability on this data. Without labeled samples, uMSOM has sensibly placed the 4 cluster-maps into the high dimensional space with the exploitation of high dependencies between the adjacent bands and over the whole spectral domain. The sub-map level captures the major cluster structures as the most meaningful regularities of this data (shown in Fig.3), while the unit level can be used to produce more detailed structures. It shows that the uMSOM has clearly discriminated the various ground objects in four classes. It is also observed that with the increase of the dimensions the computation time increases only linearly in relation to the dimensionality. For comparison, it takes 129 seconds to process 5D of data and 3,924 seconds to process 152D of data on a slow Intel 486 computer.

Fig. 3. Hyperspectral clustering by uMSOM: 4 clusters.

3.2   Joint Spatio-Temporal Classification

A bitemporal TM scene with two July and September sets (referred to as two J2/S2 temporal fields) is used to demonstrate the jMSOM model for spatio-temporal classification. Only 5 bands (TM2-5 and 7) of the TM data are used. The data comes with ground truth (Fig.4a) and training coordinates (Fig.4cd) for four classes of Corn, Soybeans, Wheat and Alfalfa/Oats displayed in four greylevels, from dark to bright (black is null on the truth and training images). Fig.4b illustrates a clustering result, while Fig.4e-h show several classification results.

Using the overall KIA metric (OKIA), Table I shows that both jSOMa and jMSOMa outperform GMLC (indicating that the classes are non-Gaussian) if only the raw (x, y) is used. All jSOMd and jMSOMd and jSOMl and jMSOMl outperform jSOMa and jMSOMa, indicating the effectiveness of using interpixel CCVs over either data or label spatial domains. Both jSOMt and jMSOMt outperform jSOMa and jMSOMa indicating the usefulness of the temporal dimension. Finally, jSOMf and jMSOMf that use all spatio-temporal contexts substantially outperform all the submodels. The above results demonstrate the effectiveness of joint modeling by jMSOM. Moreover, MSOM always outperforms SOM in extraction of class-specific discrimination information despite the fact that sometimes the results of jSOMf appear better than those of jMSOMf in OKIAs. This turns out to be due to a mistaken selection of the second training site for Alfalfa/Oats on S2 (Fig.4d), which indicates a class transition on that site from Wheat to Alfalfa/Oats between J2 and S2. The jMSOM's result (Fig.4f) has clearly captured such a temporal change of classes. In addition, jMSOM always produces an intermediate clustering result (Fig.4b), showing that the six clusters have basically matched the major class patterns of the four classes in the scene. This graphically illustrates why MSOM always discriminates better than SOM does.

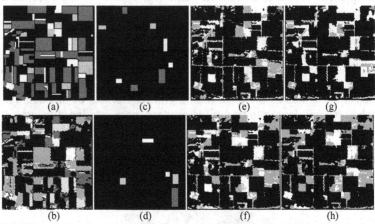

| (a) | (c) | (e) | (g) |
| (b) | (d) | (f) | (h) |

Fig. 4 JMSOM experiment with bi-temporal site: a) ground truth; b) jMSOMf (6 clusters) for joint J2-S2; c), d) training images for J2-S2 (note site for Alfalfa/Oats on S2 instroduces mistakes); e), f) jMSOMf calssification images for J2-S2 (note transfer of classes on that one Alfalfa/Oats site); g), h) jSOMf class images.

Table 1. Classification Comparison: * is affected by a mistake in selection of a site.

OKIA (%)	J2	S2
GMLC	44.81	48.89
jSOM/jMSOMa	52.87/52.81	52.78/53.39
jSOM/jMSOMd	55.32/56.40	53.54/54.68
jSOM/jMSOMl	58.32/60.14	53.18/57.76
jSOM/jMSOMt	67.00/65.10*	67.72/63.03*
jSOM/jMSOMf	70.37/72.85	69.59/68.36*

In addition, we have used the ground truth to train the same jMSOMf and achieved a match of 98.23/98.84% against 100% as an expected perfect match to the truth for J2/S2. Compare this to the match of 70.37/72.85% when using 6% of the truth as training samples (including mistakes). This shows that, for this particular site, supplying more samples or more sources provides more discrimination information so that the jMSOMf is capable of exploring the full capacity of that discrimination information by joint modeling of the spatio-temporal contexts over both input and output domains.

4   Conclusion

From the above experiments, we have demonstrated the following. (1) The MSOM is a versatile design scheme, able to handle all supervised, unsupervised and hybrid design situations. The MSOM architectures and operations are simple, which allows them to process easily various sample and modeling situations. (2) Various MSOMs, uMSOM in particular, have a better representation structure and discrimination capacity than that of the SOM. This allows uMSOM (and other MSOMs) to exploit discrimination information from the data itself without the necessity for comprehensive labeled samples. (3) MSOM has an effective representation of high-order statistics of high dimensional and complex data, where every dimension is maintained and processed by all of the multiple maps in a joint association with other dimensions. No source and dimension related dependency information is necessarily lost in the model configuration. The computation is efficient in regard to the dimensionality. Finally, (4) the jMSOM is a compound modeling scheme that is able to model a joint vector that augments all of the possible spectral, geographic, spatial and temporal features. jMSOM is able to exploit all of the source and domain dependencies from the joint vector for joint spatio-temporal classification and multisource fusion. The model is especially flexible in dealing with temporal processing, where partial temporal samples can be used to form a temporal contextual model, sequentially and incrementally, over the time slots. Such a contextual model can be used, for example, for crop monitoring and precise yield estimation purposes. To summarize, the MSOM is a powerful and flexible MCS scheme for classification or estimation applications.

We have demonstrated the great potential of the proposed MSOM approach to complex remote sensing classification problems. In the new era of remote sensing, we need to establish an industry-strength MCS scheme with essential machine-intelligence capabilities that can be used to automatically explore the massive amount and rich variety of data for joint classification and estimation applications. To conclude, we believe we have provided a strong basis for further research in searching for such a statistically sustainable solution for the remote sensing industry.

Acknowledgements

We gratefully acknowledge that the first author was supported by an ADCSS and a University College scholarship and thank Xiuping Jia for assistance on AVIRIS data and David Landgrebe for the supply of bitemporal data.

References

1. Benediktsson, J.A., and Kanellopoulos, I., 1999, "Decision Fusion Methods in Classification of Multisource and Hyperdimensional Data", *IEEE Trans. on Geo. And Remote Sens.* 37: 1367-1377, May 1999.
2. Benediktsson, J.A., and Swain, P.H., 1992, "Consensus Theoretic Classification Methods", *IEEE Trans. on System, Man and Cyber.* 22: 688-704.
3. Kohonen, T. 1989. Self-Organizing and Associative Memory. 3rd Edition, Springer-Verlag.
4. Carpenter, G.A. and Grossberg, S., Eds. 1991, Pattern Recognition by Self-Organizing Neural Networks. MIT.
5. Wan, W. and Fraser, D., 1994. "Multiple Kohonen SOMs: supervised and unsupervised formation", Proc. *ACNN'94*: 17-20. Brisbane, Australia.
6. Wan, W. and Fraser, D., 1999. "Multisource data fusion with multiple self-organizing maps". *IEEE Trans. on Geo. and Remote Sens.* 37:1344-9.
7. Wan, W. 1995. A multiple self-organizing map framework for pattern classification and scene analysis, Ph.D. dissertation, University of New South Wales.

Use of Lexicon Density in Evaluating Word Recognizers

Petr Slavík and V. Govindaraju

Center for Excellence in Document Analysis and Recognition (CEDAR)
Department of Computer Science & Engineering
University at Buffalo, Amherst, NY 14228, USA
{slavik,govind}@cedar.buffalo.edu
Fax: (716) 645-6176

Abstract. We have developed the notion of lexicon density as the true metric to measure expected recognizer accuracy. This metric has a variety of applications, among them evaluation of recognition results, static or dynamic recognizer selection, or dynamic combination of recognizers. We show that the performance of word recognizers increases as lexicon density decreases and that the relationship between the performance and lexicon density is *independent* of lexicon size. Our claims are supported by extensive experimental validation data.

1   Introduction

The ability of a recognizer to distinguish among the entries in a lexicon clearly depends on how "similar" the lexicon entries are. The "similarity" among entries depends not only on the entries themselves but also on the recognizer. Assume for example that we have a naive word recognizer that recognizes only the first character of each word. Performance of such a recognizer would certainly be poor on a lexicon where all entries start with the same letter and good on lexicons where starting letters of all entries are different. Similarly, a simple recognizer that would estimate the length of each word would perform well on lexicons where entries differ significantly in their length and poorly on lexicons with entries of the same length.

Previously, only lexicon size was used to measure how difficult it is for a recognizer to distinguish entries of a given lexicon [1]. Even though this is clearly not ideal, researchers have correctly observed that recognizers have more difficulty with large lexicons. The reason for this observation is simple—when lexicons are large, their entries are more likely to be "similar", hence on average the lexicon size appears to be an adequate measure of lexicon difficulty for a given recognizer.

The concept of lexicon density and the strong correlation between lexicon density and performance of word recognizers opens many opportunities for improving efficiency and performance of recognition systems.

Consider for example an application where the lexicon is fixed with several different recognizers to choose from. An example of such an application could

J. Kittler and F. Roli (Eds.): MCS 2000, LNCS 1857, pp. 310–319, 2000.

be a system for recognizing words in the legal amount of bankchecks [2]. An easy way to determine which recognizer would most likely perform the best is to compute the lexicon density with respect to each recognizer and use a table similar to Table 1 to determine expected performance of each recognizer and then choose the one(s) with best expected performance.

one	two	three	four	five
six	seven	eight	nine	ten
eleven	twelve	thirteen	fourteen	fifteen
sixteen	seventeen	eighteen	nineteen	twenty
thirty	forty	fifty	sixty	seventy
eighty	ninety	hundred	thousand	dollars
dollar	and	only		

Fig. 1. Handwritten legal amount recognition involves the recognition of each word in the phrase matched against a static lexicon of 33 words.

A different application with dynamically generated lexicons is the street name recognition in Handwritten Address Interpretation (HWAI). Here, lexicons are generally comprised of street name candidates generated from the knowledge of the ZIP Code and the street number. In fact, it is in such cases that the notion of lexicon density holds the greatest promise. If there are several recognizers to choose from, there should be a control mechanism that dynamically determines in any given instance which recognizer must be used. The determination can be based on the quality of the image, the time available, and the lexicon density. It could be decided, for instance, that if the image is noisy a particular recognizer should be favored based on training data. Similarly, a specific recognizer might be rendered ineffective if the lexicon density is high. This could happen if the recognizer depends heavily on a feature, say the length, and all the lexical entries have the same length.

Another application of lexicon density is in dynamic classifier combination. Consider the combination architecture in Figure 2. Let us say that for speed reasons we have determined that a particular recognizer goes first (position of classifier1 in Figure 2). On any given image instance, the lexicons that are fed to the remaining two classifiers are changing dynamically, *albeit* they are some subset of the original lexicon. By using the lexicon density of the various "sub-lexicons" that are fed forward, a decision can be dynamically made as to which recognizer takes the position of classifier2 and which one takes the position of classifier3.

Other possible use of lexicon density is in evaluating recognition results. Imagine that we have to assign some confidence to the first choice. We could compare

Fig. 2. The choice of which classifier becomes classifier2 and which one becomes classifier3 can be dynamically determined using the notion of lexicon density.

the matching scores of the first and second choices to determine how confident we are in our answer. It would however be more meaningful to also consider how likely it is for the top few choices to be confused by the recognizer, i.e. compute the "local" density. In such a case we could use additional information obtained during recognition (like number of segments or the optimal character segmentations) to reduce the number of possible combinations.

1.1   Our Results

In this paper, we propose a new, more accurate measure of difficulty of a given lexicon with respect to a given recognizer that we call the *lexicon density*. We define the lexicon density as a quantity that depends both on the entries in the lexicon and on a given recognizer. Intuitively, the higher the lexicon density the more difficult it is for the recognizer to select the correct lexicon entry.

We show that it is indeed the lexicon density and *not* the lexicon size that determines the difficulty of a lexicon for a given recognizer. Our experiments show clearly that recognizer performance is closely correlated with lexicon density and independent of lexicon size. Our evaluation methods are quite robust. We have tested the dependence between recognizer performance and lexicon density on a set of 3000 images, for each image generating 10 lexicons of size 5, 10 lexicons of size 10, 10 lexicons of size 20, and 10 lexicons of size 40.

We obtained our experimental results using a segmentation-based recognizer of handwritten words called WMR (the Word Model Recognizer [3]). However, our results can be readily generalized to almost any recognizer of handwritten or printed words.

1.2   Other Measures

The speech recognition community realized the need for a measure that captured the difficulty of the recognition task in a given instance. The notion of perplexity was introduced in [1]. Perplexity is defined in terms of the information theoretic concept of entropy. $S(w) = 2^{H(w)}$, where S is the perplexity and H is the entropy for a word w.

2   Recognizer-Dependent Distance

Before defining the lexicon density, let us first discuss the concept of a distance between two ASCII words with respect to a given recognizer. Having two words,

w_1 and w_2, we would like to measure how far word w_2 is from word w_1, or better yet how difficult it would be for a given recognizer to confuse words w_1 and w_2. One way to determine a distance between two ASCII words with respect to a segmentation based recognizer is to use the minimum edit distance between w_1 and w_2—see for example [5]. This approach can be used with recognizers that are able to correctly segment a word image into characters *without* recognizing the characters first, as is the case for recognizers of printed words. In such a case, one can use samples of training words and training characters to determine the cost of elementary edit operations (deletion, insertion, and substitution) with respect to a given recognizer.

In this paper, our focus is on recognizers of handwritten words and phrases (even though the ideas presented here could be modified for any word recognizer). Such recognizers typically combine character segmentation with recognition and hence the minimum edit distance cannot be used. To compute a lexicon density that depends on a specific recognizer (WMR in our case), we will use the recognizer-dependent image-independent *slice distance* introduced in [4].

In what follows, we will briefly describe computation of the slice distance for WMR. Interested reader can find the details in [4]. Given an image of handwritten word, WMR first oversegments the image into subcharacters. Then in the recognition phase, given a word from the lexicon, the segments are dynamically combined into characters so as to obtain the best possible match between the word and the image; that is, to minimize the total distance between features of character templates corresponding to the letters in the ASCII word and the features of segment combinations from the image. Figure 3 shows a typical example of an image of a handwritten word together with segmentation points determined by WMR.

Fig. 3. Segmented handwritten image in contour representation

Imagine now, that WMR is presented with this image and the lexicon consists of two entries—"Wilson" and "Amherst". After dynamically checking all the possible segment combinations, WMR would correctly determine that the best way to match the image and the word "Wilson" is to match segments 1-4 with "W", segment 5 with "i", segment 6 with "l", etc. The best way to match the image against "Amherst" would be to match segment 1 with "A", segments 2-5 with "m", segment 6 with "h", segment 7 with "e", segment 8-9 with "r", segment 10 with "s", and finally segment 11 with "t"—see Figure 4. Clearly the score of the second matching would be worse then the score of the first matching, hence the recognizer would correctly choose "Wilson" as its first choice.

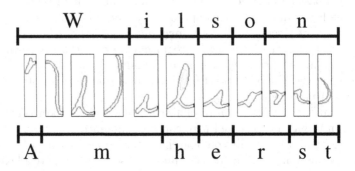

Fig. 4. Matching of ASCII words with image

Figure 4 illustrates how confusions could possibly arise in determining the best possible answer. Letter "A" was matched with the same part of the image as the left part of letter "W", left part of letter "m" was matched with the same "slice" of the image as the right part of "W", right part of letter "m" was matched with the same slice of the image as letter "i", etc. Hence to determine how difficult it would be to confuse "Wilson" and "Amherst" we have to first determine, how difficult it is to confuse "A" with the left part of "W", left part of "m" with the right part of "W", right part of "m" with "i", etc. Thus in general we must have information about how easy it is to confuse a slice of one character with a slice of another character. And not only that. Since we do not know the image before hand (and we want the distance to be image independent) we have to consider all the possible ways of confusing "Wilson" with "Amherst"; i.e. we have to consider all possible segmentation points of a hypothetical image and all possible ways of matching words "Wilson" and "Amherst" with the segments of such image. Then we choose the worst-case scenario (i.e. the smallest distance) among all possible combinations. This would be the measure of confusion between "Wilson" and "Amherst".

Elementary distances between slices of different characters can be computed during the training phase of WMR and stored in several 26 by 26 slice-confusion matrices. These matrices are a natural generalization of confusion matrices between whole characters [4]. To compute the slice distance between two ASCII words w_1 and w_2, we consider all the possible meaningful (depending on words w_1 and w_2) numbers of segments, and all possible ways of combining the segments to match individual characters of each word. Character boundaries from each word determine the boundaries of slices. The slice distance between words w_1 and w_2 is then the minimum sum of elementary slice distances for each such combination. We denote the minimum slice distance between two ASCII words

w_1 and w_2 by $msd(w_1, w_2)$. The dynamic program described in [4] computes the minimum slice distance in time $O(|w_1| \cdot |w_2| \cdot (|w_1| + |w_2|))$.

3 Lexicon Density

We are faced with a problem of determining density in a discrete space of points (=words). Notice that in our case, there is really no concept of dimension of the space (in fact the dimension of our space is infinity) which makes our task only more difficult.

Consider the following hypothetical situation. We have n points that are exactly distance 1 apart. This is easy to imagine for 2, 3, or 4 points—see Figure 5. Clearly, the density should be different for a different number of points, in fact, it should increase with the number of points. Thus in this particular case, one would want to define the density as $\rho = f(n)$ where $f(n)$ is an increasing function of n. The function $f(n)$ depends on a particular recognizer and has to be determined from experimental data.

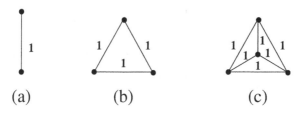

(a) (b) (c)

Fig. 5. Visualization of the special case where all the points are distance 1 apart: (a) 2 points, (b) 3 points, (c) 4 points.

Given a word recognizer R, we denote by $d_R(w1, w2)$ an image independent recognizer dependent distance between two ASCII words $w1$ and $w2$. Such distance should measure the difficulty of confusing words $w1$ and $w2$ by recognizer R. Our split distance $msd(w1, w2)$ is an example of such function.

Based on the considerations given above, we can define lexicon density in the following way.

Given a recognizer R and a lexicon L with words $w_1, \ldots, w_n$, we define the density of lexicon L with respect to recognizer R as

$$\rho(L) = \rho_R(L) = \frac{n(n-1)}{\sum_{i,j=1}^{n} d_R(w_i, w_j)} f_R(n) \tag{1}$$

where $f_R(n)$ is some increasing recognizer-dependent function.

Thus lexicon density is defined as the reciprocal of the average distance between lexicon entries multiplied by function $f_R(n)$.

We have experimented with several definitions of function $f(n)$. Setting $f(n) = \log \frac{n}{2} = \log_{10} \frac{n}{2}$ led to a complete independence of performance and lexicon size. The experimental data and the corresponding graph for this choice of $f(n)$ are shown in Table 1 and Figure 6. These results seem to be conforming to the intuitive notion of lexicon density we set out to define. Recognition accuracy decreases with increasing lexicon density and if the density is the same, although the lexicon sizes may be different, the recognition accuracy stays about the same.

4 Experiments

We have designed simple yet very effective procedure to evaluate the dependence of the performance of WMR on the lexicon density and on the lexicon size. We have used a set of 3,000 images from the "bha" series (CEDAR CDROM)—this set contains images of words extracted from handwritten addresses on U.S. mail and is used as a standard for evaluating performance of word recognizers by the research community at large.

For each image we have randomly generated 10 lexicons of sizes 5, 10, 20 and 40. Each lexicon contained the truth (the correct answer). For a specific size, the lexicons were divided into 10 groups depending on their density—the most dense lexicons for each image were collected in the first group, second most dense lexicons for each image were collected in the second group, the least dense lexicons for each image were collected in the tenth group[1]. We have tested the performance of WMR on each of these groups.

Table 1 shows the performance of WMR on 40 different groups of lexicons for $f(n) = \log n/2$. Figure 6 shows the corresponding graph. Each column corresponds to different lexicon size, groups of lexicons in each column are ordered by decreasing density. Each cell of the table shows the average lexicon density for a particular group of lexicons together with the percentage of first choice of WMR being correct and the percentage of the correct answer among the first two choices.

The results clearly indicate a strong correlation between lexicon density and recognition performance and show that the performance of WMR is in fact independent of lexicon size.

5 Acknowledgements

The authors would like to thank our colleagues at CEDAR, in particular Evie, Jaehwa, and Krasi, for numerous discussions and feedback.

---

[1] The term "dense" is used as per our definition above.

References

1. L. R. Bahl, F. Jelinek, and R. L. Mercer. A maximum likelihood approach to continuous speech recognition. *IEEE Transactions on Pattern Analysis and Machine Intelligence*, 5(2), Mar. 1983.
2. G. Kim and V. Govindaraju. Bank check recognition using cross validation between legal and courtesy amounts. *International Journal of Pattern recognition and Artificial Intelligence*, 11(4):657–674, 1997.
3. G. Kim and V. Govindaraju. A lexicon driven approach to handwritten word recognition for real-time applications. *IEEE Transactions on Pattern Analysis and Machine Intelligence*, 19(4):366–379, Apr. 1997.
4. P. Slavík. Slice distance. Technical Report 2000-04, Department of Computer Science, SUNY at Buffalo, Apr. 2000. http://www.cse.buffalo.edu/tech-reports/.
5. R. A. Wagner and M. J. Fischer. The string-to-string correction problem. *J. ACM*, 21(1):168–173, Jan. 1974.

Table 1. Performance of WMR on lexicons of different size and different average densities using $f(n) = \log n/2$. The corresponding graph for this table is shown in Figure 6

Lexicon Size	5	10	20	40
Density	110.9	114.5	199.9	247.4
1st correct	83.12	72.37	60.03	47.58
1st or 2nd correct	95.93	89.82	81.01	68.57
Density	89.0	111.9	181.2	229.4
1st correct	85.72	76.04	62.60	49.42
1st or 2nd correct	96.96	91.36	81.92	70.24
Density	76.6	110.2	165.6	211.0
1st correct	87.82	78.24	66.87	53.89
1st or 2nd correct	97.63	92.89	84.65	72.51
Density	67.1	108.7	151.9	197.4
1st correct	89.22	81.01	68.70	53.69
1st or 2nd correct	97.56	93.43	85.82	74.24
Density	58.4	93.0	126.8	161.1
1st correct	91.12	85.55	74.81	64.83
1st or 2nd correct	98.23	95.63	89.72	81.21
Density	52.0	83.6	115.8	150.1
1st correct	92.29	85.82	78.14	67.27
1st or 2nd correct	98.37	95.96	91.73	83.85
Density	46.4	68.6	103.0	132.0
1st correct	93.16	88.72	82.98	74.61
1st or 2nd correct	98.73	96.56	93.83	87.22
Density	41.4	67.8	94.7	123.2
1st correct	95.10	90.52	85.22	76.14
1st or 2nd correct	98.87	97.26	94.26	89.62
Density	36.4	53.7	85.3	110.5
1st correct	95.66	92.13	86.59	80.38
1st or 2nd correct	99.03	97.60	94.43	91.32
Density	36.4	53.7	85.3	110.5
1st correct	96.70	93.49	88.29	82.32
1st or 2nd correct	99.27	97.73	95.63	92.26

Accuracy vs Density

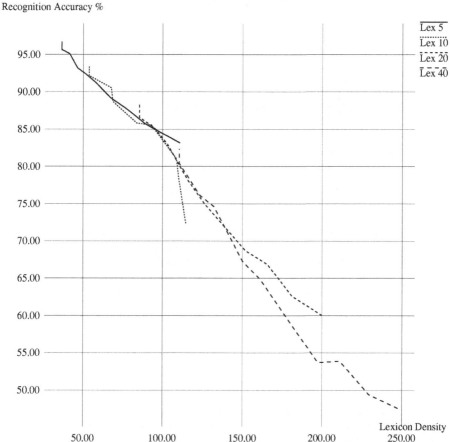

Fig. 6. Dependence of the performance of WMR on lexicon density for $f(n) = \log n/2$. Recognition accuracy decreases as lexicon density increases. Note that while lexicon sizes are different, as long as the density is approximately the same, the recognition accuracy also stays approximately the same.

A Multi-expert System for Dynamic Signature Verification

V. Di Lecce[1], G. Dimauro[2], A. Guerriero[1], S. Impedovo[2], G. Pirlo[2], and A. Salzo[2]

[1] Dipartimento di Ingegneria Elettronica, Politecnico di Bari, Via Re David , 70126 Bari,
Italy

[2] Dipartimento di Informatica, Università degli Studi di Bari, via Orabona 4, 70126 Bari,
Italy

Abstract. This paper presents a multi-expert system for dynamic signature verification. The system combines three experts whose complementar behaviour is achieved by using both different features and verification strategies. The first expert uses shape-based features and performs signature verification by a wholistic analysis. The second and third expert uses speed-based features and performs signature verification by a regional analysis. Finally, the verification responses provided by the three experts are combined by majority voting.

1 Introduction

The use of electronic computers in gathering and processing information on geographic communication networks makes the problem of high-security access basically important in many applications. For this purpose, several systems for automatic personal verification can be used [1]:
➢ physical mechanisms belonging to the individual (i.e. key or badge);
➢ information based systems (i.e. password, numeric string, key-phrase);
➢ personal characteristics (i.e. speech, finger-print, palm-print, signature).

Among others, personal characteristics are the most interesting since they cannot be lost, stolen or forgotten. Moreover, signature is the common form used for legal attestation and the customary way of identifying an individual in our society, for banking transactions and fund transfers. Therefore, automatic signature verification is of great interest also for commercial benefits due to the wide range of applications in which signature verification systems can be involved.

Signature is the result of a complex process based on a sequence of actions stored into the brain and realised by the writing system of the signer (arms and hands) through ballistic-like movements. More than other forms of writings, signatures of the same person can be very different depending on both physical and psychological condition of the writer: *short–period variability* is evident on a day-to-day basis, it is mainly due to the psychological condition of the writer and on the writing conditions

J. Kittler and F. Roli (Eds.): MCS 2000, LNCS 1857, pp. 320-329, 2000.
© Springer-Verlag Berlin Heidelberg 2000

(posture of the writer, type of pen and paper, size of the writing area, etc.); *long-period variability* is due to the modifications of the physical writing system of the signer as well as of the sequence of actions stored in his/her brain [2].

Therefore, the development of signature verification systems is not a trivial task since it involves many biophysical and psychological aspects related to human behaviour as well as many engineering issues [3, 4, 5].

Recently, many important results have been achieved toward a deeper understanding of the human behaviour related to hand-written signature generation [6,7,8], and several powerful tools (dynamic time warping [9], propagation classifiers [10], neural networks [11, 12]) and emerging strategies (regional-oriented comparison strategy [13], multi-expert approach [14,15]) have been successfully applied to signature verification [16,17].

In this paper, a new system for dynamic signature verification is presented. The system combines three experts for signature verification. The first expert uses shape-based features and performs signature verification by a wholistic analysis. The second and third expert uses speed-based features and performs signature verification by a regional analysis. Each stroke of the segmented signature is processed individually and its genuinity is verified. Successively, the verification responses for the entire set of strokes are averaged to judge the genuinity of the input specimen. The verification responses provided by the three experts are finally combined by majority voting.

The paper is organised as follows: Section 2 describes the process for signature verification. The architecture of the new system for signature verification is presented in Section 3. Section 4 presents the three experts for signature verification and the rules for decision combination. The experimental results are presented in Section 5.

2   The Process of Signature Verification

Figure 1 shows the main phases of the signature verification process [16]. The first phase concerns with the acquisition of the input signature. If on-line signature are considered, data acquisition is performed by graphic tablets or integrated graphic-tablet displays. The second phase concerns preprocessing, whose aim is to remove noise and to prepare the input data for further processing. In this phase, the segmentation of signature into basic components and strokes is performed, depending on the particular strategy used for signature comparison. In the feature extraction phase, relevant features for the verification aims are extracted from the preprocessed signature. In the comparison phase, the extracted features are used to match the input signature and the reference specimens. The result is used to judge the authenticity of the input signature. Two types of errors can occur in signature verification: type I errors (false-rejection) caused by the rejection of genuine signatures, and type II errors (false-acceptance) caused by the acceptance of forgeries [16,17].

The information in the reference database (RD) about signatures of the writers enrolled into the system plays a fundamental role in the process of signature verification and must be carefully organised. RD is generally realised during controlled training sessions according to two main approaches. The first approach is based on the selection of an average prototype of the genuine signatures together with additional information about writer variability in signing. [18]. The second approach uses as reference information one or more genuine specimens. Even if this approach implies time-consuming verification procedures it is more suitable for modelling the singular process of signing whose nature is extremely variable [9].

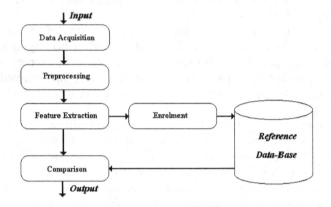

Fig. 1. The process of Signature Verification.

3   Strategies for Signature Comparison

In the comparison phase, the test signature S^t is compared against the N^r reference signatures S^r, $r=1,2,...,N^r$ which are available in the reference database. This phase produces a single response R which states the authenticity of the test signature:

$$R = \begin{cases} 0 & iff \quad \text{the test signature is a forgery} \\ 1 & iff \quad \text{the test signature is genuine.} \end{cases}$$

In order to face the enormous variability in hand-written signatures, different strategies for signature matching have been used. They can be classified into two main categories: [16]: *wholistic* and *regional*.

➢   _Wholistic matching._ In this case the test signature S^t , considered as a whole, is matched against each one of the N^r reference signatures S^1, S^2,...,S^{N^r}. Of course this approach does not allow any regional evaluation of the signature. In fact, each matching of S^t with S^r produces the response R^r:

$$R^r = \begin{cases} 0 & iff \quad S^t \text{ results a forgery when compared to } S^r \\ 1 & iff \quad S^t \text{ results genuine when compared to } S^r. \end{cases}$$

Then, the final response R is defined as:

$$R = \begin{cases} 0 & \text{iff} \quad \forall\, r = 1,2,\dots,N^r \; : \; R^r = 0 \\ 1 & \text{otherwise.} \end{cases}$$

➤   *Regional matching*. In this case both the test signature S^t and the reference signature S^r are split into n segments $(S^t_1, S^t_2, \dots, S^t_k, \dots, S^t_n)$ and $(S^r_1, S^r_2, \dots, S^r_k, \dots, S^r_n)$, respectively. The matching between S^t and S^r is performed by evaluating the local responses R^r_k obtained by matching S^t_k against S^r_k, for $k=1,2,\dots,n$:

$$R^r_k = \begin{cases} 0 & \text{iff} \quad S^t_k \text{ results a forgery when compared to } S^r_k \\ 1 & \text{iff} \quad S^t_k \text{ results genuine when compared to } S^r_k. \end{cases}$$

This approach allows a regional analysis of the signature, but it is carried out in a one-by-one comparison process: i.e. the test signature is judged to be a genuine specimen if and only if a reference signature exists for which, in the comparison process, a suitable number of segments of the test signature are found to be genuine.

An improved regional strategy for signature comparison is the *multiple regional* [13,14,16]. In this case each segment S^t_k of the test signature is matched against the entire set of the corresponding segments $(S^1_k, S^2_k, \dots, S^{N^r}_k)$ of the N^r reference signatures $S^1, S^2, \dots, S^{N^r}$. Therefore for each segment S^t_k of the test signature, a local verification response R^t_k is obtained as:

$$R^r_k = \begin{cases} 0 & \text{iff} \quad \forall r = 1,2,\dots, N^r : S^t_k \text{ results a forgery when compared to } S^r_k \\ 1 & \text{otherwise.} \end{cases}$$

The test signature is judged to be a genuine specimen if a suitable number of segments are found to be genuine. This approach allows a regional evaluation of the signature without requiring a large set of reference signatures [16].

4. A Multi-expert System for Signature Verification

The system for signature verification presented in this paper is based on a multi-expert verification procedure which combines the responses of three experts by majority voting. The experts differ in terms of both strategies for signature comparison and feature type. The first expert performs a wholistic analysis of the signature by evaluating the effectiveness of the segmentation procedure. Shape-based features are used for this purpose. The second and third expert performs signature verification by a regional analysis based on speed-based features. A multiple regional matching strategy is adopted for this purpose. In the following the three experts are described and the combination rule is illustrated.

4.1 The First Expert (E1)

The first expert evaluates the genuinity of the test signature by the analysis of the segmentation results. For the purpose, a recent segmentation technique based on a dynamic splitting procedure is used [19]. It segments the test signature according to the characteristics of the reference signatures. The segmentation procedure consists of four steps.

❖   First, the procedure detects the local maxima (CSP^{MAX}) and minima (CSP^{MIN}) in the vertical direction of the signatures. These two sets of points are considered as Candidate Splitting Points (CSP) and a simple procedure is adopted to identify the points of CSP^{MAX} and CSP^{MIN} for the splitting. In the following we discuss the procedure for the set CSP^{MAX} (the procedure for CSP^{MIN} is similar). Figure 2a shows three reference specimens S^1, S^2, S^3 and a test signature S^t. The $CSPs^{MAX}$ are marked with "*".

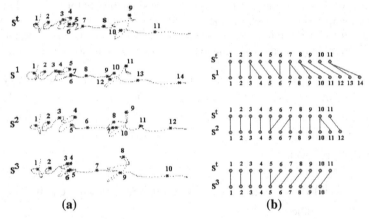

(a)   (b)

Fig.2. Matching between test and reference signatures

❖   In the second step, the procedure determines the warping function between the $CSPs^{MAX}$ of each reference signature and those of the test signature which satisfies the *monotonicity*, *continuity* and *boundary* conditions [20], and which minimises the quantity

$$D = \sum_{k=1}^{K} d(c_k),$$

where $c_k=(i_k,j_k)$, (k=1,2,...,K) is the sequence of indexes coupling $CSPs^{MAX}$ of the reference and test signature, and $d(c_k) = d(z^r(i_k), z^t(j_k))$ a distance measure in the representation space of the signatures. Figure 2b shows the best coupling sequences for the signatures in figure 2a.

❖   In the third step, the sequence of indexes $c_k=(i_k,j_k)$, k=1,2,...,K, is used to detect the CSPs^{MAX} of the reference and test signatures that are directly matched; i.e. that are one-by-one coupled [19]. Table 1 reports the set of CSP^{MAX} directly matched to points of the test signature (see Figure 2b).

Table 1. Set of CSP^{MAX} directly matched

1st Reference Signature	1,2,3,4,6,7,8,9,10
2nd Reference Signature	1,2,3,4,8,9,12
3rd Reference Signature	1,2,5,11,12

❖   In the fourth step the CSPs^{MAX} of the test signature that are always directly matched to all the reference signatures are used to segment the test and the reference signatures.

Table 2. Set of splitting points.

Test Signature	1	2	4	9
1st Reference Signature	1	2	4	8
2nd Reference Signature	1	2	4	9
3rd Reference Signature	1	2	5	11

For instance, the CSP^{MAX} number 1,2,4 and 9 of S^t are always directly matched to points of S^1, S^2 and S^3. Therefore the CSP^{MAX} number 1,2,4 and 9 are the splitting point for the signature S^t. The corresponding splitting points for S^1,S^2,S^3 are reported in Table 2.

On the basis of the segmentation results, the expert computes the following index to evaluate the genuinity of the test signature:

$$R_1 = \frac{\text{Number of splitted strokes of the test signature}}{\text{Number of Candidate Splitting Points of the test signature}}.$$

The verification rule is the following:
- if $R_1 < T^1_1$ then: Test signature = "False"
- if $T^1_1 \leq R_1 \leq T^1_2$ then: Test signature = "Rejected"
- if $T^1_2 < R_1$ then: Test signature = "Genuine"

where T^1_1 and T^1_2 are two personal thresholds (different from writer to writer) detected from analysis of the minimum and maximum value of the index R_1 for the set of genuine specimens.

4.2 The Second Expert (E2)

The second expert adopts a multiple regional verification strategy and an elastic matching procedure for the verification of each segment of the test signature. The authenticity of each stroke of the test signature is evaluated by matching the stroke against the corresponding stroke of each reference signature. In our system, a speed-based dissimilarity measure is used to match couple of genuine specimens S^r and S^t:

$$D = \sum_{k=1}^{K} d(c_k)$$

where $d(c_k) = d(z^r(i_k), z^t(j_k))$, and $v^r(i_k)$ and $v^t(j_k)$ is the velocity of the tip of the pen (computed from the displacement vectors) of the signatures S^r and S^t, at points i_k and j_k, respectively. The stroke is considered a genuine sample if and only if the least value of the dissimilarity measure is lower than the regional threshold which is the worst dissimilarity measure obtained by matching all the pairs of coupled strokes of the reference signatures [9,19]. This procedure provides the vector of local verification responses for the strokes of the test signature $(R'_1, R'_2, ...R'_{Nt})$ where, for each stroke S'_k, the local verification response R'_k is:

$$R^r_k = \begin{cases} 0 & \text{iff } \forall r = 1,2,..., N^r : S^t_k \text{ results a forgery when compared to } S^r_k \\ 1 & \text{otherwise.} \end{cases}$$

From the vector of local verification responses, the second expert computes the index:

$$R_2 = \frac{\text{length of genuine strokes of the test signature}}{\text{length of the test signature}}.$$

The verification rule is the following:
- if $R_2 < T^2_1$ then: Test signature = "False"
- if $T^2_1 \leq R_2 \leq T^2_2$ then: Test signature = "Rejected"
- if $T^2_2 < R_2$ then: Test signature = "Genuine"

where thresholds T^2_1 and T^2_2 are detected from analysis of the range of variability of R_2 for set of genuine specimens.

4.3 The Third Expert (E3)

The vector of the local verification responses $(R'_1, R'_2, ...R'_{Nt})$ is also used by the third expert. The verification index for this expert is:

$$R_3 = \frac{\text{Number of genuine strokes of the test signature}}{\text{Number of strokes of the test signature}}.$$

The verification rule is the following:
- if $R_3 < T^3_1$ then: Test signature = "False"
- if $T^3_1 \leq R_3 \leq T^3_2$ then: Test signature = "Rejected"
- if $T^3_2 < R_3$ then: Test signature = "Genuine"

also in this case the threshold values T^3_1 and T^3_2 are detected from analysis of the range of variability of R_3 for set of genuine specimens.

4.4 The Combination Criterion (E-MV)

The decisions of the three experts are combined by majority voting [15,16]:
➢ if at least two decisions are "genuine" the final response is "genuine";
➢ if at least two decisions are "false" the final response is "false";
➢ otherwise the final response is "rejected".

5   Experimental Results

For the experimental phase, fifteen writers have collected the genuine signatures and other fifteen persons have produced the forged samples in daily writing sessions. In each session, the writer has had about ten minutes to practice himself with the electronic tablet and five minutes to affix up to five signatures. The forgers attended the writing sessions and training themselves in imitating the genuine signatures. After enrolment, for each writer a database of fifty genuine signature and fifty forgeries were available. All specimens have been suitably normalised [19]. Five additional genuine specimens have been collected for each writer and used to find out the optimal set of three specimens for reference, according to a correlation-based analysis on the local stability [21,22].

S^t_1 S^t_2 S^t_3 S^t_4 S^t_5

Fig.3. Verification result of a test signature

Figure 3 reports a test signature (genuine signature of writer #1). For this specimen the system provide the correct result since the verification responses of the three experts are:
⇒ (E1) (global analysis) Verification Response=G
⇒ (E2) (regional analysis) Verification Response=G
⇒ (E3) (regional analysis) Verification Response=G
(The local responses for E2 and E3 are: S^t_1=**G**; S^t_2=**F**; S^t_3=**G**; S^t_4=**G**; S^t_5=**R**).

Table 3a. Verification responses: signer #1 - genuine signatures

n.	1	2	3	4	5	6	7	8	9	10	11	12	13	14	15	16	17	18	19	20	21	22	23	24	25	26	27	28	29	30	31	32	33	34	35	36	37	38	39	40	41	42	43	44	45	46	47	48	49	50
E1	G	R	F	G	G	G	G	R	G	G	G	G	G	G	G	F	G	G	G	G	R	G	G	G	G	R	G	G	G	G	F	F	G	G	G	G	R	G	G	G	R	G	G	G	G	G	G	G	G	G
E2	G	G	F	G	G	R	G	G	G	G	G	G	G	G	G	G	G	G	F	G	G	G	G	G	G	G	G	G	G	G	G	G	G	G	G	G	G	G	F	G	G	G	G	G	R	G	F	G		
E3	G	G	G	G	G	G	G	R	G	G	G	G	G	G	R	G	G	G	G	F	G	G	G	F	G	G	G	G	G	G	G	G	G	G	G	F	G	G	G	G	G	G	G	G	G	F	G			
E-MV	G	G	F	G	G	G	G	G	G	G	G	G	G	G	G	G	G	G	G	G	G	G	G	F	G	G	G	G	G	G	G	G	G	G	G	G	G	G	R	G	G	G	G	G	G	G	G	G	F	G

Table 3b. Verification responses: signer #1 - false signatures

n.	1	2	3	4	5	6	7	8	9	10	11	12	13	14	15	16	17	18	19	20	21	22	23	24	25	26	27	28	29	30	31	32	33	34	35	36	37	38	39	40	41	42	43	44	45	46	47	48	49	50
E1	F	F	F	G	F	F	R	R	F	F	F	F	R	R	R	F	F	F	F	F	F	F	F	F	F	G	F	F	F	F	F	G	F	G	F	F	F	F	F	F	F	F	F	R	F	G	F	F	F	R R

Table 3b. Verification responses: signer #1 - false signatures

(Verification response table, rows E1, E2, E3, E-MV over columns n. 1–50, values F/G/R — see original.)

The verification responses for signer #1 are reported in Table 3a (genuine signatures), and 3b (forgeries). This result shows to what extent the three expert are complementary. Precisely, E2 and E3 agree more times (88/100) than E1 and E2 (72/100), and E1 and E3 (71/100). In fact, E2 and E3 use speed-based features while E1 uses shape-based features and a different comparison strategy.

For the 15 writers, the performances for E1 are Type I Error = 5.1%, Type II Error = 0.75%, Rejection = 7.2%; for E2 are Type I Error = 4.5%, Type II Error = 1.05%, Rejection = 6.5%; for E3 are Type I Error = 5.7%, Type II Error = 0.95%, Rejection = 6.2%. When the decisions of the three experts are combined, the performances are reported in Table 4. The net result is Type I Error=3.2%, Type II Error=0.55%, Rejection=3.2%.

Table 4. System Performance

Signer	#1	#2	#3	#4	#5	#6	#7	#8	#9	#10	#11	#12	#13	#14	#15
Type I	6%	4%	4%	0%	2%	6%	2%	4%	2%	4%	0%	4%	2%	4%	4%
Type II	2%	0%	2%	0%	0%	0%	0%	2%	0%	2%	0%	2%	0%	0%	0%
Rejection	4%	2%	4%	2%	4%	2%	2%	4%	8%	2%	4%	2%	2%	2%	4%

6 Conclusion

A multi-expert system for dynamic signature verification is presented in this paper. The system combines three experts by majority voting. The experts are based on different features and verification strategies. Complementarity among experts has been achieved by different feature sets and classification strategies. The first expert uses shape-based features and performs signature verification by a wholistic analysis. The second and third expert uses speed-based features and performs signature verification by a regional analysis.

References
1. *Proc. of Securtech*, Washington D.C., April 7-9, 1992.
2. J. Duvernoy and D. Charraut, "Stability and Stationarity of Cursive Handwriting", *Pattern Recognition*, Vol. 11, pp. 145-154, 1979.

3. R. Plamondon and F.J. Maarse, "An Evaluation of Motor Models of handwriting", *IEEE Trans. Syst. Man Cybern.*, vol. 19, n. 5, pp. 1060-1072, 1989.

4. M.C. Fairhurst and P. S. Brittan, "An evaluation of parallel strategies for feature vector construction in automatic signature verification systems", *Int. J. Pattern Recog. Artif. Intell.* 8, 3 (1994) 661-678.

5. M.C. Fairhurst, P. S. Brittan and K.D. Cowley, Parallel realisation of feature selection for a high performance signature verification system, PACTA 1992, Barcellona.

6. R. Plamondon, "A Kinematic Theory of Rapid Human Movements: Part I: Movement Representation and generation", *Biological Cybernetics*, vol. 72, 4, 1995, pp. 295-307.

7. R. Plamondon, "A Kinematic Theory of Rapid Human Movements: Part II: Movement Time and Control", *Biological Cybernetics*, vol. 72, 4, 1995, pp. 309-320.

8. R. Plamondon, "A Kinematic Theory of Rapid Human Movements: Part III: Kinetic Outcomes", *Biological Cybernetics*, Jan. 1997.

9. I. Yoshimura and M. Yoshimura, "On-line signature verification incorporating the direction pen movement - An experimental examination of the effectiveness", in *From Pixels to Features III - Frontiers in Handwriting Recognition*, S. Impedovo and J.C. Simon eds., Elsevier Publ., pp. 353-362, 1992.

10. Sabourin and J.P. Drouhard, "Off-line signature verification using directional PDF and neural networks", in *Proc. of 11th Int. Conf. on Pattern Recognition*, 1992, pp.321-325.

11. Barua, "Neural Networks and their applications to computer security", in *Proc. SPIE-Int. Society for Optical Engineering*, 1992, pp. 735-742.

12. Tseng and T.H. Huang,"An on-line Chinese signature verification scheme based on the ART1 neural network", *Proc. of Int. J. Conf. on N.N.*, Maryland, 1992, pp. 624-630.

13. Dimauro, S. Impedovo, G. Pirlo, "Component-oriented algorithms for signature verification", *Int. J. Pattern Recog. Artif. Intell.* **8**, 3 (1994) 771-794.

14. Dimauro, S. Impedovo, G. Pirlo, A. Salzo, "A multi-expert signature verification system for bankcheck processing", *International Journal of Pattern Recognition and Artificial Intelligence*, Vol.11, N.5, World Scientific Publ., Singapore, 1997.

15. R.Plamondon, P.Yergeau and J.J.Brault, "A multi-level signature verification system", in *From Pixels to Features III - Frontiers in Handwriting Recognition*, S.Impedovo and J.C.Simon eds., Elsevier Publ., pp. 363-370, 1992.

16. G. Pirlo, "Algorithms for Signature Verification", Proc. of NATO-ASI *"Fundamentals in Handwriting Recognition"*, Springer-Verlag, pp. 139-152, 1994.

17. F. Leclerc, R. Plamondon, "Signature verification: The state of the Art 1989-1994", *Int. J. Pattern Recognition and Artificial Intelligence, Special Issue on Signature Verification*, vol. 8, no.3, pp. 643-660.

18. B. Wirtz, "Average Prototypes for Stroke-Based Signature Verification", Proc. ICDAR 95, August 1997, Ulm, Germany, pp. 268-272.

19. G. Dimauro, S. Impedovo, G. Pirlo, "On-line Signature Verification through a Dynamical Segmentation Technique", Proc. of the *Third International Workshop on Frontiers in Handwriting Recognition*, Buffalo - NY, USA, pp. 262-271, 1993.

20. L.R.Rabiner, S.E.Levinson, "Isolated and connected word recognition . Theory and Selected applications", *IEEE TC*, Vol. 29, No. 5, 1981, pp. 621-659.

21. G. Congedo, G. Dimauro, S. Impedovo, G. Pirlo, "Selecting Reference Signatures for On-Line Signature Verification", in *Image Analysis and Processing, Lecture Notes in Computer Science*, vol. 974, ed. by C. Braccini et oth., Springer Verlag, Berlin, 1995, pp. 521-526.

22. V. Di Lecce, G. Dimauro, A. Guerriero, S. Impedovo, G. Pirlo, A. Salzo, L. Sarcinella, "Selection of Reference Signatures for Automatic Signature Verification", Proc. ICDAR 99, Bangalore, India, 1999, pp. 597-600.

A Cascaded Multiple Expert System for Verification

L. P. Cordella[1], P. Foggia[1], C. Sansone[1], F. Tortorella[2], and M. Vento[1]

[1] Dipartimento di Informatica e Sistemistica - Università degli Studi di Napoli "Federico II"
Via Claudio 21, I-80125 Napoli, Italy
{cordel, foggiapa, carlosan, vento}@unina.it
http://amalfi.dis.unina.it

[2] Dip. di Automazione, Elettromagnetismo, Ing. dell'Informazione e Matematica Industriale
Università degli Studi di Cassino
Via G. Di Biasio 43, I-03043 Cassino, Italy
tortorella@unicas.it

Abstract. In this paper we propose a multi-expert architecture, particularly suited for verification systems, which attempts to offer the performance advantages of a serial approach while retaining the reliability of a parallel combination scheme. In this framework, criteria for evaluating the reliability of both the intermediate answers and the final response are provided, together with a method for the determination of an optimal reject option. This architecture has been tested on a signature verification application, confirming the effectiveness of the proposed approach.

1 Introduction

In many complex classification problems, a decision must be taken between two alternative classes. Applications such as automated cancer diagnosis, signature verification, and fraud detection fall in this category. In these cases, frequently the distributions of the two classes is so skew (with one class much less frequent and largely overlapping with the other one) that it is necessary to employ a large set of different features to reliably distinguish between samples coming from distinct classes. However, the excessive size of the feature vector could make impracticable the construction of reliable classifiers and thus it could be advisable to split the features among different feature sets and consider a different expert for each of the feature sets individuated. In this way, each expert is tailored on a particular feature set, and can employ the most appropriate learning techniques and classification algorithms. In the general case, the whole classification system is thus accomplished by combining the outputs of the various experts with some suitable rule so as to take the final decision on the basis of all the single decisions [1].

A situation which allows the construction of classification systems particularly efficient is when it is possible to establish a hierarchy among the feature sets obtained such that, by examining the feature sets in a proper order, it could be possible to decide about one of the classes without considering the remaining features. An example

J. Kittler and F. Roli (Eds.): MCS 2000, LNCS 1857, pp. 330-339, 2000.

of this case is given by the systems for verification and/or validation [2]. A verification system is a specialized type of classifier devoted to ascertain in a dependable manner whether an input sample belongs to a given category; a typical use of this kind of systems is for authentication purposes (e.g. validation of a signature on a check, identity verification of fingerprints or retinal patterns). Such systems usually have only two possible output classes: the input sample can either be recognized as a genuine instance of the category (it will be termed a *positive* sample), or it can be considered as extraneous (a *negative* sample). Some systems make also provisions for a third possible kind of outcome: the system realizes its inadequacy for classifying in a reliable way the sample at hand, and abdicates the task invoking the intervention of a more powerful system, if available, or of a human operator; in this case we say that the sample is *rejected* by the system.

In most applications of verification systems the role played by the two classes (positive and negative samples) are very far from being symmetrical: usually the costs incurred when a negative sample is misclassified as positive (the sample is a *false positive*) are dramatically higher than those of a positive sample treated as negative (*false negative*). Thus, a conservative strategy is to assign a sample to the positive class only if there is a very strong supporting evidence, while the assignment to the negative class can be based on a somewhat weaker ground.

A typical approach for this kind of systems is to organize the experts in a decision tree [3,4] so as to minimize the number of experts employed to reach the final decision. A serious drawback of such approach is that a possible error in the first layers of the tree could propagate up to the final stage. This can heavily affect the classification performance in applications where the main goal is to obtain a very reliable decision, possibly coupled with an assessment of the confidence of the decision.

In this paper, we propose a suitable combining architecture, the Cascaded Multiple Expert System (CMES), in which the experts are serially connected according to the hierarchy established. Each expert considers a particular feature set and, for each incoming sample, provides an output class together with a reliability estimate of its classification act. After each expert, a decider determines if a decision sufficiently reliable has been reached, thus stopping the analysis of the remaining features. In the opposite case, the decider activates the following experts in the cascade, forwarding to them the partial decision and the associated reliability. In this way, only the experts necessary to ensure a decision sufficiently reliable are activated. The decision of stopping the analysis or activating the following stages is made according to a threshold on the reliability value. The threshold is chosen so as to ensure, on the basis of the requirements of the application domain, the best tradeoff between rejects (which imply the activation of the successive experts in the CMES) and errors.

The proposed architecture represents a hybrid solution between a pure serial topology and a parallel one. A similar approach is proposed by Rahman and Fairhurst [5], which describe a generalized serial topology (the Modified Distributed Tree Classifier). The main difference that distinguishes our approach from that of Rahman and Fairhurst is that this latter relies, for its final decision, on the response of only one expert, the last activated. In our proposal, instead, all the partial decisions taken by the intermediate experts are considered and used to reach and strengthen the final decision and to evaluate the final reliability.

The proposed architecture has been tested on a signature verification application, employing a large database of signatures produced by 49 different writers. The results obtained confirm the effectiveness of the presented method.

2 The Proposed Approach

The proposed architecture is made up of a cascade of stages: all but the last stage are *decision stages* which consider different set of features, while the final stage, which is a *combination stage*, intervenes only if the previous stages were not able to take a decision. An overview of the system is given in Fig. 1.

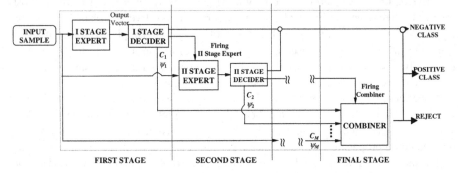

Fig. 1.   The proposed architecture for a verification system

Each decision stage is made of an expert, devoted to the classification of an input sample, and of a decider. The expert is a two-class classifier (positive or negative). The decider, on the basis of the output vector provided by the corresponding expert estimates, by a suitably defined parameter, the reliability of the classification decision and isolates all the samples that can be reliably considered as negatives. On the other hand, if either the sample is considered positive or the classification reliability is not sufficient, the sample is forwarded to the next stage. If none of the decision stages was able to assign the sample to the negative class, the last stage (combination stage) receives their answers (including the estimated reliabilities), and on their basis chooses the most appropriate class. Notice that while the attribution to the negative class can be done by a single expert, a sample can be assigned to the positive class only after taking into account the results of all the decision stages.

Before going in details about the flow of the decision process, we briefly explain the used notation: we will denote as M the number of decision stages, so the total number of stages is $M+1$. The reliability parameters, whose values range from 0 to 1, are in general indicated with ψ, and the reliability thresholds (formally defined hereafter) with σ. These symbols have a subscript denoting the stage they refer to. So $\psi_1, \ldots, \psi_M$, and ψ_c respectively denote the reliability evaluated in the intermediate decision stages and in the final (combination) stage, and $\sigma_1, \dots, \sigma_M$ and σ_c are the corresponding thresholds.

The verification process starts by presenting the input sample to the first stage. If its response is that the sample is negative and the reliability ψ_1 associated to this decision is higher than a suitably fixed reliability threshold σ_1, the system concludes that the sample is negative and the process stops. Otherwise the sample is forwarded to the next stage, where the same process takes place, until either the sample is recognized as negative or the final stage is reached. The samples forwarded up to the last stage are those recognized as positives by the preceding stages, no matter the associated reliability, or those recognized as negatives, but with reliability lower than the threshold. The final stage combines the information regarding the decisions taken by the previous stages, i.e. the class the sample was tentatively attributed to (in the following called vote) and the reliabilities associated to each vote. The combination stage takes the final decision according to a weighted voting criterion, i.e., by performing a sum of the votes for each class, each weighted by the corresponding reliability, and attributing the signature to the class that achieves the highest score. This stage can decide for a reject if the reliability ψ_c associated to the winner class (see Section 2.2) is below a threshold σ_c.

Section 2.1 illustrates the criteria used for evaluating the reliability of the classification decisions and for determining the optimal values of the reject thresholds for the decision stages, while section 2.2 will present with more detail the combination rule of the final stage and the corresponding reliability definition.

2.1 The Decision Stages

As discussed in [6], the low reliability of a classification can be traced back to one of the following situations: *a*) the considered sample is significantly different from those present in the training set; *b*) the point which represents the sample considered in the feature space lies where the regions pertaining to different classes overlap.

To distinguish between classifications which are unreliable because a sample is of type *a* or *b*, let us define two reliability parameters, ψ^a and ψ^b, whose values vary between 0 (completely unreliable) and 1 (very reliable). The two parameters are associated with each expert and each parameter is a function of the expert output vector. Suitable definitions of the reliability parameters for some classifier types can be found in [6,7].

A parameter ψ providing an inclusive measure of the reliability of a classification can be computed by combining the values of ψ^a and ψ^b. The form chosen for ψ is:

$$\psi = \min\{\psi^a, \psi^b\}.$$

This is certainly a conservative choice because it implies that a low value for only one of the parameters is sufficient to consider unreliable the whole classification. However, this is consistent with the kind of classification system considered, which is aimed at achieving the highest reliability.

We will now describe the method for determining the optimal values of the thresholds; the rationale of this method has already been described in [6], but with some restriction that will be removed in the present paper. We will first present the method in its most general form; then we will show its application to the decision stages.

It is assumed that an effectiveness function P is defined which, taking into account the requirements of the particular application, evaluates the quality of the classification in terms of correct recognition, misclassification and rejection rates, where, for the decision stages, rejection simply means that the following stage has to be activated. Under this assumption the optimal reject threshold value, determining the best trade-off between reject rate and misclassification rate, is the one for which the function P reaches its absolute maximum.

The requirements of the particular application domain are specified by attributing costs to misclassifications, rejects and correct classifications. In [6] it is assumed that these costs are invariant with the classes; in this paper the method is generalized to the case in which the cost of an error is different as a function of the actual class.

To operatively define the function P, let us refer to a general classification problem. Suppose that the samples to be classified can be assigned to one of N+1 classes with labels 0, 1, ..., N, where 1, ..., N are the labels of the real classes and 0 is a fictitious class label indicating the reject of the sample. For each class $i=1,...,N$ let us call R_{ii} the percentage of samples correctly classified, R_{ij} the percentage of samples erroneously assigned to the class j (with $j\neq i$) and R_{i0} the percentage of rejected samples. For the same class i, let R_{ii}^0 and R_{ij}^0 indicate respectively the percentage of samples correctly classified and the percentage of samples erroneously assigned to the class j, when the classifier is used at 0-reject. If we assume for P a linear dependence on R_{ii}, R_{ij} and R_{i0}, its expression is given by:

$$P = \sum_{i=1}^{N} C_{ii}\left(R_{ii} - R_{ii}^0\right) - \sum_{i=1}^{N}\sum_{\substack{j=1 \\ j\neq i}}^{N} C_{ij}\left(R_{ij} - R_{ij}^0\right) - \sum_{i=1}^{N} C_{i0}R_{i0} . \tag{2}$$

In other words, P measures the actual effectiveness improvement when the reject option is introduced, with respect to the performance of the expert at 0-reject. The quantity C_{ij} denotes the cost of assigning to the class j a sample belonging to the class i. It is worth noting that, for $j=0$, we indicate the cost of rejecting a sample coming from the class i, while, when $j=i$, the cost represents actually the gain associated to a correct classification. Obviously, for each class i, the following relation must hold:

$$C_{ij} \geq C_{i0} \quad \forall j \neq 0, j \neq i \tag{3}$$

Since R_{ii}, R_{ij} and R_{i0} depend on the value of the reject threshold σ, P is also a function of σ. Starting from the results presented in [6] it is possible to show that the following relation holds:

$$P(\sigma) = \sum_{\substack{i=1}}^{N} \sum_{\substack{j=1 \\ j \neq i}}^{N} \left(C_{ij} - C_{i0} \right) \int_0^\sigma D_{ij}(\psi) d\psi - \sum_{i=1}^{N} \left(C_{ii} + C_{i0} \right) \int_0^\sigma D_{ii}(\psi) d\psi \qquad (4)$$

where $D_{ii}(\psi)$ and $D_{ij}(\psi)$ (with $j \neq i$) are respectively, the occurrence density curves of correctly classified and misclassified samples for the class i as a function of the value of ψ. In other words, $D_{ij}(\psi) d\psi$ is the fraction of samples of class i assigned to class j with a reliability in the interval $[\psi, \psi + d\psi]$.

The optimal value σ^* of the reject threshold σ is the one for which the function P gets its maximum value. In practice, the functions $D_{ij}(\psi)$ are not available in their analytical form and therefore, for evaluating σ^*, they should be experimentally determined in tabular form on a set of labeled samples, adequately representative of the target domain. The optimal threshold σ^* can be eventually determined by means of an exhaustive search among the tabulated values of $P(\sigma)$. It is easy to show that, in case of costs independent of the classes the results coincide with those reported in [6].

In the case of the decision stages of our verification system, the number N of classes is equal to two and we can use the index 1 to denote the positive class and the index 2 for the negative class. It is worth recalling that the system uses σ only if the sample is assigned to class 2; hence we actually do not need to define the costs C_{11} and C_{21}. Since the samples which are rejected by an intermediate stage are re-examined by the following stages, we can assume that rejecting a sample has a negligible cost, thus having $C_{10} = C_{20} = 0$. The definition of the gain for correct recognition C_{22} is based on the estimation of the advantage deriving from the reduction of the number of samples that need to be passed to successive stages if the current one can safely assign them to the negative class. This advantage is not limited only to the computational cost improvement, as it might seem. Also the overall recognition rate can benefit from the sample filtering done in early stages, since the successive experts have to deal only with a subset of the possible kinds of negative samples, and thus their training becomes simpler. Finally, the misclassification cost C_{12} is used to take into account the penalty incurred by the system if a positive sample is mistakenly considered negative. It is usually strongly dependent on the application requirements; for example, in interactive applications it is often simply a measure of the nuisance perceived by the user for having to repeat the verification process, while in off-line applications it might be the actual cost of a check performed by a human operator. In typical applications we expect that $C_{12} \gg C_{22}$, thus forcing the system to choose a σ which permits only a very low misclassification rate.

In order to make each expert able to specialize on those cases that are not dealt with properly by the preceding stages, the expert training is performed in a sequential fashion. The expert of the stage k is trained only after the expert of the stage $(k-1)$ has been trained and the optimal threshold of its decider has been determined. Furthermore, for training the expert of stage k only those samples of the training set are used which are not definitely classified as negatives by the preceding decision stages. In this way, the task of determining the class boundaries becomes simpler, since only a subset of the possible variants of negative samples has to be taken into account; furthermore, the classification can be based on specialized features which are particularly effective on this subset, while might be not equally appropriate in the general case. The determination of the optimal threshold also requires a set of labeled samples, as we have pointed out before. For similar reasons, also for this set we consider at each stage only the samples that have been passed through by the preceding stages.

2.2 The Combination Stage

The combination stage receives as its input the classes guessed by the decision stages and the corresponding reliabilities; that is, for each stage k it receives a pair (C_k, ψ_k). These results are combined by means of a weighted voting scheme, using as weights the ψ of each stage scaled by a constant factor which takes into account the overall reliability attributed to that stage. More formally, for each class j a vote V_j is computed as follows:

$$V_j = \sum_{C_k = j} W(k, C_k) \cdot \psi_k \tag{5}$$

where the factor $W \in [0,1]$ depends on both the stage and the guessed class. The combiner then assigns the sample to the class C_c that received the maximum vote. Notice that the behavior of the scheme proposed in [5] correspond to having $W(k, C_k) = 0$ for $k \neq M$. In the general case the values of W can be determined on the basis of the classification performance of each stage on a representative data set, for example by estimating the *a posteriori* probability that the expert k is right when it guess the class C_k.

Once the class C_c has been determined, the combiner has to evaluate the reliability ψ_c of this response on the basis of the ψ of the intermediate stages. The definition of the reliability is given, according to the considerations in the preceding section, in terms of two parameters, ψ_c^a and ψ_c^b, which characterize the two possible situations that give rise to unreliable classifications.

First we define two auxiliary quantities, which represent the degree of confidence of the decision stages with respect to the two classes:

$$\pi_1 = \max_k \left\{ W(k, C_k) \cdot \psi_k | C_k = C_c \right\} \quad \pi_2 = \max_k \left\{ W(k, C_k) \cdot \psi_k | C_k \neq C_c \right\} \cup \{0\} \tag{6}$$

that is, π_1 represents the maximum weighted reliability for the winning class, and π_2 is the maximum weighted reliability for the other class (or 0 if all the decision stages agree on the winner class).

Given these definitions, the reliability factors can be evaluated as follows:

$$\psi_c^a = \pi_1, \quad \psi_c^b = 1 - \pi_2 / \pi_1, \quad \psi_c = \min\left\{ \psi_c^a, \psi_c^b \right\} \tag{7}$$

Once we have determined the reliability of the combiner output, we can apply to the final stage the method presented in subsection 2.1 for defining an optimal reject threshold.

It is worth recalling that this time the threshold is used for both the classes, and not only for the negative samples. In fact, the final stage has three possible outcomes: the sample is assigned with high reliability to the positive class, the sample is assigned with high reliability to the negative class, or the system decides that it is not able to classify the sample with sufficient reliability.

It follows that for the final stage the whole cost matrix C_{ij} has to be defined. We may assume that the gain for correct classification and the cost of a reject are not dependent on the class of the sample, that is $C_{11} = C_{22}$ and $C_{10} = C_{20}$. On the other hand, we can expect that the costs of a misclassification are quite different for the two classes; in particular, for most applications of a verification system $C_{21} \gg C_{12}$. Moreover, since the combination stage is the last stage of the system, errors in its outputs cannot be easily detected and recovered later, so the misclassification costs for both classes are probably quite higher than the cost of a reject.

In section 3 we will illustrate an experimental testing of our method for a typical application of a verification system (off-line signature verification). In that context, an example of reasonable values for all the application dependent parameters will be given.

3. Experimental Results

The proposed method has been tested on a signature verification application for which reliable techniques are currently requested. In signature verification three different types of forgeries should be taken into account: *random forgeries*, produced without knowing neither the name of the signer nor the shape of its signature, *simple forgeries* produced knowing the name of the signer but without having a sample of his signature, and *skilled forgeries* produced by imitating the shape of the original signature. Since both random and simple forgeries can be very different from genuine signatures, because in both cases the writer does not know the model of the genuine signature, it seems reasonable to consider random and simple forgeries as one category. Consequently, the proposed system is made up of three stages: the first one will cope mostly with random and simple forgeries, the second one mostly with skilled forgeries, and the final stage will consider the cases about which the two previous stages were not able to take a decision.

The features used have been selected among those well known in the literature and extensively used in other signature verification systems. We have considered two of the descriptions proposed by Huang and Yan in [8]: the projections of the outline of the signature and the high pressure regions. We have defined for the first one a feature vector of 120 elements, and for the second one a feature vector of 30 elements. The first feature set, as documented in [8], is able to detect most of random and simple forgeries, even if a number of skilled forgeries can deceive it. On the contrary, the second feature set revealed extremely discriminant for distinguishing between skilled forgeries and genuine signatures.

Both the experts in the first and the second stage are based on neural classifiers (Multi-Layer Perceptron Networks with three layers of neurons).

The database used contains 1960 signatures produced by 49 writers, selected in inhomogeneous social and cultural contexts and differing in sex, age and profession. For each writer, 20 genuine signatures, 10 simple forgeries and 10 skilled forgeries have been included. Skilled forgeries have been produced by writers after a preliminary training phase in which they tried to reproduce each signature about twenty times.

To have an estimate of the performance of the proposed system, we report the experimental results, in terms of FAR (False Acceptance Rate, i.e. the percentage of forgeries classified as genuine) and FRR (False Rejection Rate, i.e. the percentage of the genuine signatures classified as forgeries). We consider: *i*) the two experts working stand-alone; *ii*) the experts working according to the proposed architecture at 0-reject, i.e. without reject in the third stage (σ_c=0) and, finally, *iii*) considering the reject option. Results regarding *i*) and *ii*) are reported in Table 1, while results regarding *iii*) are in Table 2. For cases *ii*) and *iii*), the cost coefficients used for the decision stages are $C_{22} = 1$ and $C_{12} = 10$.

Table 1 highlights that the performance of the two experts working separately is not particularly good; in fact, both the FAR of the first stage (*Outline*) on skilled forgeries and the FRR of the second stage (*High Pressure Regions*) is significantly high. The use of the experts according to the architecture proposed, operating at 0-reject (this is obtained by fixing the threshold σ_c to zero) allows the performance to be significantly improved on the forgeries, as it is evident from the last row of Tab. 1. In fact, the FAR is, as wanted, significantly lower than the one of each single expert used (about 67% less on random, 40% less on simple and 20% less on skilled forgeries). However, in this case the FRR of the overall system is over twice the FRR of the first stage working alone (5.71% vs. 2.65%). This is due to the fact that the FRR of the second stage (*High Pressure Regions*) of the whole system is very high, i.e. 12.04%, and this limits the possibility of obtaining good results in terms of the whole FRR.

Table 1. Results in terms of FRR and FAR obtained by the experts constituting the first and the second stage, working separately, and by the proposed system without the reject option in the third stage. Last row reports the percentage relative improvement of the FAR and the FRR obtained by using the system without reject option, with respect to the best single expert.

	FRR	FAR		
		Random	Simple	Skilled
Outline (First Stage expert)	2.65	0.09	7.14	38.98
High Pressure Regions (Second Stage expert)	12.04	0.86	12.45	26.12
Proposed CMES (without reject option)	5.71	0.03	4.29	20.82
Relative improvement	-115.47%	66.67%	39.92%	20.29%

The addition of the reject option to the third stage, with cost coefficients $C_{11} = C_{22} = 1$, $C_{10} = C_{20} = 2$, $C_{12} = 4$ and $C_{21} = 10$, determines a significant performance improvement, as evident in Table 2. In fact, the FRR becomes less than that of the best single expert working separately (2.04 vs. 2.65) and the FAR on random and skilled forgeries further decreases. Particularly effective is the result on random forgeries, whose relative FAR is almost zero. In conclusion, the system obtains a relative reduction of 23% in terms of FRR and of 51%, in the average, in terms of FAR.

Table 2. Results in terms of FRR, FAR and reject rate (RR) obtained by the proposed CMES on the whole database.

Genuine		Random		Simple		Skilled	
FRR	RR	FAR	RR	FAR	RR	FAR	RR
2.04	3.67	0.01	0.02	4.29	0.00	19.80	1.22

4. Conclusions

In this paper we have presented a multi-expert architecture particularly suited for verification systems. For this architecture, we have given some criteria for evaluating the reliability of the response and a method for the determination of an optimal reject option. The effectiveness of our proposal has been experimentally evaluated in the context of a signature verification application, where a significant improvement in the reliability of the system has been demonstrated.

References

1. J. Kittler, M. Hatef, R.P.W. Duin, J. Matas, "On Combining Classifiers", *IEEE Trans. Pattern Anal. and Mach. Intell.*, vol. 20, no. 3, pp. 226-239, 1998.
2. R. Plamondon, F. Leclerc, "Automatic signature verification: the state of the art 1989-1993", *Int. Journ. of Pattern Recogn. and Artif. Intell.*, vol. 8, no. 3, pp. 643-659, 1994.
3. P. Argentiero, R. Chin, P. Beaudet, "An Automated Approach to the Design of Decision Tree Classifiers", *IEEE Trans. Pattern Anal. and Mach. Intell.*, vol. 4, pp. 51-57, 1982.
4. Q.R. Wang, C.Y. Suen, "Analysis and Design of a Decision Tree Based on Entropy Reduction and its Application to Large Character Set Recognition", *IEEE Trans. Pattern Analysis and Machine Intelligence*, vol. 6, no. 4, pp. 406-414, 1984.
5. A.F.R. Rahman, M.C. Fairhurst, "Serial Combination of Multiple Experts: A Unified Evaluation", *Pattern Anal. & Applications*, vol. 2, no. 4, pp. 292-311, 1999.
6. L.P. Cordella, C. Sansone , F. Tortorella, M. Vento, C. De Stefano, "Neural Networks Classification Reliability", in C.T. Leondes (ed.). Academic Press theme volumes on Neural Network Systems, Techniques and Applications. Academic Press 1998, 5: 161-199.
7. L.P. Cordella, P. Foggia, C. Sansone, F. Tortorella, M. Vento, "Reliability Parameters to Improve Combination Strategies in Multi-Expert Systems", *Pattern Anal. and Applications*, vol. 3, no. 2, pp. 205-214, 1999
8. K. Huang, H. Yan, "Off-line signature verification based on geometric feature extraction and neural network classification", *Pattern Recognition*, vol. 30, no. 1, pp. 9-17, 1997.

Architecture for Classifier Combination Using Entropy Measures

Kr. Ianakiev and V. Govindaraju

Center for Excellence in Document Analysis and Recognition (CEDAR)
Department of Computer Science & Engineering
University at Buffalo, Amherst, NY 14228, USA
{ianakiev,govind}@cedar.buffalo.edu
Fax: (716) 645-6176

Abstract. In this paper we emphasize the need for a general theory of combination. Presently, most systems combine recognizers in an *ad hoc* manner. Recognizers can be combined in series and/or in parallel. Empirical methods can become extremely time consuming, given the very large number of combination possibilities. We have developed a method of systematically arriving at the optimal architecture for combination of classifiers that can include both parallel and serial methods. Our focus in this paper, however, will be on serial methods. We also derive some theoretical results to lay the foundation for our experiments. We show how a greedy algorithm that strives for entropy reduction at every stage leads to results superior to combination methods which are *ad hoc*. In our experiments we have seen an advantage of about 5% in certain cases.

1 Introduction

Machine recognition of isolated handwritten words, especially cursive script, is a difficult problem. The problem is made tractable only when constrained by a *lexicon*, a list of words that includes the truth of the image as one of its elements. Research in handwritten word recognition (HWWR) has traditionally focused on relatively small lexicons, typically comprised of 10 - 1000 entries. Features extracted from the image are matched against every lexicon entry by an expensive matching algorithm, and a confidence value is computed for each lexicon entry [5]. The lexicon entries are ranked in decreasing order of confidence. While this paradigm has proven to be sufficient for many applications from check amounts to street names in mail addresses, there are other applications wherein the lexicons are large (of the order of 10,000 entries or more) and it is no longer practical to compare the features extracted from the image with every lexicon entry. Some means of rapidly eliminating large parts of the lexicon as being unlikely matches is called for. This process is called lexicon reduction, and serves to rapidly trim the original lexicon down to a tractable size for a word classifier. It is a known fact that classifier performance declines with increasing size of lexicon. This may be attributed to the presence in large lexicons of several entries that the classifier finds difficult to distinguish from the reference. By eliminating some of these entries, lexicon reduction results in improved recognition performance. Classifiers can combine in either series or in parallel. Figure 1 shows the architectures possible. This paper is about developing a general theory for combination of classifiers. In particular, we want to discuss the theoretical and complexity

J. Kittler and F. Roli (Eds.): MCS 2000, LNCS 1857, pp. 340–350, 2000.

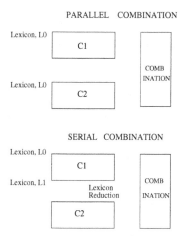

Fig. 1. Two Classifier Combination Models. Parallel Combination methods can have the classifiers acting independently in terms of both looking at the same original lexicon. Serial methods are clearly dependent on each other as the second classifier in the series depends on the results of the first classifier.

issues pertaining to lexicon reduction and the serial combination of classifiers. Let us assume for the discussion in this paper that the word recognizer is the classifier and the lexical entries are the classes. Further, let us begin by discussing the case of two classifiers. We shall later see how the methodology developed can be readily generalized to any number of classifiers. The method of parallel combination of classifiers would submit the same lexicon to both classifiers and combine the results using a variety of methods, such as logistic regression and Borda Count [3,7]. On the other hand, in serial combination, classifiers that operate later in the engine deal with smaller lexicons. In fact, lexicon reduction is central to the serial combination methods.

Table 1 shows a few serial combination methods using 3 classifiers. We take note of the fact that the number of possibilities is very large. First, if there are 3 classifiers, they can be ordered in $3! = 6$ ways. Further, given the original lexicon L_0 of length $|L_0|$, the reduced lexicon output by classifier C_1 can be of $|L_0 - 2|$ different sizes (not counting the cases when the entire lexicon or just 1 entry are returned). For $L_0 = 2768$, it amounts to $6 \times 2766 = 16,596$ possible configurations for the architecture.

The motivation for this paper stems from the difficulty confronted by a designer in choosing the correct architecture. Empirical methods are typically used by researchers. However, as the number of classifiers increases and the size of the lexicon (L_0) increases, the situation quickly gets out of hand. Our objective is to develop the theory that will provide the guidelines for choosing the best method of serial combination.

If one were to consider parallel combination methods as well, the possible configurations increase further. Table 1 shows how different architectures can be configured mixing the notion of serial and parallel combination. We have

Table 1. There are $n!$ different ways in which n classifiers can be arranged in series. A_x indicates the accuracy of reduction after first stage of classification with classifier1 and A_y after the second stage. x and y are the sizes of the reduced lexicons.

Architecture	A_x	A_y	A_1
2768 → classifier 1 → 50 → classifier 2 → 10 → classifier 3 → 1	$A_{50} = 70.87\%$	$A_{10} = 39.23\%$	34.40%
2768 → classifier 2 → 500 → classifier 1 → 50 → classifier 3 → 1	$A_{500} = 62.77\%$	$A_{50} = 60.77\%$	46.60%
2768 → classifier 1 → 50 → classifier 3 → 1		$A_{50} = 70.87\%$	52.40%
2768 → classifier 1 → 10 → classifier 3 → 1		$A_{10} = 66.43\%$	53.83%

shown just a few examples. It should be apparent that the possibilities are very large. We will describe a universal combination architecture that will allow us to enumerate every possible configuration. Searching for the optimal choice of

Table 2. Various configurations are possible when parallel and serial methods are mixed. A_x, A_y, and A_z have the same meaning as above.

Architecture	A_x	A_y	A_z	A_1
2768 → classifier 2 → 50 → union of lexicons → classifier 3 → 1; 500 → classifier 1 → 10	$A_{500} = 62.77\%$	$A_{50} = 26.80\%$	$A_{10} = 57.10\%$	46.83%
2768 → classifier 1 → 50 → union of lexicons → classifier 3 → 1; 50 → classifier 2 → 5	$A_{100} = 70.87\%$	$A_{10} = 70.87\%$	$A_5 = 27.77\%$	52.40%

the architecture is clearly an open research problem. We will develop a greedy algorithm that uses entropy measures to search the optimal architecture. We have experimented with 3 classifiers and present our results (Table 1).

2   Universal Combinator

Let us consider the following model for possible combinations of N classifiers C_1, C_2, ..., C_N (Figure 2). Without loss of generality we can assume that the clas-

Table 3. The GREEDY algorithm described in this paper performs better than the traditionally used parallel combination methods and the *ad hoc* serial combination methods.

Architecture		A_1
1704 classifier 1		
	linear regresion 1	
1704 classifier 3		
		79.08%
1704 classifier 1		
	borda count 1	
1704 classifier 3		
		79.74%
1704 classifier 1 5 classifier 3 1		
		83.01%
GREEDY (our method described here)		84.31%

sifiers are running in the same order as they are enumerated. Given an unknown pattern x and a lexicon L_1, the run of the first classifier C_1 produces a ranked list R_1 of the words in the lexicon and their associated probabilities. A part R_1^0 of that ranked list is sent to the final decision maker, a part R_1^2 contributes to the lexicon (for a UNION and/or INTERSECTION with other parts of the lexicon) of the second classifier C_2, while another part R_1^3 is used for building the lexicon of the third classifier C_3, and so on.

Parts R_1^2, R_1^3, ..., R_1^N of the ranked list R_1, that was output from the run of the first classifier, are used in building lexicons for the classifiers, that run after the first one, R_1^2 for C_2, R_1^3 for C_3, ..., R_1^N for C_N. Now, when the run of the first classifier is over, it is the turn of the second classifier C_2 to run with lexicon L_2 built from part R_1^2 of the ranked list, produced by the first classifier C_1, that is sent to C_2. The result of the run of the second classifier C_2, as before, is a ranked list R_2 of the words in the lexicon L_2 and their associated probabilities. A part R_2^0 of that ranked list is sent to the final decision maker, a part R_2^3 contributes to the lexicon of the third classifier C_3, while another part R_2^4 is used to build the lexicon of the fourth classifier C_4, and so on. When the run of the second classifier is over, the third classifier C_3 run with lexicon L_3 built from R_1^3 part of the ranked list, produced by the first classifier C_1, and part R_2^3 of the ranked list, produced by the second classifier C_2. The output is a ranked list R_3 of the words in the lexicon L_3 and their associated probabilities, parts of which are used to build lexicons for following classifiers. The same procedure is repeated for all classifiers that follow in the recognition engine. The final decision maker outputs the final decision as a ranked list or the top choice.

Our conjecture is that the universal classifier combination model with suitably chosen parameters $R_1^0, R_1^2, R_1^3, \ldots, R_1^N, R_2^0, R_2^3, \ldots, R_2^N, \ldots, R_{N-1}^0, R_{N-1}^N$ represents all possible classifier combination of N classifiers. The model gets its power from the fact that certain R_p^q values can be 0. In fact, if the only non-zero values are accorded to $R_1^0 \ldots R_{N-1}^0$, then the classifiers only contribute to the final decision combinator (Figure 2) and the architecture becomes purely parallel. Further details of the universal combinator will be reserved for another paper in preparation [4].

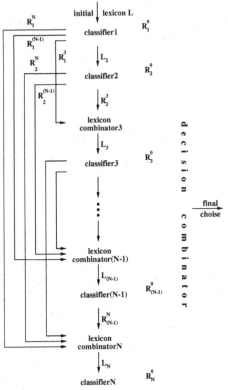

L_i - denotes the lexicon used by classifier(i)

R_i^j - denotest the part of rank list, produced by classifier(i), used in forming of lexicon L_j

Fig. 2. Universal Classifier Combination Model

3   Entropy Measure

Given a lexicon L_i, an unknown pattern x, and a classifier C_i which assigns a probability p_w to each word (w) in the lexicon, the initial entropy of the system is given by

$$E_1 = - \sum_{w \in L_1} p_w \ln p_w \ .$$

Our conjecture is that the entropy monotonically reduces as the lexicon keeps getting smaller. There are two cases to be considered. We will show here that the conjecture holds if the classifiers are error free. That is at every stage, the classifier preserves the true choice in the reduced lexicon. Since the last classifier in a serial engine returns just 1 choice, this case assumes that the final recognition choice returned by the cascade of classifiers is correct. In fact, the conjecture holds for cases when the classifier is not necessarily error-free. We will skip the proof of this second case for now.

Lexicon L_1 is split into L_2 and $L_1 \setminus L_2$. H_2 is the entropy associated with the lexicon L_2 (with the corresponding *a posteriori* probabilities) and G_2 is the entropy associated with the complement $L_1 \setminus L_2$. The total entropy of the system is given by

$$E_2 = \alpha_2 H_2 + (1 - \alpha_2)G_2 \ ,$$

where α_2 is a parameter.

Lexicon L_2 is split into L_3 and $L_2 \setminus L_3$. H_3 is the entropy associated with the lexicon L_3 and G_3 is the entropy associated with the complement $L_2 \setminus L_3$. The total entropy of the system is given by

$$E_3 = \alpha_2(\alpha_3 H_3 + (1 - \alpha_3)G_3) + (1 - \alpha_2)G_2 \ ,$$

where α_2 and α_3 are parameters.

We can prove that the entropy of the system keeps decreasing as the lexicon gets reduced (under certain conditions), provided the reduced lexicon always contains the true choice[1].

If after application of classifier C_i the lexicon is reduced to $L_1 = \{c_1, \ldots, c_k\}$ then the new probability of x to be the word c_i is $\bar{p}_i = \dfrac{p_i}{p_1 + \ldots + p_k}$.

Let the initial entropy of the system be $E_0 = -\sum\limits_{i=1}^{n} p_i \ln(p_i)$. Since the classifier C_i is error-free, we can choose $\alpha_1 = 1$. The entropy of the system after the reduction is

$$E_1 = -\sum_{i=1}^{k} \frac{p_i}{p_1 + \ldots + p_k} \ln\left(\frac{p_i}{p_1 + \ldots + p_k}\right) =$$

---

[1] We use the following two results,

Corollary 1:

$$(x + y) \ln \frac{x + y}{2} \le x \ln x + y \ln y \le (x + y) \ln(x + y)$$

Corollary 2:

A. $x_1 \ln x_1 + x_2 \ln x_2 + \ldots + x_n \ln x_n \le (x_1 + x_2 + \ldots + x_n) \ln(x_1 + x_2 + \ldots + x_n)$

B. $x_1 \ln x_1 + x_2 \ln x_2 + \ldots + x_n \ln x_n \ge (x_1 + x_2 + \ldots + x_n) \ln \dfrac{x_1 + x_2 + \ldots + x_n}{n}$

$$= \frac{1}{p_1 + \ldots + p_k} \sum_{i=1}^{k} p_i \ln(p_i) - \ln(p_1 + \ldots + p_k)$$

Let $S = p_1 + \ldots + p_k$, then
$$E_0 - E_1 =$$

$$(\frac{1}{p_1 + \ldots + p_k} - 1) \sum_{i=1}^{k} p_i \ln(p_i) - \sum_{i=k+1}^{n} p_i \ln(p_i) - \ln(p_1 + \ldots + p_k)$$

which is greater than

$$(\frac{1}{p_1 + \ldots + p_k} - 1)(p_1 + \ldots + p_k) \ln \frac{p_1 + \ldots + p_k}{k} -$$
$$-(1 - (p_1 + \ldots + p_k)) \ln(1 - (p_1 + \ldots + p_k)) - \ln(p_1 + \ldots + p_k)$$

Hence,
$$E_0 - E_1 \geq -S \ln S - (1 - S) \ln k - (1 - S) \ln(1 - S)$$

Let us define $f(y)$ (Figure 3).

$$f(y) = -y \ln y - (1 - y) \ln k - (1 - y) \ln(1 - y)$$

$$f'(y) = \ln \frac{k(1 - y)}{y}$$

Note that if $S \geq r_k$, then $E_0 \geq E_1$, i.e entropy is decreasing

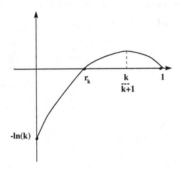

Fig. 3. Graph of $f(y)$

3.1   Probability Values for Lexical Entries

Most methods take the image of a handwritten word and a lexicon of possible words, and rank the lexicon based on the "goodness" of match between each lexicon entry and the word image. Typically, the word recognizer computes a measure of "similarity" between each lexicon entry and the word image and uses this measure to sort the lexicon in descending order of the similarity measure. The lexicon entry with the highest similarity is the top choice of the recognizer. The top m choices are often referred to as the confusion set as it contains the lexicon entries that are "similar" to the actual lexicon entry that matches the truth in some feature space.

We have developed elsewhere [1] the groundwork for the use of Bayesian methodology in integration of recognizers with any subsequent processing by deriving meaningful probabilistic measures from recognizers. This allows us to compute the entropy values.

4   Greedy Algorithm

We have developed a "greedy" algorithm to dynamically construct a combinator of N classifiers. Given a test pattern x and a lexicon L, we first apply the classifier with the best recognition rate on lexicons of size $|L|$. We reduce the lexicon in order to minimize the entropy. This reduced lexicon is sent to the next classifier. We continue the process until we cannot reduce the entropy any more or the last classifier is exhausted. The top choice of the last classifier used is the final recognition choice.

Algorithm

- input: pattern x, lexicon L,
- for (i = 1; i ≤ N; i++) {
    1. choose from un-used classifiers the one with the best accuracy performance on a lexicon of size $|L|$
    2. perform the classification and create a ranked list R from the words in the lexicon L according to their confidences
    3. if (i == N) {
        - return the first entry of R
        - exit }
    4. for (k = 1; k ≤ $|L|$; k++) {
        - R_1 is formed from the first k words of the ranked list R with new *a posteriori* probabilities
        - R_2 is formed from the rest of the words of the ranked list R with new *a posteriori* probabilities
        - choose appropriate α
        (for example: probability of the true choice to be present in the lexicon R_1)
        - compute the entropy H_k }
    5. find the minimal entropy among H_k , $2 < k < |L|$
    6. if ($H_{|L|}$ is the minimum) {
        - mark the classifier as used, but do not use it in the combination
        - keep the same lexicon L }
    7. if (H_1 is the minimum) {
        - return the first entry of R

```
           – exit }
     8. if (H_m is the minimum) {
           – mark the classifier as used, but do not use it in the combination
           – keep in the lexicon L only the first m words of the ranked list R}
           }
```

5   Experiments

Three word classifiers - CMWR (Character Model Word Recognizer) [2] is Classifier$_1$, WMWR (Word Model Word Recognizer)[5] is classifier$_2$ and HOL (Holistic) [6] is classifier$_3$ in our experiments. Each of them takes as input a binary image and an ASCII lexicon, computes a probability each lexicon entry and ranks the lexicon by decreasing probabilities.

WMR is a fast lexicon-driven analytical classifier that operates on the chain-coded description of the street name image. Following slant normalization and smoothing, the image is "oversegmented" at likely character segmentation points. The resulting segments are grouped and the extracted features matched against letters in each lexicon entry using a dynamic programming algorithm.

CMR adopts a different approach. After preprocessing and oversegmentation, segments are grouped in various ways and OCR is performed on the groups to obtain a graph of possible character candidates. For each lexicon entry, the best path through the graph is then determined. CMR is computationally more expensive than WMR. The two recognizers are sufficiently orthogonal in approach as well as features used to be useful in a combination strategy.

HOL does not perform any segmentation, but uses holistic information such as length, ascenders and descenders to classify the image.

The individual performances of CMR and WMR are shown in Figure 4. The Oracle represents the method of combination where a correct result is obtained in the top choice if either of the recognizers has it correct. Tables 4&5 show how the entropy of the system reduces with lexicon reduction. In this case the classifiers are not error free. However, the entropy still goes down. Table 6 shows that the GREEDY method finds the lowest entropy when compared to other *ad hoc* methods of determining the architecture of combination.

6   Conclusions

Research in handwritten word recognition has traditionally concentrated on small lexicons of 10 - 1000 words. Several real-world applications, such as the recognition of English prose, involve large lexicons of 10,000 - 50,000 words. Existing classifiers may still be used for these tasks if preceded by a *lexicon reduction* step. The task of lexicon reduction is that of rapidly discarding from the original lexicon entries that are unlikely to match the given image. The resulting two-stage architecture is a *serial combination* or *cascading* of classifiers, and is an effective method of dealing with large lexicons in real-life word recognition scenarios. Moreover, by discarding entries that may potentially confuse

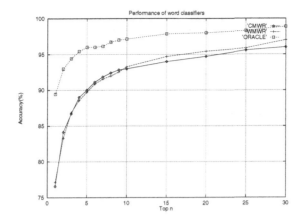

Fig. 4. Oracle combination shows the best possible results that one could obtain from the combination of WMR and CMR

Table 4. Note the reduction in entropy after each stage of lexicon reduction on 6 example image samples for two different architectures.

Image Samples	1704 classifier 1 · 10 classifier 2 · 5 classifier 3 · 1			1704 classifier 1 · 50 classifier 2 · 10 classifier 3 · 1		
	after C_1	after C_2	final entropy	after C_1	after C_2	final entropy
1	5.577219	3.614541	2.814851	6.294333	4.193750	3.366025
2	5.265298	3.447350	2.646646	5.946801	4.045334	3.217013
3	5.537880	3.594105	2.793283	6.250293	4.175640	3.347035
4	5.047477	3.328180	2.530059	5.701441	3.938757	3.112000
5	5.549012	3.598829	2.799862	6.263592	4.180160	3.352859
6	5.577230	3.615262	2.814670	6.294185	4.194074	3.365882

Table 5. Note the reduction in entropy after each stage of lexicon reduction on 6 example image samples for two different architectures.

Image Sampeles	1704 classifier 1 · 5 classifier 3 · 1		1704 classifier 1 · 10 classifier 3 · 1	
	after C_1	final entropy	after C_1	final entropy
1	3.730102	2.761246	4.064764	2.783761
2	3.554187	2.584103	3.897464	2.615539
3	3.708750	2.738524	4.044601	2.762236
4	3.428433	2.461479	3.778463	2.498956
5	3.713430	2.745451	4.049117	2.768770
6	3.730988	2.761039	4.065277	2.783551

Table 6. Final entropy on various image samples using the GREEDY method and other *ad hoc* architectures. Note that the GREEDY method usually has the final lowest entropy.

Image Samples	"Greedy"	1704 classifier 1 — 5 — classifier 3 — 1	1704 classifier 1 — 10 — classifier 3 — 1	1704 classifier 1 — 10 — classifier 2 — 5 — classifier 3 — 1
1	2.76	2.76	2.78	2.81
2	2.58	2.58	2.62	2.65
3	2.74	2.74	2.76	2.79
4	2.46	2.46	2.50	2.53
5	2.75	2.75	2.77	2.80
6	2.76	2.76	2.78	2.81
7	2.65	2.66	2.69	2.72

the classifier, lexicon reduction results in improved recognition performance. In this paper, we have presented an overview of lexicon reduction as a problem in its own right, and discussed some of the issues relating to the design and construction of different combination methods. We have presented a method of serial combination of classifiers using a GREEDY algorithm that strives for minimal entropy of the system. Its recognition accuracy is superior to other *ad hoc* combination methods.

We have shown theoretically that if the classifiers are error free, the entropy of the system must reduce as the lexicon size keeps reducing.

We have introduced the notion of the universal combinator.

References

1. D. Bouchaffra, V. Govindaraju, and S. Srihari. A methodology for mapping scores to probabilities. *IEEE Transactions on Pattern Analysis and Machine Intelligence*, 21(9):923–927, 1999.
2. J. Favata and S. Srihari. Off-line recognition of handwritten cursive words. In *SPIE Symposium on Electronic Imaging Science and Technology*, San Jose, CA, 1992.
3. T. Ho, J. Hull, and S. Srihari. Desicion combination in multiple classifier systems. *IEEE Transactions on Pattern Analysis and Machine Intelligence*, 16(1):66–75, 1994.
4. K. Ianakiev and V. Govindaraju. The universal combinaton methodology. *In preparation*, 2000.
5. G. Kim and V. Govindaraju. A lexicon driven approach to handwritten word recognition for real-time applications. *IEEE Transactions on Pattern Analysis and Machine Intelligence*, 19(4):366–379, Apr. 1997.
6. S. Madhvanath, E. Kleinberg, and V. Govindaraju. Holistic verification for handwritten phrases. *IEEE Transactions on Pattern Analysis and Machine Intelligence*, 21(12):1344–1356, 1999.
7. L. Xu, A. Krzyzak, and C. Suen. Methods of combining multiple classifiers and their applications to handwritting recognition. *System Man and Cybernatics*, 22(3):418–435, May/June 1992.

Combining Fingerprint Classifiers

Raffaele Cappelli, Dario Maio, and Davide Maltoni

DEIS, CSITE - CNR, Università di Bologna, viale Risorgimento 2, 40136 Bologna - Italy
{rcappelli,dmaio,dmaltoni}@deis.unibo.it

Abstract. This paper explores several ways of combining the MASKS and MKL-based classifiers which we specifically designed for the fingerprint classification task. The advantages of coupling these distinct techniques are well evident; in particular, in the case of exclusive classification, the FBI challenge requiring a classification error $\leq 1\%$ at 20% rejection was broken on NIST-DB14.

1 Introduction

The huge amount of data of the large fingerprint databases (several million fingerprints) seriously compromises the efficiency of the fingerprint identification task in AFIS (Automated Fingerprint Identification Systems) for both forensic and civil applications. Adopting a classification approach is a common strategy to reduce the number of comparisons during fingerprint retrieval and, consequently, to improve the response time of the identification process.

According to the typology of fingerprints, five classes (Arch, Left loop, Right loop, Whorl and Tented arch) are commonly used by exclusive classification techniques. Unfortunately, exclusive classification approaches suffer from the non-uniform distribution of the fingerprints among the classes (approximately 90% of fingerprints belong to only three classes) and from the existence of "ambiguous" fingerprints, whose exclusive membership cannot be reliably stated even by human experts.
We recently proved [12] [3] that a continuous classification approach, where each fingerprint is characterized by a numerical vector used for indexing the database, outperforms exclusive classification both in terms of accuracy and efficiency.

The fingerprint classification problem has aroused a great interest in the scientific community due to its relevance and intrinsic difficulty, and many papers have been published on this topic [2] [3] [4] [6] [8] [9] [10] [13]. In some recent works, different classifiers are combined to achieve better results: for example, in [2], a probabilistic neural network classifier is coupled with an auxiliary ridge-tracing module and in [8] a k-NN classifier is combined with a set of ten neural networks.

The aim of this work is to investigate the advantages of coupling the MASKS and MKL-based classifiers, which we recently introduced:

- MASKS [3] is a structural approach where the fingerprint directional image is partitioned into homogeneous regions, as the result of an optimization process driven by a set of dynamic masks.

J. Kittler and F. Roli (Eds.): MCS 2000, LNCS 1857, pp. 351-361, 2000.
© Springer-Verlag Berlin Heidelberg 2000

- The MKL-based approach [4] relies on a generalization of the KL transform [7] (which we call Multi-space KL transform or MKL [5]), where multiple subspaces are used for representing and classifying the patterns.

2   MASKS Classifier

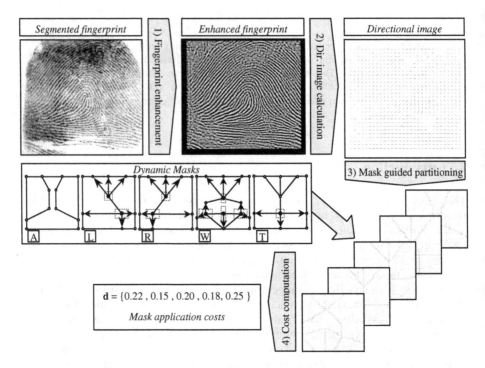

Fig. 1. Functional schema of the fingerprint classifier MASKS

Fig. 1 shows a functional schema of the dynamic masks approach (MASKS): the fingerprint is initially located and cropped from the whole image (*segmentation*), then its quality is enhanced through a filtering in the frequency domain and the *directional image* is calculated. A directional image is a discrete matrix whose elements represent the local average directions of the fingerprint ridge lines.

The basic idea of the method consists in deriving a compact version of the directional image by partitioning it into homogeneous regions (that is having a low variance in the orientations of the directional elements), thus obtaining a synthetic representation. A set of dynamic masks, directly derived from the five fingerprint classes (A, L, R, W, T), is used for the partitioning step, where each mask is independently adapted to best fit the directional image, according to a cost function. The resulting costs constitute a numerical vector ($\mathbf{d}$) which can be directly used as an access key for similarity searches in a continuous classification approach, or can be processed by a neural or statistical classifier to obtain an exclusive classification.

The reader should refer to [3] for a thorough treatment of the dynamic masks approach.

3 MKL-Based Classifiers

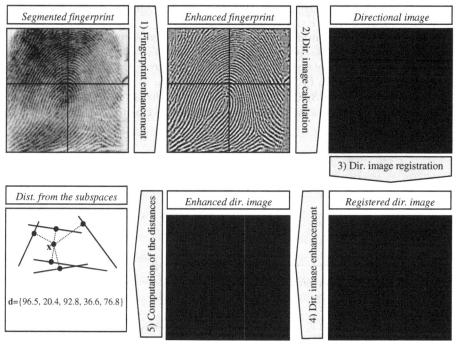

Fig. 2. Functional schema of the MKL-based classifiers

The MKL-based fingerprint classifier relies on a generalization of the KL transform called MKL (which we introduced in a more general context [5]), where multiple subspaces are used for representing and classifying multidimensional patterns.

Fig. 2 shows a functional schema of this approach [4]. The first two steps are the same as in MASKS; the third step is the *registration* of the directional image, which performs an alignment with respect to the *core point* in order to reduce the amount of translational variation. An enhancement step is then executed to reduce the effects of noise and to increase the importance of the discriminant elements. The enhanced directional image is treated as a single vector of n elements (by simply postponing its rows); in the following we will indicate with x_i the n-dimensional vector obtained from a generic fingerprint i.

The underlying idea of the approach is to find, for each class, one or more KL subspaces which are well-suited in representing the fingerprints belonging to them. These subspaces are created according to an optimization criterion which attempts to minimize the average mean-square reconstruction error over a representative training set; the reader should refer to [5] for a formal discussion of the MKL related concepts.

With respect to the general MKL formulation, which is an unsupervised technique over a global training set, the MKL classifier is implemented here in a two-layer way: first, a "supervised" MKL partitions the training set according to the class information, then for each partition an "unsupervised" MKL is applied to calculate a set of KL subspaces. The number of subspaces for each class is fixed a priori according to the class "complexity"; in particular, more subspaces are created for complex classes (i.e. whorl), where the MKL ability to handle non-linear spaces[1] allows a more effective indexing to be achieved.

The classification of an unknown pattern is performed according to its distances from all the KL subspaces. For example, in fig. 3, three KL subspaces (S_1, S_2, S_3) have been calculated from a training set containing elements from the two classes A and B: subspaces S_1 and S_2 have been obtained from the elements in A, while S_3 has been obtained from those in B. Given a new pattern **x**, the distances from the three subspaces (d_1, d_2 and d_3) contain useful information for its classification.

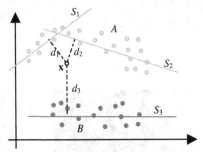

Fig. 3. A two-dimensional example of MKL transform, where two subspaces (S_1, S_2) and one subspace (S_3) are used to represent classes A and B, respectively

More formally, let P be a training set of fingerprints, $P \subset \mathfrak{R}^n$, whose classes (A,L,R,W and T) induce a partitioning of P into 5 subsets: P_A, P_L, P_R, P_W, P_T; let $K = \{k_A, k_L, k_R, k_W, k_T\}$ be a set of scalars specifying, for each class, the dimensionality of the subspaces associated to that class and let $N = \{n_A, n_L, n_R, n_W, n_T\}$ be a set of scalars determining the number of subspaces to be created for each class; then the set of KL subspaces $S = \{S_{A_1}, ..., S_{A_{n_A}}, S_{L_1}, ..., S_{L_{n_L}}, S_{R_1}, ..., S_{R_{n_R}}, S_{W_1}, ..., S_{W_{n_W}}, S_{T_1}, ..., S_{T_{n_T}}\}$ is obtained by generating, for each training subset P_c ($c \in \{A,L,R,W,T\}$), the set of n_c KL subspaces $\{S_{c_1}, ..., S_{c_{n_c}}\}$ through the MKL optimization procedure described in [5].

Given a vector **x** corresponding to an unknown fingerprint, the feature vector (of dimensionality $n_A + n_L + n_R + n_W + n_T$) used for the classification is:

$$\mathbf{d} = [d_{FS}(\mathbf{x},S_{A_1}), ..., d_{FS}(\mathbf{x},S_{A_{n_A}}), ..., d_{FS}(\mathbf{x},S_{T_1}), ..., d_{FS}(\mathbf{x},S_{T_{n_T}})]$$

where $d_{FS}(\mathbf{x},S_i)$ denotes the distance between the vector **x** and the subspace S_i.

---

[1] MKL operates according to a divide-et-impera decomposition which produces a piecewise linear approximation of the input data.

- As to continuous classification, the vector itself is used as an access key.

- As to exclusive classification, two simple criteria are used:

  1. Minimum distance classifier (MKL-MIN): the fingerprint is assigned to the class c^* such that:

$$c^* = arg \min_{c \in \{A,L,R,W,T\}} \left(\min_{i=1..n_c} d_{FS}\left(\mathbf{x}, S_{c_i}\right) \right)$$

  2. K-Nearest Neighbor classifier (MKL-KNN): the fingerprint is classified according to the k-NN rule.

In order to provide a rejection option, a confidence value in [0,1] is associated to each fingerprint by the above classifiers:

  1. MKL-MIN: the confidence is the normalized difference between the two smallest distances d_1 and d_2:

$$conf = |d_1 - d_2| / (d_1 + d_2)$$

  2. MKL-KNN: the confidence is the normalized difference between the number of occurrences (n_1 and n_2) of the two most frequent classes among the k nearest neighbors:

$$conf = |n_1 - n_2| / (n_1 + n_2)$$

4 Combining Classifiers for Exclusive Classification

Since MASKS was specifically conceived for continuous classification, its exclusive classification accuracy is substantially lower than those of the two MKL-based classifiers and, in this specific case, no significant improvement was obtained by combining MASKS with the two MKL-based classifiers; hence, in the exclusive classification results, only combinations of MKL-MIN and MKL-KNN classifiers are reported.

Several classification schemes may be adopted for combining classifiers in the case of exclusive classification [11] [1]; some of the most popular are: simple and weighted averaging, voting schemes [16] and non-linear combinations using rank-based estimators such as the median. In our experimentation, a simple *majority vote rule* proved to be an effective technique:

let $C = \{C_1, C_2, ..., C_{NC}\}$ be a set of NC classifiers and

$$\theta_{ij} = \begin{cases} 1 & \text{if } j \text{ is the class hypothesized by } C_i \\ 0 & \text{otherwise} \end{cases} \quad (1 \le i \le NC, 1 \le j \le 5)$$

then the fingerprint is assigned to the class t such that:

$$t = \max_{j=1}^{5} \left(\sum_{i=1}^{NC} \theta_{ij} \right)$$

In order to provide a rejection criterion, the confidence of the combined classifier is defined as the average of the individual classifier confidences. The rejection criterion simply consists in discarding fingerprints whose confidence is lower than a fixed threshold.

4.1 Experimental Results

The experimentation was performed on NIST Special Database 14 (DB14) [14], which consists of 54000 fingerprint images from 27000 fingers. Two different fingerprint instances (named "F" and "S") are present for each finger: the images are numbered from F00001 to F27000 and from S00001 to S27000.

In accordance with the testing rules adopted by PCASYS developers [2], we tested the classifier on the last 2700 fingerprints (S24301-S27000). Fingerprints F00001-F24300 and S00001-S24300 (48600 images) can be used for training the classifiers; we did not use fingerprints F24301-F27000 for training, since they are impressions of the same fingers used in the test set.

Three disjoint training sets (TR1, TR2 and TR3), each 9720 fingerprints wide, were assembled from a subset (3/5) of the available 48600 images. Both MKL-MIN and MKL-KNN classifiers were trained over TR1, TR2 and TR3, thus obtaining six different classifiers (see table 1). The classifier MKL-COMB is obtained by coupling the six classifiers according to the majority vote rule. The parameters used are: $K = \{26,28,28,29,28\}$, $N = \{1,2,2,3,1\}$; the number k of neighbors for the MKL-KNN classifiers is 5. In table 1, the error rates of the different classifiers are reported; it should be noted that the MKL-COMB error rate is 5.6%, which constitutes a 18% improvement with respect to the average error of the individual classifiers (6.8%); the performance of the PCASYS hybrid classifier (probabilistic neural network with auxiliary pseudo-ridge tracer) is 7.8% [2].

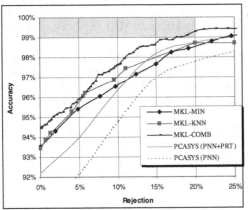

Table 1. Errors of the different classifiers

Classifier	Error
MKL-KNN 1	6.6%
MKL-KNN 2	6.7%
MKL-KNN 3	7.0%
MKL-MIN 1	7.0%
MKL-MIN 2	6.5%
MKL-MIN 3	7.1%
MKL-COMB	5.6%
PCASYS	7.8%

Average: 6.8%

Fig. 4. Accuracy versus rejection curves. The PCASYS performance was manually sampled from the graph printed in [2]

The graph in fig. 4 shows the accuracy of the classifiers as a function of the percentage of rejected fingerprints; the results of MKL-COMB and of the best MKL-MIN and the best MKL-KNN classifiers are reported; the remaining two curves show the accuracy of the PCASYS system, when used with and without the auxiliary classifier (PRT) respectively. The gray area of the graph highlights the region where the FBI requirement (99% accuracy with 20% rejection rate) is met. It should be noted that only MKL-COMB crosses this region; in particular, a 99% accuracy is quoted at 17.5% rejection rate. To the best of our knowledge, no other classification approach met the FBI requirement on NIST databases.

We would like to remark that the particular training and test set used were chosen for a fair comparison with [2], but very close performances (sometimes better) were measured on different sets over DB14. Finally, NIST DB4 [15] (4000 fingerprints wide), which is another common classification benchmark, was not used here since it does not contain enough fingerprints to train several classifiers on different sets. However, a single MKL-based classifier performed 92.2% at 0% rejection on that database [4].

5 Combining Classifiers for Continuous Classification

In continuous classification, each fingerprint is characterized by a feature vector in a multidimensional space. Assuming that similar fingerprints are mapped into close points, the retrieval problem can be dealt with as a nearest neighbor search. This approach enables the problem of exclusive membership of "ambiguous" fingerprints to be avoided and the system reliability to be regulated by adjusting the size of the neighborhoods considered.

Combining the two classifiers MASKS and MKL in the case of continuous classification requires a substantially different approach with respect to that introduced in the exclusive case. In fact, instead of combining decisions, here we have to couple continuous measures indicating the distance or "dissimilarity" between fingerprints.

Let $d_{MASKS}(i,j)$ and $d_{MKL}(i,j)$ be the distances between fingerprint i and j as associated by MASKS and the MKL-based approach, respectively; defining the combined distance $d_{COMB}(i,j)$ as a simple or weighted average of $d_{MASKS}(i,j)$ and $d_{MKL}(i,j)$ is in general not satisfactory, since they are usually defined over different ranges. A trivial normalization with respect to their minimum and maximum measured values is still not effective due to the presence of outliers. Furthermore, an "alignment" between the two distance distributions is necessary in order to establish a common operating point.

The approach here presented re-maps the two distances into a common domain by means of a double sigmoid function; then, a weighted average is taken according to a coefficient w, which denotes the individual classifier performance.

$$d_{COMB}(i,j) = (1-w) \cdot bisigm(d_{MKL}(i,j), m_{MKL}, s1_{MKL}, s2_{MKL}) +$$
$$w \cdot bisigm(d_{MASKS}(i,j), m_{MASKS}, s1_{MASKS}, s2_{MASKS})$$

$$\text{where } bisigm(d,m,s1,s2)=\begin{cases} \dfrac{1}{1+\exp\left(-2\cdot\dfrac{(d-m)}{s1}\right)} & \text{if } d<m \\[2em] \dfrac{1}{1+\exp\left(-2\cdot\dfrac{(d-m)}{s2}\right)} & \text{otherwise} \end{cases}$$

Fig. 5 gives an example of the *bisigm* function, where the meaning of the input parameters m, $s1$ and $s2$ is graphically explained. In particular, m indicates a "reference" operating point (which is mapped to 1/2), $s1$ and $s2$ denote respectively the left and right intervals where the function exhibits a near-linear shape. The choice of such a mapping function allows:

1. the distances lower than (m-$s1$) to be only softly penalized; this is reasonable since, in real pattern recognition applications, perfect matching is almost impossible;
2. the distances between [m-$s1$, m+$s2$] to be near-linearly mapped;
3. the distances higher than (m+$s2$), which should be attributed to outliers, to be not too penalized.

An effective way of choosing appropriate values for m, $s1$ and $s2$, for a given classifier, is to select reference points over the curve denoting the complementary cumulative distribution of the genuine[2] distances; given the distribution $f_g(d)$ of the genuine distances, the complementary cumulative distribution $\overline{F}_g(d)$ is defined as:

$$\overline{F}_g(d)=1-\int_0^d f_g(t)\,dt$$

$\overline{F}_g(d)$ indicates the percentage of fingerprint pairs whose distance is greater than d.

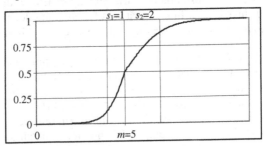

Fig. 5. The *bisigm* function plot for m=5, $s1$=1 and $s2$=2

In our experimentation, m, $s1$ and $s2$ are chosen such that:

- $\overline{F}_g(m)=0.6$
- $\overline{F}_g(m-s1)=0.95$
- $\overline{F}_g(m+s2)=0.05$.

---

[2] By "genuine" we denote distances between different impressions of the same finger.

Fig. 6 shows the histograms of the genuine distances distributions $f_g(d)$ and the corresponding $\overline{F}_g(d)$ curves both for MKL-based and MASKS classifiers. While the values 0.95 and 0.05 are reasonable choices, according to the above mentioned aims 1 and 3, the empirical choice of the m reference point (0.6) derives from the visual inspection of both the histograms in fig. 6, which exhibit a maximum close to this value.

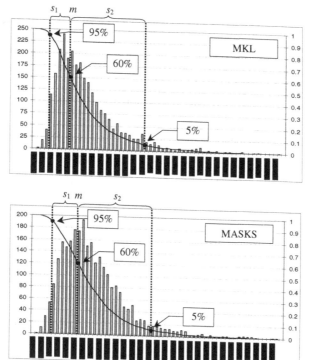

Fig. 6. $f_g(d)$ and $\overline{F}_g(d)$ for MKL and MASKS; the reference points are marked with vertical dashed lines

5.1 Experimental Results

NIST DB14 was used as a workbench:

- TR1 (as defined in section 4.1) is used to train the MKL-based classifier and to adjust MASKS parameters; m_{MKL}, $s1_{MKL}$, $s2_{MKL}$, m_{MASKS}, $s1_{MASKS}$, $s2_{MASKS}$ were tuned over TR2; the weight w is determined according to the relative global performance of the MKL-based approach and MASKS over TR2.
- Fingerprints F24301-F27000 and S24301-S27000 constitute the test set.

The parameter values used for the tests are: $K = \{26,29,29,29,29\}$, $N = \{2,3,3,4,1\}$, $w = 0.4$.

Continuous classification performance is provided in accordance with methodologies MA and MB defined in [3]. Methodology MA assumes an error-free classification and is carried out by retrieving the fingerprints which are less far than a prefixed tolerance ρ from the searched one. Methodology MB allows for misclassifications to be taken into account; to this aim, the search is incrementally extended until a valid matching is found (eventually up to the whole database), avoiding any possible retrieval error. Fingerprints are processed according to their distance from the searched one, in increasing order.

As to methodology MA, the graph in fig. 7 shows the accuracy versus efficiency tradeoff. The combined classifier clearly outperforms the individual classifiers for errors greater than 2%, while it collapses to MKL performance otherwise.

As far as methodology MB is concerned, table 2 summarizes the average portion of database searched for the individual and the combined classifiers. A significant improvement (35% over the average of the individual performances) is achieved by COMB.

Table 2. Methodology MB: average portion of searched database

MASKS	MKL	COMB
6.4%	4.9%	3.7%

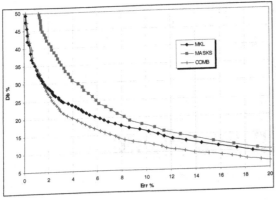

%DB	%Err		
	MKL	MASK	COMB
10%	18.4%	21.0%	13.2%
15%	11.1%	12.7%	7.2%
20%	6.2%	8.2%	4.0%
25%	3.2%	5.9%	2.3%

Fig. 7. Tradeoff between the portion of database searched and the retrieval error, varying the tolerance ρ, for the individual and the combined classifiers. Some specific values are highlighted in the table on the right

6   Conclusions

In this work classifier combination has been investigated for fingerprint classification, which is a real challenging task. Several combinations of the MASKS and MKL-based classifiers have been tested in both exclusive and continuous classification scenarios. A heuristic approach to combine distance measures between feature vectors (produced by different methods) has been proposed; the approach has been designed to address the problem of distance normalization and "alignment".

In both exclusive and continuous classification, the combined classifier outperforms the individual ones; in particular, as to exclusive classification, better accuracy (94.4%) than those published so far in the literature on NIST DB14 is obtained, while, in the continuous classification case, a remarkable result (3.7% of database searched) is achieved for MB. In order to further improve the performance, we believe that an interesting research direction is to study the combination of the methods presented here with other classifiers which exploit features other than the directional image (on which both MKL and MASKS are based).

References

1. E.S. Bigun, J. Bigun, B. Duc and S. Fisher, "Expert Conciliation for Multi Modal Person Authentication Systems by Bayesian Statistics", *in proceedings First Int'l Conf. Audio Video-Based Personal Authentication*, pp. 327-334, Crans-Montant, Switzerland, March 1997.
2. G.T. Candela et. al. "PCASYS - A Pattern-Level Classification Automation System for Fingerprints", *NIST tech. report* NISTIR 5647, August 1995.
3. R. Cappelli, A. Lumini, D. Maio and D. Maltoni, "Fingerprint Classification by Directional Image Partitioning", *IEEE Transactions on Pattern Analysis Machine Intelligence*, v. 21, no. 5, pp. 402-421, 1999.
4. R. Cappelli, D. Maio and D. Maltoni, "Fingerprint Classification based on Multi-space KL", in *proceedings AutoID'99*, Summit (NJ), pp.117-120, October 1999.
5. R. Cappelli, D. Maio and D. Maltoni, "Multi-space KL for pattern representation and classification", *DEIS internal report*, University of Bologna, March 1999.
6. M.M.S. Chong et. al., "Geometric Framework for Fingerprint Image Classification", *Pattern Recognition*, v. 30, no. 9, pp. 1475-1488, 1997.
7. K. Fukunaga, *Introduction to Statistical Pattern Recognition*, Academic Press, San Diego, 1990.
8. A.K. Jain, S. Prabhakar, and L. Hong, "A Multichannel Approach to Fingerprint Classification", *IEEE Transactions on PAMI*, Vol.21, No.4, pp. 348-359, April 1999.
9. K. Karu and A.K. Jain, "Fingerprint Classification", *Pattern Recognition*, v. 29, no. 3, pp. 389-404, 1996.
10. M. Kawagoe and A. Tojo "Fingerprint Pattern Classification", *Pattern Recognition*, v. 17, no. 3, pp. 295-303, 1984.
11. J. Kittler, M. Hatef and R.P.W. Duin, "Combining Classifiers", *in proceedings 13th ICPR*, Vienna 96, pp. 897-901, August 1996.
12. A. Lumini, D. Maio and D. Maltoni, "Continuous vs Exclusive Classification for Fingerprint Retrieval", *Pattern Recognition Letters*, v. 18, no. 10, pp. 1027-1034, 1997.
13. D. Maio and D. Maltoni, "A Structural Approach to Fingerprint Classification", *in proceedings 13th ICPR*, Vienna 96, August 1996.
14. C.I. Watson, *Nist Special Database 14, Fingerprint Database*. U.S. National Institute of Standards and Technology, 1993.
15. C. I. Watson and C. L. Wilson, "Nist Special Database 4, Fingerprint Database". U.S. National Institute of Standards and Technology, 1992.
16. Y.A. Zuev and S.K. Ivanonv, "The Voting as a Way to Increase the Decision Reliability", *in Proc. Foundations of Information/Decision Fusion With Applications to Eng. Problems*, pp. 206-210, Washington D.C., August 1996.

Statistical Sensor Calibration for Fusion of Different Classifiers in a Biometric Person Recognition Framework

Bernhard Fröba, Constanze Rothe, and Christian Küblbeck

Fraunhofer Institute for Integrated Circuits,
Departement of Applied Electronics
Am Weichselgarten 3, D-91058 Erlangen,Germany
{bdf,cro,kue}@iis.fhg.de

Abstract. Biometric person authentication is a secure and user-friendly way of identifying persons in a variety of everyday applications. In order to achieve high recognition rates, we propose an audio-visual person recognition system based on voice, lip motion and still image. The combination of these three data sources (called sensor fusion) may be performed in several ways. We present a method for a sensor normalization based on statistical properties which we call sensor calibration. The final fusion simplifies to a multiplication or addition of the outputs of each sensor. This approach is evaluated on a large database of 170 people with a total of 6315 recordings which were recorded in at least two sessions per person.

1 Introduction

With electronic communication starting to dominate large areas of everyday life, a safe method of identifying users is essential to prevent data misuse. Home-banking, tele-shopping and internet services are being used by an increasing number of people. In these business relationships the partner is only virtually present which means that identifying him or her by a reliable identification system becomes necessary.

Identification systems, however, are only acceptable if all participants can rely on the safe identification of the people involved. A password and a PIN number alone do not meet this heightened need for security. Biometric methods, that is the evaluation of persona-specific data, may, however, increase the protection of the user and at the same time improve the convenience of operation.

With the person authentication system SESAM (Synergetic Recognition by still image, acoustics and motoricity[1]) [1] biometric information from several different sensor sources are put together to form a common decision.

In this paper we focus on the sensor fusion within the SESAM system. We present a method for obtaining normalized sensor output independent of preprocessing and classification algorithms being used. This is done by using a statistical description estimated from a training sample. We refer to this whole procedure as sensor calibration.

This paper is devided into six sections. The next section describes the basic system outline and the feature extraction and classification methods used for each biometric

---

[1] the abbreviation comes from the German translation **S**ynergetische **E**rkennung mittels **S**tandbild, **A**kustik und **M**otorik

cue. In section 3 a method for statistical sensor calibration is presented. In section 4 we describe our database used for the experiments. The results obtained and the testing protocol is described in section 5. In the last section an outlook on further work is presented.

2 System Outline

The basic concept behind our system is shown in figure 2. This concept was originally described in [1]. It utilizes one static and two dynamic biometric modalities for recognition. The modalities are:

- a still image of a person's face
- acoustic features of a person's voice
- the mimic information of the mouth region.

The features are calculated from a short video sequence which is captured while the person under test is pronouncing a short code word, for example his/her last name. The recording interval is one second and the code word is fixed, as we use a text dependent speaker and mimic-recognition.

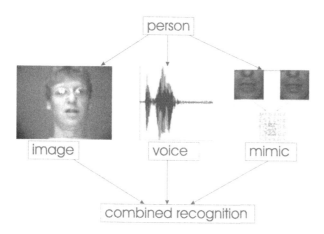

Fig. 1. Multi-sensory person recognition based on audio and visual sensor sources.

In order to test the system, two different frameworks come into question: a verification and an identification framework. In the verification case a user provides his identity and is then approved by the system to really be that person. This can be said to be a "two-class decision". On the other side, when identifying a person, the system has to choose which person out of a more or less large pool of persons known to the system. This can be called a "multi-class decision". We use an identification framework to measure the performance of our algorithms.

The algorithms used for the processing and classification in each sensor cue are detailed in the next sections.

2.1   Face Processing

Detecting and locating faces in gray-level images is the first step in a real-world face recognition system. For our experiments presented in this paper our database is manually labeled so that we know the face positions in advance.

The face processing consists of a spatial normalization step where the faces are scaled to a size of 64 × 64 pixel. The facial organs such as the eyes and the mouth are spatially aligned. This is necessary because our classification algorithm is view-based.

To become robust against different lighting conditions the aligned and normalized face image undergoes an edge extraction step. The edge information is calculated using a standard sobel edge operator [2]. This edge image is reordered into a vector and used as a feature vector for the classification.

For recognition of the face features we use the synergetic computer. A detailed description of the algorithm can be found in [3] and [4].

2.2   Mimic Processing

For motion analysis of the lip movements a sequence of sub-images containing only the mouth area is extracted from the video sequence. A window centered on the located mouth positions in each of the original images of the video sequence is used. The mouth area is normalized to a size of 128 × 128 pixel. We use only 17 consecutive frames (frame-rate 25 fps) for feature extraction.

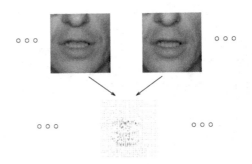

Fig. 2. Feature calculation from a lip sequence with optical flow analysis.

An optical flow analysis using the method of Horn and Schunk [5] is applied to the generated mouth sequence. This algorithm extracts the motion in an image sequence in a quick and robust manner. The optical flow is calculated between every two consecutive frames and stored in 16 vector fields of 32 × 32 vectors. In order to guarantee invariance with respect to spatial and temporal shifts, the power spectrum from the three-dimensional motion field is calculated. This is then used as the feature vector in the classification process. In this branch we also use the synergetic computer for classification.

2.3   Speech Processing

As we have a fixed codeword for each person we use a text dependent approach for speaker recognition. The first processing step is to window the speech signal using a hamming window of 22msec length and 11msec overlap. Each of the i obtained windows w_i of length $N = 1924$ samples is then input for a fourier based cepstrum calculation. The fourier cepstrum c_i is defined as follows [6]:

$$c_i(0) = \sqrt{\frac{1}{N} \sum_{\nu=0}^{N/2-1} \log |W_i(\nu)|}, \tag{1}$$

$$c_i(q) = \frac{1}{N} \sum_{\nu=0}^{N/2-1} \log |W_i(\nu)| \cos \frac{\pi q(2\nu + 1)}{N},$$

$$q = 1, \cdots, N/2, \tag{2}$$

where $|W_i|$ is the power spectrum calculated from the i-th speech window w_i

$$W_i = DFT \{w_i\}. \tag{3}$$

The ensemble of feature vectors c_i is used for classification. The classification itself is done with a vector quantizer (VQ) [7] approach. For each person a codebook consisting of 2 code vectors is built during training. Given a sample of i feature vectors c_i obtained from a spoken code word we obtain the score by computing the euclidian distance of the sample to each personal codebook.

3   Sensor Fusion

The purpose of sensor fusion is to determine which class a given sample of biometric data belongs to. We assume that the combination of several biometric cues that can be measured independently and therefore make independent errors leads to a superior classification performance compared to each single sensor.

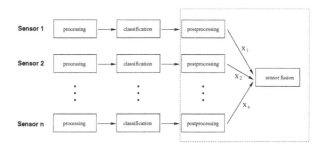

Fig. 3. Schematic diagram of sensor fusion.

Figure 3 shows the schematic flow diagram of sensor fusion. At first the three sensors work independently. Each sensor performs data acquisition, then the data is processed (as described in detail in sections 2.1, 2.2, 2.3). Next the extracted features are passed on to the classifier. This process is also independent from the classifiers in the other sensor branches. Each classifier returns a class result and a score for that class.

In the post processing step, the results of the classifiers can be scaled and combined in several different ways as explained in the following sections.

3.1   Distance Measures

The classification algorithms used here are the two mentioned in section 2, namely the synergetic computer for face and mimic classification and the VQ for speech classification. Here we want to discuss how to generate a similarity measure in an identification task that can be used for both methods. Suppose we have K persons trained to the system. If a person is classified, K distances have to be calculated. In a naive approach one would say that the person is assigned to the class with the best distance (using min or max decision rule due to the used classifier). It is not possible to reject a person as unknown because there always exists one "best" distance.

To overcome this we can use a security threshold for the absolute distance (Distance To Prototype, DTP) or define a relative score measure that allows the introduction of a robust security threshold [1]. Both can be used as input for the sensor calibration and fusion introduced in the next sections.

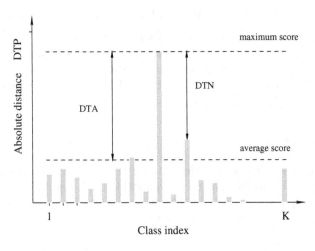

Fig. 4. Example for the three proposed distance measures DTP, DTA, DTN (see text for definition) displayed for the best score according to the maximum rule

We reorder the K distances in descending (ascending in case of minimum rule) rank order $S(r)$, with $r = 0, 1 \ldots, K-1$, so that $S(0)$ gets the best score while $S(K-1)$ gets the worst. We define the Distance To Next (DTN) score measure as

$$DTN(r) = |S(0) - S(r)| \quad r \in [1, K-1] \tag{4}$$

Of special interest is the relative distance between the best and the second score $DTN(0)$.

Another score measure that takes the distance between the average score and the best score is called Distance to Average (DTA) and is defined as

$$DTA(r) = S(r) - \frac{1}{K} \sum_{\rho=0}^{K-1} S(\rho); \tag{5}$$

While the DTN measure always is positive, the DTA measure will change sign for large r. These values indicate a bad match and so all classes which have other-signed values can be ignored in the sensor fusion step. Tests for the two proposed score measures DTP and DTA are reported in section 5.

3.2   Sensor Calibration

As the results of the sensors come from different classifiers and feature distributions, they cannot be compared in that form. Therefore we want to estimate a statistical description so that each sensor calculates a probability for a measurement to belong to a certain class. The data handled to the fusion module then consists of a set of class labels and dedicated confidence values. We consider the case of a single sensor first and look at the decision fusion later.

Given a binary event ω which describes whether the class label k estimated from the sensor measurement X_i^k points to the correct class ($\omega = \omega_0$) or not ($\omega = \omega_1$). X_i^k is measured using one of the score measures (DTP, DTA, DTN) presented in the last section. The subscript i denotes the number of the sensor, in our case $i \in \{1, 2, 3\}$. We are especially interested in the two probability density functions $p(X_i^k \mid \omega_0)$ which describes the probability for a measurement X_i^k being associated with the correct class (that is k in that case) and $p(X_i^k \mid \omega_1)$ the opposite event.

The probability density function (PDF) for X_i^k can be written as

$$p(X_i^k) = p(X_i^k \mid \omega_0)p_i(\omega_0) + p(X_i^k \mid \omega_1)p_i(\omega_1); \tag{6}$$

where the a-priory probability $p_i(\omega_0)$ is the recognition rate or ground truth of the classifier and $p_i(\omega_1) = 1 - p_i(\omega_0)$ is the miss classification rate in the sensor branch i. This probabilities can be estimated from a training data set. We use the results reported in a former published paper on this biometric identification framework [1].

The (PDF) is calculated from histograms which are obtained from a training data set. Figure 5 shows an example of such histograms.

The probability of assigning the right class label to a measurement is according to Bayes' theorem:

$$p(\omega_0 \mid X_i^k) = \frac{p(X_i^k \mid \omega_0)}{p(X_i^k)} p_i(\omega_0); \tag{7}$$

The Probability Density Functions (PDF) $p(X_i^k \mid \omega_0)$ and $p(X_i^k \mid \omega_1)$ are estimated on the training database. The corresponding strategies are detailed in the next paragraph.

To calibrate the sensor we use the confidence

$$P(\omega_0 \mid X_i^k) = \int_{-\infty}^{X_i^k} p(\omega_0 \mid X)dX. \tag{8}$$

for a match to the right class for mapping the K classifier scores in the i-th branch X_i^k.

3.3   Decision Fusion

The final step in our fusion approach is the combination of the results obtained from the normalized sensors. In order to do so simple fusion approaches are used. We evaluate the sum rule (SUM) which is defined as

$$S_k = \frac{1}{3} \sum_i P(\omega_0 \mid X_i^k) \tag{9}$$

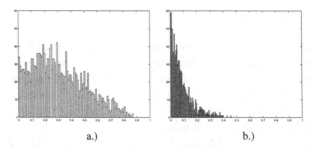

a.)   b.)

Fig. 5. Example for a measured histogram of the distance measure DTN obtained from 2000 trials in the face recognition branch. The first histogram shows the distribution for true customers while the second was obtained from impostor trials. The two PDFs $p(X_i \mid \omega_0)$ and $p(X_i \mid \omega_1)$ are estimated using such histograms.

and the product rule (PROD)

$$S_k = \sqrt[3]{\prod_i P(\omega_0 \mid X_i^k)}. \tag{10}$$

The maximal score after the combination calculated with one of the distance measures DTN or DTA is compared with a safety threshold. If the score survives the threshold the person is classified to the associated class, if not it is rejected as unknown. The threshold allows to parameterize the system with regards to specific safety requirements.

4   Testing Protocol

4.1   Database

The database used for the test of our proposed sensor calibration consists of 6315 samples taken from 170 persons. The samples of each person is recorded in at least two sessions. Each sample consists of an audio and video sequence showing a person saying the code word. The data set is divided into two subsets.

Table 1. Data sets used for fusion experiments.

set	persons	recordings person	recordings total
TOTAL	170	25-60	6315
TRAIN	170	8	1360
TEST	170	17-52	4955

Table 1 gives an overview over our database. The set TRAIN is used to train the classifiers and to estimate the PDFs for the sensor calibration. The set TEST is classified to evaluate the system.

4.2   Estimating the Calibration Data

The sensor fusion experiments are conducted with an identification task. Here all persons are trained to the system. For recognition no identity claim is made by the user. The system has to decide whether the user belongs to the set of known persons and has to assign a class label to him or not. The two PDFs used for sensor calibration are computed from the training set for each sensor individually. We usually use three to five samples per person to train the system. Each sensor is trained independently from the others except for the fact that the data stems from the same sample. To measure the calibration data we train the system using a leave-one-out method.

To estimate $p(X_i \mid \omega_0)$ we leave out one sample of all persons and train the remaining ones. The left out samples are classified. This is done repeatedly for all training shots.

For the estimation of $p(X_i \mid \omega_1)$ we leave out all training samples of one person. The remaining persons are trained and the samples of the left out person are classified. This is repeated for all persons.

The results are counted in two histograms (one for ω_0 and one for ω_1). This histograms are transformed into corresponding PDFs by smoothing and normalization.

5   Performance Evaluation

The rates presented here are the false rejection rate (FRR) and the false acceptance rate (FAR). These rates are dependent on a certain threshold that can be adjusted when classifying: when lowering this safety threshold, the FRR is decreased, while the FAR is increased. The rate where both error rates are the same is called EER and is used in the following section as a measurement for the quality of a certain configuration.

We have analyzed the influence of the number of sensors and the type of combination. In table 2 and 3 we show on the one hand the EER and on the other hand the maximal recognition rate when no safety threshold is applied.

Table 2. Error rates when using only one, two or three sensors for classification, using the sensor calibration and the fusion method SUM and the score measure DTN.

Sensor	EER max
single sensor	
audio	5.8% 89.9%
flow	5.9% 90.4%
face	9.5% 83.2%
two sensors	
flow and audio	2.7% 95.5%
face and flow	3.2% 94.9%
face and audio	5.9% 89.9%
three sensors	
flow, audio and face	2.4% 96.2%

Table 3 shows the same rates that can be achieved using different sensor fusion methods. The lowest rates are achieved using the sum fusion. For this case figure 6

Table 3. Error rates when using all three sensors for classification, and different fusion methods and distance measures.

distance measure	fusion method	EER	max
DTN	SUM	2.4%	96.2%
	PROD	2.5%	96.0%
DTA	SUM	2.3%	96.2%
	PROD	2.5%	96.0%

shows the curves for the FAR and FRR rates. From the intersection point of these curves the EER can be estimated. The overall computing time required to record and evaluate a person's data is about 1,5 secounds on a Pentium 200 Mhz.

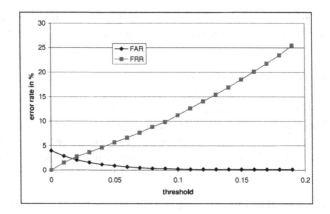

Fig. 6. The recognition curves for the combined three sensor results using SUM fusion rule and DTN measure. The EER is the crossover point of the two error curves.

6   Conclusions and Future Work

We have presented a scheme for normalization of a sensor independent from the others for a sensor fusion architecture. The term sensor calibration refers to the physical sensor and the feature extraction and classification. Provided there is enough data to estimate the sensor specific statistics needed for calibration as it is the case in a large identification system where there are usually many customers, the system performs very well.

Future work is directed towards the comparison of this method with other proposed fusion schemes, also an extension to person verification is planned. There the sensor normalization must be done for each person individually or at least a personal adaption step must be included.

7 Acknowledgements

This research was partly funded by the German Federal Ministry of Education and Research (BMBF) under the project EMBASSI.

References

1. U. Dieckmann, P. Plankensteiner, R. Schamburger, B. Fröba, and S. Meller, "Sesam: A biometric person identification system using sensor fusion," in *AVBPA97*, pp. 301–310, March 1997.
2. K. R. Castelman, *Digital Image Processing*. New Jersey: Prentice Hall, 1996.
3. U. Dieckmann, P. Plankensteiner, and T. Wagner, "Multisensory pattern analysis for person identification with synergetic computers," in *International Workshop on Automated Face- and Gesture-Recognition*, pp. 368–371, 1995.
4. R. W. Frischholz, F. Böbel, and K. P. Spinnler, "Face recognition with the synergetic computer," in *Proceedings of the First International Conference on Applied Synergetic and Synergetic Engineering*, (Erlangen), pp. 100–106, 1994.
5. B. Horn and B. Schunk, "Determining optical flow," *Artificial Intelligence*, vol. 17, pp. 185–, 1981.
6. E. G. Schukat-Talamazzini, *Automatische Spracherkennung*. BraunschweigWiesbaden: Vieweg, 1995.
7. Y. Linde, A. Buzo, and R. M. Grey, "An algorithm for vector quantizer design," *IEEE Transactions on Communication*, pp. 84–95, January 1980.
8. S. Ben-Yacoub, Y. Abdeljaoued, and E. Mayoraz, "Fusion of face and speech data for person identity verification," IDIAP-RR 03, IDIAP, 1999.
9. L. A. Klein, *Sensor and Data Fusion Concepts and Applications*. SPIE Press, 1999.
10. J. Kittler, Y.P.Li, J. Matas, and M. U. Ramos Sanchez, "Combining evidence in multimodal person identity recognition systems," in *AVBPA97*, pp. 327–334, March 1997.
11. T. Choudhury, B. Clarkson, T. Jebara, and A. Pentland, "Multimodal person recognition using unconstrained audio and video," in *AVBPA99*, pp. 176–181, March 1999.
12. A. Jain, L. Hong, and Y. Kulkarni, "A multimodal biometric system using fingerprint, face and speech," in *AVBPA99*, pp. 182–187, March 1999.
13. R. Inguva and G. Garrison, "Fusion of lwir sensor data by bayesian methods," in *Sensor Fusion: Architectures, Algorithms, and Applications II*, (Orlando, Florida), pp. 161–172, SPIE, April 1998.
14. Y. Abdeljaoued, "Fusion of person authentication probabilities by bayesian statistics," in *AVBPA99*, pp. 172–175, March 1999.
15. J. Kittler, M. Hatef, R. P. Duin, and J. Matas, "On combining classifiers," *IEEE Transactions on Pattern Analysis and Machine Intelligence*, 1998.

A Modular Neuro-Fuzzy Network for Musical Instruments Classification

Anna Maria Fanelli, Giovanna Castellano, and C. Alessandro Buscicchio

Università degli Studi di Bari - Dipartimento di Informatica, Via E. Orabona 4,
70126, Bari, Italy
{fanelli, castellano}@di.uniba.it, alebus@libero.it

Abstract. A modular neuro-fuzzy network is proposed for the classification of musical instruments from the sound they produce. Each module, which is inherently a fuzzy inference system with the capability of learning fuzzy rules from data, operates on a distinct subset of input features. All sub-networks are separately initialized and trained by a two-phase strategy. First, a fuzzy clustering algorithm is applied to establish the structure of each sub-network as well as the initial values of its parameters. Then, each sub-network enters a supervised learning phase for optimal adjustment of its parameters. After learning, each sub-network encodes in its structure the knowledge learned in the form of fuzzy if-then rules. The various sub-networks are then combined in a single modular network that is able to face the complete classification task. Preliminary experimental results compare favorably with human performance on the same task and demonstrate the utility of the modular approach.

1 Introduction

Recognizing sound sources in a complex environment is arguably the primary function of the human auditory system. Recognition is possible, in part, because acoustic features of sounds often betray physical properties of their sources. While humans can become skilled at identifying the types of sound sources, no artificial system, to date, has been built that can demonstrate the same competence. As a consequence, much attention of the research is devoted to create artificial systems that can learn to recognize the sound sources in a complex auditory environment. There are many applications in which automatic sound source identification would be useful. For example, it would be useful to build intelligent systems that can annotate [1] or transcribe music [2], [3] to build up safety systems based on the recognition of particular sound sources (e.g. human voice), for sound data compression, for studies about the human processes of sound source recognition.

Current research in this area is still mainly based on the Helmholtz's study [4] concerning the definition of musical "timbre" and the relative perceptual importance of various acoustic features of musical instrument sound. However, traditional approaches of computer science in general [5] and Artificial Intelligence [6] in particular do not offer good solutions in a world such as the musical one, characterized by its subjective and irrational character.

J. Kittler and F. Roli (Eds.): MCS 2000, LNCS 1857, pp. 372–382, 2000.
© Springer-Verlag Berlin Heidelberg 2000

The goal of this work is to develop an artificial system that automatically classifies and recognizes musical instruments from the sounds they produce. The work has two objectives. From a scientific point of view, it intends to deepen the knowledge about music interpretation through its modelization via adaptive techniques. From an engineering point of view, it is an attempt to build a piece of an artificial system for annotation/transcription of musical sounds.

In particular, in this paper we focus on the classification of orchestral musical instruments into families using a modular neuro-fuzzy network. Both the classification problem and the network architecture are divided. The classification task is split into a number of simpler sub-tasks and as many sub-networks are trained on separate training sets corresponding to different sub-regions of the feature space. The structure and the weights of each sub-network are first initialized by a fuzzy clustering algorithm. Then each network enters a supervised learning phase for optimal adjustment of its parameters. After learning, each sub-network encodes in its structure the knowledge learned in form of fuzzy rules and processes information according to a fuzzy reasoning scheme. The various sub-networks are then combined in a single modular network that is able to face the complete classification task. The use of such a modular approach, also justified on neurobiological grounds [7], would permit the formation of high-order computational units that can perform complex tasks such as that of musical instrument identification. Moreover, one key advantage is the reduction of the computational complexity of the learning process, which is globally more affordable with respect to training a single large network to solve the task as a whole. In addition, the integration of a fuzzy reasoning scheme and a neural network helps to develop explicit rather than implicit classification schemes and to quantify vagueness can exist both in musical sounds themselves and in rules governing the classification mechanism.

The paper is organized as follows. Section II describes the preprocessing of musical data and feature extraction. Section III illustrates the architecture of the proposed modular neural-fuzzy network. In section IV the learning algorithm is described. Section V presents the experimental results followed by conclusions in Section VI.

2 Data Pre-processing and Features Extraction

Given a musical instrument, we want to classify it into the correct instrument family (i.e strings, woodwinds, brass) by processing any instrument tone's sound signal, properly sampled at a given frequency. Typically, in a sound waveform four regions can be identified according to its energy (Fig. 1). Since the sound waveform is not so "regular" in time, it is important to take into account spectral features and the time in which they occur in the signal. Then, both temporal and spectral features should be extracted from the sampled signal.

To perform this time-frequency analysis we use the *short-time Fourier transform* (STFT) which is equivalent to a filterbank where the filter channels are linearly spaced in center frequency and all channels have the same bandwidth. STFT is computed by dividing the original signal $x(t)$ into S segments (called *frames*), and then by computing the Fourier transform $X_s(f)$ of each segment $s = 1,...,S$. The result is a *spectrogram*, which provides the spectrum of the signal in every frame. See Fig. 2 for an illustrative example.

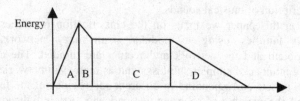

Fig. 1. Typical trend of energy for a sound waveform produced by a traditional musical instrument. Regions: (A) *attack*, (B) *decay*, (C) *sustain*, (D)*release*.

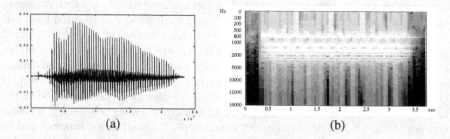

Fig. 2. (a) Tone of a horn (the sound signal $x(t)$ is sampled with a sampling frequency of 32 KHz). (b) Spectrogram of the signal. The horizontal axis is time, the vertical axis is frequency, the gray intensity is the harmonic magnitude at a given frequency and time.

The spectrogram provides a very large amount of frequency-time information. We extract a smaller number of spectral features by considering some particular frequency bands of biological relevance. Precisely, by simulating the frequency response of the human cochlea, we divide the range of frequencies $U = [100, 16000]$ Hz (see Figure 3) by means of the *Equivalent Rectangular Bandwidth* (ERB) scale [8], [9] into 24 bands, on the same line of the *Critical Bandwidth* (CB) scale [10]. The spectral information is reduced by integrating the spectral magnitude envelope of the s-th segment, i.e. $|X_s(f)|$, over the frequencies within each ERB band. Hence, for each frame $s = 1,..., S$ and for each ERB band $b = 1,..., B$ we compute the *band loudness*:

$$L_s^b = \int_{f_b - \Delta_b/2}^{f_b + \Delta_b/2} |X_s(f)| df \tag{1}$$

where f_b and Δ_b are the center and the width of the b-th band, respectively. L_s^b can be regarded as the intensity of the sound signal within a window of frequencies having the width of a ERB band.

Moreover, we consider only 1 sec of the sampled signal $x(t)$ (i.e. since sampling frequency is 32 KHz, we get the first 32000 sound samples) and compute the STFT with a window's width of 1/20 sec (i.e. 1600 samples). An overlap of 6.25 msec (i.e. 200 samples) between windows is also taken. As a result, we obtain $S = 20$ frames. This is not so restrictive, because typically a classical musical instrument's sound reaches its "steady state" energy in less than 1 sec. The result is a *cochleagram* (Figure 4) which represents, in the time domain, the loudness of the sound signal within all the 24 critical bands. Hence, the total amount of resulting features is $24 \times 20 = 480$.

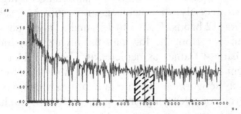

Fig. 3. Partitioning of U into 24 ERB critical bands. The vertical lines show the bands' centers. The computation of L_1^{22} (for frame s=1 and band b=22 having center frequency f_b =9739.51 Hz) is also shown in a geometrical sense.

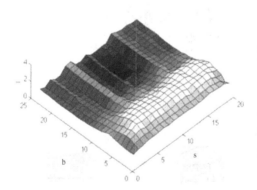

Fig. 4. Cochleagram of the signal in fig. 2a., where s is the frame number, b is the band number, l is the band loudness. Each square region of the surface represents a feature.

3   The Modular Neuro-Fuzzy Network

In this section we describe the modular neuro-fuzzy network designed for musical instruments classification. The task of classifying musical instruments can be formalized as follows. We assume that P patterns $\bar{x}^p = \left(x_1^p,...,x_N^p\right), p=1,...,P$ are available. Each pattern represents the cochleagram of the note's sound performed by an instrument belonging to one of m classes (families) $C_1,...,C_m$ of musical instruments. The classification task involves assigning a given pattern $\bar{x}$ to one of the m possible classes based on its features, hence it can be represented as a mapping $\varphi : X^N \rightarrow \{0,1\}^m$ where $\varphi(\bar{x})=\bar{c}=(c_1,...,c_m)$ such that $c_l=1$ and $c_j=0, j=1,...,m, j \neq l$.

To perform this task we propose the use of a modular neuro-fuzzy network. The architecture is composed of a number of modules (sub-networks) that operate on disjoint subsets of the input features without communicating each other. Each module is a neurofuzzy network capable of classifying a pattern according to a region defined on the input features. Precisely, the cochleagram is split into sub-regions: a "low" part comprising the first 12 bands (from 1 to 12), and a "high" part comprising the last 12 bands (from 13 to 24). Both the low and the high part is further divided into 5 regions, each comprising 4 frames as depicted in Figure 5. Hence, 10 sub-networks are used; each of them specializes itself by learning a region of the input space made of 48 features. The sub-network outputs are then properly combined by an integrating unit which has the role of averaging among the different modules to produce the desired classification response.

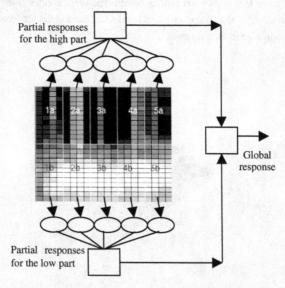

Fig. 5. Architecture of the modular neuro-fuzzy network. The cochleagram is split into 10 regions that are inputs for sub-networks (here represented by circles). Their responses are averaged to give the final response.

3.1 Sub-network Structure

In this section the structure of a single sub-network is described. Such structure is designed to match the inference mechanism of a multi-input multi-output (MIMO) fuzzy classifier with the form of a zero-order TSK model, i.e. based on a collection of K rules of the form:

$$R_k : \text{IF}(x_1 \text{ is } A_1^k) \text{ AND...AND}(x_n \text{ is } A_n^k) \text{ THEN}(c_1 \text{ is } v_{k1}) \text{ AND...AND}(c_m \text{ is } v_{km})$$

for $k = 1,...,K$, where R_k is the k-th rule, A_i^k are fuzzy sets defined on the input variable x_i, $i = 1,...,n$. They are represented by Gaussian membership functions $\mu_{ik}(x_i) = \exp\{-(x_i - w_{ik})^2/\sigma_{ik}^2\}$ where w_{ik} and σ_{ik} are the center and the width of the Gaussian function, respectively. The consequents v_{kj} are fuzzy singletons defined on the output variable c_j representing the membership value of pattern $\bar{x}$ to class C_j. They can be regarded as the center of a symmetric membership function with its width neglected during the defuzzification process.

By adopting singleton fuzzification, discrete center-of-gravity defuzzification method and rule inference with the Larsen's product operator for fuzzy conjunction and sum as aggregation., the inferred crisp output values (i.e. the class membership values) for an input pattern $\bar{x}^0 = (x_1^0, x_2^0,...,x_n^0)$, are calculated as:

$$\hat{c}_j = \sum_{k=1}^{K} \mu_k(\bar{x}^0) \cdot v_{kj} \Big/ \sum_{k=1}^{K} \mu_k(\bar{x}^0) \qquad j = 1,...,m \qquad (2)$$

where $\mu_k(\bar{x}^0) = \prod_{i=1}^{n} \mu_{ik}(x_i^0)$ is the activation strength of the k-th rule. Thus the outputs $\hat{c}_j \in [0,1]$ of the fuzzy classifier represent the membership degree of the pattern to class C_j. This yields to a "soft" (fuzzy) classification.

The topology of each sub-network, designed according to the working process of such a fuzzy system, comprises three layers:

1. *Layer L_1*. Nodes in this layer receive the feature values $(x_1, x_2,...,x_n)$ and act as fuzzy sets defined on the corresponding input variable. They are arranged into n groups; each group comprises fuzzy terms of a single input variable. Each node $i_k \in L_1$ receives the input variable concerned, *i.e.* x_i, and computes the membership value $\mu_{ik}(x_i)$ which specifies the degree to which the input value x_i belongs to the fuzzy set A_i^k. The output of node $i_k \in L_1$ is computed by the following function:

$$f_{ik}^{(1)} = \exp\{-(x_i - w_{ik})^2/\sigma_{ik}^2\}$$

2. *Layer L_2*. The number of nodes in this layer is equal to the number of fuzzy rules. A node in this layer represents a fuzzy rule; for each node, there are n fixed links from the input term nodes representing the premise part of a fuzzy rule. The kth node performs precondition matching of the kth rule by computing its activation strength, thus its output is:

$$f_k^{(2)} = \prod_{i=1}^{n} f_{ik}^{(1)}$$

3. *Layer* L_3. Nodes in this layer correspond to the output variables. Each node j acts as a defuzzifier and computes the output values $\hat{c}_j$ according to (2) :

$$f_j^{(3)} = \sum_{k=1}^{K} f_k^{(2)} v_{kj} \bigg/ \sum_{k=1}^{K} f_k^{(2)}$$

The weights of the network are $\{w_{ik}\}$, $\{\sigma_{ik}\}$ and $\{v_{kj}\}$ representing the parameters of the Gaussian membership functions $\{\mu_{ik}\}$ and the consequent values of fuzzy rules, respectively. Hence the neuro-fuzzy network encodes a set of fuzzy rules in its topology, and processes information in a way that matches the fuzzy reasoning scheme adopted. The structure of this neuro-fuzzy network is depicted in Fig. 6.

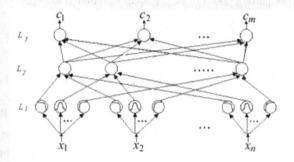

Fig. 6. Structure of a single sub-network.

3.2 Integrating Units

Finally, one important issue is how to combine the outputs of the ten sub-networks to form the final output of the classification system. The interconnectivity of a modular network is usually tuned to the application domain by using some integrating units that perform the function of mediating among the sub-networks. In our case, two integrating units are used, one to combine the outputs of the five sub-networks processing part "low" of the feature space, and the other to combine the sub-networks processing part "high". The outputs of each integrating unit is a weighted average, as follows:

$$\hat{c}_j^{Low} = \sum_{r \in Low} \alpha^{(r)} \hat{c}_j^{(r)} \bigg/ \sum_{r \in Low} \alpha^{(r)} \qquad \hat{c}_j^{High} = \sum_{r \in High} \alpha^{(r)} \hat{c}_j^{(r)} \bigg/ \sum_{r \in High} \alpha^{(r)} \qquad (3)$$

where $\hat{c}_j^{(r)}$ is the j-th output of the sub-network processing the r-th sub-region, and $\alpha^{(r)}$ are the associated weights. Such weights are chosen so as to give more importance to the output of modules processing the first frames. Indeed, it has been demonstrated experimentally that the attack has a great influence in the recognition of a sound source (if we discard the onset of a sound, the recognition becomes difficult even for humans). In fact, many sound timbre characteristics are stronger in the early vibrations than in the last ones (i.e. more in the sound onset than in his "steady state"). As a consequence, the weights have been chosen according to the following decreasing function: $\alpha^{(r)} = \frac{c}{r}$, $r=1,...,5$ where c is a constant value, here set to 3.0. However, such weights can also be modified as part of the learning by implementing the integrating unit as a gating network [11].

The final output of the modular classifier is obtained as a simple average of the partial outputs produced by the two parts of sub-networks.

$$\hat{c}_j = \tfrac{1}{2}\left(\hat{c}_j^{low} + \hat{c}_j^{high}\right) \tag{4}$$

Note that each sub-network gives a "soft" classification response, and the average of them is also "soft". To obtain hard classification, the highest component of the final output vector is mapped to 1 while other components are mapped to 0. In other words, the pattern $\bar{x}^0$ is assigned to the class C_t such that $\hat{c}_t = \max\{\hat{c}_1,...,\hat{c}_m\}$.

4 Sub-network Learning

Each sub-network is initialized and trained by a two-phase strategy. The first phase clusters the feature space to find rules parameters. The second phase uses a supervised scheme for rule premise and consequent adaptation.

Given a training set $S = \{(\bar{x}^p, \bar{c}^p), p=1,...,P\}$ of P patterns, the weights of the network are initialized by clustering the input space and defining the logical relationship between the cluster membership values and the class labels. The fuzzy c-means (FCM) algorithm [12] is applied to find clusters in the input space. When clustering is completed, a collection of K cluster centers, together with cluster membership values for each training pattern, hereafter denoted by $\{\varpi_{pk}\}$, are available. Each cluster center $\bar{w}_k = (w_{1k}, w_{2k},...,w_{nk})$ is a prototypical data point in the feature space X^n that represents the antecedent of the kth fuzzy rule, hence its components are used to initialize the weights $\{w_{ik}\}$ representing the centers of the Gaussian membership functions in the premise part of the kth rule. Initial weights $\{\sigma_{ik}\}$ representing the widths of the membership functions are obtained using the N-first-nearest-neighbor heuristic: $\sigma_{ik} = \|\bar{w}_k - \bar{w}_h\|/r$, $i=1,...,n$ where $\bar{w}_h$ is the closest cluster center to $\bar{w}_k$ and r is an overlap parameter ranging in $[1.0, 2.0]$. Finally, initial values of $\{v_{kj}\}$ are obtained by taking into account how much patterns belonging to class C_j are covered by the k-th cluster. This is done by using the cluster membership values ϖ_{pk}, directly available from the FCM algorithm, and the class label vectors $\bar{c}^p = (c_1^p,...,c_m^p)$, for all training patterns $p = 1,...,P$. as follows:

$$v_{kj} = \sum_{p=1}^{P} \varpi_{pk} c_j^p \bigg/ \sum_{p=1}^{P} \varpi_{pk} \qquad j=1,...,m$$

After weight initialization, the network enters the supervised learning phase to optimally adjust the parameters. A gradient method performing the steepest descent on a surface in the network parameter space is used [13]. Given the training set, the goal is to adjust weights so as to minimize an overall error function $e = \frac{1}{P}\sum_{p=1}^{P} E_p$ with

$E_p = \frac{1}{2}\sum_{j=1}^{m}(c_j^p - \hat{c}_j^p)^2$, where $\hat{c}_j^p$ is the j-th output of the neuro-fuzzy network for the

current pattern $\bar{x}^p$ and c_j^p is the corresponding desired class label. For the sake of simplicity, the subscript p indicating the current pattern will be dropped in the following. The general update formula for a generic weight α is $\Delta\alpha = -\eta \partial E/\partial\alpha$ where η is the learning rate. Starting at the first layer, a forward pass is used to compute the activity levels of all the nodes in the network to obtain the current output values. Then, starting at the output nodes, a backward pass is used to compute $\partial E/\partial\alpha$ for all the nodes. In summary, the complete learning algorithm is as follows.

1. Initialization: initialize weights $\{w_{ik}\}$ and $\{\sigma_{ik}\}$ with center and width of membership functions determined by clustering, and weights $\{v_{kj}\}$ with rule consequent derived after clustering.
2. Input: Select the next sample $(\bar{x},\bar{c})$ from S
3. Forward step: propagate $\bar{x}$ through the network and determine the class membership values $(\hat{c}_1,...,\hat{c}_m)$
4. Backward step: compute error terms for units $j \in L_3$, $k \in L_2$ and $i_k \in L_1$

$$\delta_j^{(3)} = -\frac{\partial E}{\partial f_j^{(3)}} = c_j - \hat{c}_j \;, \qquad \delta_k^{(2)} = -\frac{\partial E}{\partial f_k^{(2)}} = -\sum_{j=1}^{m}\frac{\partial E}{\partial f_j^{(3)}}\frac{\partial f_j^{(3)}}{\partial f_k^{(2)}} = \sum_{j=1}^{m}\delta_j^{(3)}\left(v_{kj} - f_j^{(3)}\right)$$

$$\delta_{ik}^{(1)} = -\frac{\partial E}{\partial f_{ik}^{(1)}} = -\frac{\partial E}{\partial f_k^{(2)}}\frac{\partial f_k^{(2)}}{\partial f_{ik}^{(1)}} = \delta_k^{(2)} \cdot \frac{\partial f_k^{(2)}}{\partial f_{ik}^{(1)}}$$

5. Adjustment: update weights $\{v_{kj}\}$, $\{w_{ik}\}$ and $\{\sigma_{ik}\}$ respectively according to:

$$\Delta v_{kj} = \eta \delta_j^{(3)} \cdot \frac{f_k^{(2)}}{\sum_{t=1}^{K} f_t^{(2)}}, \quad \Delta w_{ik} = \eta \delta_{ik}^{(1)}\left[\frac{2(x_i - w_{ik})}{\sigma_{ik}^2}\right]f_{ik}^{(1)}, \quad \Delta\sigma_{ik} = \eta \delta_{ik}^{(1)}\left[\frac{2(x_i - w_{ik})^2}{\sigma_{ik}^3}\right]f_{ik}^{(1)}$$

6. If $E < \varepsilon$ then go to step 7. else go to step 2.
7. End.

4 Experimental Results

To perform the task of classifying musical instruments into families, we used a dataset of 500 sound samples of 12 orchestral instruments played on their entire pitch ranges, belonging to three different families: strings (viola, violin), woodwinds (bassoon, oboe, clarinet, flute, piccolo), brass (tuba, horn, trumpet, flugelshorn, muted trumpet). The sound dataset was supplied by K. D. Martin of the MIT Media Laboratory Machine Listening Group, Cambridge MA, USA.

In these preliminary experiments, all sub-networks were initialized with the same structure by applying the FCM algorithm with 15 clusters. Each sub-network was trained for 1000 epochs on 70% of the samples, leaving 30% as test samples. All sub-networks were cross-validated with 20 different 70%-30% splits, providing a classification rate on the training set ranging from 93% to 98%. The average generalization results for the single sub-networks as well as for the whole modular network are summarized in Table I, while Table II shows a breakdown of the generalization results in terms of musical families.

Reading such results, it can be seen that the whole modular network provides a better classification rate on the test set with respect to single sub-networks. This is due to the effect of the integration unit that averages all the partial outputs: if a sub-network fails, some others can compensate for its mistake, thus allowing the whole network to provide a good final response.

Table I. Average classification results of the single sub-networks and the modular network on the test set for 20 trials using different 70%-30% splits

	Sub-networks				
	1	2	3	4	5
Part Low	82,25	64,66	65,63	69,19	64,61
Part High	76,61	75,63	76,12	75,07	72,28
Modular Network	87,61				

Table II. Average classification results of the modular network with a breakdown into families

	Strings (26 samples)	Woodwinds (53 samples)	Brass (63 samples)	Whole Test Set (142 samples)
Ave.	80,96	85,84	91,82	87,61
St. Dev.	7,54	3,88	2,80	2,83

6 Conclusions

A modular neuro-fuzzy network for musical instrument classification has been proposed. Each sub-network is a connectionist model of a fuzzy classifier, which can find its optimal structure and parameters automatically. Preliminary experimental results showed that the proposed modular network is able classify instruments into the correct family with a success rate that compares favorably with human performance on the same task. Of course, further work is in progress to improve the classification results. For example, we are studying the effect of using different structure sizes for the sub-networks and different types of integrating unit on the modular network performance. This work represents the first step towards the development of a system which identifies individual instruments after a first classification into families. The use of such a taxonomic hierarchy should provide strong computational advantages over direct classification of musical instruments.

References

1. Wold, E., Blum,T., Keislar, D., Wheaton, J.: Content-based classification, search, and retrieval of audio. IEEE Multimedia (1996) 27-36
2. Vercoe, B.L., Gardner, W.G., Scheirer, E.D.: Structured audio: the creation, transmission and rendering of parametric sound representations. Proc. IEEE **85** (5) 922-940
3. Martin, K.D.: Toward automatic sound source recognition: identifying musical instruments. Proc. NATO Computational Hearing Advanced Study Institute. Il Ciocco, Italy (1998)
4. Helmholtz, H.: On the sensations of tone as a physiological basis for the theory of music. A.J. Allis, Trans., Dover (1954)
5. Dannenberg, R.B.: Real-time scheduling and computer accompaniment. In: Mathews, Pierce (eds.): Current Directions in Computer Music Research. The MIT Press, Cambridge MA (1989)
6. Marvin, M., Laske, O.: Foreword: a conversation with Marvin Minsky. In: Balaban, Ebciagly, Laske (eds.): Understanding Music with AI. Perspective on Music Cognition. The AAAI Press/MIT Press, Cambridge, MA (1992)
7. Houk, J.C.: Learning in modular networks. In: Proc. of Seventh Yale Workshop on Adaptive and Learning Systems, New Haven, CT: Yale University, (1992) 80-84
8. Moore, B.C.J., Glasberg, B.R.: A Revision of Zwicker's Loudness Model. ACTA Acoustica **82** (1996) 335–345
9. Slaney, M.: An efficient implementation of the Patterson-Holdsworth auditory filter-bank. Apple Computer Technical report #35 (1993)
10. Zwicker, E., Fastl, H.: Psychoacoustics, Facts and Models. Springer Verlag, Berlin (1990)
11. Jacobs, R.A., Jordan, M.I., Nowlan, S.J., Hinton, G.E.: Adaptive mixtures of local experts. Neural Computation **3**(1) (1991) 79-87.
12. Bezdek, J.C.: Pattern Recognition with Fuzzy Objective Function Algorithms. Plenum Press, New York (1981)
13. Lin, C., Lee, C.S.G.: Neural-network-based fuzzy logic control and decision system. IEEE Trans. Comput. **40**(12) (1991) 1320-1336

Classifier Combination for Grammar-Guided Sentence Recognition

Xiaoyi Jiang, Keren Yu, and Horst Bunke

Department of Computer Science, University of Bern
Neubrückstrasse 10, CH-3012 Bern, Switzerland
Email: {jiang,yu,bunke}@iam.unibe.ch

Abstract. In this paper we consider a category of classification tasks, where the classification results are sentences of words subject to a given grammar. The particular nature of grammar-guided sentence recognition makes classifier combination rules known from the literature not applicable any longer. We propose a conceptually new approach to classifier combination that consists of three main components: class set reduction, inconsistency localization, and resolution. The proposed algorithm represents a framework for classifier combination in grammar-guided sentence recognition that is applicable to a variety of different tasks. Experimental results will be shown for the task of spoken email command recognition, where an acoustic and a visual classifier are combined.

1 Introduction

Traditionally, the classification decision made by a classifier represents an atomic entity, i.e. a single class name, which is regarded correct or wrong as a whole. In this paper we investigate a different category of classification tasks, where the classification results are sentences of words subject to a given grammar. Examples of this kind of classification tasks are email commands [3] and legal amount recognition in check reading [1]. If we consider each sentence possibly generated by the grammar as an individual class, we are faced with a very high number of classes (possibly infinite) which makes the recognition task difficult. Moreover, each class, i.e. each sentence, consists of a (possibly large) number of basic words. Thus if only one of the words is misrecognized, the whole sentence is not correctly classified. As the number of words in a sentence may vary, for the same input signal, from one classifier to the other, combination strategies developed earlier for the classification of atomic entities are not applicable for grammar-guided classification tasks.

We propose a conceptually new approach to classifier combination dedicated to grammar-guided sentence recognition. It consists of three main components: class set reduction, inconsistency localization and resolution. We first introduce the general concept of grammar-guided sentence recognition. Then, an outline of the classifier combination algorithm is given in Section 3, followed by a description of the three main components in Sections 4-6. Finally, we conclude the paper by a discussion of the application of the proposed classifier combination approach to recognition of spoken email commands in Section 7 and by a summary of the work in Section 8.

J. Kittler and F. Roli (Eds.): MCS 2000, LNCS 1857, pp. 383–392, 2000.

2   Grammar-Guided Sentence Recognition

A grammar $G = (N, T, P, S)$ is defined by its finite sets of nonterminals N, terminals T, productions P, and the unique initial nonterminal $S \in N$. The terminals T are the basic words from which a sentence of the language can be constructed by concatenation, while the nonterminals N correspond to higher level concepts. The productions P describe how complete sentences of the language are built from simpler parts. $L(G)$ is the language generated by G.

In the rest of the paper we will illustrate the various definitions and steps of the classifier combination algorithm by using the grammar $G = (N, T, P, S)$:

$N = \{$ COMMAND, VERB, NUMBER, DIGIT $\}$
$T = \{$ display, reply, forward, delete, message, one, two, ..., nine, zero, oh $\}$
$S =$ COMMAND;
$P = \{$ COMMAND $\rightarrow$ VERB message NUMBER,
         VERB $\rightarrow$ display | reply | forward | delete,
         NUMBER $\rightarrow$ DIGIT | DIGIT DIGIT,
         DIGIT $\rightarrow$ one | two | three | $\cdots$ | nine | zero | oh $\}$

which is a simplified version of the email command grammar defined in [3].

Classifiers can be constructed to recognize sentences subject to a given grammar. For instance, hidden Markov models are able to incooperate grammatical knowledge. In this case the output of the classifier will be an ordered list of N legal sentences of the grammar, each being possibly associated with a recognition confidence value. Such a classifier therefore solves the two subproblems of a sentence recognition task:

- segmentation of an input signal, resp. its representation in terms of feature vectors, into individual parts, each corresponding to a single word, and
- classification of each individual part

in a unified framework. The integration of a grammar makes sure that the output sentences can all be produced by the grammar.

3   Outline of Classifier Combination Approach

The prerequisite for classifier combination is k classifiers, each of which provides, for an input signal, a sorted list of N candidate sentences. If we assume that the correct sentence appears in the lists of all classifiers, we can apply, for example, the Borda count combination rule which basically sums up the rank of each candidate sentence in all k ranking lists. Unfortunately, the usual case in real life is that the correct sentence may not appear at all among the N top candidates of neither classifier. However, if the majority of the atomic classes (i.e. the individual words that make up the sentence) output by each classifier is correct, we may be able to recover the correct sentence by classifier combination. For this combination the first question is which candidate among the N to choose from each classifier. In accordance with the Borda count rule we

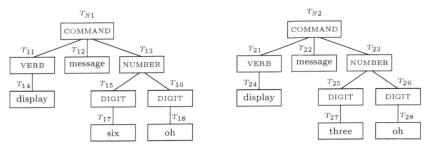

Fig. 1. Syntax tree for sentence *display message six oh* (left) and *display message three oh* (right), respectively.

certainly prefer candidates with high confidence (low ranks). On the other hand, we should select, from the different classifiers, only candidates that are similar to each other. By considering both criteria we define a score function to select one candidate sentence from the output of each classifier, see Section 4.

The next step consists of localizing the differences between the selected candidate sentences (Section 5) and resolving the inconsistencies (Section 6). The inconsistency localization is done by comparing the corresponding syntax trees of the candidate sentences. After the inconsistent parts within each sentence have been identified, a second round of classification is initiated. It is focused on the inconsistent parts only and includes classifier combination again. Thus classifier combination is applied in a recursive way.

As an example, let's assume that there are two classifiers and two candidate sentences *display message six oh / display message three oh*, one from each classifier, are selected based on the score function. The corresponding syntax trees are shown in Figure 1. Their comparison reveals that the two sentences differ only in the subsentences *six / three*, both of which are derived from the nonterminal *DIGIT*. This inconsistency is then resolved by applying the classifiers and the classifier combination procedure again to the localized inconsistent subsentences.

In the following sections all components of the classifier combination procedure will be discussed. For description clarity we assume $k = 2$ and a formal description for a generalization to $k > 2$ classifiers can be found in [4].

4   Class Set Reduction

Given two ranked lists of N candidate sentences, we are concerned with selecting the one candidate from each list that is most likely to be a distorted version of the correct sentence. As stated in Section 3, two criteria are involved here: rank (in accordance with the Borda count rule) and distance of candidate sentences.

4.1   Distance of Sentences

A candidate sentence is a string of terminal symbols of the given grammar. As such, the distance, or dissimilarity, of two candidate sentences may be defined as the string edit distance [2]. From the information theoretic point of view, however, a sentence goes beyond a simple string of symbols because it is subject to grammatical rules in a way specified by the corresponding syntax tree of the sentence. Therefore, we have to take this structural information source into consideration. In this work we assume that the grammar is unambiguous. That is, there exists a unique syntax tree for each sentence derived from the grammar[1].

The syntax tree of a sentence is an ordered labeled tree whose nodes are labeled by nonterminal/terminal symbols of the grammar and in which the left-to-right order among siblings is significant. By incooperating structural information, a sentence, or equivalently its syntax tree, can be represented by a sequence consisting of all subtrees of the root node. The order of the subtrees is exactly the same as that in the syntax tree from left to right. Given two sentences we therefore have two sequences of subtrees. By considering subtrees as symbols, the standard dynamic programming technique [2] can be used to compute a matching score between the two sequences, i.e. the two given sentences. For this purpose we only need to specify the cost function $c(t^1 \rightarrow t^2)$, where t^1 (t^2) corresponds to either a subtree of the first (second) syntax tree or an empty tree Λ. (The cost function will be discussed later in this section.) Note that this notation implies the cost for all standard edit operations insertion, deletion, and substitution. As the result of matching the two sequences of subtrees we obtain a matching score and the corresponding optimal mapping Π from the first sequence $t_1^1 t_2^1 \cdots t_m^1$ to the second sequence $t_1^2 t_2^2 \cdots t_n^2$, where t_i^k represents the i-th subtree of the syntax tree of the k-th sentence generated by the classifier. The mapping Π consists of pairs (t_i^1, t_j^2), (Λ, t_j^2), and (t_i^1, Λ), which correspond to edit operations substitution, insertion, and deletion, respectively.

Recall that our goal is to define a distance function between two sentences taking into regard the structural information. The matching score resulting from sequence matching may serve this purpose. However, it suffers from the problem that the real difference between two sentences is not described in proportion to their overall size. For instance, two sentences $t_1^1 t$ and $t_1^2 t$ with common tail t will be assigned the same distance value independent of the size of t. This effect is definitely undesired. Our solution to this problem is to set the different parts of two sentences, resp. the corresponding syntax trees, in relation to their overall size. Given two sentences $T_1 = t_1^1 t_2^1 \cdots t_m^1$ and $T_2 = t_1^2 t_2^2 \cdots t_n^2$, each represented by the sequence of their subtrees, let $\Pi_{T_1 T_2}$ denote the optimal mapping from T_1 to T_2. Then, the number of common nodes, $n(T_1, T_2)$, of T_1 and T_2 can be counted by:

$$
n(T_1, T_2) = \begin{cases} 0; & T_1 = \Lambda \text{ or } T_2 = \Lambda \\ 0; & \text{root labels of } T_1 \text{ and } T_2 \text{ are different} \\ 1 + \sum_{(t_i, t_j) \in \Pi_{T_1 T_2}} n(t_i, t_j); & \text{otherwise} \end{cases}
$$

---

[1] From the practical point of view, this is not a real limitation usually.

Finally, we define the distance of two sentences T_1 and T_2 by:

$$d(T_1, T_2) = \begin{cases} 0; & T_1 = \Lambda \text{ and } T_2 = \Lambda \\ 1 - \frac{n(T_1, T_2)}{\max(|T_1|, |T_2|)}; & \text{otherwise} \end{cases}$$

where $|T|$ denotes the number of nodes in T. Obviously, this distance function maps two sentences to a real number within $[0, 1]$ and the value zero is only taken for the case of two identical sentences.

In the dynamic programming technique described above the cost function $c(t^1 \rightarrow t^2)$ is still not defined. Generally, this function models the likelihood that, due to distortions, t^1 is transformed into t^2. Therefore, it is directly related to the difference between t^1 and t^2. We propose to use

$$c(t^1 \rightarrow t^2) = d(t^1, t^2).$$

Implicitly, this specifies the cost for insertion and deletion

$$c(\Lambda \rightarrow t^2) = c(t^1 \rightarrow \Lambda) = 1$$

as well.

In summary the computation of sentence distance includes the following steps. The two involved sentences are represented by $T_1 = t_1^1 t_2^1 \cdots t_m^1$ and $T_2 = t_1^2 t_2^2 \cdots t_n^2$ in terms of their subtrees. The dynamic programming technique is applied to compute a matching score and the corresponding optimal mapping $\Pi_{T_1 T_2}$ from T_1 to T_2. Then, the number $n(T_1, T_2)$ of common nodes of T_1 and T_2 is determined based on $\Pi_{T_1 T_2}$, which finally leads to the distance $d(T_1, T_2)$. Note that the cost function for the edit operation substitution is defined by the distance value of the two involved subtrees. Consequently, the procedure of distance computation described above is recursively called in the dynamic programming algorithm.

For our example of the two sentences and their corresponding syntax trees T_{S1} and T_{S2} in Figure 1 the dynamic programming technique will provide the optimal mapping:

$$\Pi_{T_{S1} T_{S2}} = \{(T_{11}, T_{21}), (T_{12}, T_{22}), (T_{13}, T_{23})\} \tag{1}$$

To illustrate the procedure of distance computation we consider $c(T_{13} \rightarrow T_{23}) \equiv d(T_{13}, T_{23})$, which is required for computing $d(T_{S1}, T_{S2})$. The dynamic programming produces a matrix for $T_{13} = T_{15} T_{16}$ and $T_{23} = T_{25} T_{26}$, see Figure 2. Here we need, among others, the cost $c(T_{15} \rightarrow T_{25})$ ($\equiv d(T_{15}, T_{25})$), which is again solved by the dynamic programming technique, see Figure 2. For this purpose we need further $c(T_{17} \rightarrow T_{27})$ which is simply 1 because $n(T_{17}, T_{27}) = 0$ holds. Moreover, an insertion and deletion operation with cost one each are involved. We then obtain $\Pi_{T_{15} T_{25}} = \{(T_{17}, T_{27})\}$ from the matrix. This leads to:

$$n(T_{15}, T_{25}) = 1 + n(T_{17}, T_{27}) = 1$$

and

$$c(T_{15} \rightarrow T_{25}) = d(T_{15}, T_{25}) = \frac{1}{2}.$$

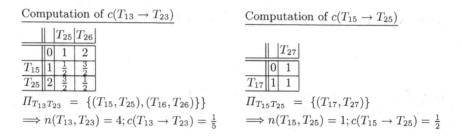

Fig. 2. Example of distance computation.

Similarly, we are able to derive $n(T_{16}, T_{26}) = 2$ and $c(T_{16} \to T_{26}) = d(T_{16}, T_{26}) = 0$. Based on $c(T_{15} \to T_{25})$ and $c(T_{16} \to T_{26})$ we easily get:

$$\Pi_{T_{13}T_{23}} = \{(T_{15}, T_{25}), (T_{26}, T_{26})\}$$

from the dynamic programming which results in:

$$n(T_{13}, T_{23}) = 1 + n(T_{15}, T_{25}) + n(T_{16}, T_{26}) = 4.$$

Finally, the cost $c(T_{13} \to T_{23})$ is determined to be $\frac{1}{5}$. It can be verified in a similar way that $d(T_{S1}, T_{S2}) = \frac{1}{9}$.

4.2   Sentence Selection

Recall that the reason for deriving the distance function of two sentences is the operation of class set reduction. It selects one sentence from each of two ranked lists of N candidate sentences that is most likely to be a distorted version of the correct sentence.

As stated earlier, two criteria are investigated for this purpose: rank (in accordance with the Borda count rule) and distance of candidate sentences. We consider pairs of candidate sentences, one from each classifier. Each pair (T_1, T_2) is evaluated by a score function:

$$S(T_1, T_2) = w \cdot \frac{(r(T_1) - 1) + (r(T_2) - 1)}{2(N - 1)} + (1 - w) \cdot d(T_1, T_2)$$

where $r()$ denotes the rank of a sentence and takes a value out of $\{1, 2, \cdots, N\}$. The first term represents a variation of the Borda count, while the second term brings the distance of the two sentences into consideration. The two terms are weighted by the factor $w \in [0, 1]$. The pair (T_1, T_2) with the smallest score is accepted to be distorted versions of the correct sentence and fed to the inconsistency localization and resolution step (described in Sections 5 and 6). In case of multiple pairs, all having the same minimum score, we compare the respective $d()$ of these pairs and select the pair with the smallest $d()$ value. If ambiguity remains even in this case, we need some more sophisticated resolution rule.

Currently, we simply generate a reject, with the consequence that the overall classifier combination algorithm terminates immediately and outputs a reject.

In our illustration example we simply assume that the sentence pair shown in Figure 1 will be assigned the smallest score among all possible pairs and therefore forwarded to the inconsistency localization and resolution step.

5 Inconsistency Localization

Given a pair of candidate sentences determined by the class set reduction step, we are faced with two possible situations. The two candidates may be identical. In this case no further action is needed. The classifier combination algorithm terminates immediately and outputs the sentence as the combination result.

For the case of the two candidate sentences being not identical there exists at least one identical nonterminal symbol R in the corresponding syntax trees which has different derivations under the two classifiers. Let T_1 and T_2 denote the tree below R (including R) in the two syntax trees, respectively. Further we assume $\Pi_{T_1 T_2}$ being the optimal mapping from T_1 to T_2. Then, $\Pi_{T_1 T_2}$ must contain one edit operation of the type:

- $(t^1, \Lambda) \in \Pi_{T_1 T_2}$, or
- $(\Lambda, t^2) \in \Pi_{T_1 T_2}$, or
- $(t^1, t^2) \in \Pi_{T_1 T_2}$, where the root labels of t^1 and t^2 are not identical.

Such a nonterminal symbol indicates an inconsistency in the recognition results of the two classifiers and must be identified. For this purpose we consider two syntax tress T_1 and T_2, both with the same root node label R, and establish a list of inconsistencies (LOI). At the beginning T_1 and T_2 are given by the entire syntax trees T_{S1} and T_{S2}, respectively, and R is simply the initial nonterminal symbol S of the grammar. The discussions above lead to the following simple rules:

1. If $|T_1| = 1$ and $|T_2| = 1$, then LOI$(T_1, T_2)=\emptyset$.
2. If the optimal mapping $\Pi_{T_1 T_2}$ from T_1 to T_2 contains one edit operation of one of the three types listed above, then the derivation corresponding to T_1 is different from the derivation corresponding to T_2, i.e. LOI$(T_1, T_2) = \{(T_1, T_2)\}$.
3. Otherwise, LOI$(T_1, T_2) = \cup_{(t^1, t^2) \in \Pi_{T_1 T_2}}$ LOI(t^1, t^2).

Here the first rule stops the process of determining LOI(T_1, T_2). Note that if $|T_1| = 1$, then $|T_2| = 1$ must be true as well. Otherwise, T_1 has a single (root) node labeled by a terminal, while T_2 has a nonterminal root node. Since T_1 and T_2 have root nodes with different labels, the process must have terminated at the father node of the two root nodes. Therefore, no other termination rules other than the first one are needed. After applying these rules, the list LOI(T_{S1}, T_{S2}) contains all inconsistencies that occur in the recognition results of the two classifiers.

For the example sentence pair shown in Figure 1 the optimal mapping $\Pi_{T_{S1}T_{S2}}$ is given in (1). In this case we obtain:

$$\mathrm{LOI}(T_{S1}, T_{S2}) = \mathrm{LOI}(T_{11}, T_{21}) \cup \mathrm{LOI}(T_{12}, T_{22}) \cup \mathrm{LOI}(T_{13}, T_{23})$$
$$= \mathrm{LOI}(T_{11}, T_{21}) \cup \mathrm{LOI}(T_{12}, T_{22}) \cup \{\mathrm{LOI}(T_{15}, T_{25}) \cup \mathrm{LOI}(T_{16}, T_{26})\}$$

Obviously, $\mathrm{LOI}(T_{15}, T_{25}) = \{(T_{15}, T_{25})\}$ holds since $\Pi_{T_{15}T_{25}}$ contains (T_{17}, T_{27}) only and the two trees T_{17} and T_{27} have different root labels. Without explicit derivation we observe that $\mathrm{LOI}(T_{11}, T_{21}) = \mathrm{LOI}(T_{12}, T_{22}) = \mathrm{LOI}(T_{16}, T_{26}) = \emptyset$. Finally, we get $\mathrm{LOI}(T_{S1}, T_{S1}) = \{(T_{15}, T_{25}\}$. That is, the single inconsistency in this example results from two different interpretations of the nonterminal *DIGIT*.

6   Inconsistency Resolution

There is one situation where no inconsistency resolution is possible. If the list $\mathrm{LOI}(T_{S1}, T_{S2})$ only contains one entry (T_{S1}, T_{S2}), then the inconsistency occurs at the initial nonterminal symbol S. In this case the classifier combination algorithm immediately terminates with a reject.

In all other cases, all inconsistencies in $\mathrm{LOI}(T_{S1}, T_{S2})$ detected by the localization process will be independently resolved. Each inconsistency $(T_1, T_2) \in \mathrm{LOI}(T_{S1}, T_{S2})$ corresponds to a common nonterminal symbol R and a corresponding subpart P_1 resp. P_2 of the entire input signal to the two classifiers. We propose to resolve the inconsistency by applying the classification and combination procedure again locally to P_1 and P_2. This process consists of two steps. First, we need to extract the subparts P_1 and P_2 from the original input signals and compute the features of P_1 and P_2 that are fed to the classifiers. Here we can include a preprocessing of P_1 and P_2 in a way locally adapted to these subparts. In handwritten text reading, for instance, this preprocessing could be a local slant correction constrained to P_1 resp. P_2 only. Under consideration of the possibly non-uniform slant of text lines this kind of local preprocessing operations potentially helps us resolve the inconsistencies [1]. A second preparation step concerns the grammar used by the classifiers to guide the classification. The initial nonterminal symbol S should be replaced by R now, resulting in a new grammar (N, T, P, R), which generally generates a subset of the original language only.

For each $(T_1, T_2) \in \mathrm{LOI}(T_{S1}, T_{S2})$, the application of the classification and combination cycle provides a unique result or the combination procedure terminates with a reject. In the former case the inconsistency positions in the recognition results of the two classifiers are replaced by the unique result from the inconsistency resolution procedure.

For the two example sentences the inconsistency resolution step implies that the parts of the input signal corresponding to T_{15}/T_{25}, i.e. the word *six/three*, are extracted and their features, possibly after a proper local preprocessing, are fed to a new cycle of classification and combination. Notice that in this new cycle, the input signal is smaller, and the grammar is more constrained. Thus, it

Input: ranked list of candidate sentences L_1 and L_2 from two classifiers
Output: a sentence or reject
/* Class set reduction */
select one sentence C_1 (C_2) from each L_1 (L_2);
if selection not successful **then** terminate with reject;
if $C_1 = C_2$ **then** terminate with C_1 as result;
/* Inconsistency localization */
compute LOI(T_{S1}, T_{S2}) for (C_1, C_2);
/* Inconsistency resolution */
if LOI(T_{S1}, T_{S2})=$\{(T_{S1}, T_{S2})\}$ **then** terminate with reject;
for each (T_1, T_2) $\in$ LOI(T_{S1}, T_{S2}) **do**
    resolve inconsistency (T_1, T_2) by applying a new classification/combination cycle;

Fig. 3. Classifier combination algorithm Combiner(L_1, L_2).

can be expected that this new round of classification is more robust and reliable than the previous one. If the inconsistency can be successfully resolved, then the resulting word will replace the initial inconsistent part in the sentence and generate the final combined classification result.

Now we are able to give an overall description of the classifier combination algorithm, see Figure 3. This description highlights the three main components, i.e. class set reduction, inconsistency localization and resolution.

7 Application and Experimental Results

In this section we briefly describe an application of the classifier combination approach proposed in this paper to a lipreading task of understanding spoken email commands. A detailed description of the lipreading task including the grammar which generates the email commands is given in [5]. The total number of classes, i.e. sentences generated by the grammar in this application is more than thirty thousand.

Two classifiers are designed using acoustic and visual signals, respectively. Both the acoustic and visual classifier are based on hidden Markov models (HMM). For each basic word of the vocabulary (terminals of G) an HMM is constructed. These basic HMMs are then concatenated according to the grammar G, resulting in a complex HMM that is able to recognize any sentence generated by G. For acoustic and visual recognition, linear prediction coefficients and 2D-FFT coefficients are used as features, respectively.

The experimental data were collected by a single person speaking sentences following the grammar G. The training set consists of 222 sentences, which contain 976 instances of the 44 basic words (terminals) while the testing set has a size of 106 sentences with a total of 322 word instances. The ground truth labeling of the training data was made manually.

We define rejection and error rate as

$$\text{rejection rate} = \frac{\text{rejections}}{\text{total tests}}; \quad \text{error rate} = \frac{\text{total tests} - \text{rejections} - \text{correct tests}}{\text{total tests} - \text{rejections}}$$

respectively. The recognition results at sentence level from both classifiers and from classifier combination are

	acoustic	visual	combination	
	error	error	error	rejection
rate	27.4%	39.6%	19.5%	17.9%

The rejection rate of each of the two individual classifiers is zero. Here we can see that the error rate is significantly reduced by means of classifier combination. Obviously, this reduction of the error rate can be achieved only if part of the input data is rejected. However, such a behavior of the classifier may be desired in applications where the cost of a wrong decision is high compared to a rejection.

8   Conclusion

Earlier works on multiple classifier combination are concerned with classification tasks in which the classification decision represents an atomic entity. In the present paper we have considered classifier combination in the framework of grammar-guided sentence recognition. Its particular nature makes simple combination rules such as Borda count not applicable any longer. We have proposed a conceptually new approach to classifier combination that consists of three main components: class set reduction, inconsistency localization and resolution. The proposed algorithm is general enough to be adapted to various applications. Examples of grammar-guided sentence recognition include email commands and legal amount recognition in check reading. The classification combination algorithm proposed in the present paper has been applied to the email command recognition problem combining two classifiers that operate on acoustic and visual signals, respectively, and achieved encouraging results.

References

1. G. Kaufmann,H. Bunke, Error localization and correction in check processing, Proc. of 6th Int. Workshop on Frontiers in Handwriting Recognition, Taejon, 77–87, 1998.
2. R.A. Wagner and M.J. Fischer, The string-to-string correction problem, JACM, 21: 168–173, 1974.
3. K. Yu, X. Jiang, and H. Bunke, Automatic lipreading of sentences combining hidden Markov models and grammars, Proc. of 2nd Int. Conf. on Audio- and Video-Based Biometric Person Authentication, 90–95, Washington D.C., 1999.
4. K. Yu, Methods for Lipreading: Classification of Isolated Words, Sentence Recognition, and Classifier Combination, PhD. thesis, University of Bern, 1999.
5. K. Yu, X. Jiang, and H. Bunke, Combining acoustic and visual classifiers for the recognition of spoken sentences, 2000. (submitted for publication)

Shape Matching and Extraction by an Array of Figure-and-Ground Classifiers

Itsuo Kumazawa

Department of Computer Science
Tokyo Institute of Technology
Tokyo, Japan, 152-8552
kumazawa@cs.titech.ac.jp

Abstract. For matching a template to a target object in an image under influences from obstructing objects, a two dimensional array of figure-and-ground classifiers is introduced. Each classifier in the array observes a corresponding point in an image and determines if the point belongs to the target object (figure) or its background (ground). Neighboring classifiers communicate via local connections. The local communication is used to transmit the shape transformation parameter values so that the neighboring classifiers interpret their observing points under continuous and topology preserving shape transformation. Some basic experiments were conducted to evaluate the performance of the method and the method's effectiveness was confirmed.

1 Introduction

A number of shape matching techniques have been developed and applied to pattern recognition and computer vision related problems. For example, Hough transform and its generalized version for arbitrary shapes [1], have been used to match a parameterized template shape to target shapes under noises and obstructing background objects. Hough transforms only deal with uniform and geometric transformations such as shift, rotation and dilation. To cope with irregular and non-geometric shape deformations, which occur due to various observing conditions, deformable template techniques have been developed [2] [12] [5] [11]. The deformable template techniques are more sensitive to the influences from background obstacles than the techniques based on Hough transforms. In addition, their computation cost increases in a combinatorial order in terms of the number of deformation factors. As there is no theoretical solution to reduce the computation cost, heuristic approaches have been taken but the matching procedure tends to get stuck at a local optimum.

Although their applications are limited to relatively simple problems, Markov Random Field (MRF) models [4] and cellular neural networks [9] provide an interesting framework which deals with image processing tasks by an array of locally connected simple processing units. In these frameworks, each processing unit observes only a point or a small portion in an image. Global information is obtained only through the interaction among neighboring processing units

J. Kittler and F. Roli (Eds.): MCS 2000, LNCS 1857, pp. 393–400, 2000.

as there is neither a unit observing a whole image nor a connection between distant units. In the MRF models, the local connections are used to constrain the gray levels of connected pixels to be continuous when these pixels belong to an identical region. This constraint is turned off when the connected pixels belong to different regions.

The method presented in this paper, inspired by the frameworks of Hough transforms and MRF models, uses an array of classifiers and performs shape matching or object extraction by finding an optimal set of shape transformation parameters for a registered template of the object. Each classifier in the array observes a point in an image and judges if the point belongs to the object or not. The classifier consists of a shape representation neural network and, as its preprocessing part, an Affine transformation neural network. The template shape is represented by the shape representation neural network which is designed to output 1 when the coordinates (x, y) of a point inside the template shape are inputted and to output 0 when the coordinates (x, y) of a point outside the template shape are inputted. As the neural network is composed by sigmoid functions, the actual output value takes a gray level in the range $(0, 1)$. However, the binary representation is obtained when the gain parameters of the sigmoid functions take sufficiently large numbers. When the gain parameters take small values, a blurred shape is represented. An output value closer to 1 means that the inputted point is more plausibly classified as an inside point and an output value closer to 0 means that the inputted point is more plausibly classified as an outside point.

Each classifier in the array, at first, transforms the coordinates of its observing point by Affine transformation, and then, by applying the shape representation neural network, classifies the transformed point to inside or outside of the object. As in the MRF models, a continuity constraint operates so that the Affine transformation parameters are kept constant or continuous within the same object region. This constraint is implemented using local connections and used to keep the shape's topological structure. Under this continuity constraint, each classifier in the array repeatedly updates its Affine transformation parameters so that its output becomes close to 1 when the intensity level of its observing pixel is high and 0 when the intensity level is low, where we assume the input images are otained by a sensing system which gives high intensity levels for the pixels corresponding to the object regions. This framework works in a similar fashion to the Hough transform as it finds a set of pixels which are mapped to the template shape by the same or close Affine transformation parameter values.

In our previous works, the Affine transformation parameter values were fixed inside a windowed area [7] or their continuity were controlled so that the neighboring pixels belonging to the same object were mapped using the same or close Affine parameters, while the pixels in the background and the pixels in the object were mapped using different Affine parameters area [8]. The former failed in shape detection when the windowed area contained obstructing objects in its large portion. In the latter, variables to control the continuity of Affine parameters were introduced so that the constraint of continuity was turned off along the boundary between the object and the background. Unfortunately, this made the method very complicated and required careful adjustment of system parameters depending on input images. It also required an impractical amount of computation. In this paper, a simple averaging operator is shown to be effective to reduce the effects of obstructing objects with a small amount of computation.

2   Shape Representation and Figure-and-Ground Classification

The shape extraction method presented in this paper, uses a template represented in a parametric fashion [11], that is, as a function: $g = F(x, y, P)$ which, with a set of transformation parameters: P, specifies a gray level $g \in (0, 1)$ of the template image for any given position (x, y). In this representation, different from the pixel-based template representation which specifies gray levels for discrete positions, gray levels can be specified for any continuous positions. Transformed shapes are represented by using different parameter values for P. By searching values of P with which transformed template matches a target shape in an input image, shape extraction is performed.

The function $F(x, y, P)$ is constituted by a three layer feed forward neural network (Shape representation network) and, as its pre-processor, an Affine transformation network. Use of 6 inputs: x^2, y^2, xy, x, y and 1 to the Shape representation network is proven to be effective to represent shapes. The overall structure of the network is illustrated in Fig.1 (a). A template is represented by the part framed as Shape Representation Net. A unit in the first layer represents a basic shape component by a linear combination of the six inputs. For example, the unit in Fig.1 (b) represents a half plane region with a boundary along a line $ax + by + c = 0$. The unit in Fig.1 (c) represents an ellipse region with its contour represented by $ax^2 + by^2 + cxy + dx + ey + f = 0$. The unit in the second layer (output layer) represents a template shape by combining the shape components represented in the first layer and inputting their weighted sum to a sigmoid function. For example, a square is represented by combining four half planes represented in the first layer. By using ellipses in the combination, a shape with curved edges is also represented. The neural network formalized in this fashion is called Shape Representation Net. Each unit in the first layer and in the second layer is called Edge Unit and Combining Unit respectively. The shape representation neural network shows the result of figure-and-ground classification with its output 1 for a point inside the shape and 0 for a point outside the shape. Fig.2 shows how these figure-and-ground classifiers are arrayed in the entire system. In the following discussion, we assume use of a classifier for each pixel which observes the corresponding pixel value.

Before executing shape matching, a template shape for the target object needs to be represented (prepared) by determining the connection weights of the shape representation net. This determination is executed by the back-propagation learning algorithm. As an example, we show an airplane shape represented by a shape representation net with 8 edge description units in Fig.3, where the upper left is a bit map image used for learning and the upper right is its representation by the shape representation net. The lower graph shows the convergence curve (decrease of squared errors with respect to the number of parameter updating) during the back propagation learning.

By changing the parameter σ (gain) in the sigmoid function used in each unit:

$$sigmoid(s, \sigma) = \frac{1}{1 + e^{-\sigma s}}, \tag{1}$$

the represented shapes can be blurred and the convergence property of shape matching can be improved.

3 Shape Transformation and Matching

The set of parameters P to describe topology preserving shape transformations, such as Affine transformation, can be implemented by adding a preprocessing neural network to the shape representation net, which is already trained to represent a specific template shape. The preprocessing network maps the original coordinates (x', y') to the Affine-transformed coordinates (x, y) by using equations:

$$x = M \quad \cos \theta \quad x' - M \quad \sin \theta \quad y' + a, \tag{2}$$
$$y = M \quad \sin \theta \quad x' + M \quad \cos \theta \quad y' + b. \tag{3}$$

The set of Affine parameters $P = (M, \theta, a, b)$ is stored among the connection weights of the preprocessing network as shown in Fig.1(a). This preprocessing network is called Affine Transform Net. During the course of shape matching, these parameters are repeatedly updated by the back-propagation algorithm so that the transformed shape of a template matches a target shape included in an input image. Although the back-propagation algorithm is known to be slow and tend to get stuck at a local minimum, the procedure during the matching process, which updates only a part of weights for shape transformation, fixing other parts of weights for shape representation, is expected to show a better performance.

4 Shape Extraction by an Array of Figure-and-Ground Classifiers

The Affine transformation parameters (M, θ, a, b) should be constant throughout the mapping of all the points constituting an object shape in order to keep the original shape of the object. However, to deal with irregular but topology preserving distortions which often occur in practical situations, continuous change should be allowed for Affine transformation parameters. By allowing such a change, influences from nearby obstructing objects are also reduced. To cope with the changes in Affine transformation parameters, in stead of using a unique set of parameters for a whole shape, we can use a set of parameters for each pixel and, each of which can determine the mapping of the pixel position in the shape. By allowing parameters of nearby points to take different but close values, irregular but topology preserving shape distortions can be dealt with. In addition, the influences from obstructing objects are reduced as the transformation parameters of the object and the obstructing objects can take independent values.

For this purpose, an array of figure-and-ground classifiers, shown in Fig.2, can be introduced. In this array, each figure-and-ground classifier has the constitution shown in Fig.1(a). Each classifier observes a point in an image and, with its own Affine parameters, maps the coordinates (x', y') of its observing point to the coordinates (x, y). The coordinates (x, y) is inputted to the shape representation net and its output, which evaluates if the point is inside or outside the template shape, is computed. The Affine parameters of the classifier are updated so that the output becomes close to 1 when the point (x', y') is inside the object and 0 when the point (x', y') is outside the object. For this updating, the input image, which indicates the target object with high intensity levels of its pixels, is referenced to judge if the pixel is inside the object region or not. As the image usually contains obstructing objects and noises and they are also indicated with high intensity pixel values, we need to separate these erroneous information by controlling the continuity of Affine parameters while updating them in the above procedure.

5   Implementation of Continuity Constraint by an Averaging Operator

As described in the previous section, we use an independent set of Affine transformation parameters for each pixel. However, if each pixel is mapped with completely different transformation parameter values, the topology of the original shape is not preserved. In order to preserve the topology of the shape, Affine transformation parameters should change continuously inside the target region. In order to implement this continuity requirement, we use an averaging operator. This operator works as follows. After Affine transformation parameters of every classifier are updated by the procedure described in the previous section, each classifier obtains Affine transformation parameter values of its 8 neighboring classifiers and compute the average of these 8 and its own for each component of P. Then these averaged values substitute their previous values. This simple averaging operation is alternately and repeatedly applied while the parameter updating procedure described in the previous section proceeds. As demonstrated in the next section, the continuity constraint implemented by this averaging operator is shown to be effective to reduce the influences from obstructing objects and noises.

In the array of figure-and-ground classifiers, as shown in Fig.2, only neighboring classifiers can communicate through local connections. This so-called cellular architecture is suitable for each classifier to get parameter values from neighboring classifiers and makes its own parameter values close to them by applying the averaging operation at its own site.

6   Experiments

The performance of the array of figure-and-ground classifiers on a shape extraction task is examined and compared with our previous method [7] which used a common set of Affine transformation parameter values over a windowed area.

Prior to the shape extraction experiments, a three layer shape representation net is constructed and its connection weights are determined by the backpropagation algorithm to represent an airplane shape. The image used for the training and the represented shape are shown in Fig.3 along with the convergence curve during the training. As shown in the result, a rough silhouette of a toy airplane is represented by a compact shape representation network with 8 edge describing units. The training was repeated for 500 times per pixel.

Shape extraction experiments were conducted using the template represented by the shape representation neural network and three different image samples. Each sample was a square region of 32×32 pixels windowed from a larger image so that it contained a target shape. In each of Fig.4 -7, the results for the three samples are shown in sub-figures of (a),(b) and (c). In each sub-figure, the top left image is the input image with the resolution of 32 by 32 pixels, the top right image shows the shape extraction result with the gray level of each pixel indicating the output of the figure-and-ground classifier. The bright pixels mean they were classified as inside the object and the dark pixels mean they were classified as outside the object. The bottom graph shows the convergence curve.

In the first series of experiments, three images which were noisy but did not include a large obstructing area were used. Fig.4 shows the results by our previous method which uses a common set of Affine transformation parameter values throughout a whole image. It is observed that the target shape was successfully extracted in any image. Fig.5 shows the results by the array of figure-and-ground classifiers. As the Affine transformation parameters can differ for each pixel under the continuity constraint introduced by the averaging operator, the template shape was deformed to meet with the irregular deformation of the target shape. However, some noises were also classified as parts of the target object.

In the second series of experiments, three images including a large obstructing area were used. In Fig.6 and 7, the obstructing areas are observed as white areas at one of the corners in the top left images of sub-figures (a),(b) and (c). Fig.6 shows the results by our previous method. As the Affine transformation parameters must be constant throughout a whole image, the obstructing region affects the entire result and the target shape was not extracted correctly in any image. Fig.7 shows the results by the array of figure-and-ground classifiers. As the Affine transformation parameters for the target region are influenced by the obstructing area only through the continuity constraint, and they can take different values in distant areas, the target object was successfully extracted in every image. It should be noted that, in any extraction result, the obstructing areas had bright intensity levels. This means that these obstructing areas were also interpreted as parts of target object. This seems like a classification failure but actually a result faithful to the method's principle. In our method, any white region can be classified as a part of the target object as far as its shape is approximated by a part of Affine-transformed template shape. When an object is partially observed through the restricted view of the windowed area, the observed part is likely to match a part of the template shape and be classified as a part of the target.

7 Conclusion

An array of figure-and-ground classifiers was introduced for shape matching and extraction purposes. Compared with our previous method, which maps all the points in a windowed region using a common set of Affine transformation parameters, the new method, which allows continuous change in the Affine transformation parameters, showed a better performance when the windowed region included obstructing objects. To constrain the Affine transformation parameters of neighboring classifiers to take close values, a simple averaging operator was effectively introduced with a reduced computation cost. As the current method extracts any region as far as it is approximated by a part of Affine transformed template shape, an extraction error occurs in such cases that an isolated white pixel is approximated by an extremely reduced template or the shape of a partially observed object in the windowed area is approximated by a part of the Affine transformed template. Some posterior criteria should be introduced to evaluate the appropriateness of the obtained Affine transformation parameters to exclude these cases.

References

1. Ballard,D.H.: Generalizing the Hough Transform to Detect Arbitrary Shapes. Pattern Recognition 13, (2),(1981) 111–122.
2. Bardinet, E., Cohen, L.D.: A Parametric Deformable Model to Fit Unstructured 3D Data. Computer Vision and Image Understanding 71,(1),(1998) 39–54.
3. Ben-Arie, J., Rao, J.K., Wang,Z.: A Neural Network Approach for Shape Description and Invariant Recognition. Proc. 1994 Image Understanding Workshop. Monterey, CA, II, (1994) 863–870.
4. Geman,D., Geman,S.: Stochastic relaxation, Gibbs distribution, and the Bayesian restoration of images. IEEE Trans. on Pattern Analysis and Machine Intelligence, PAMI-6(6), (1984) 721–741.
5. Jain, A.K., Zhong,Y., Lakshmanan, S.: Object Matching Using Deformable Templates.IEEE Trans. Pattern Analysis and Machine Intelligence 18, (3), (1996) 267–278
6. Kumazawa,I.: Shape extraction by cellular Hough transform, Technical report of IEICE, PRMU96–105, (1996) 9-16

7. Kumazawa,I.: Learning and Tracking Target Shapes by Compact Neural Network, Proceedings of ICONIP/ANZIIS/ANNES'99 International Workshop, (1999) 41–44

8. Kumazawa,I.: A cellular neural network framework for shape representation and matching, Proceedings of Third International Conference on Kowledge-based Intelligent Information Engineering Systems, (1999) 178–181

9. Roska,T., Vandewalle,J. (eds.): Cellular Neural Networks, John Wiley & Sons, Inc. (1993)

10. Suzuki,M., Kumazawa,I.: Functional representation of template and cellular parallel computing model for shape extraction, Technical report of IEICE, PRMU97-144, (1997) 117–124.

11. Staib, L.H., Duncan, J.S.:
Parametrically deformable contour models. Computer Vision and Pattern Recognition. IEEE Computer Society Press, (1989) 98–103.

12. Shum, H.Y., Hebert, M., Ikeuchi, K., Reddy, R.: An Integral Approach to Free-Form Object Modeling, IEEE Trans. Pattern Analysis and Machine Intelligence 19, (12), (1997) 1,366–1,375.

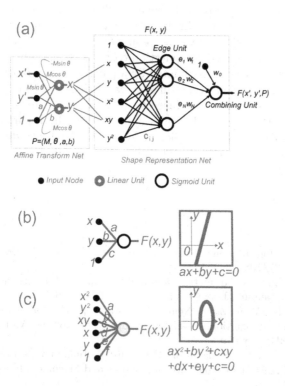

Fig. 1. (a) A figure-and-ground classifier. (b) A half plane with a linear edge represented by an Edge unit. (c) An ellipse region with a curved edge represented by an Edge unit.

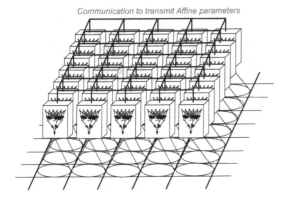

Fig. 2. The array of figure-and-ground classifiers. Each classifier observes a point in an input image and is connected with neighboring classifiers.

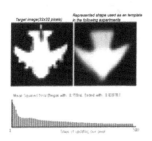

Fig. 3. (a) An image used for training. (b) An template shape represented by a shape representation net which is trained using the image in (a).

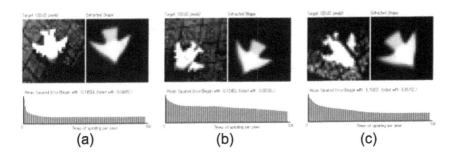

Fig. 4. Shape extraction results when a common set of Affine transformation parameters was applied over an entire image which did not include obstructing objects.

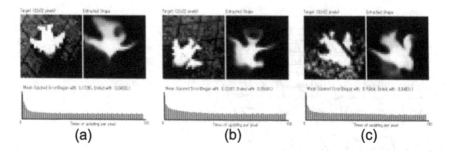

Fig. 5. Shape extraction results when Affine transformation parameters were allowed to vary continuously over an image which did not include obstructing objects.

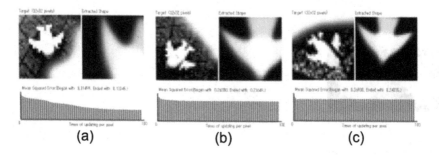

Fig. 6. Shape extraction results when a common set of Affine transformation parameters was applied over an entire image which included obstructing objects.

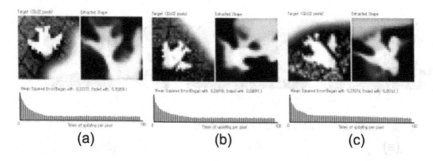

Fig. 7. Shape extraction results when Affine transformation parameters were allowed to vary continuously over an image which included obstructing objects.

Author Index

Alonso González, C.J.   210

Benediktsson, J.A.   280
Bock, P.   137
Bruzzone, L.   290
Bunke, H.   383
Buscicchio, C.A.   372

Cappelli, R.   351
Castellano, G.   372
Chandroth, G.O.   30
Cohen, S.   147
Conversano, C.   167
Cordella, L.P.   330
Cossu, R.   290
Crawford, M.   270

Debeir, O.   200
Decaestecker, C.   200
Di Lecce, V.   320
Dietterich, T.G.   1
Dimauro, G.   320
Duin, R.P.W.   16, 117, 190

Fanelli, A.M.   372
Foggia, P.   330
Fraser, D.   300
Fröba, B.   362
Furlanello, C.   220

Gerecke, U.   30
Ghosh, J.   270
Giacinto, G.   177
Govindaraju, V.   310, 340
Griffith, N.   250
Grim, J.   157
Guerriero, A.   320

Happel, M.D.   137
Ho, T.K.   97

Ianakiev, K.   340
Impedovo, S.   230, 320
Intrator, N.   147

Jiang, W.   87
Jiang, X.   383

Jones, P.   240

Kittler, J.   157
Kleinberg, E.M.   67
Küblbeck, C.   362
Kumar, S.   270
Kumazawa I. ,   393

Lam, L.   52, 77
Latinne, P.   200

Maio, D.   351
Maltoni, D.   351
Masulli, F.   107
Merler, S.   220
Mola, F.   167

Partridge, D.   240, 250
Pękalska , E.   117
Pirlo, G.   320
Prieto, D.F.   290
Pudil, P.   157

Rodriguez Diez, J.J.   210
Roli, F.   177
Rothe, C.   362

Salzo, A.   230, 320
Sansone, C.   330
Sato, A.   127
Sharkey, A.J.C.   30
Sharkey, N.E.   30
Siciliano, R.   167
Skurichina, M.   117, 190

Slavík, P.   310
Somol, P.   157
Srihari, S.N.   45
Suen, C.Y.   52
Sveinsson, J.R.   280

Takahashi, K.   127
Tax, D.M.J.   16
Tortorella, F.   330

Valentini, G.   107
Vento, M.   330

Wan, W.   300
Wang, W.   240
Windeatt, T.   260

Yu, K.   383